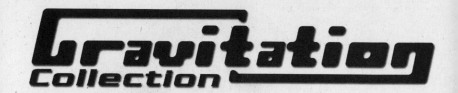

# Gravitation Collection

Volume 6

By
Maki Murakami

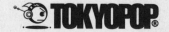

HAMBURG // LONDON // LOS ANGELES // TOKYO

*Gravitation Collection Volume 6*
by Maki Murakami

Translation - Ray Yoshimoto
English Adaptation - Jamie S. Rich
Retouch and Layout - Michael Paolilli
Production Artist - Michael Paolilli
Graphic Designer - Louis Csontos


Original Editor - Paul Morrissey
Editor - Cindy Suzuki
Print Production Manager - Lucas Rivera
Managing Editor - Vy Nguyen
Senior Designer - Louis Csontos
Art Director - Al-Insan Lashley
Director of Sales and Manufacturing - Allyson De Simone
Associate Publisher - Marco F. Pavia
President and C.O.O. - John Parker
C.E.O. and Chief Creative Officer - Stu Levy

A 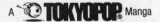 Manga

TOKYOPOP and 🐸 are trademarks or registered trademarks of TOKYOPOP Inc.

TOKYOPOP Inc.
5900 Wilshire Blvd. Suite 2000
Los Angeles, CA 90036

E-mail: info@TOKYOPOP.com
Come visit us online at www.TOKYOPOP.com

ISBN: 978-1-4278-1658-0

First TOKYOPOP printing: November 2010
10  9  8  7  6  5  4  3  2  1
Printed in the USA

# Gravitation

Volume 6

CONTENTS

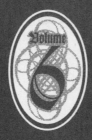

# Volume 6

# Gravitation

*Maki Murakami*

# THE MEMBERS OF THE GRAVITATION BAND

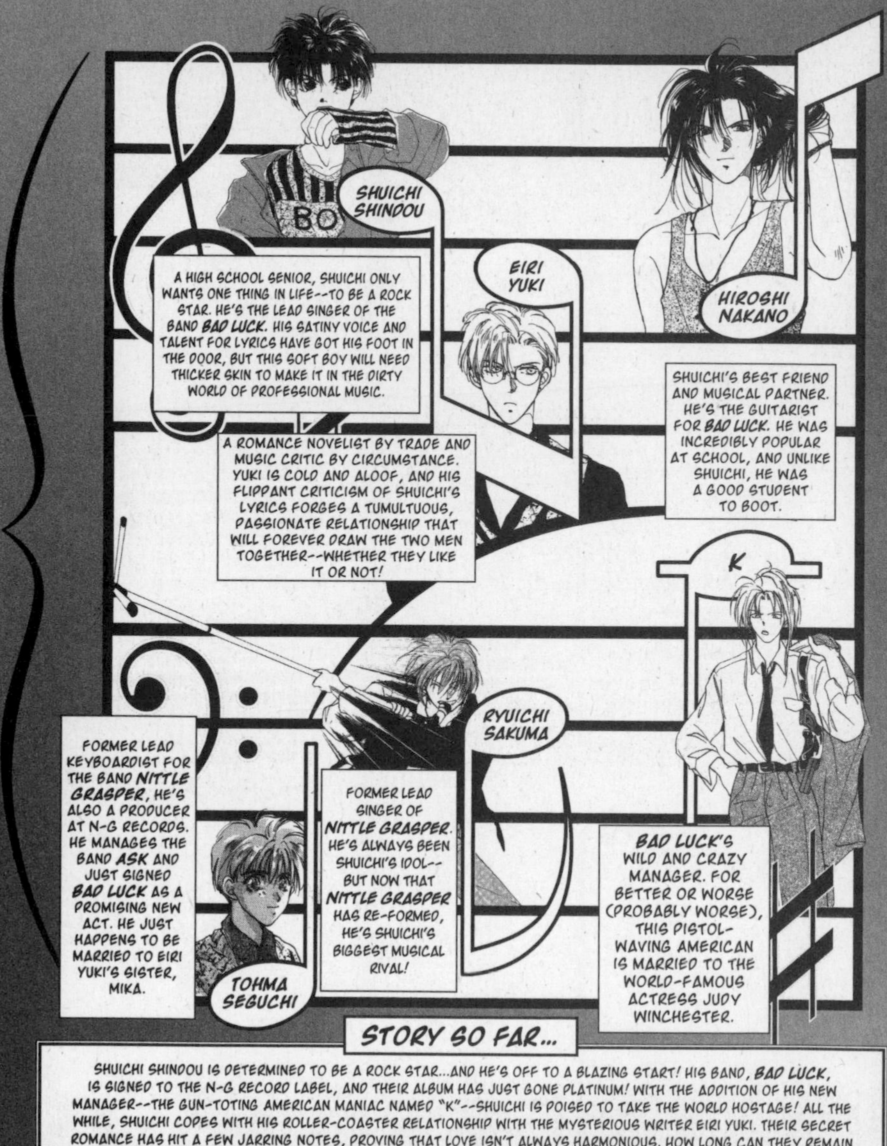
SHUICHI SHINDOU
A HIGH SCHOOL SENIOR, SHUICHI ONLY WANTS ONE THING IN LIFE--TO BE A ROCK STAR. HE'S THE LEAD SINGER OF THE BAND BAD LUCK. HIS SATINY VOICE AND TALENT FOR LYRICS HAVE GOT HIS FOOT IN THE DOOR, BUT THIS SOFT BOY WILL NEED THICKER SKIN TO MAKE IT IN THE DIRTY WORLD OF PROFESSIONAL MUSIC.
EIRI YUKI
A ROMANCE NOVELIST BY TRADE AND MUSIC CRITIC BY CIRCUMSTANCE. YUKI IS COLD AND ALOOF, AND HIS FLIPPANT CRITICISM OF SHUICHI'S LYRICS FORGES A TUMULTUOUS, PASSIONATE RELATIONSHIP THAT WILL FOREVER DRAW THE TWO MEN TOGETHER--WHETHER THEY LIKE IT OR NOT!
HIROSHI NAKANO
SHUICHI'S BEST FRIEND AND MUSICAL PARTNER. HE'S THE GUITARIST FOR BAD LUCK. HE WAS INCREDIBLY POPULAR AT SCHOOL, AND UNLIKE SHUICHI, HE WAS A GOOD STUDENT TO BOOT.
K
BAD LUCK'S WILD AND CRAZY MANAGER. FOR BETTER OR WORSE (PROBABLY WORSE), THIS PISTOL-WAVING AMERICAN IS MARRIED TO THE WORLD-FAMOUS ACTRESS JUDY WINCHESTER.
RYUICHI SAKUMA
FORMER LEAD SINGER OF NITTLE GRASPER. HE'S ALWAYS BEEN SHUICHI'S IDOL--BUT NOW THAT NITTLE GRASPER HAS RE-FORMED, HE'S SHUICHI'S BIGGEST MUSICAL RIVAL!
TOHMA SEGUCHI
FORMER LEAD KEYBOARDIST FOR THE BAND NITTLE GRASPER, HE'S ALSO A PRODUCER AT N-G RECORDS. HE MANAGES THE BAND ASK AND JUST SIGNED BAD LUCK AS A PROMISING NEW ACT. HE JUST HAPPENS TO BE MARRIED TO EIRI YUKI'S SISTER, MIKA.

## STORY SO FAR...

SHUICHI SHINDOU IS DETERMINED TO BE A ROCK STAR...AND HE'S OFF TO A BLAZING START! HIS BAND, ***BAD LUCK***, IS SIGNED TO THE N-G RECORD LABEL, AND THEIR ALBUM HAS JUST GONE PLATINUM! WITH THE ADDITION OF HIS NEW MANAGER--THE GUN-TOTING AMERICAN MANIAC NAMED "K"--SHUICHI IS POISED TO TAKE THE WORLD HOSTAGE! ALL THE WHILE, SHUICHI COPES WITH HIS ROLLER-COASTER RELATIONSHIP WITH THE MYSTERIOUS WRITER EIRI YUKI. THEIR SECRET ROMANCE HAS HIT A FEW JARRING NOTES, PROVING THAT LOVE ISN'T ALWAYS HARMONIOUS. HOW LONG CAN THEY REMAIN INEXORABLY INTERTWINED, HELD TOGETHER BY A FORCE AS STRONG AS GRAVITY? CONFRONTED BY A VORACIOUS PACK OF REPORTERS, YUKI SURPRISINGLY ADMITS TO A SHOCKED WORLD THAT HE AND SHUICHI ARE INDEED LOVERS! FUELED BY JEALOUSLY, SEGUCHI ORDERS SHUICHI TO BREAK UP WITH EIRI. SHUICHI CONTEMPLATES LEAVING N-G IN ORDER TO SALVAGE HIS ROMANCE, BUT ALL IS FOR NAUGHT--IN A SHOCKING MOVE, EIRI DUMPS ***HIM***! K TRIES IN VAIN TO HELP A DEVASTATED SHUICHI RECOVER, BUT THE SURPRISES JUST KEEP COMING: SHUICHI IS KIDNAPPED...AND PUT ON A PLANE TO R-O-C-K IN THE U.S.A.! SHUICHI'S NEW MANAGER AT XMR RECORDS--THE VOLATILE REIJI (A.K.A. RAGE)--IS DETERMINED TO MAKE HIM AN AMERICAN SUPERSTAR. ALTHOUGH SHUICHI CONTEMPLATES NORTH AMERICAN FAME, HIS UNDYING LOVE FOR YUKI ULTIMATELY LEADS HIM BACK TO JAPAN. THERE'S JUST ONE PROBLEM: THE INSANELY JEALOUS RAGE HAS DECIDED TO FOLLOW HIM BACK HOME--IN HER GIANT, ROBOTIC FLYING PANDA!

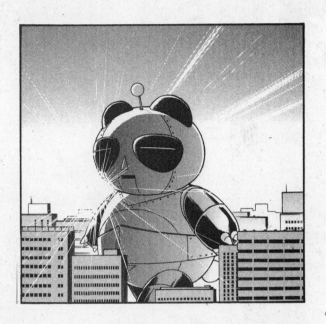

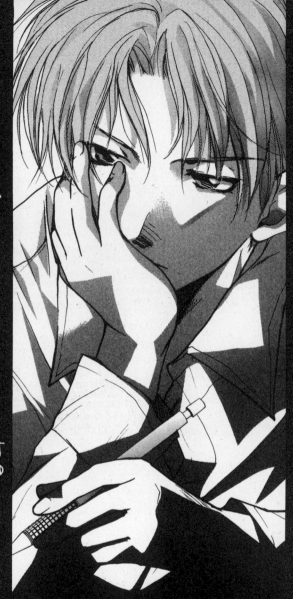

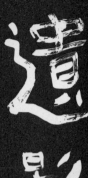

PORTRAIT
OF A DEAD
MAN

track45

Gravitation

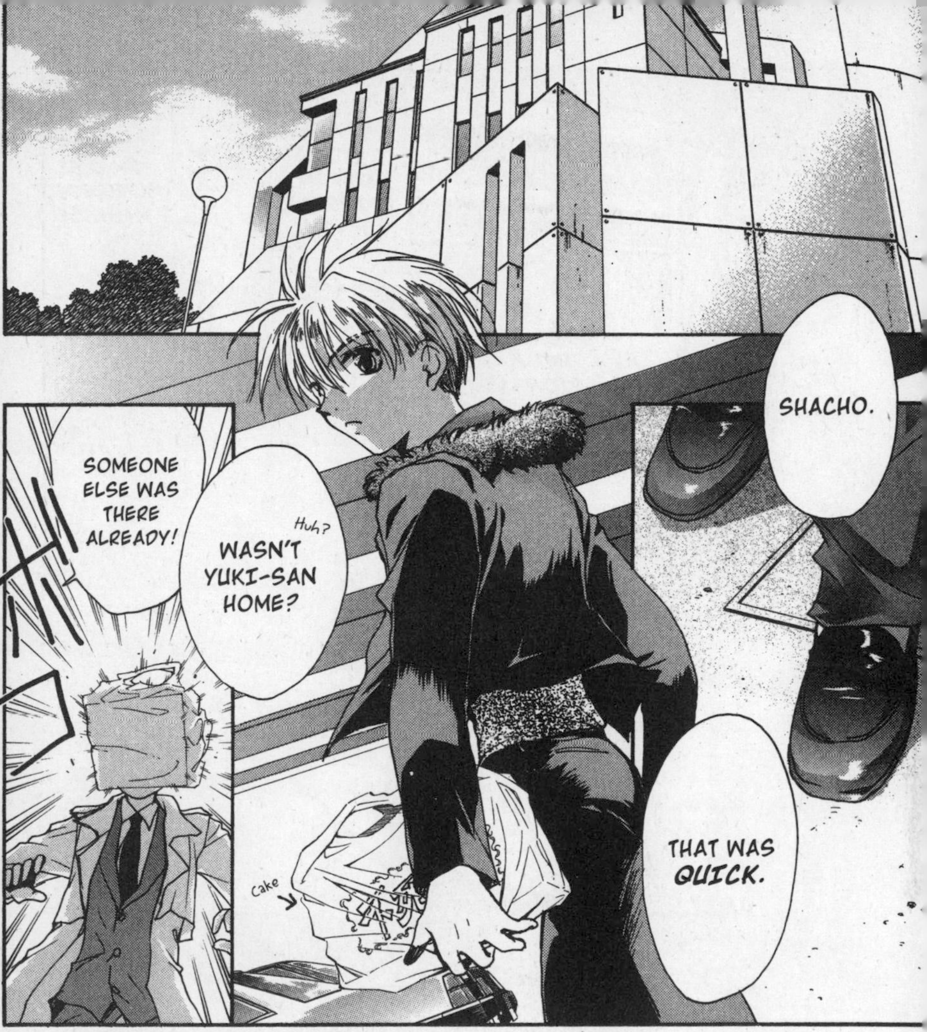
SHACHO.
THAT WAS QUICK.
Huh?
WASN'T YUKI-SAN HOME?
Cake
SOMEONE ELSE WAS THERE ALREADY!

## ABOUT GRAVITATION TRACK 45

I've gotten used to using this autograph pen, and at first glance you might not even recognize my writing. What do you think? I also use a specialized G pen, but I have a hard time writing with that one, too. After all, they're autograph pens! But it's a pretty cheap way to go. Each pen costs about 100 yen, and it'll last about 100 pages. But it's not something to brag about. This is just a last resort, since I have nothing to write about in this space.

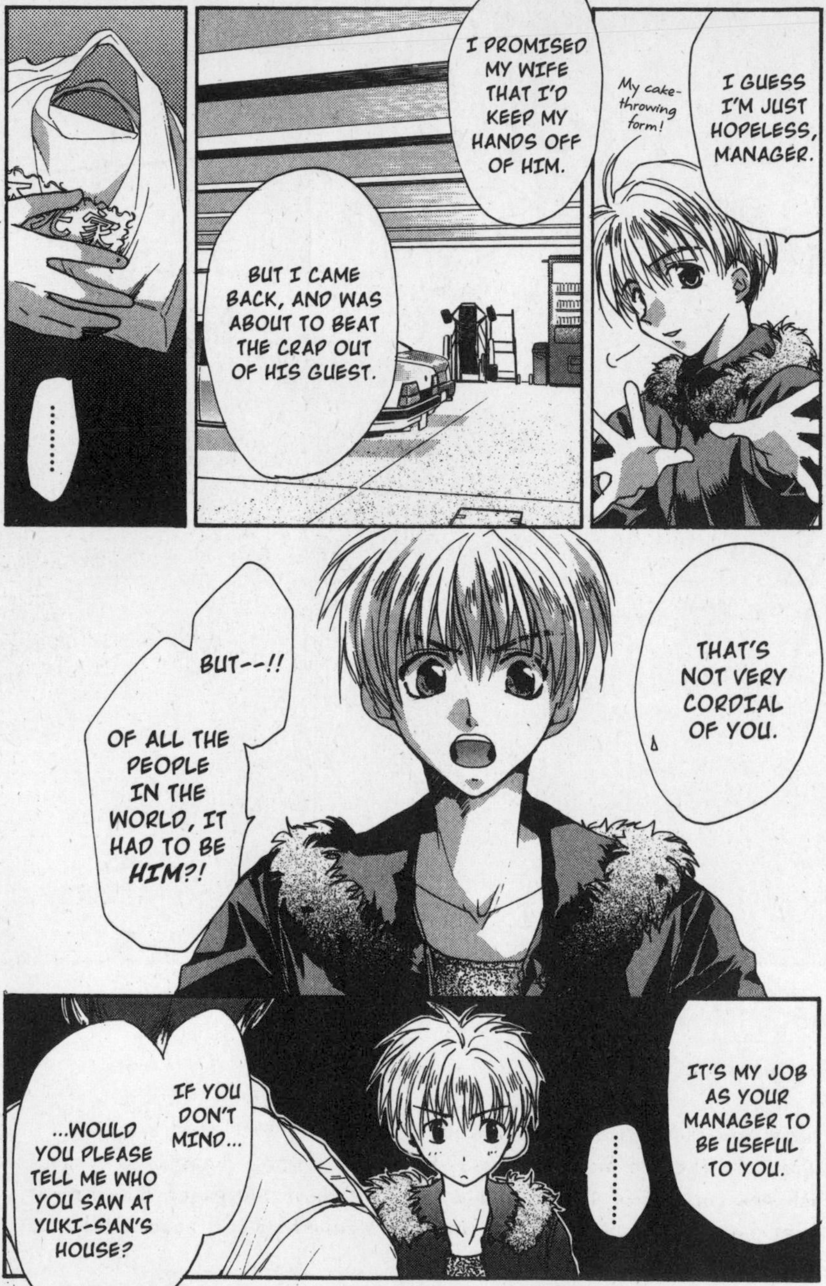

I GUESS I'M JUST HOPELESS, MANAGER.
My cake-throwing form!
I PROMISED MY WIFE THAT I'D KEEP MY HANDS OFF OF HIM.
BUT I CAME BACK, AND WAS ABOUT TO BEAT THE CRAP OUT OF HIS GUEST.
......
THAT'S NOT VERY CORDIAL OF YOU.
BUT--!!
OF ALL THE PEOPLE IN THE WORLD, IT HAD TO BE *HIM*?!
IT'S MY JOB AS YOUR MANAGER TO BE USEFUL TO YOU.
......
IF YOU DON'T MIND...
...WOULD YOU PLEASE TELL ME WHO YOU SAW AT YUKI-SAN'S HOUSE?

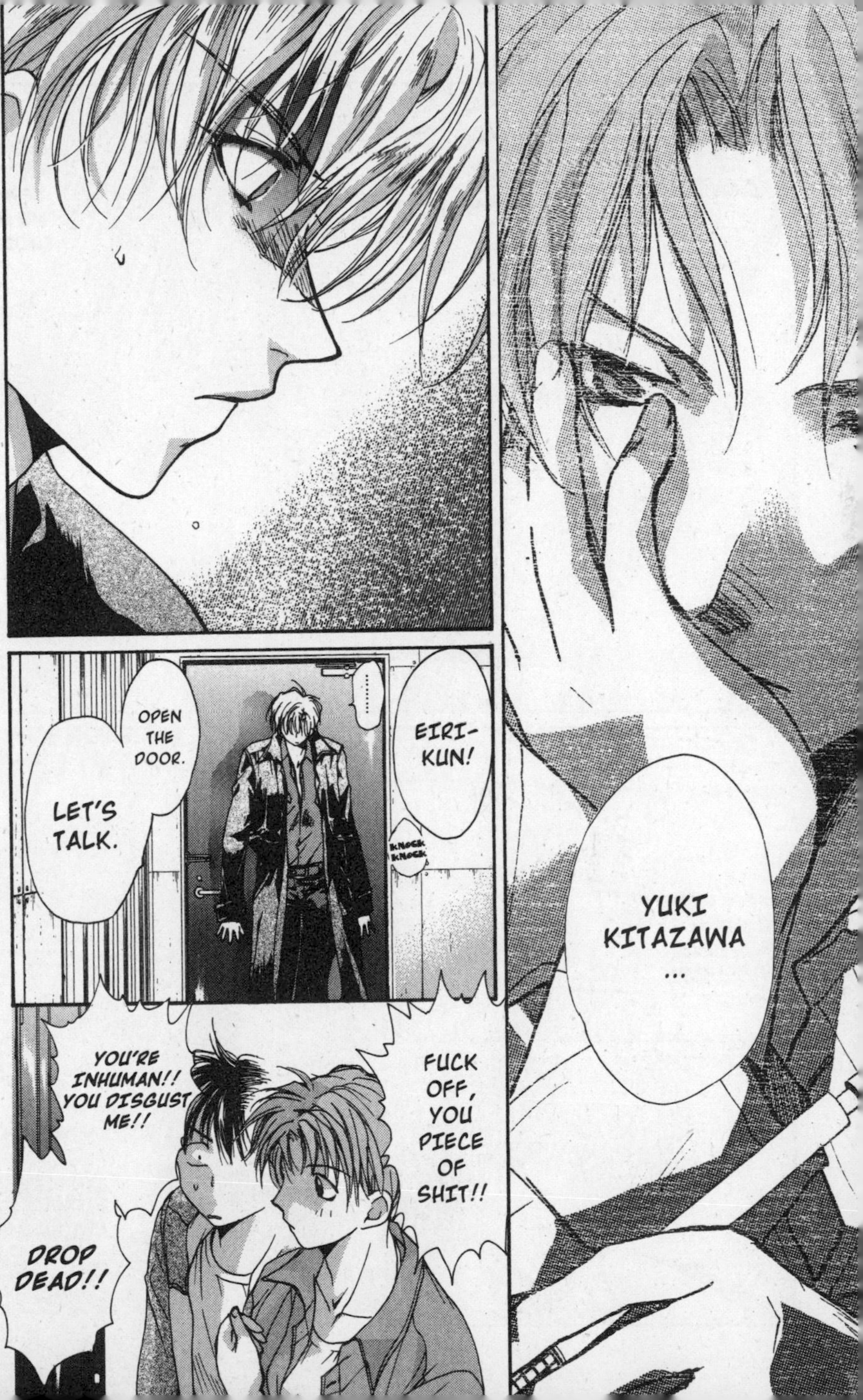
YUKI KITAZAWA ...
EIRI-KUN!
......
KNOCK KNOCK
OPEN THE DOOR.
LET'S TALK.
FUCK OFF, YOU PIECE OF SHIT!!
YOU'RE INHUMAN!! YOU DISGUST ME!!
DROP DEAD!!

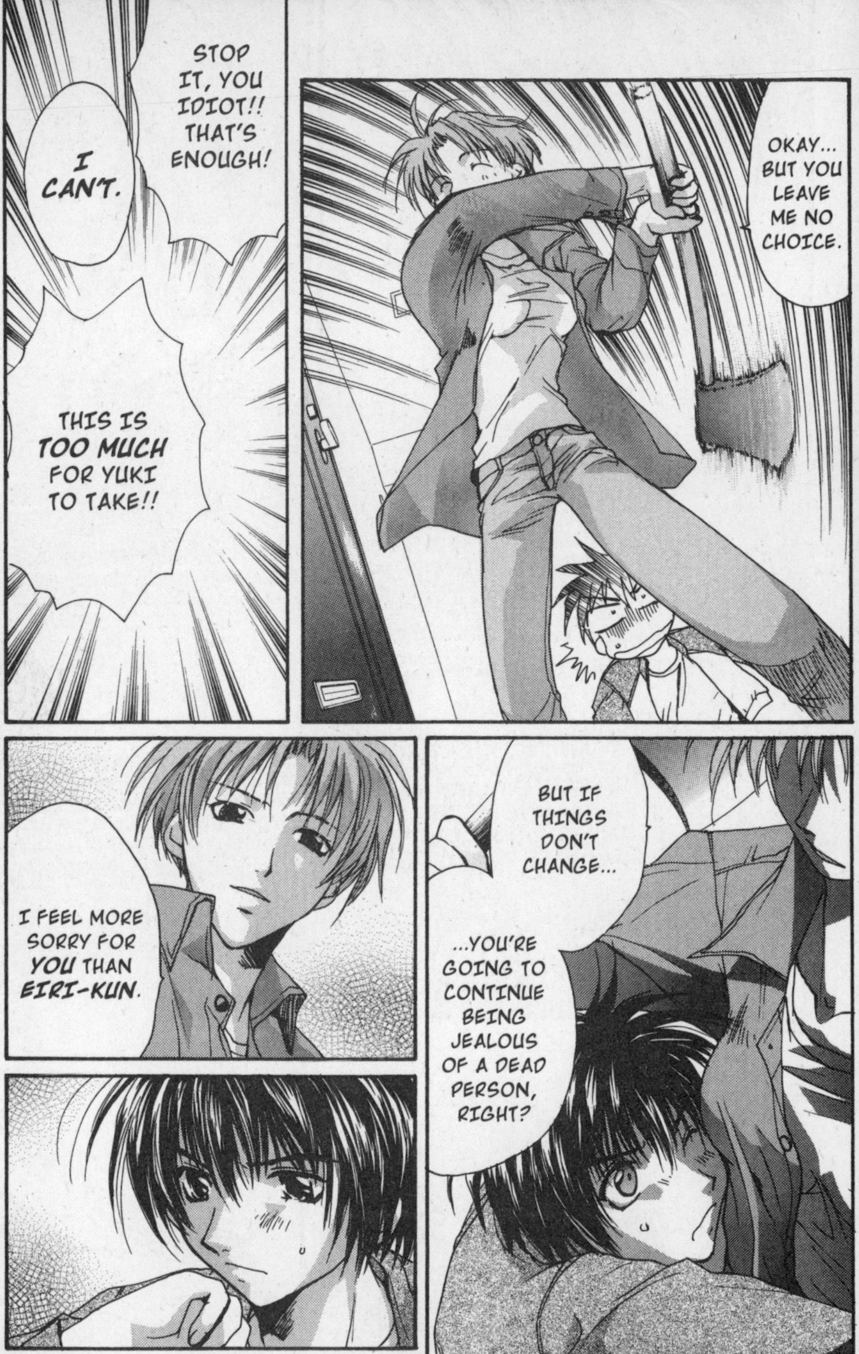
OKAY... BUT YOU LEAVE ME NO CHOICE.
STOP IT, YOU IDIOT!! THAT'S ENOUGH!
I CAN'T.
THIS IS TOO MUCH FOR YUKI TO TAKE!!
BUT IF THINGS DON'T CHANGE...
...YOU'RE GOING TO CONTINUE BEING JEALOUS OF A DEAD PERSON, RIGHT?
I FEEL MORE SORRY FOR YOU THAN EIRI-KUN.

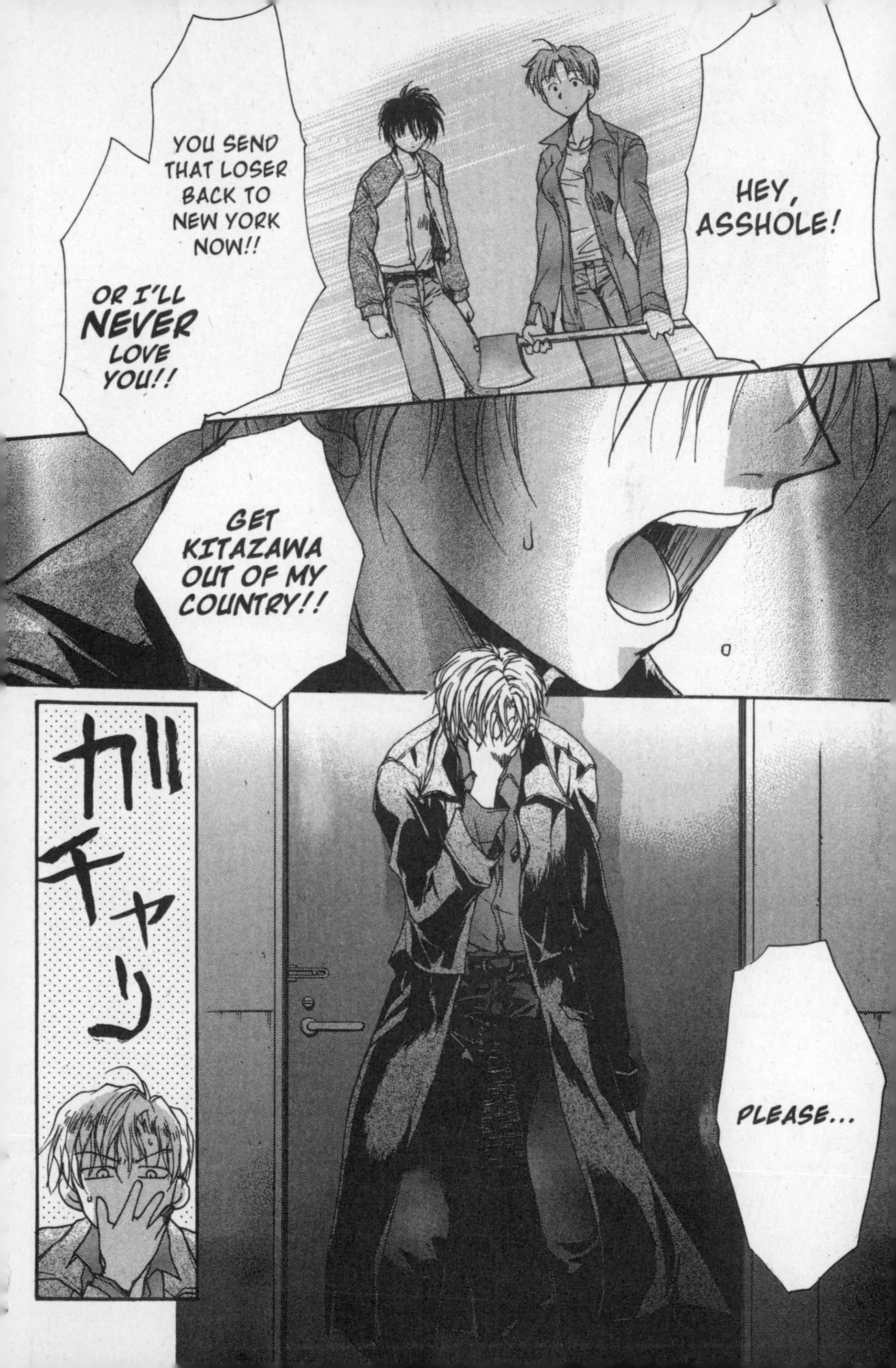
HEY, ASSHOLE!
YOU SEND THAT LOSER BACK TO NEW YORK NOW!!
OR I'LL NEVER LOVE YOU!!
GET KITAZAWA OUT OF MY COUNTRY!!
PLEASE...
ガチャリ

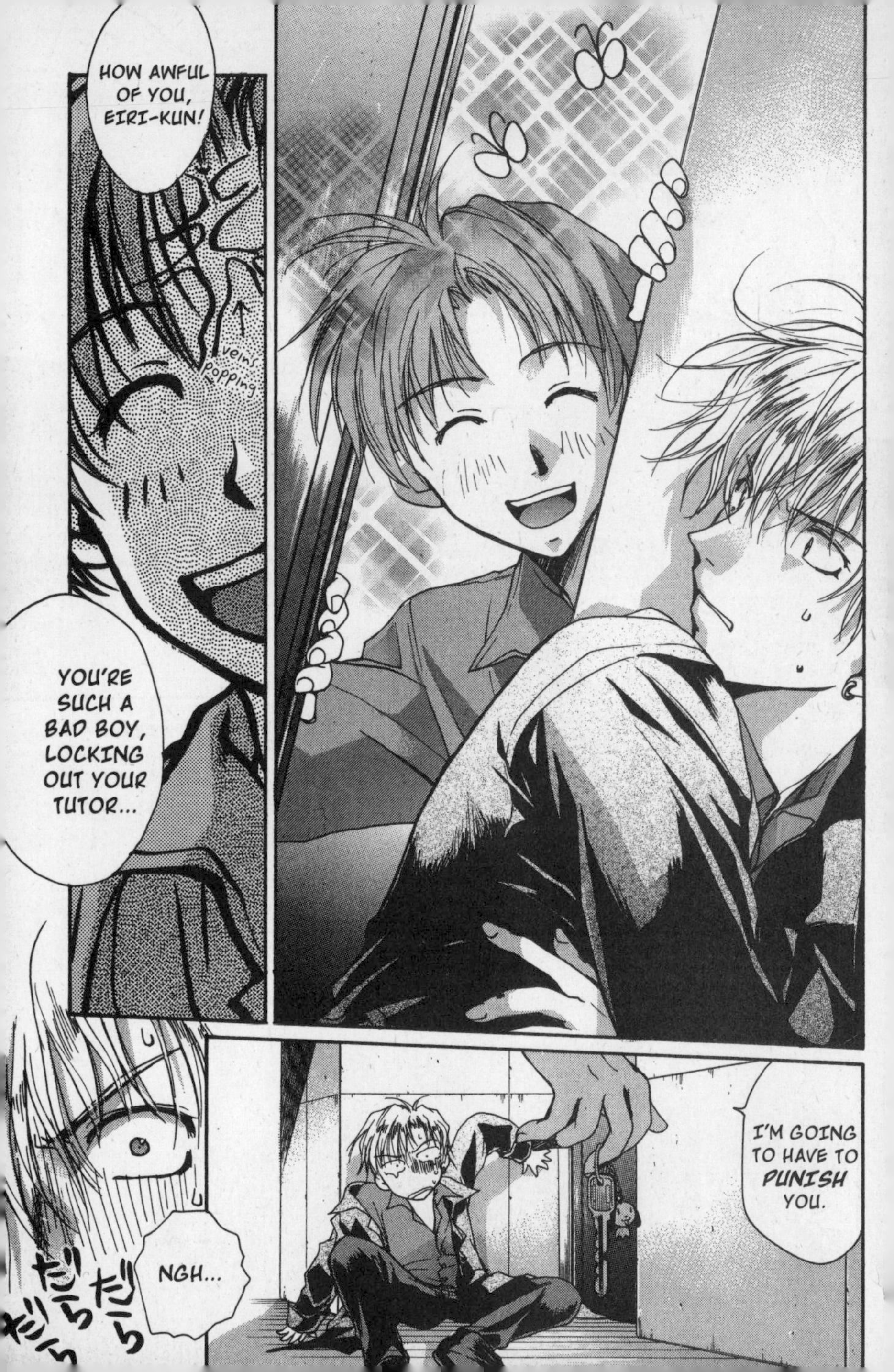
HOW AWFUL OF YOU, EIRI-KUN!
veins popping
YOU'RE SUCH A BAD BOY, LOCKING OUT YOUR TUTOR...
I'M GOING TO HAVE TO *PUNISH* YOU.
NGH...
だらだら だらだら

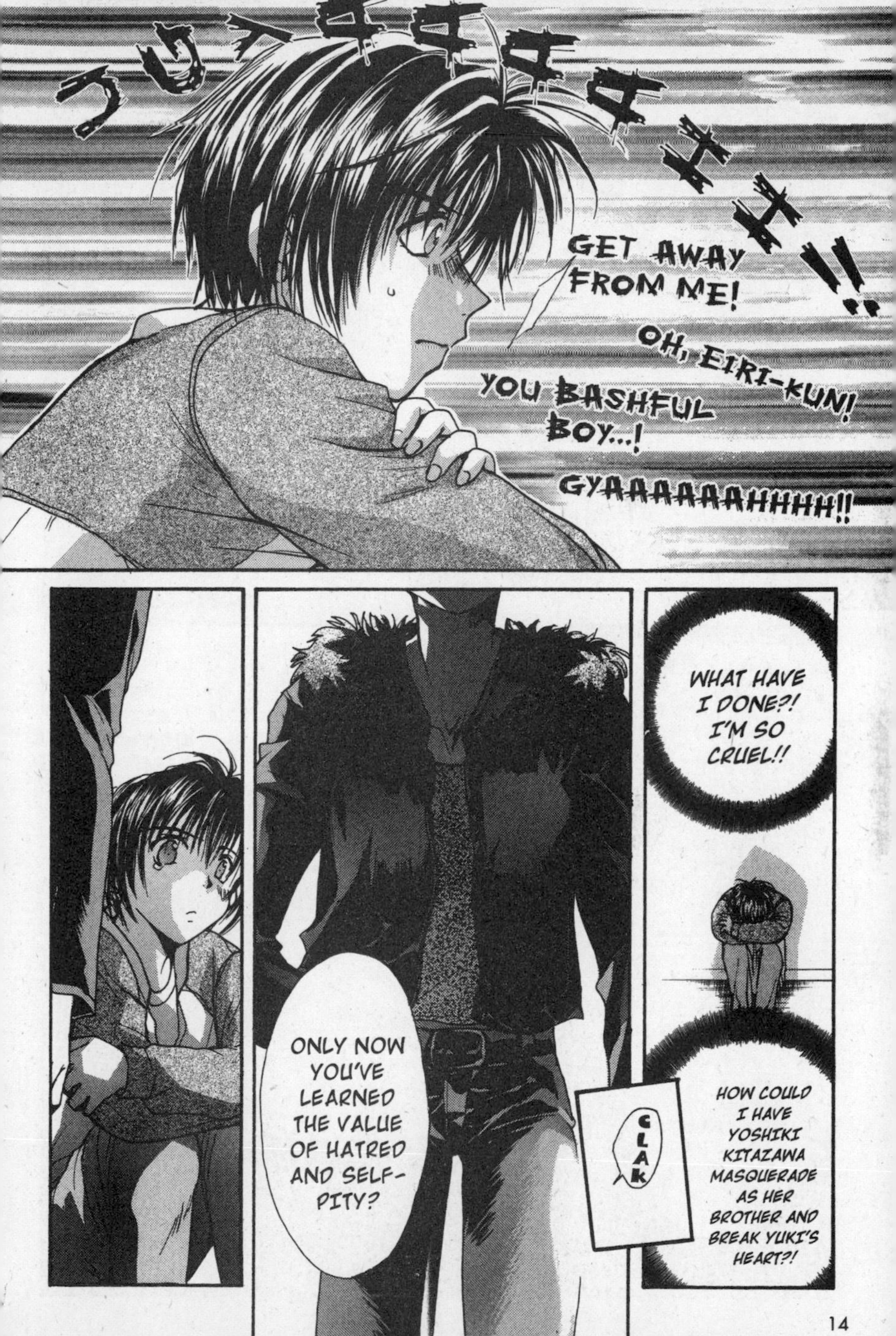
GET AWAY FROM ME!
OH, EIRI-KUN! YOU BASHFUL BOY...!
GYAAAAAAAHHHH!!
WHAT HAVE I DONE?! I'M SO CRUEL!!
HOW COULD I HAVE YOSHIKI KITAZAWA MASQUERADE AS HER BROTHER AND BREAK YUKI'S HEART?!
CLAK
ONLY NOW YOU'VE LEARNED THE VALUE OF HATRED AND SELF-PITY?

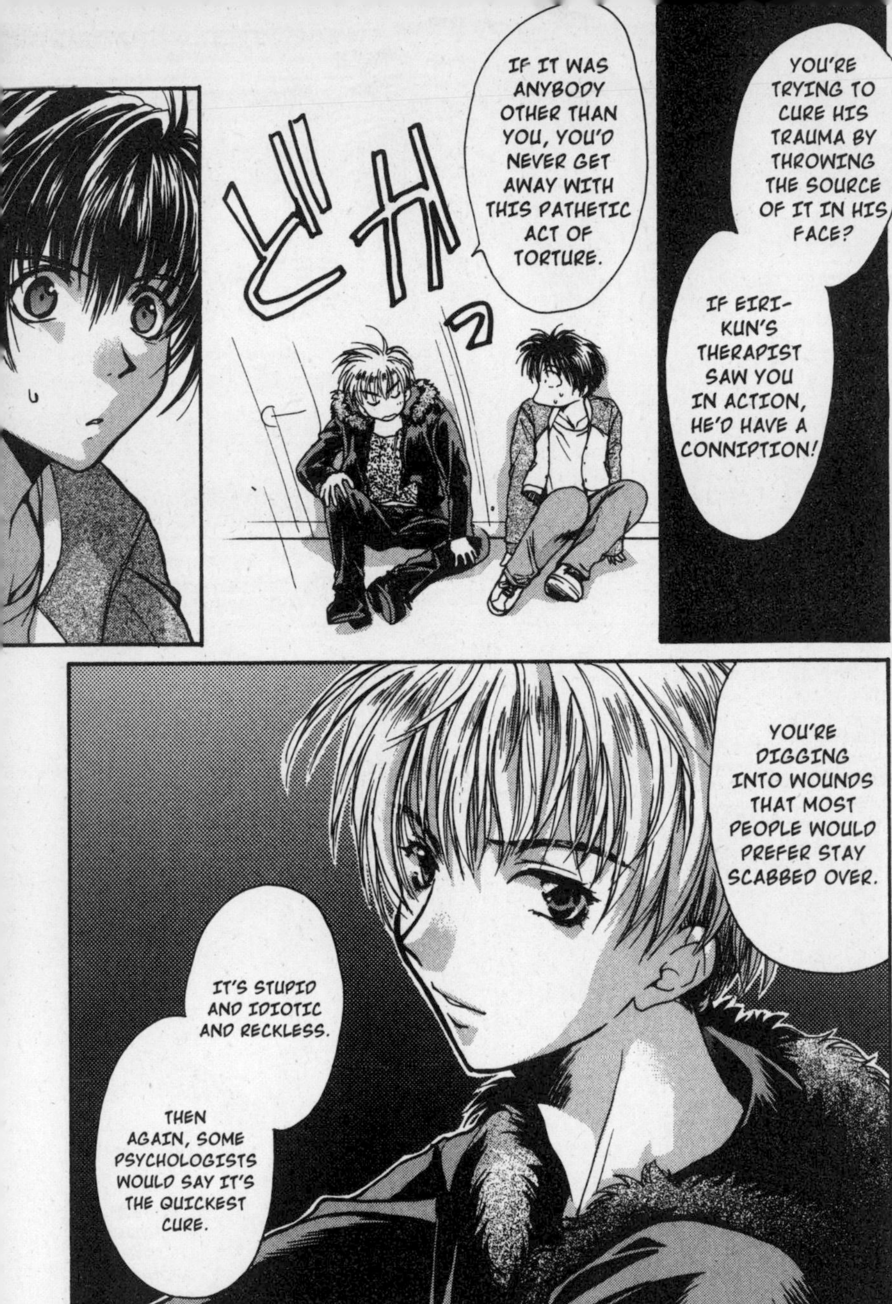

YOU'RE TRYING TO CURE HIS TRAUMA BY THROWING THE SOURCE OF IT IN HIS FACE?
IF EIRI-KUN'S THERAPIST SAW YOU IN ACTION, HE'D HAVE A CONNIPTION!
どカっ
IF IT WAS ANYBODY OTHER THAN YOU, YOU'D NEVER GET AWAY WITH THIS PATHETIC ACT OF TORTURE.
YOU'RE DIGGING INTO WOUNDS THAT MOST PEOPLE WOULD PREFER STAY SCABBED OVER.
IT'S STUPID AND IDIOTIC AND RECKLESS.
THEN AGAIN, SOME PSYCHOLOGISTS WOULD SAY IT'S THE QUICKEST CURE.

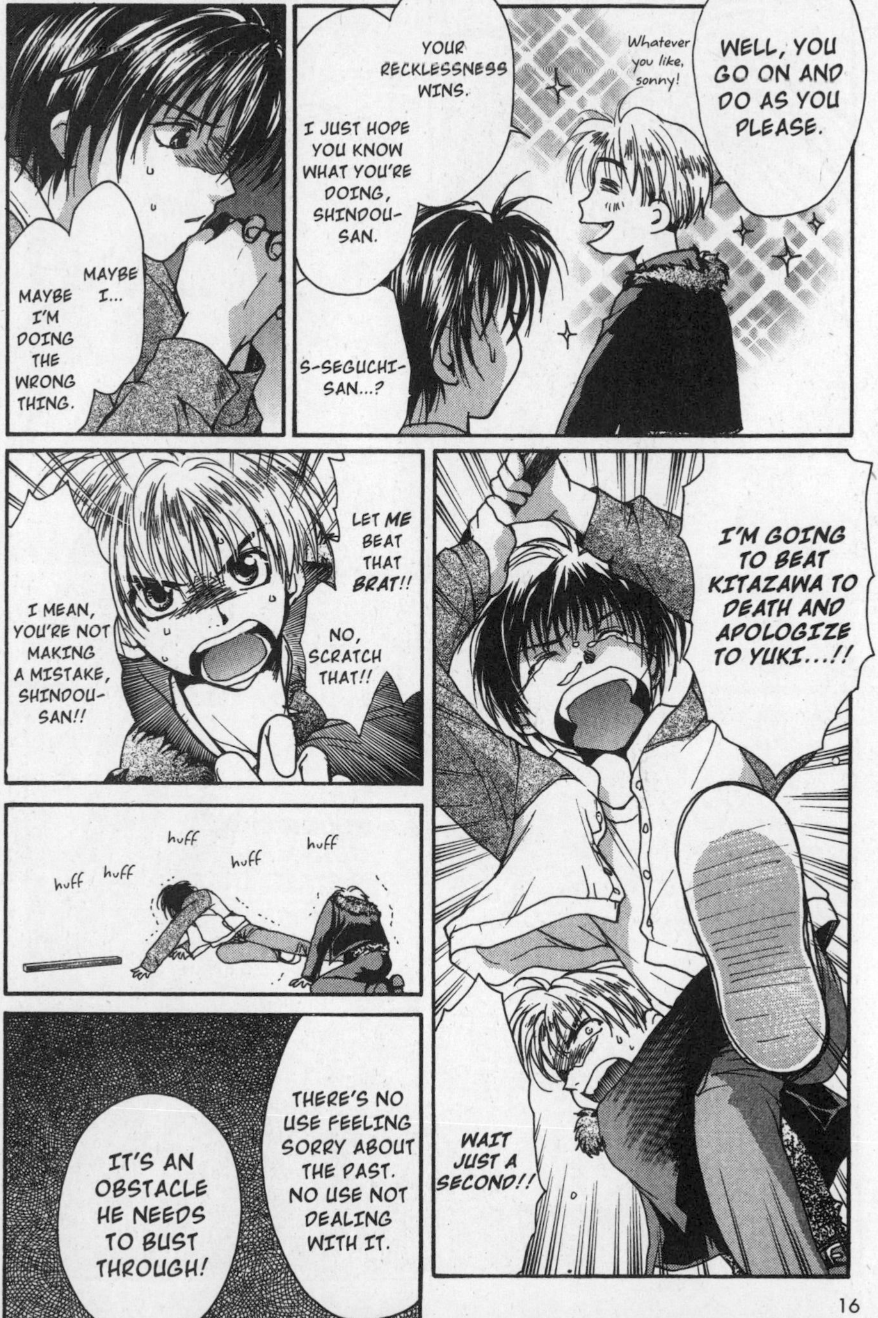
WELL, YOU GO ON AND DO AS YOU PLEASE.
Whatever you like, sonny!
YOUR RECKLESSNESS WINS.
I JUST HOPE YOU KNOW WHAT YOU'RE DOING, SHINDOU-SAN.
S-SEGUCHI-SAN...?
MAYBE I...
MAYBE I'M DOING THE WRONG THING.
I'M GOING TO BEAT KITAZAWA TO DEATH AND APOLOGIZE TO YUKI...!!
WAIT JUST A SECOND!!
LET ME BEAT THAT BRAT!!
NO, SCRATCH THAT!!
I MEAN, YOU'RE NOT MAKING A MISTAKE, SHINDOU-SAN!!
huff
huff
huff
huff
huff
THERE'S NO USE FEELING SORRY ABOUT THE PAST. NO USE NOT DEALING WITH IT.
IT'S AN OBSTACLE HE NEEDS TO BUST THROUGH!

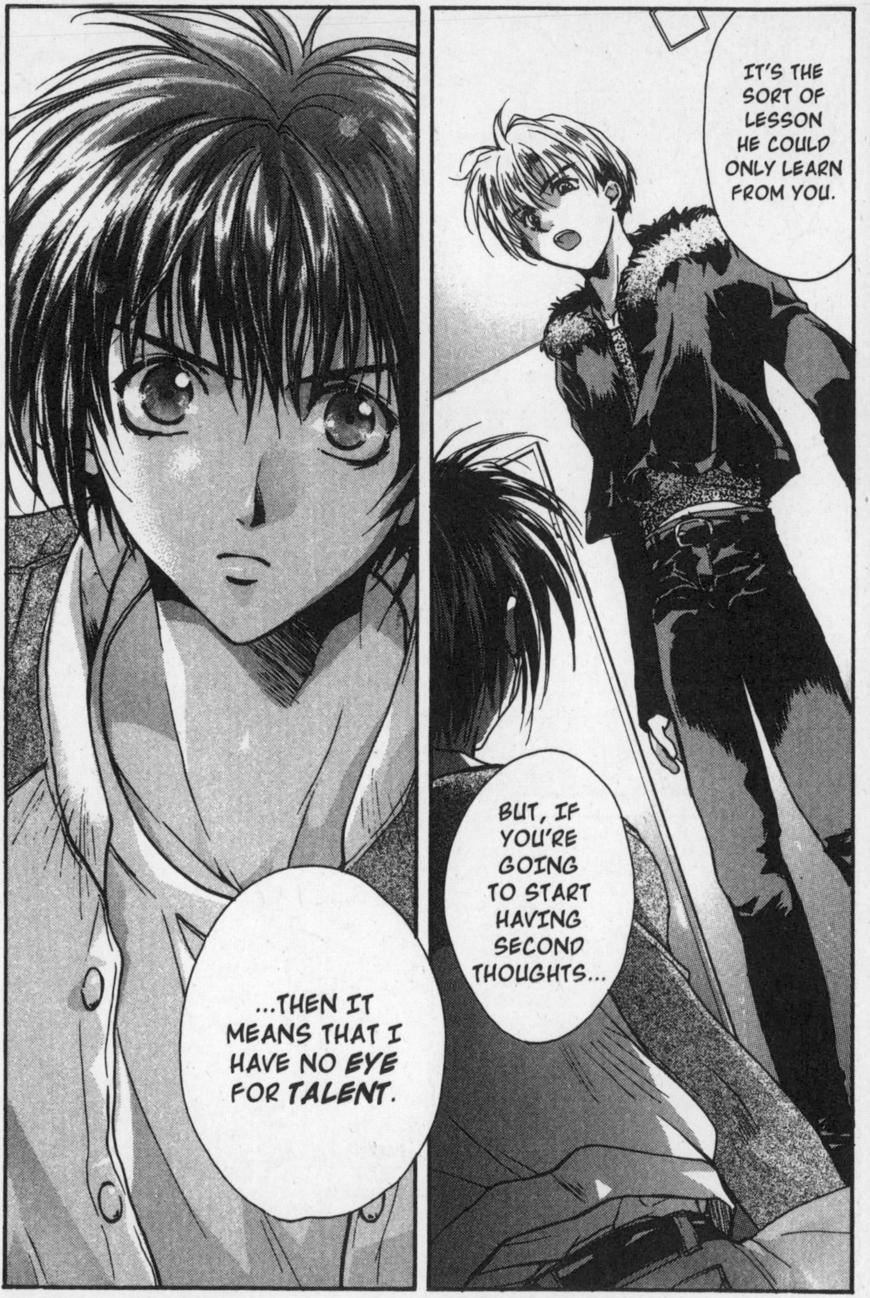
IT'S THE SORT OF LESSON HE COULD ONLY LEARN FROM YOU.
BUT, IF YOU'RE GOING TO START HAVING SECOND THOUGHTS...
...THEN IT MEANS THAT I HAVE NO *EYE* FOR *TALENT*.

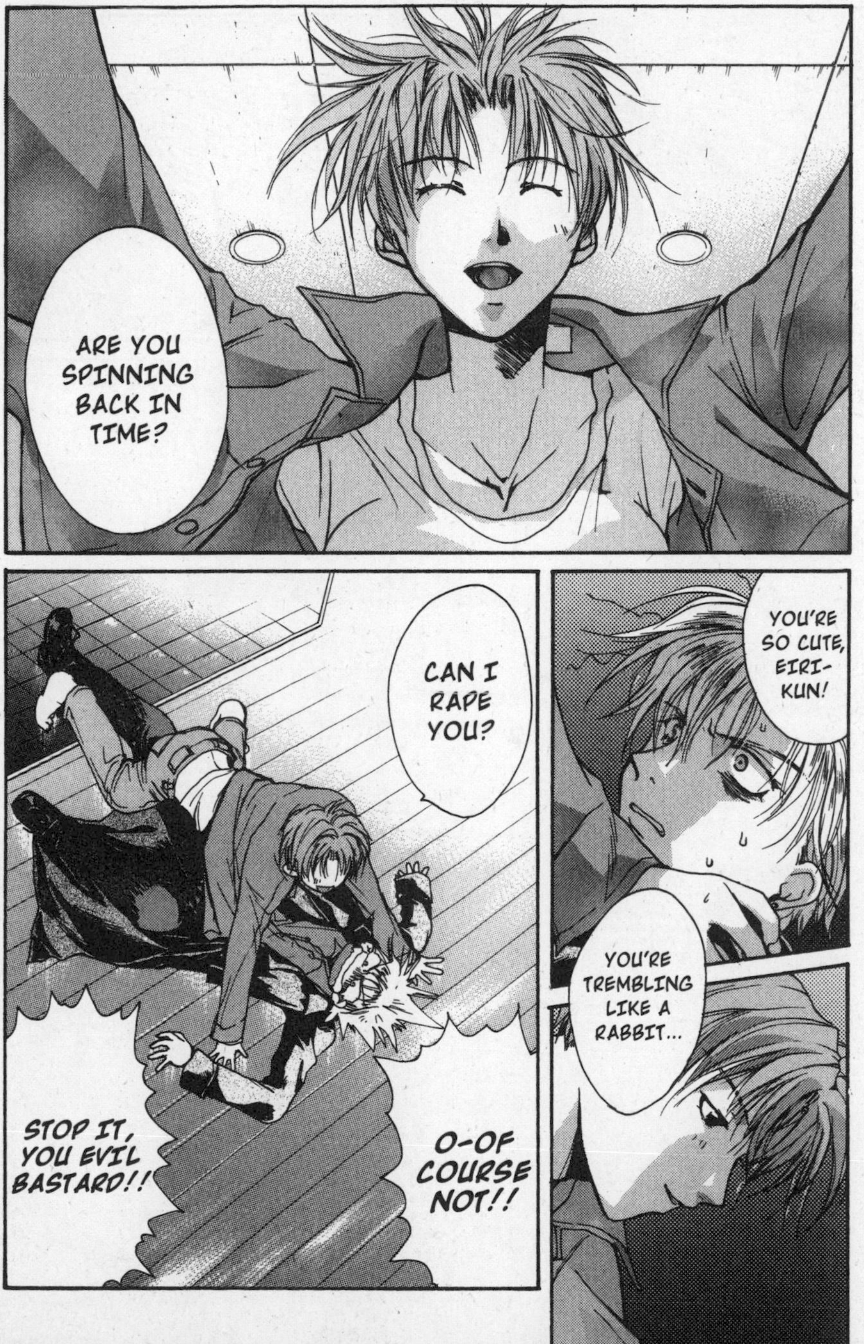
ARE YOU SPINNING BACK IN TIME?
YOU'RE SO CUTE, EIRI-KUN!
YOU'RE TREMBLING LIKE A RABBIT...
CAN I RAPE YOU?
O-OF COURSE NOT!!
STOP IT, YOU EVIL BASTARD!!

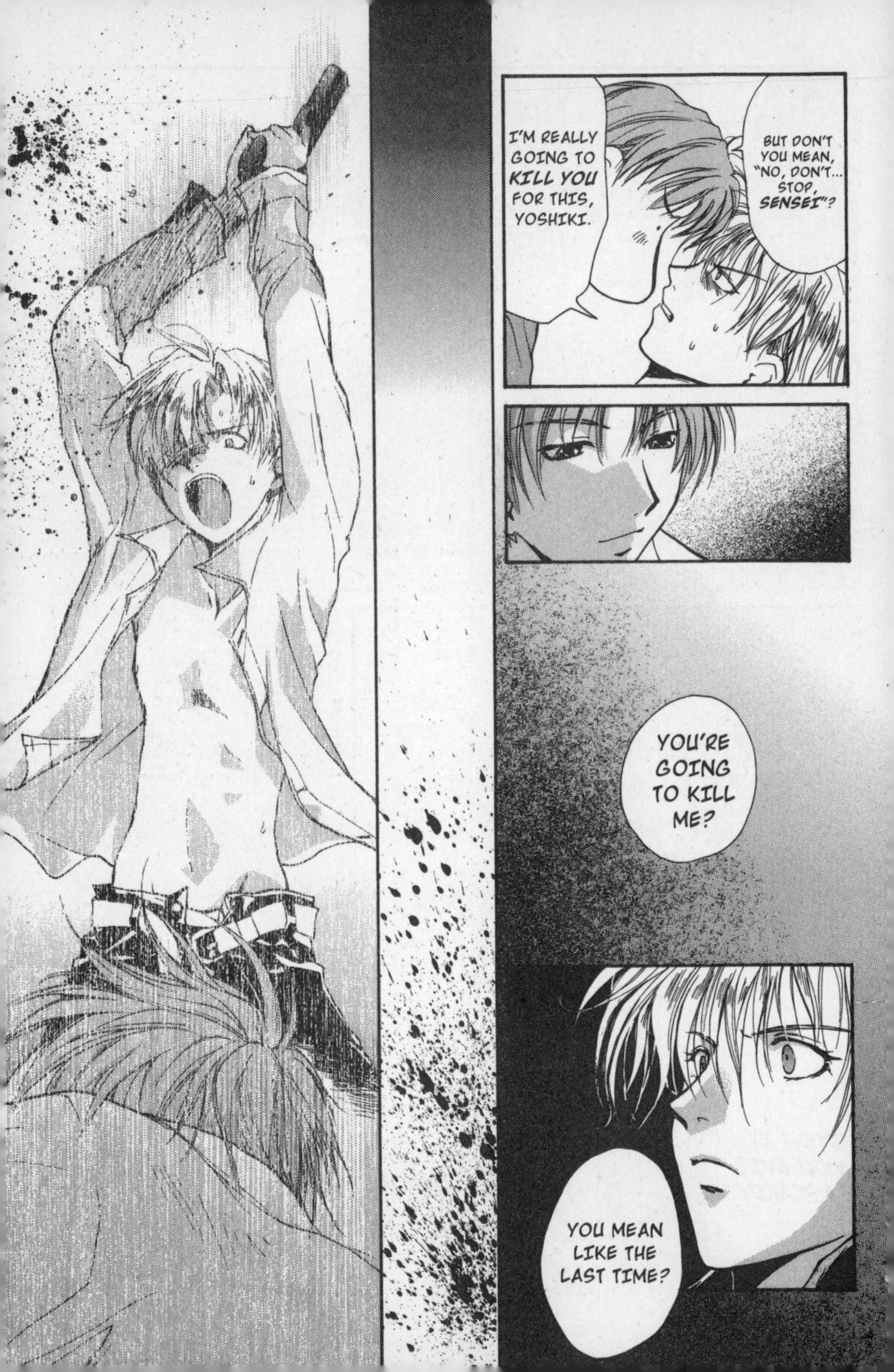
BUT DON'T YOU MEAN, "NO, DON'T... STOP, SENSEI"?
I'M REALLY GOING TO KILL YOU FOR THIS, YOSHIKI.
YOU'RE GOING TO KILL ME?
YOU MEAN LIKE THE LAST TIME?

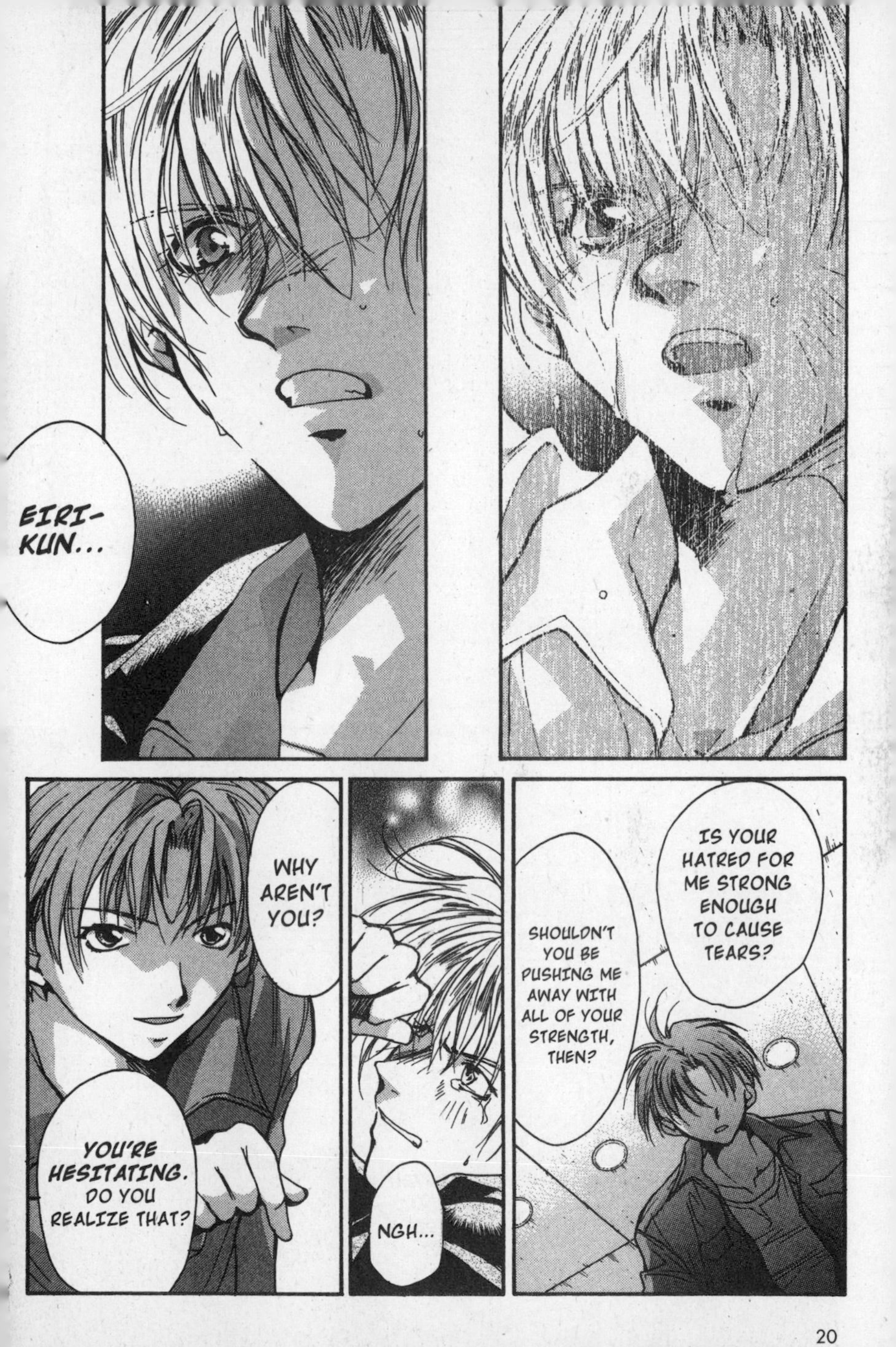
EIRI-KUN...
IS YOUR HATRED FOR ME STRONG ENOUGH TO CAUSE TEARS?
SHOULDN'T YOU BE PUSHING ME AWAY WITH ALL OF YOUR STRENGTH, THEN?
NGH...
WHY AREN'T YOU?
YOU'RE HESITATING. DO YOU REALIZE THAT?

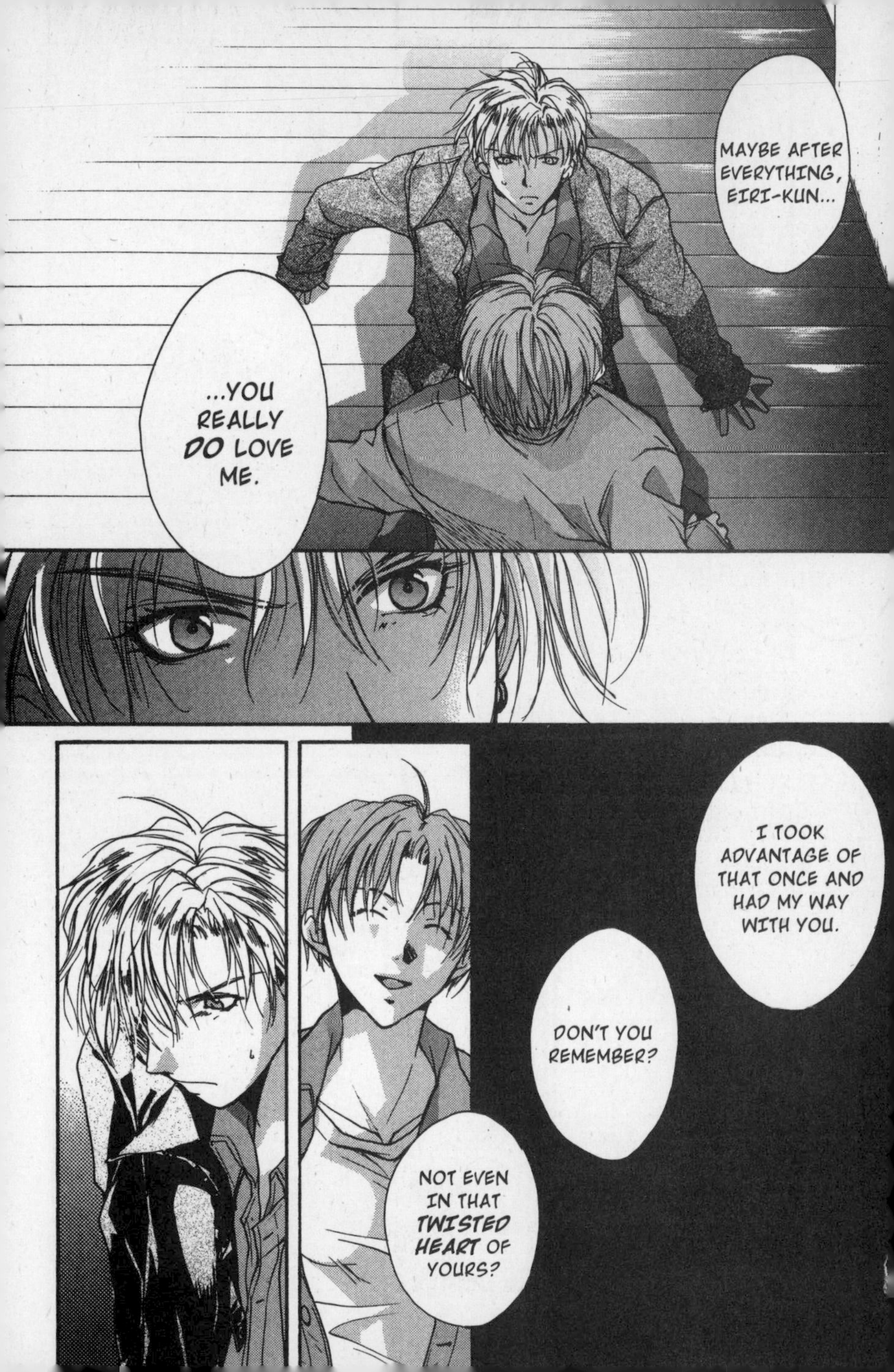
MAYBE AFTER EVERYTHING, EIRI-KUN...
...YOU REALLY DO LOVE ME.
I TOOK ADVANTAGE OF THAT ONCE AND HAD MY WAY WITH YOU.
DON'T YOU REMEMBER?
NOT EVEN IN THAT TWISTED HEART OF YOURS?

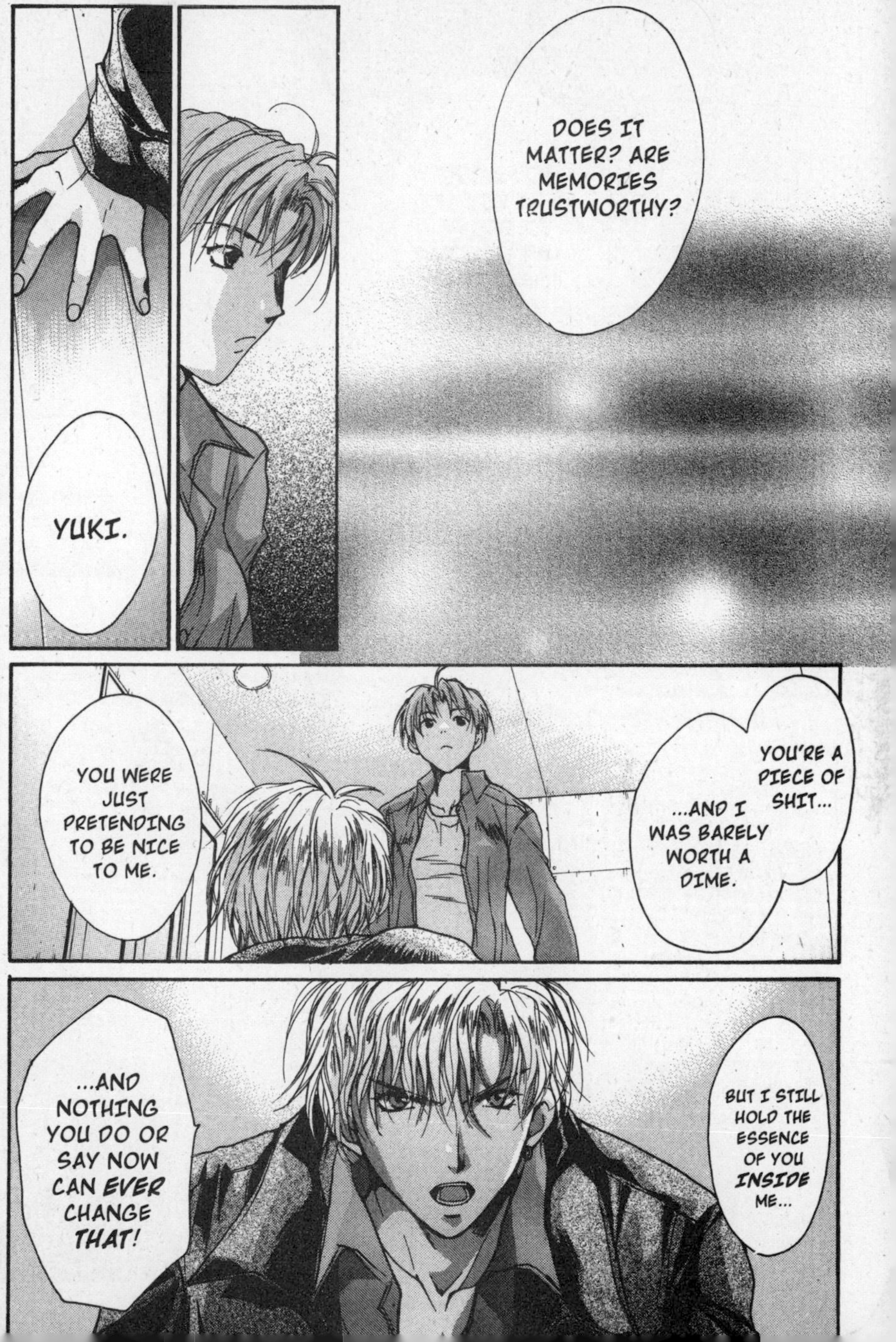
DOES IT MATTER? ARE MEMORIES TRUSTWORTHY?
YUKI.
YOU'RE A PIECE OF SHIT...
...AND I WAS BARELY WORTH A DIME.
YOU WERE JUST PRETENDING TO BE NICE TO ME.
BUT I STILL HOLD THE ESSENCE OF YOU INSIDE ME...
...AND NOTHING YOU DO OR SAY NOW CAN EVER CHANGE THAT!

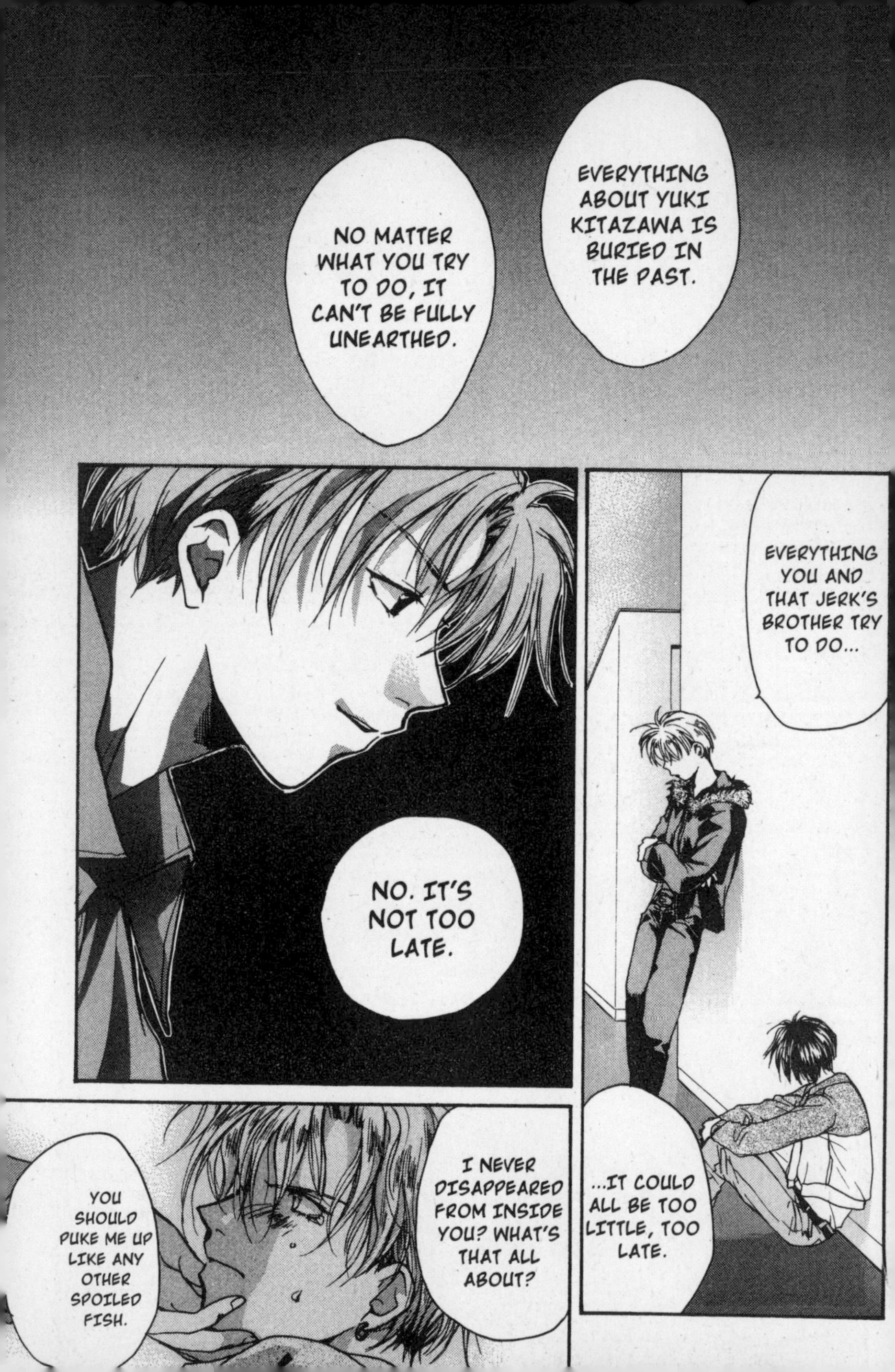
EVERYTHING ABOUT YUKI KITAZAWA IS BURIED IN THE PAST.
NO MATTER WHAT YOU TRY TO DO, IT CAN'T BE FULLY UNEARTHED.
EVERYTHING YOU AND THAT JERK'S BROTHER TRY TO DO...
...IT COULD ALL BE TOO LITTLE, TOO LATE.
NO. IT'S NOT TOO LATE.
I NEVER DISAPPEARED FROM INSIDE YOU? WHAT'S THAT ALL ABOUT?
YOU SHOULD PUKE ME UP LIKE ANY OTHER SPOILED FISH.

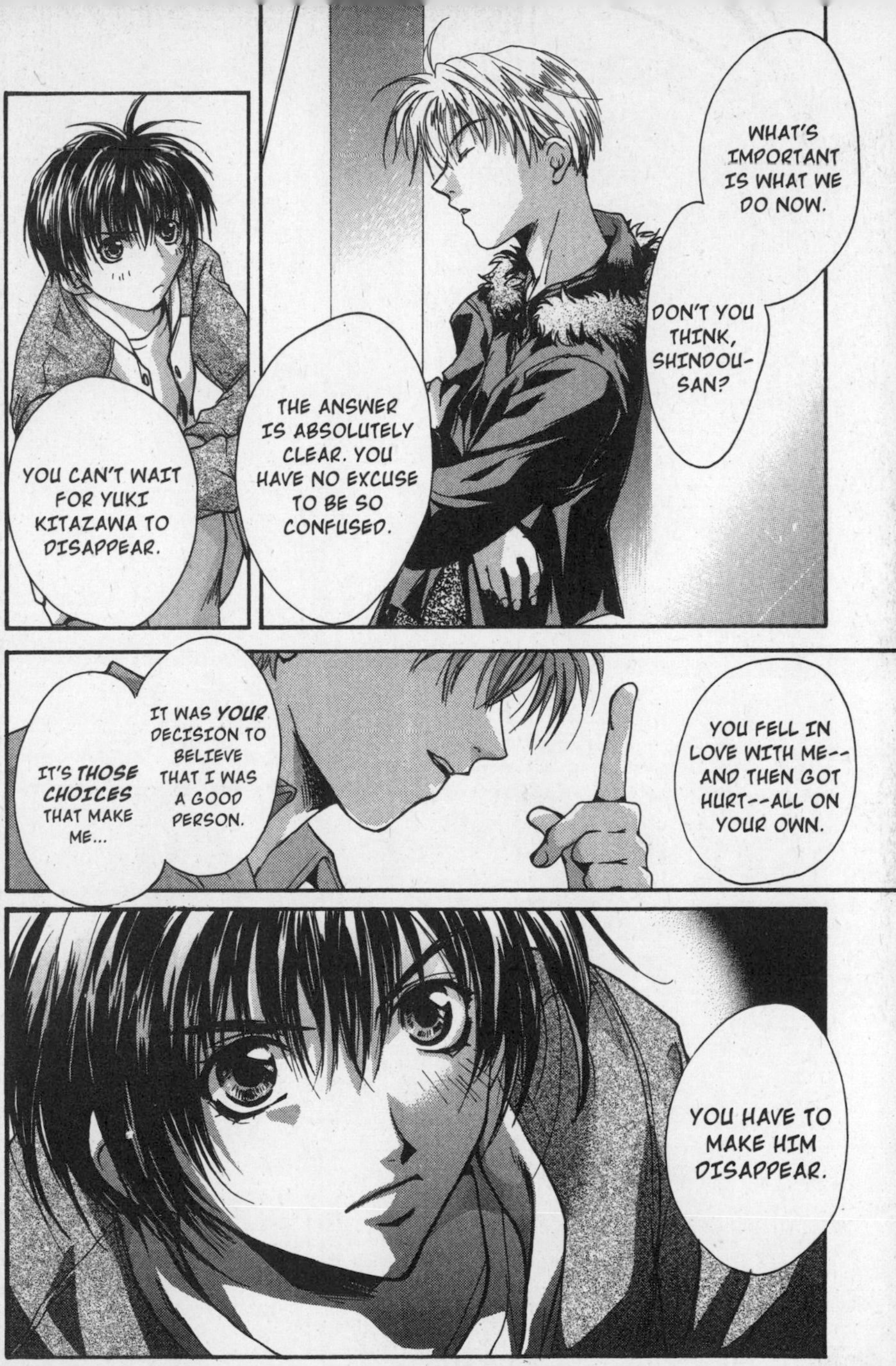
WHAT'S IMPORTANT IS WHAT WE DO NOW.
DON'T YOU THINK, SHINDOU-SAN?
THE ANSWER IS ABSOLUTELY CLEAR. YOU HAVE NO EXCUSE TO BE SO CONFUSED.
YOU CAN'T WAIT FOR YUKI KITAZAWA TO DISAPPEAR.
YOU FELL IN LOVE WITH ME--AND THEN GOT HURT--ALL ON YOUR OWN.
IT WAS *YOUR* DECISION TO BELIEVE THAT I WAS A GOOD PERSON.
IT'S *THOSE CHOICES* THAT MAKE ME...
YOU HAVE TO MAKE HIM DISAPPEAR.

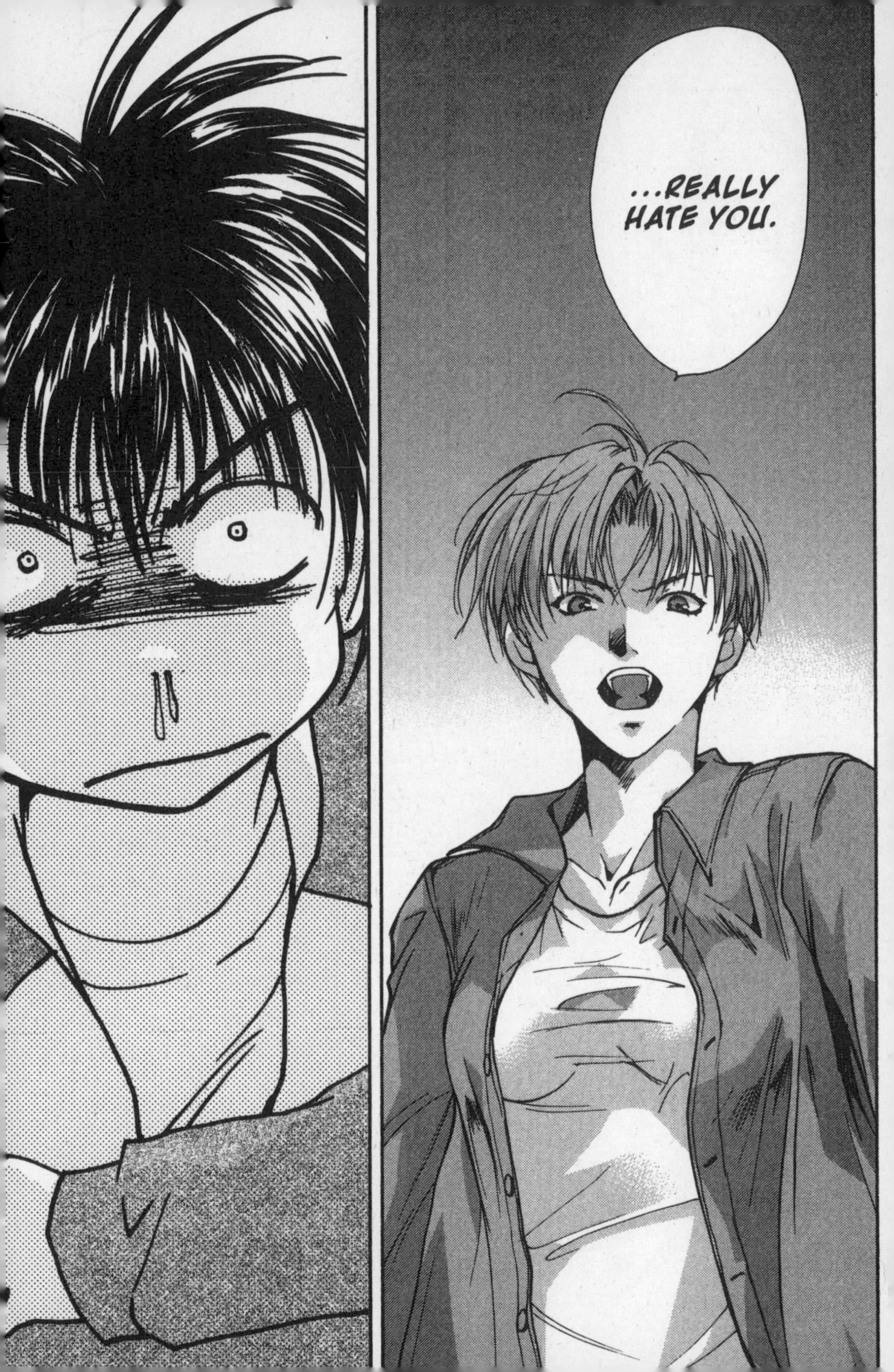
...REALLY HATE YOU.

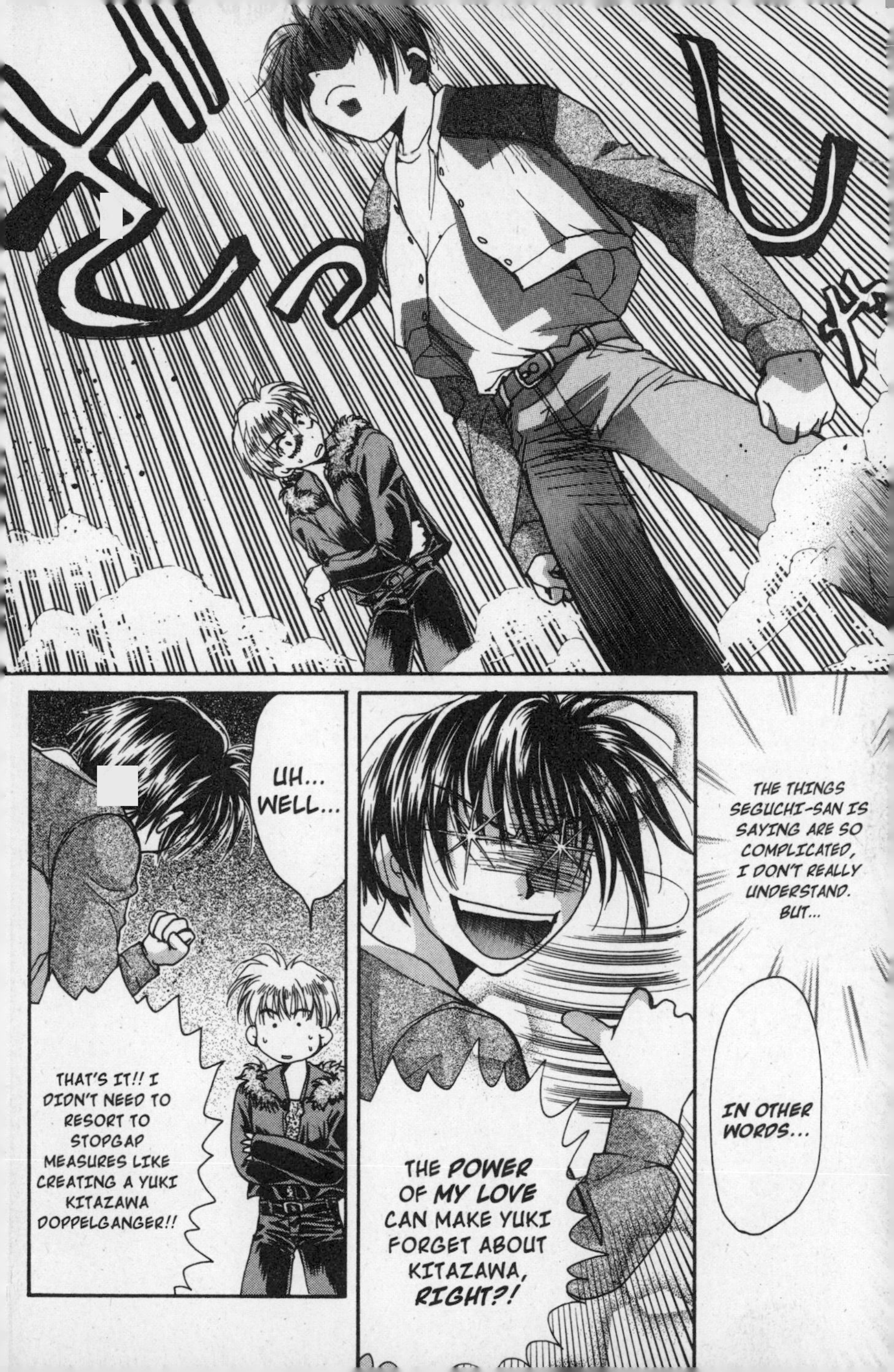
THE THINGS SEGUCHI-SAN IS SAYING ARE SO COMPLICATED, I DON'T REALLY UNDERSTAND. BUT...
IN OTHER WORDS...
THE POWER OF MY LOVE CAN MAKE YUKI FORGET ABOUT KITAZAWA, RIGHT?!
UH... WELL...
THAT'S IT!! I DIDN'T NEED TO RESORT TO STOPGAP MEASURES LIKE CREATING A YUKI KITAZAWA DOPPELGANGER!!

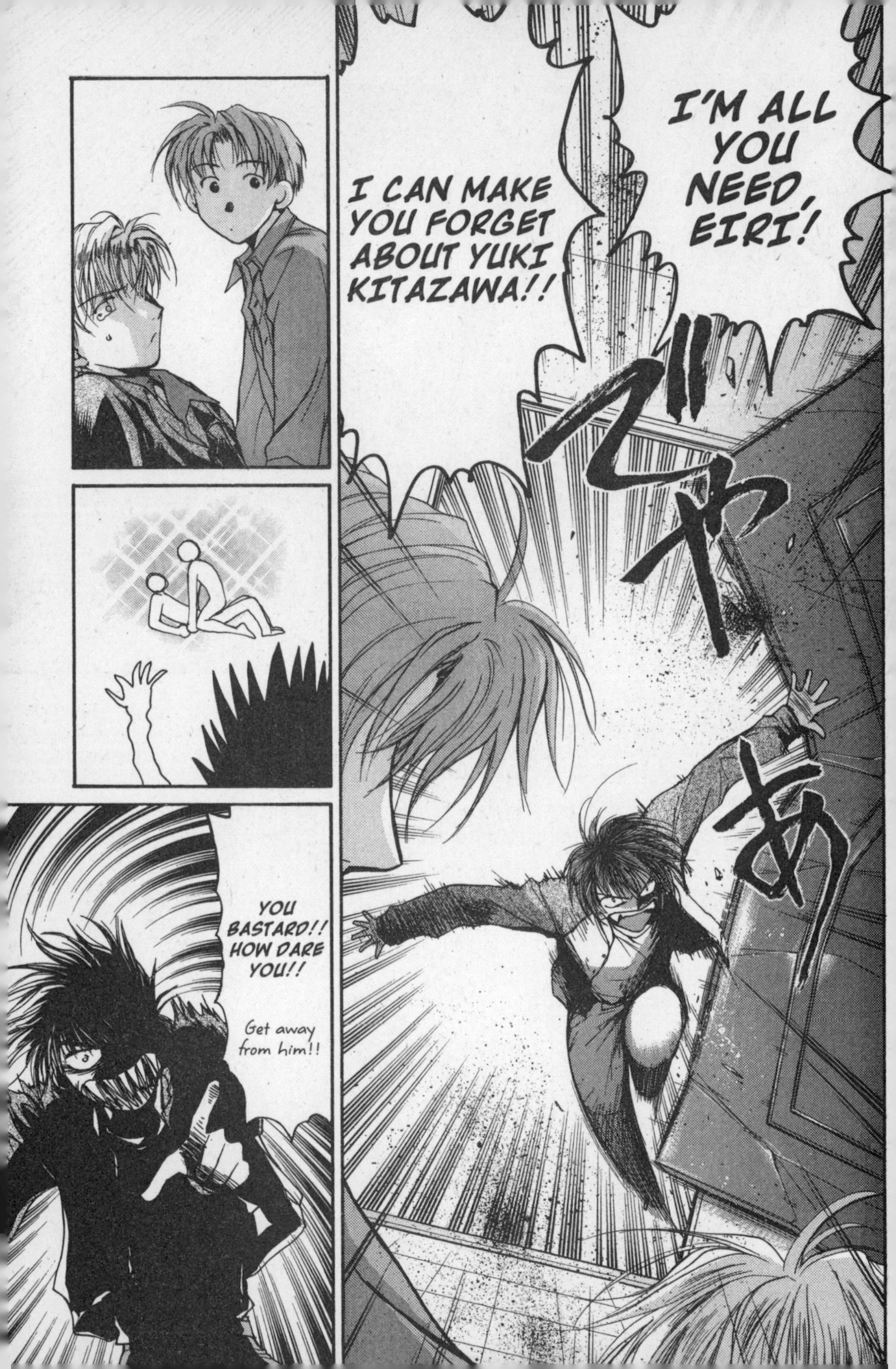
I'M ALL YOU NEED, EIRI!
I CAN MAKE YOU FORGET ABOUT YUKI KITAZAWA!!
YOU BASTARD!! HOW DARE YOU!!
Get away from him!!

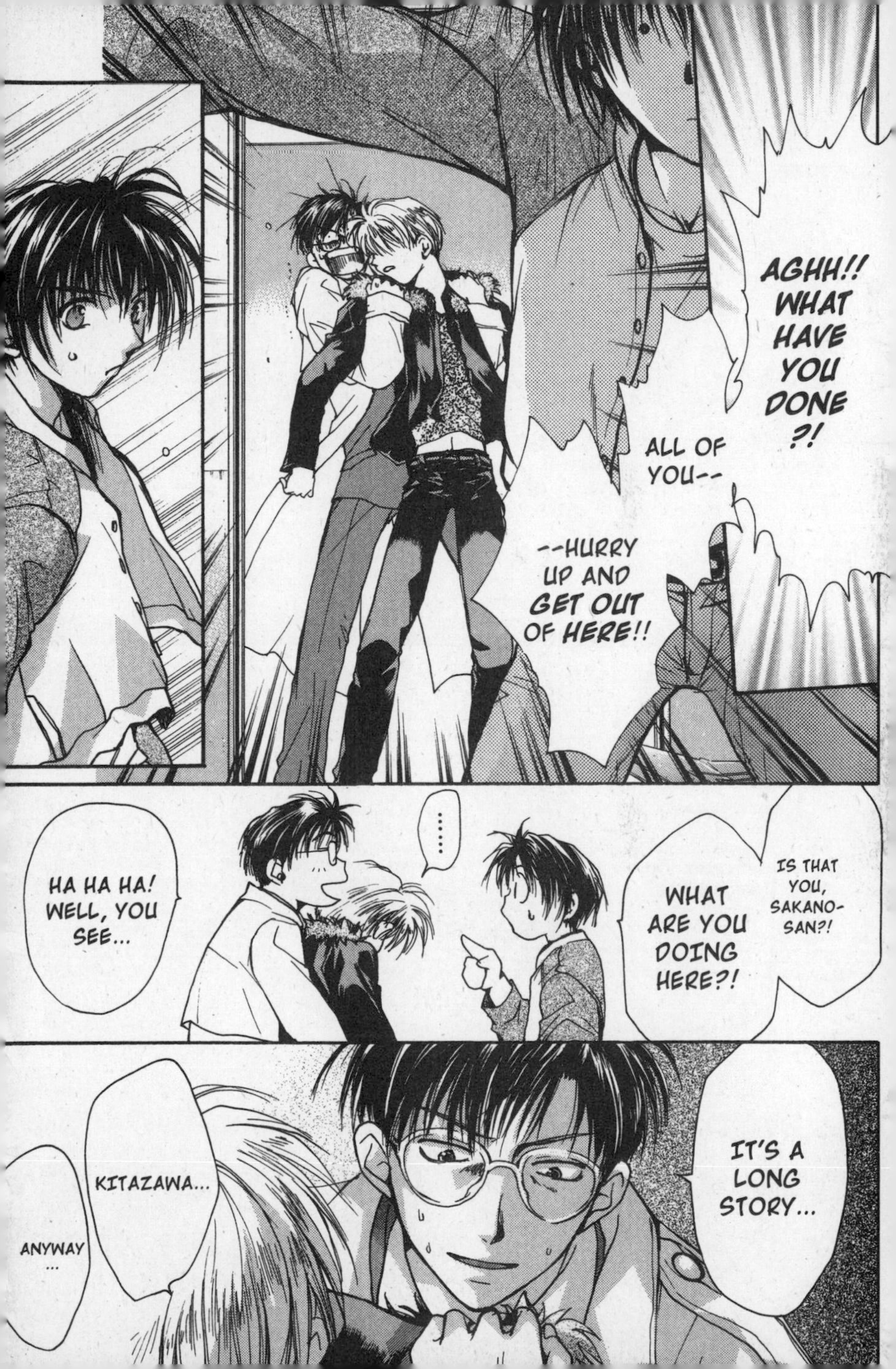
AGHH!! WHAT HAVE YOU DONE?!
ALL OF YOU--
--HURRY UP AND GET OUT OF HERE!!
IS THAT YOU, SAKANO-SAN?!
WHAT ARE YOU DOING HERE?!
......
HA HA HA! WELL, YOU SEE...
IT'S A LONG STORY...
KITAZAWA...
ANYWAY ...

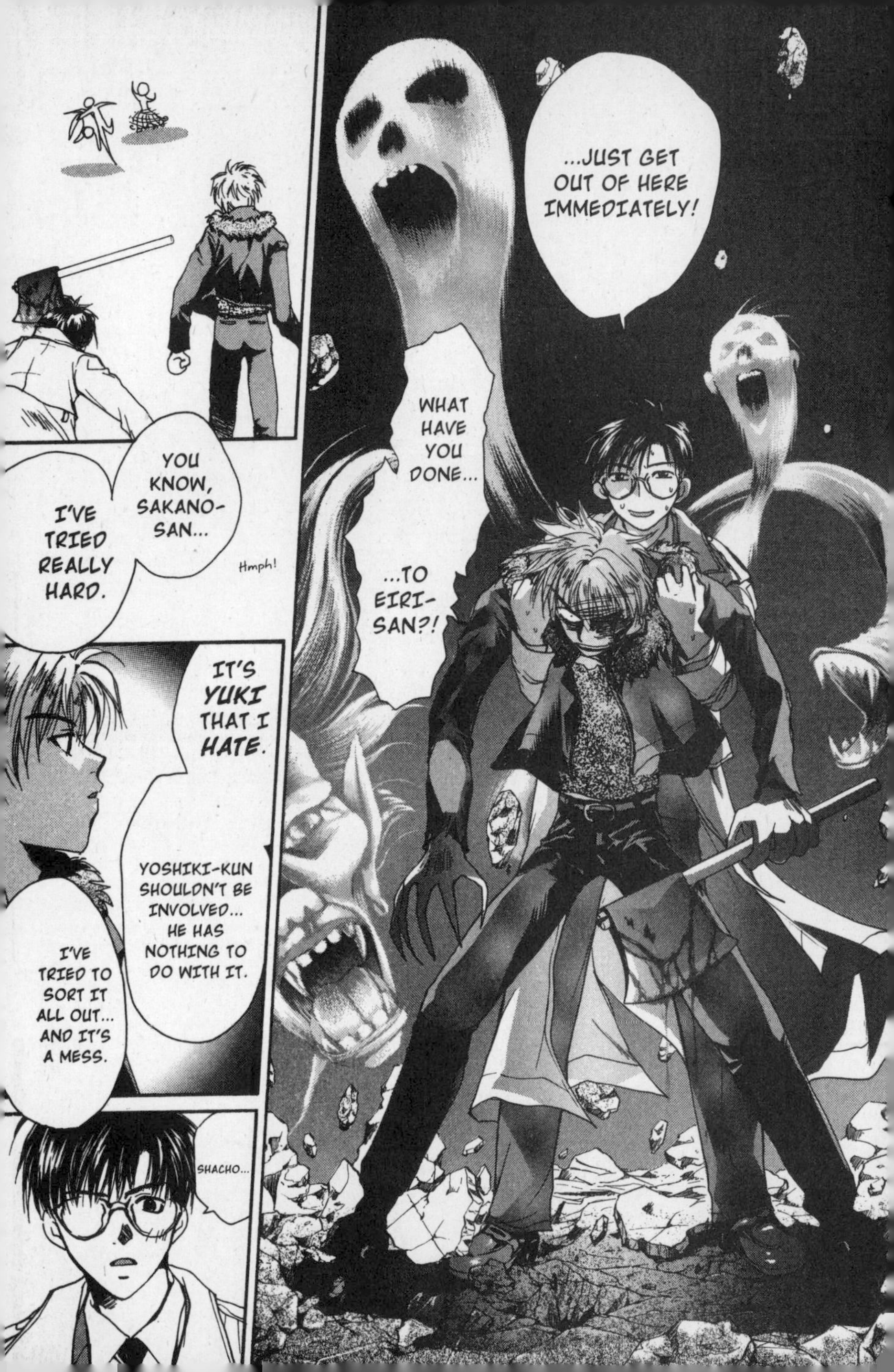
...JUST GET OUT OF HERE IMMEDIATELY!
WHAT HAVE YOU DONE...
...TO EIRI-SAN?!
YOU KNOW, SAKANO-SAN...
Hmph!
I'VE TRIED REALLY HARD.
IT'S YUKI THAT I HATE.
YOSHIKI-KUN SHOULDN'T BE INVOLVED... HE HAS NOTHING TO DO WITH IT.
I'VE TRIED TO SORT IT ALL OUT... AND IT'S A MESS.
SHACHO...

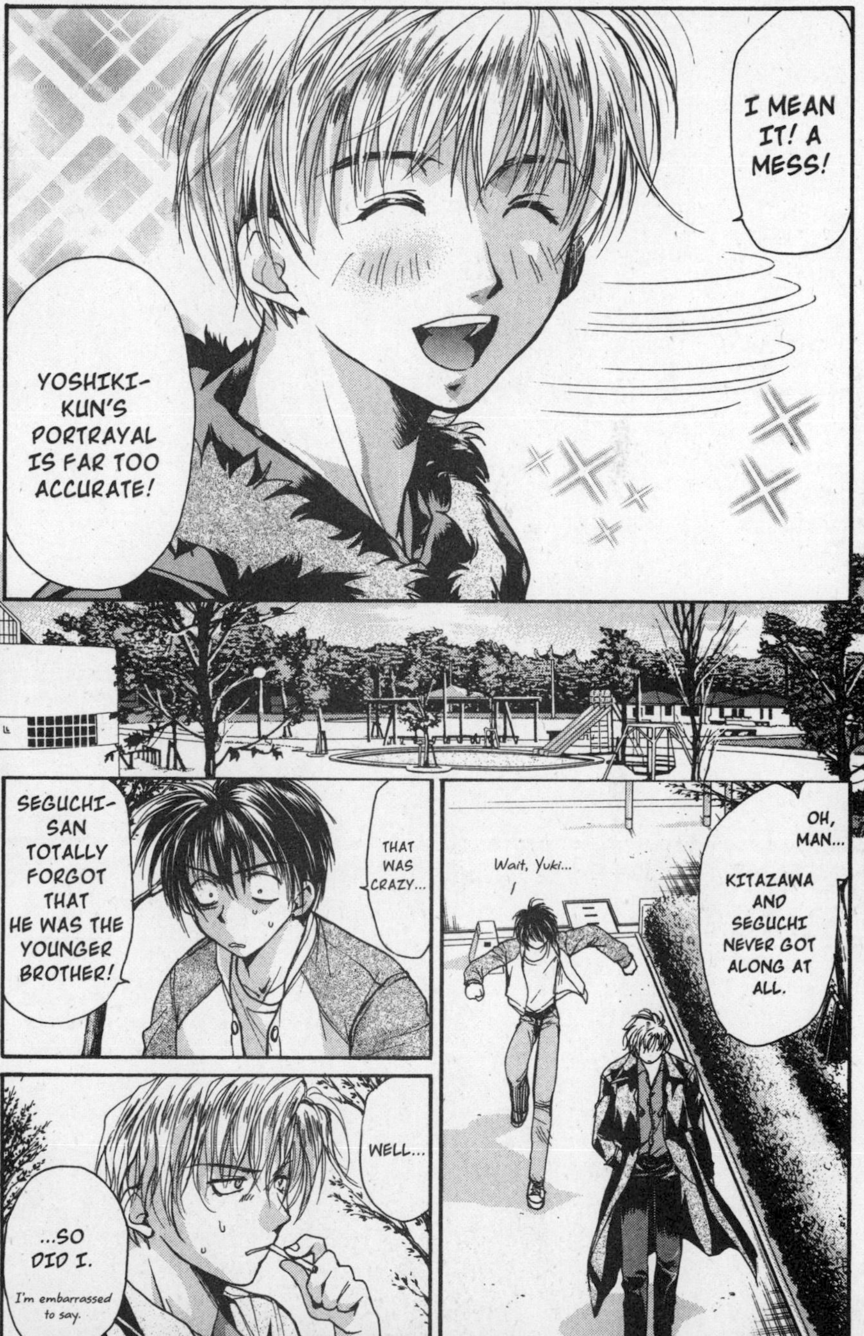
I MEAN IT! A MESS!
YOSHIKI-KUN'S PORTRAYAL IS FAR TOO ACCURATE!
OH, MAN...
KITAZAWA AND SEGUCHI NEVER GOT ALONG AT ALL.
Wait, Yuki...
THAT WAS CRAZY...
SEGUCHI-SAN TOTALLY FORGOT THAT HE WAS THE YOUNGER BROTHER!
WELL...
...SO DID I.
I'm embarrassed to say.

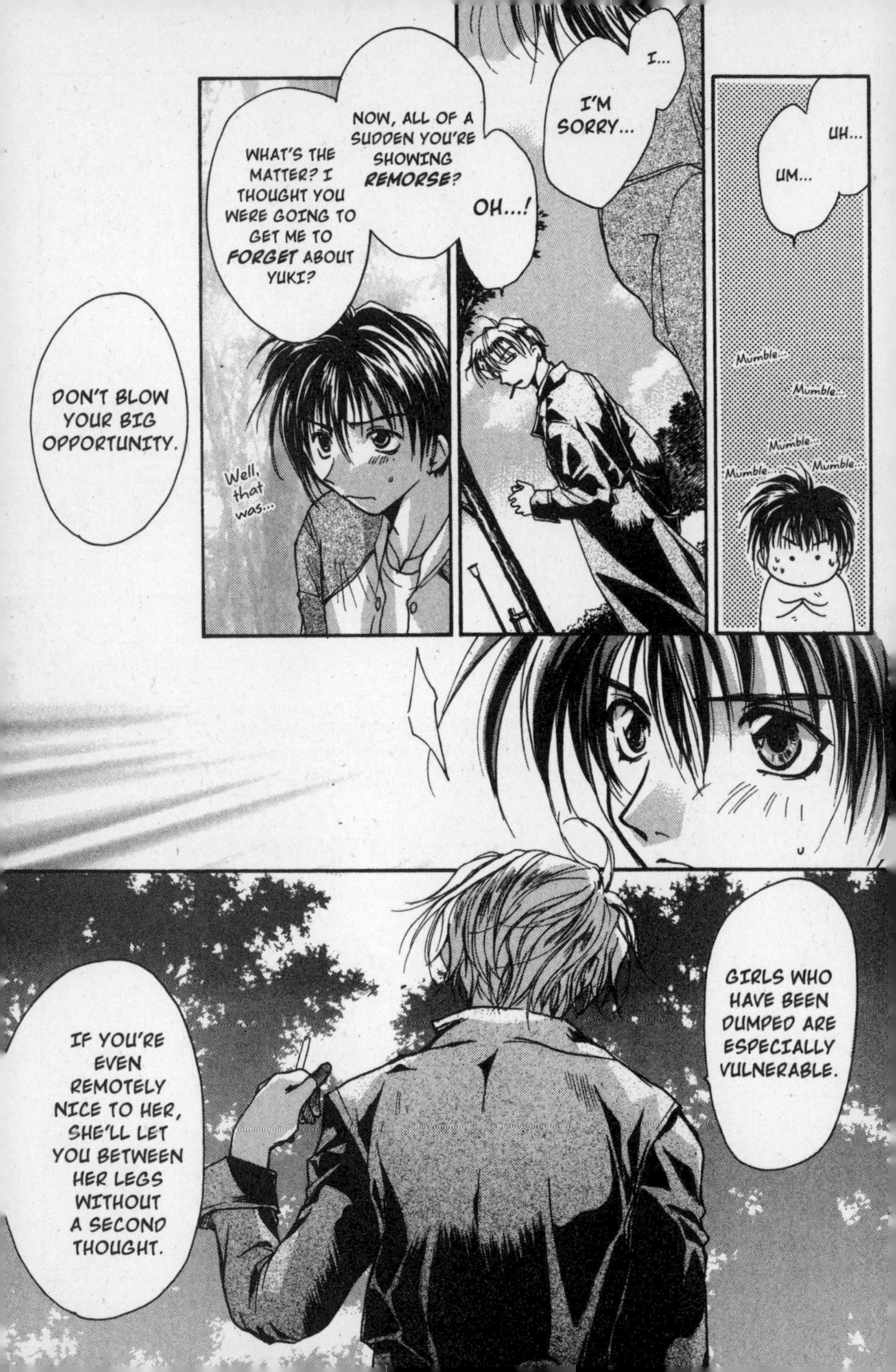
UH...
UM...
Mumble... Mumble... Mumble... Mumble...
I...
I'M SORRY...
OH...!
NOW, ALL OF A SUDDEN YOU'RE SHOWING REMORSE?
WHAT'S THE MATTER? I THOUGHT YOU WERE GOING TO GET ME TO FORGET ABOUT YUKI?
Well, that was...
DON'T BLOW YOUR BIG OPPORTUNITY.
GIRLS WHO HAVE BEEN DUMPED ARE ESPECIALLY VULNERABLE.
IF YOU'RE EVEN REMOTELY NICE TO HER, SHE'LL LET YOU BETWEEN HER LEGS WITHOUT A SECOND THOUGHT.

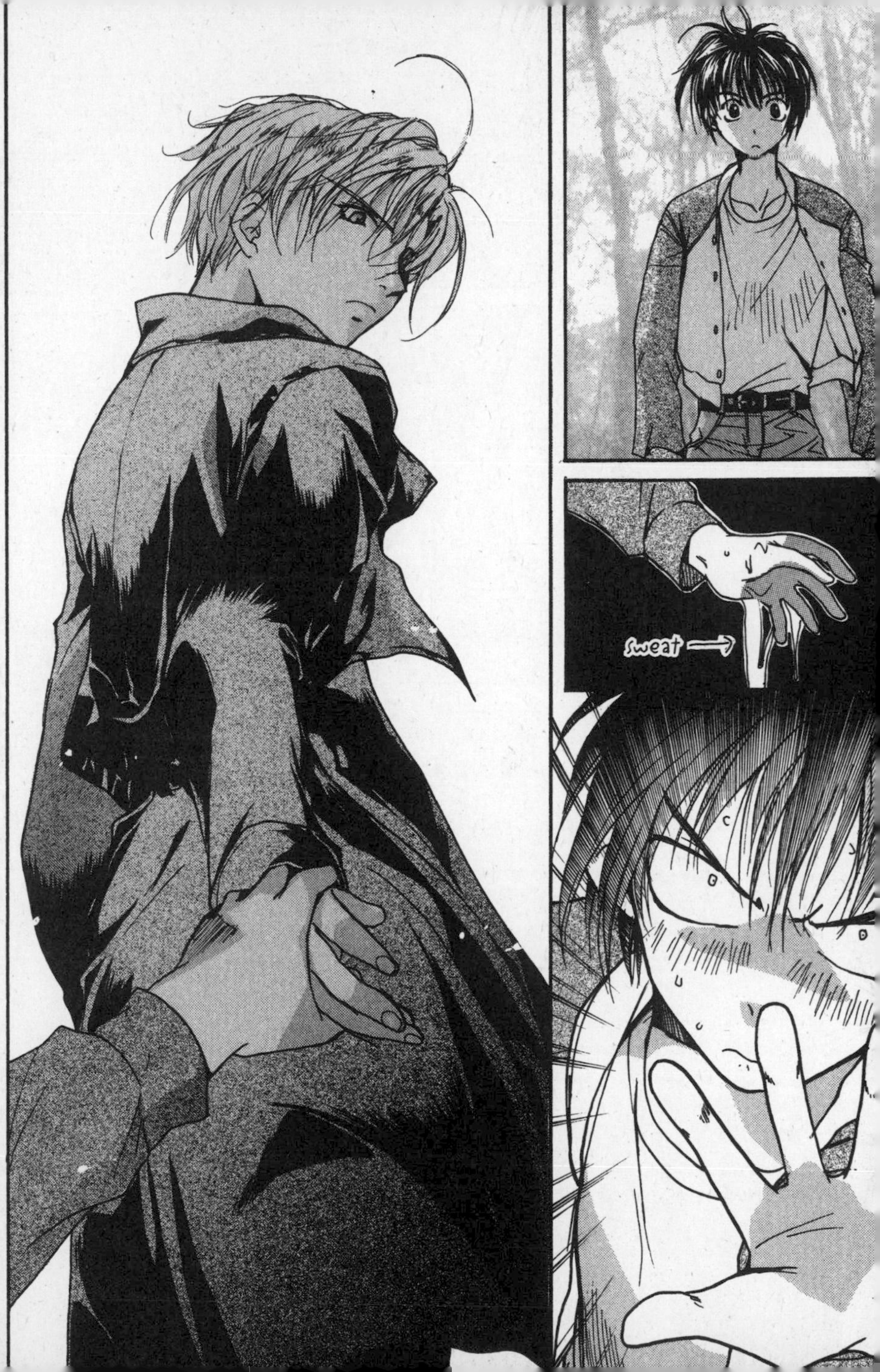
sweat

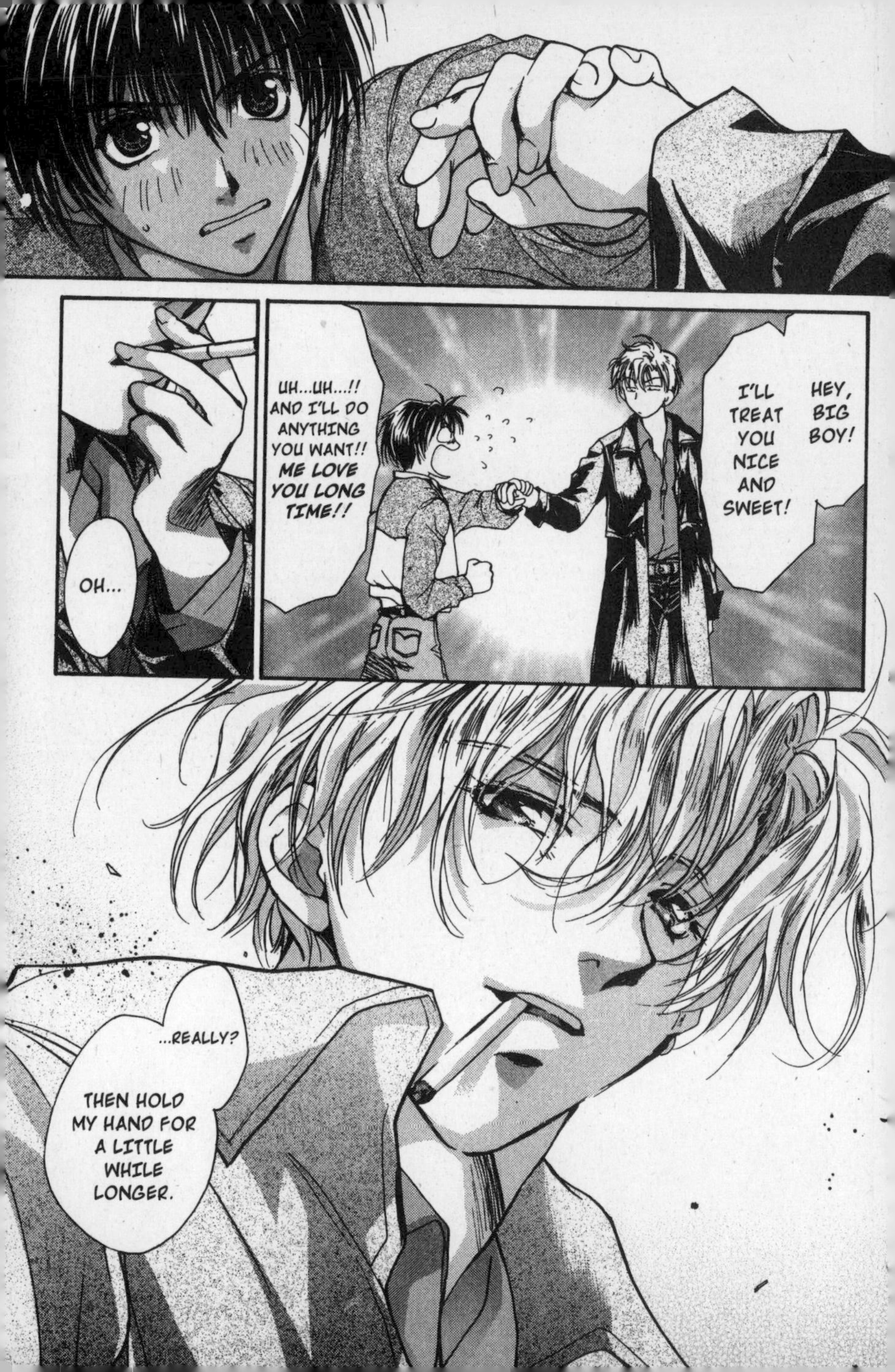
HEY, BIG BOY!
I'LL TREAT YOU NICE AND SWEET!
UH...UH...!! AND I'LL DO ANYTHING YOU WANT!! ME LOVE YOU LONG TIME!!
OH...
...REALLY?
THEN HOLD MY HAND FOR A LITTLE WHILE LONGER.

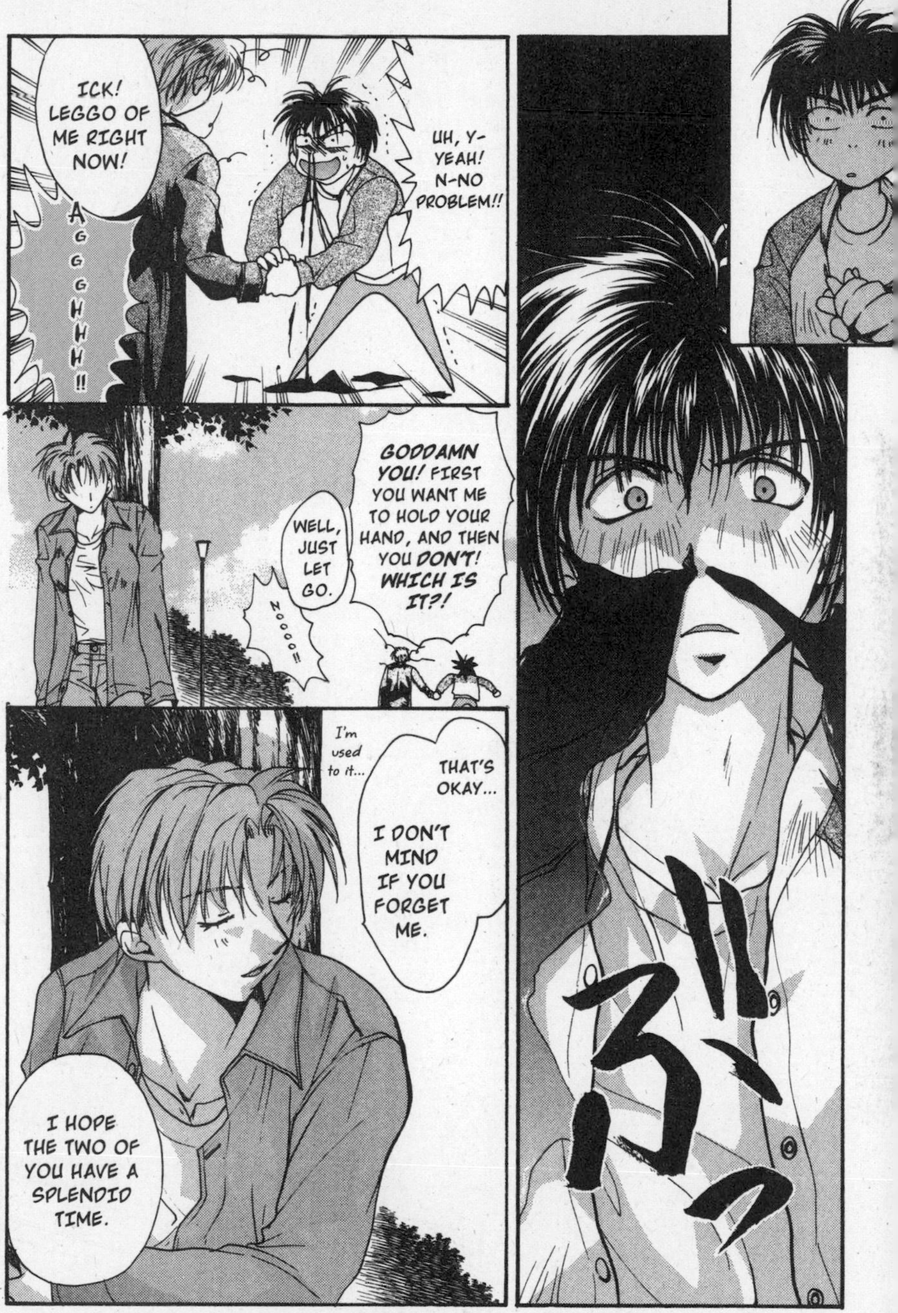
UH, Y-YEAH! N-NO PROBLEM!!
ICK! LEGGO OF ME RIGHT NOW!
AGGGHHHH!!
GODDAMN YOU! FIRST YOU WANT ME TO HOLD YOUR HAND, AND THEN YOU DON'T! WHICH IS IT?!
WELL, JUST LET GO.
NOOOOO!!
THAT'S OKAY...
I DON'T MIND IF YOU FORGET ME.
I'm used to it...
I HOPE THE TWO OF YOU HAVE A SPLENDID TIME.

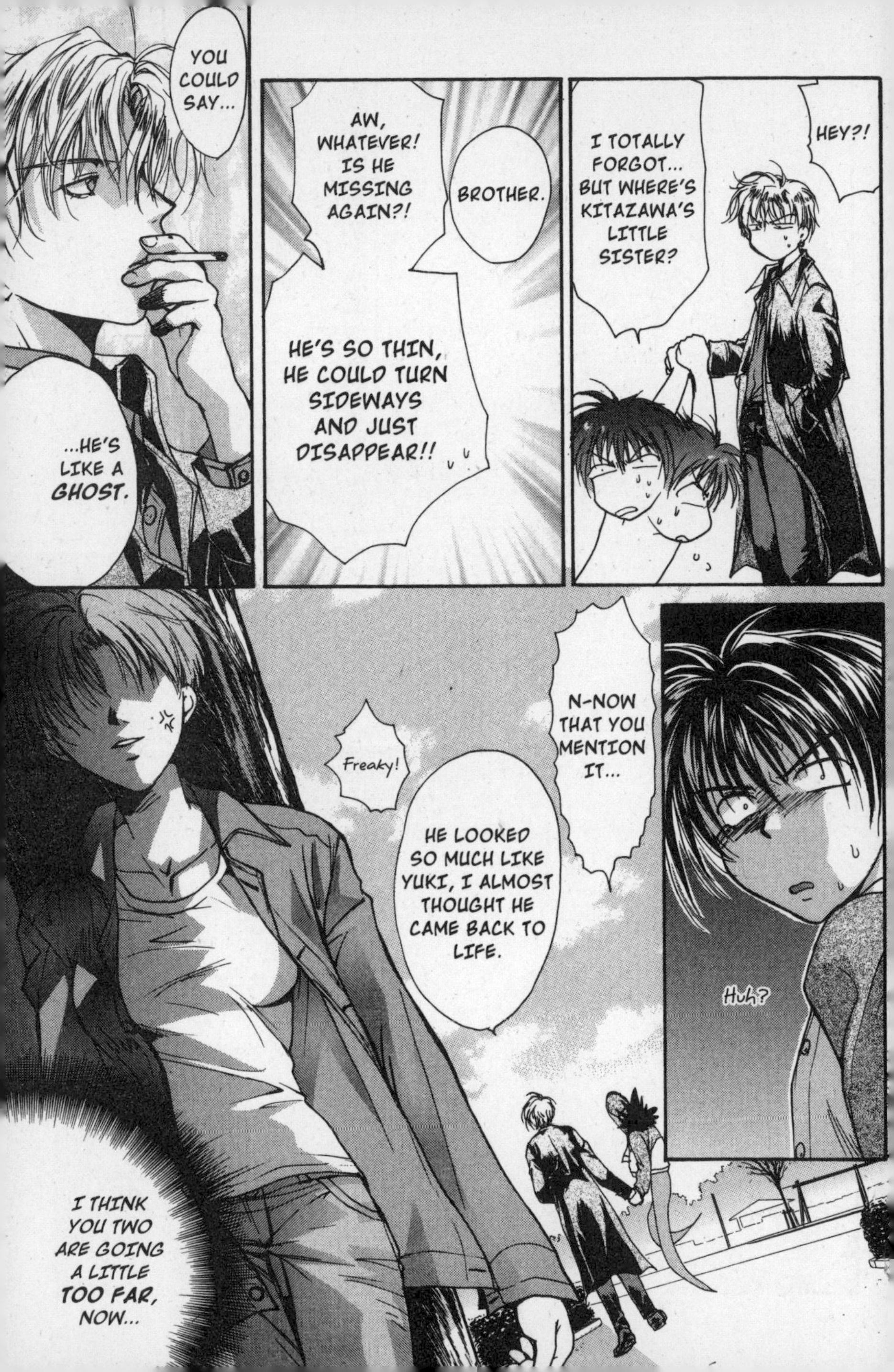
HEY?!
I TOTALLY FORGOT... BUT WHERE'S KITAZAWA'S LITTLE SISTER?
BROTHER.
AW, WHATEVER! IS HE MISSING AGAIN?!
HE'S SO THIN, HE COULD TURN SIDEWAYS AND JUST DISAPPEAR!!
YOU COULD SAY...
...HE'S LIKE A GHOST.
N-NOW THAT YOU MENTION IT...
Huh?
Freaky!
HE LOOKED SO MUCH LIKE YUKI, I ALMOST THOUGHT HE CAME BACK TO LIFE.
I THINK YOU TWO ARE GOING A LITTLE TOO FAR, NOW...

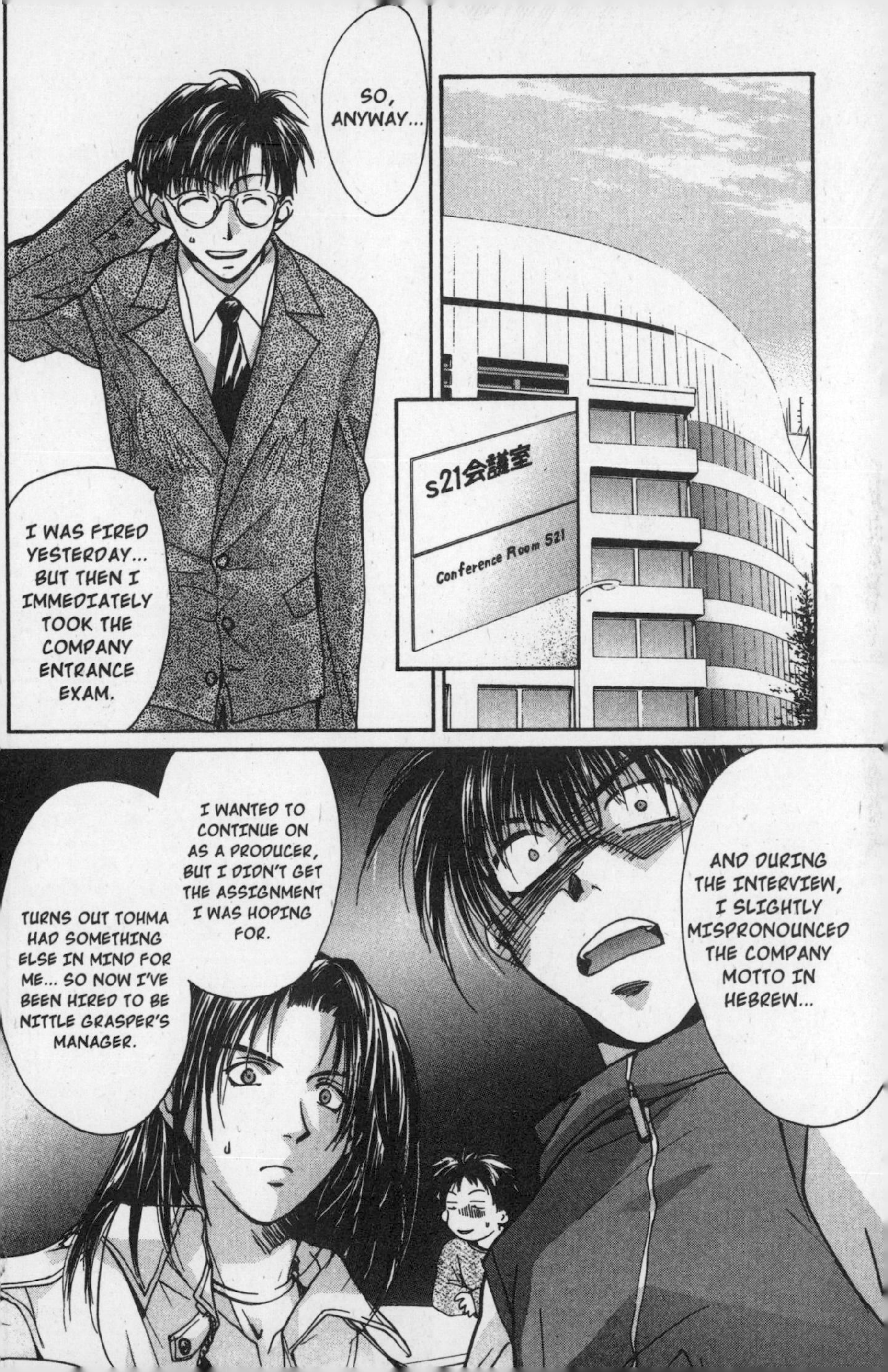
s21会議室
Conference Room S21
SO, ANYWAY...
I WAS FIRED YESTERDAY... BUT THEN I IMMEDIATELY TOOK THE COMPANY ENTRANCE EXAM.
AND DURING THE INTERVIEW, I SLIGHTLY MISPRONOUNCED THE COMPANY MOTTO IN HEBREW...
I WANTED TO CONTINUE ON AS A PRODUCER, BUT I DIDN'T GET THE ASSIGNMENT I WAS HOPING FOR.
TURNS OUT TOHMA HAD SOMETHING ELSE IN MIND FOR ME... SO NOW I'VE BEEN HIRED TO BE NITTLE GRASPER'S MANAGER.

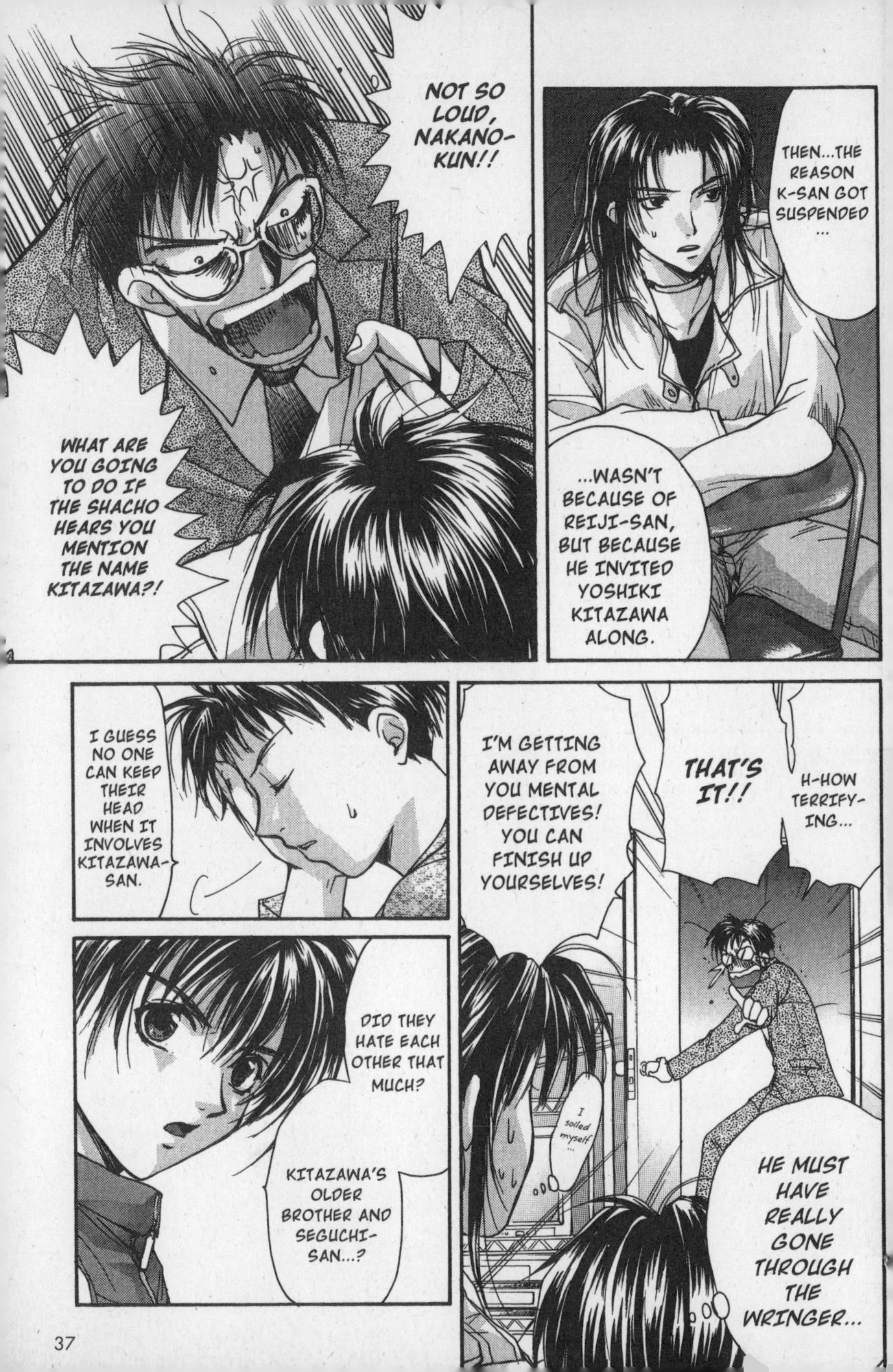
THEN...THE REASON K-SAN GOT SUSPENDED ...
...WASN'T BECAUSE OF REIJI-SAN, BUT BECAUSE HE INVITED YOSHIKI KITAZAWA ALONG.
NOT SO LOUD, NAKANO-KUN!!
WHAT ARE YOU GOING TO DO IF THE SHACHO HEARS YOU MENTION THE NAME KITAZAWA?!
H-HOW TERRIFY-ING...
THAT'S IT!!
I'M GETTING AWAY FROM YOU MENTAL DEFECTIVES! YOU CAN FINISH UP YOURSELVES!
I soiled myself ...
HE MUST HAVE REALLY GONE THROUGH THE WRINGER...
I GUESS NO ONE CAN KEEP THEIR HEAD WHEN IT INVOLVES KITAZAWA-SAN.
DID THEY HATE EACH OTHER THAT MUCH?
KITAZAWA'S OLDER BROTHER AND SEGUCHI-SAN...?

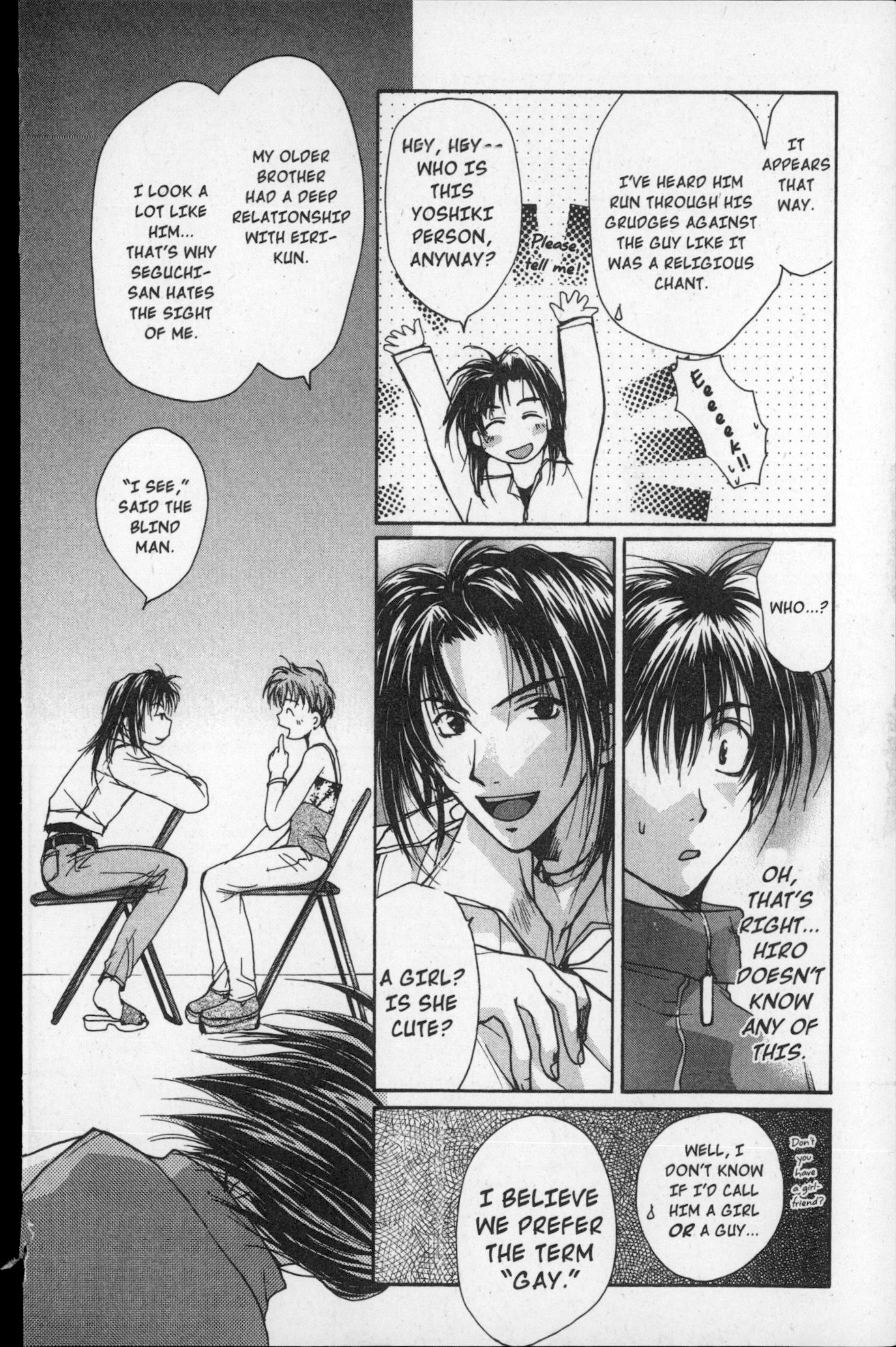
IT APPEARS THAT WAY.
I'VE HEARD HIM RUN THROUGH HIS GRUDGES AGAINST THE GUY LIKE IT WAS A RELIGIOUS CHANT.
HEY, HEY-- WHO IS THIS YOSHIKI PERSON, ANYWAY?
Please tell me!
Eeeeek!!
WHO...?
OH, THAT'S RIGHT... HIRO DOESN'T KNOW ANY OF THIS.
A GIRL? IS SHE CUTE?
Don't you have a girlfriend?
WELL, I DON'T KNOW IF I'D CALL HIM A GIRL OR A GUY...
I BELIEVE WE PREFER THE TERM "GAY."
MY OLDER BROTHER HAD A DEEP RELATIONSHIP WITH EIRI-KUN.
I LOOK A LOT LIKE HIM... THAT'S WHY SEGUCHI-SAN HATES THE SIGHT OF ME.
"I SEE," SAID THE BLIND MAN.

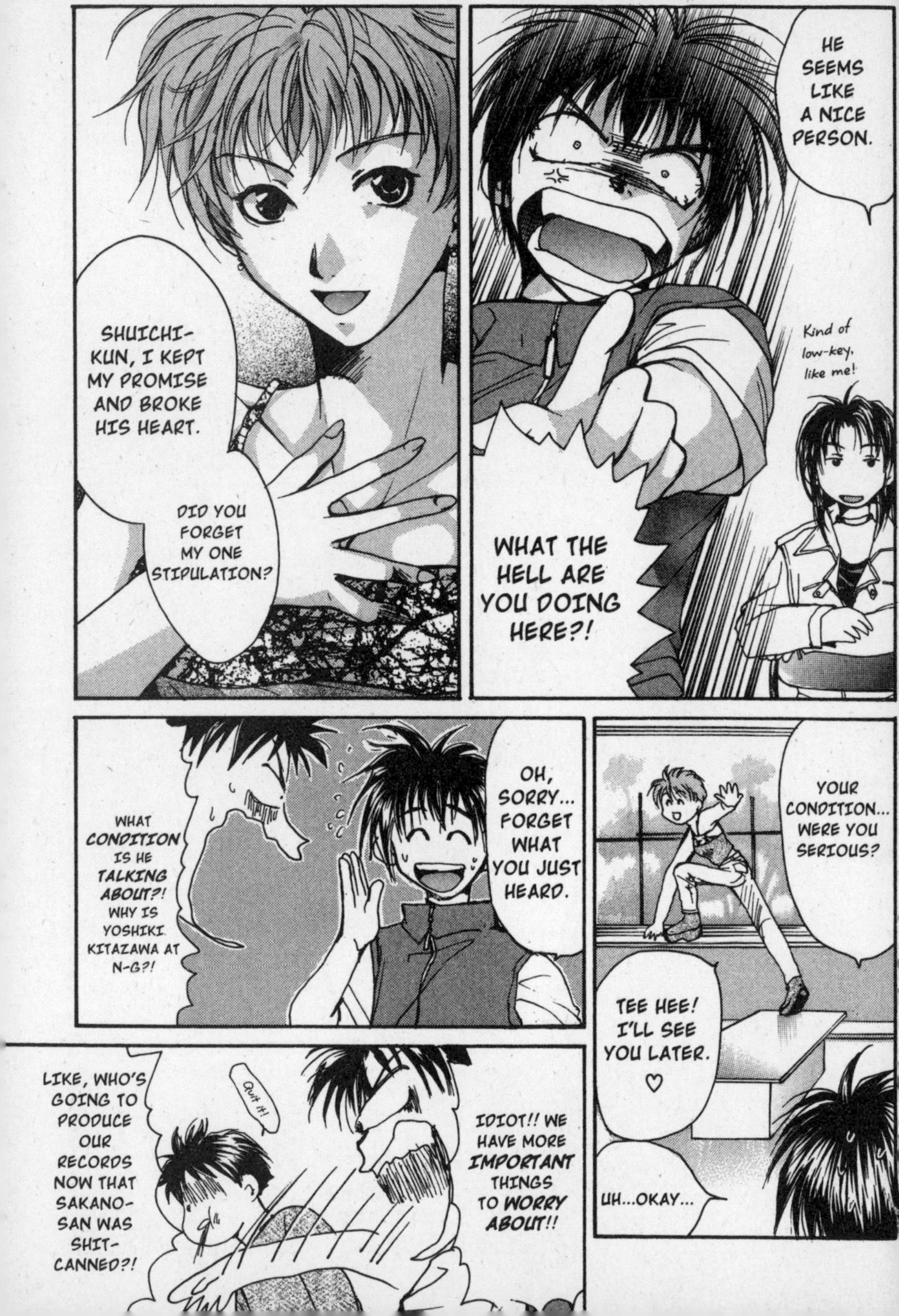
HE SEEMS LIKE A NICE PERSON.
Kind of low-key, like me!
WHAT THE HELL ARE YOU DOING HERE?!
SHUICHI-KUN, I KEPT MY PROMISE AND BROKE HIS HEART.
DID YOU FORGET MY ONE STIPULATION?
YOUR CONDITION... WERE YOU SERIOUS?
TEE HEE! I'LL SEE YOU LATER. ♡
UH...OKAY...
OH, SORRY... FORGET WHAT YOU JUST HEARD.
WHAT CONDITION IS HE TALKING ABOUT?! WHY IS YOSHIKI KITAZAWA AT N-G?!
IDIOT!! WE HAVE MORE IMPORTANT THINGS TO WORRY ABOUT!!
Quit it!
LIKE, WHO'S GOING TO PRODUCE OUR RECORDS NOW THAT SAKANO-SAN WAS SHIT-CANNED?!

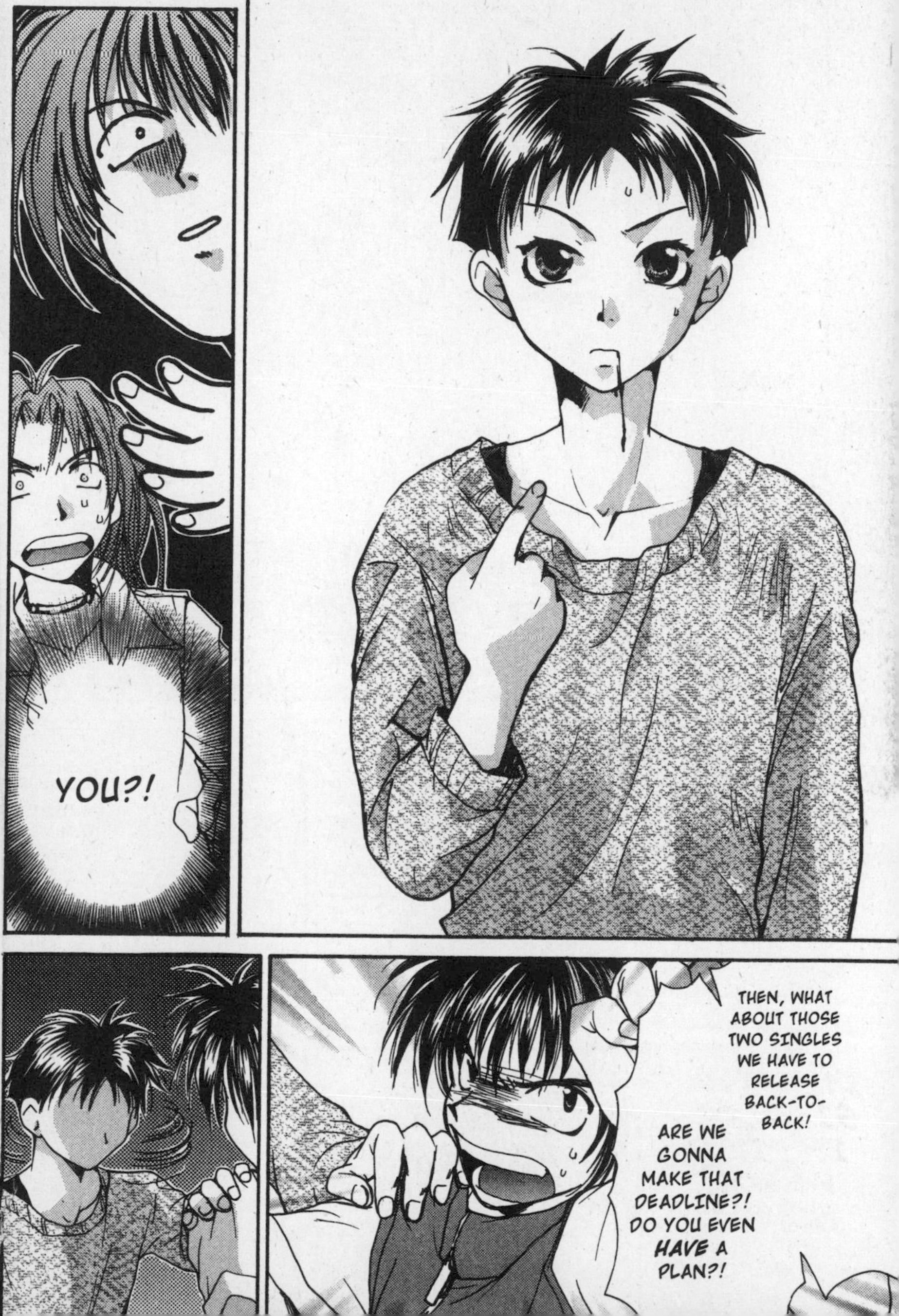
YOU?!
THEN, WHAT ABOUT THOSE TWO SINGLES WE HAVE TO RELEASE BACK-TO-BACK!
ARE WE GONNA MAKE THAT DEADLINE?! DO YOU EVEN *HAVE* A PLAN?!

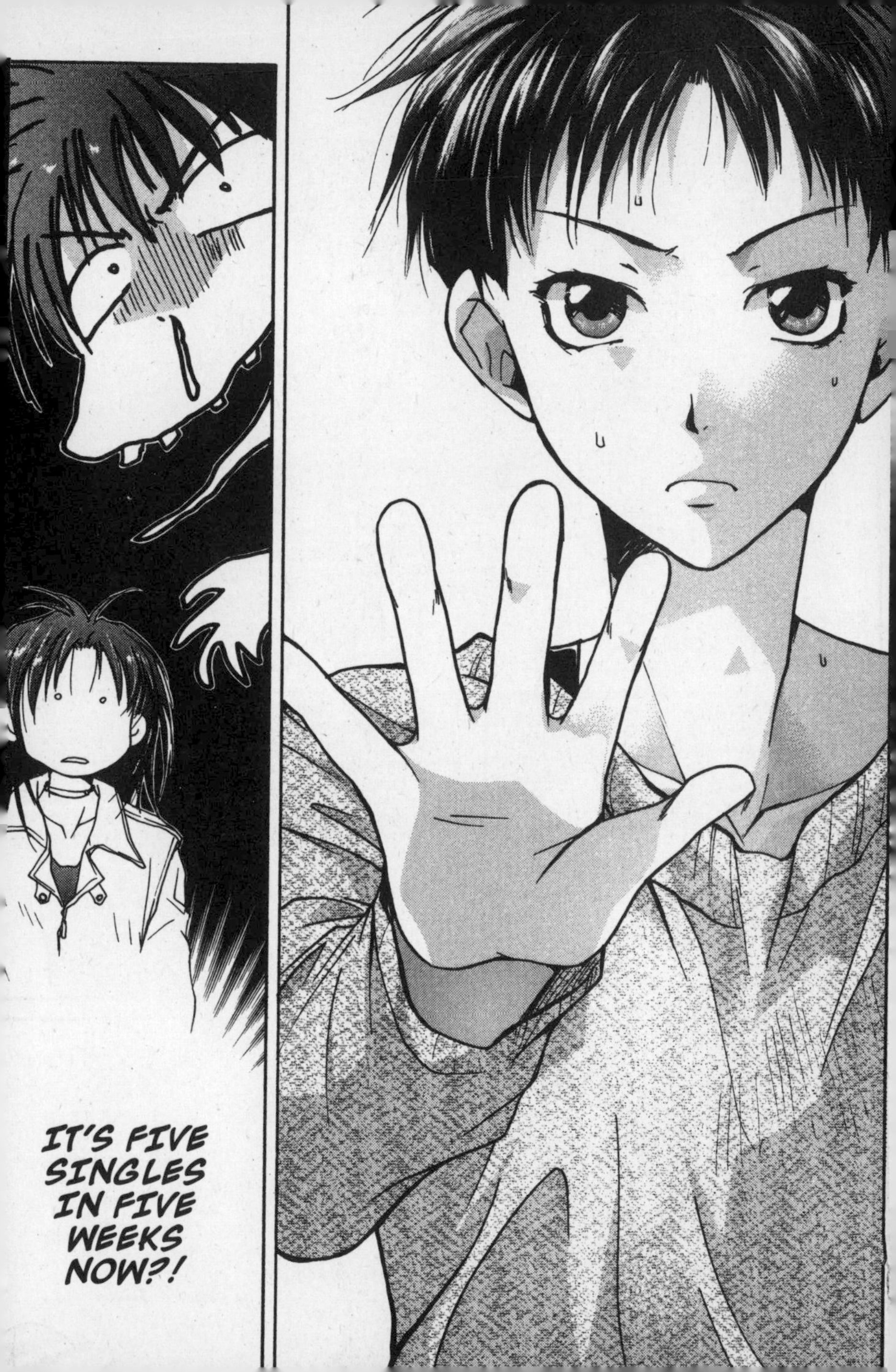
IT'S FIVE SINGLES IN FIVE WEEKS NOW?!

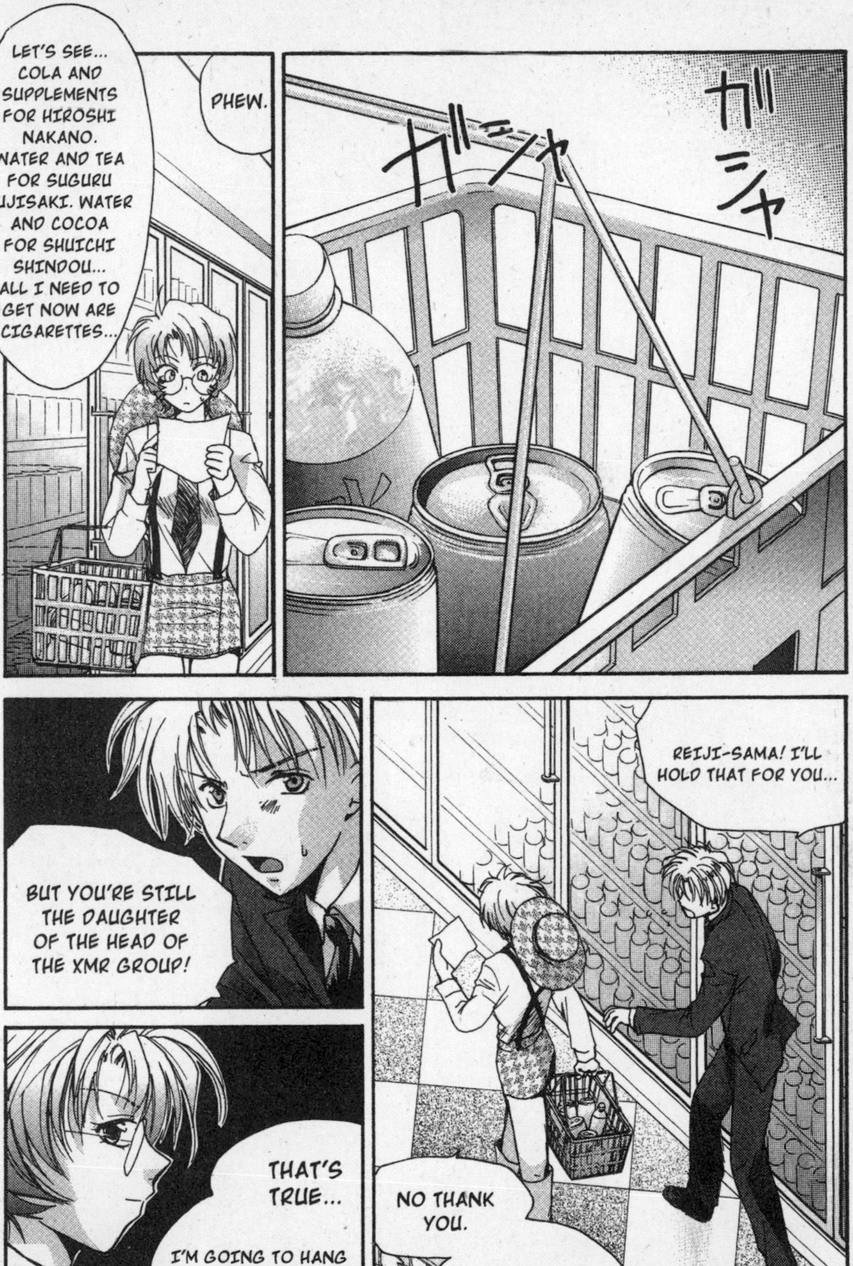

ガシャ
ガシャ
PHEW.
LET'S SEE... COLA AND SUPPLEMENTS FOR HIROSHI NAKANO. WATER AND TEA FOR SUGURU FUJISAKI. WATER AND COCOA FOR SHUICHI SHINDOU... ALL I NEED TO GET NOW ARE CIGARETTES...
REIJI-SAMA! I'LL HOLD THAT FOR YOU...
NO THANK YOU.
THIS IS PART OF MY JOB AS MANAGER.
BUT YOU'RE STILL THE DAUGHTER OF THE HEAD OF THE XMR GROUP!
THAT'S TRUE...
I'M GOING TO HANG ON TO THAT PRESTIGE A LITTLE LONGER.

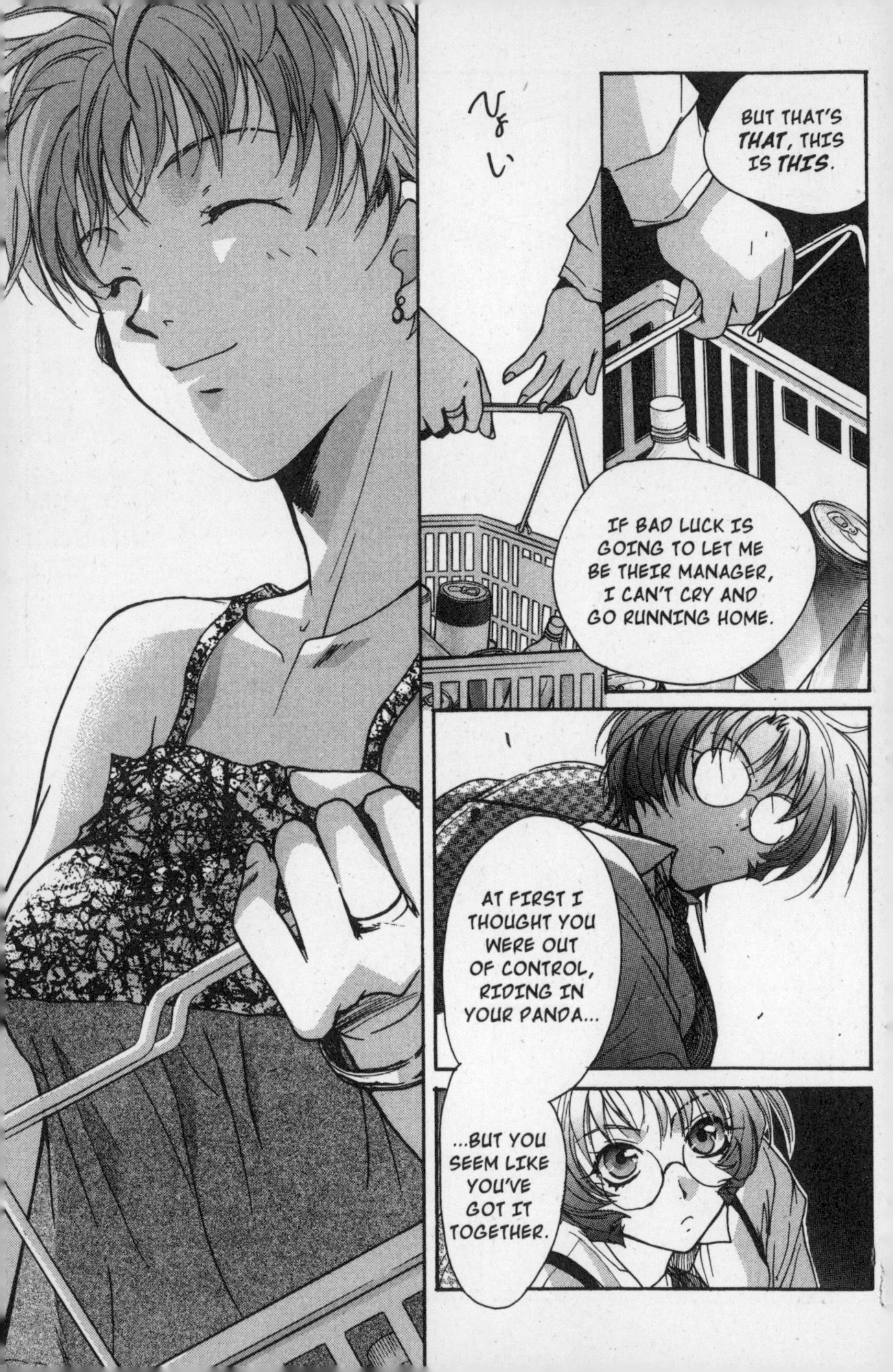
BUT THAT'S THAT, THIS IS THIS.
IF BAD LUCK IS GOING TO LET ME BE THEIR MANAGER, I CAN'T CRY AND GO RUNNING HOME.
AT FIRST I THOUGHT YOU WERE OUT OF CONTROL, RIDING IN YOUR PANDA...
...BUT YOU SEEM LIKE YOU'VE GOT IT TOGETHER.

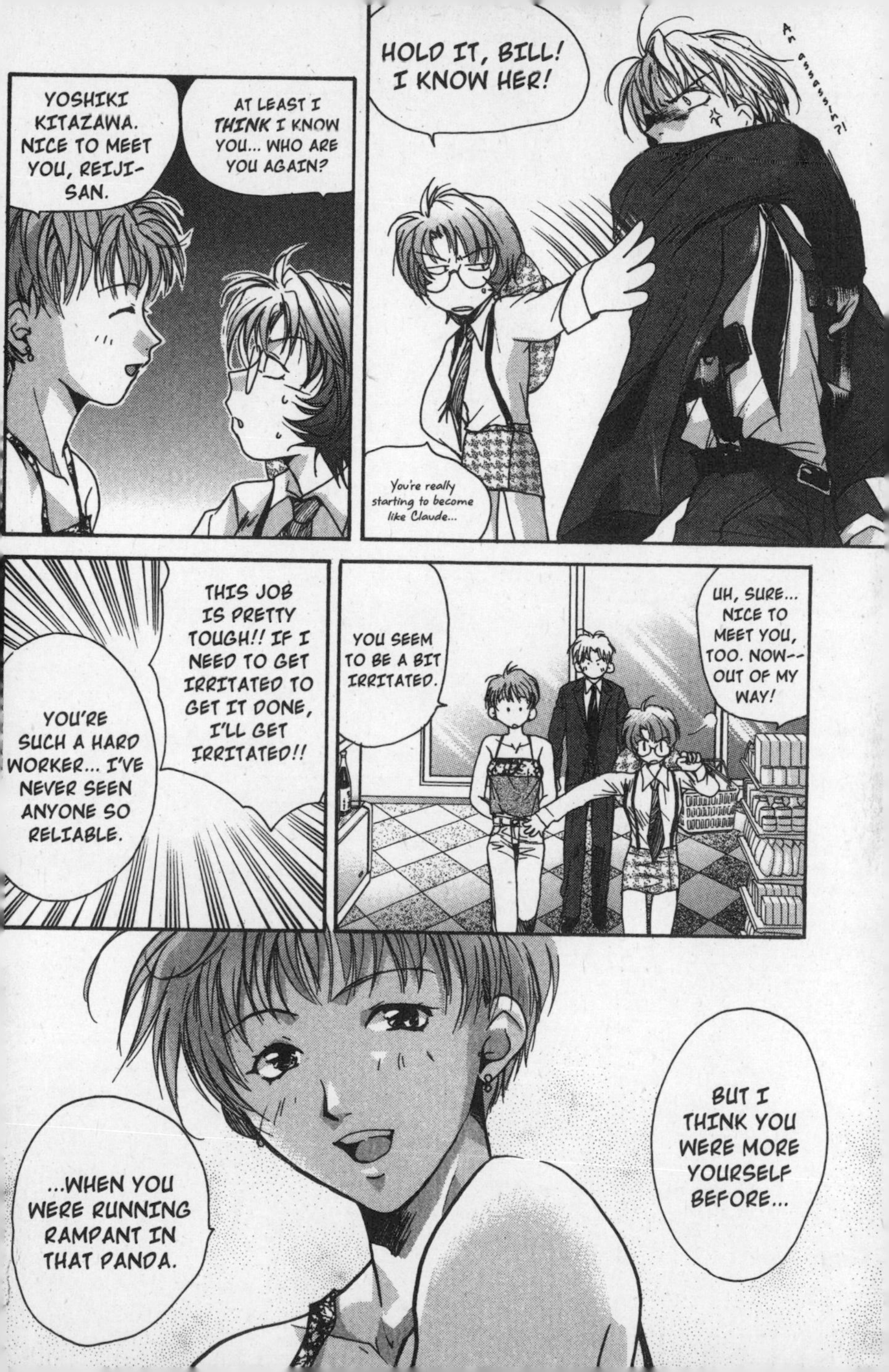
HOLD IT, BILL! I KNOW HER!
An assassin?!
You're really starting to become like Claude...
AT LEAST I THINK I KNOW YOU... WHO ARE YOU AGAIN?
YOSHIKI KITAZAWA. NICE TO MEET YOU, REIJI-SAN.
UH, SURE... NICE TO MEET YOU, TOO. NOW--OUT OF MY WAY!
YOU SEEM TO BE A BIT IRRITATED.
THIS JOB IS PRETTY TOUGH!! IF I NEED TO GET IRRITATED TO GET IT DONE, I'LL GET IRRITATED!!
YOU'RE SUCH A HARD WORKER... I'VE NEVER SEEN ANYONE SO RELIABLE.
BUT I THINK YOU WERE MORE YOURSELF BEFORE...
...WHEN YOU WERE RUNNING RAMPANT IN THAT PANDA.

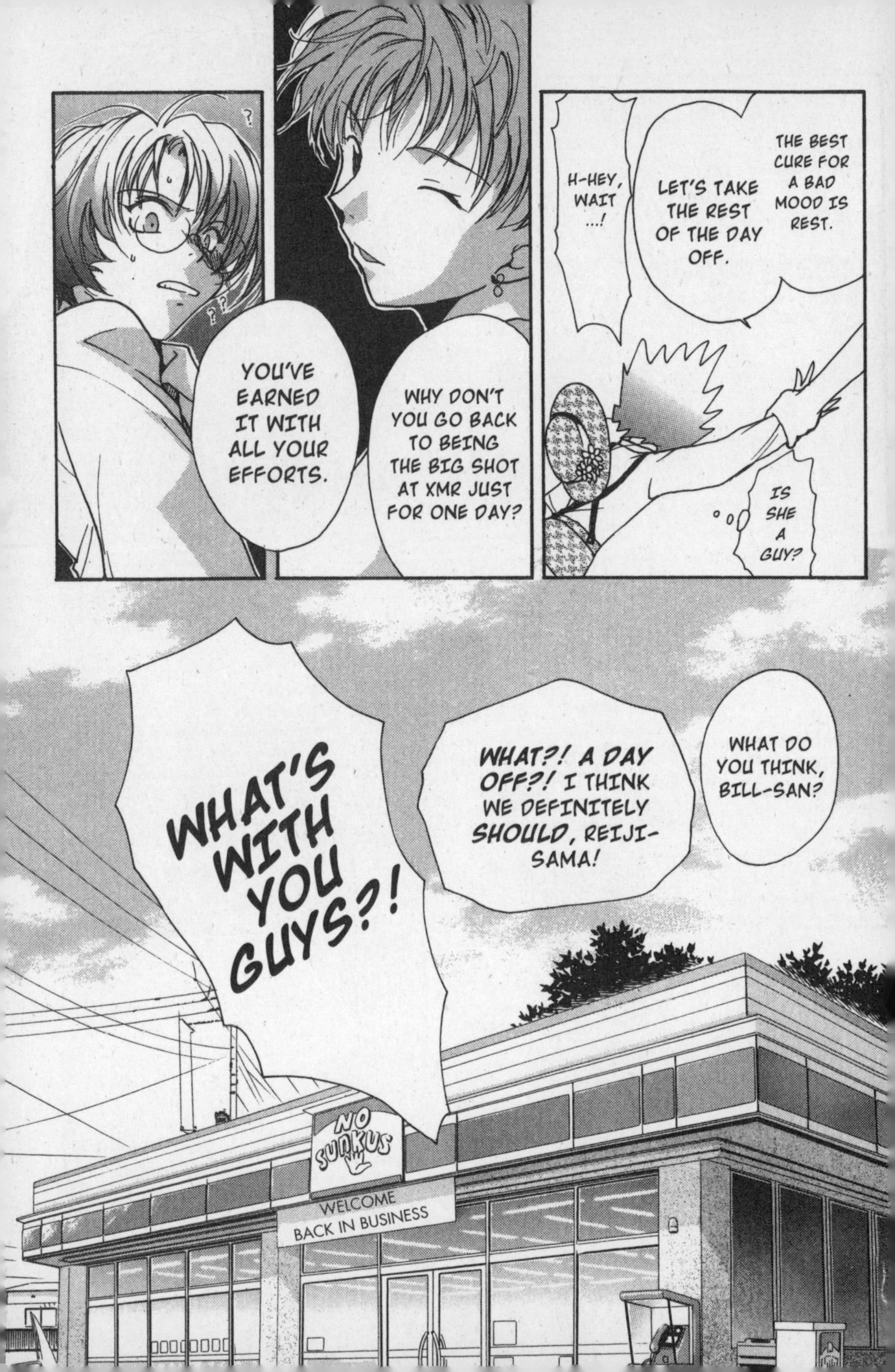
THE BEST CURE FOR A BAD MOOD IS REST.
LET'S TAKE THE REST OF THE DAY OFF.
H-HEY, WAIT ...!
IS SHE A GUY?
WHY DON'T YOU GO BACK TO BEING THE BIG SHOT AT XMR JUST FOR ONE DAY?
YOU'VE EARNED IT WITH ALL YOUR EFFORTS.
WHAT DO YOU THINK, BILL-SAN?
WHAT?! A DAY OFF?! I THINK WE DEFINITELY SHOULD, REIJI-SAMA!
WHAT'S WITH YOU GUYS?!
NO SUNKUS
WELCOME BACK IN BUSINESS

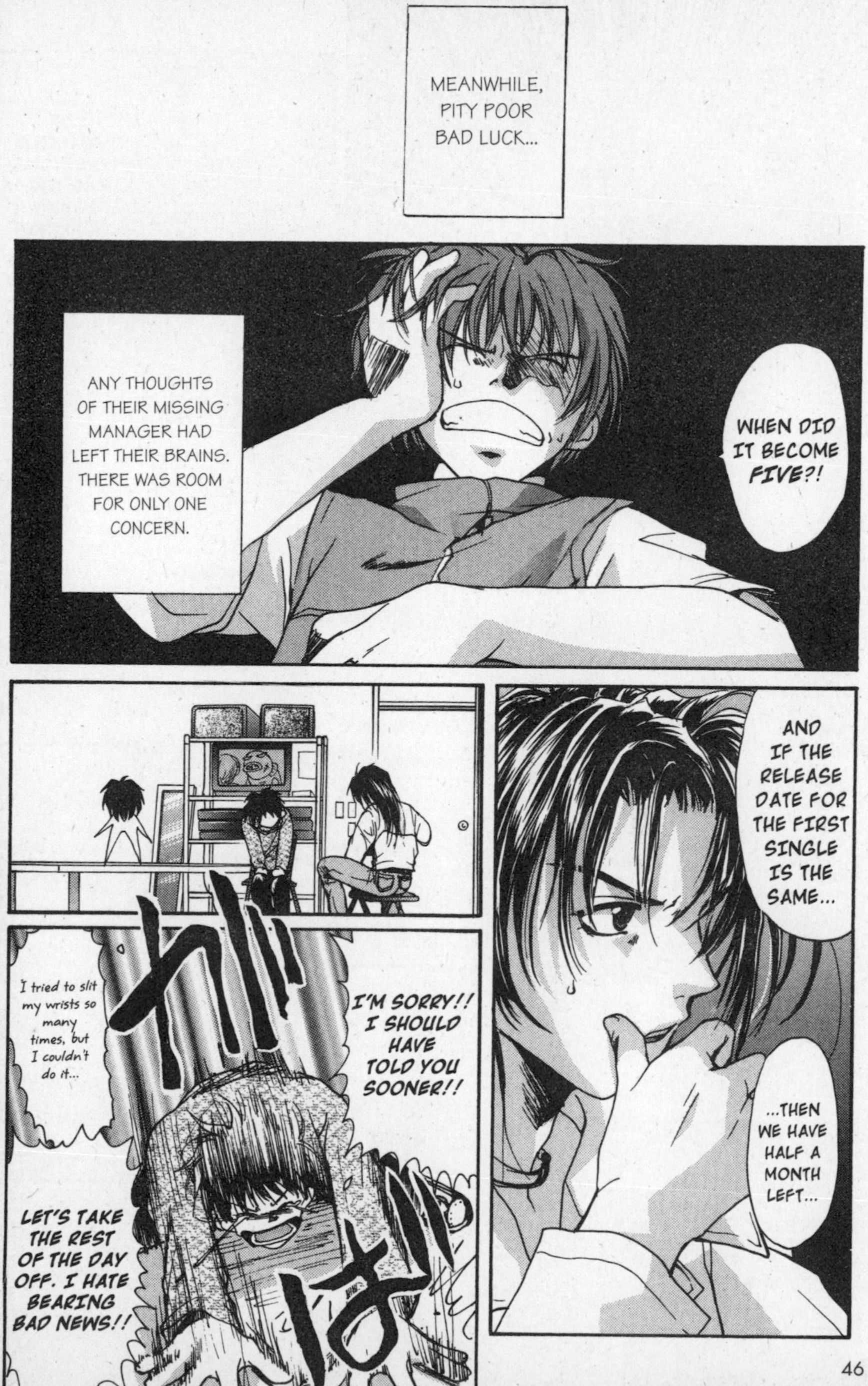
MEANWHILE, PITY POOR BAD LUCK...
ANY THOUGHTS OF THEIR MISSING MANAGER HAD LEFT THEIR BRAINS. THERE WAS ROOM FOR ONLY ONE CONCERN.
WHEN DID IT BECOME *FIVE*?!
AND IF THE RELEASE DATE FOR THE FIRST SINGLE IS THE SAME...
...THEN WE HAVE HALF A MONTH LEFT...
I'M SORRY!! I SHOULD HAVE TOLD YOU SOONER!!
I tried to slit my wrists so many times, but I couldn't do it...
LET'S TAKE THE REST OF THE DAY OFF. I HATE BEARING BAD NEWS!!

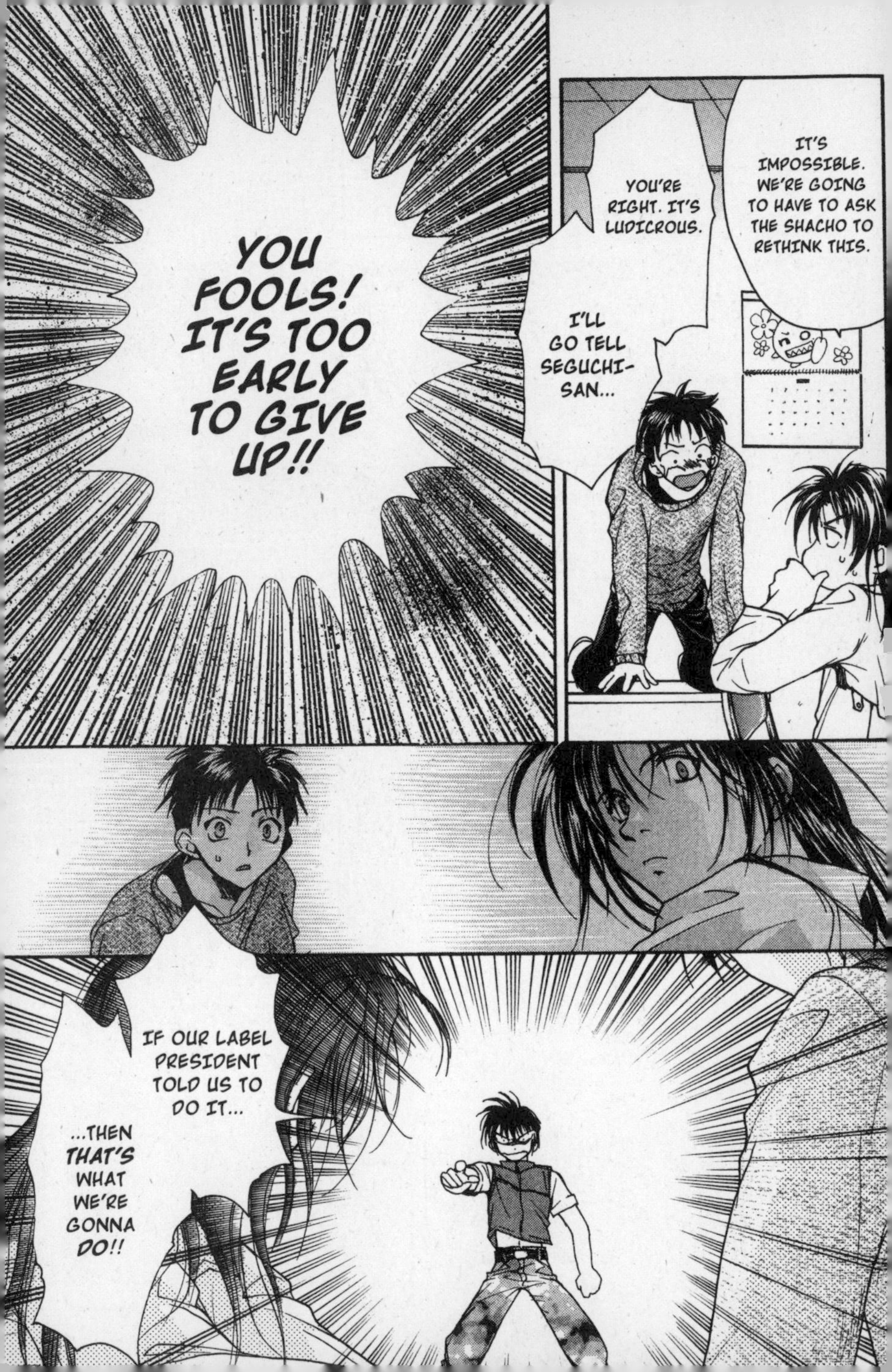

IT'S IMPOSSIBLE. WE'RE GOING TO HAVE TO ASK THE SHACHO TO RETHINK THIS.
YOU'RE RIGHT. IT'S LUDICROUS.
I'LL GO TELL SEGUCHI-SAN...
YOU FOOLS! IT'S TOO EARLY TO GIVE UP!!
IF OUR LABEL PRESIDENT TOLD US TO DO IT...
...THEN THAT'S WHAT WE'RE GONNA DO!!

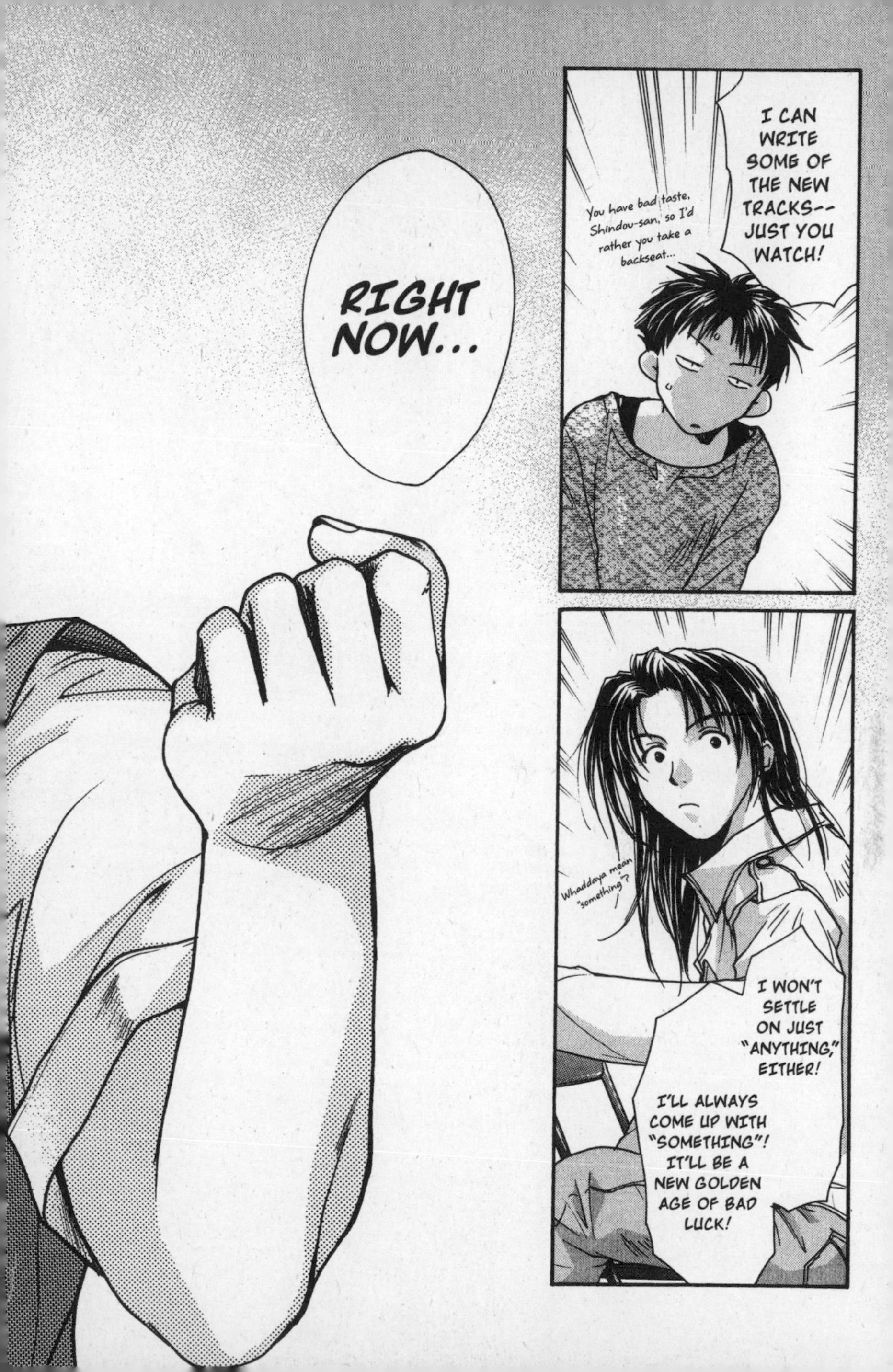
I CAN WRITE SOME OF THE NEW TRACKS-- JUST YOU WATCH!
You have bad taste, Shindou-san, so I'd rather you take a backseat...
I WON'T SETTLE ON JUST "ANYTHING," EITHER!
I'LL ALWAYS COME UP WITH "SOMETHING"! IT'LL BE A NEW GOLDEN AGE OF BAD LUCK!
Whaddaya mean "something"?
RIGHT NOW...

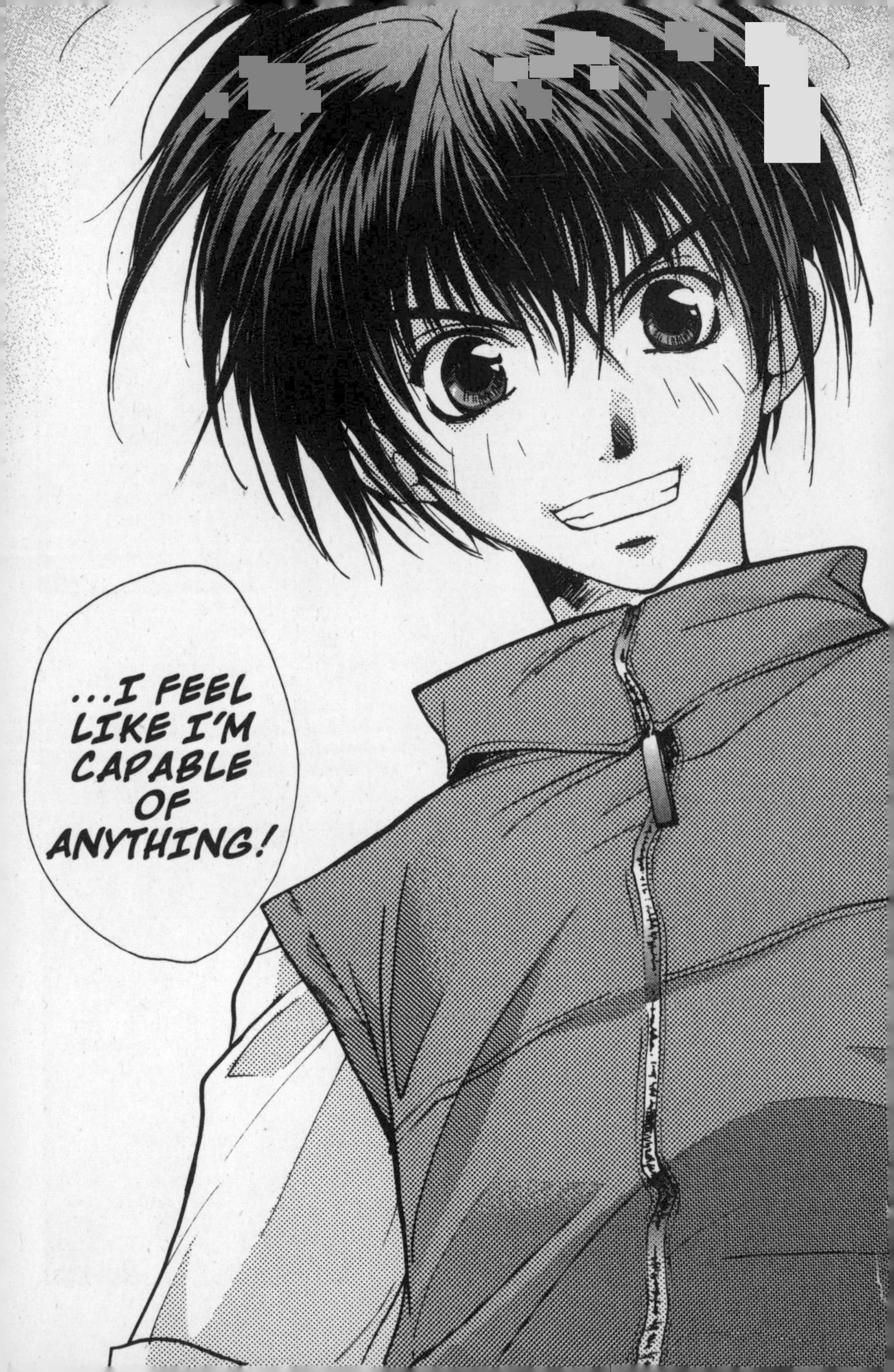
...I FEEL LIKE I'M CAPABLE OF ANYTHING!

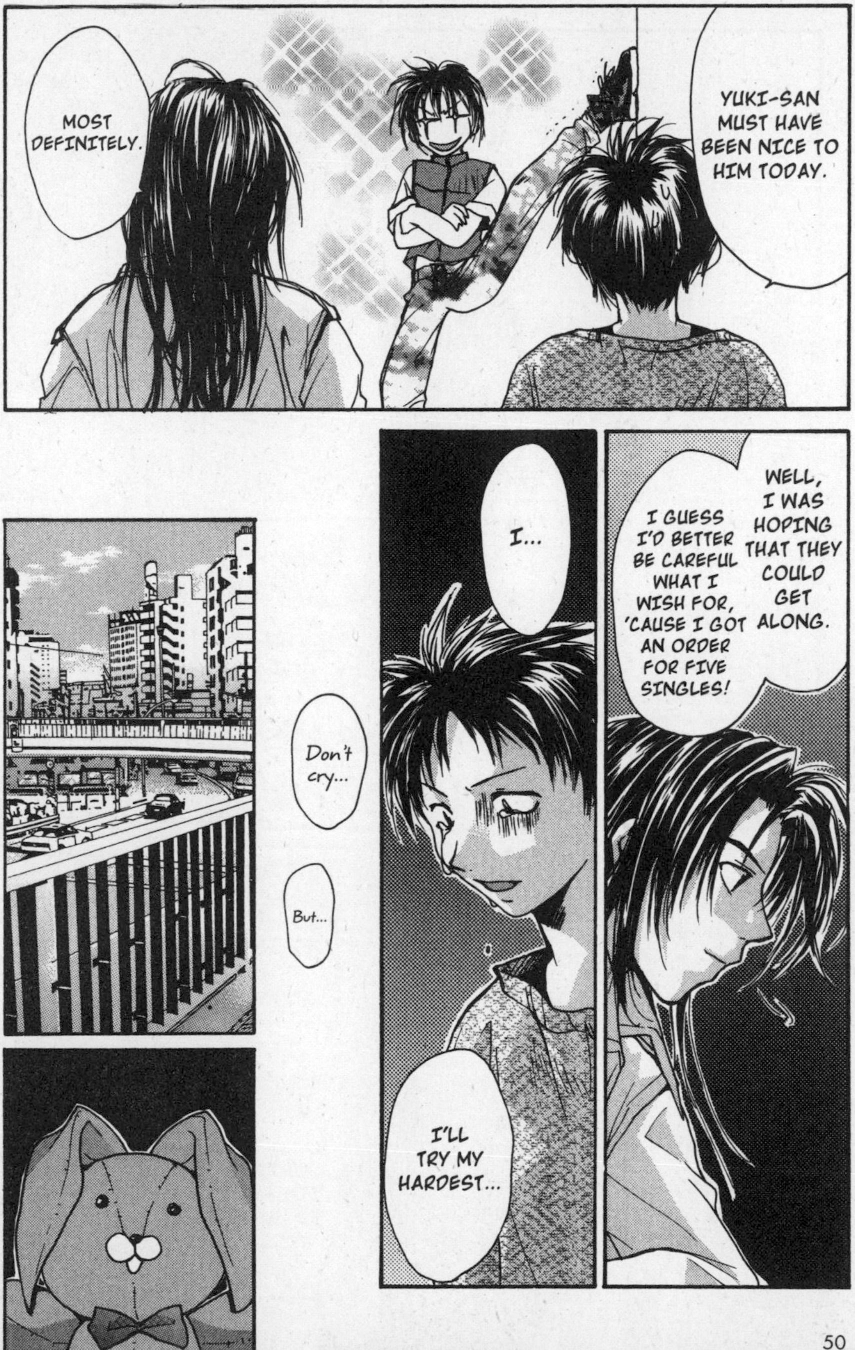
YUKI-SAN MUST HAVE BEEN NICE TO HIM TODAY.
MOST DEFINITELY.
WELL, I WAS HOPING THAT THEY COULD GET ALONG.
I GUESS I'D BETTER BE CAREFUL WHAT I WISH FOR, 'CAUSE I GOT AN ORDER FOR FIVE SINGLES!
I...
I'LL TRY MY HARDEST...
Don't cry...
But...

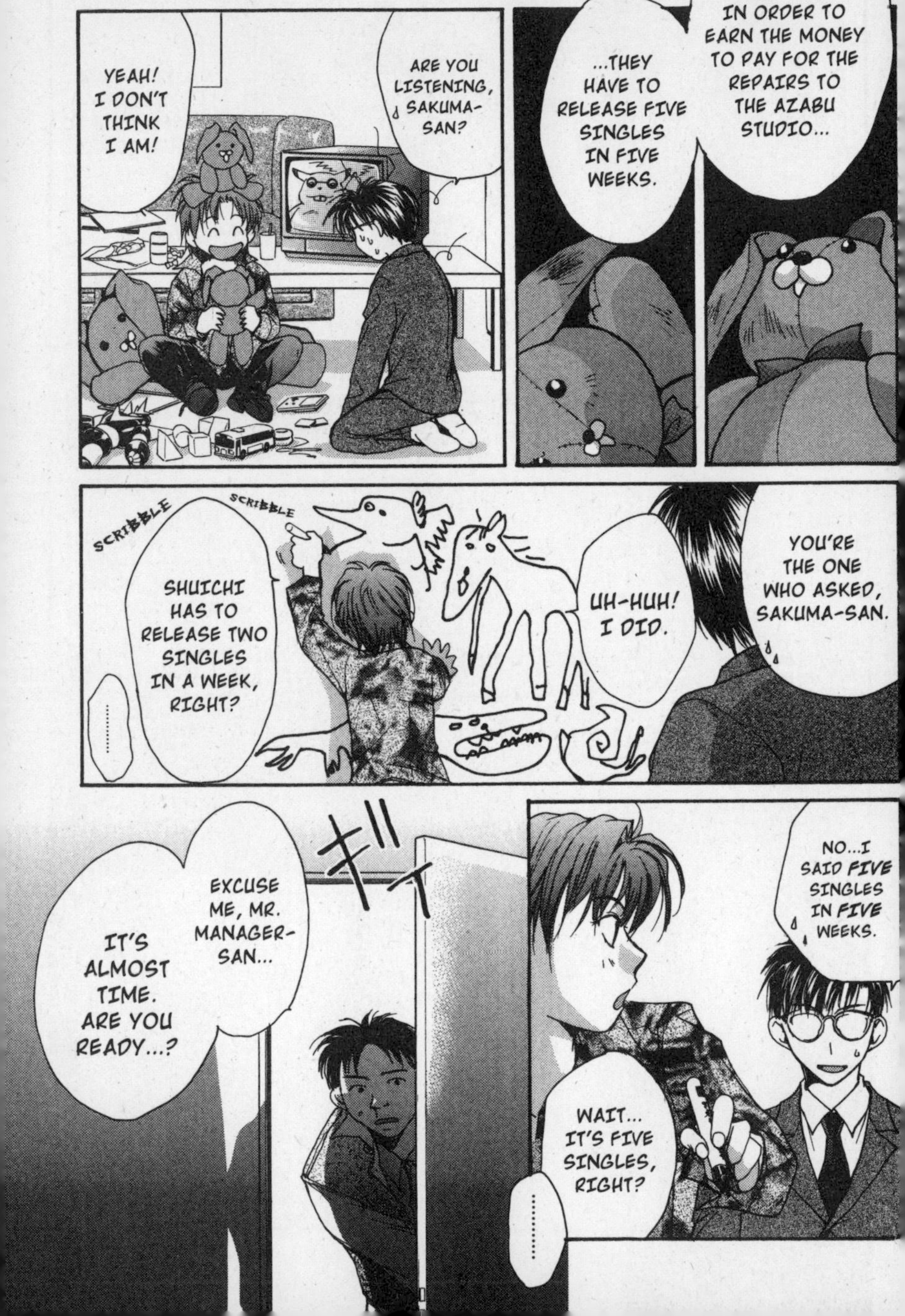
AND SO, IN ORDER TO EARN THE MONEY TO PAY FOR THE REPAIRS TO THE AZABU STUDIO...
...THEY HAVE TO RELEASE FIVE SINGLES IN FIVE WEEKS.
ARE YOU LISTENING, SAKUMA-SAN?
YEAH! I DON'T THINK I AM!
YOU'RE THE ONE WHO ASKED, SAKUMA-SAN.
UH-HUH! I DID.
SCRIBBLE
SCRIBBLE
SHUICHI HAS TO RELEASE TWO SINGLES IN A WEEK, RIGHT?
......
NO...I SAID *FIVE* SINGLES IN *FIVE* WEEKS.
WAIT... IT'S FIVE SINGLES, RIGHT?
......
ギイ
EXCUSE ME, MR. MANAGER-SAN...
IT'S ALMOST TIME. ARE YOU READY...?

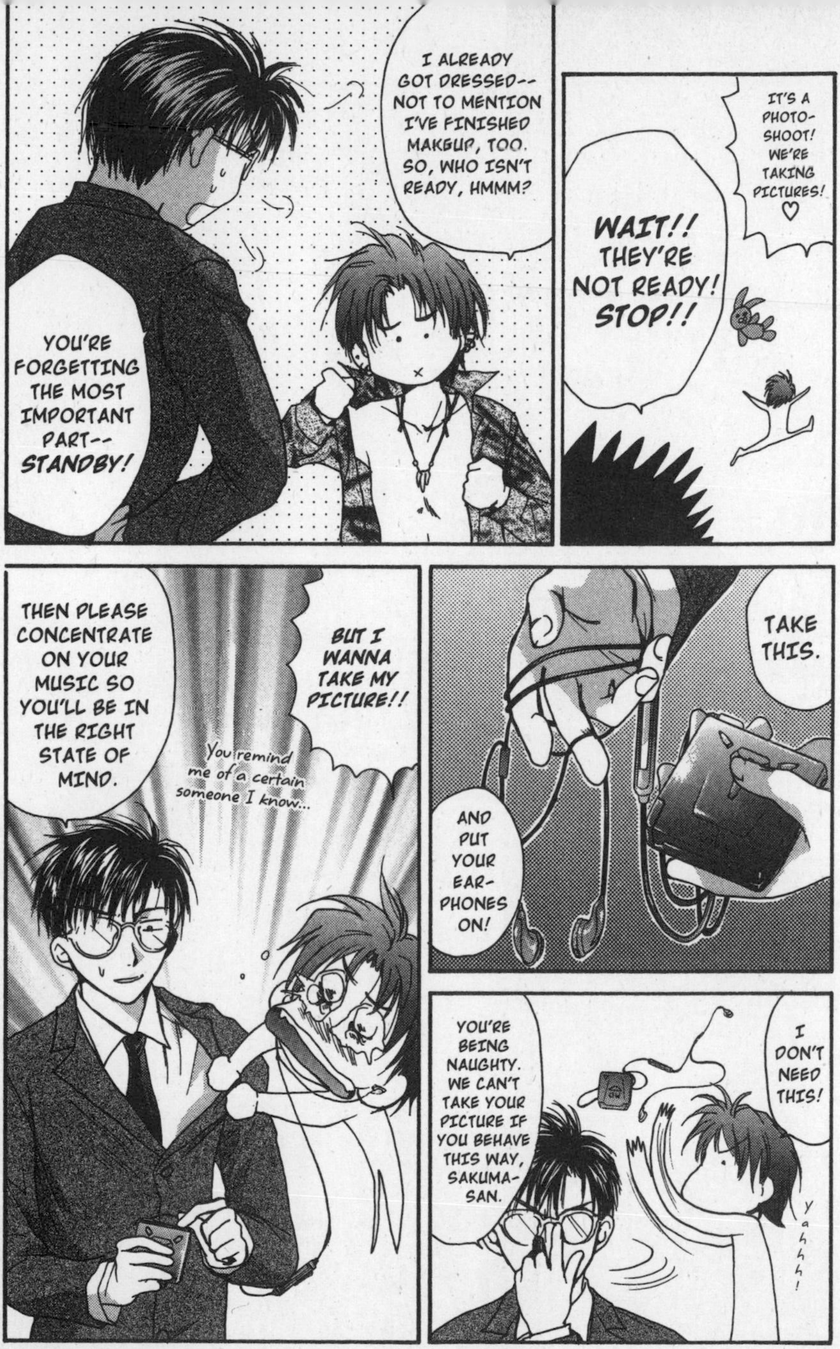
IT'S A PHOTO-SHOOT! WE'RE TAKING PICTURES! ♡
WAIT!! THEY'RE NOT READY! STOP!!
I ALREADY GOT DRESSED-- NOT TO MENTION I'VE FINISHED MAKEUP, TOO. SO, WHO ISN'T READY, HMMM?
YOU'RE FORGETTING THE MOST IMPORTANT PART-- STANDBY!
TAKE THIS.
AND PUT YOUR EAR-PHONES ON!
I DON'T NEED THIS!
YOU'RE BEING NAUGHTY. WE CAN'T TAKE YOUR PICTURE IF YOU BEHAVE THIS WAY, SAKUMA-SAN.
Yahhh!
BUT I WANNA TAKE MY PICTURE!!
THEN PLEASE CONCENTRATE ON YOUR MUSIC SO YOU'LL BE IN THE RIGHT STATE OF MIND.
You remind me of a certain someone I know...

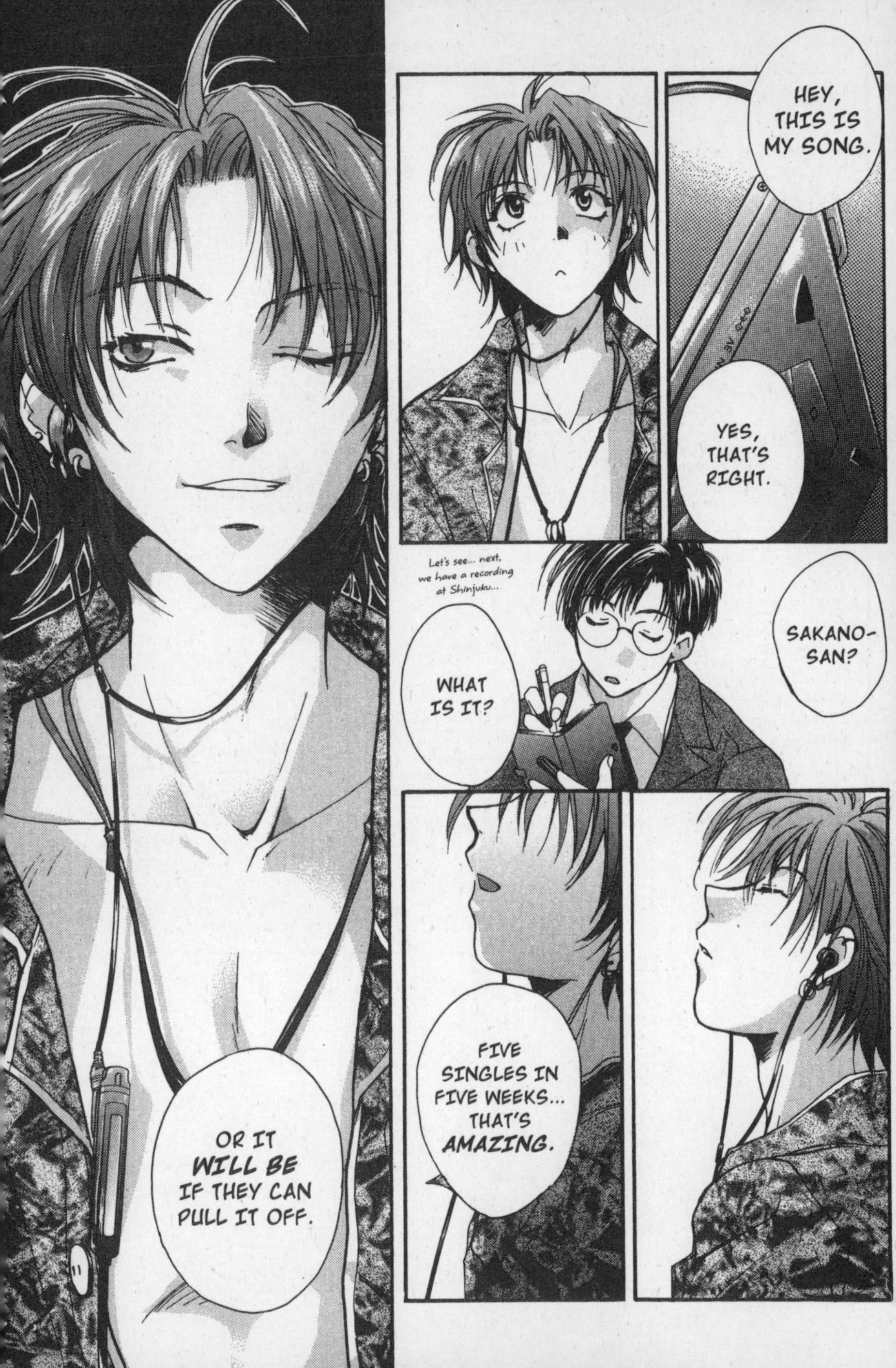
HEY, THIS IS MY SONG.
YES, THAT'S RIGHT.
SAKANO-SAN?
Let's see... next, we have a recording at Shinjuku...
WHAT IS IT?
FIVE SINGLES IN FIVE WEEKS... THAT'S AMAZING.
OR IT WILL BE IF THEY CAN PULL IT OFF.

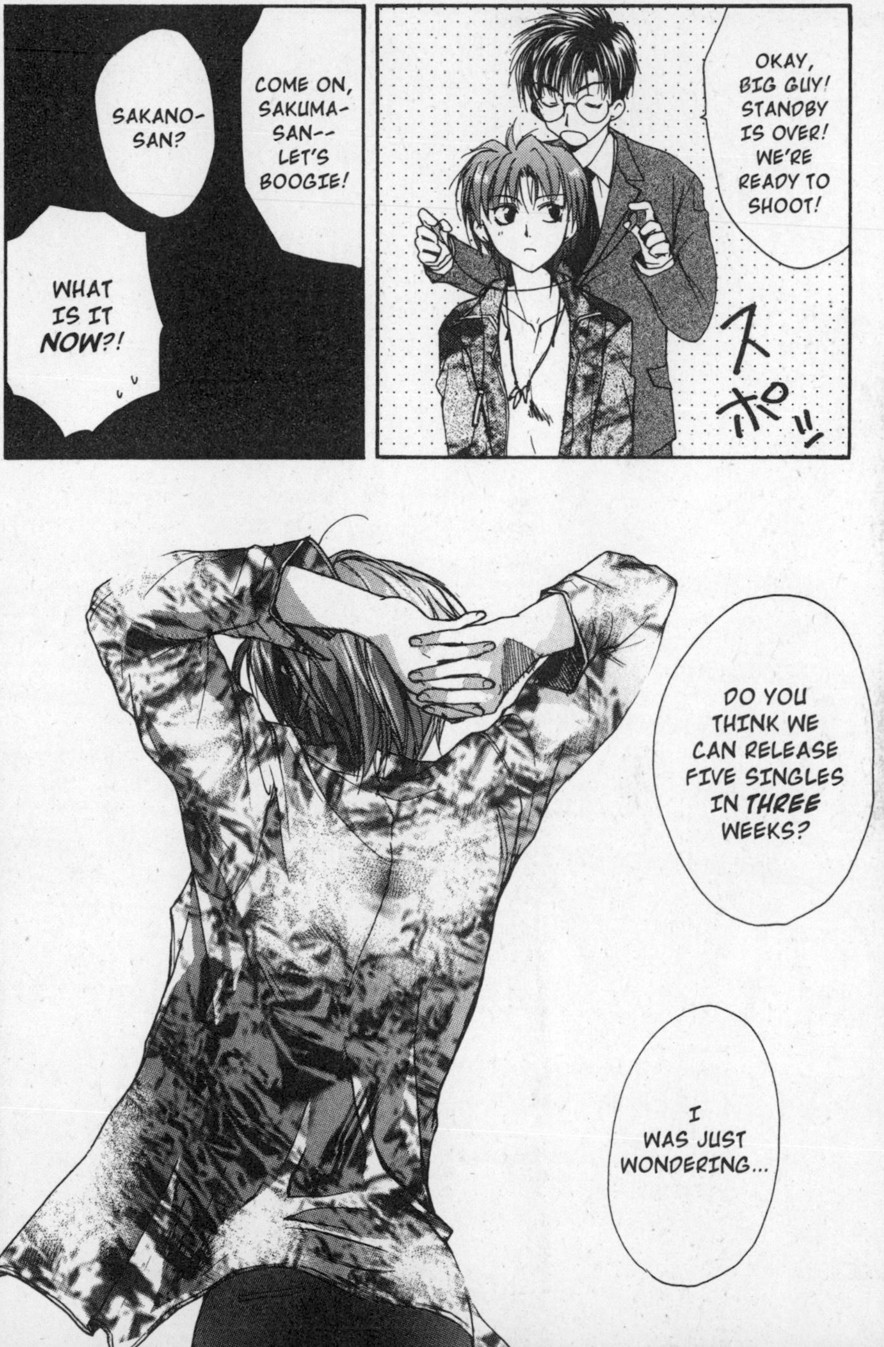
OKAY, BIG GUY! STANDBY IS OVER! WE'RE READY TO SHOOT!
スポッ
COME ON, SAKUMA-SAN-- LET'S BOOGIE!
SAKANO-SAN?
WHAT IS IT *NOW*?!
DO YOU THINK WE CAN RELEASE FIVE SINGLES IN *THREE* WEEKS?
I WAS JUST WONDERING...

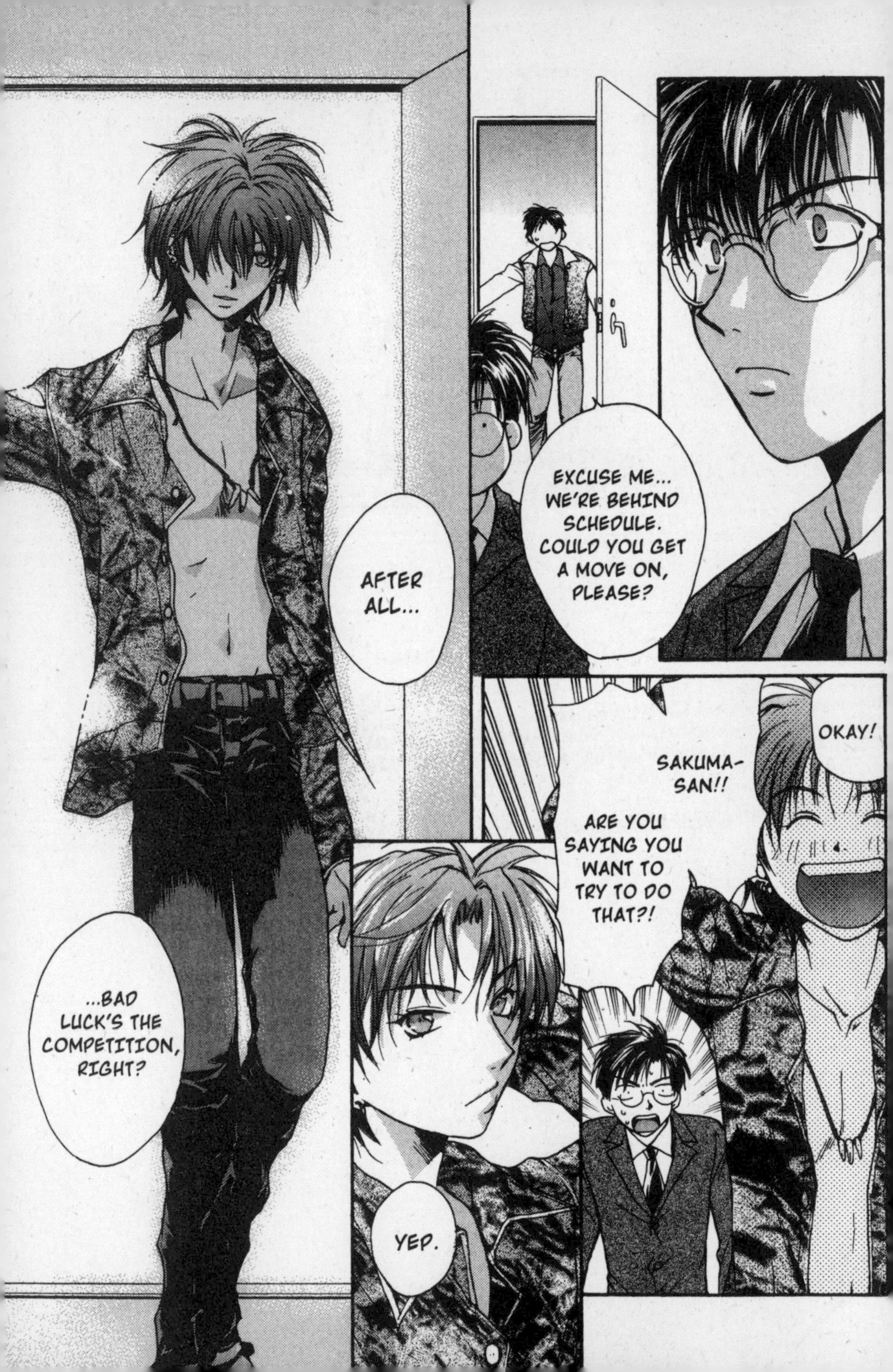
EXCUSE ME... WE'RE BEHIND SCHEDULE. COULD YOU GET A MOVE ON, PLEASE?
OKAY!
SAKUMA-SAN!!
ARE YOU SAYING YOU WANT TO TRY TO DO THAT?!
YEP.
AFTER ALL...
...BAD LUCK'S THE COMPETITION, RIGHT?

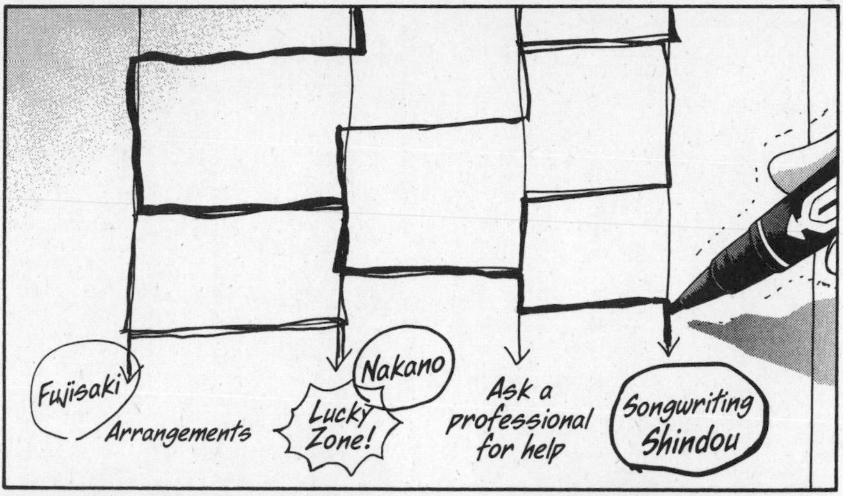
Songwriting Shindou
Ask a professional for help
Nakano
Lucky Zone!
Fujisaki
Arrangements

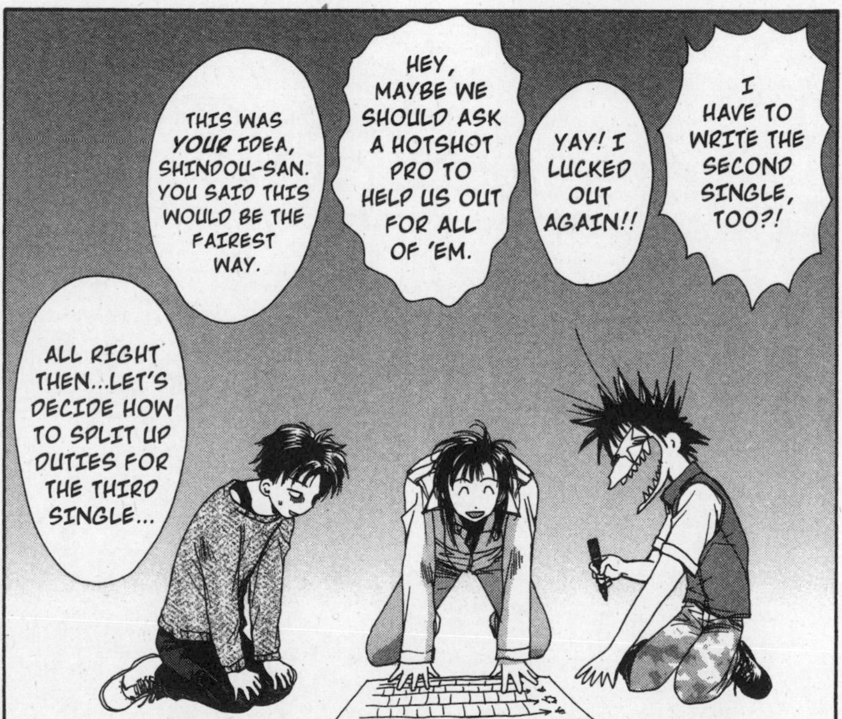
I HAVE TO WRITE THE SECOND SINGLE, TOO?!
YAY! I LUCKED OUT AGAIN!!
HEY, MAYBE WE SHOULD ASK A HOTSHOT PRO TO HELP US OUT FOR ALL OF 'EM.
THIS WAS YOUR IDEA, SHINDOU-SAN. YOU SAID THIS WOULD BE THE FAIREST WAY.
ALL RIGHT THEN...LET'S DECIDE HOW TO SPLIT UP DUTIES FOR THE THIRD SINGLE...

track45 ▶ END

GRAVITATION

Special Edition

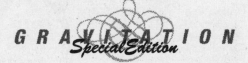

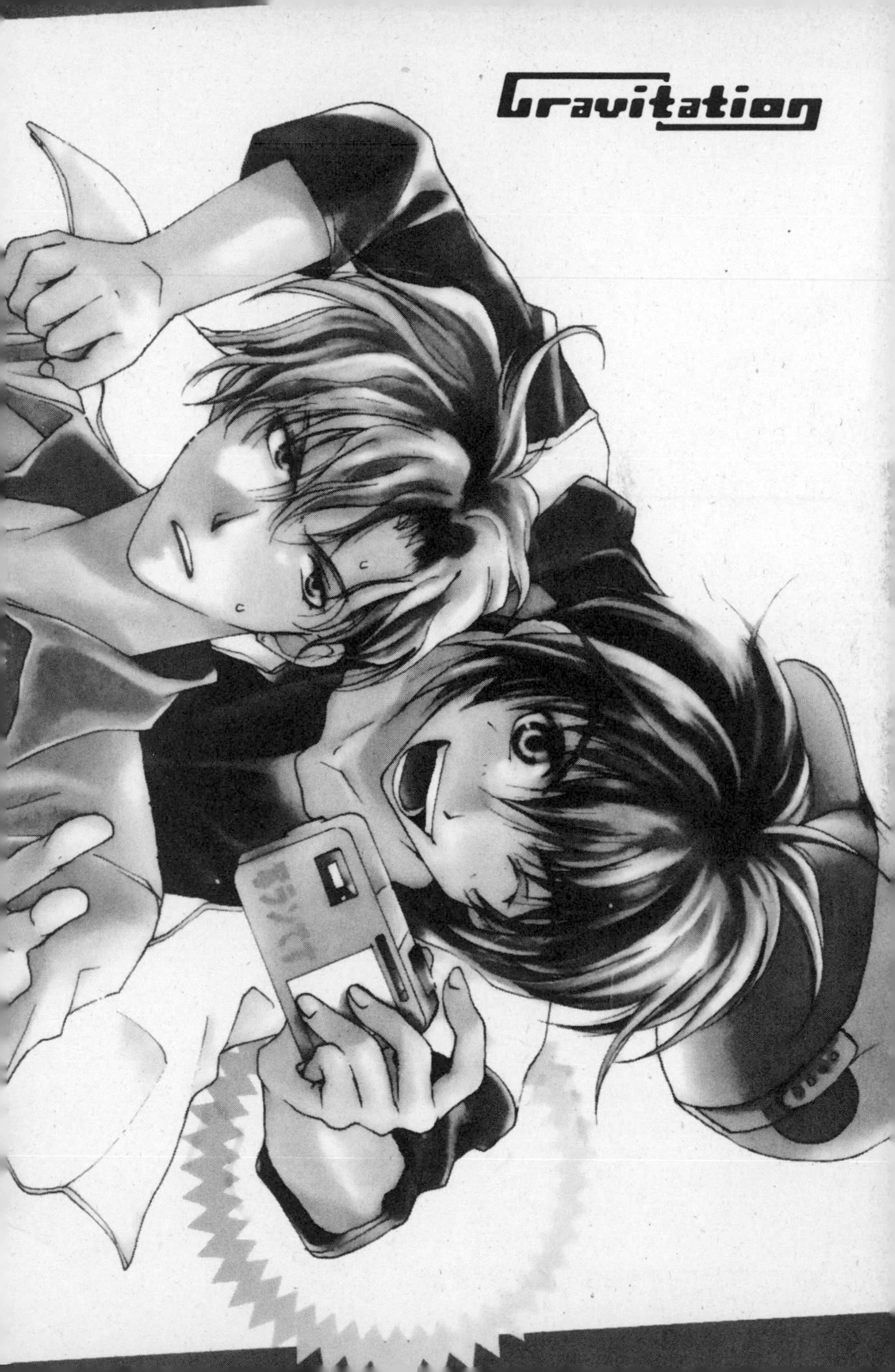
Gravitation

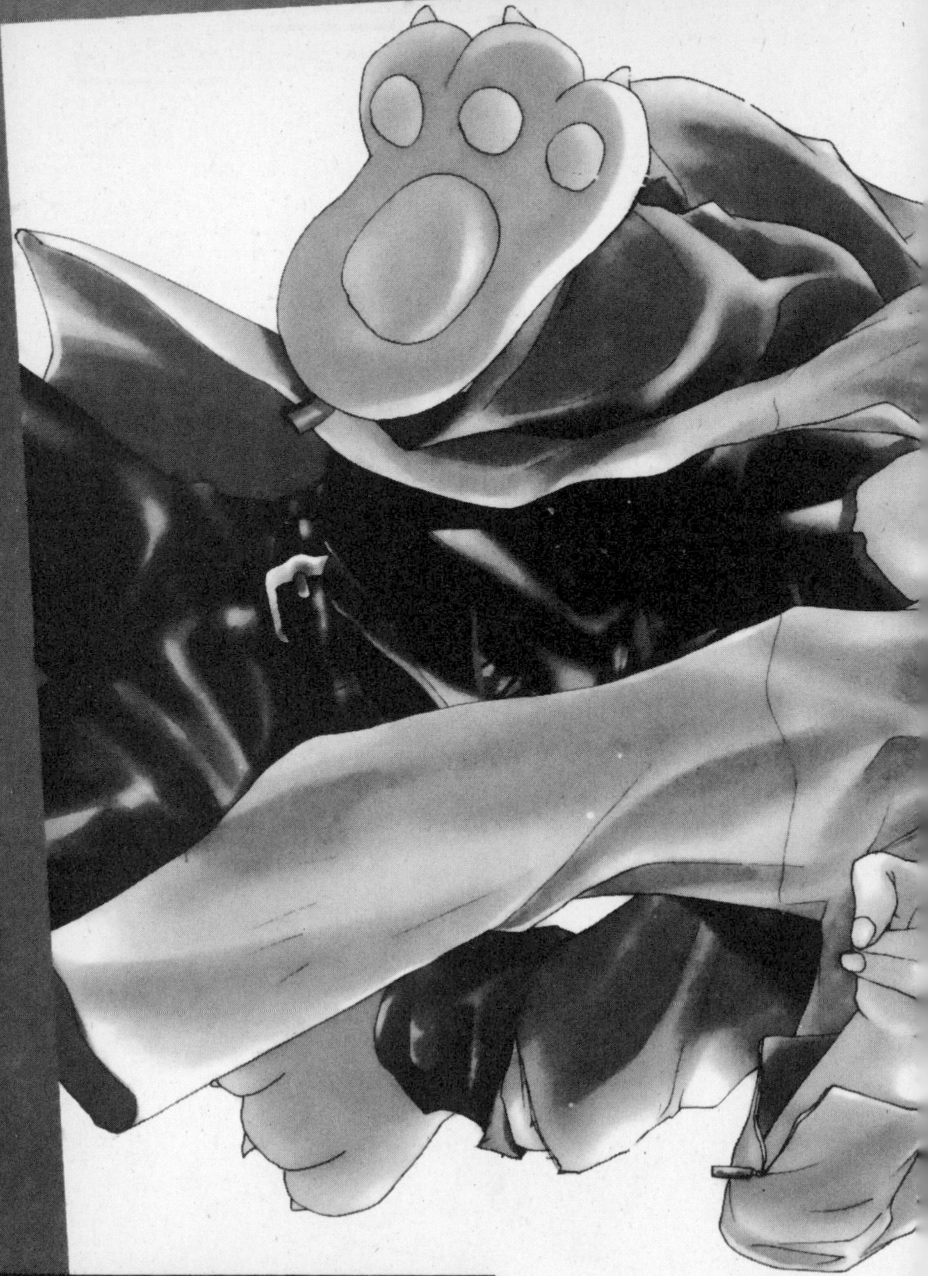

# track 46

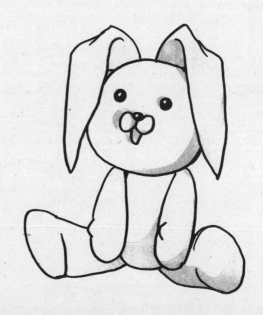

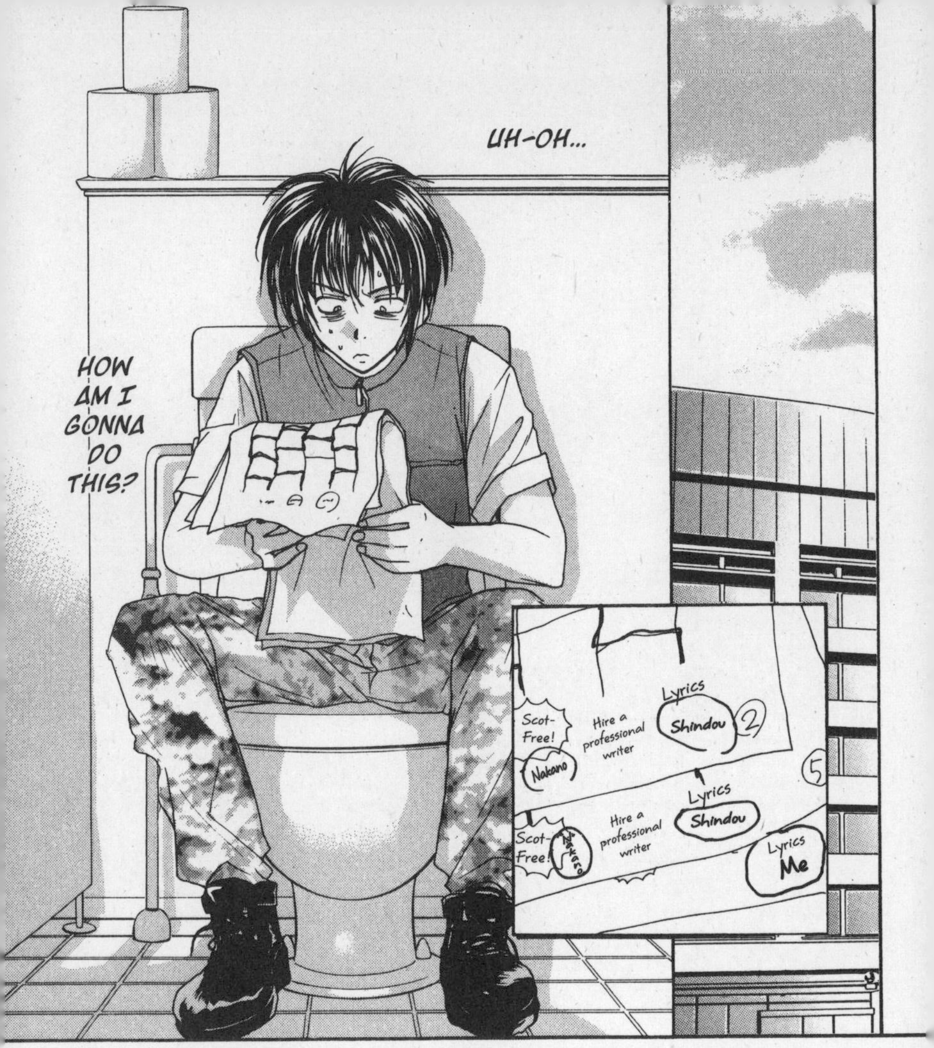
UH-OH...
HOW AM I GONNA DO THIS?
Lyrics
Shindou
2
Hire a professional writer
Scot-Free!
Nakano
5
Lyrics
Shindou
Hire a professional writer
Scot-Free!
Nakano
Lyrics
Me

## ABOUT GRAVITATION TRACK 46

Hello! Long time no see! This is your favorite female manga artist here, who also raises a breed of grasshopper named Tonosama Batta. (Ugh!) Yup, you guessed it--it's me, Maki Murakami. Or maybe I'm not...maybe I'm actually a guy... (Double ugh!) Anyway, I present to you the 46th chapter of *Gravitation*. This manga just keeps going, and going, and going... And just when you think it's coming to an end, it doesn't! Oh, the anxiety of it all...ugh!! We're into a new storyline now, so I hope you'll like it. I'll try to heat up all this cold anxiety with *Gravitation*'s new direction. Cheers!

p.s. - Then again, if it doesn't work and you have a hard time reading this one, I'm sorry. Boy, it sure is cold in here...

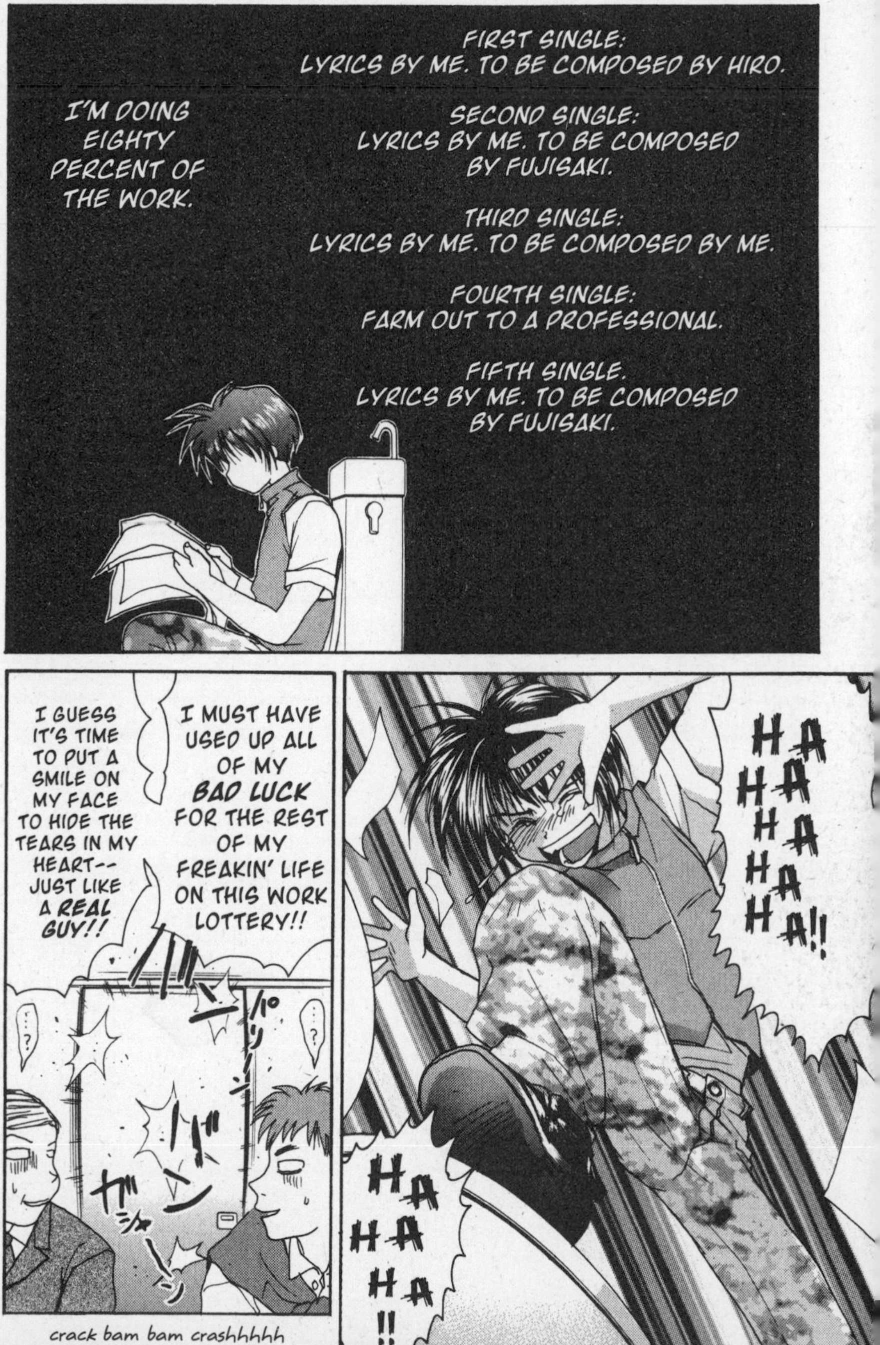
FIRST SINGLE:
LYRICS BY ME. TO BE COMPOSED BY HIRO.
SECOND SINGLE:
LYRICS BY ME. TO BE COMPOSED BY FUJISAKI.
THIRD SINGLE:
LYRICS BY ME. TO BE COMPOSED BY ME.
FOURTH SINGLE:
FARM OUT TO A PROFESSIONAL.
FIFTH SINGLE.
LYRICS BY ME. TO BE COMPOSED BY FUJISAKI.
I'M DOING EIGHTY PERCENT OF THE WORK.
HA HA HA HA HA HA HA HA HA HA!!
HA HA HA HA !!
I MUST HAVE USED UP ALL OF MY BAD LUCK FOR THE REST OF MY FREAKIN' LIFE ON THIS WORK LOTTERY!!
I GUESS IT'S TIME TO PUT A SMILE ON MY FACE TO HIDE THE TEARS IN MY HEART-- JUST LIKE A REAL GUY!!
...?
...?
パリン
ガシャーン
crack bam bam crashhhhh

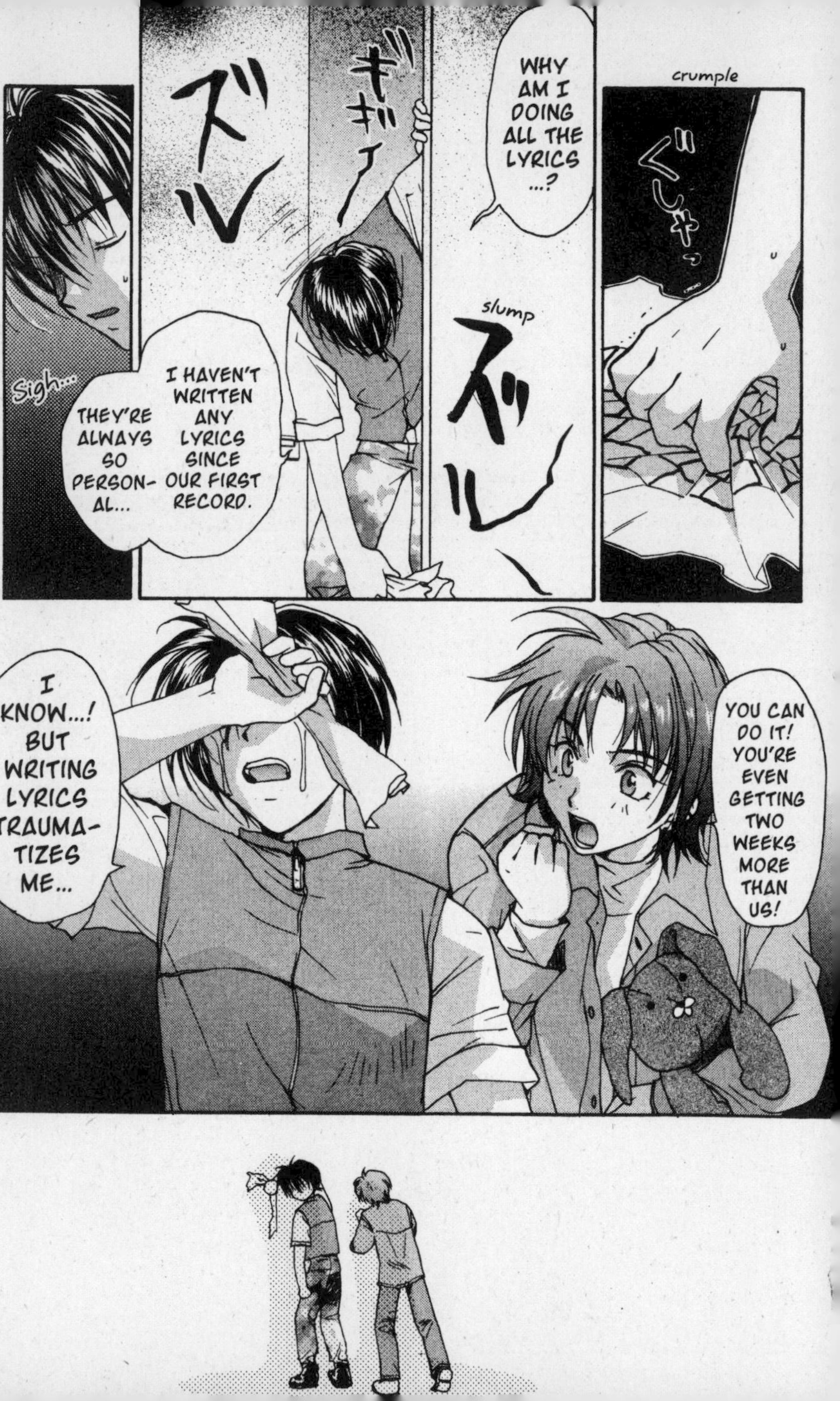
crumple
ぐしゃっ
WHY AM I DOING ALL THE LYRICS ...?
slump
ズッル
ギギィ
ズル
I HAVEN'T WRITTEN ANY LYRICS SINCE OUR FIRST RECORD.
THEY'RE ALWAYS SO PERSON-AL...
Sigh...
YOU CAN DO IT! YOU'RE EVEN GETTING TWO WEEKS MORE THAN US!
I KNOW...! BUT WRITING LYRICS TRAUMA-TIZES ME...

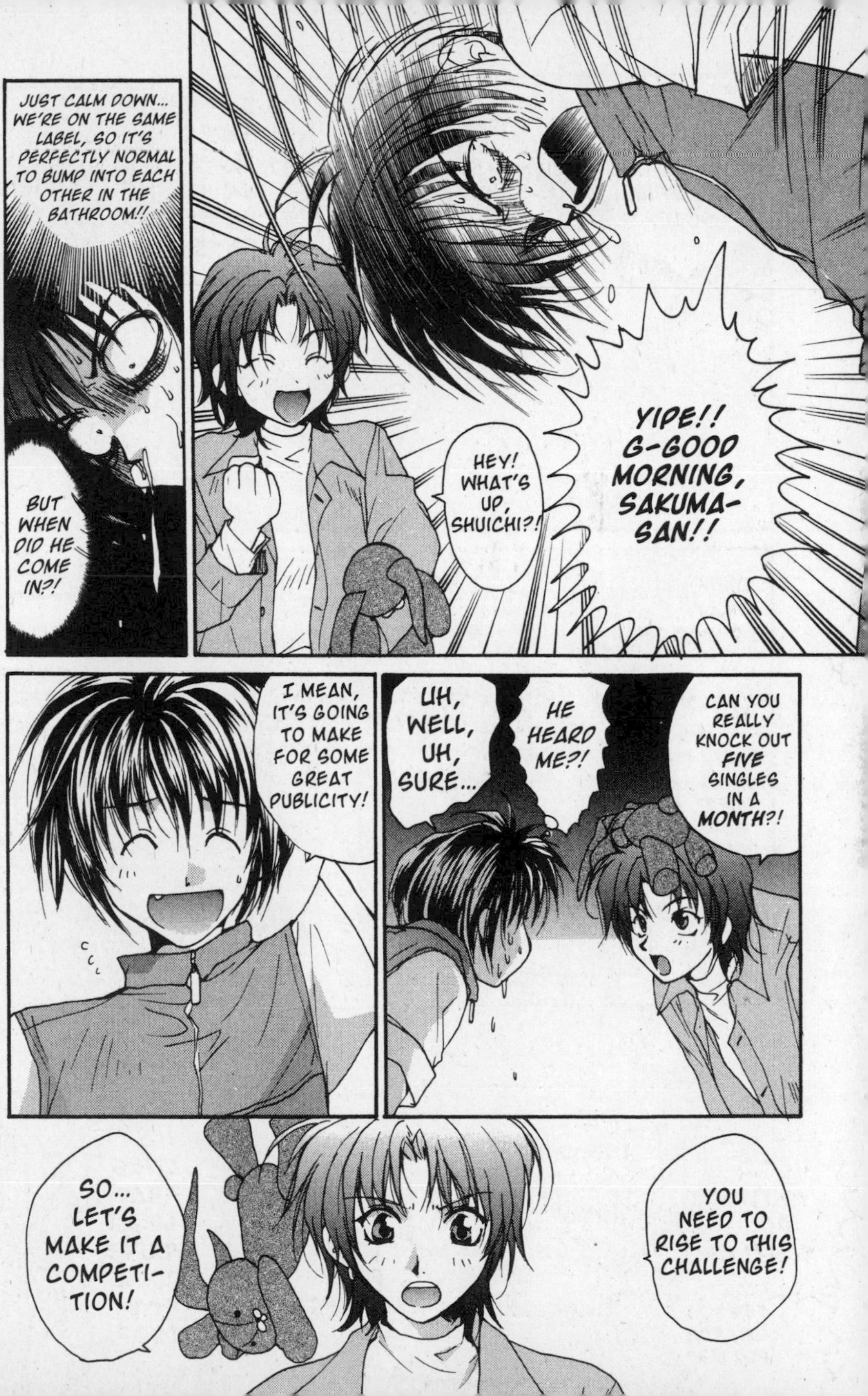
YIPE!! G-GOOD MORNING, SAKUMA-SAN!!
HEY! WHAT'S UP, SHUICHI?!
JUST CALM DOWN... WE'RE ON THE SAME LABEL, SO IT'S PERFECTLY NORMAL TO BUMP INTO EACH OTHER IN THE BATHROOM!!
BUT WHEN DID HE COME IN?!
CAN YOU REALLY KNOCK OUT FIVE SINGLES IN A MONTH?!
HE HEARD ME?!
UH, WELL, UH, SURE...
I MEAN, IT'S GOING TO MAKE FOR SOME GREAT PUBLICITY!
YOU NEED TO RISE TO THIS CHALLENGE!
SO... LET'S MAKE IT A COMPETITION!

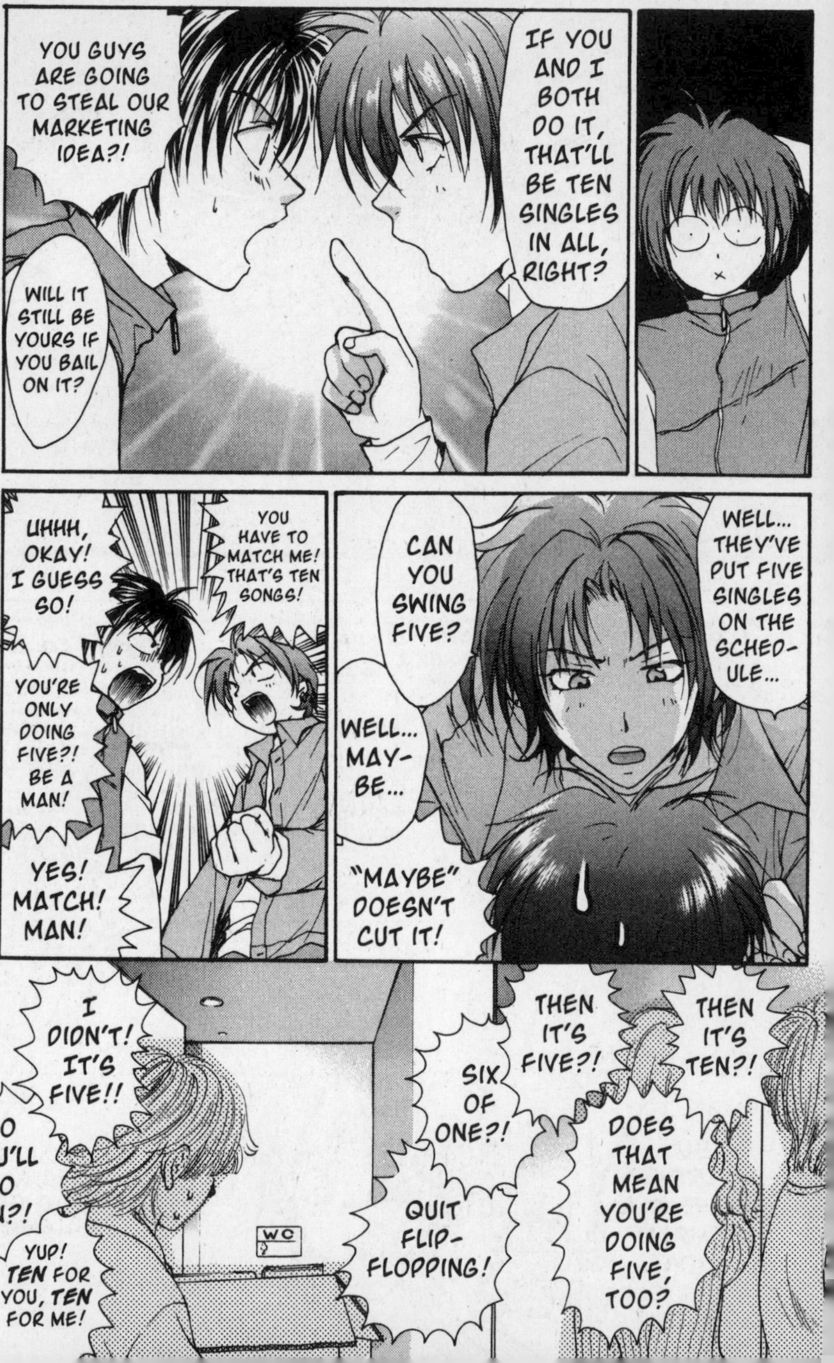
IF YOU AND I BOTH DO IT, THAT'LL BE TEN SINGLES IN ALL, RIGHT?
YOU GUYS ARE GOING TO STEAL OUR MARKETING IDEA?!
WILL IT STILL BE YOURS IF YOU BAIL ON IT?
WELL... THEY'VE PUT FIVE SINGLES ON THE SCHEDULE...
CAN YOU SWING FIVE?
WELL... MAYBE...
"MAYBE" DOESN'T CUT IT!
YOU HAVE TO MATCH ME! THAT'S TEN SONGS!
UHHH, OKAY! I GUESS SO!
YOU'RE ONLY DOING FIVE?! BE A MAN!
YES! MATCH! MAN!
THEN IT'S TEN?!
THEN IT'S FIVE?!
SIX OF ONE?!
DOES THAT MEAN YOU'RE DOING FIVE, TOO?
QUIT FLIP-FLOPPING!
I DIDN'T! IT'S FIVE!!
SO YOU'LL DO TEN?!
YUP! **TEN** FOR YOU, **TEN** FOR ME!
WC

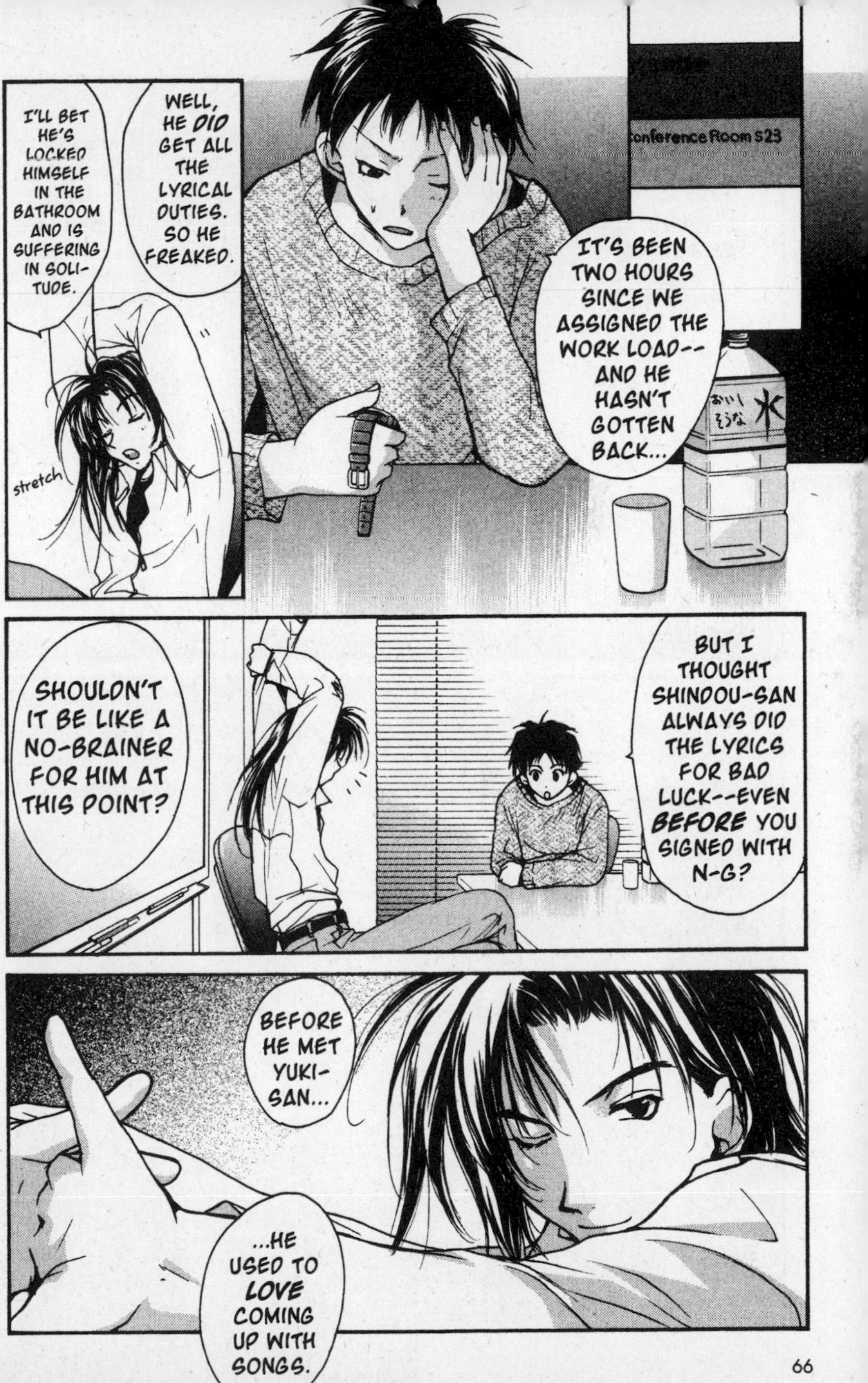

conference Room S23
IT'S BEEN TWO HOURS SINCE WE ASSIGNED THE WORK LOAD-- AND HE HASN'T GOTTEN BACK...
おいしそうな水
WELL, HE *DID* GET ALL THE LYRICAL DUTIES. SO HE FREAKED.
I'LL BET HE'S LOCKED HIMSELF IN THE BATHROOM AND IS SUFFERING IN SOLI-TUDE.
stretch
BUT I THOUGHT SHINDOU-SAN ALWAYS DID THE LYRICS FOR BAD LUCK--EVEN ***BEFORE*** YOU SIGNED WITH N-G?
SHOULDN'T IT BE LIKE A NO-BRAINER FOR HIM AT THIS POINT?
BEFORE HE MET YUKI-SAN...
...HE USED TO ***LOVE*** COMING UP WITH SONGS.

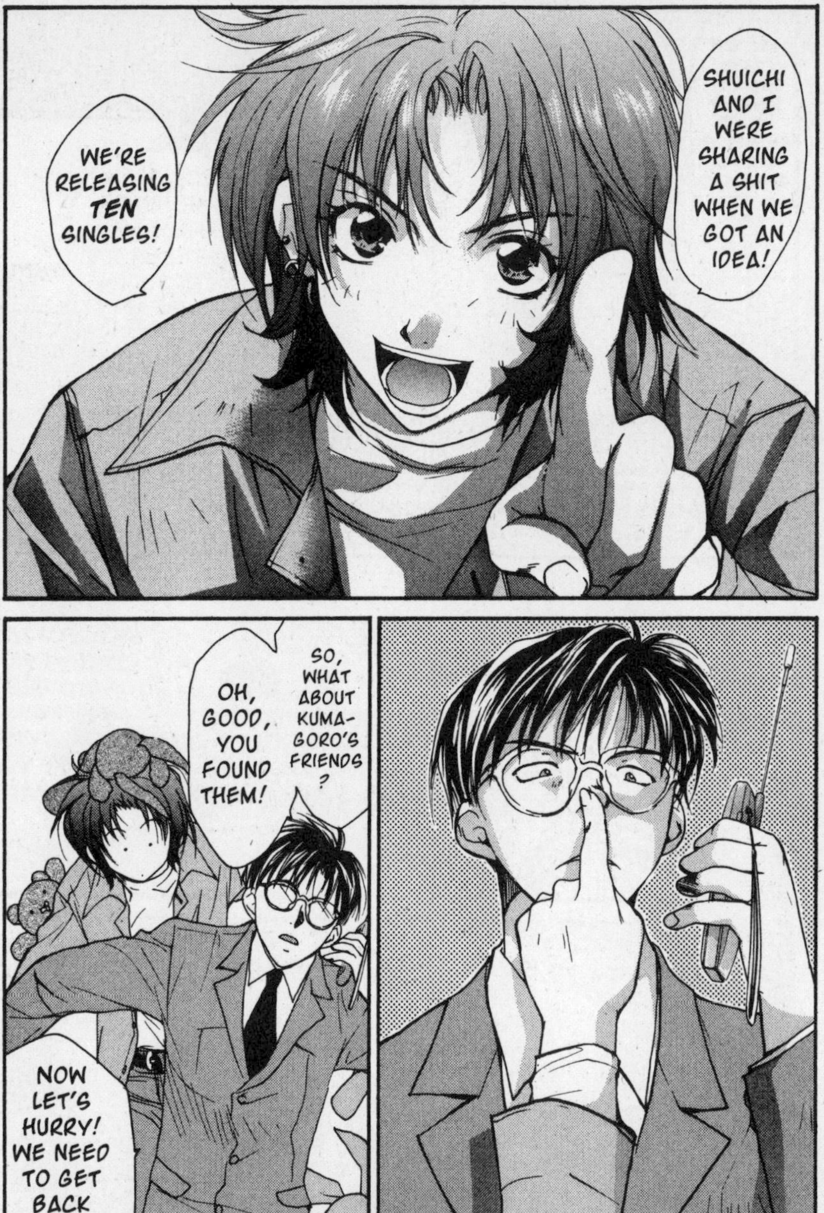
SHUICHI AND I WERE SHARING A SHIT WHEN WE GOT AN IDEA!
WE'RE RELEASING TEN SINGLES!
SO, WHAT ABOUT KUMAGORO'S FRIENDS?
OH, GOOD, YOU FOUND THEM!
NOW LET'S HURRY! WE NEED TO GET BACK TO THE SHOOT!

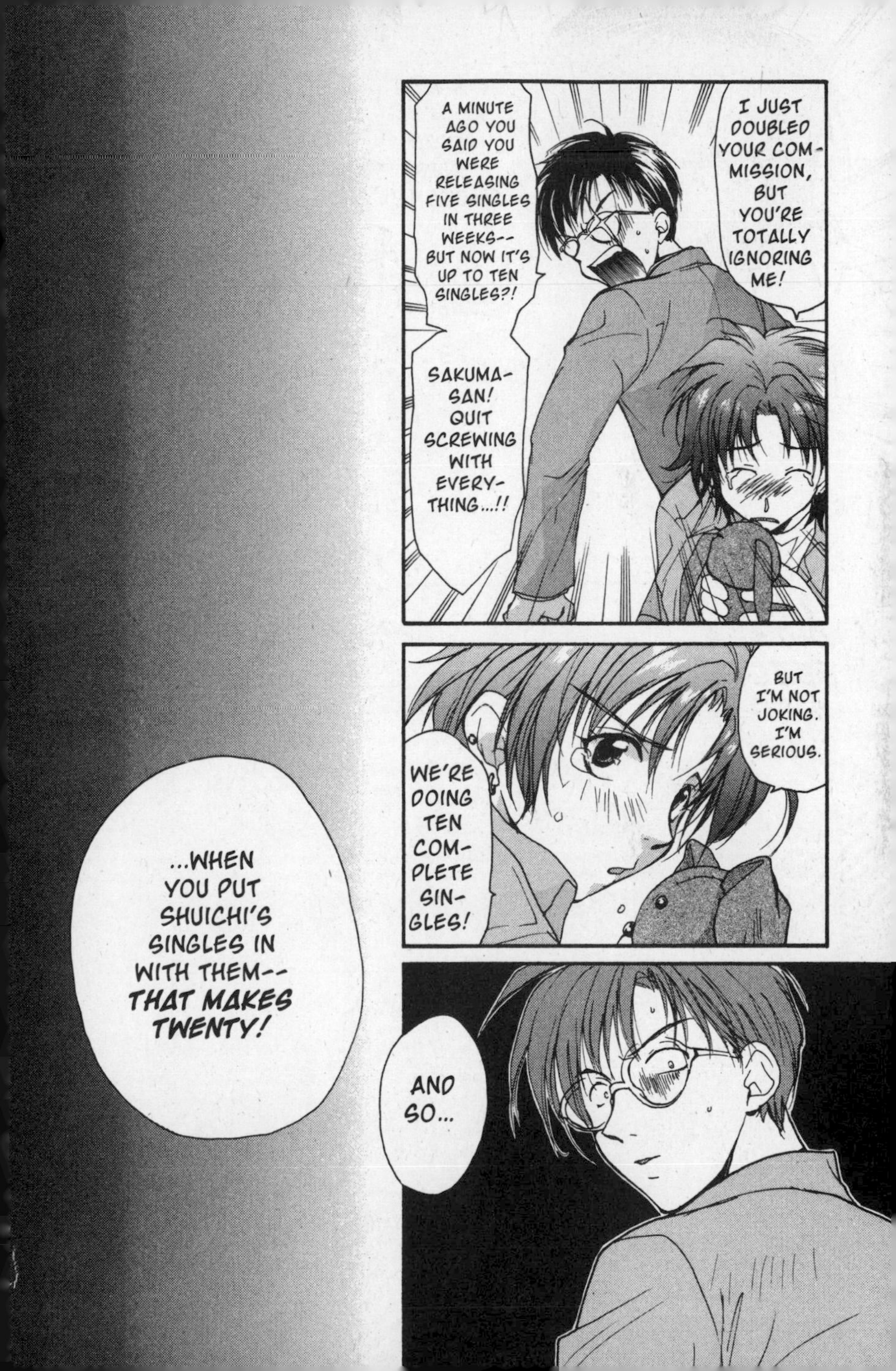
I JUST DOUBLED YOUR COM-MISSION, BUT YOU'RE TOTALLY IGNORING ME!
A MINUTE AGO YOU SAID YOU WERE RELEASING FIVE SINGLES IN THREE WEEKS-- BUT NOW IT'S UP TO TEN SINGLES?!
SAKUMA-SAN! QUIT SCREWING WITH EVERY-THING...!!
BUT I'M NOT JOKING. I'M SERIOUS.
WE'RE DOING TEN COM-PLETE SIN-GLES!
AND SO...
...WHEN YOU PUT SHUICHI'S SINGLES IN WITH THEM-- THAT MAKES TWENTY!

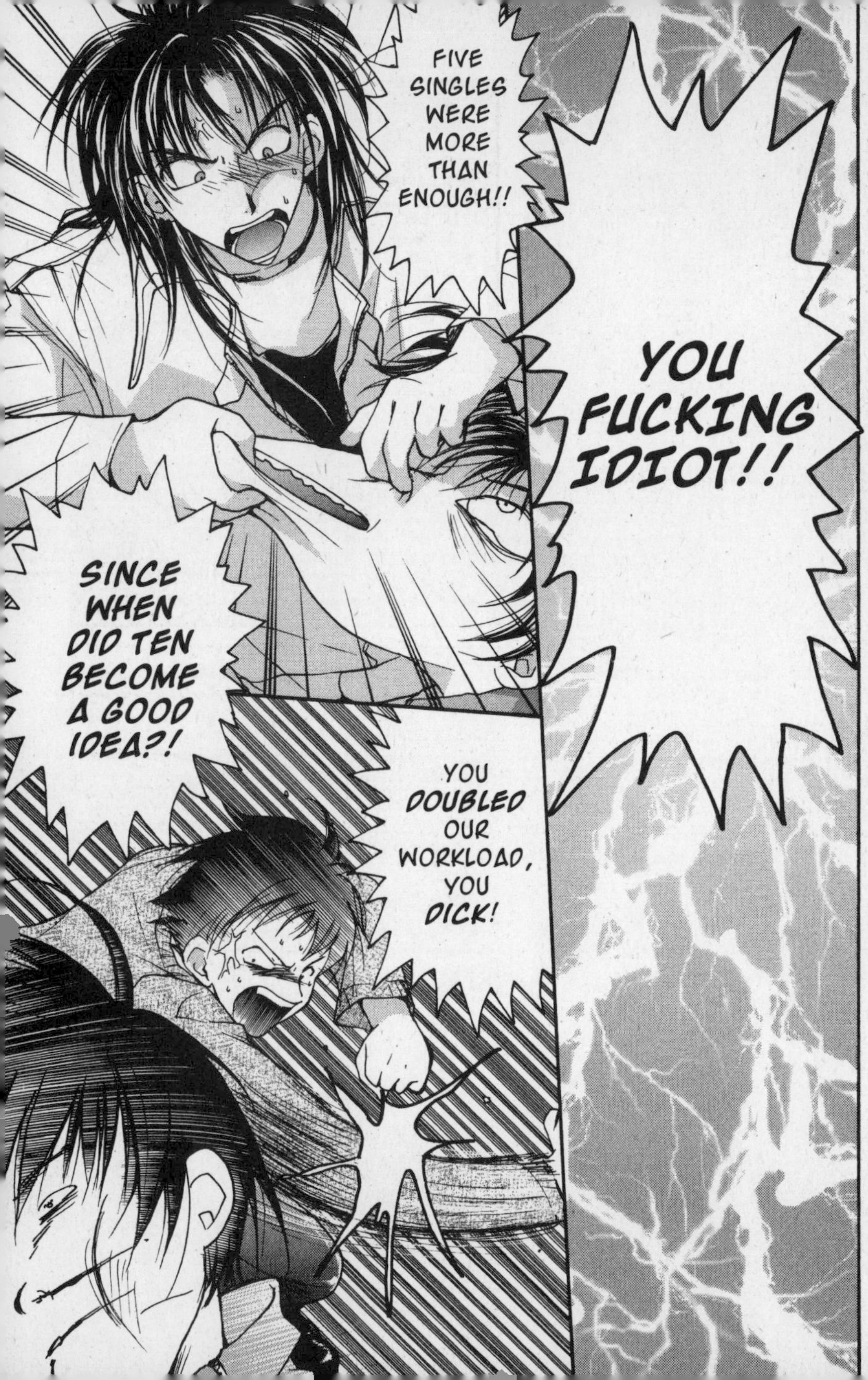
YOU FUCKING IDIOT!!
FIVE SINGLES WERE MORE THAN ENOUGH!!
SINCE WHEN DID TEN BECOME A GOOD IDEA?!
YOU DOUBLED OUR WORKLOAD, YOU DICK!

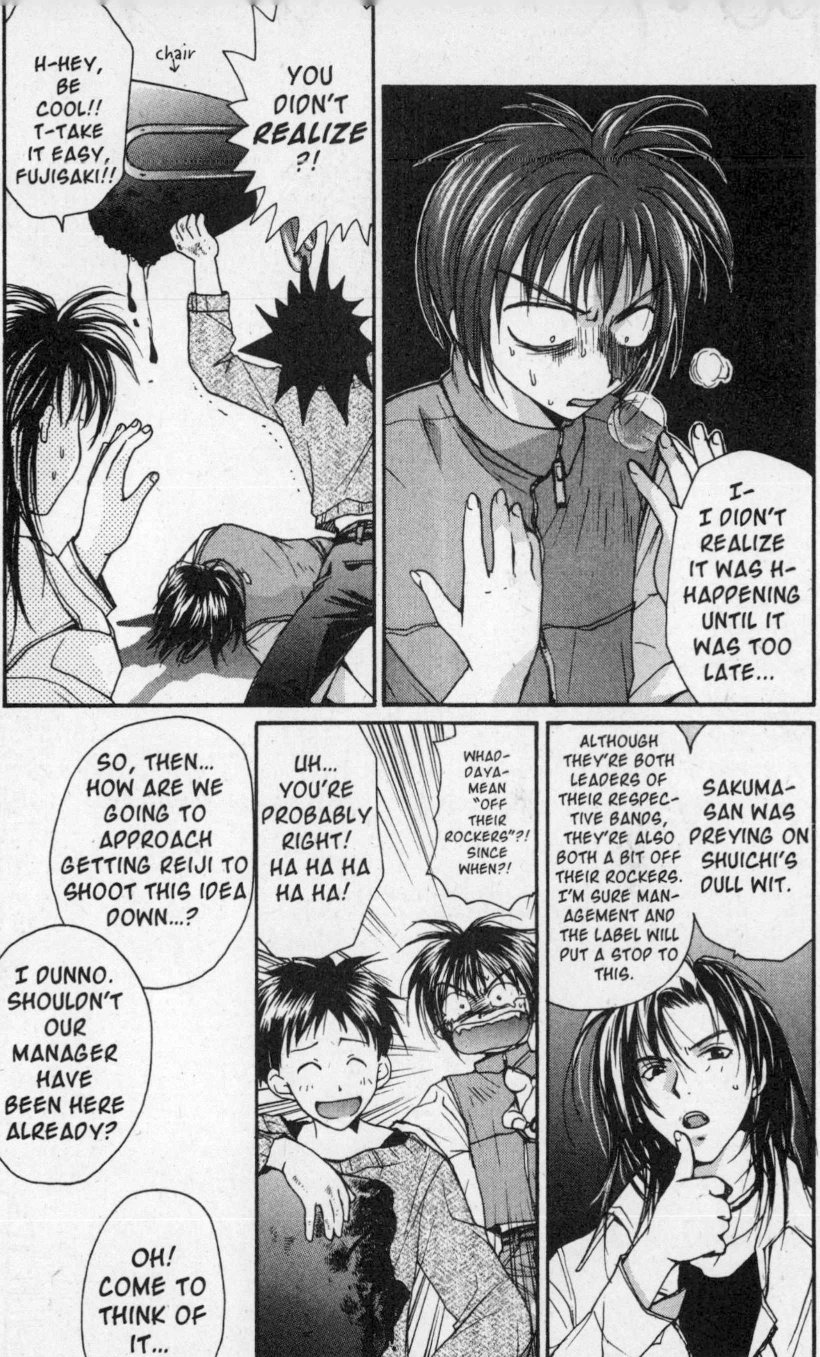
I-
I DIDN'T REALIZE IT WAS H-HAPPENING UNTIL IT WAS TOO LATE...
YOU DIDN'T REALIZE ?!
chair
H-HEY, BE COOL!! T-TAKE IT EASY, FUJISAKI!!
SAKUMA-SAN WAS PREYING ON SHUICHI'S DULL WIT.
ALTHOUGH THEY'RE BOTH LEADERS OF THEIR RESPEC-TIVE BANDS, THEY'RE ALSO BOTH A BIT OFF THEIR ROCKERS. I'M SURE MAN-AGEMENT AND THE LABEL WILL PUT A STOP TO THIS.
WHAD-DAYA-MEAN "OFF THEIR ROCKERS"?! SINCE WHEN?!
UH... YOU'RE PROBABLY RIGHT! HA HA HA HA HA!
SO, THEN... HOW ARE WE GOING TO APPROACH GETTING REIJI TO SHOOT THIS IDEA DOWN...?
I DUNNO. SHOULDN'T OUR MANAGER HAVE BEEN HERE ALREADY?
OH! COME TO THINK OF IT...

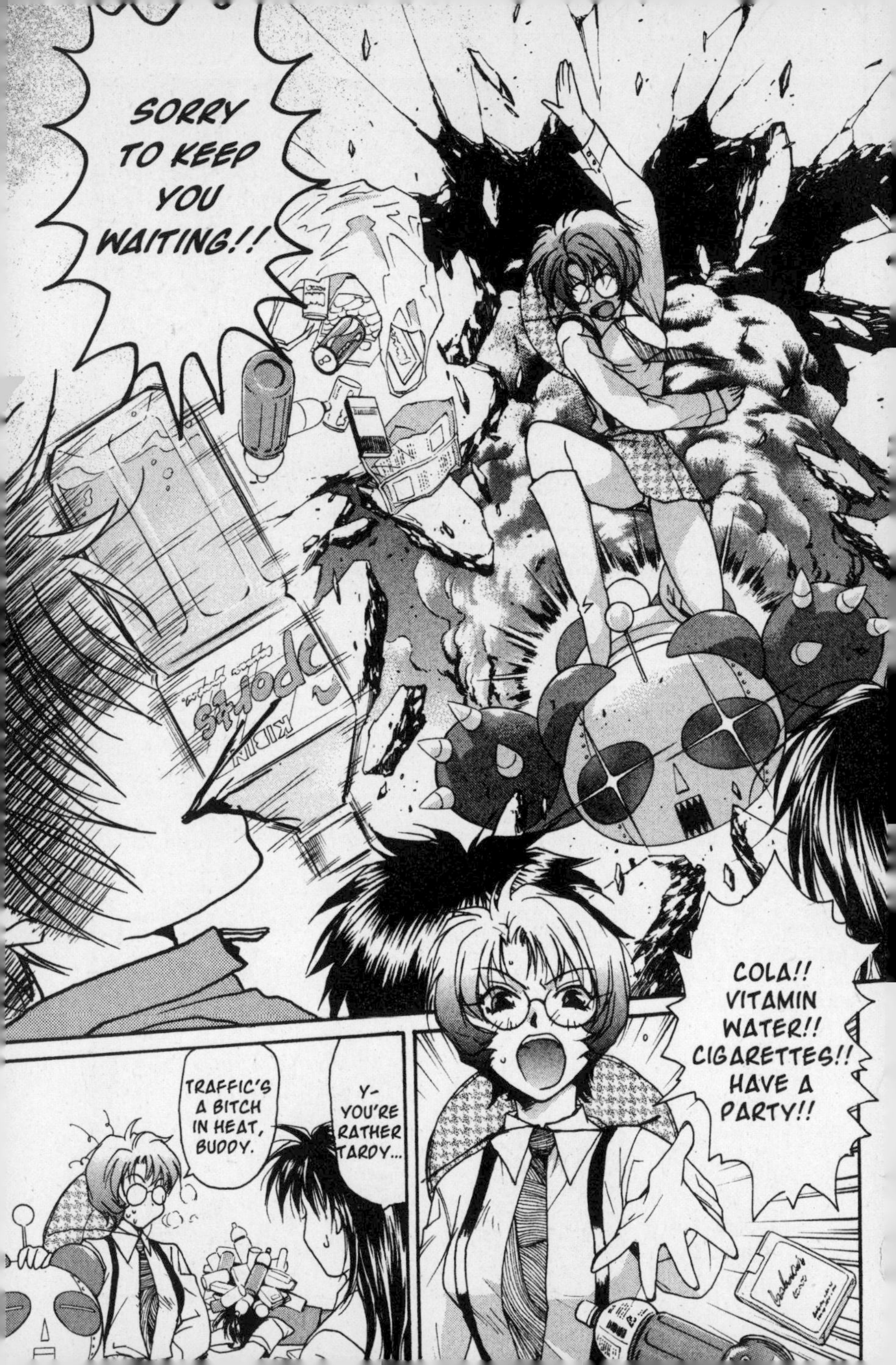
SORRY TO KEEP YOU WAITING!!
COLA!! VITAMIN WATER!! CIGARETTES!! HAVE A PARTY!!
Y- YOU'RE RATHER TARDY...
TRAFFIC'S A BITCH IN HEAT, BUDDY.

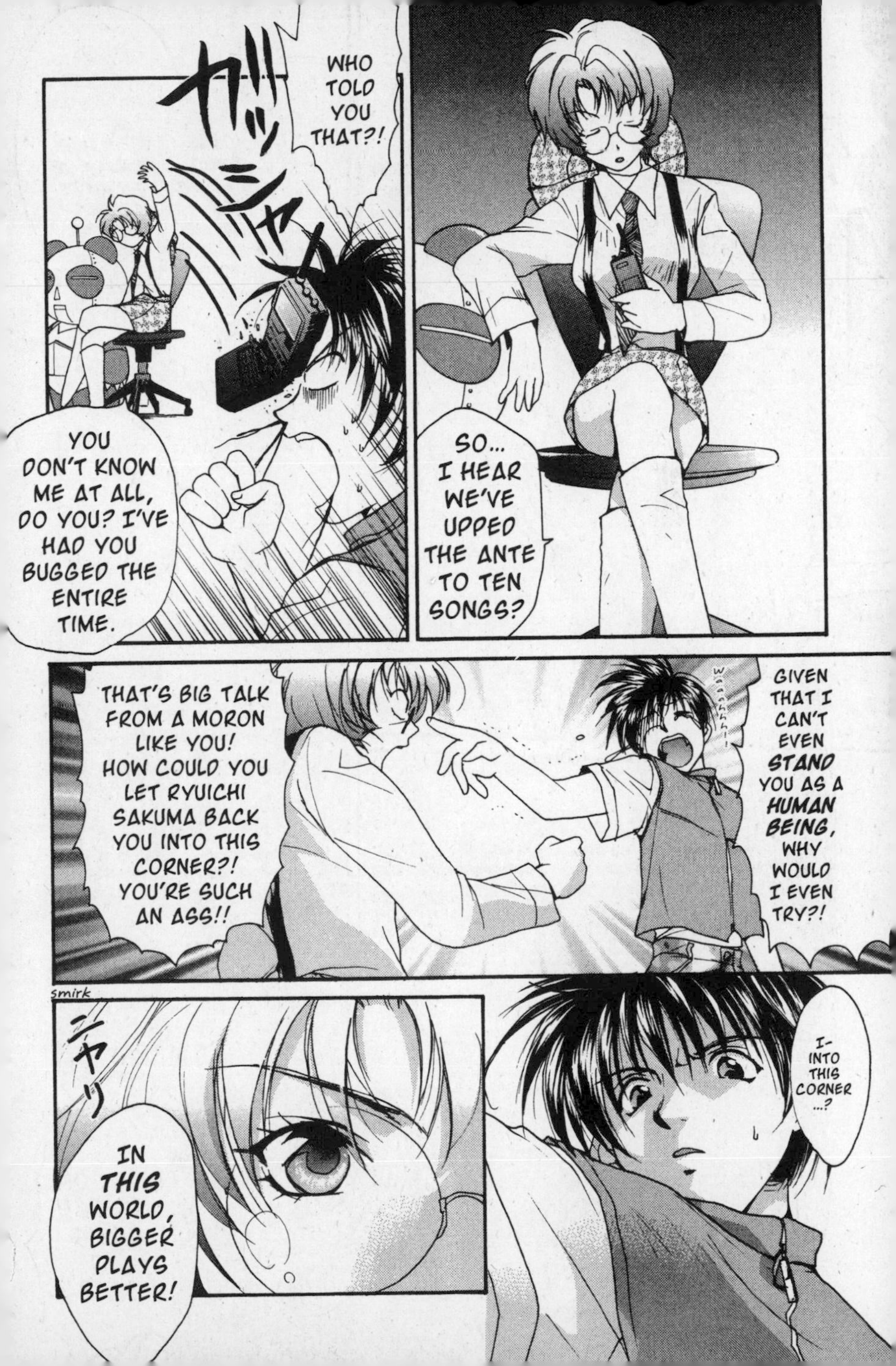
SO... I HEAR WE'VE UPPED THE ANTE TO TEN SONGS?
WHO TOLD YOU THAT?!
YOU DON'T KNOW ME AT ALL, DO YOU? I'VE HAD YOU BUGGED THE ENTIRE TIME.
GIVEN THAT I CAN'T EVEN STAND YOU AS A HUMAN BEING, WHY WOULD I EVEN TRY?!
THAT'S BIG TALK FROM A MORON LIKE YOU! HOW COULD YOU LET RYUICHI SAKUMA BACK YOU INTO THIS CORNER?! YOU'RE SUCH AN ASS!!
I- INTO THIS CORNER ...?
smirk
IN THIS WORLD, BIGGER PLAYS BETTER!

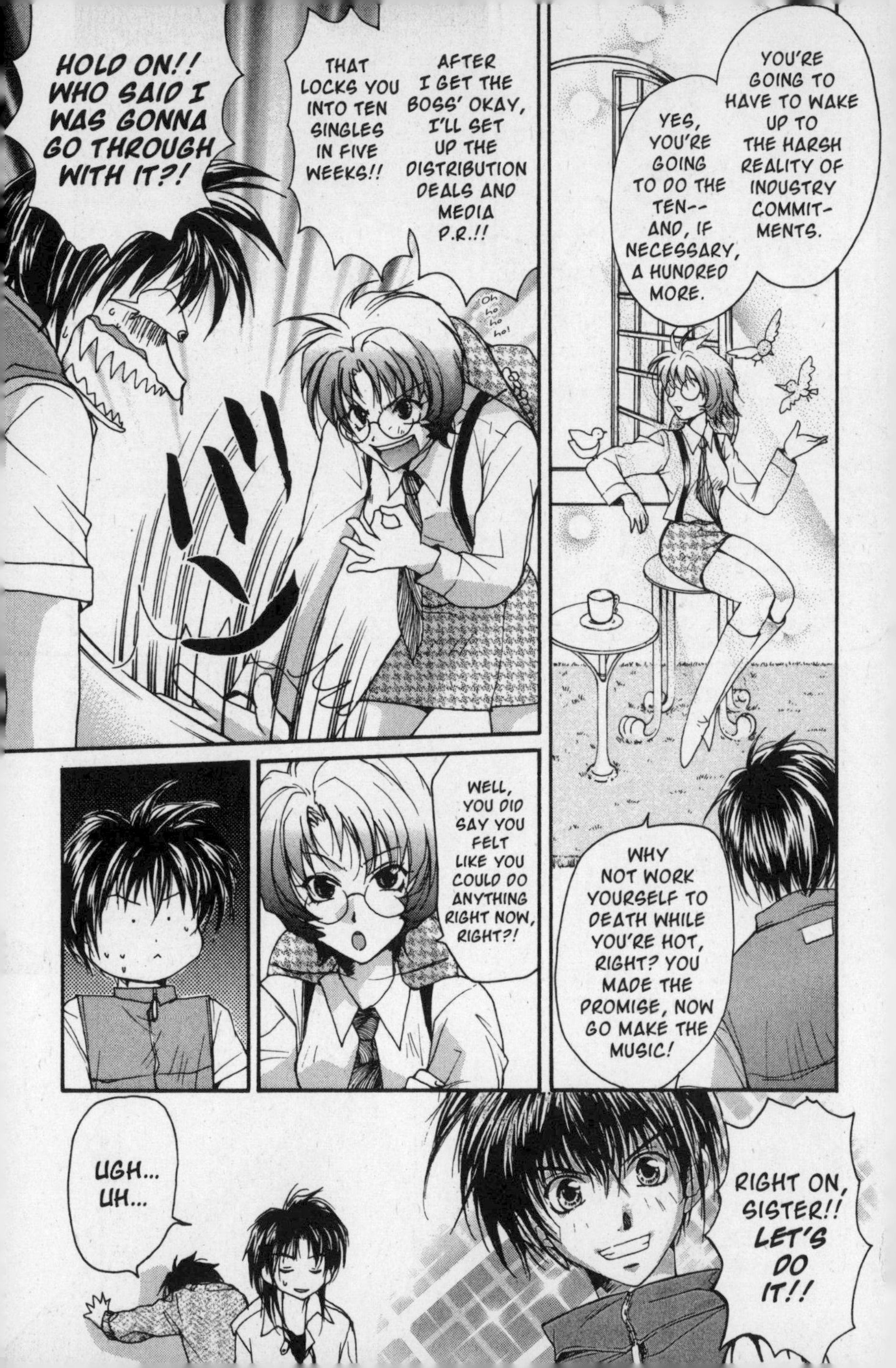

HOLD ON!! WHO SAID I WAS GONNA GO THROUGH WITH IT?!
THAT LOCKS YOU INTO TEN SINGLES IN FIVE WEEKS!!
AFTER I GET THE BOSS' OKAY, I'LL SET UP THE DISTRIBUTION DEALS AND MEDIA P.R.!!
Oh ho ho ho!
YES, YOU'RE GOING TO DO THE TEN-- AND, IF NECESSARY, A HUNDRED MORE.
YOU'RE GOING TO HAVE TO WAKE UP TO THE HARSH REALITY OF INDUSTRY COMMIT-MENTS.
WELL, YOU DID SAY YOU FELT LIKE YOU COULD DO ANYTHING RIGHT NOW, RIGHT?!
WHY NOT WORK YOURSELF TO DEATH WHILE YOU'RE HOT, RIGHT? YOU MADE THE PROMISE, NOW GO MAKE THE MUSIC!
UGH... UH...
RIGHT ON, SISTER!! LET'S DO IT!!

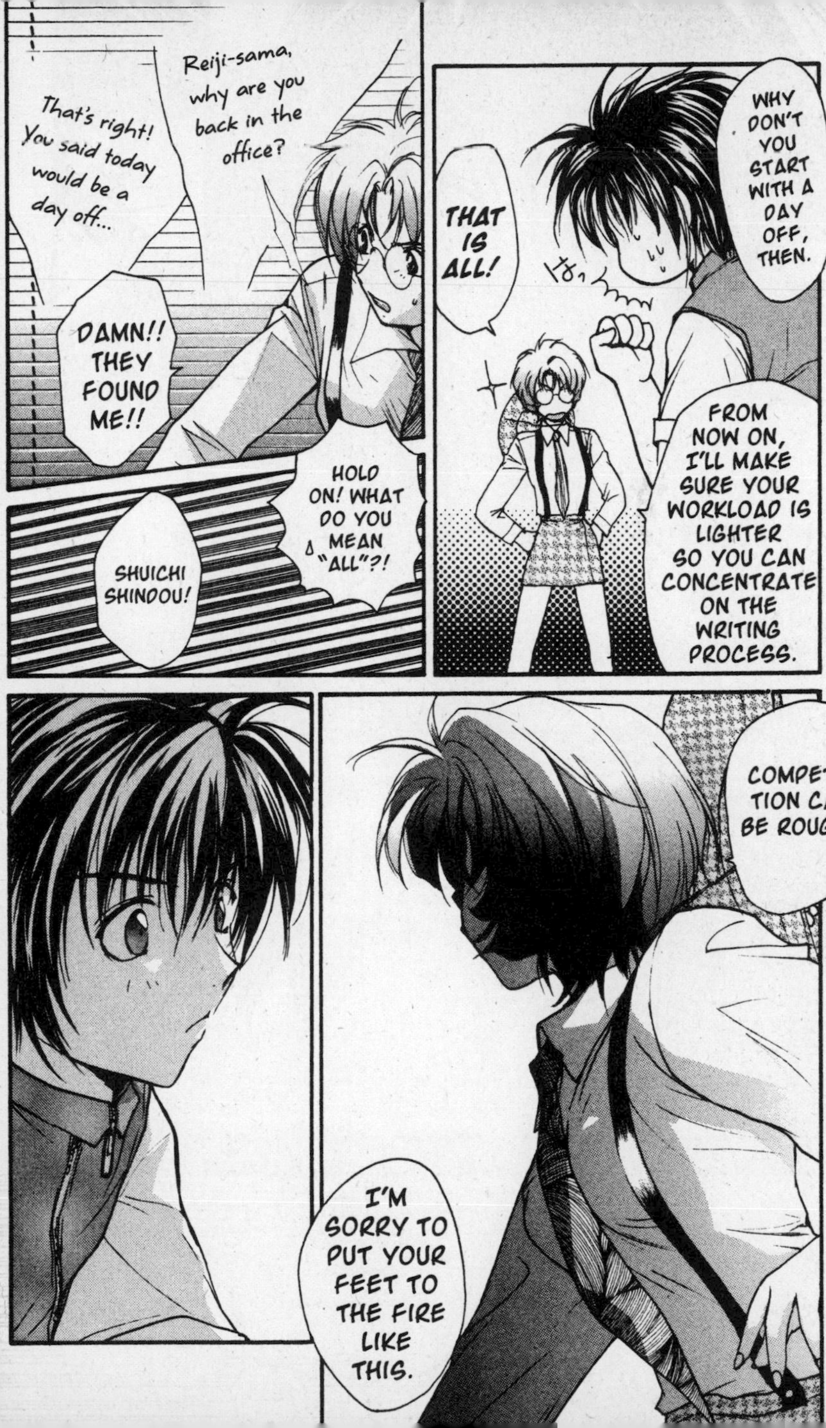
WHY DON'T YOU START WITH A DAY OFF, THEN.
THAT IS ALL!
FROM NOW ON, I'LL MAKE SURE YOUR WORKLOAD IS LIGHTER SO YOU CAN CONCENTRATE ON THE WRITING PROCESS.
Reiji-sama, why are you back in the office?
That's right! You said today would be a day off...
DAMN!! THEY FOUND ME!!
HOLD ON! WHAT DO YOU MEAN "ALL"?!
SHUICHI SHINDOU!
COMPETITION CAN BE ROUGH.
I'M SORRY TO PUT YOUR FEET TO THE FIRE LIKE THIS.

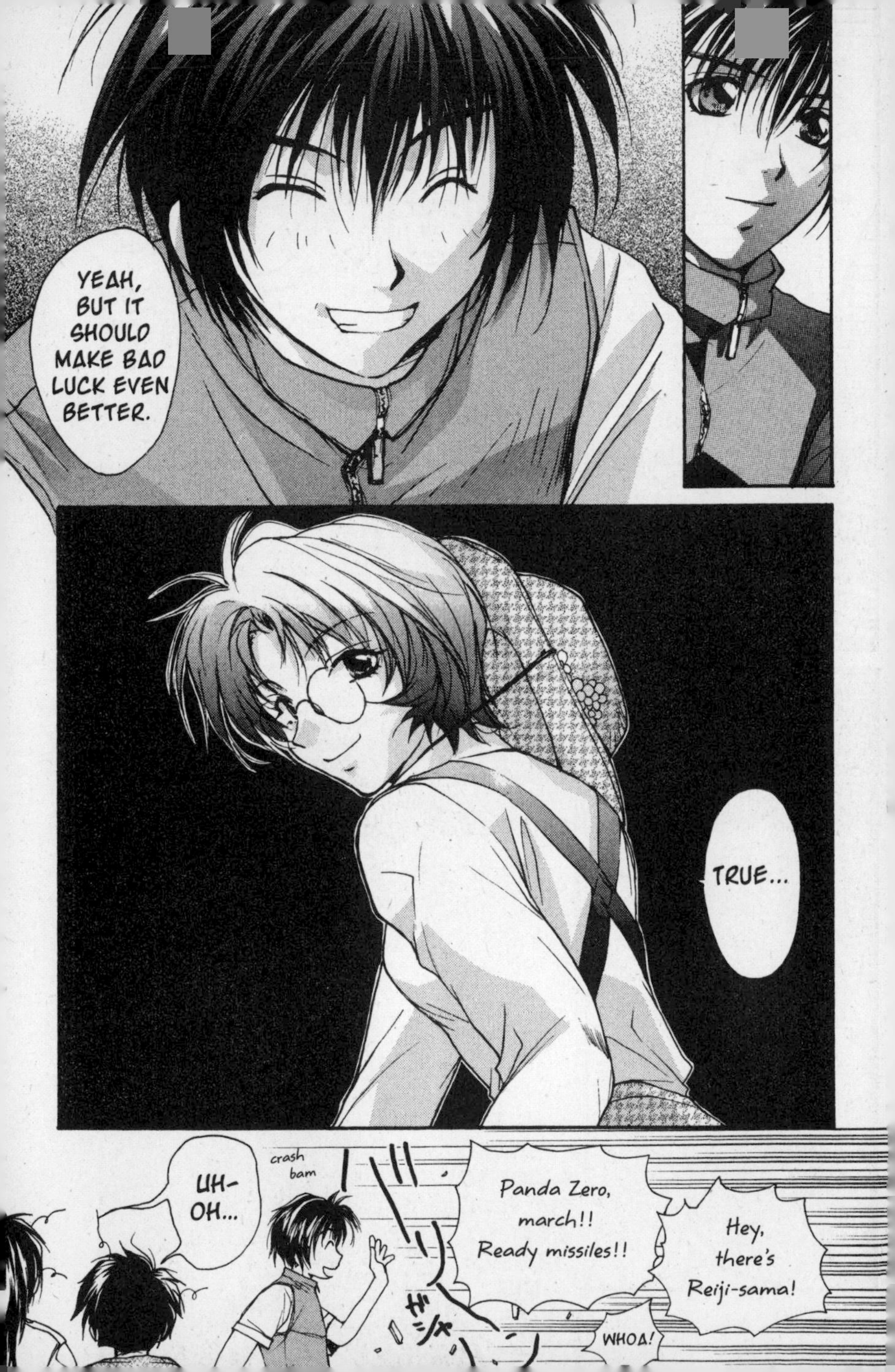
YEAH, BUT IT SHOULD MAKE BAD LUCK EVEN BETTER.
TRUE...
Hey, there's Reiji-sama!
Panda Zero, march!! Ready missiles!!
WHOA!
ガシャ
crash bam
UH-OH...

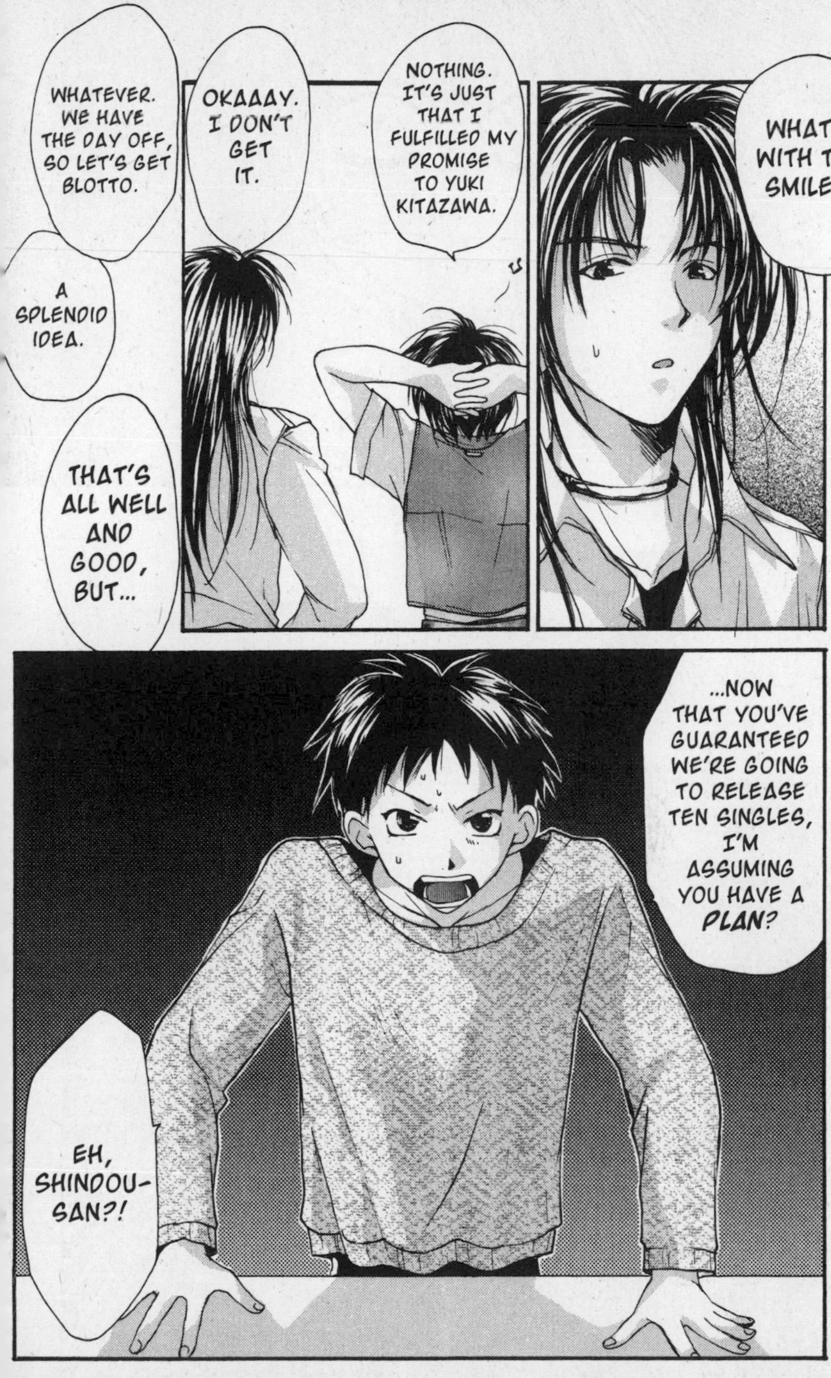
WHAT'S WITH THE SMILE?
NOTHING. IT'S JUST THAT I FULFILLED MY PROMISE TO YUKI KITAZAWA.
OKAAAY. I DON'T GET IT.
WHATEVER. WE HAVE THE DAY OFF, SO LET'S GET BLOTTO.
A SPLENDID IDEA.
THAT'S ALL WELL AND GOOD, BUT...
...NOW THAT YOU'VE GUARANTEED WE'RE GOING TO RELEASE TEN SINGLES, I'M ASSUMING YOU HAVE A *PLAN*?
EH, SHINDOU-SAN?!

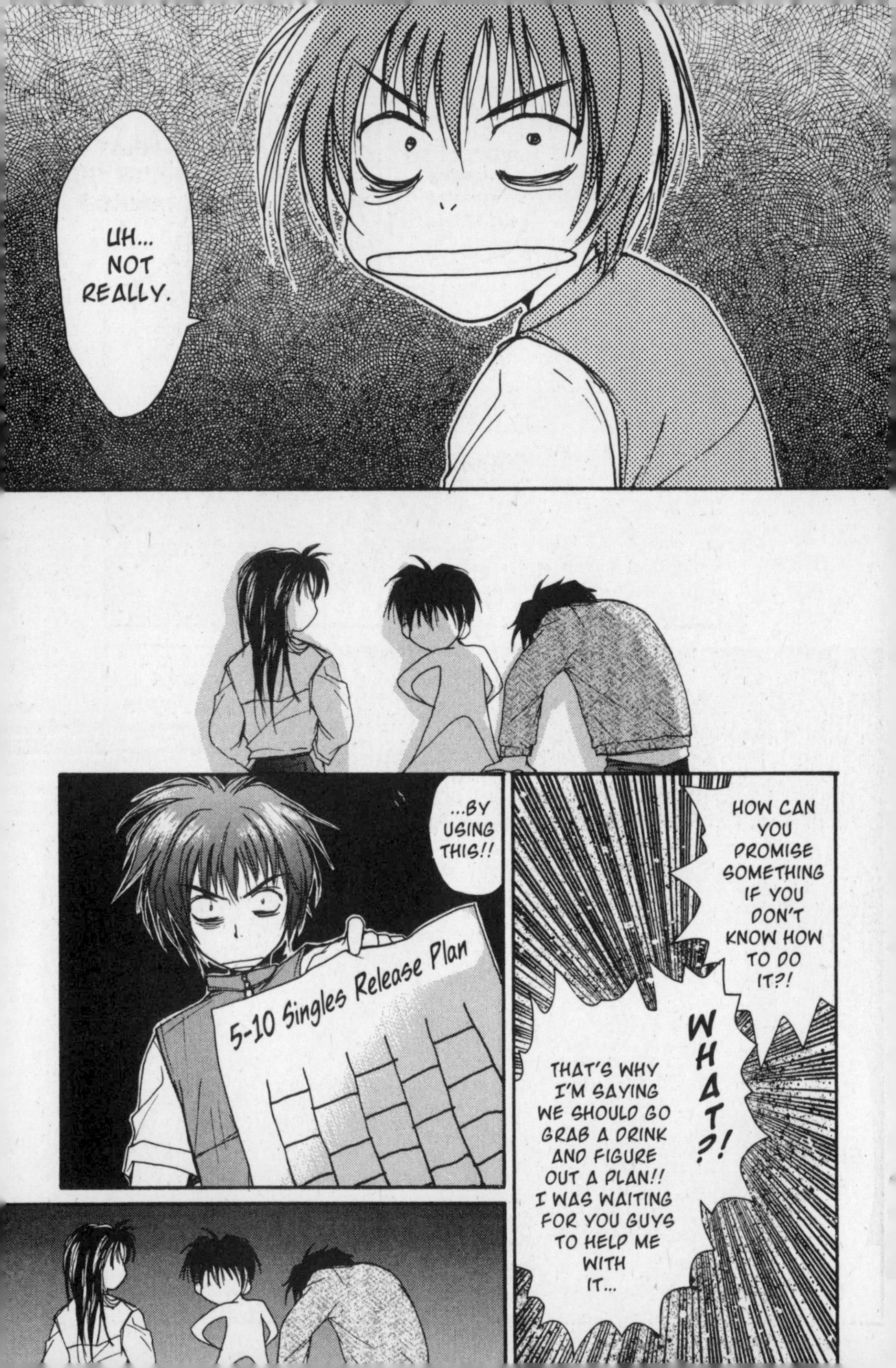
UH... NOT REALLY.
HOW CAN YOU PROMISE SOMETHING IF YOU DON'T KNOW HOW TO DO IT?!
WHAT?!
THAT'S WHY I'M SAYING WE SHOULD GO GRAB A DRINK AND FIGURE OUT A PLAN!! I WAS WAITING FOR YOU GUYS TO HELP ME WITH IT...
...BY USING THIS!!
5-10 Singles Release Plan

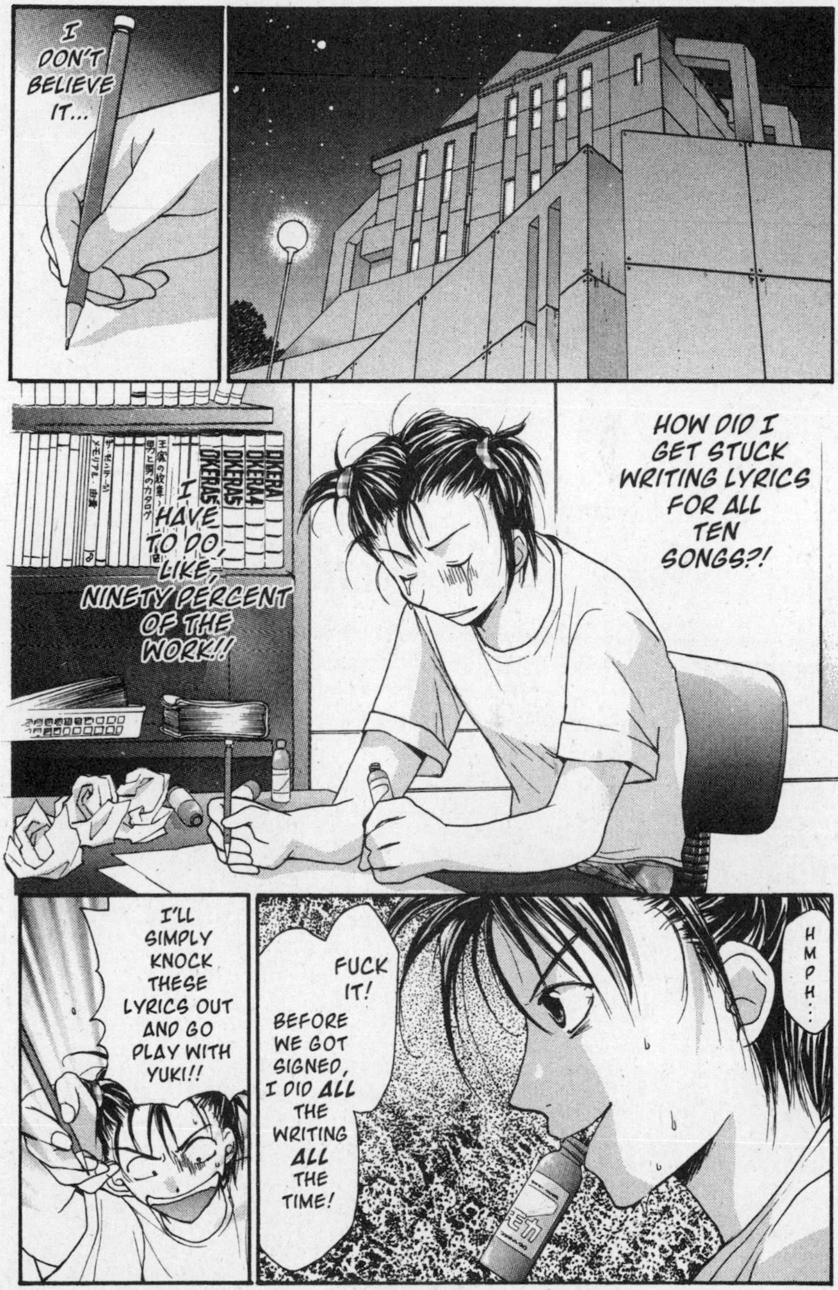
I DON'T BELIEVE IT...
HOW DID I GET STUCK WRITING LYRICS FOR ALL TEN SONGS?!
I HAVE TO DO, LIKE, NINETY PERCENT OF THE WORK!!
HMPH...
FUCK IT!
BEFORE WE GOT SIGNED, I DID ALL THE WRITING ALL THE TIME!
I'LL SIMPLY KNOCK THESE LYRICS OUT AND GO PLAY WITH YUKI!!

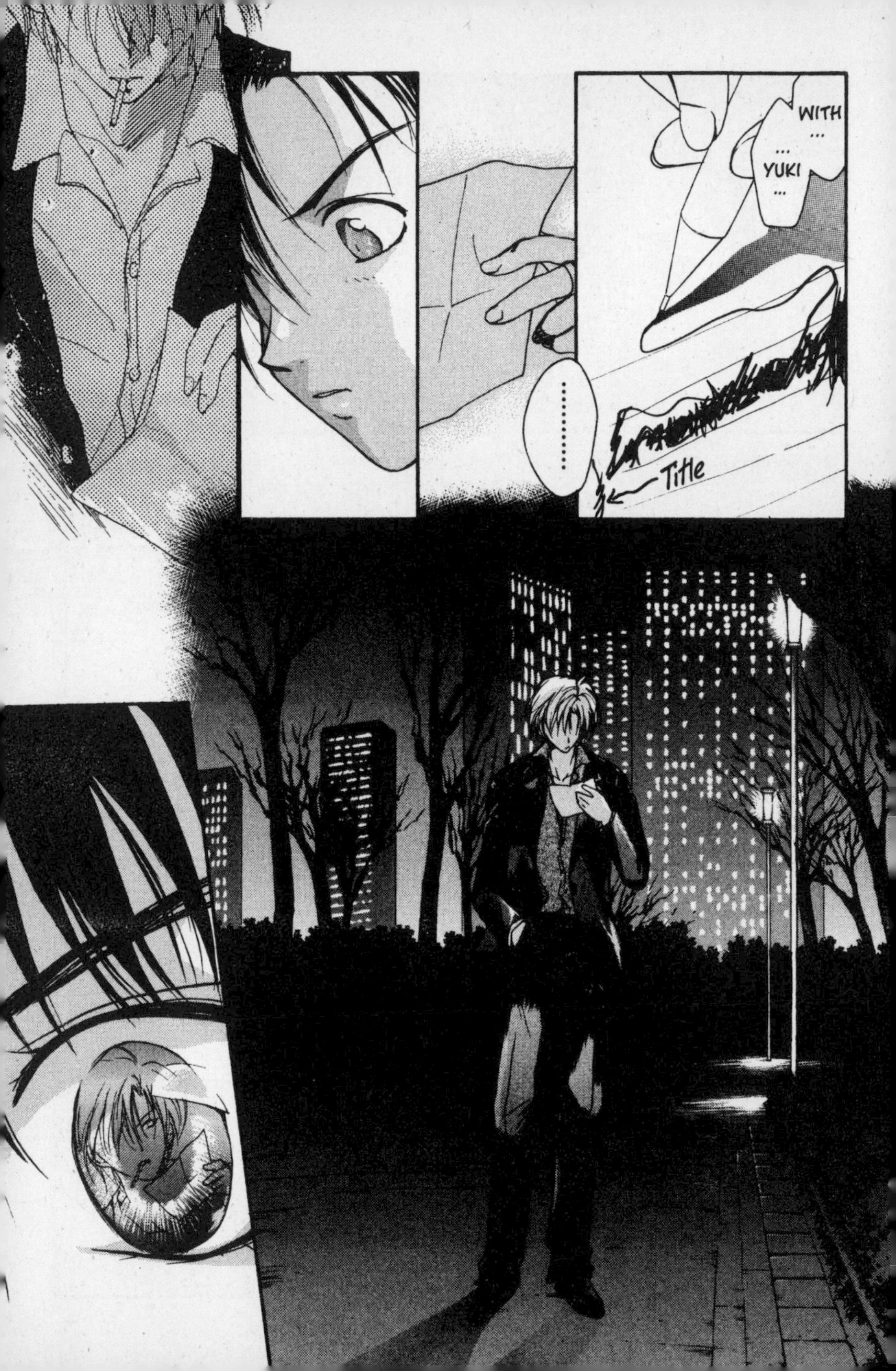
WITH ... ... YUKI ...
Title
......

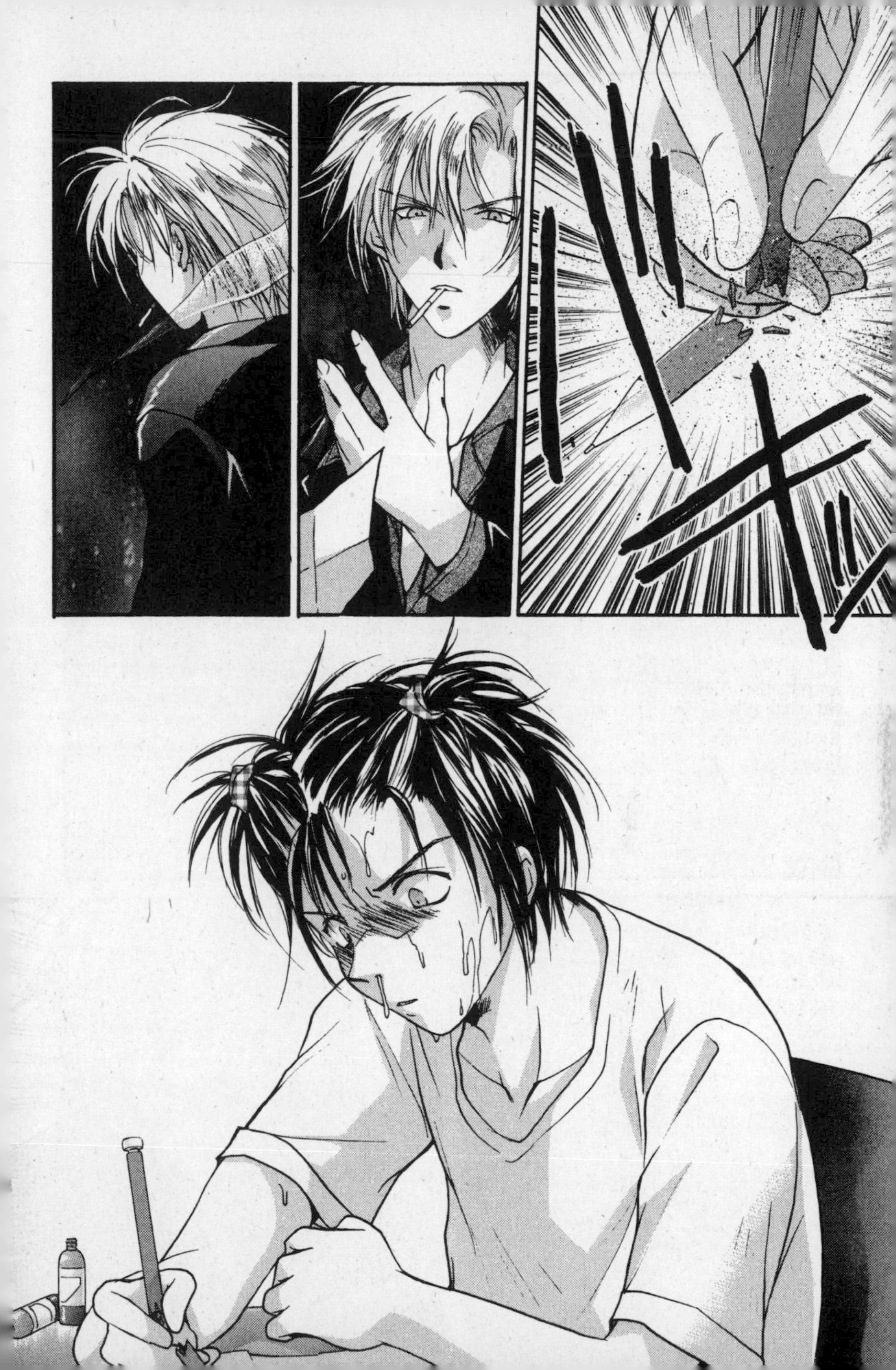

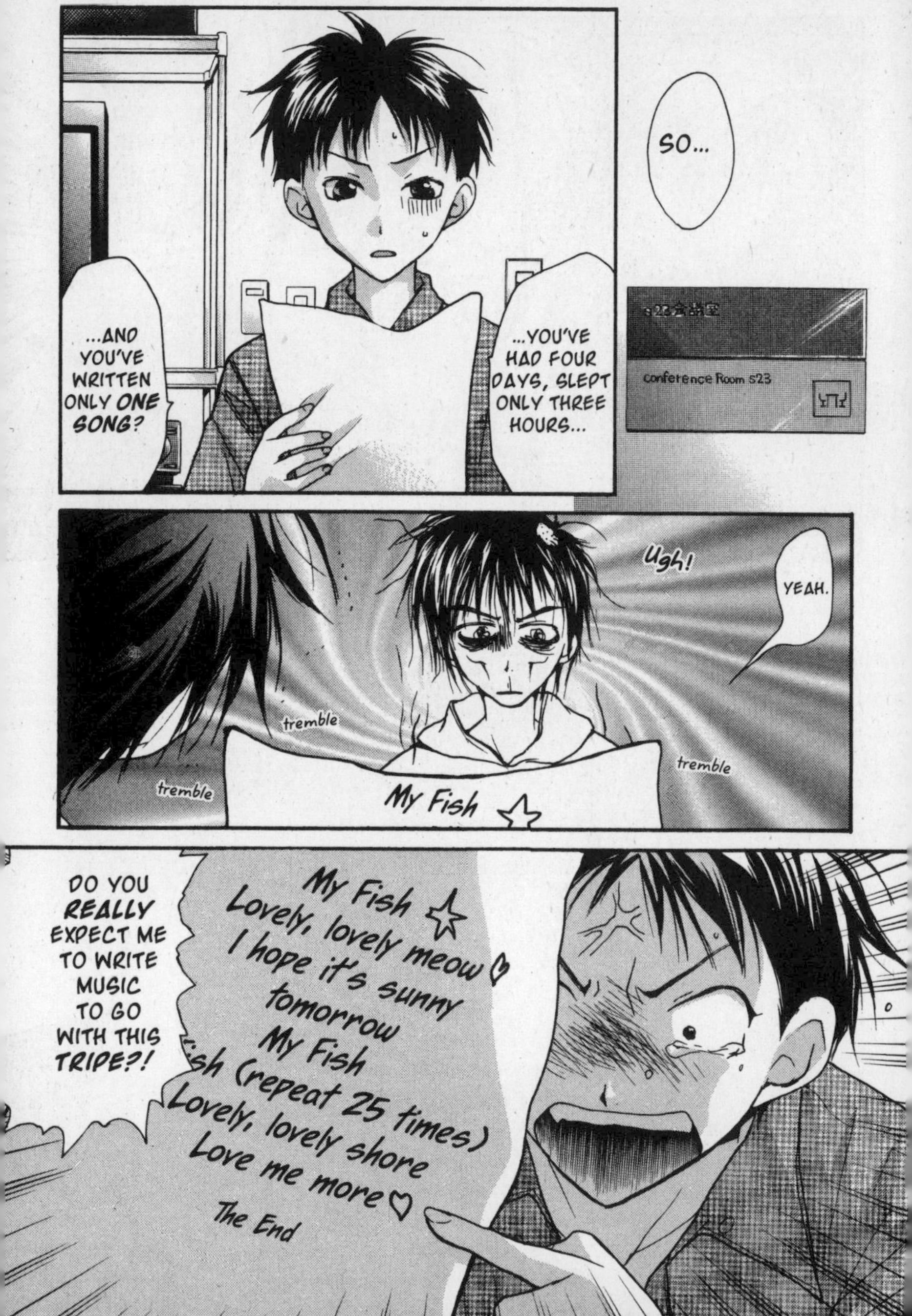
SO...
conference Room s23
...YOU'VE HAD FOUR DAYS, SLEPT ONLY THREE HOURS...
...AND YOU'VE WRITTEN ONLY ONE SONG?
YEAH.
Ugh!
tremble
tremble
tremble
My Fish
My Fish ☆
Lovely, lovely meow ♡
I hope it's sunny
tomorrow
My Fish
ish (repeat 25 times)
Lovely, lovely shore
Love me more ♡
The End
DO YOU REALLY EXPECT ME TO WRITE MUSIC TO GO WITH THIS TRIPE?!

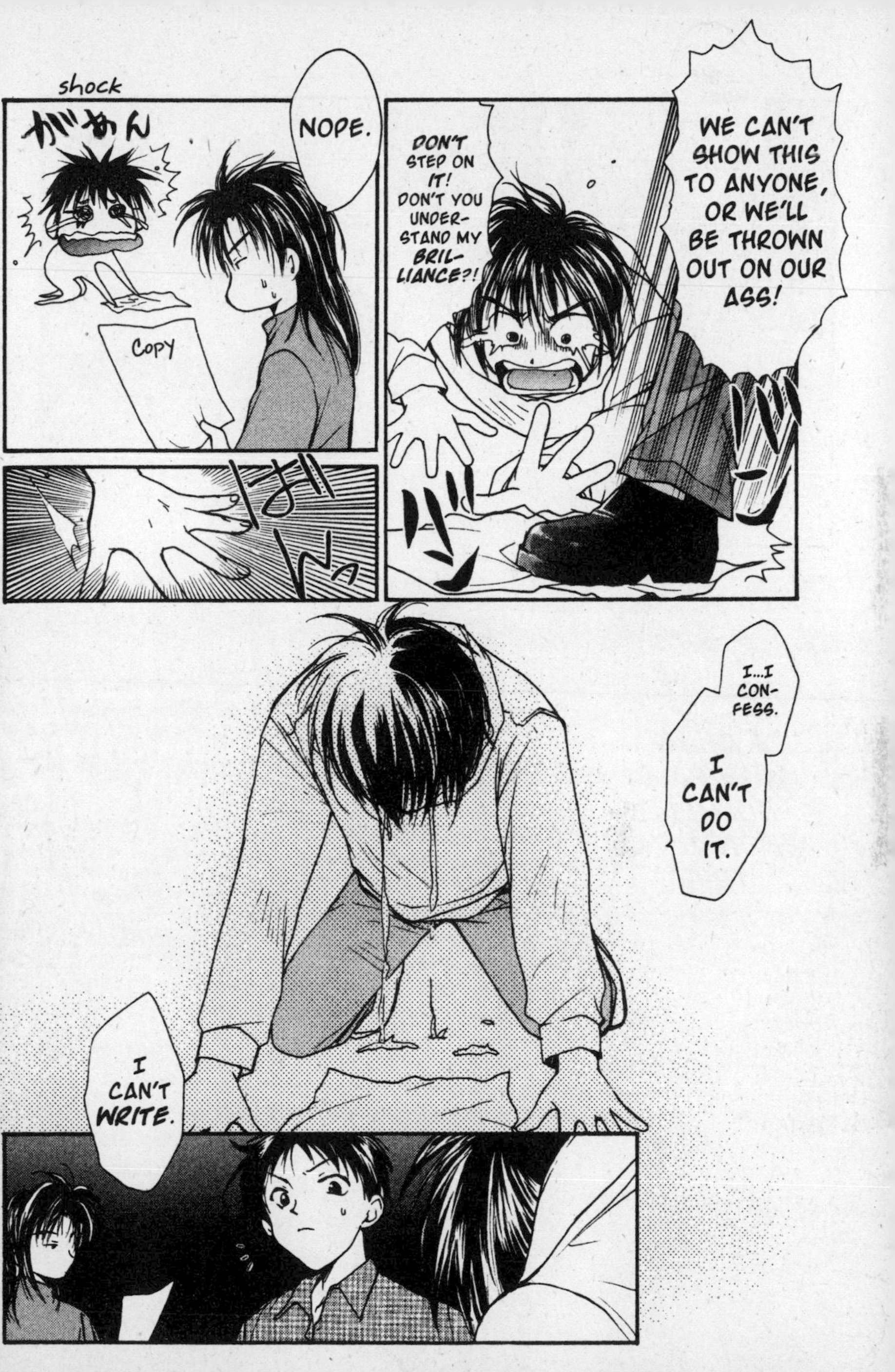
WE CAN'T SHOW THIS TO ANYONE, OR WE'LL BE THROWN OUT ON OUR ASS!
DON'T STEP ON IT! DON'T YOU UNDER-STAND MY BRIL-LIANCE?!
NOPE.
shock
Copy
I...I CON-FESS.
I CAN'T DO IT.
I CAN'T WRITE.

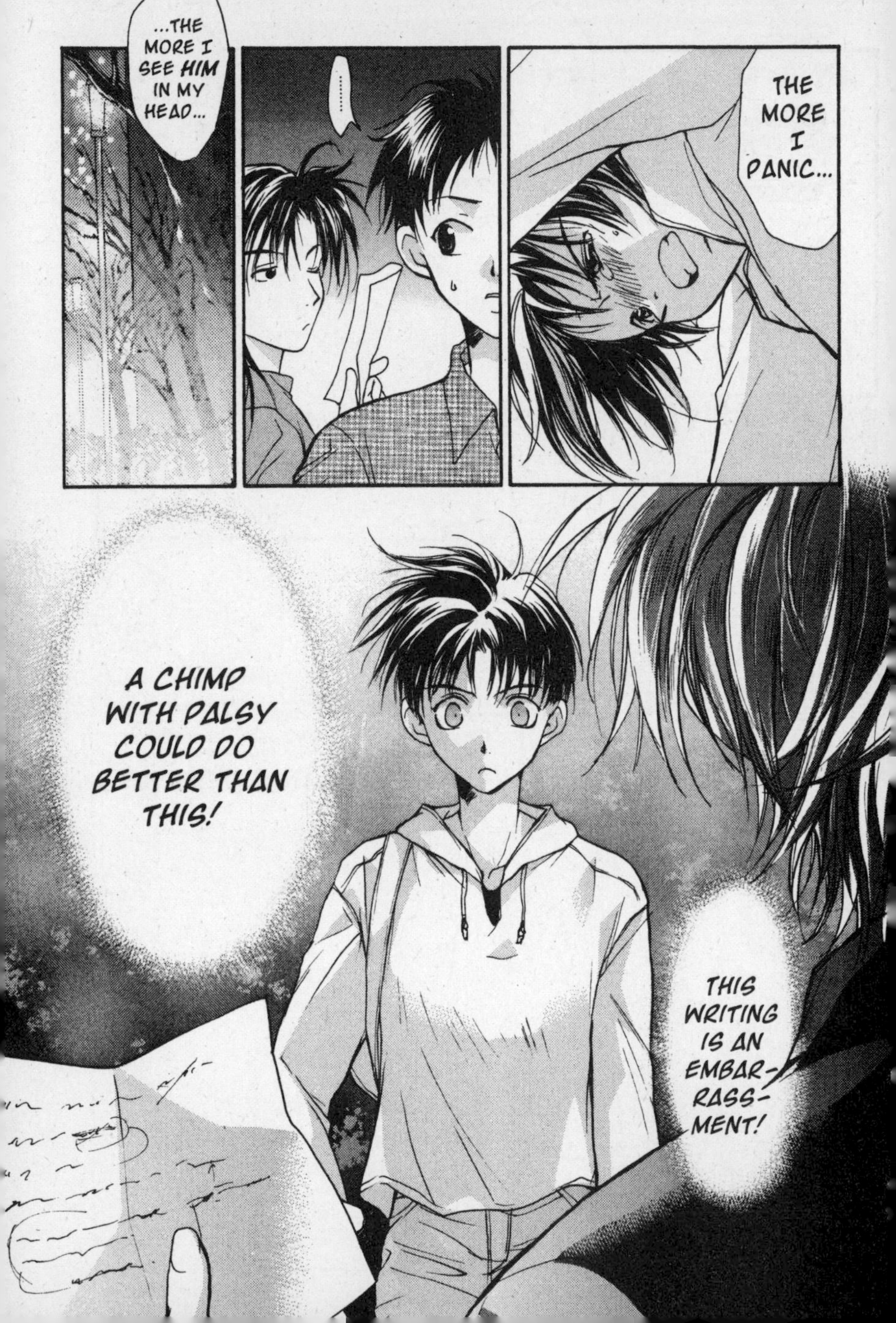
THE MORE I PANIC...
......
...THE MORE I SEE HIM IN MY HEAD...
THIS WRITING IS AN EMBARRASSMENT!
A CHIMP WITH PALSY COULD DO BETTER THAN THIS!

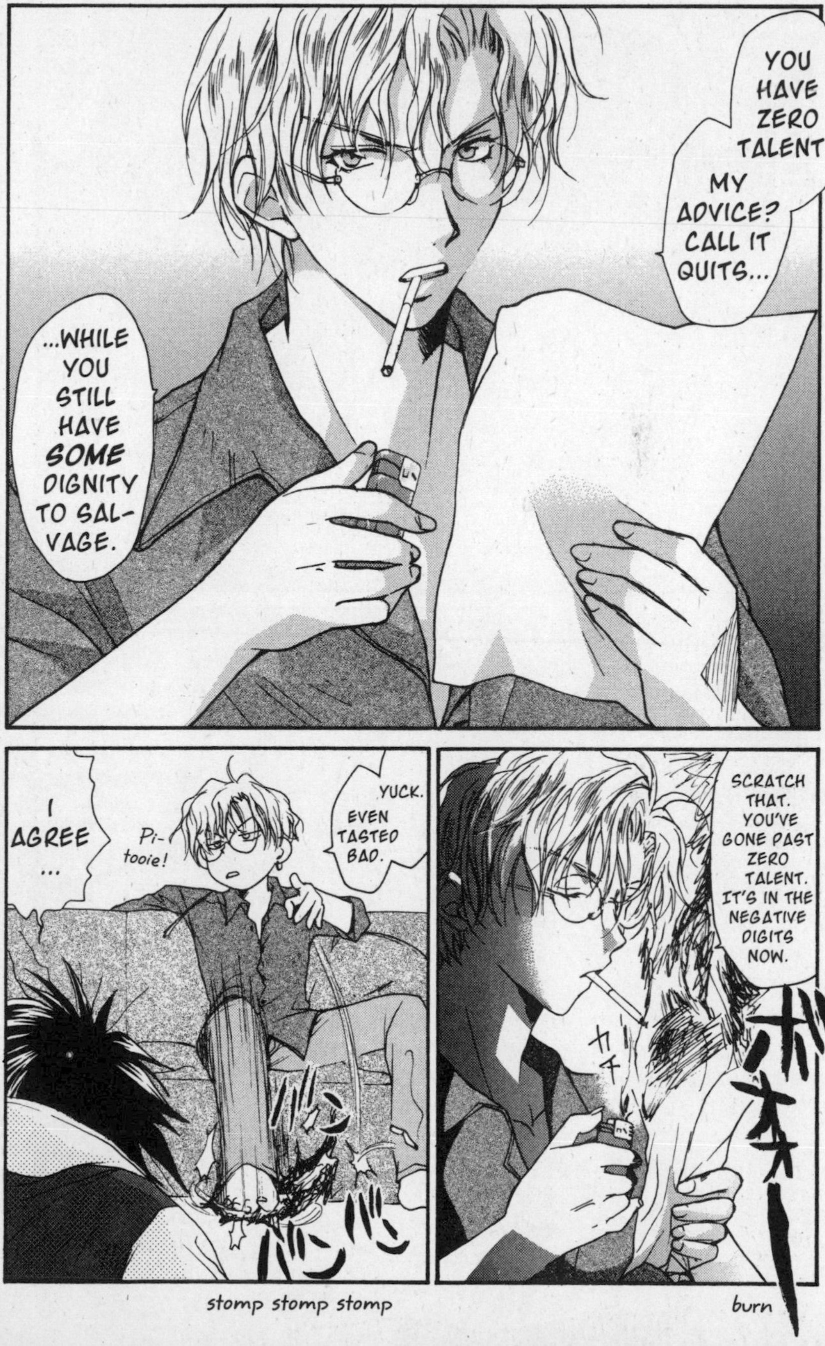
YOU HAVE ZERO TALENT.
MY ADVICE? CALL IT QUITS...
...WHILE YOU STILL HAVE **SOME** DIGNITY TO SAL-VAGE.
SCRATCH THAT. YOU'VE GONE PAST ZERO TALENT. IT'S IN THE NEGATIVE DIGITS NOW.
カチ
burn
YUCK.
EVEN TASTED BAD.
Pi-tooie!
I AGREE ...
stomp stomp stomp

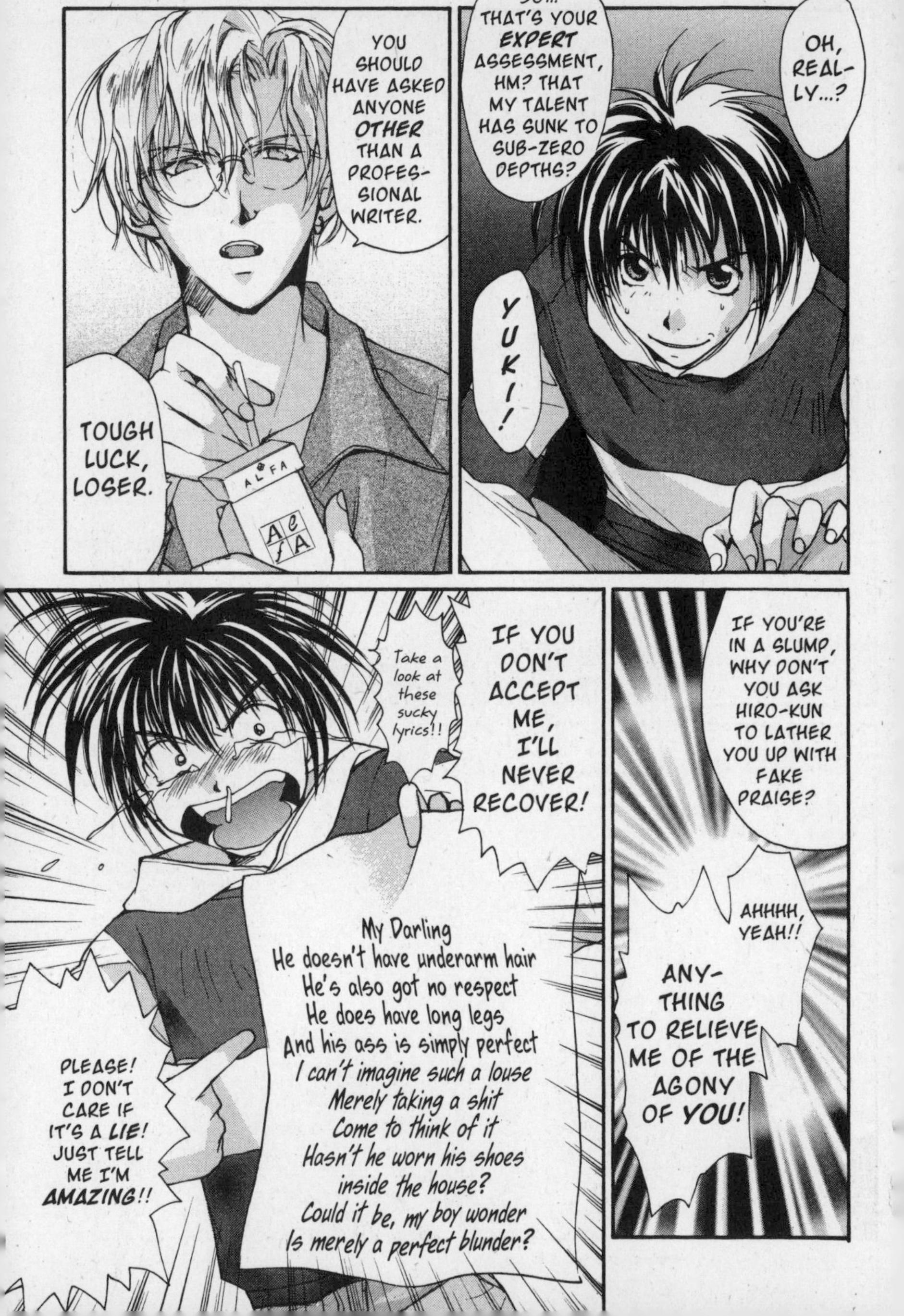
OH, REALLY...?
SO... THAT'S YOUR EXPERT ASSESSMENT, HM? THAT MY TALENT HAS SUNK TO SUB-ZERO DEPTHS?
YUKI!
YOU SHOULD HAVE ASKED ANYONE OTHER THAN A PROFESSIONAL WRITER.
TOUGH LUCK, LOSER.
IF YOU'RE IN A SLUMP, WHY DON'T YOU ASK HIRO-KUN TO LATHER YOU UP WITH FAKE PRAISE?
AHHHH, YEAH!!
ANYTHING TO RELIEVE ME OF THE AGONY OF YOU!
IF YOU DON'T ACCEPT ME, I'LL NEVER RECOVER!
Take a look at these sucky lyrics!!
My Darling
He doesn't have underarm hair
He's also got no respect
He does have long legs
And his ass is simply perfect
I can't imagine such a louse
Merely taking a shit
Come to think of it
Hasn't he worn his shoes
inside the house?
Could it be, my boy wonder
Is merely a perfect blunder?
PLEASE! I DON'T CARE IF IT'S A LIE! JUST TELL ME I'M AMAZING!!

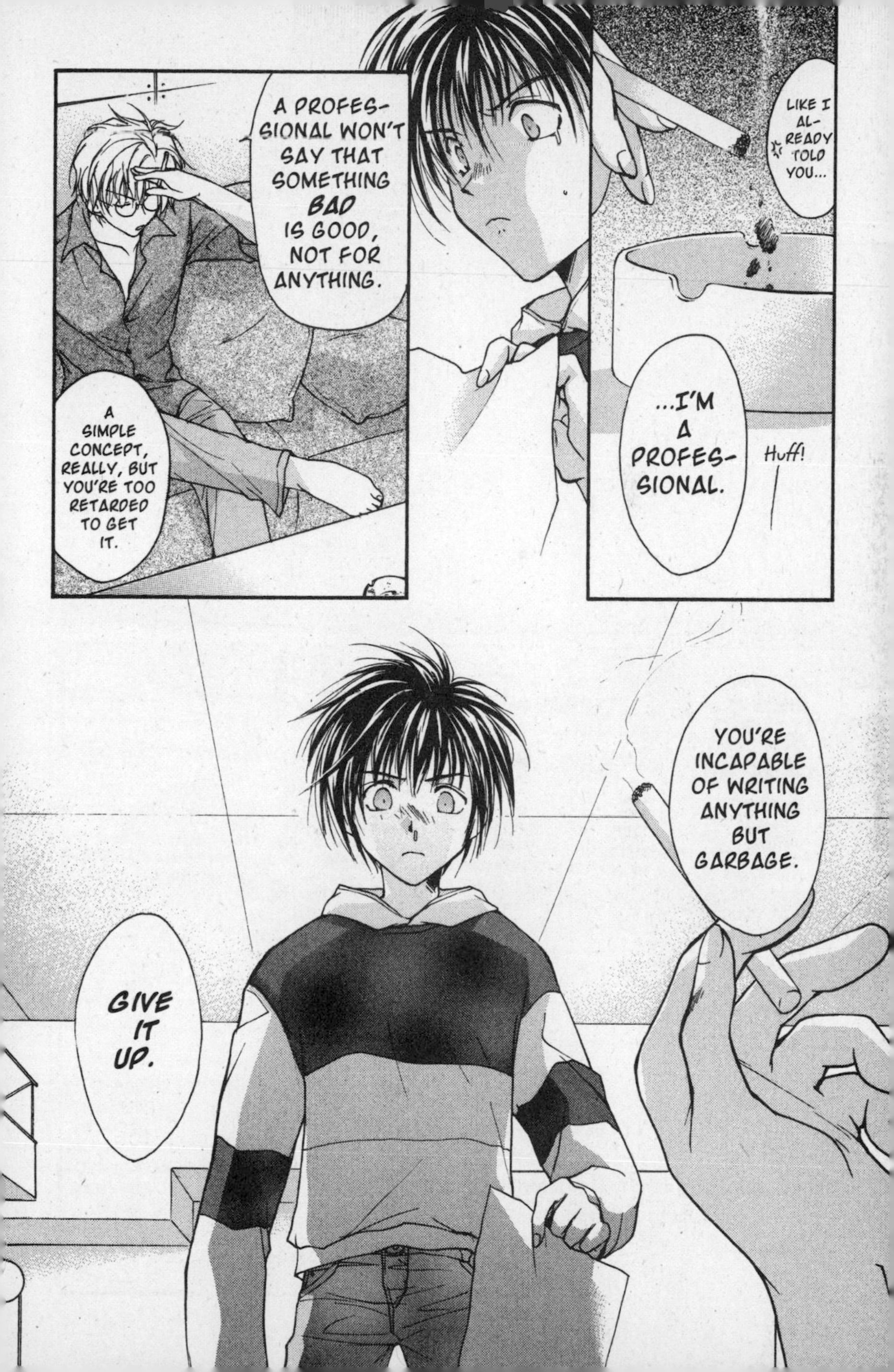
LIKE I AL-READY TOLD YOU...
...I'M A PROFES-SIONAL.
Huff!
A PROFES-SIONAL WON'T SAY THAT SOMETHING BAD IS GOOD, NOT FOR ANYTHING.
A SIMPLE CONCEPT, REALLY, BUT YOU'RE TOO RETARDED TO GET IT.
YOU'RE INCAPABLE OF WRITING ANYTHING BUT GARBAGE.
GIVE IT UP.

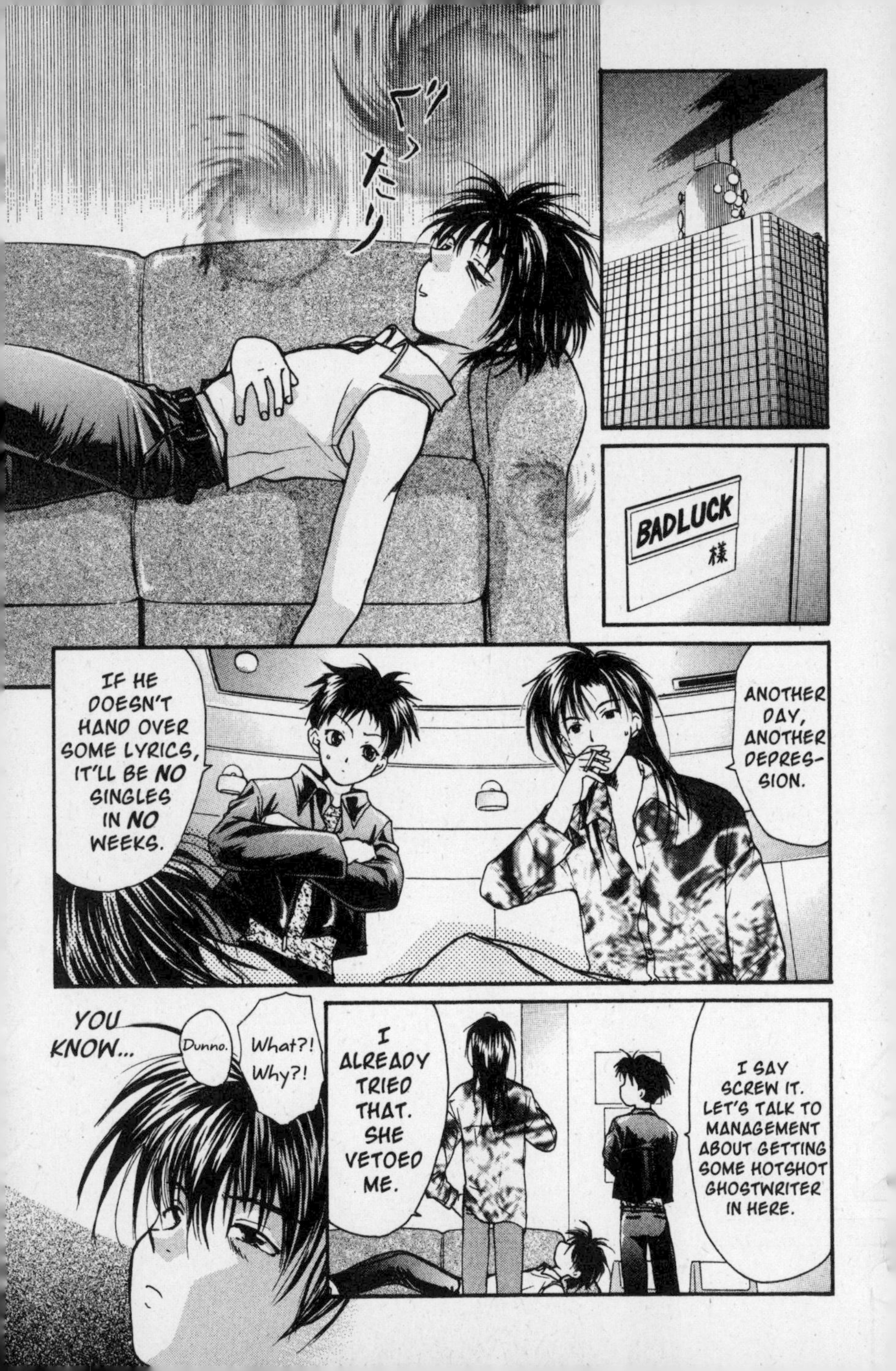
BADLUCK
様
ぐったり
ANOTHER DAY, ANOTHER DEPRESSION.
IF HE DOESN'T HAND OVER SOME LYRICS, IT'LL BE **NO** SINGLES IN **NO** WEEKS.
I SAY SCREW IT. LET'S TALK TO MANAGEMENT ABOUT GETTING SOME HOTSHOT GHOSTWRITER IN HERE.
I ALREADY TRIED THAT. SHE VETOED ME.
What?! Why?!
Dunno.
YOU KNOW...

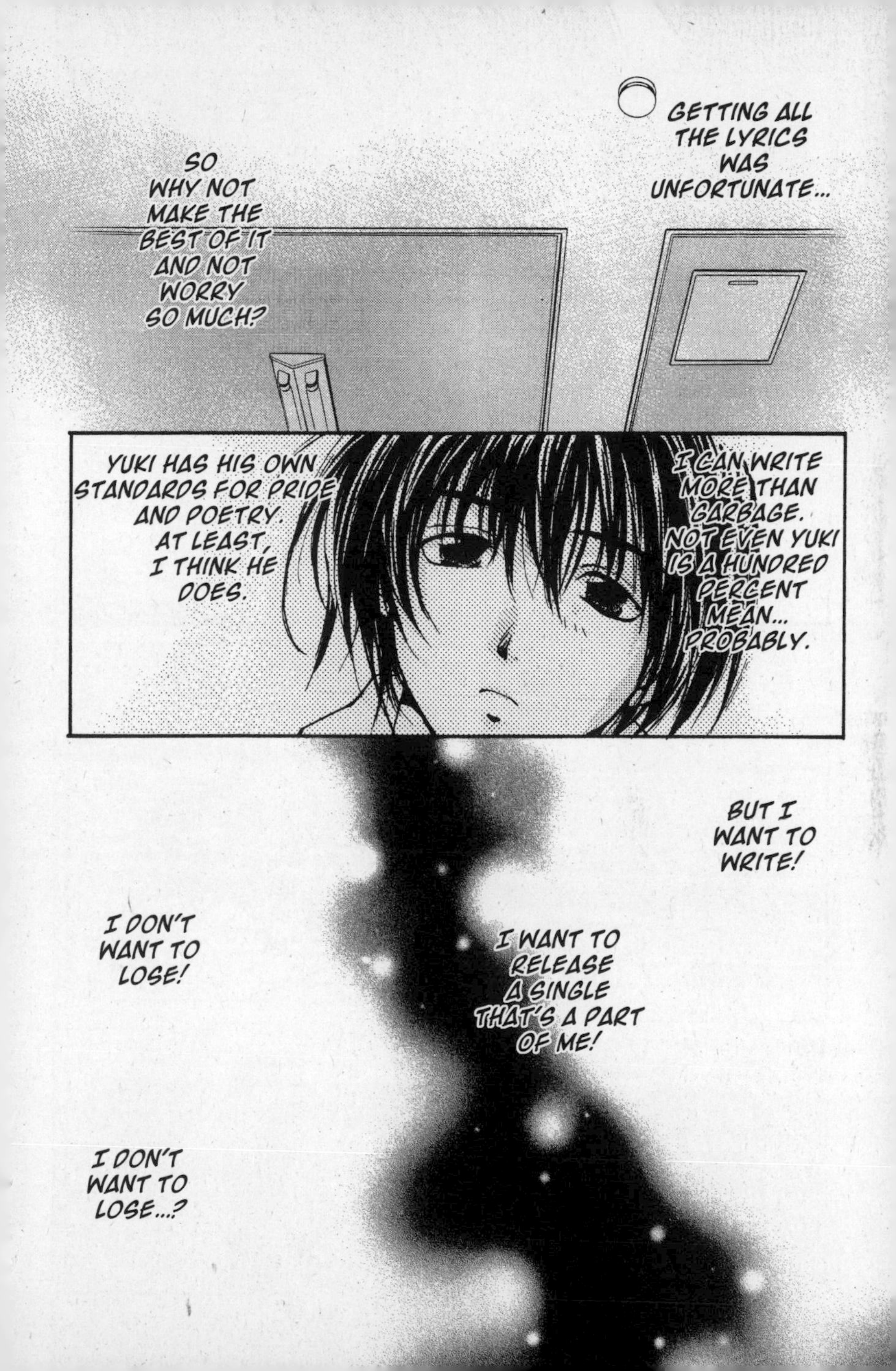
GETTING ALL THE LYRICS WAS UNFORTUNATE...
SO WHY NOT MAKE THE BEST OF IT AND NOT WORRY SO MUCH?
I CAN WRITE MORE THAN GARBAGE. NOT EVEN YUKI IS A HUNDRED PERCENT MEAN... PROBABLY.
YUKI HAS HIS OWN STANDARDS FOR PRIDE AND POETRY. AT LEAST, I THINK HE DOES.
BUT I WANT TO WRITE!
I WANT TO RELEASE A SINGLE THAT'S A PART OF ME!
I DON'T WANT TO LOSE!
I DON'T WANT TO LOSE...?

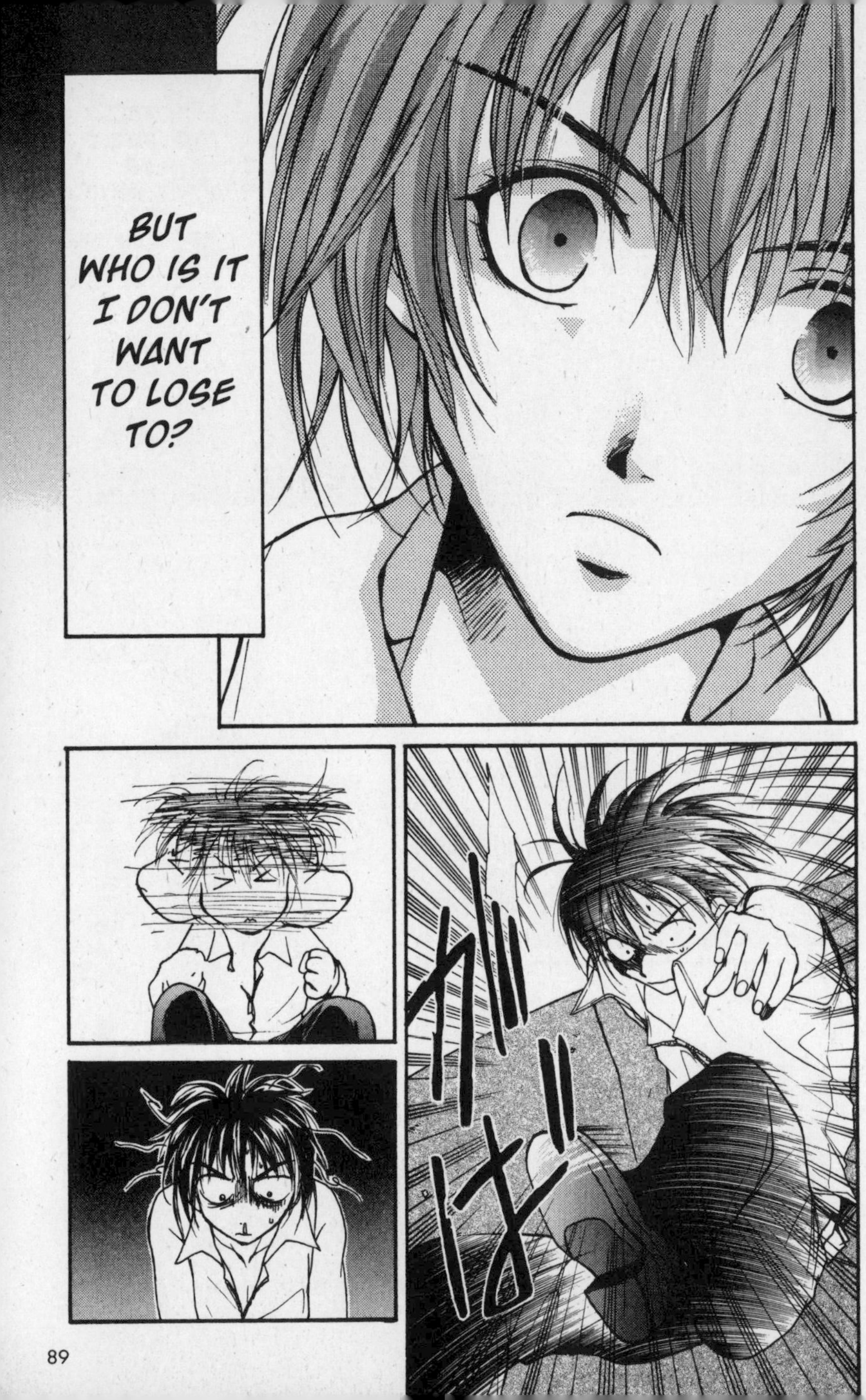
BUT WHO IS IT I DON'T WANT TO LOSE TO?

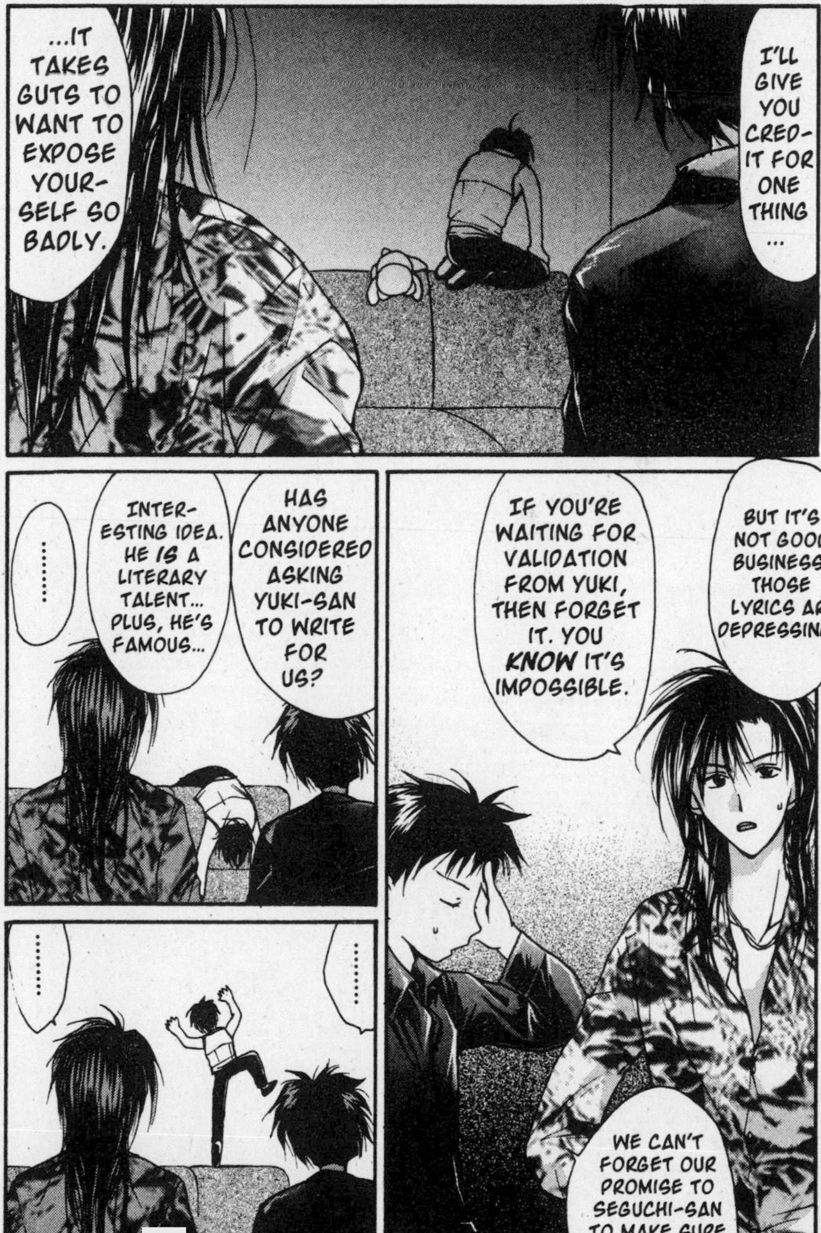
I'LL GIVE YOU CRED-IT FOR ONE THING...
...IT TAKES GUTS TO WANT TO EXPOSE YOUR-SELF SO BADLY.
BUT IT'S NOT GOOD BUSINESS. THOSE LYRICS ARE DEPRESSING.
IF YOU'RE WAITING FOR VALIDATION FROM YUKI, THEN FORGET IT. YOU *KNOW* IT'S IMPOSSIBLE.
WE CAN'T FORGET OUR PROMISE TO SEGUCHI-SAN TO MAKE SURE THESE RECORDS SELL.
HAS ANYONE CONSIDERED ASKING YUKI-SAN TO WRITE FOR US?
INTER-ESTING IDEA. HE *IS* A LITERARY TALENT... PLUS, HE'S FAMOUS...
........
........
........

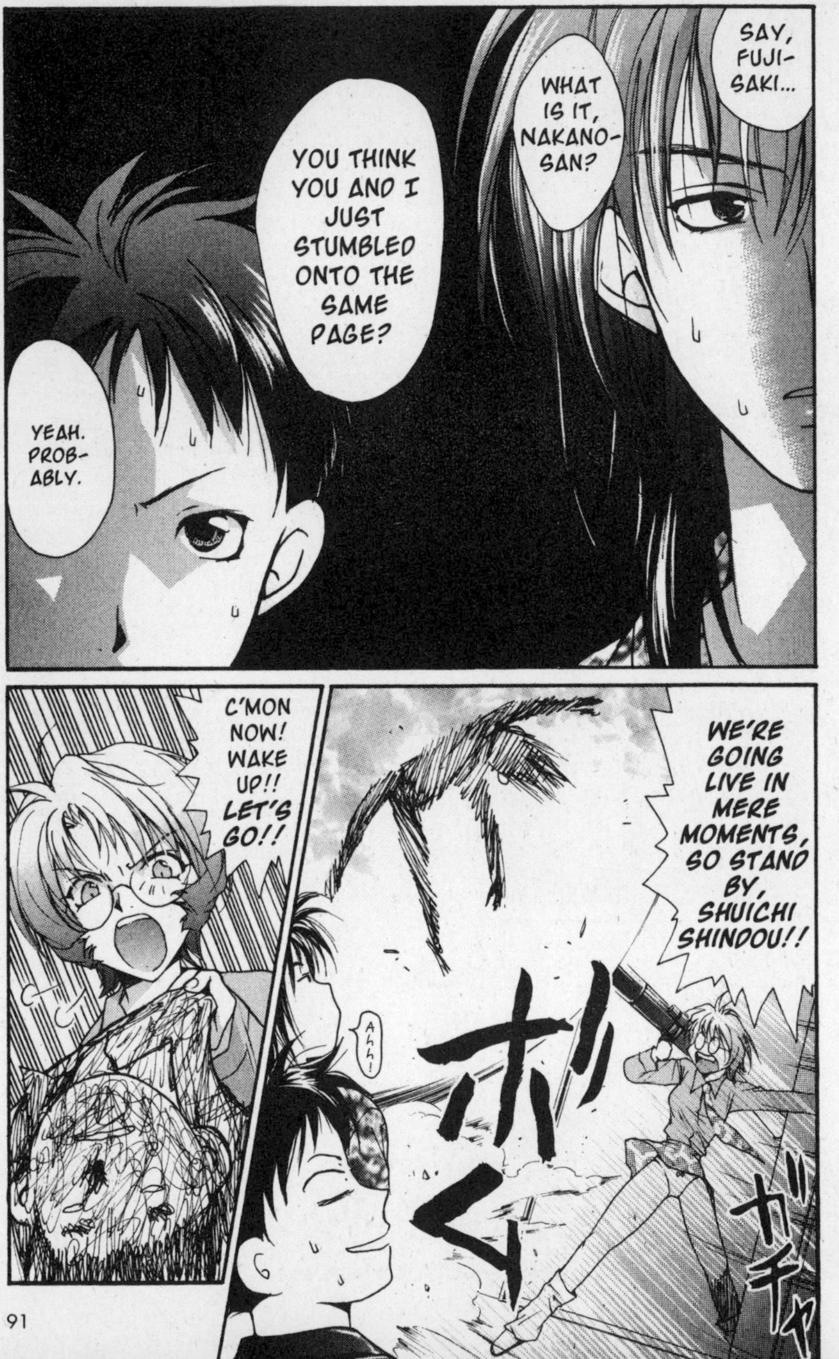
SAY, FUJI-SAKI...
WHAT IS IT, NAKANO-SAN?
YOU THINK YOU AND I JUST STUMBLED ONTO THE SAME PAGE?
YEAH. PROBABLY.
WE'RE GOING LIVE IN MERE MOMENTS, SO STAND BY, SHUICHI SHINDOU!!
Ahh!
ガチャ
C'MON NOW! WAKE UP!! LET'S GO!!

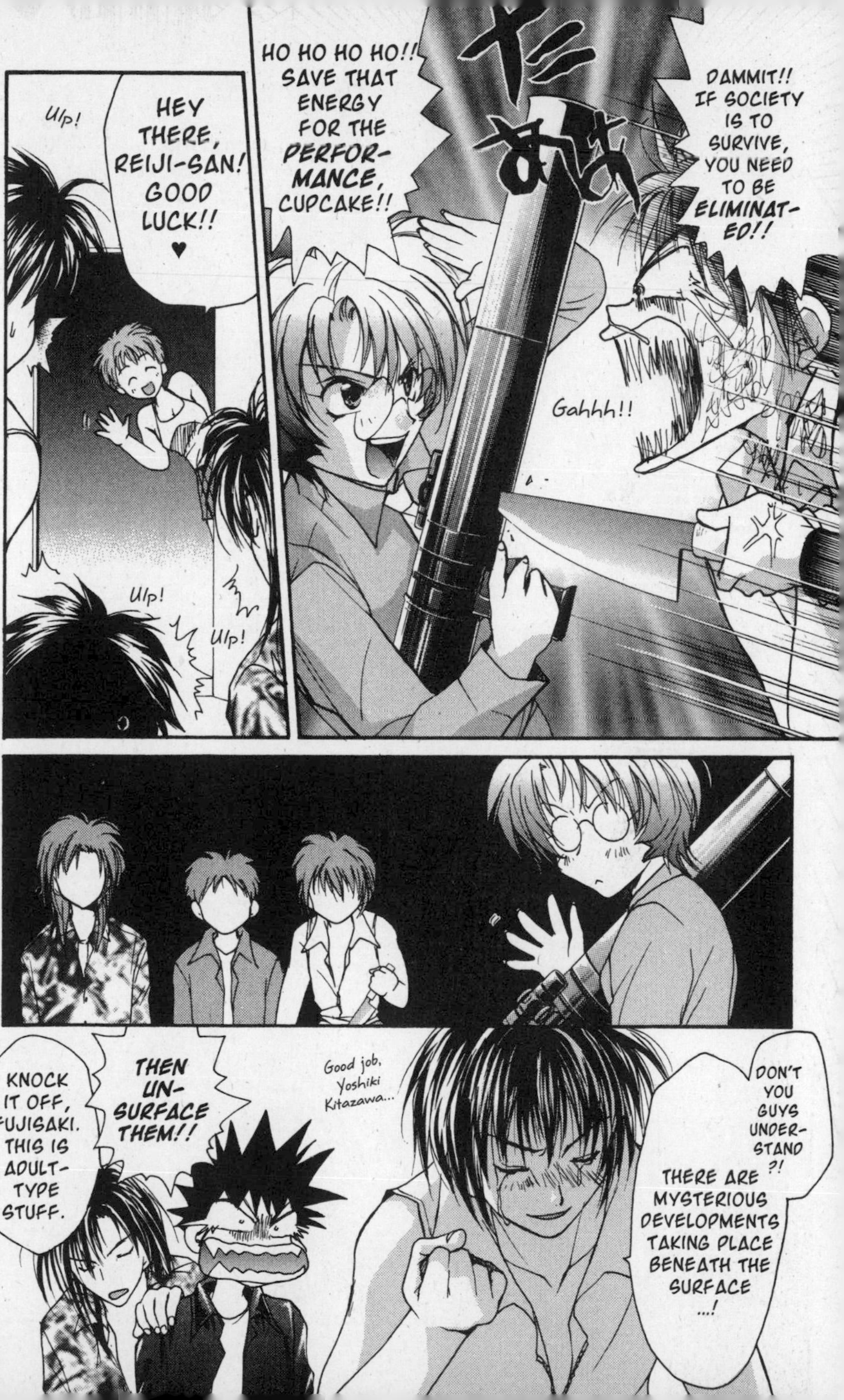
DAMMIT!! IF SOCIETY IS TO SURVIVE, YOU NEED TO BE ELIMINATED!!
HO HO HO HO!! SAVE THAT ENERGY FOR THE PERFORMANCE, CUPCAKE!!
Gahhh!!
HEY THERE, REIJI-SAN! GOOD LUCK!! ♥
Ulp!
Ulp!
Ulp!
DON'T YOU GUYS UNDERSTAND?!
THERE ARE MYSTERIOUS DEVELOPMENTS TAKING PLACE BENEATH THE SURFACE ...!
Good job, Yoshiki Kitazawa...
THEN UN-SURFACE THEM!!
KNOCK IT OFF, FUJISAKI. THIS IS ADULT-TYPE STUFF.

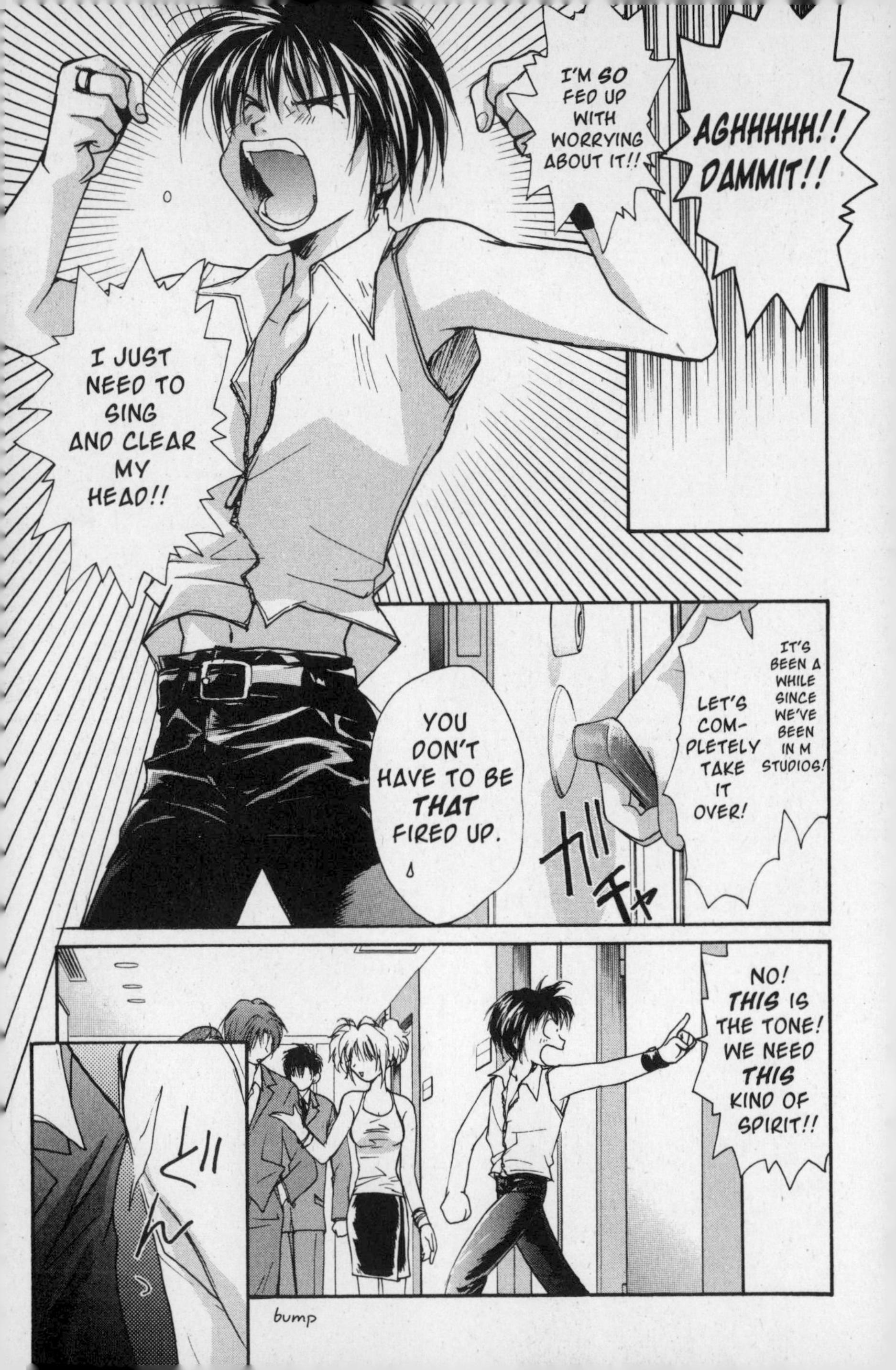
AGHHHHH!! DAMMIT!!
I'M SO FED UP WITH WORRYING ABOUT IT!!
I JUST NEED TO SING AND CLEAR MY HEAD!!
IT'S BEEN A WHILE SINCE WE'VE BEEN IN M STUDIOS!
LET'S COMPLETELY TAKE IT OVER!
ガチャ
YOU DON'T HAVE TO BE THAT FIRED UP.
NO! THIS IS THE TONE! WE NEED THIS KIND OF SPIRIT!!
どん
bump

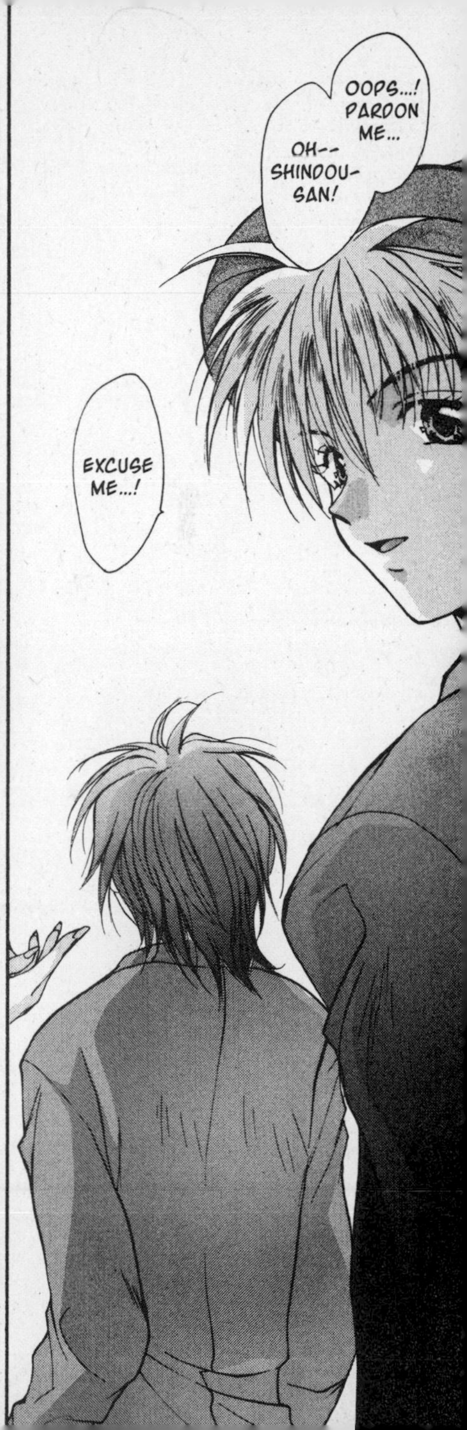
OOPS...! PARDON ME...
OH-- SHINDOU-SAN!
EXCUSE ME...!

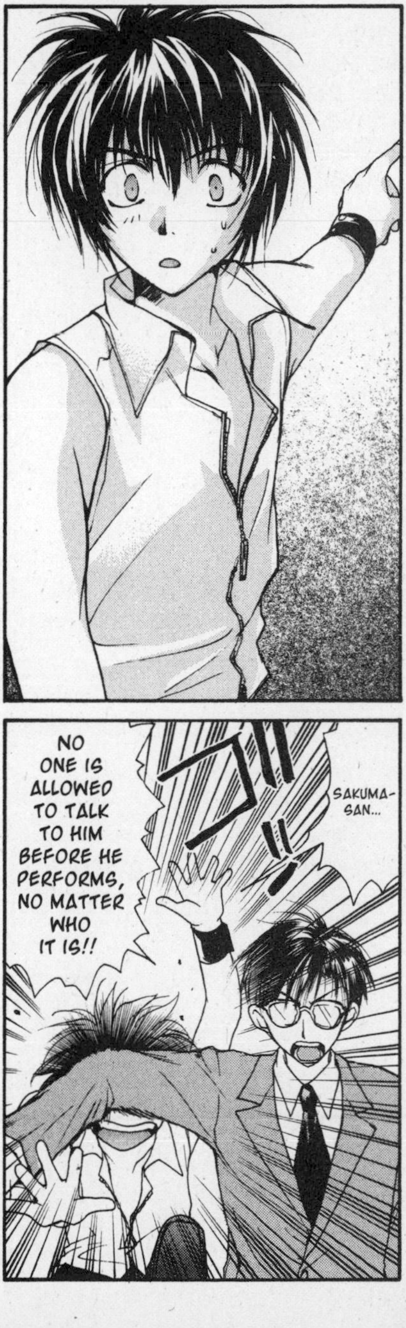
SAKUMA-SAN...
NO ONE IS ALLOWED TO TALK TO HIM BEFORE HE PERFORMS, NO MATTER WHO IT IS!!

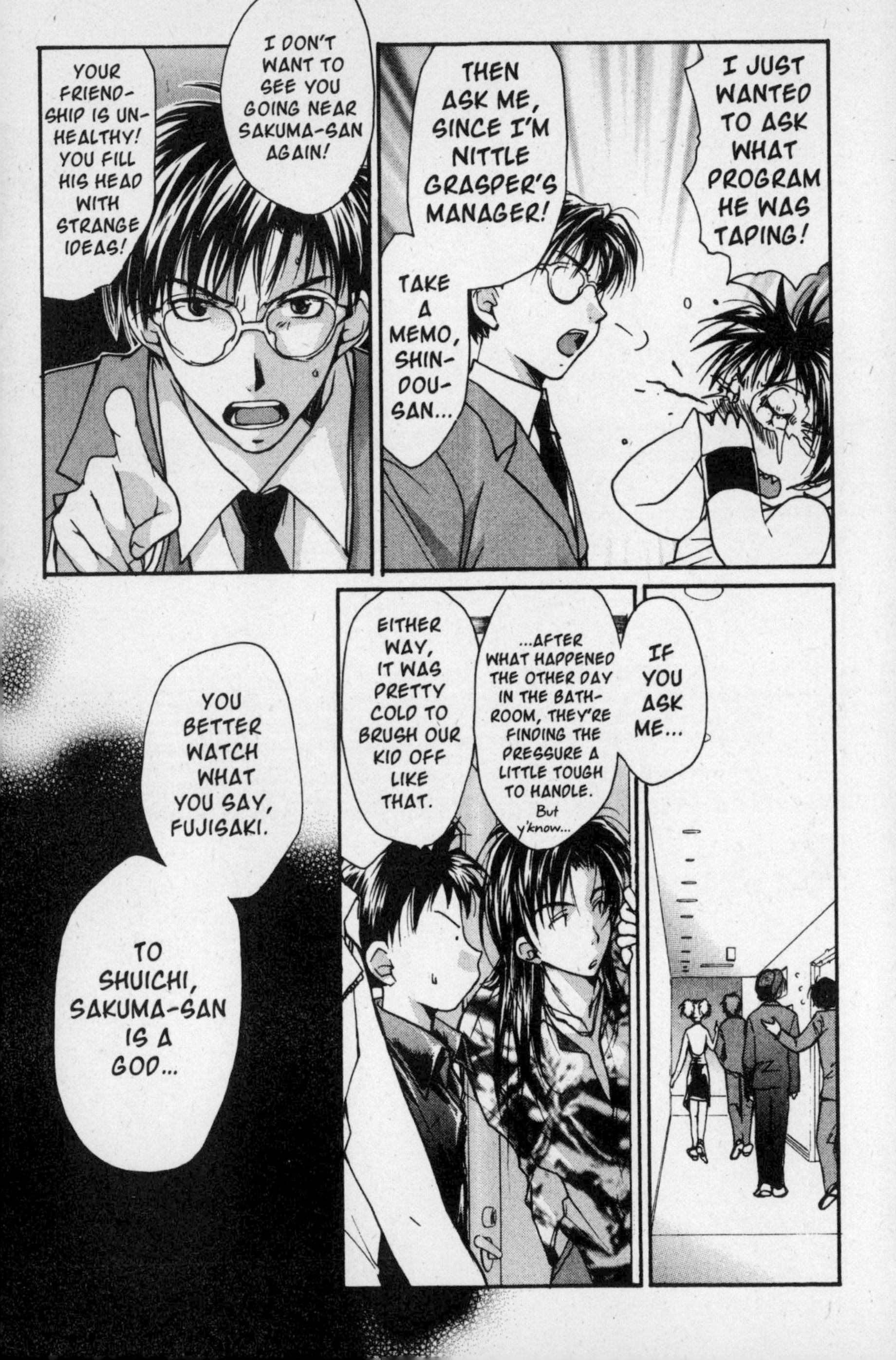
I JUST WANTED TO ASK WHAT PROGRAM HE WAS TAPING!
THEN ASK ME, SINCE I'M NITTLE GRASPER'S MANAGER!
TAKE A MEMO, SHINDOU-SAN...
I DON'T WANT TO SEE YOU GOING NEAR SAKUMA-SAN AGAIN!
YOUR FRIENDSHIP IS UNHEALTHY! YOU FILL HIS HEAD WITH STRANGE IDEAS!
IF YOU ASK ME...
...AFTER WHAT HAPPENED THE OTHER DAY IN THE BATHROOM, THEY'RE FINDING THE PRESSURE A LITTLE TOUGH TO HANDLE.
But y'know...
EITHER WAY, IT WAS PRETTY COLD TO BRUSH OUR KID OFF LIKE THAT.
YOU BETTER WATCH WHAT YOU SAY, FUJISAKI.
TO SHUICHI, SAKUMA-SAN IS A GOD...

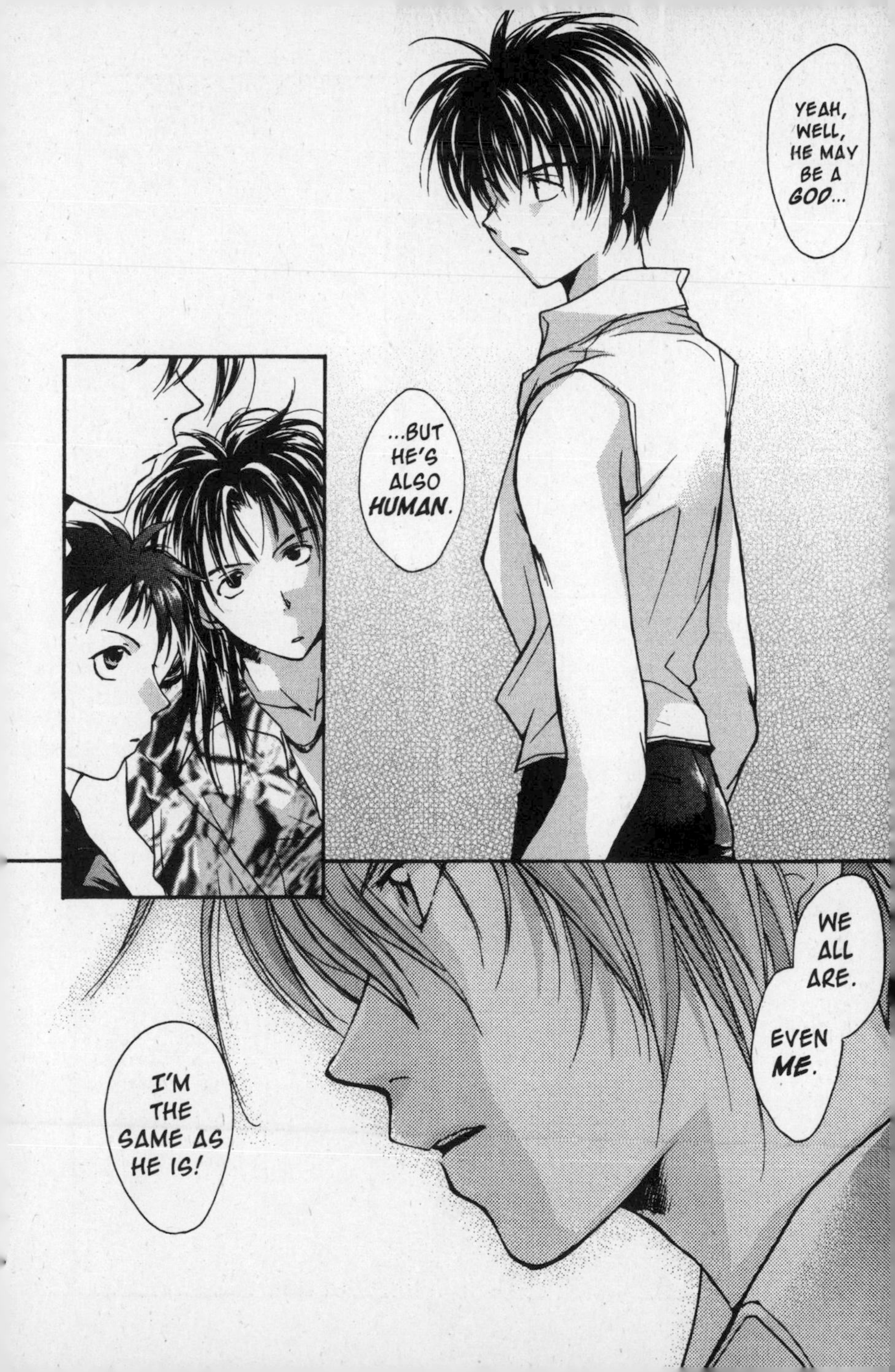
YEAH, WELL, HE MAY BE A GOD...
...BUT HE'S ALSO HUMAN.
WE ALL ARE.
EVEN ME.
I'M THE SAME AS HE IS!

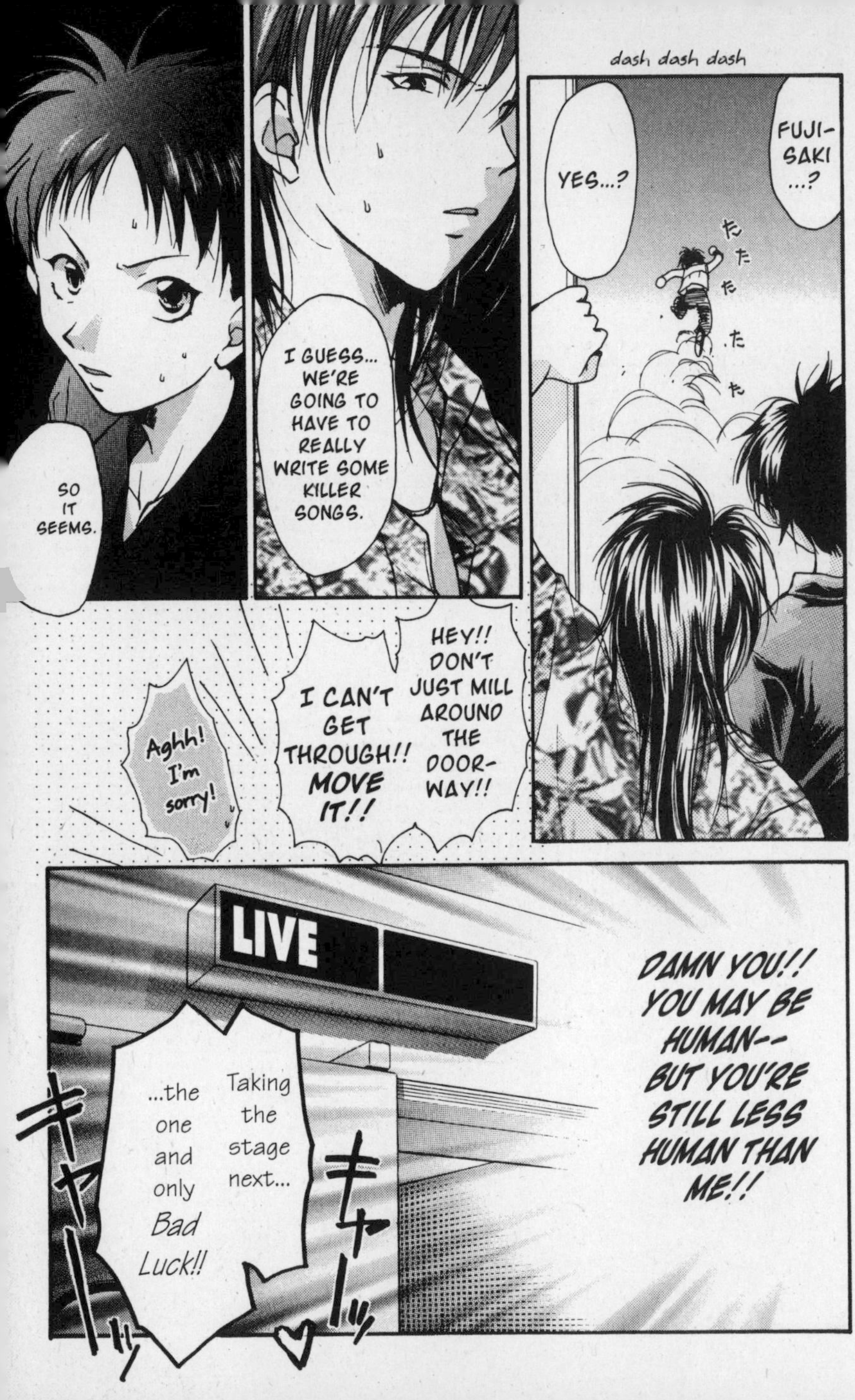
dash dash dash
FUJI-SAKI ...?
YES...?
たたたたた
I GUESS... WE'RE GOING TO HAVE TO REALLY WRITE SOME KILLER SONGS.
SO IT SEEMS.
HEY!! DON'T JUST MILL AROUND THE DOOR-WAY!!
I CAN'T GET THROUGH!! MOVE IT!!
Aghh! I'm sorry!
LIVE
DAMN YOU!! YOU MAY BE HUMAN-- BUT YOU'RE STILL LESS HUMAN THAN ME!!
Taking the stage next...
...the one and only Bad Luck!!
キャーッ
キャー

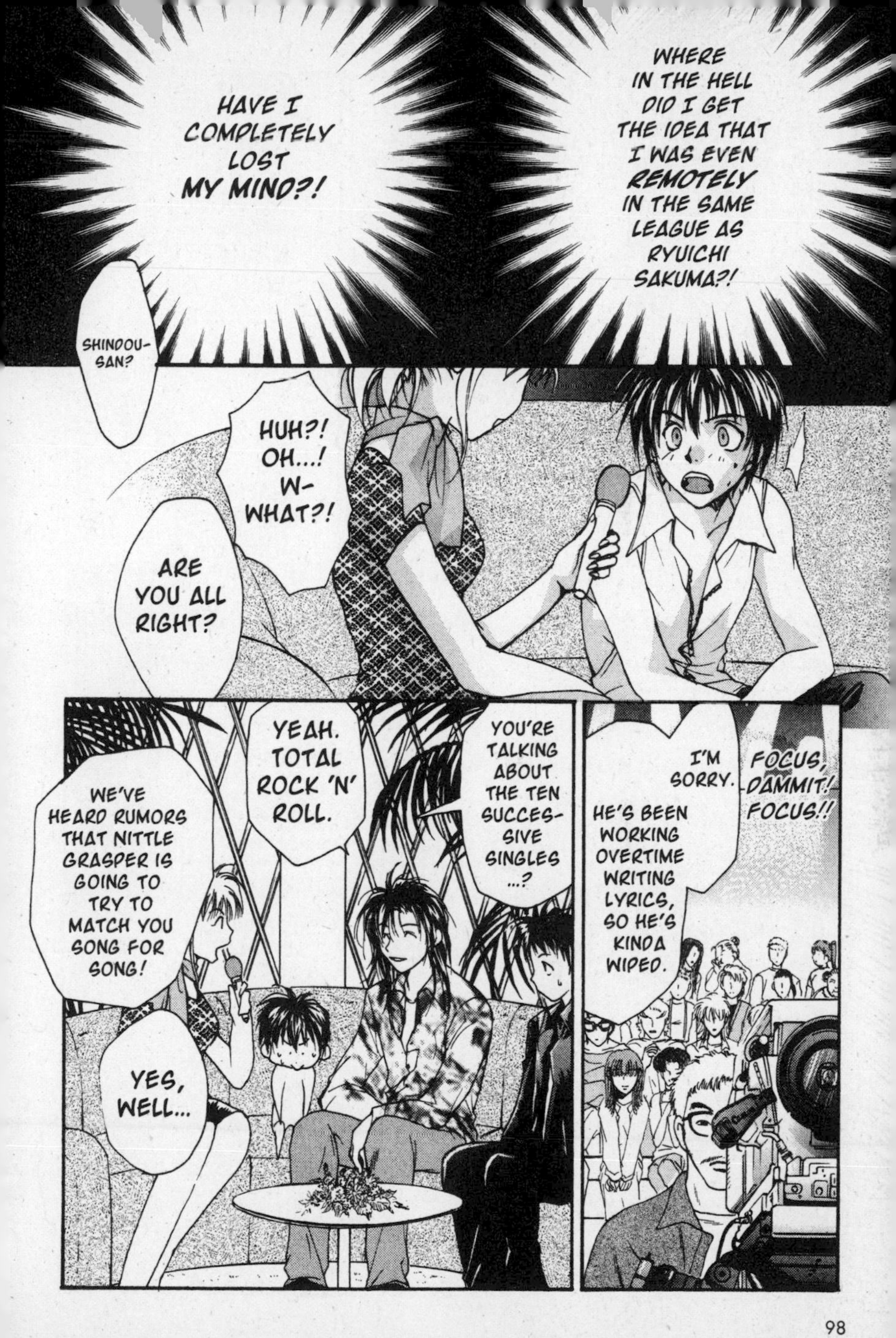
WHERE IN THE HELL DID I GET THE IDEA THAT I WAS EVEN *REMOTELY* IN THE SAME LEAGUE AS RYUICHI SAKUMA?!
HAVE I COMPLETELY LOST **MY MIND?!**
SHINDOU-SAN?
HUH?! OH...! W-WHAT?!
ARE YOU ALL RIGHT?
FOCUS, DAMMIT! FOCUS!!
I'M SORRY.
HE'S BEEN WORKING OVERTIME WRITING LYRICS, SO HE'S KINDA WIPED.
YOU'RE TALKING ABOUT THE TEN SUCCES-SIVE SINGLES ...?
YEAH. TOTAL ROCK 'N' ROLL.
WE'VE HEARD RUMORS THAT NITTLE GRASPER IS GOING TO TRY TO MATCH YOU SONG FOR SONG!
YES, WELL...

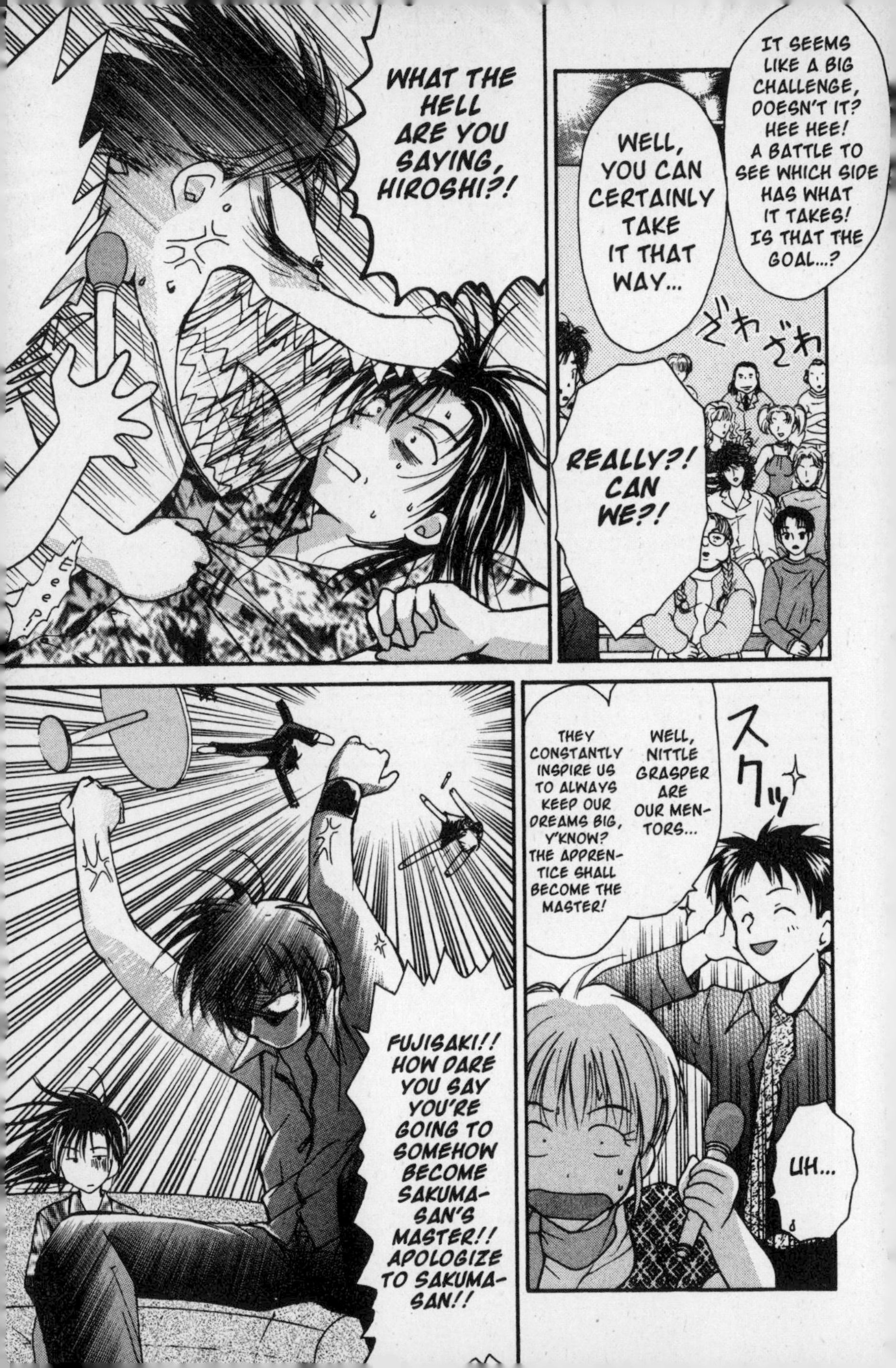
IT SEEMS LIKE A BIG CHALLENGE, DOESN'T IT? HEE HEE! A BATTLE TO SEE WHICH SIDE HAS WHAT IT TAKES! IS THAT THE GOAL...?
WELL, YOU CAN CERTAINLY TAKE IT THAT WAY...
ざわざわ
REALLY?! CAN WE?!
WHAT THE HELL ARE YOU SAYING, HIROSHI?!
Eeep!
WELL, NITTLE GRASPER ARE OUR MEN-TORS... THEY CONSTANTLY INSPIRE US TO ALWAYS KEEP OUR DREAMS BIG, Y'KNOW? THE APPREN-TICE SHALL BECOME THE MASTER!
スクッ
UH...
FUJISAKI!! HOW DARE YOU SAY YOU'RE GOING TO SOMEHOW BECOME SAKUMA-SAN'S MASTER!! APOLOGIZE TO SAKUMA-SAN!!

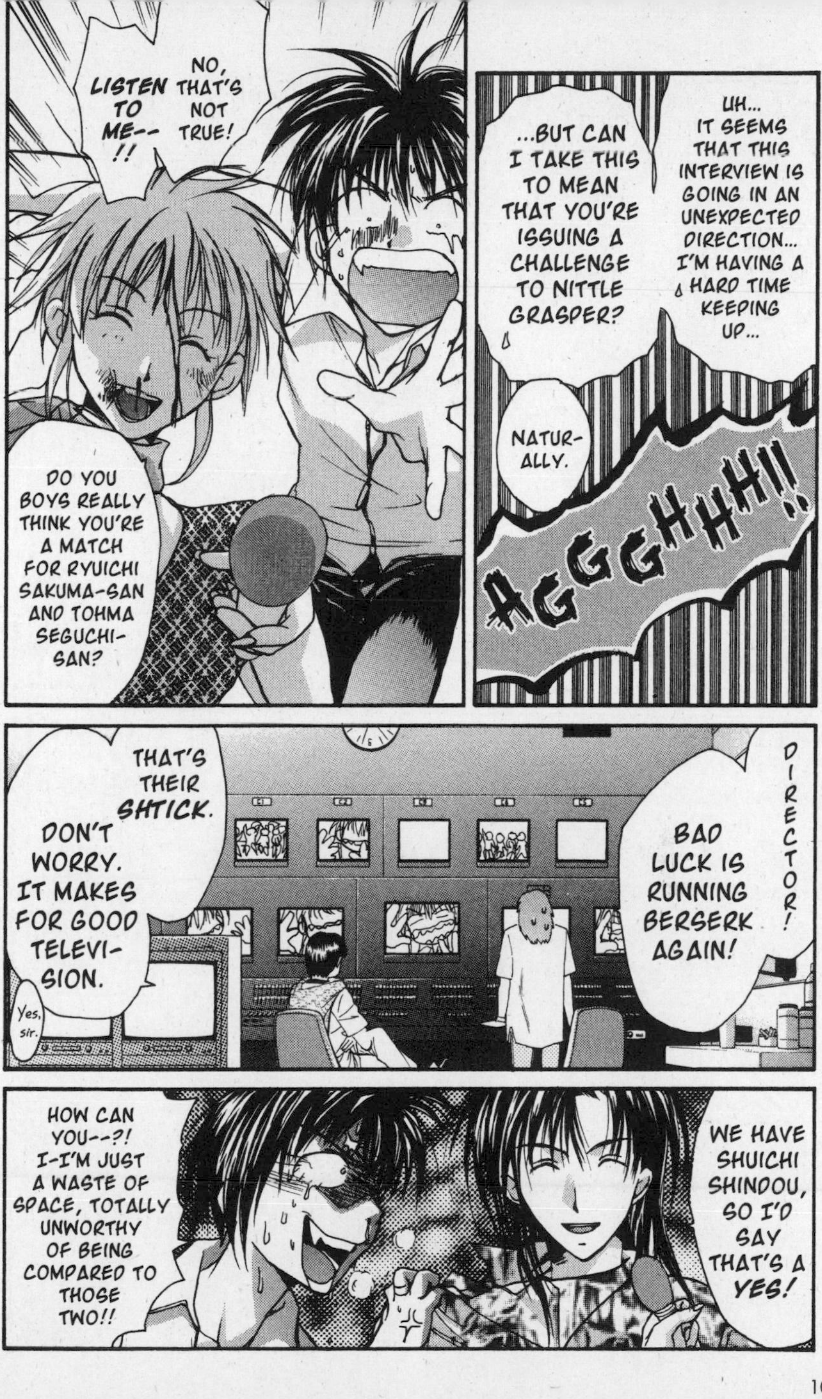
UH... IT SEEMS THAT THIS INTERVIEW IS GOING IN AN UNEXPECTED DIRECTION... I'M HAVING A HARD TIME KEEPING UP...
...BUT CAN I TAKE THIS TO MEAN THAT YOU'RE ISSUING A CHALLENGE TO NITTLE GRASPER?
NATURALLY.
AGGGHHH!!
NO, THAT'S NOT TRUE!
LISTEN TO ME--!!
DO YOU BOYS REALLY THINK YOU'RE A MATCH FOR RYUICHI SAKUMA-SAN AND TOHMA SEGUCHI-SAN?
DIRECTOR!
BAD LUCK IS RUNNING BERSERK AGAIN!
THAT'S THEIR SHTICK.
DON'T WORRY. IT MAKES FOR GOOD TELEVISION.
Yes, sir.
WE HAVE SHUICHI SHINDOU, SO I'D SAY THAT'S A YES!
HOW CAN YOU--?! I-I'M JUST A WASTE OF SPACE, TOTALLY UNWORTHY OF BEING COMPARED TO THOSE TWO!!

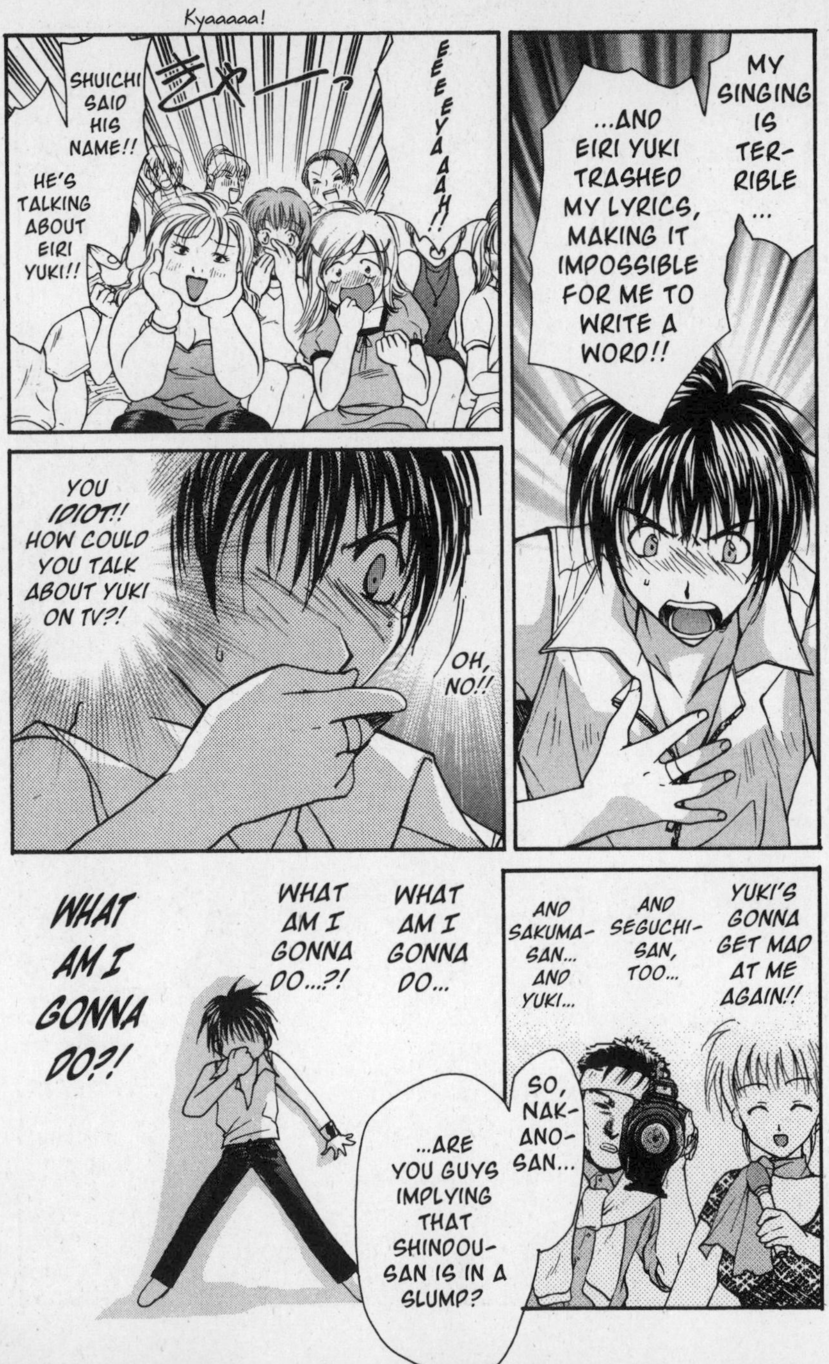
MY SINGING IS TERRIBLE...
...AND EIRI YUKI TRASHED MY LYRICS, MAKING IT IMPOSSIBLE FOR ME TO WRITE A WORD!!
Kyaaaaa!
EEEEYAAAAH!!
きゃーっ
SHUICHI SAID HIS NAME!!
HE'S TALKING ABOUT EIRI YUKI!!
OH, NO!!
YOU IDIOT!! HOW COULD YOU TALK ABOUT YUKI ON TV?!
YUKI'S GONNA GET MAD AT ME AGAIN!!
AND SEGUCHI-SAN, TOO...
AND SAKUMA-SAN... AND YUKI...
SO, NAKANO-SAN...
...ARE YOU GUYS IMPLYING THAT SHINDOU-SAN IS IN A SLUMP?
WHAT AM I GONNA DO...
WHAT AM I GONNA DO...?!
WHAT AM I GONNA DO?!

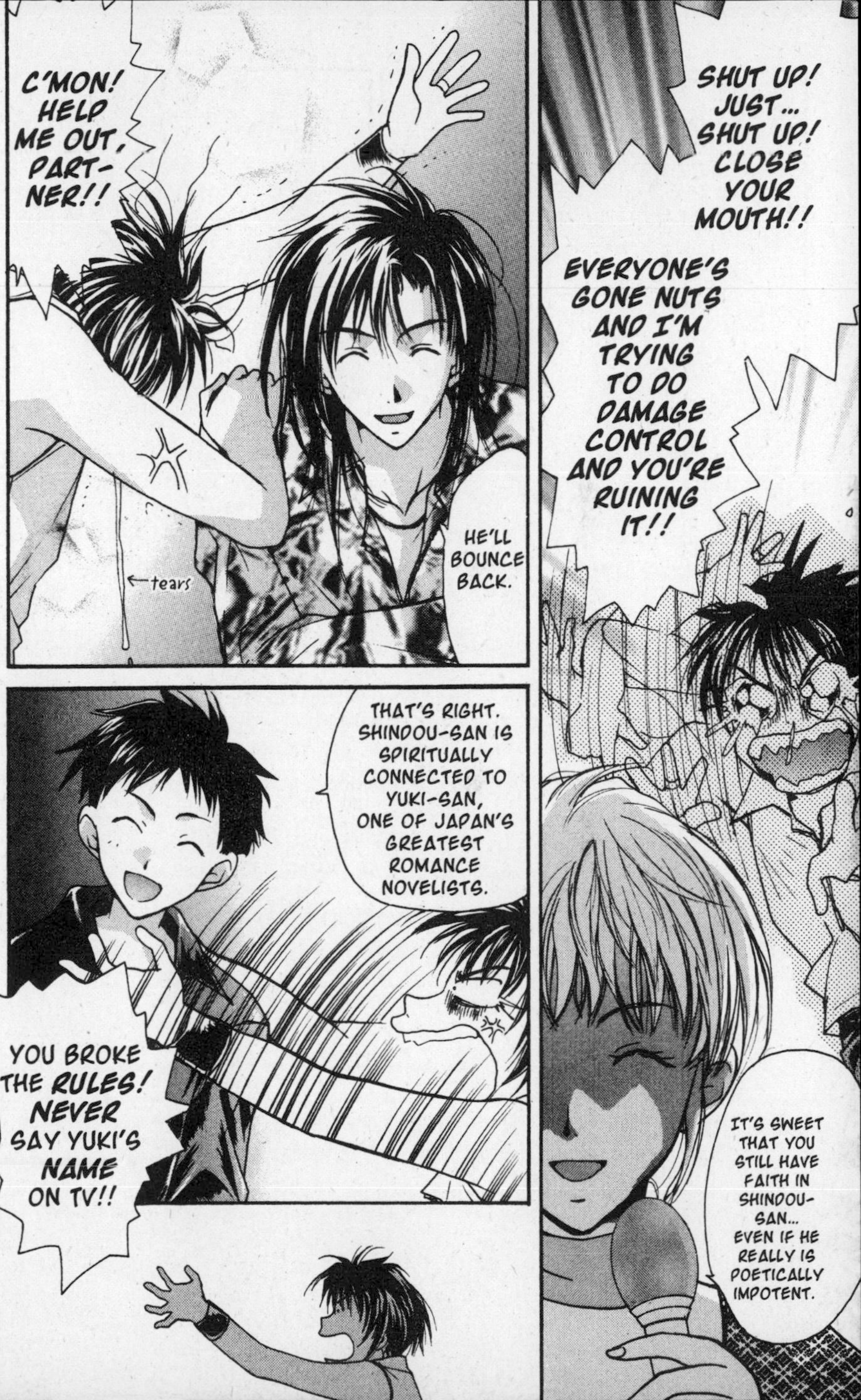
SHUT UP! JUST... SHUT UP! CLOSE YOUR MOUTH!!
EVERYONE'S GONE NUTS AND I'M TRYING TO DO DAMAGE CONTROL AND YOU'RE RUINING IT!!
IT'S SWEET THAT YOU STILL HAVE FAITH IN SHINDOU-SAN... EVEN IF HE REALLY IS POETICALLY IMPOTENT.
C'MON! HELP ME OUT, PARTNER!!
HE'LL BOUNCE BACK.
←tears
THAT'S RIGHT. SHINDOU-SAN IS SPIRITUALLY CONNECTED TO YUKI-SAN, ONE OF JAPAN'S GREATEST ROMANCE NOVELISTS.
YOU BROKE THE RULES! NEVER SAY YUKI'S NAME ON TV!!

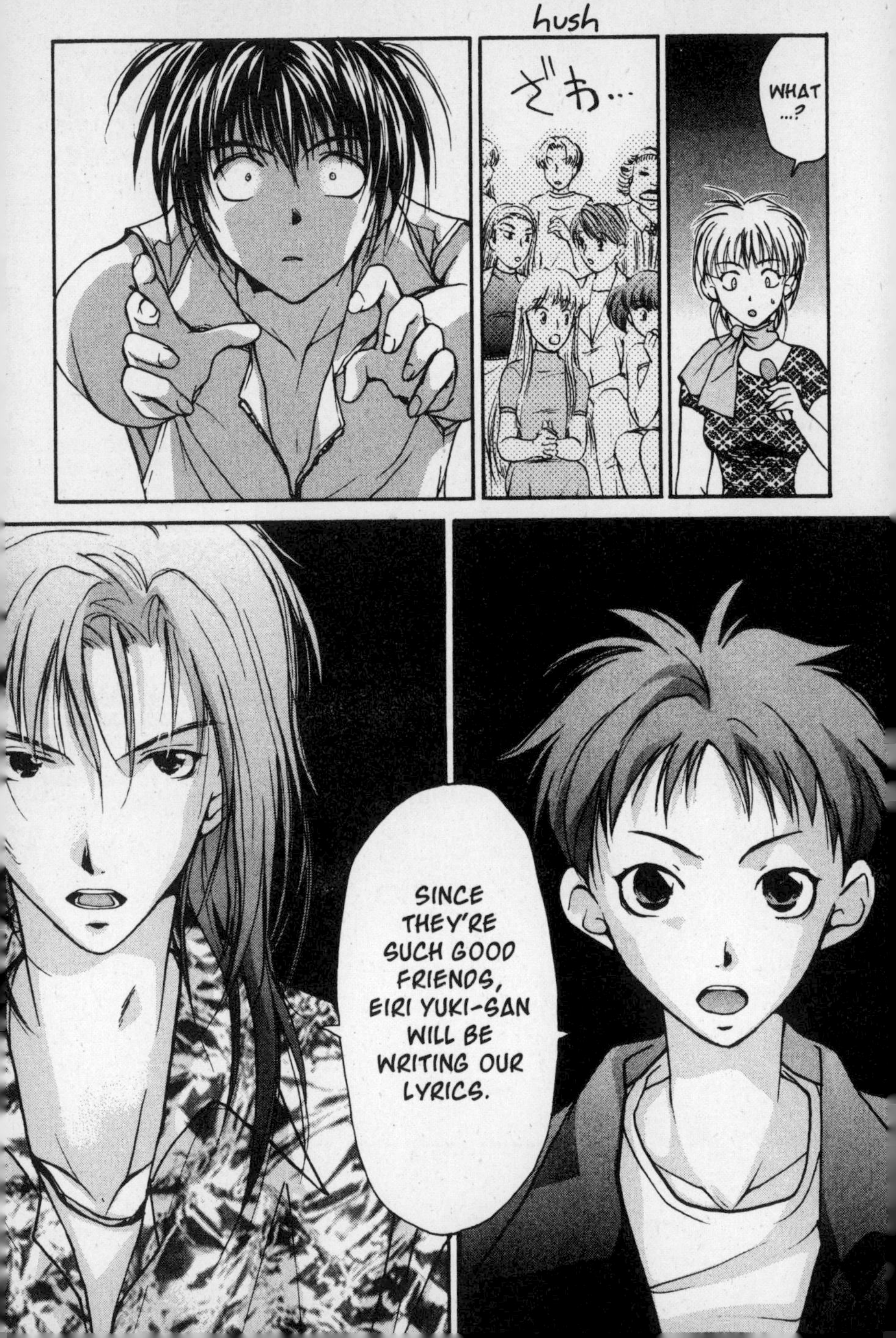
WHAT ...?
hush
ざわ…
SINCE THEY'RE SUCH GOOD FRIENDS, EIRI YUKI-SAN WILL BE WRITING OUR LYRICS.

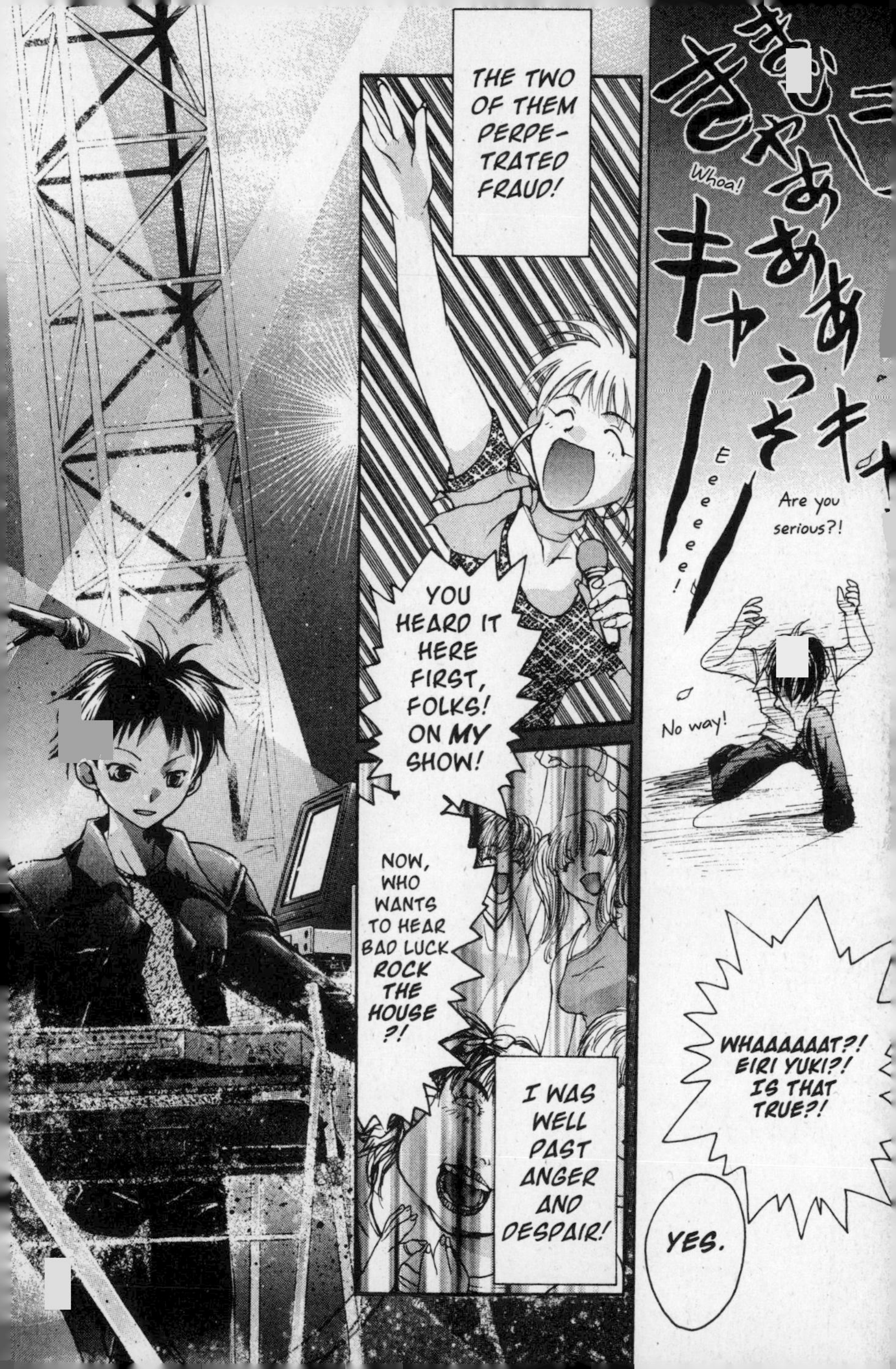
Whoa!
Eeeeee!
Are you serious?!
No way!
WHAAAAAAT?! EIRI YUKI?! IS THAT TRUE?!
YES.
THE TWO OF THEM PERPE-TRATED FRAUD!
YOU HEARD IT HERE FIRST, FOLKS! ON MY SHOW!
NOW, WHO WANTS TO HEAR BAD LUCK ROCK THE HOUSE?!
I WAS WELL PAST ANGER AND DESPAIR!

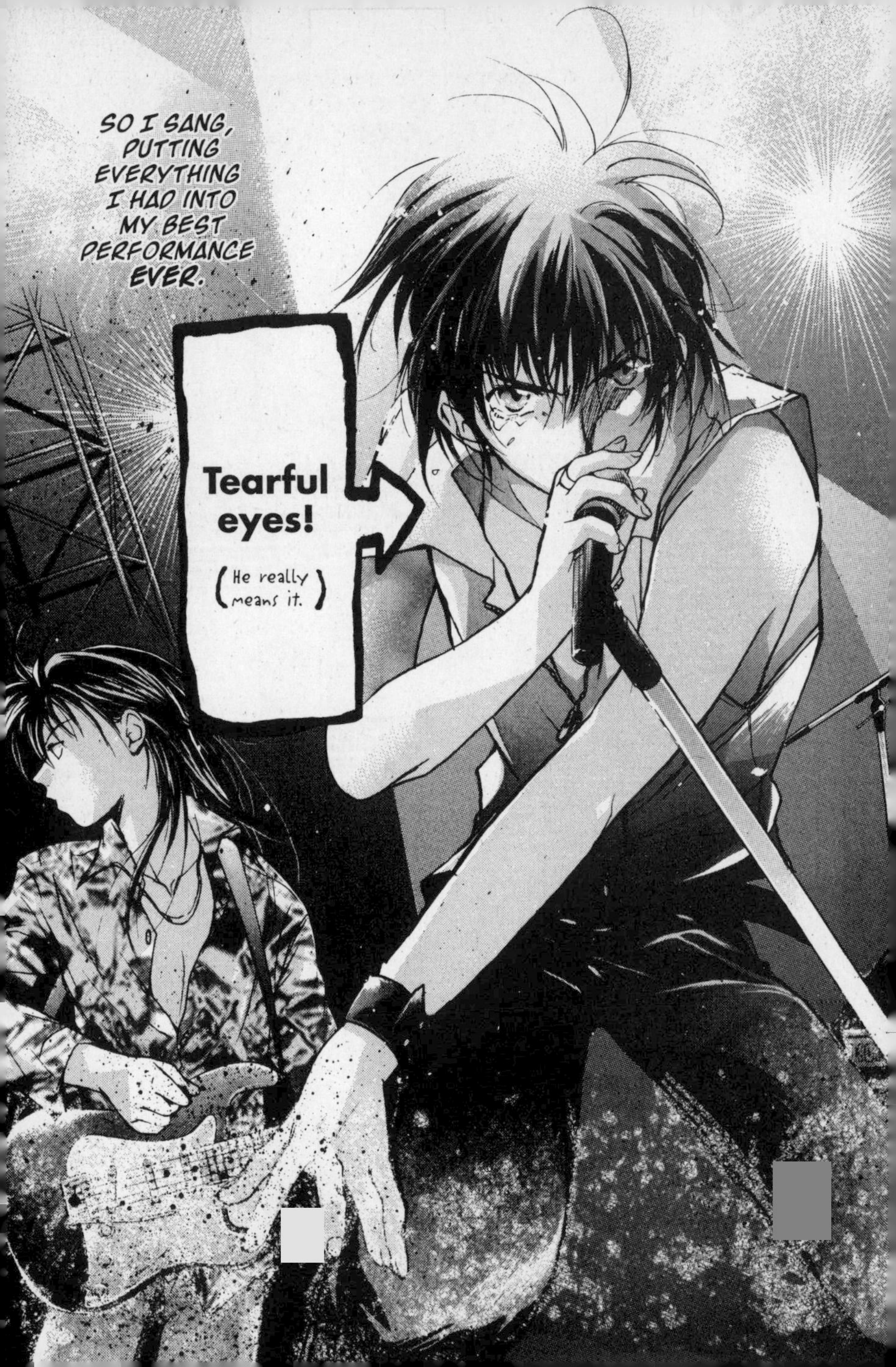
SO I SANG, PUTTING EVERYTHING I HAD INTO MY BEST PERFORMANCE EVER.
Tearful eyes!
(He really means it.)

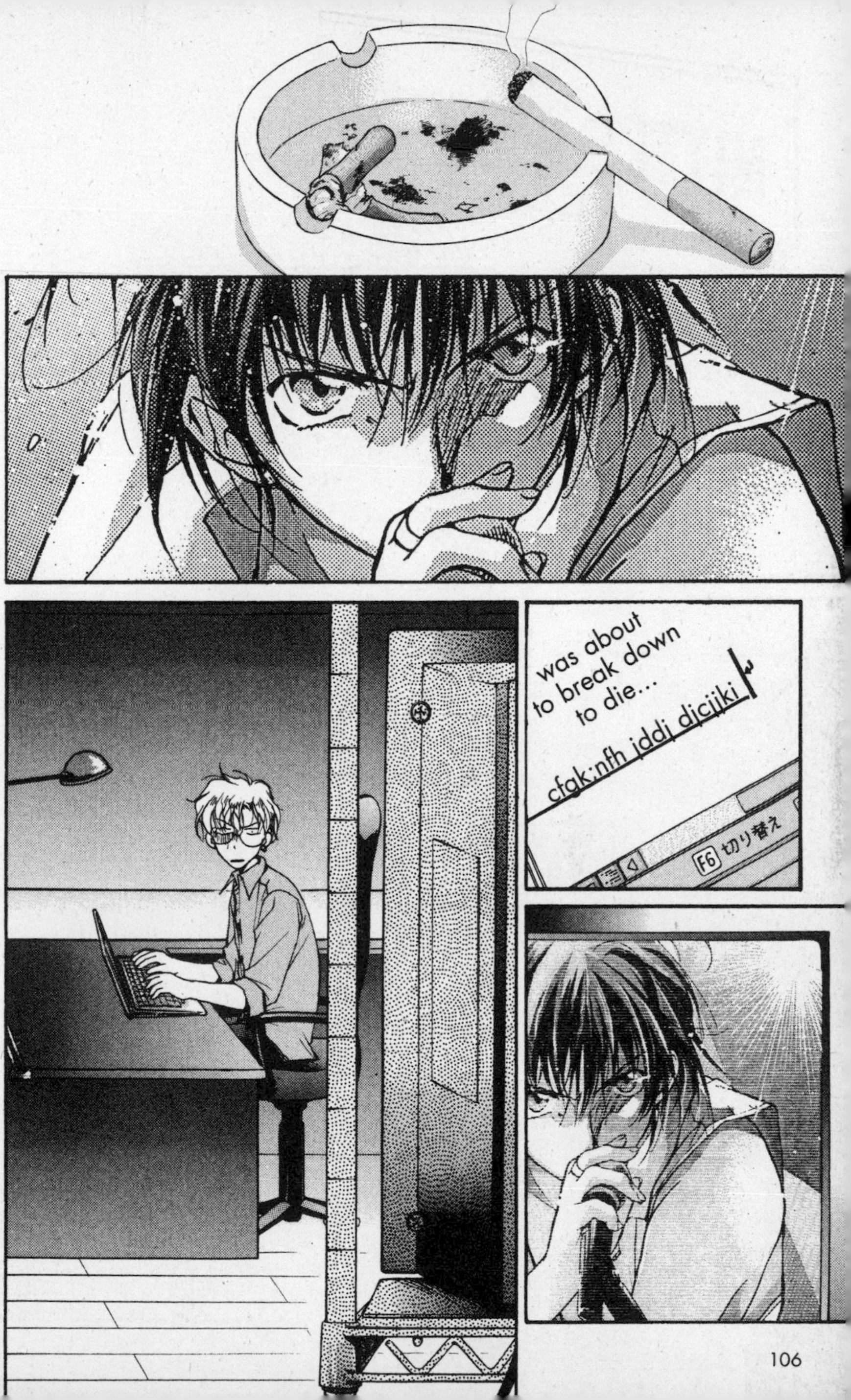
was about
to break down
to die...
cfgk:nfh iddj djcjiki
F6 切り替え

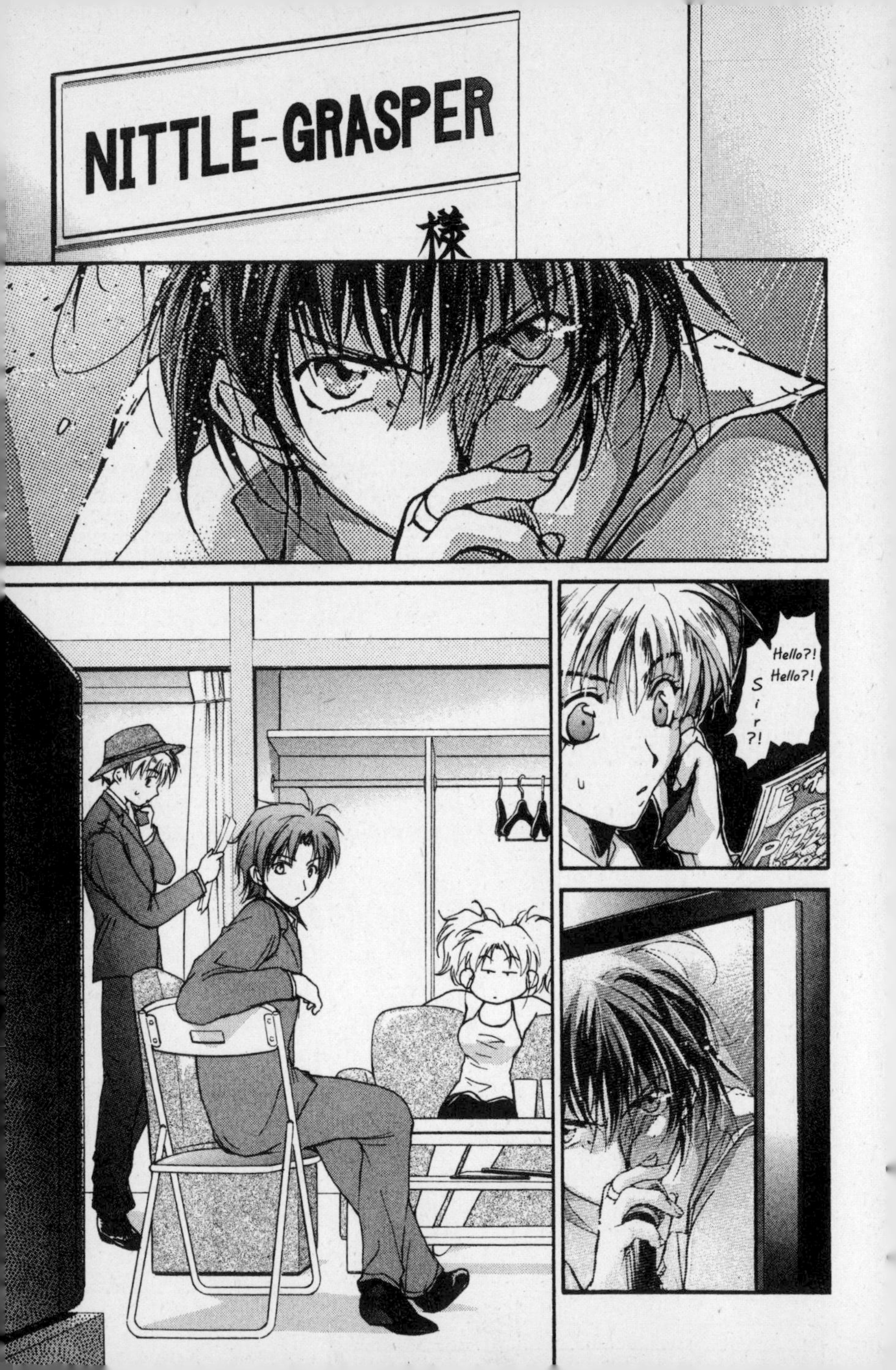
NITTLE-GRASPER
様
Hello?! Hello?!
Sir?!

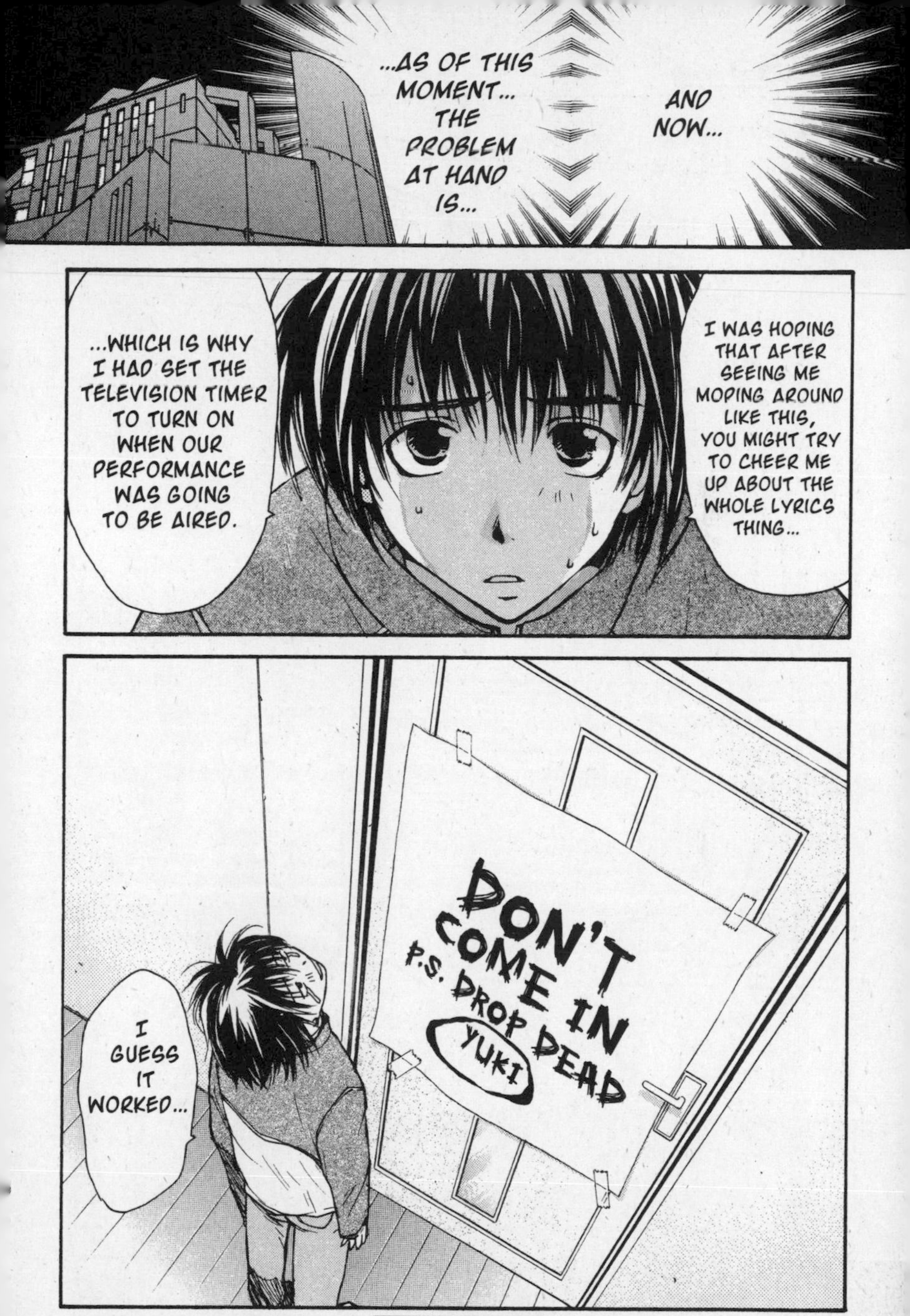
AND NOW...
...AS OF THIS MOMENT... THE PROBLEM AT HAND IS...
I WAS HOPING THAT AFTER SEEING ME MOPING AROUND LIKE THIS, YOU MIGHT TRY TO CHEER ME UP ABOUT THE WHOLE LYRICS THING...
...WHICH IS WHY I HAD SET THE TELEVISION TIMER TO TURN ON WHEN OUR PERFORMANCE WAS GOING TO BE AIRED.
DON'T COME IN
P.S. DROP DEAD
YUKI
I GUESS IT WORKED...

track46 ▶ END

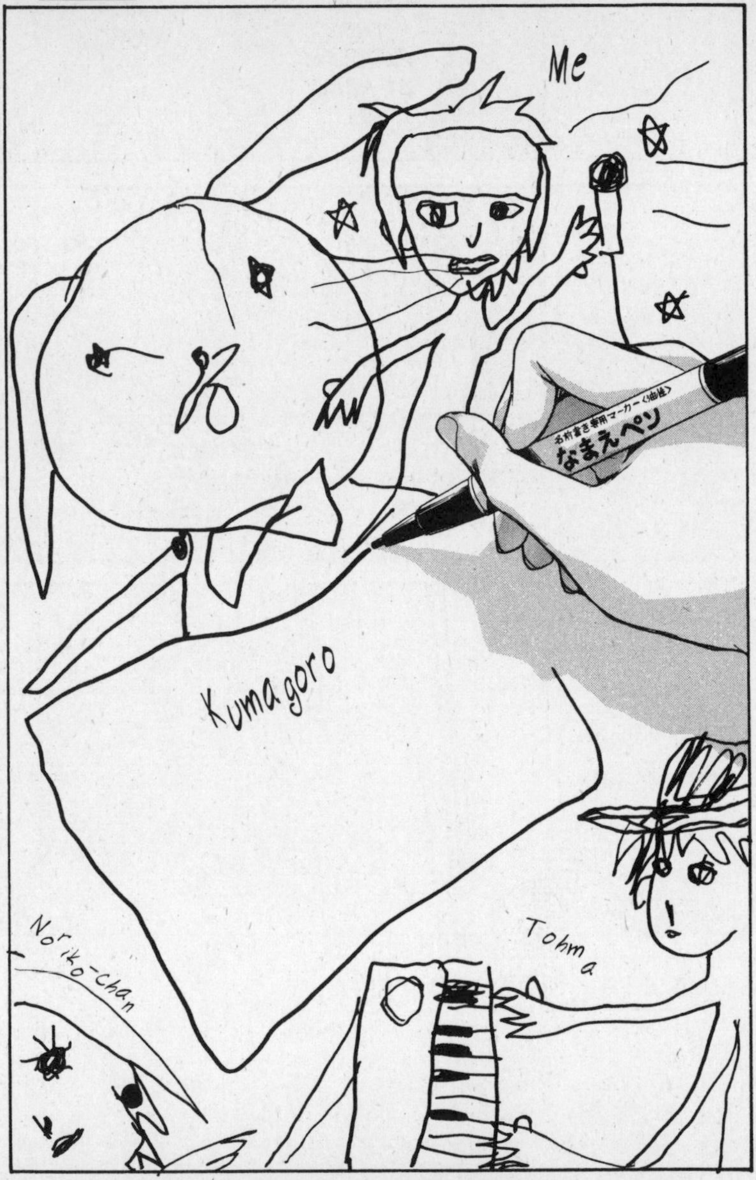
Me
名前書き専用マーカー〈油性〉
なまえペン
Kumagoro
Tohma
Noriko-chan

# track 47

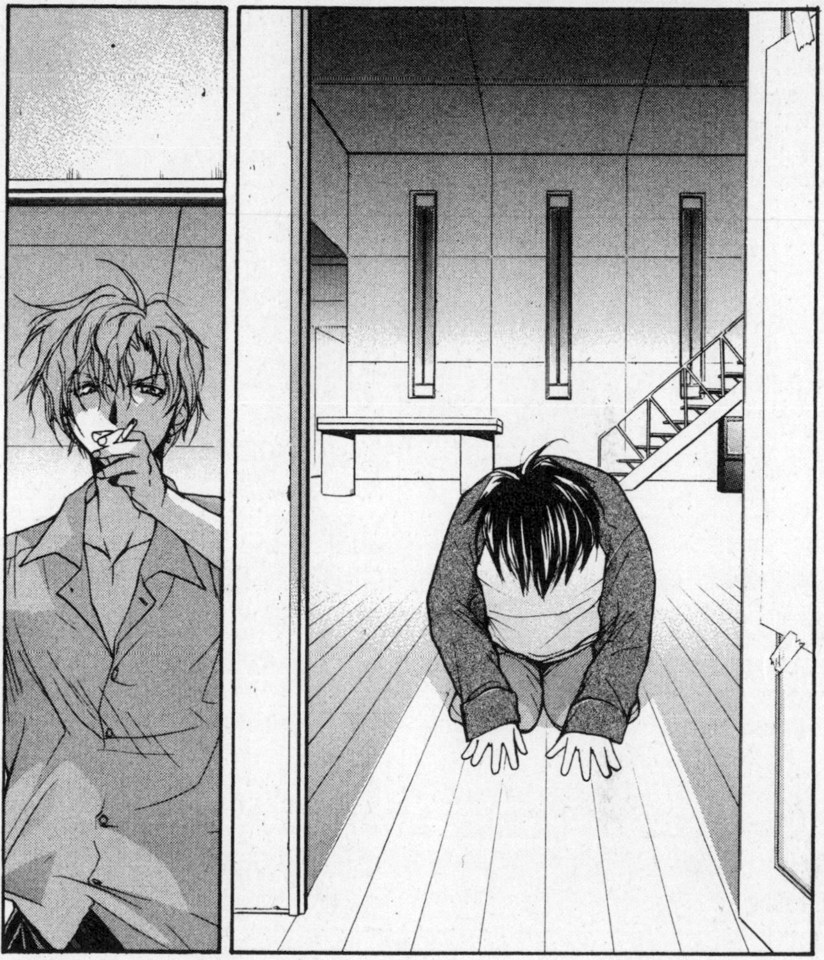

## ABOUT GRAVITATION TRACK 47

This is episode 47, which simply reeks of misery. Not just the characters', but mine. The whole thing looks like it was drawn in a panic. It's pathetic! I hate feeling like I could have done more. But it'll make me happy if you can look past that and read it for what it is. I won't blame you if you get discouraged, though. It's gotten really chilly these days. Please be careful not to catch cold. And if it's not chilly where you are...I'm sorry if things are too hot. What's good to eat over there during this kind of season? Let's go have a drink someday. But I'm not a heavy drinker. But people used to say they thought I looked like I could hold my liquor...I dunno. They also said that I looked like I could operate a combine...but I don't have a license.

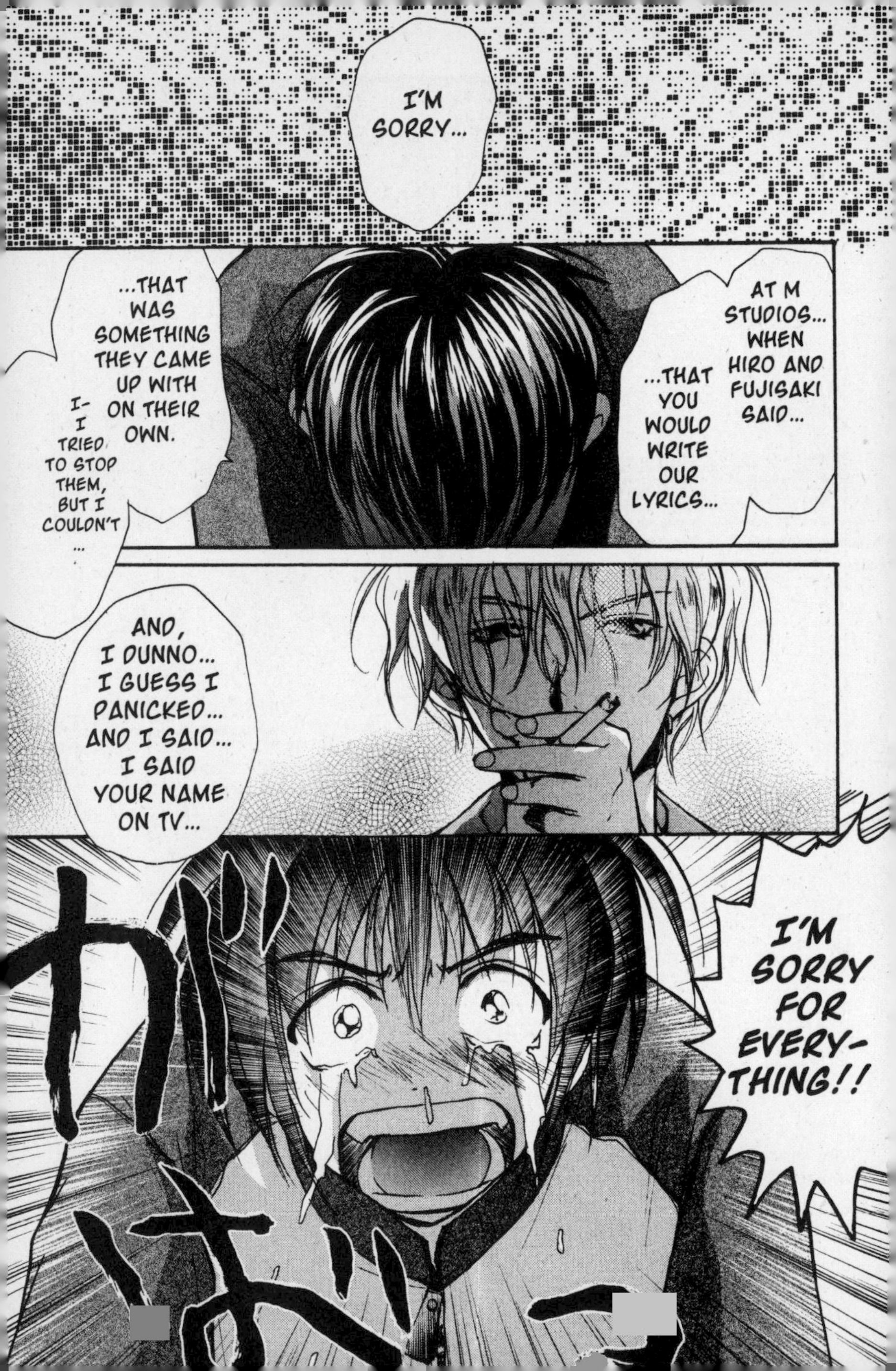
I'M SORRY...
AT M STUDIOS... WHEN HIRO AND FUJISAKI SAID...
...THAT YOU WOULD WRITE OUR LYRICS...
...THAT WAS SOMETHING THEY CAME UP WITH ON THEIR OWN.
I- I TRIED TO STOP THEM, BUT I COULDN'T ...
AND, I DUNNO... I GUESS I PANICKED... AND I SAID... I SAID YOUR NAME ON TV...
I'M SORRY FOR EVERY-THING!!

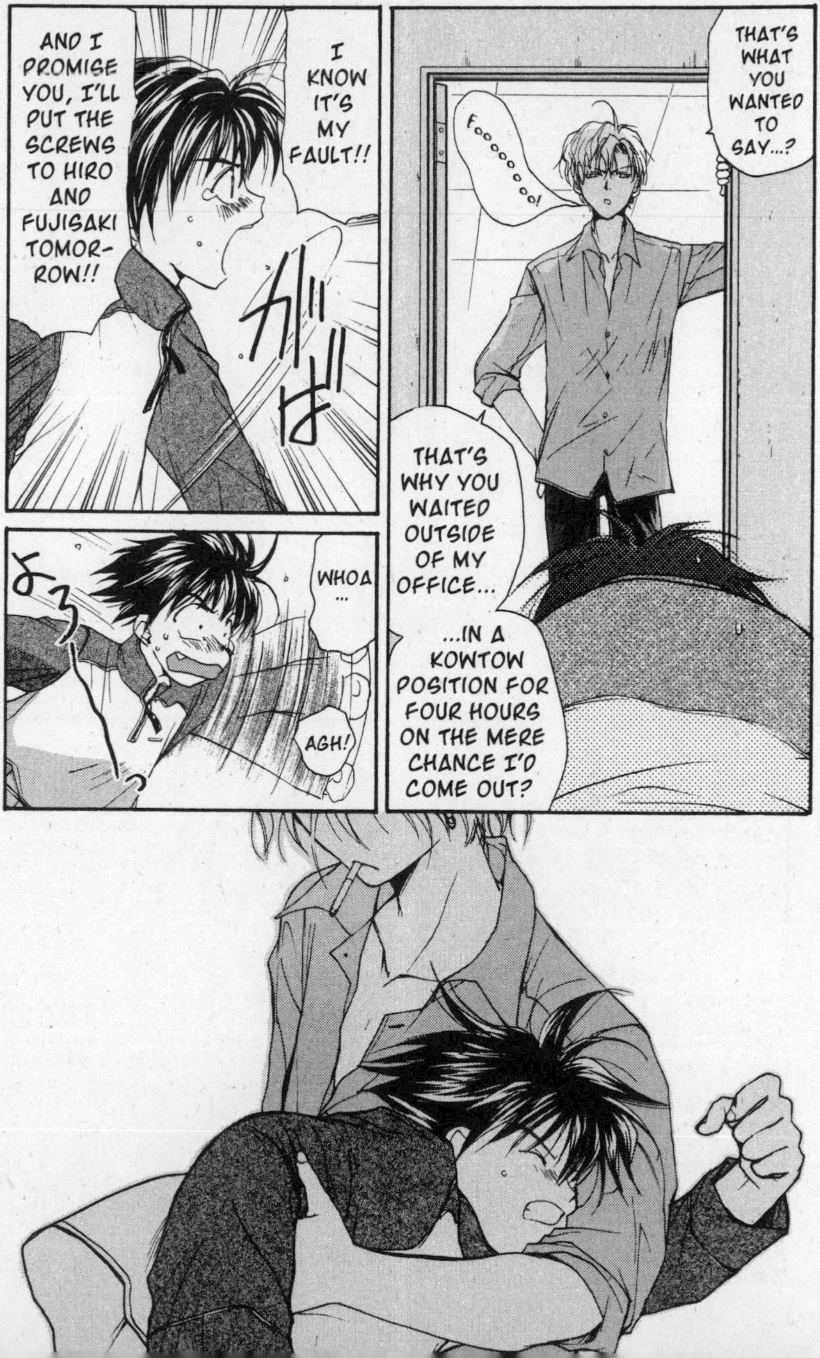
THAT'S WHAT YOU WANTED TO SAY...?
Fooooooooo!
THAT'S WHY YOU WAITED OUTSIDE OF MY OFFICE...
...IN A KOWTOW POSITION FOR FOUR HOURS ON THE MERE CHANCE I'D COME OUT?
I KNOW IT'S MY FAULT!!
AND I PROMISE YOU, I'LL PUT THE SCREWS TO HIRO AND FUJISAKI TOMOR-ROW!!
がば
WHOA ...
AGH!
よろ

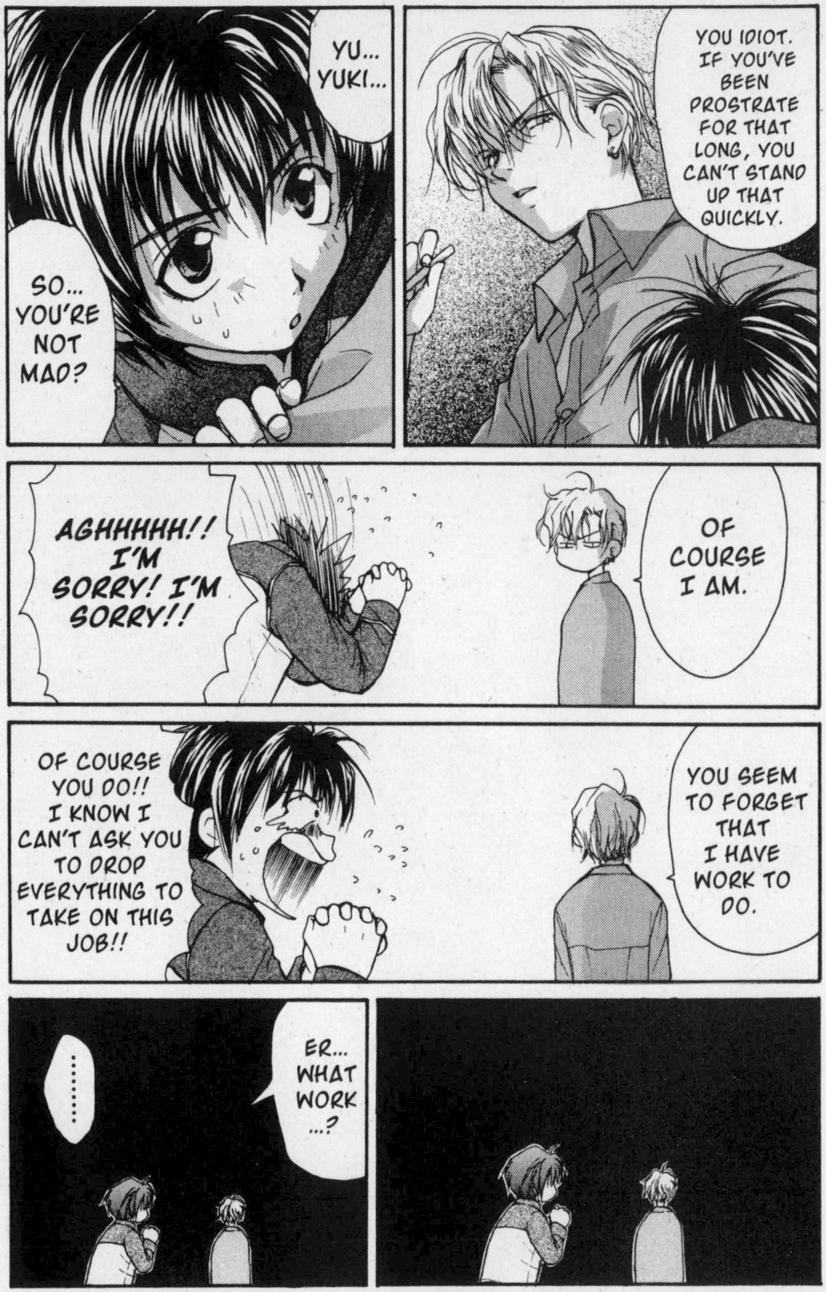
YOU IDIOT. IF YOU'VE BEEN PROSTRATE FOR THAT LONG, YOU CAN'T STAND UP THAT QUICKLY.
YU... YUKI...
SO... YOU'RE NOT MAD?
OF COURSE I AM.
AGHHHH!! I'M SORRY! I'M SORRY!!
YOU SEEM TO FORGET THAT I HAVE WORK TO DO.
OF COURSE YOU DO!! I KNOW I CAN'T ASK YOU TO DROP EVERYTHING TO TAKE ON THIS JOB!!
ER... WHAT WORK ...?
........

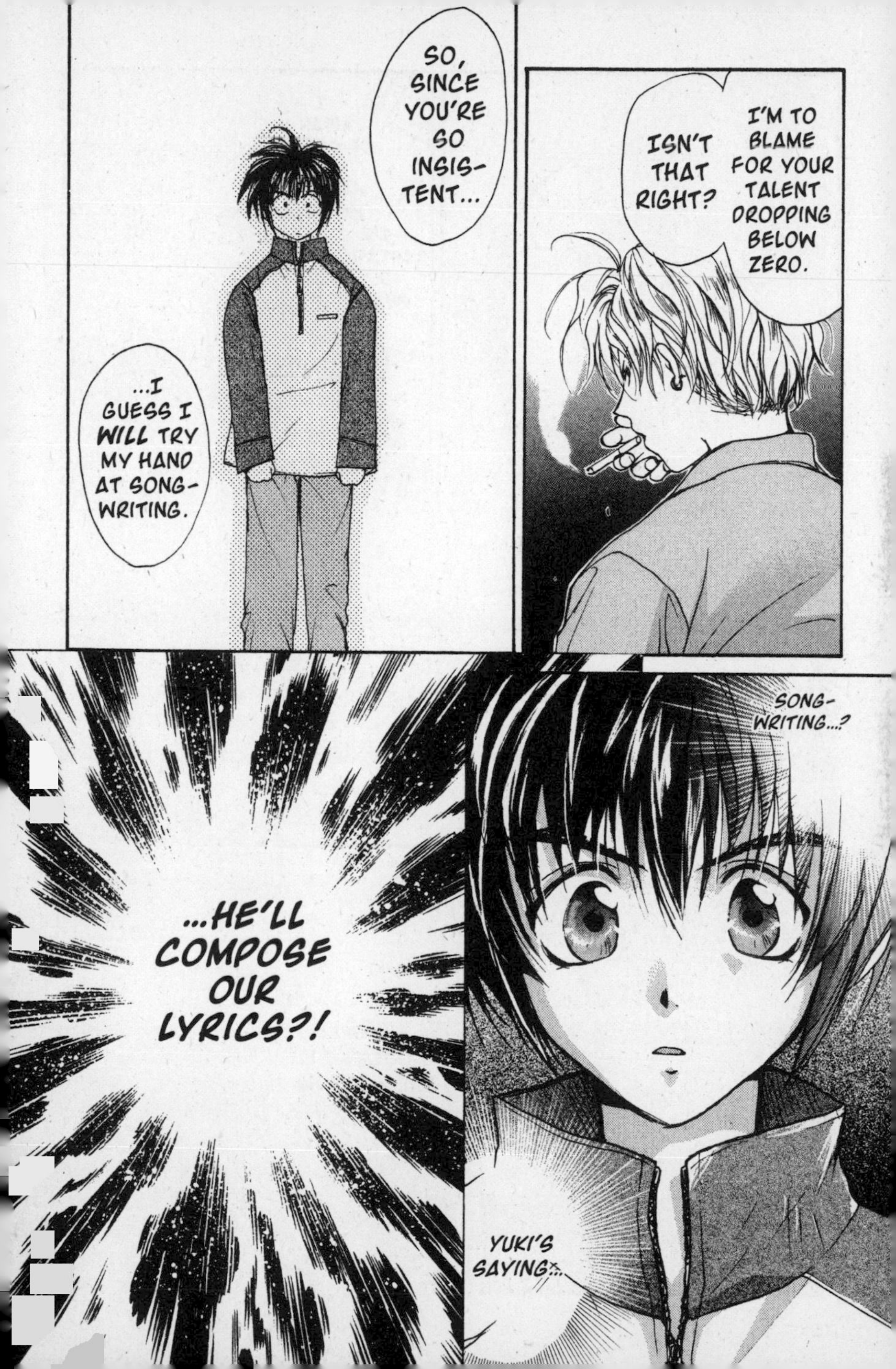
I'M TO BLAME FOR YOUR TALENT DROPPING BELOW ZERO.
ISN'T THAT RIGHT?
SO, SINCE YOU'RE SO INSIS-TENT...
...I GUESS I **WILL** TRY MY HAND AT SONG-WRITING.
SONG-WRITING...?
YUKI'S SAYING...
...HE'LL COMPOSE OUR LYRICS?!

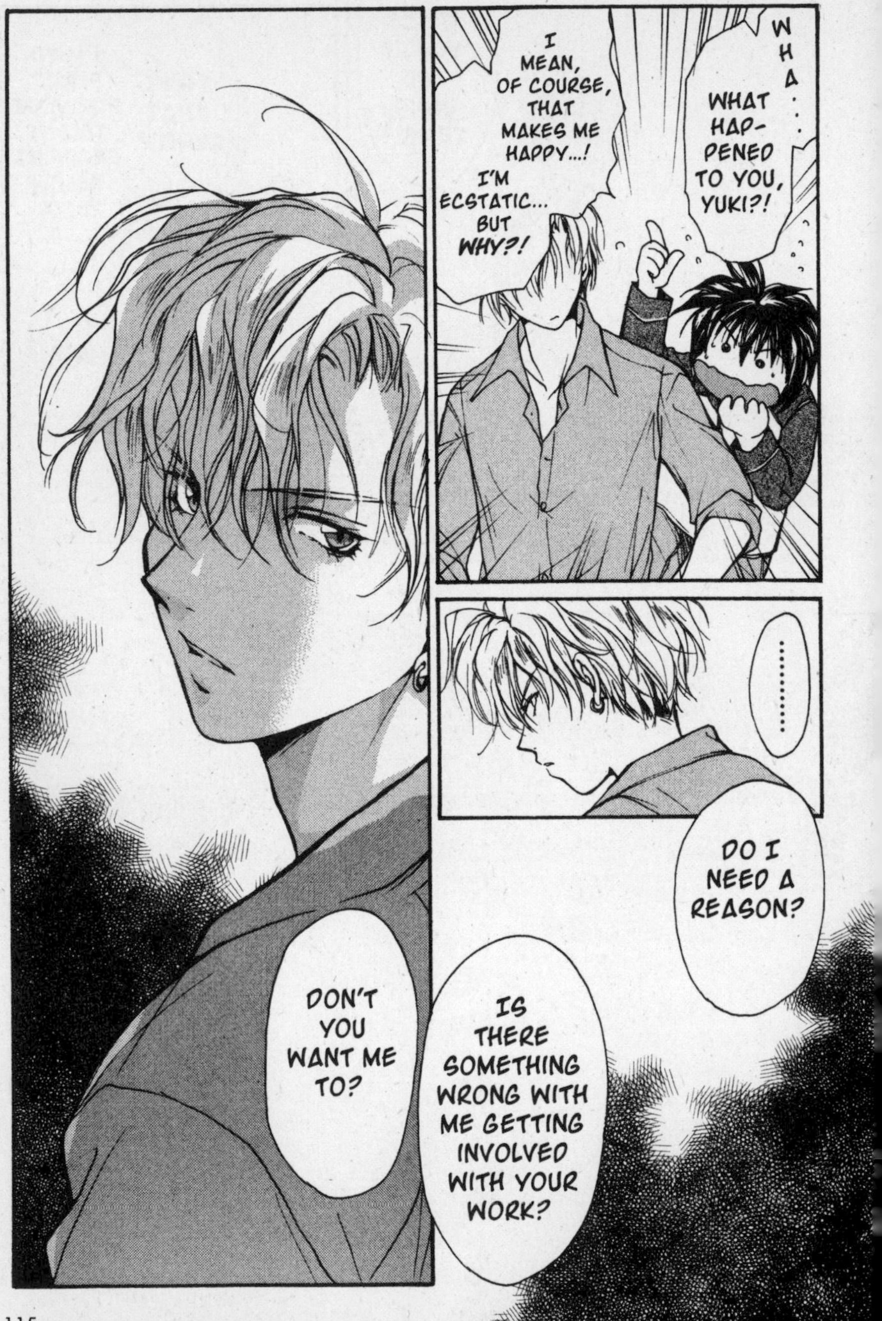

WHA...
WHAT HAP-PENED TO YOU, YUKI?!
I MEAN, OF COURSE, THAT MAKES ME HAPPY...!
I'M ECSTATIC... BUT WHY?!
......
DO I NEED A REASON?
IS THERE SOMETHING WRONG WITH ME GETTING INVOLVED WITH YOUR WORK?
DON'T YOU WANT ME TO?

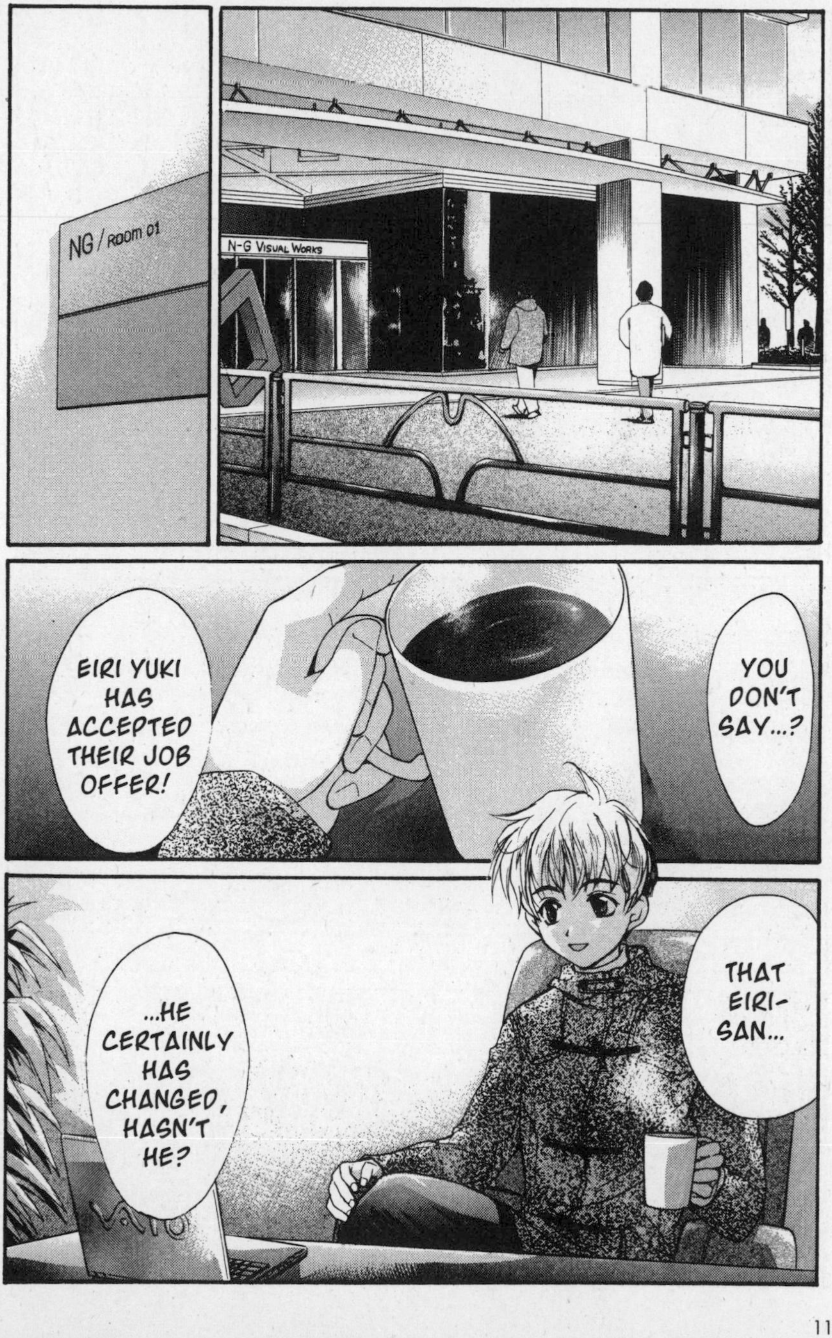
N-G VISUAL WORKS
NG / ROOM 01
YOU DON'T SAY...?
EIRI YUKI HAS ACCEPTED THEIR JOB OFFER!
THAT EIRI-SAN...
...HE CERTAINLY HAS CHANGED, HASN'T HE?

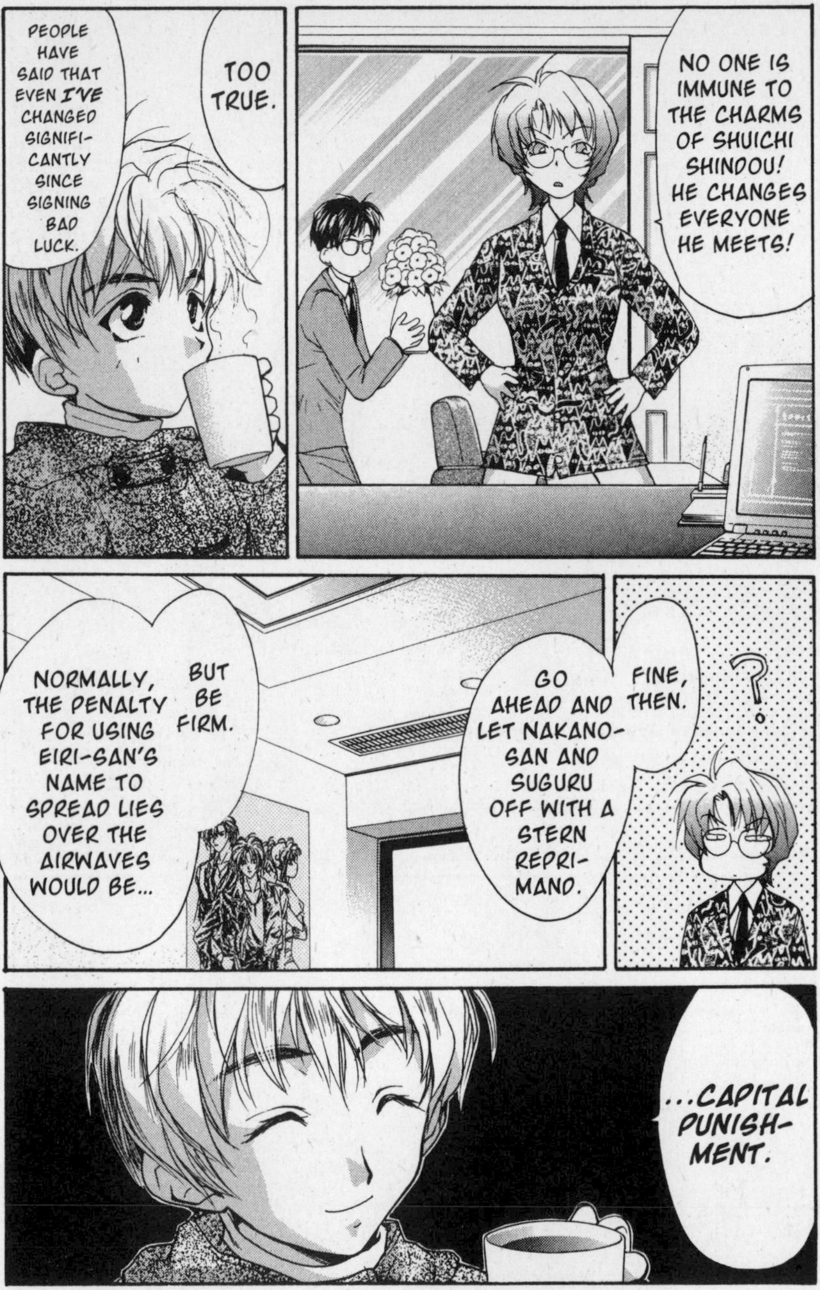
NO ONE IS IMMUNE TO THE CHARMS OF SHUICHI SHINDOU! HE CHANGES EVERYONE HE MEETS!
TOO TRUE.
PEOPLE HAVE SAID THAT EVEN *I'VE* CHANGED SIGNIFI-CANTLY SINCE SIGNING BAD LUCK.
FINE, THEN.
GO AHEAD AND LET NAKANO-SAN AND SUGURU OFF WITH A STERN REPRI-MAND.
BUT BE FIRM.
NORMALLY, THE PENALTY FOR USING EIRI-SAN'S NAME TO SPREAD LIES OVER THE AIRWAVES WOULD BE...
...CAPITAL PUNISH-MENT.

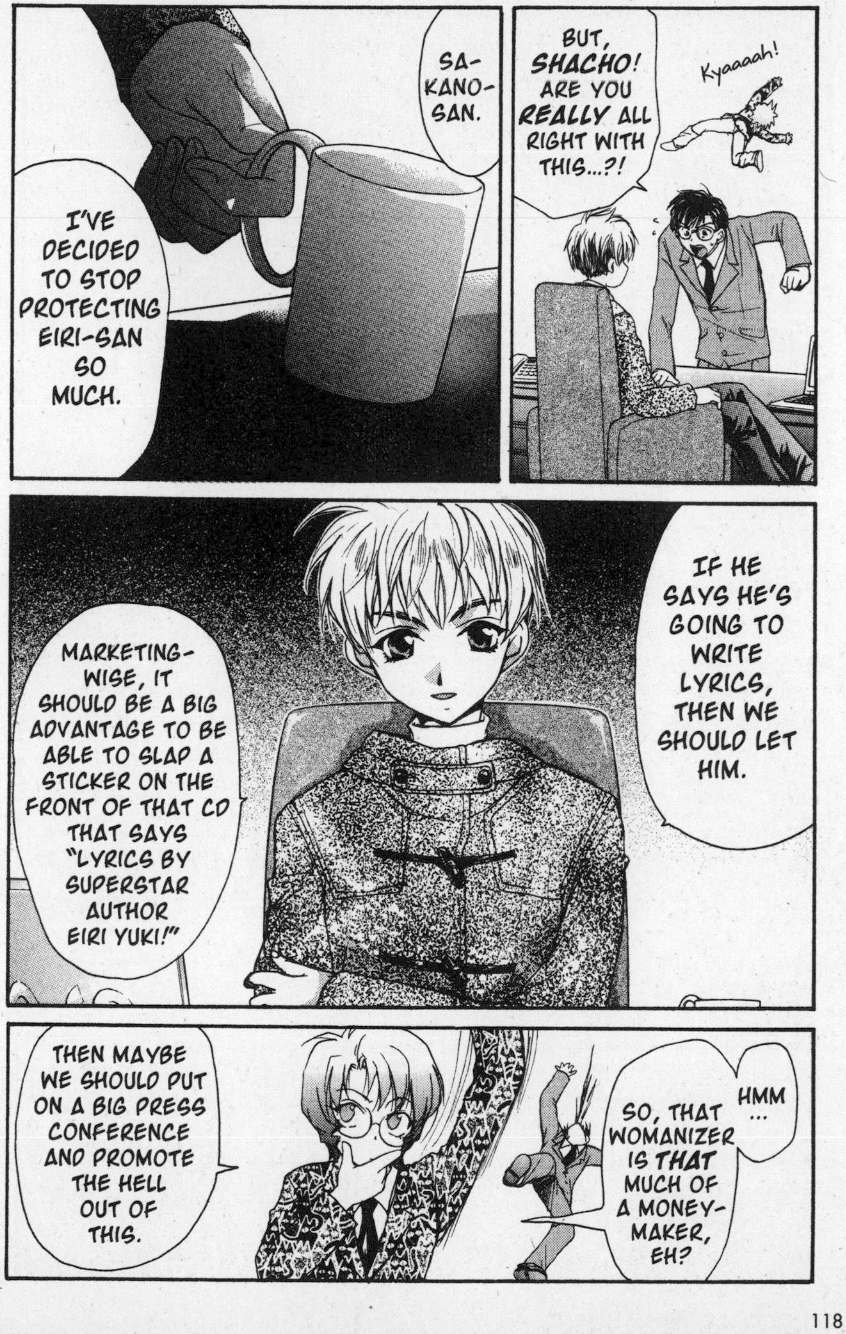
Kyaaaah!
BUT, SHACHO! ARE YOU REALLY ALL RIGHT WITH THIS...?!
SA-KANO-SAN.
I'VE DECIDED TO STOP PROTECTING EIRI-SAN SO MUCH.
IF HE SAYS HE'S GOING TO WRITE LYRICS, THEN WE SHOULD LET HIM.
MARKETING-WISE, IT SHOULD BE A BIG ADVANTAGE TO BE ABLE TO SLAP A STICKER ON THE FRONT OF THAT CD THAT SAYS "LYRICS BY SUPERSTAR AUTHOR EIRI YUKI!"
HMM ...
SO, THAT WOMANIZER IS THAT MUCH OF A MONEY-MAKER, EH?
THEN MAYBE WE SHOULD PUT ON A BIG PRESS CONFERENCE AND PROMOTE THE HELL OUT OF THIS.

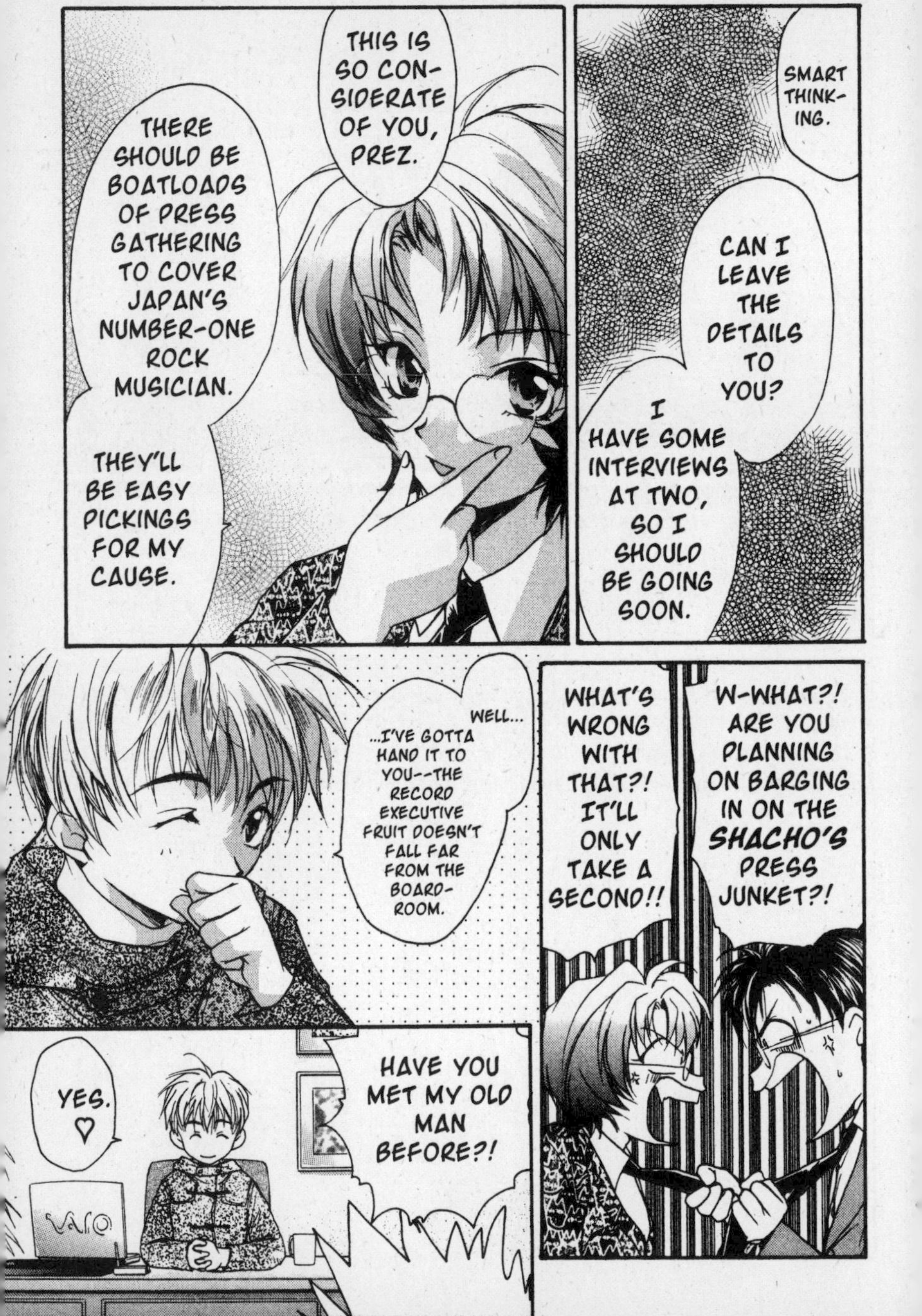
SMART THINKING.
CAN I LEAVE THE DETAILS TO YOU?
I HAVE SOME INTERVIEWS AT TWO, SO I SHOULD BE GOING SOON.
THIS IS SO CONSIDERATE OF YOU, PREZ.
THERE SHOULD BE BOATLOADS OF PRESS GATHERING TO COVER JAPAN'S NUMBER-ONE ROCK MUSICIAN.
THEY'LL BE EASY PICKINGS FOR MY CAUSE.
W-WHAT?! ARE YOU PLANNING ON BARGING IN ON THE *SHACHO'S* PRESS JUNKET?!
WHAT'S WRONG WITH THAT?! IT'LL ONLY TAKE A SECOND!!
WELL...
...I'VE GOTTA HAND IT TO YOU--THE RECORD EXECUTIVE FRUIT DOESN'T FALL FAR FROM THE BOARDROOM.
HAVE YOU MET MY OLD MAN BEFORE?!
YES. ♥
VAIO

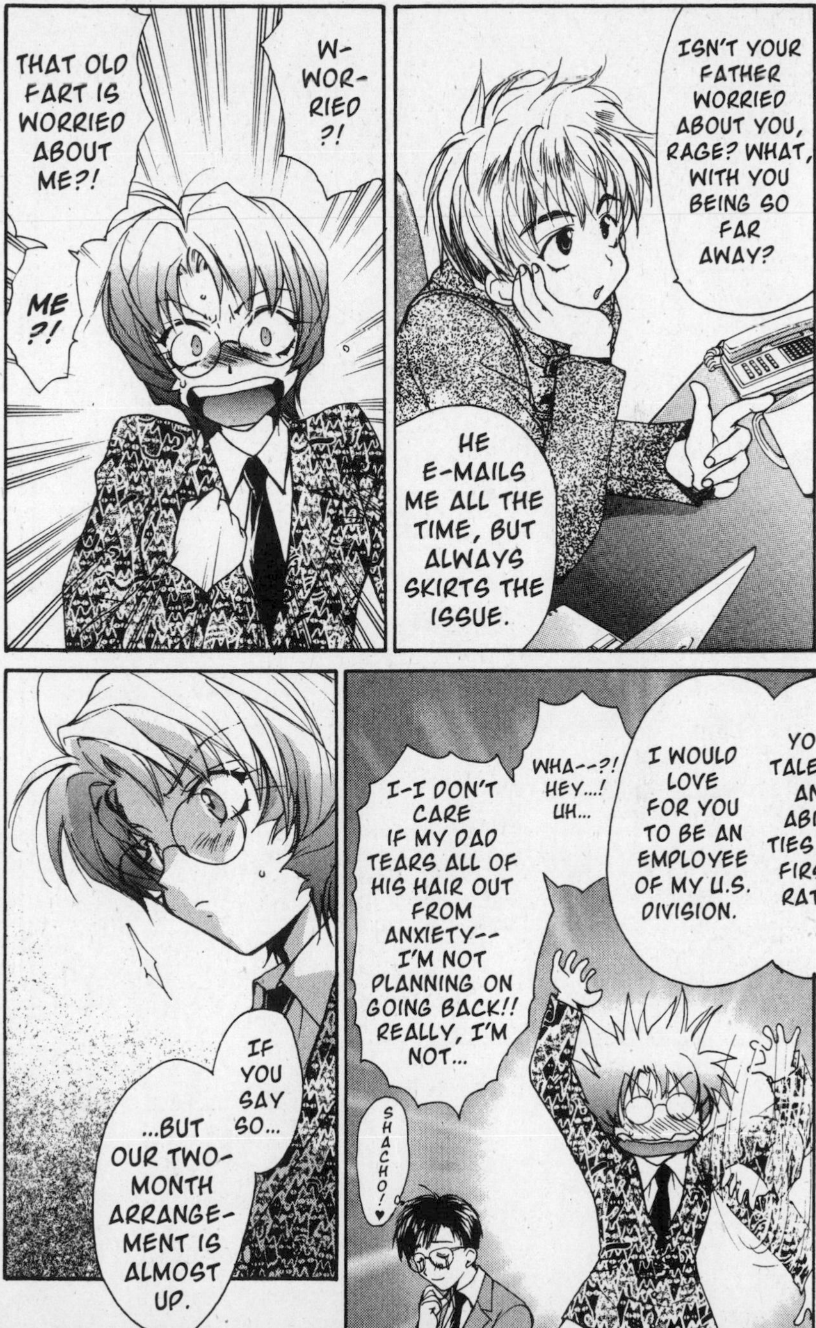
ISN'T YOUR FATHER WORRIED ABOUT YOU, RAGE? WHAT, WITH YOU BEING SO FAR AWAY?
HE E-MAILS ME ALL THE TIME, BUT ALWAYS SKIRTS THE ISSUE.
W-WOR-RIED?!
THAT OLD FART IS WORRIED ABOUT ME?!
ME?!
YOUR TALENTS AND ABILI-TIES ARE FIRST-RATE.
I WOULD LOVE FOR YOU TO BE AN EMPLOYEE OF MY U.S. DIVISION.
WHA--?! HEY...! UH...
I-I DON'T CARE IF MY DAD TEARS ALL OF HIS HAIR OUT FROM ANXIETY-- I'M NOT PLANNING ON GOING BACK!! REALLY, I'M NOT...
SHACHO!♥
IF YOU SAY SO...
...BUT OUR TWO-MONTH ARRANGE-MENT IS ALMOST UP.

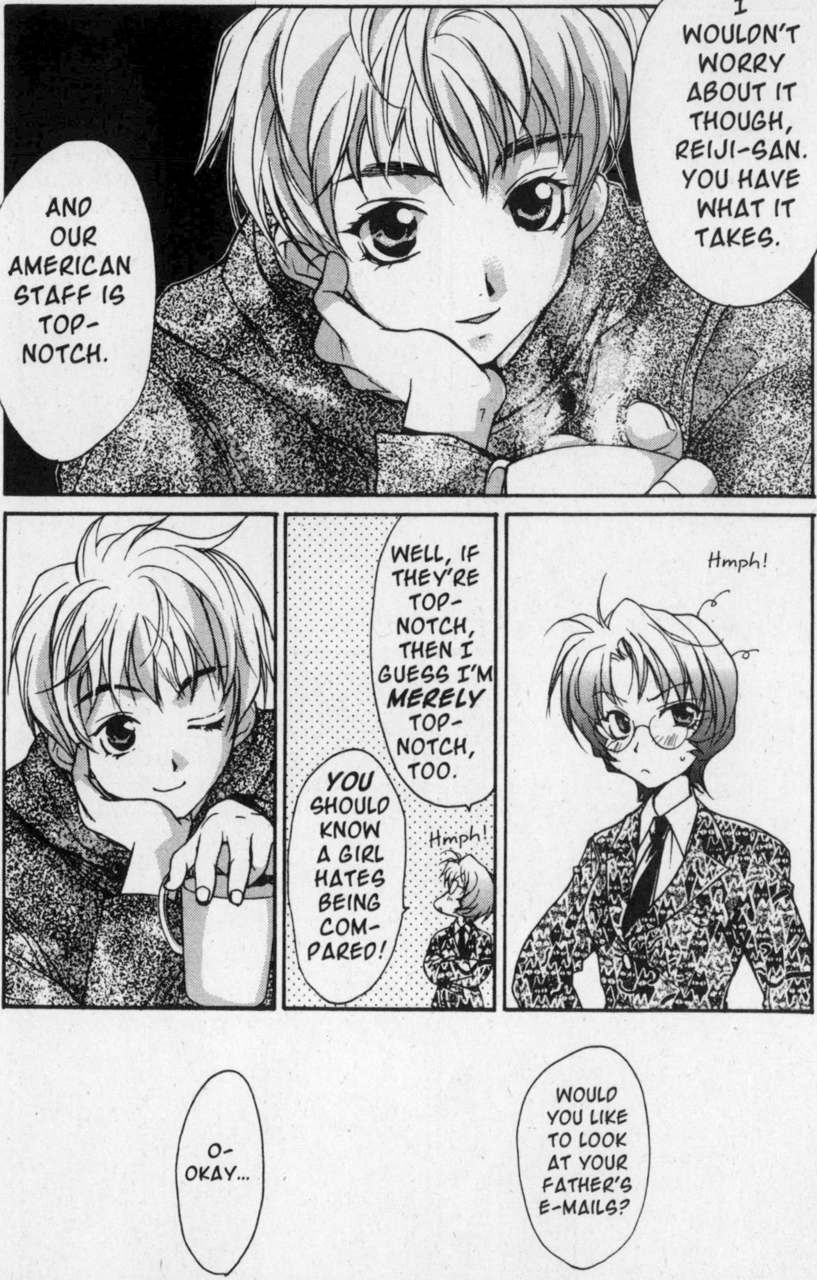
I WOULDN'T WORRY ABOUT IT THOUGH, REIJI-SAN. YOU HAVE WHAT IT TAKES.
AND OUR AMERICAN STAFF IS TOP-NOTCH.
Hmph!
WELL, IF THEY'RE TOP-NOTCH, THEN I GUESS I'M *MERELY* TOP-NOTCH, TOO.
Hmph!
*YOU* SHOULD KNOW A GIRL HATES BEING COM-PARED!
WOULD YOU LIKE TO LOOK AT YOUR FATHER'S E-MAILS?
O-OKAY...

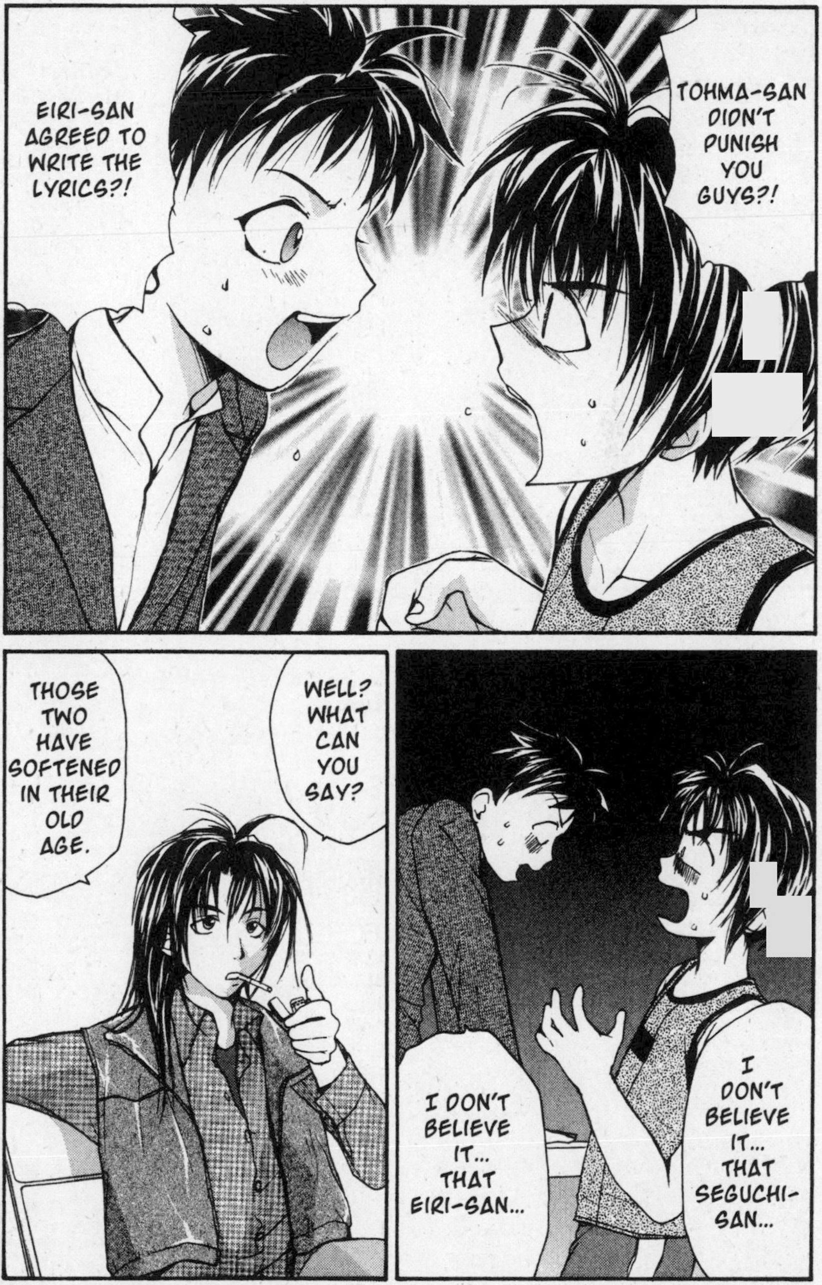
TOHMA-SAN DIDN'T PUNISH YOU GUYS?!
EIRI-SAN AGREED TO WRITE THE LYRICS?!
I DON'T BELIEVE IT... THAT SEGUCHI-SAN...
I DON'T BELIEVE IT... THAT EIRI-SAN...
WELL? WHAT CAN YOU SAY?
THOSE TWO HAVE SOFTENED IN THEIR OLD AGE.

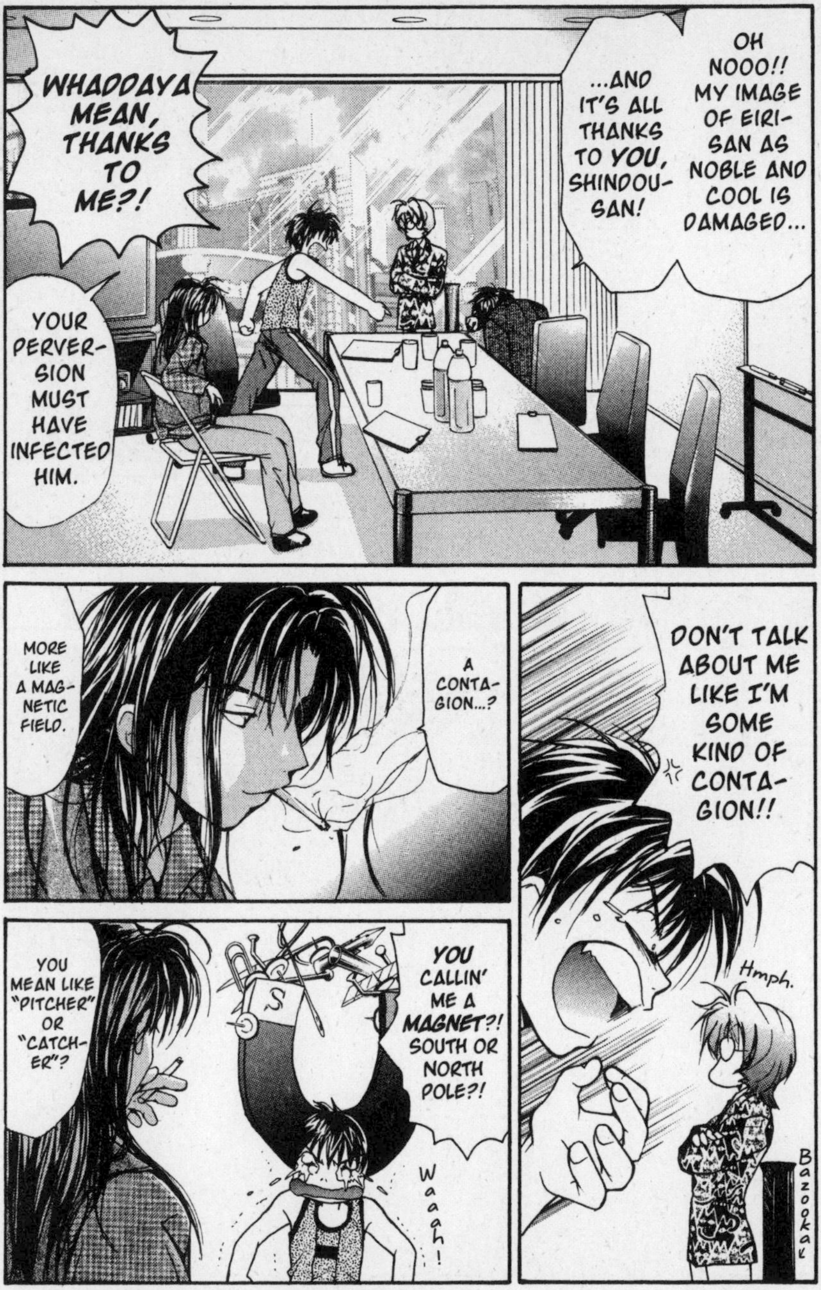
OH NOOO!! MY IMAGE OF EIRI-SAN AS NOBLE AND COOL IS DAMAGED...
...AND IT'S ALL THANKS TO *YOU*, SHINDOU-SAN!
WHADDAYA MEAN, THANKS TO ME?!
YOUR PERVERSION MUST HAVE INFECTED HIM.
DON'T TALK ABOUT ME LIKE I'M SOME KIND OF CONTAGION!!
Hmph.
Bazookak
A CONTAGION...?
MORE LIKE A MAGNETIC FIELD.
*YOU* CALLIN' ME A ***MAGNET***?! SOUTH OR NORTH POLE?!
Waaah!
YOU MEAN LIKE "PITCHER" OR "CATCHER"?

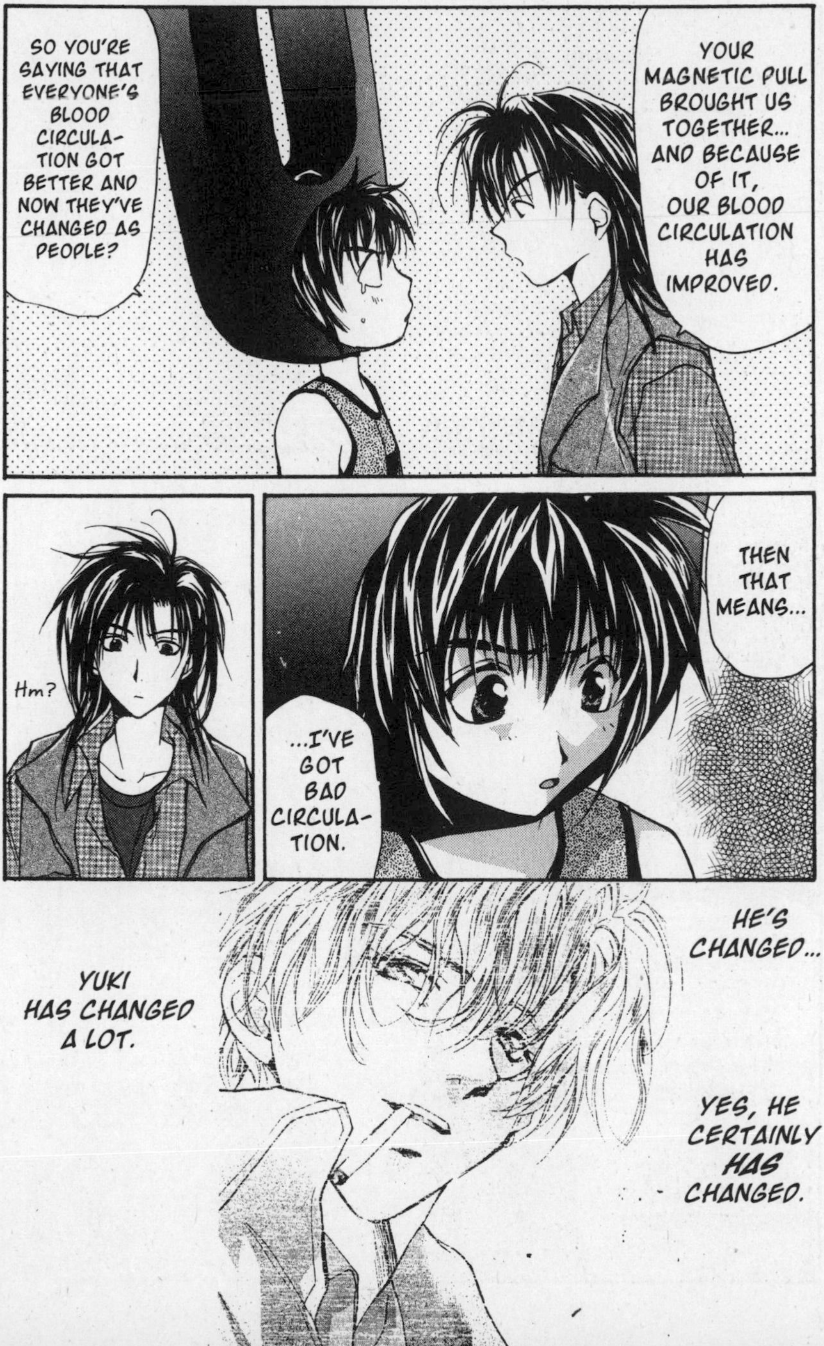
YOUR MAGNETIC PULL BROUGHT US TOGETHER... AND BECAUSE OF IT, OUR BLOOD CIRCULATION HAS IMPROVED.
SO YOU'RE SAYING THAT EVERYONE'S BLOOD CIRCULATION GOT BETTER AND NOW THEY'VE CHANGED AS PEOPLE?
THEN THAT MEANS...
...I'VE GOT BAD CIRCULATION.
Hm?
HE'S CHANGED...
YUKI HAS CHANGED A LOT.
YES, HE CERTAINLY HAS CHANGED.

BUT NOT ME...

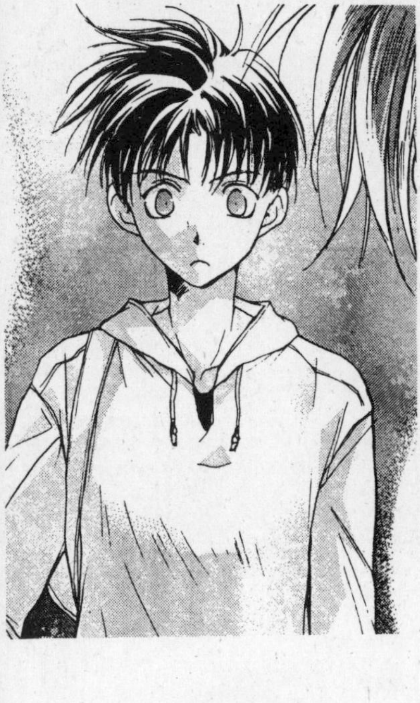

I'M STILL THE SAME...

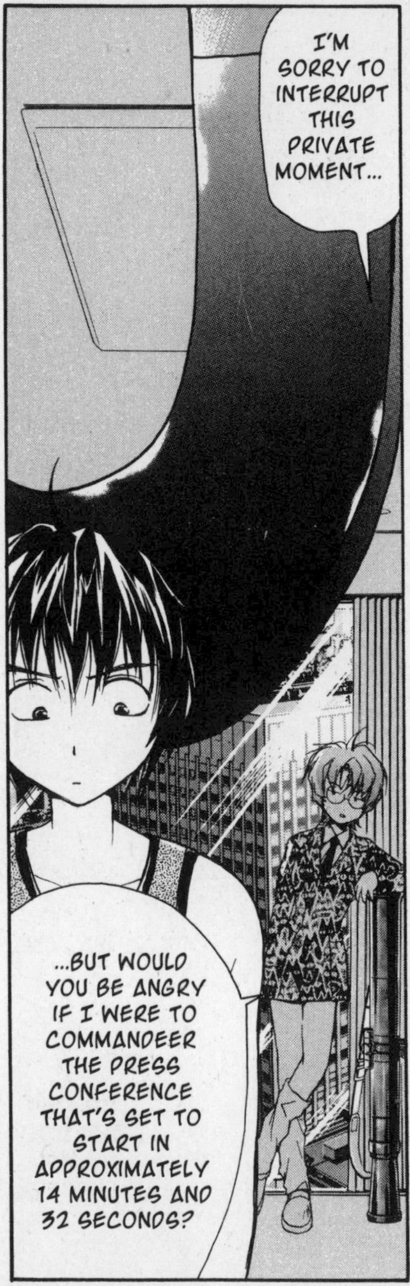
I'M SORRY TO INTERRUPT THIS PRIVATE MOMENT...
...BUT WOULD YOU BE ANGRY IF I WERE TO COMMANDEER THE PRESS CONFERENCE THAT'S SET TO START IN APPROXIMATELY 14 MINUTES AND 32 SECONDS?

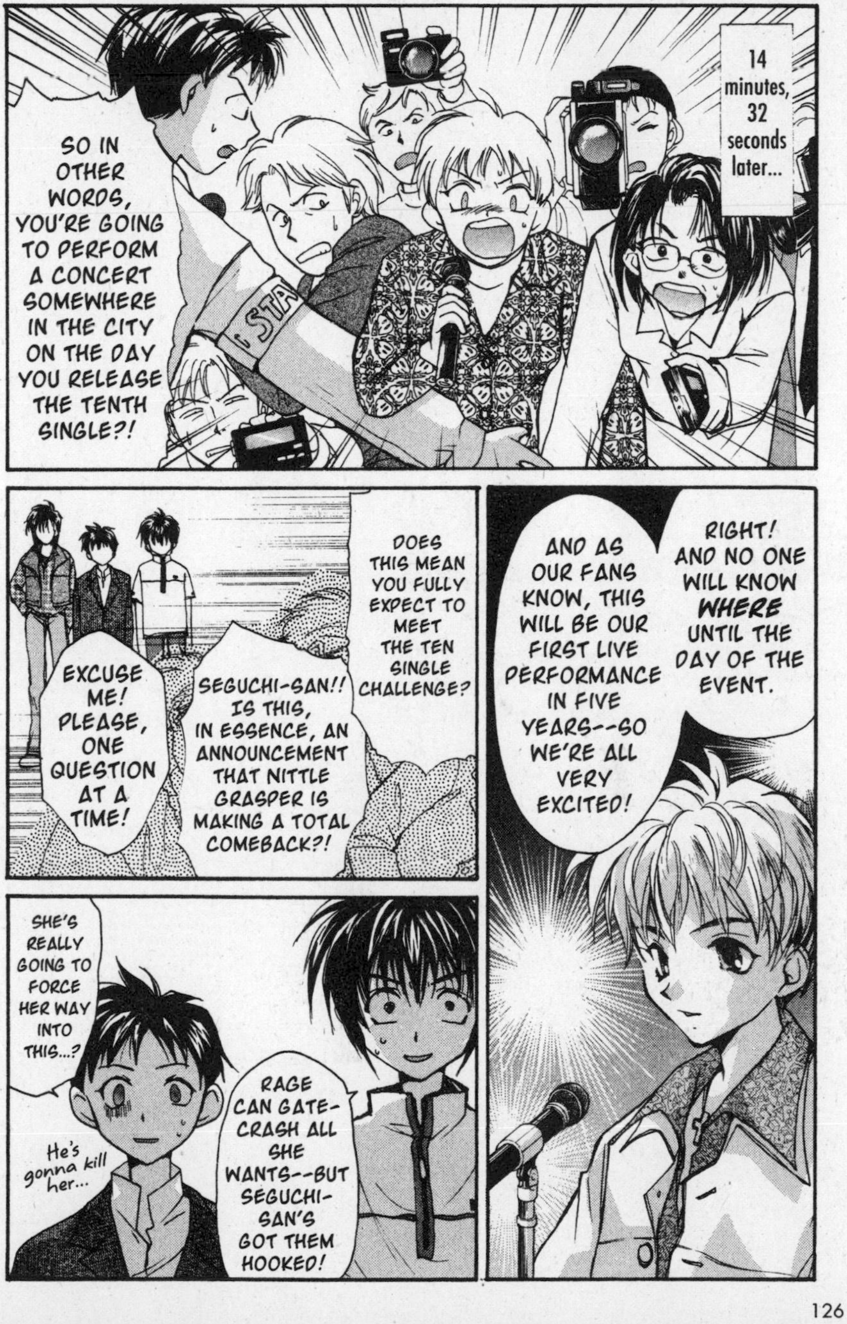
14 minutes, 32 seconds later...
SO IN OTHER WORDS, YOU'RE GOING TO PERFORM A CONCERT SOMEWHERE IN THE CITY ON THE DAY YOU RELEASE THE TENTH SINGLE?!
RIGHT! AND NO ONE WILL KNOW WHERE UNTIL THE DAY OF THE EVENT.
AND AS OUR FANS KNOW, THIS WILL BE OUR FIRST LIVE PERFORMANCE IN FIVE YEARS--SO WE'RE ALL VERY EXCITED!
DOES THIS MEAN YOU FULLY EXPECT TO MEET THE TEN SINGLE CHALLENGE?
SEGUCHI-SAN!! IS THIS, IN ESSENCE, AN ANNOUNCEMENT THAT NITTLE GRASPER IS MAKING A TOTAL COMEBACK?!
EXCUSE ME! PLEASE, ONE QUESTION AT A TIME!
RAGE CAN GATE-CRASH ALL SHE WANTS--BUT SEGUCHI-SAN'S GOT THEM HOOKED!
SHE'S REALLY GOING TO FORCE HER WAY INTO THIS...?
He's gonna kill her...

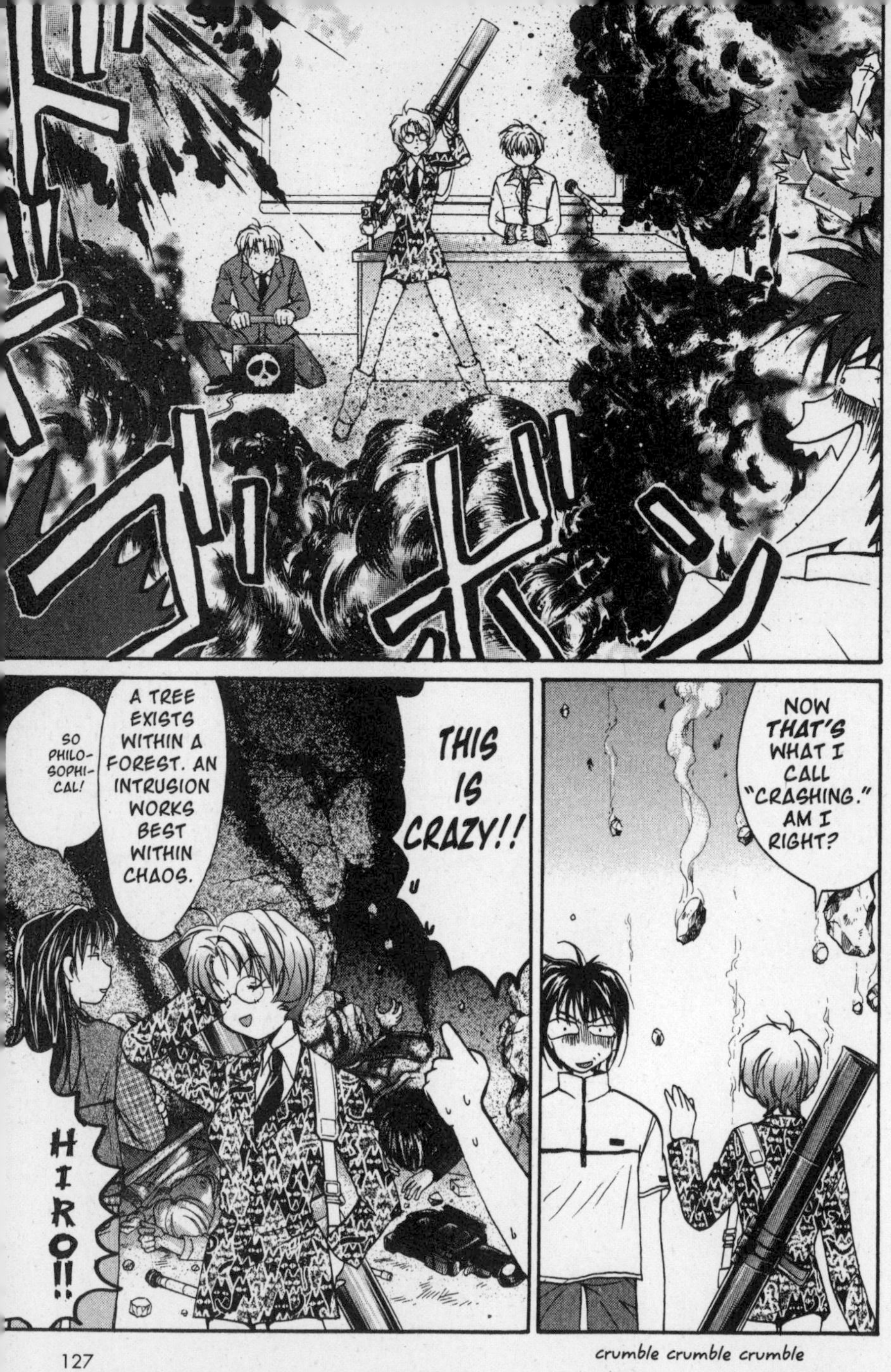
NOW THAT'S WHAT I CALL "CRASHING." AM I RIGHT?
THIS IS CRAZY!!
A TREE EXISTS WITHIN A FOREST. AN INTRUSION WORKS BEST WITHIN CHAOS.
SO PHILOSOPHICAL!
HIRO!!

crumble crumble crumble

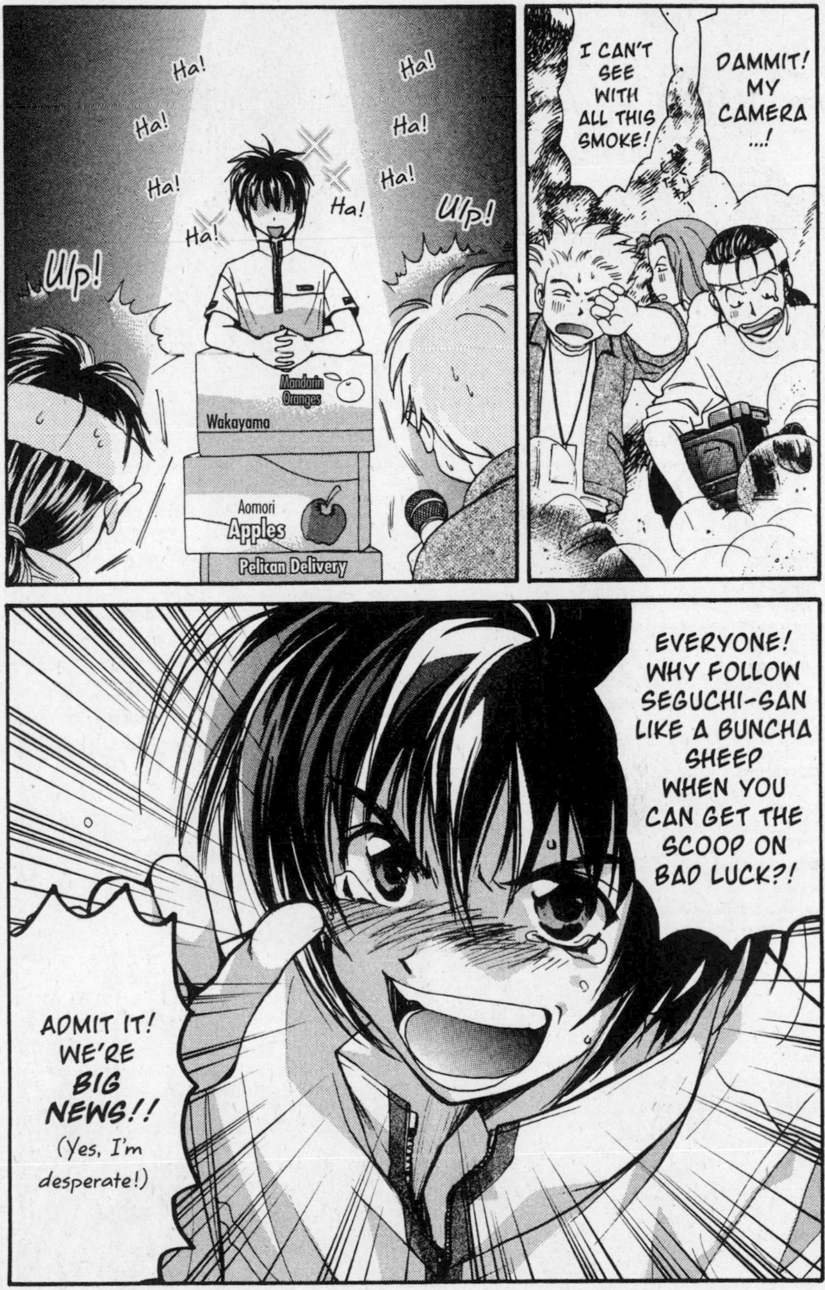
DAMMIT! MY CAMERA ...!
I CAN'T SEE WITH ALL THIS SMOKE!
Ha!
Ha!
Ulp!
Ha!
Ha!
Ha!
Ha!
Ha!
Ha!
Ulp!
Mandarin Oranges
Wakayama
Aomori Apples
Pelican Delivery
EVERYONE! WHY FOLLOW SEGUCHI-SAN LIKE A BUNCHA SHEEP WHEN YOU CAN GET THE SCOOP ON BAD LUCK?!
ADMIT IT! WE'RE BIG NEWS!!
(Yes, I'm desperate!)

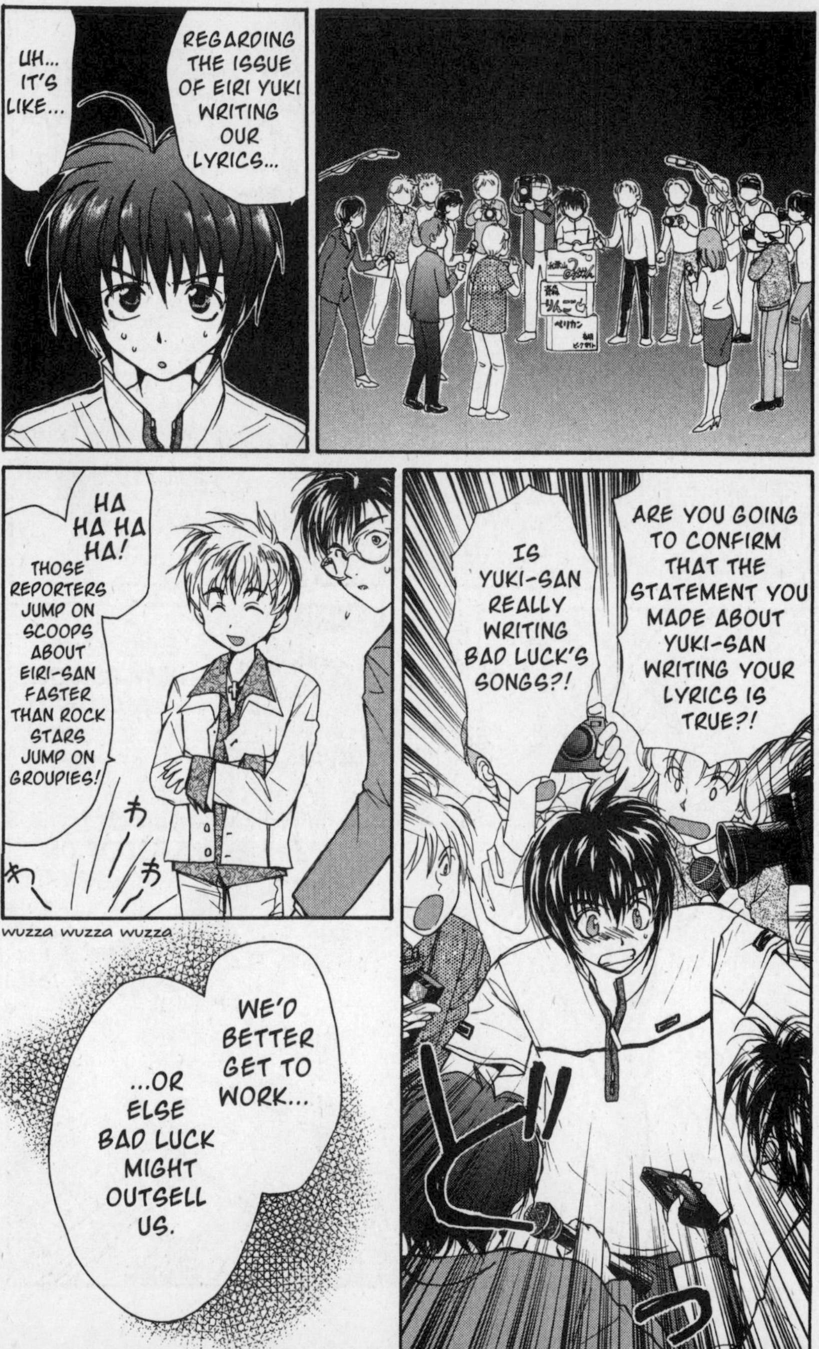
REGARDING THE ISSUE OF EIRI YUKI WRITING OUR LYRICS...
UH... IT'S LIKE...
ARE YOU GOING TO CONFIRM THAT THE STATEMENT YOU MADE ABOUT YUKI-SAN WRITING YOUR LYRICS IS TRUE?!
IS YUKI-SAN REALLY WRITING BAD LUCK'S SONGS?!
HA HA HA HA!
THOSE REPORTERS JUMP ON SCOOPS ABOUT EIRI-SAN FASTER THAN ROCK STARS JUMP ON GROUPIES!
wuzza wuzza wuzza
WE'D BETTER GET TO WORK...
...OR ELSE BAD LUCK MIGHT OUTSELL US.

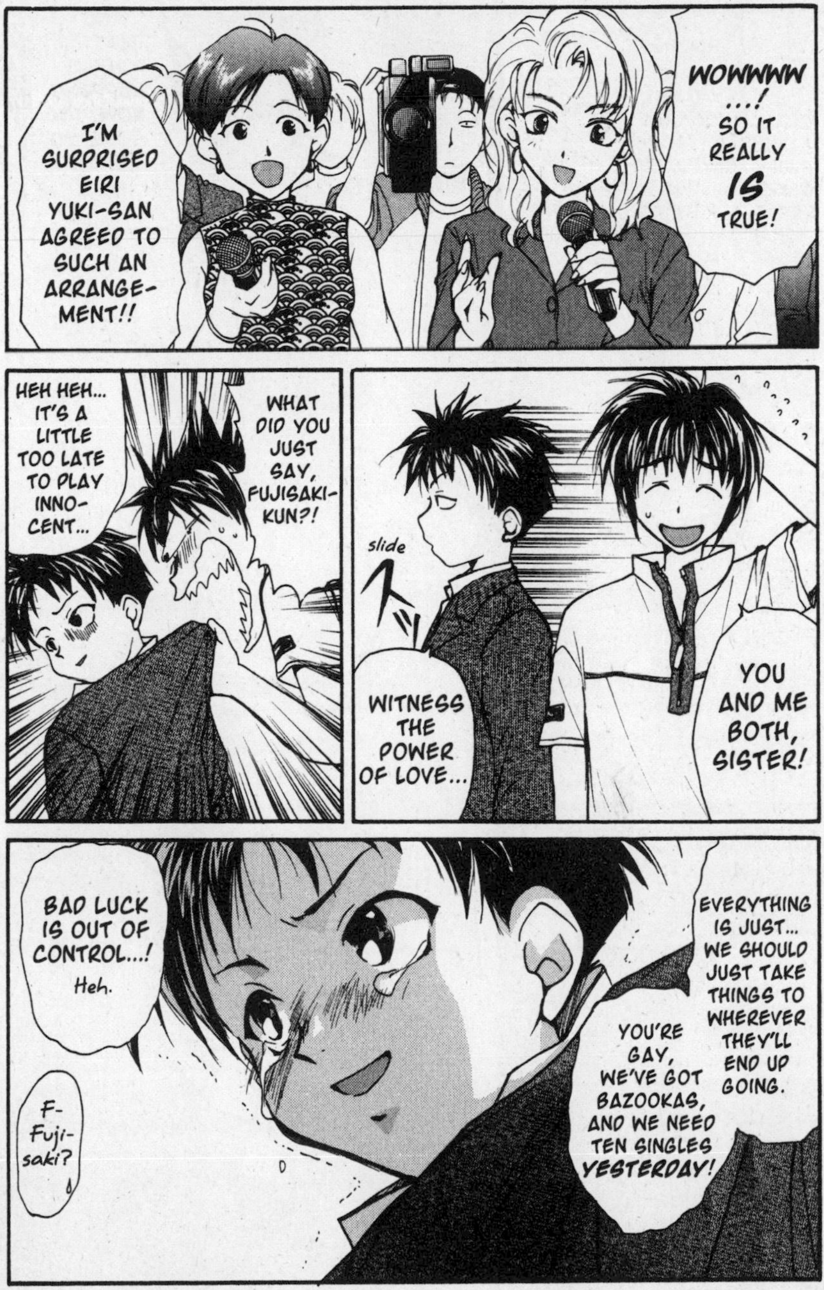
WOWWWW...! SO IT REALLY IS TRUE!
I'M SURPRISED EIRI YUKI-SAN AGREED TO SUCH AN ARRANGEMENT!!
YOU AND ME BOTH, SISTER!
slide
WITNESS THE POWER OF LOVE...
WHAT DID YOU JUST SAY, FUJISAKI-KUN?!
HEH HEH... IT'S A LITTLE TOO LATE TO PLAY INNOCENT...
EVERYTHING IS JUST... WE SHOULD JUST TAKE THINGS TO WHEREVER THEY'LL END UP GOING.
YOU'RE GAY, WE'VE GOT BAZOOKAS, AND WE NEED TEN SINGLES YESTERDAY!
BAD LUCK IS OUT OF CONTROL...!
Heh.
F-Fuji-saki?

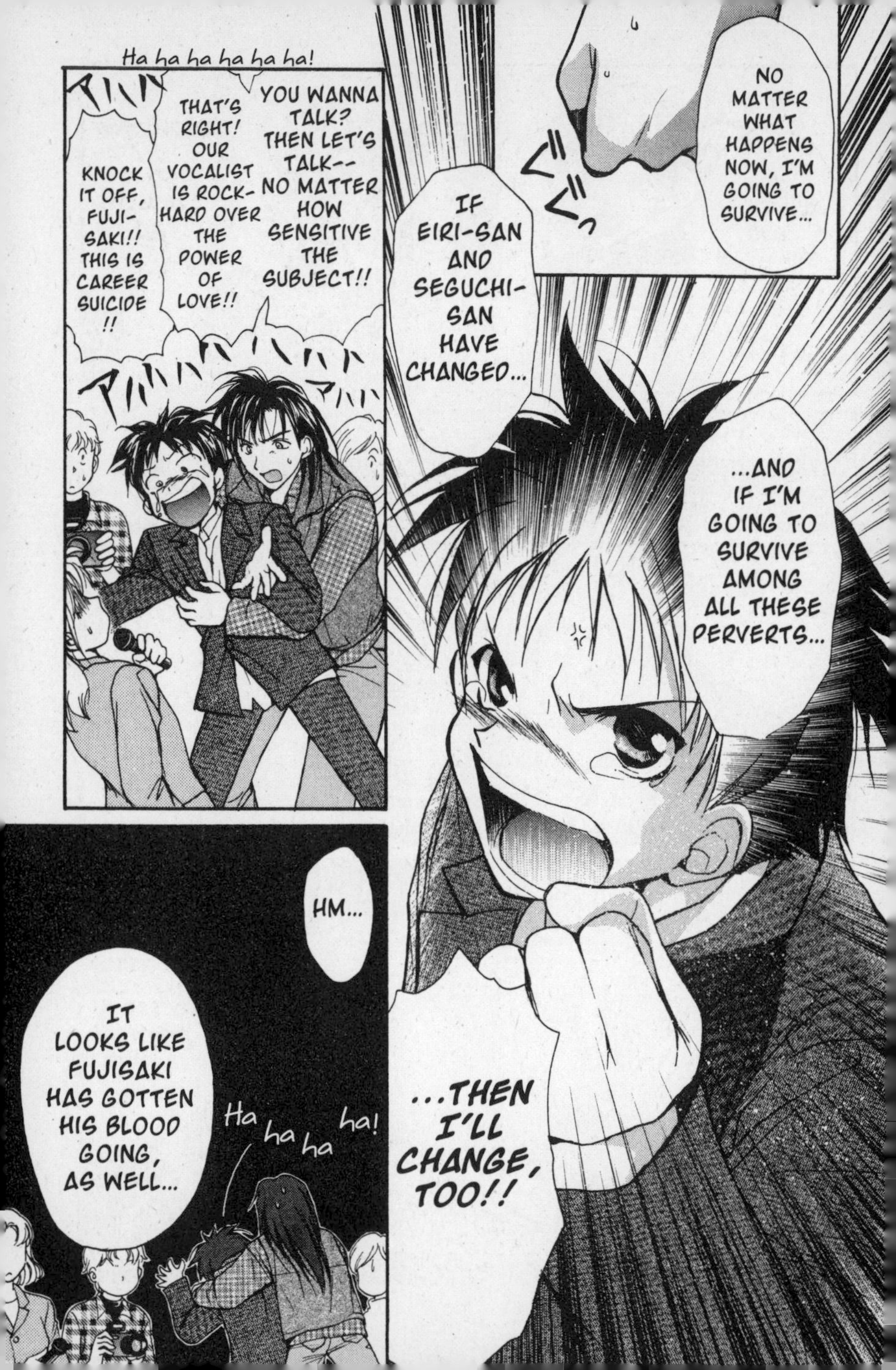

NO MATTER WHAT HAPPENS NOW, I'M GOING TO SURVIVE...
IF EIRI-SAN AND SEGUCHI-SAN HAVE CHANGED...
...AND IF I'M GOING TO SURVIVE AMONG ALL THESE PERVERTS...
...THEN I'LL CHANGE, TOO!!
Ha ha ha ha ha ha ha!
YOU WANNA TALK? THEN LET'S TALK-- NO MATTER HOW SENSITIVE THE SUBJECT!!
THAT'S RIGHT! OUR VOCALIST IS ROCK-HARD OVER THE POWER OF LOVE!!
KNOCK IT OFF, FUJI-SAKI!! THIS IS CAREER SUICIDE!!
HM...
IT LOOKS LIKE FUJISAKI HAS GOTTEN HIS BLOOD GOING, AS WELL...
Ha ha ha ha!

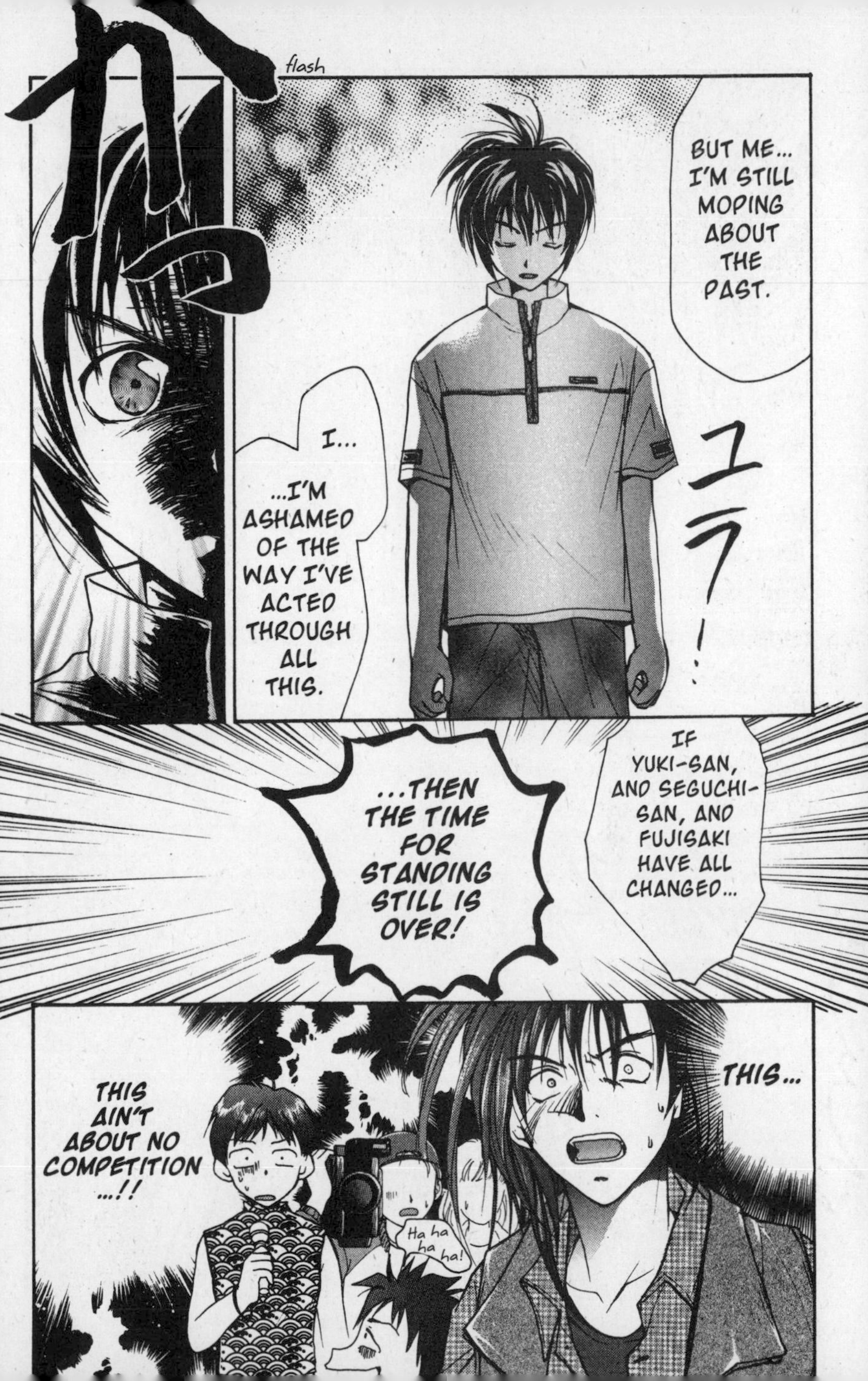
BUT ME... I'M STILL MOPING ABOUT THE PAST.
I...
...I'M ASHAMED OF THE WAY I'VE ACTED THROUGH ALL THIS.
ユラ!
かっ
flash
IF YUKI-SAN, AND SEGUCHI-SAN, AND FUJISAKI HAVE ALL CHANGED...
...THEN THE TIME FOR STANDING STILL IS OVER!
THIS...
Ha ha ha ha!
THIS AIN'T ABOUT NO COMPETITION ...!!

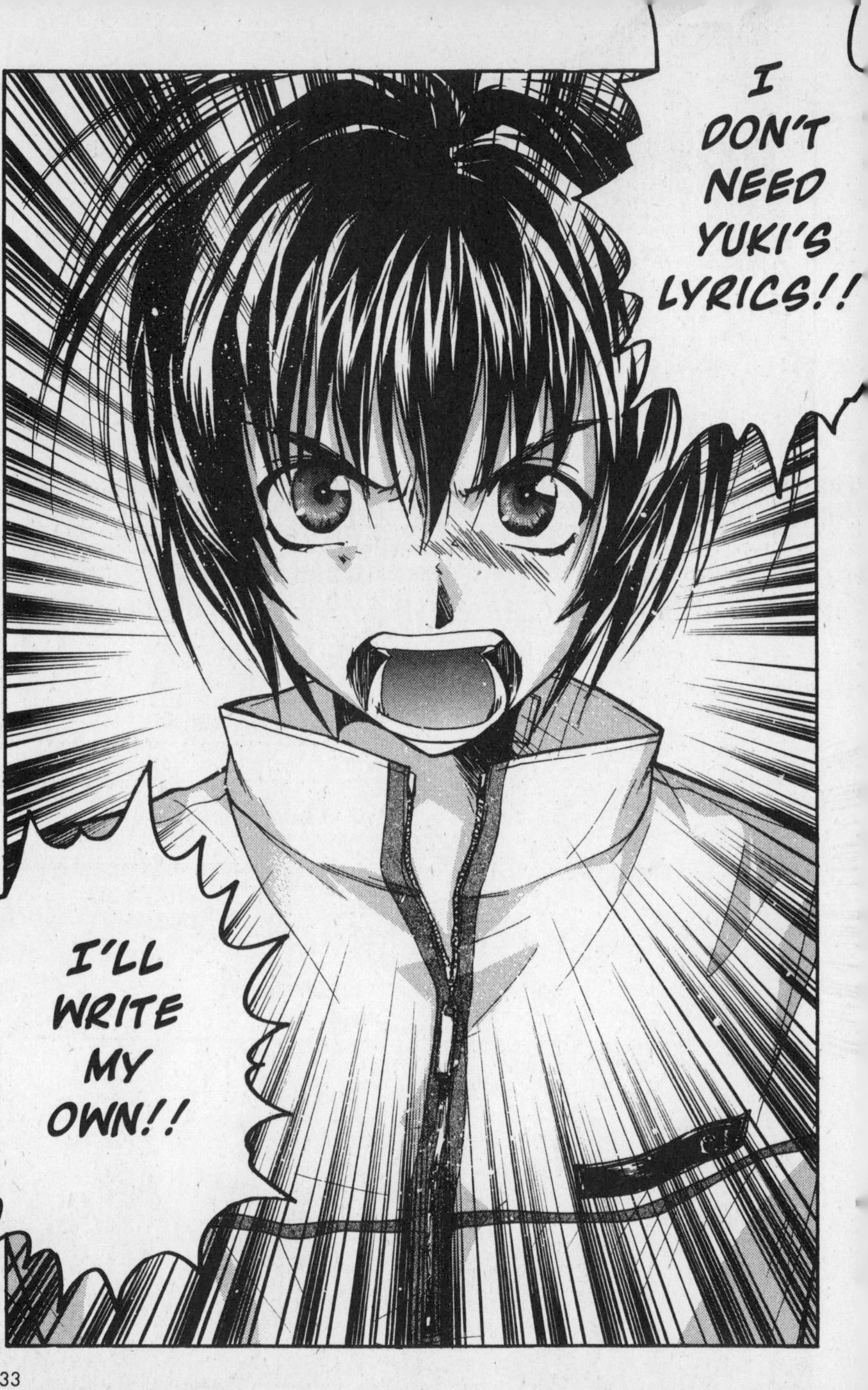
I DON'T NEED YUKI'S LYRICS!!
I'LL WRITE MY OWN!!

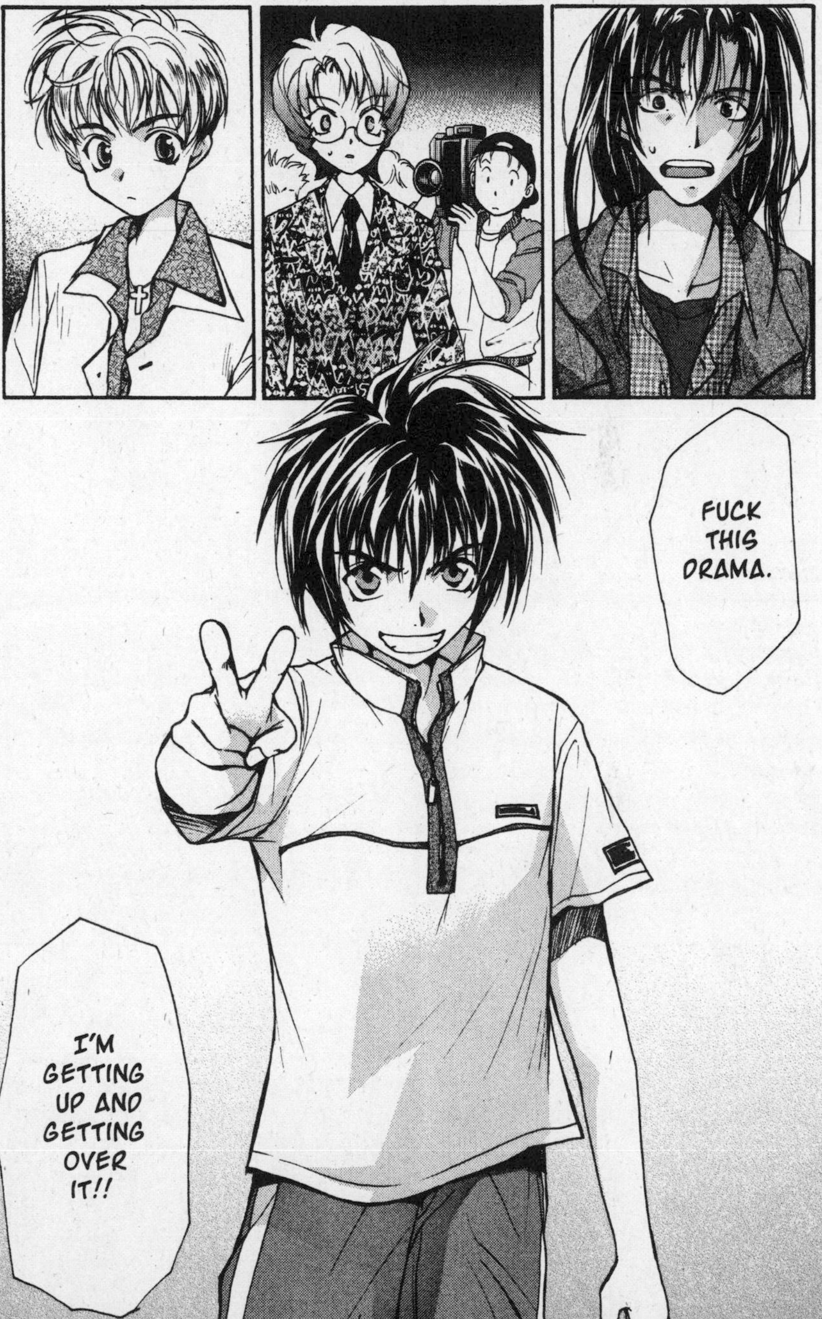
FUCK THIS DRAMA.
I'M GETTING UP AND GETTING OVER IT!!

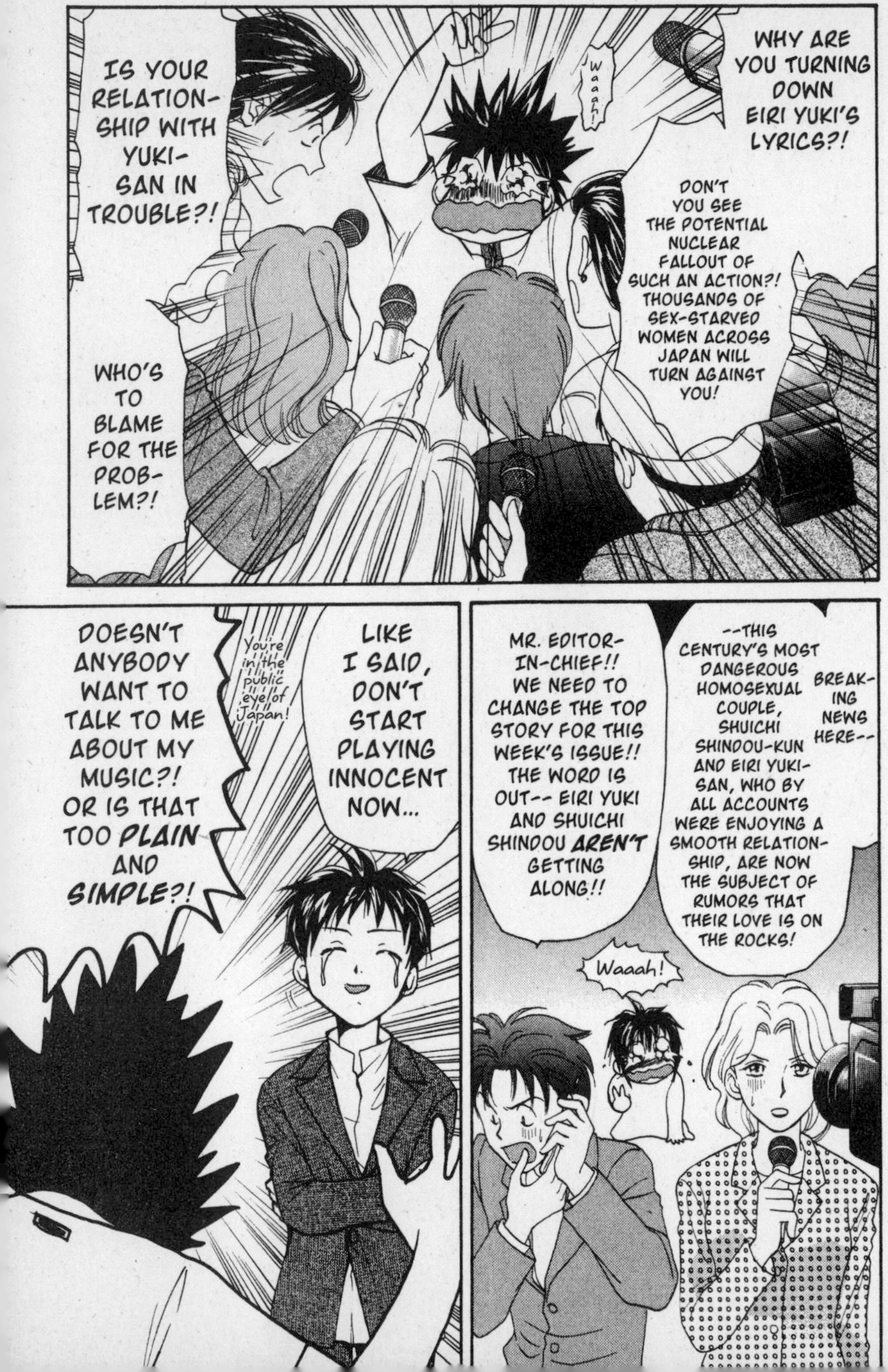
WHY ARE YOU TURNING DOWN EIRI YUKI'S LYRICS?!
Waaah!
IS YOUR RELATIONSHIP WITH YUKI-SAN IN TROUBLE?!
DON'T YOU SEE THE POTENTIAL NUCLEAR FALLOUT OF SUCH AN ACTION?! THOUSANDS OF SEX-STARVED WOMEN ACROSS JAPAN WILL TURN AGAINST YOU!
WHO'S TO BLAME FOR THE PROBLEM?!
BREAKING NEWS HERE--
--THIS CENTURY'S MOST DANGEROUS HOMOSEXUAL COUPLE, SHUICHI SHINDOU-KUN AND EIRI YUKI-SAN, WHO BY ALL ACCOUNTS WERE ENJOYING A SMOOTH RELATIONSHIP, ARE NOW THE SUBJECT OF RUMORS THAT THEIR LOVE IS ON THE ROCKS!
MR. EDITOR-IN-CHIEF!! WE NEED TO CHANGE THE TOP STORY FOR THIS WEEK'S ISSUE!! THE WORD IS OUT-- EIRI YUKI AND SHUICHI SHINDOU *AREN'T* GETTING ALONG!!
Waaah!
LIKE I SAID, DON'T START PLAYING INNOCENT NOW...
You're in the public eye of Japan!
DOESN'T ANYBODY WANT TO TALK TO ME ABOUT MY MUSIC?! OR IS THAT TOO *PLAIN* AND *SIMPLE*?!

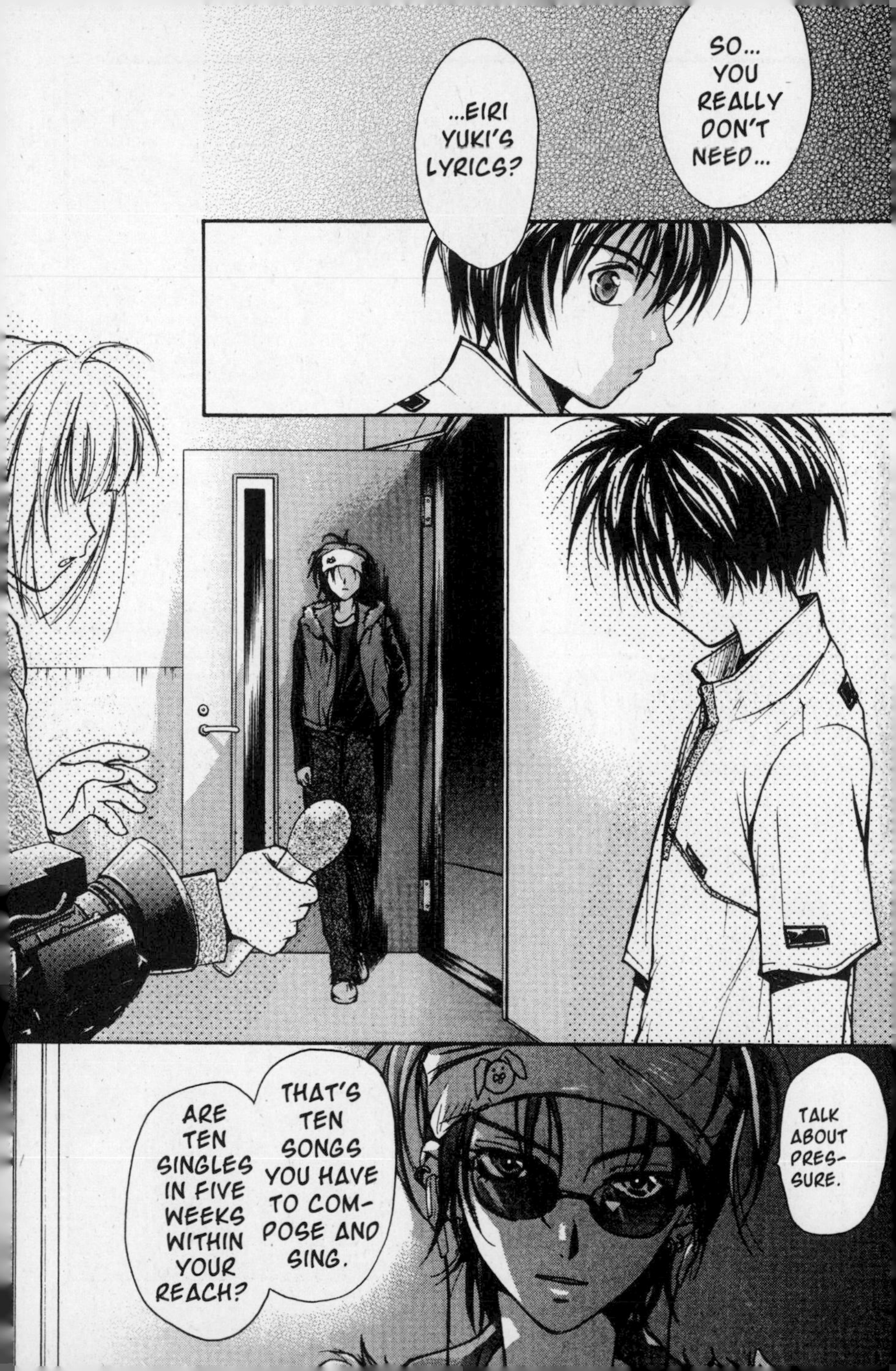
SO... YOU REALLY DON'T NEED...
...EIRI YUKI'S LYRICS?
TALK ABOUT PRES-SURE.
THAT'S TEN SONGS YOU HAVE TO COM-POSE AND SING.
ARE TEN SINGLES IN FIVE WEEKS WITHIN YOUR REACH?

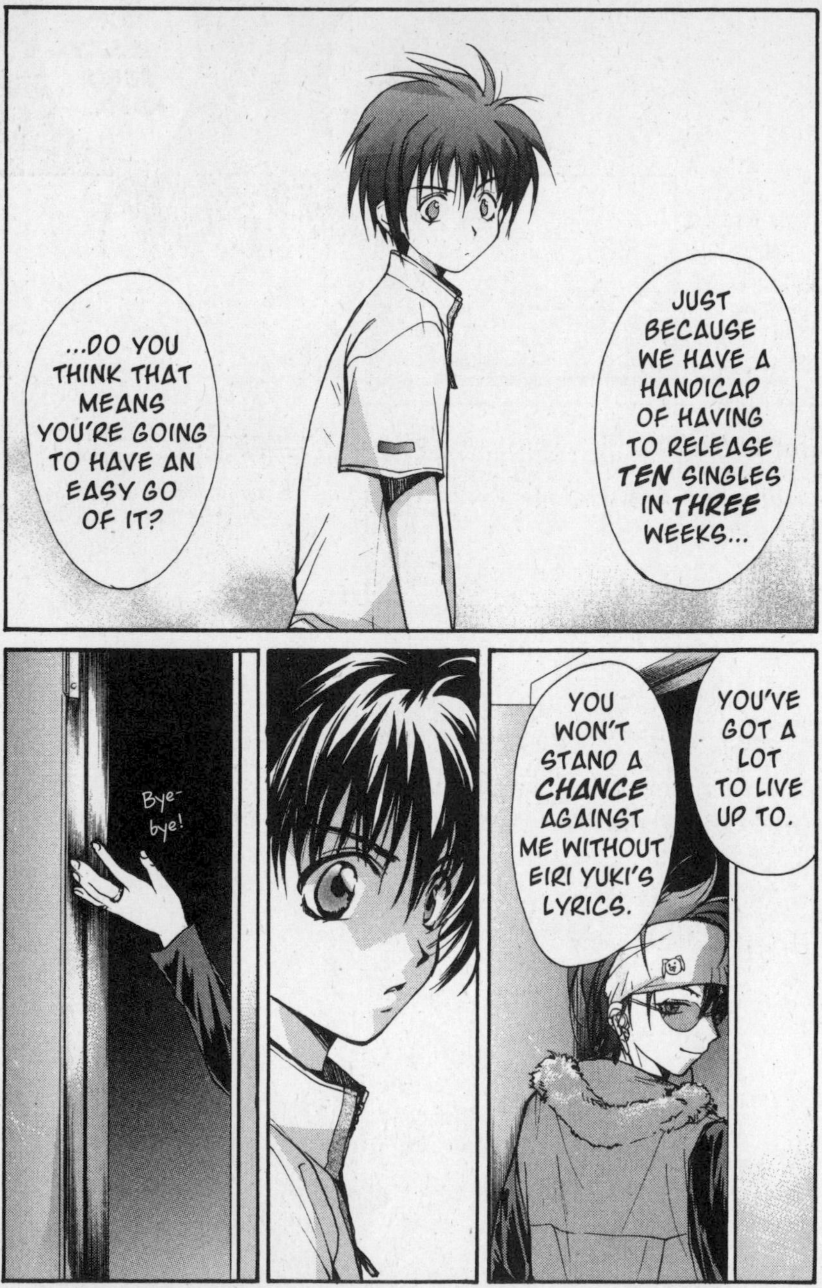
JUST BECAUSE WE HAVE A HANDICAP OF HAVING TO RELEASE TEN SINGLES IN THREE WEEKS...
...DO YOU THINK THAT MEANS YOU'RE GOING TO HAVE AN EASY GO OF IT?
YOU'VE GOT A LOT TO LIVE UP TO.
YOU WON'T STAND A CHANCE AGAINST ME WITHOUT EIRI YUKI'S LYRICS.
Bye-bye!

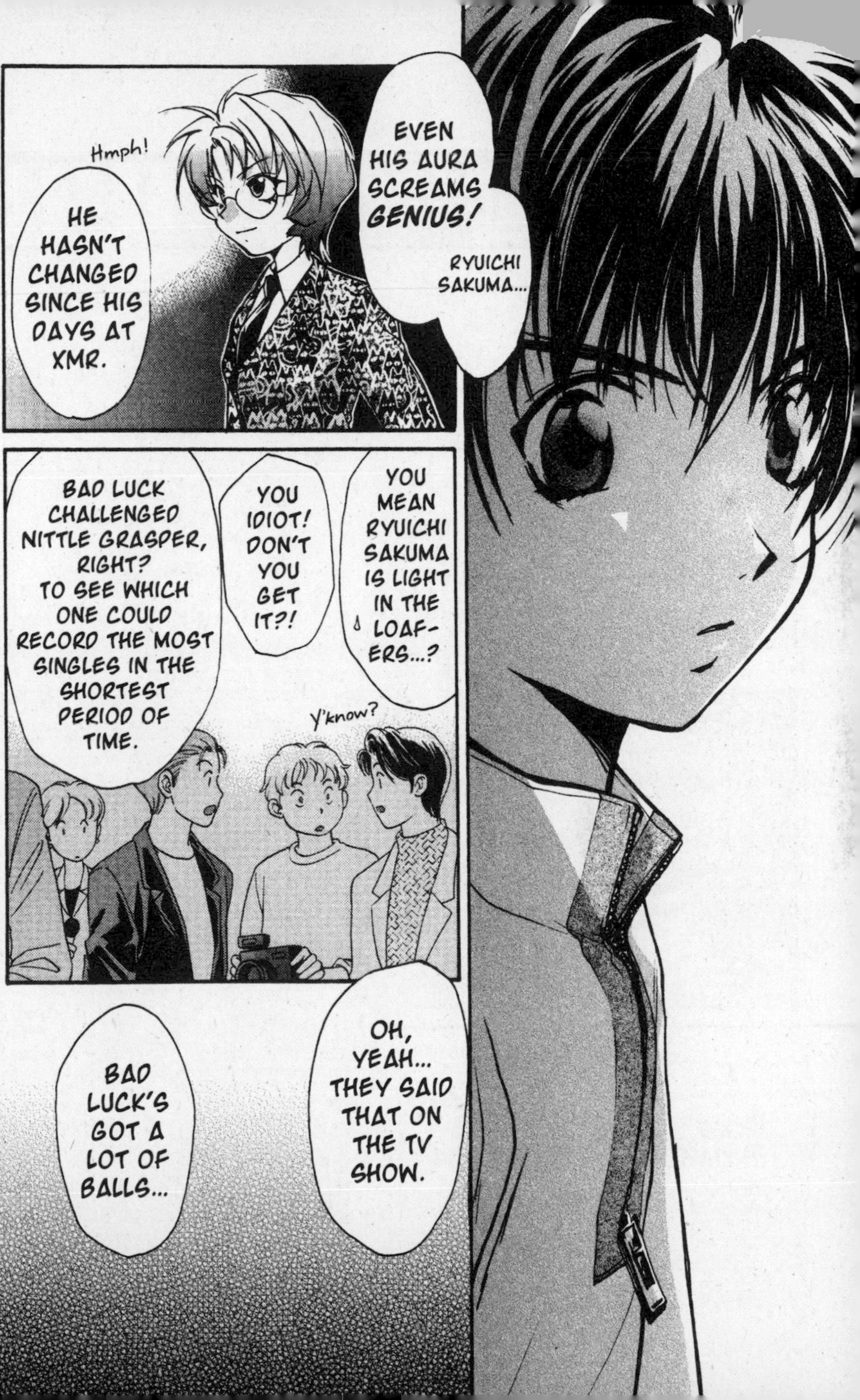
EVEN HIS AURA SCREAMS GENIUS!
RYUICHI SAKUMA...
Hmph!
HE HASN'T CHANGED SINCE HIS DAYS AT XMR.
YOU MEAN RYUICHI SAKUMA IS LIGHT IN THE LOAF-ERS...?
YOU IDIOT! DON'T YOU GET IT?!
Y'know?
BAD LUCK CHALLENGED NITTLE GRASPER, RIGHT? TO SEE WHICH ONE COULD RECORD THE MOST SINGLES IN THE SHORTEST PERIOD OF TIME.
OH, YEAH... THEY SAID THAT ON THE TV SHOW.
BAD LUCK'S GOT A LOT OF BALLS...

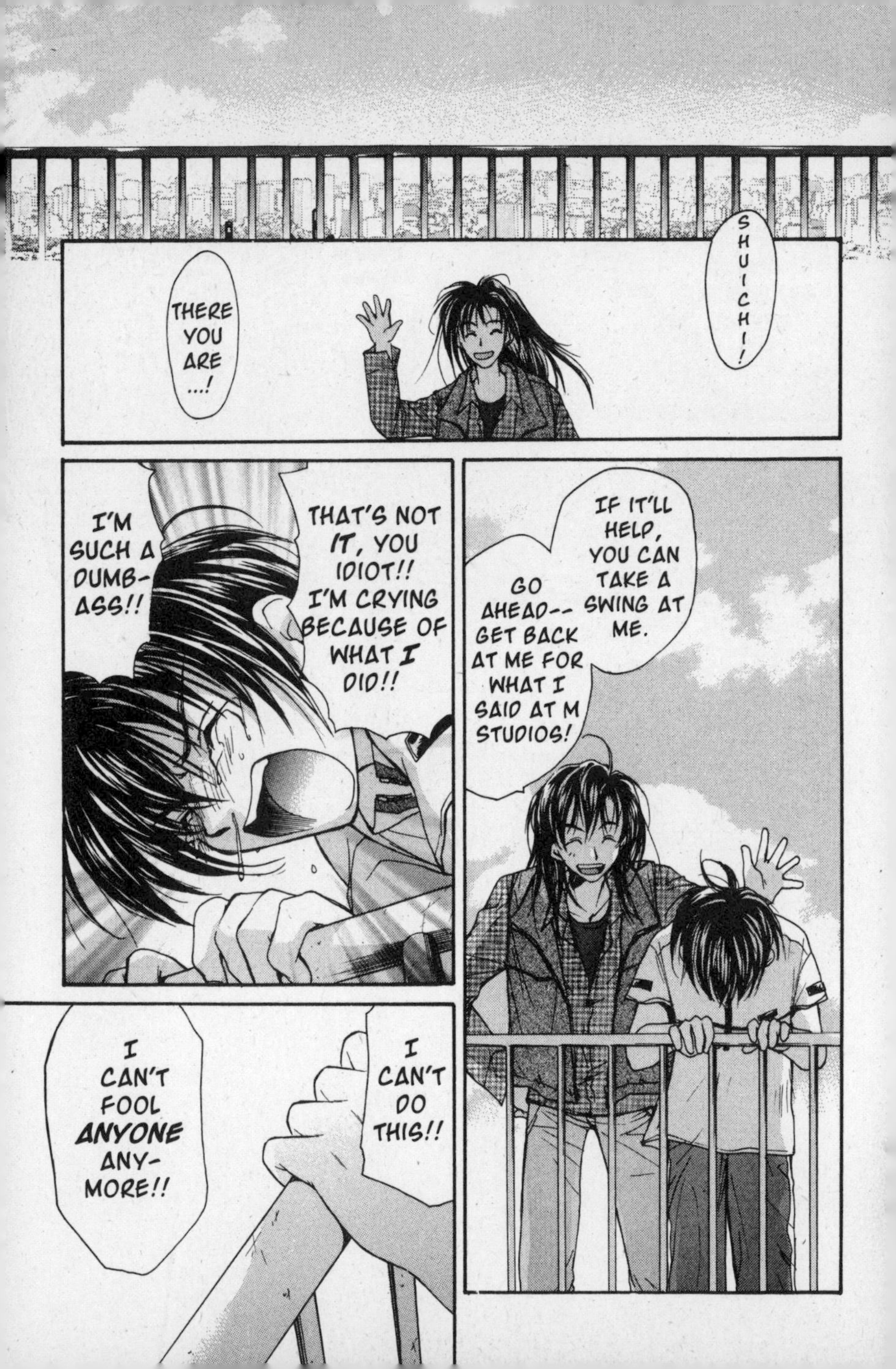
SHUICHI!
THERE YOU ARE...!
IF IT'LL HELP, YOU CAN TAKE A SWING AT ME.
GO AHEAD-- GET BACK AT ME FOR WHAT I SAID AT M STUDIOS!
THAT'S NOT IT, YOU IDIOT!! I'M CRYING BECAUSE OF WHAT I DID!!
I'M SUCH A DUMB-ASS!!
I CAN'T DO THIS!!
I CAN'T FOOL ANYONE ANYMORE!!

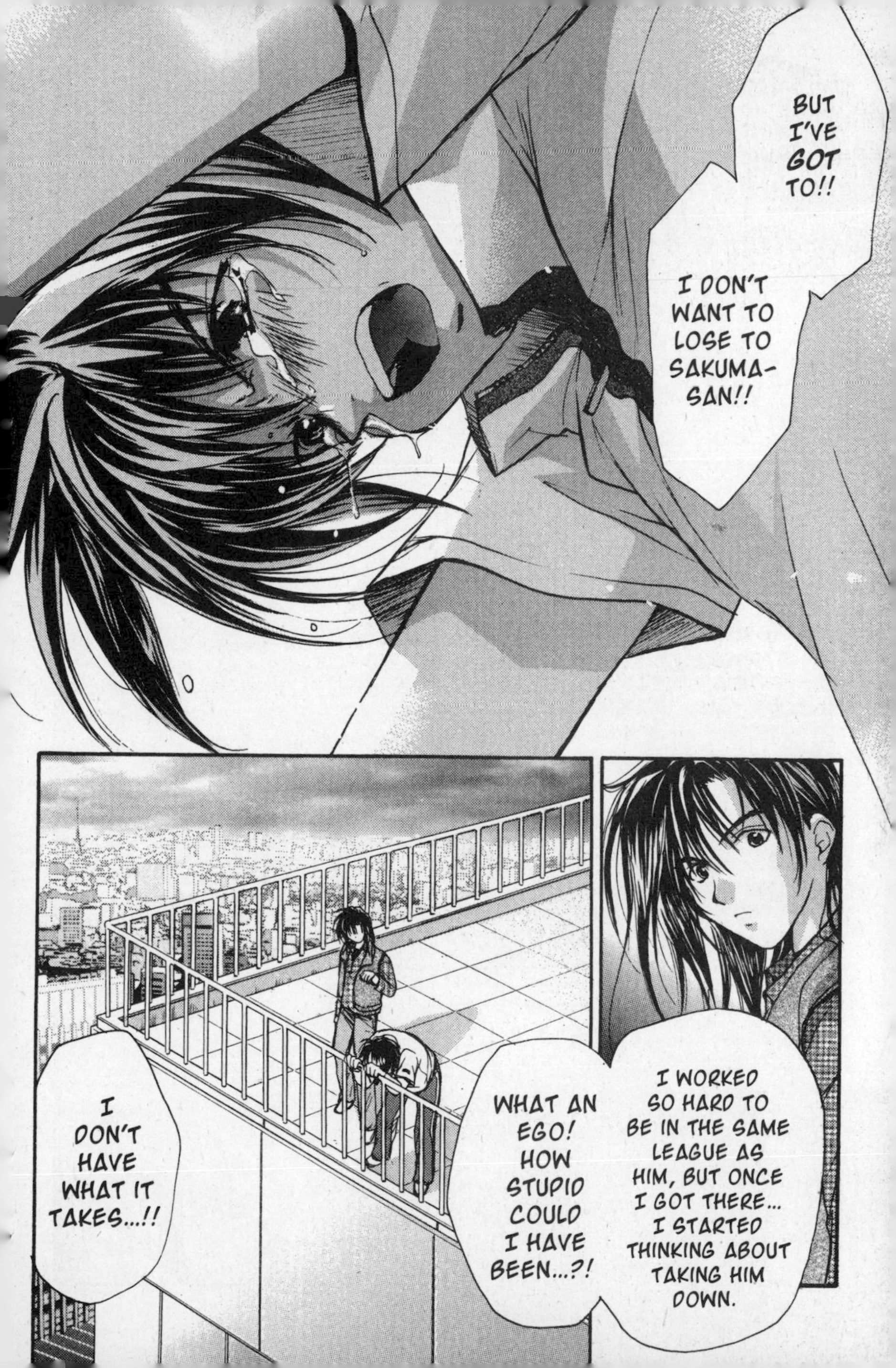
BUT I'VE GOT TO!!
I DON'T WANT TO LOSE TO SAKUMA-SAN!!
I WORKED SO HARD TO BE IN THE SAME LEAGUE AS HIM, BUT ONCE I GOT THERE... I STARTED THINKING ABOUT TAKING HIM DOWN.
WHAT AN EGO! HOW STUPID COULD I HAVE BEEN...?!
I DON'T HAVE WHAT IT TAKES...!!

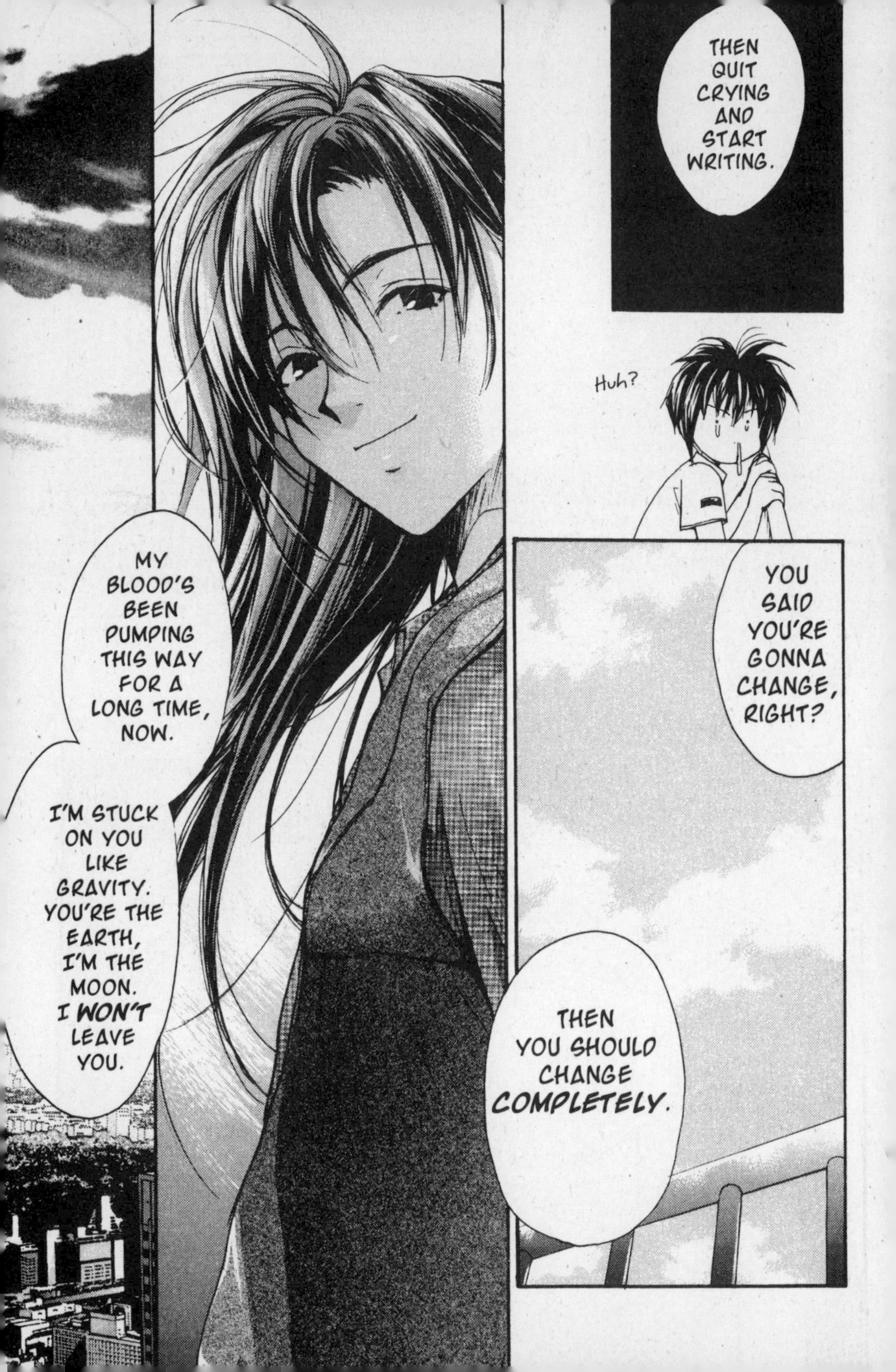

THEN QUIT CRYING AND START WRITING.
Huh?
YOU SAID YOU'RE GONNA CHANGE, RIGHT?
THEN YOU SHOULD CHANGE COMPLETELY.
MY BLOOD'S BEEN PUMPING THIS WAY FOR A LONG TIME, NOW.
I'M STUCK ON YOU LIKE GRAVITY. YOU'RE THE EARTH, I'M THE MOON. I WON'T LEAVE YOU.

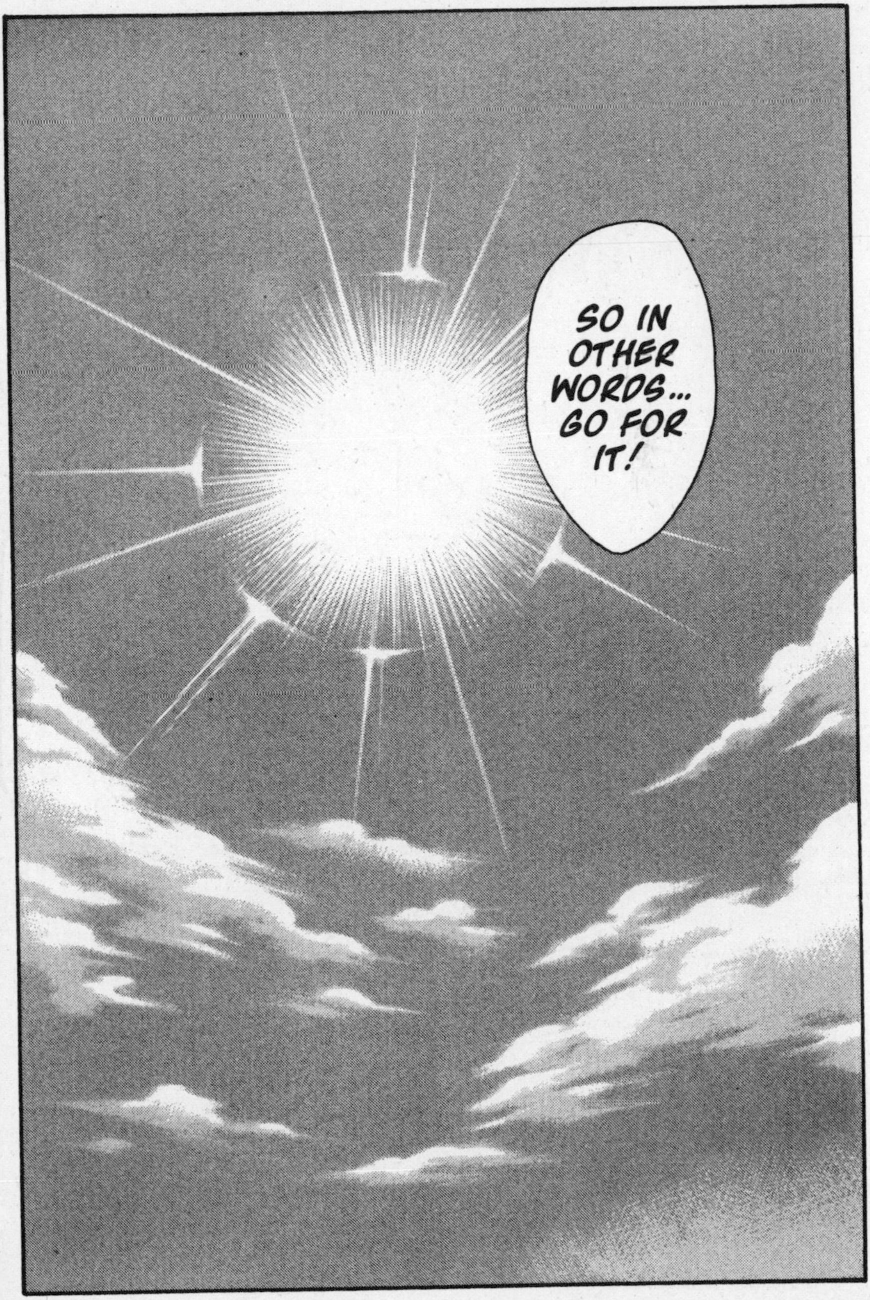
SO IN OTHER WORDS... GO FOR IT!

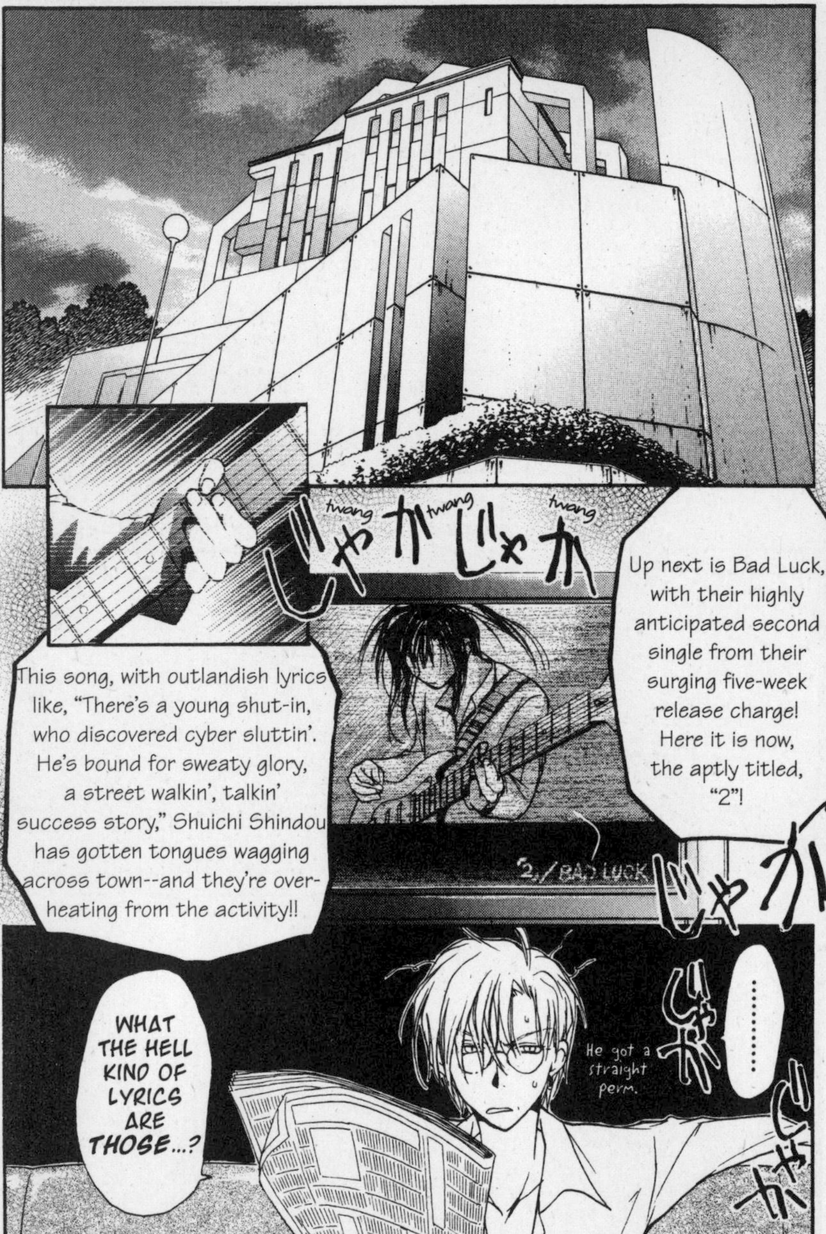

twang twang twang
じゃかじゃか
Up next is Bad Luck, with their highly anticipated second single from their surging five-week release charge! Here it is now, the aptly titled, "2"!
2 / BAD LUCK
This song, with outlandish lyrics like, "There's a young shut-in, who discovered cyber sluttin'. He's bound for sweaty glory, a street walkin', talkin' success story," Shuichi Shindou has gotten tongues wagging across town--and they're over-heating from the activity!!
じゃか
......
He got a straight perm.
WHAT THE HELL KIND OF LYRICS ARE *THOSE*...?

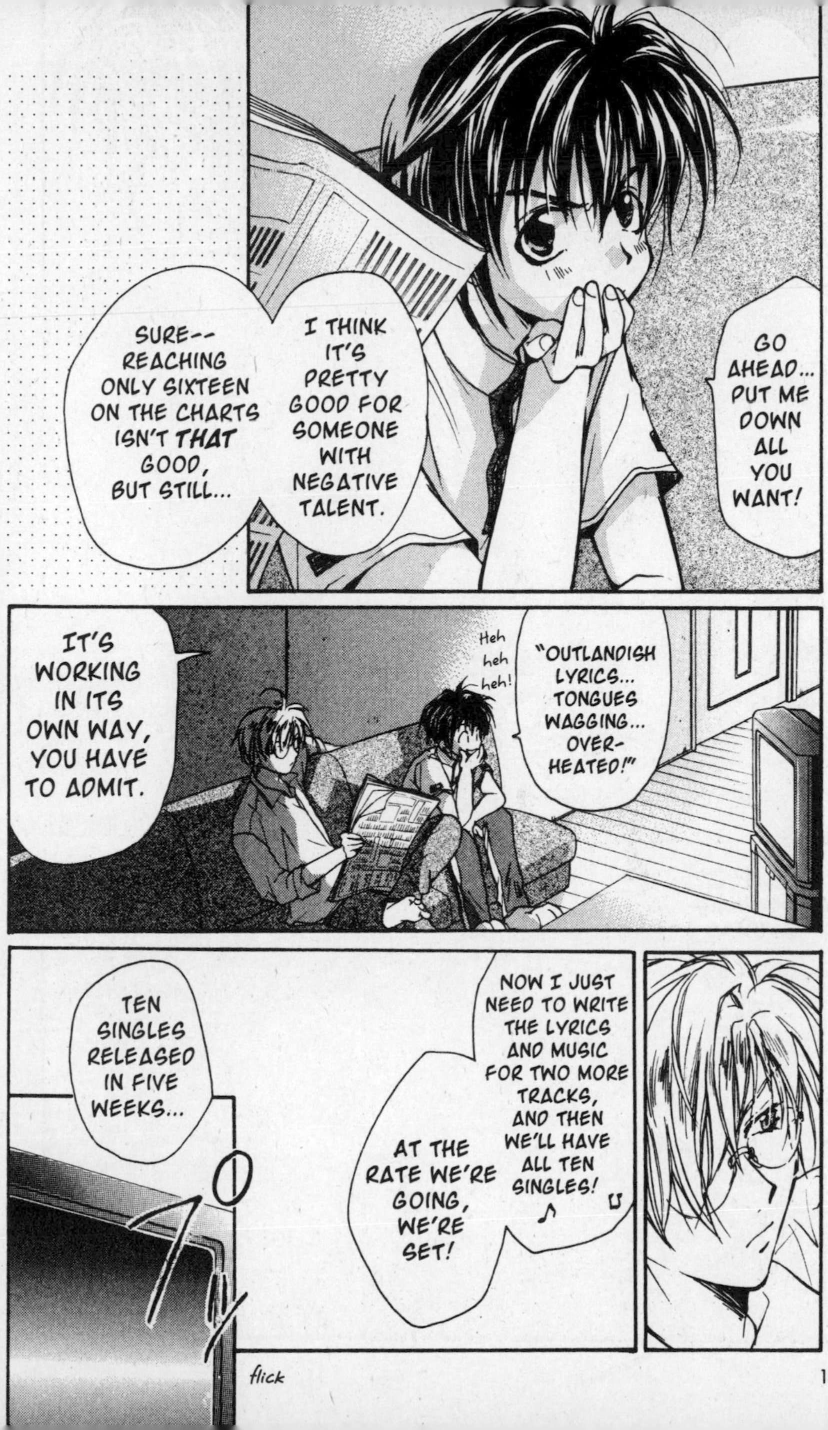
GO AHEAD... PUT ME DOWN ALL YOU WANT!
I THINK IT'S PRETTY GOOD FOR SOMEONE WITH NEGATIVE TALENT.
SURE--REACHING ONLY SIXTEEN ON THE CHARTS ISN'T THAT GOOD, BUT STILL...
Heh heh heh!
"OUTLANDISH LYRICS... TONGUES WAGGING... OVER-HEATED!"
IT'S WORKING IN ITS OWN WAY, YOU HAVE TO ADMIT.
NOW I JUST NEED TO WRITE THE LYRICS AND MUSIC FOR TWO MORE TRACKS, AND THEN WE'LL HAVE ALL TEN SINGLES!
AT THE RATE WE'RE GOING, WE'RE SET!
TEN SINGLES RELEASED IN FIVE WEEKS...
flick

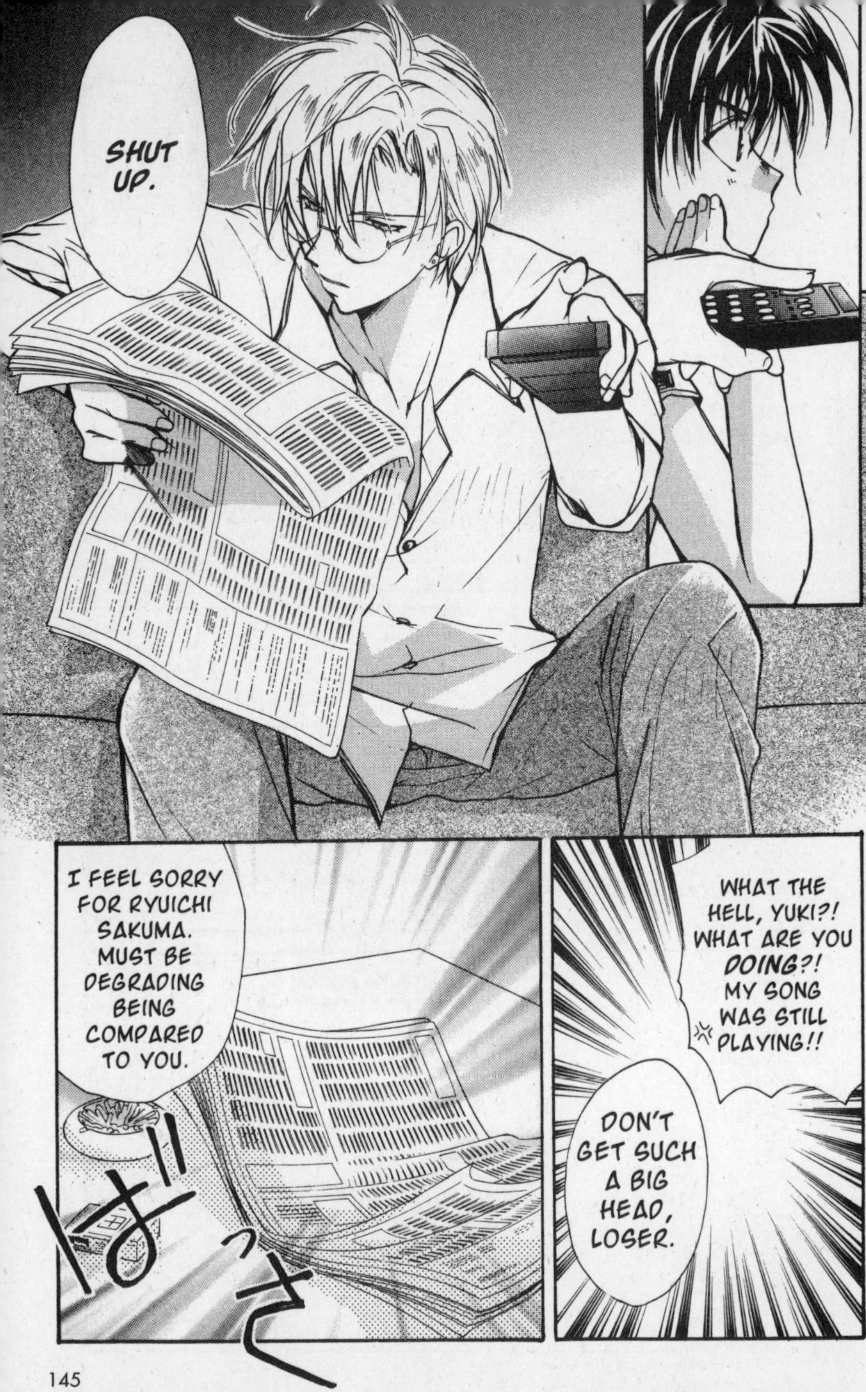
SHUT UP.
WHAT THE HELL, YUKI?! WHAT ARE YOU DOING?! MY SONG WAS STILL PLAYING!!
DON'T GET SUCH A BIG HEAD, LOSER.
I FEEL SORRY FOR RYUICHI SAKUMA. MUST BE DEGRADING BEING COMPARED TO YOU.
ばっさ

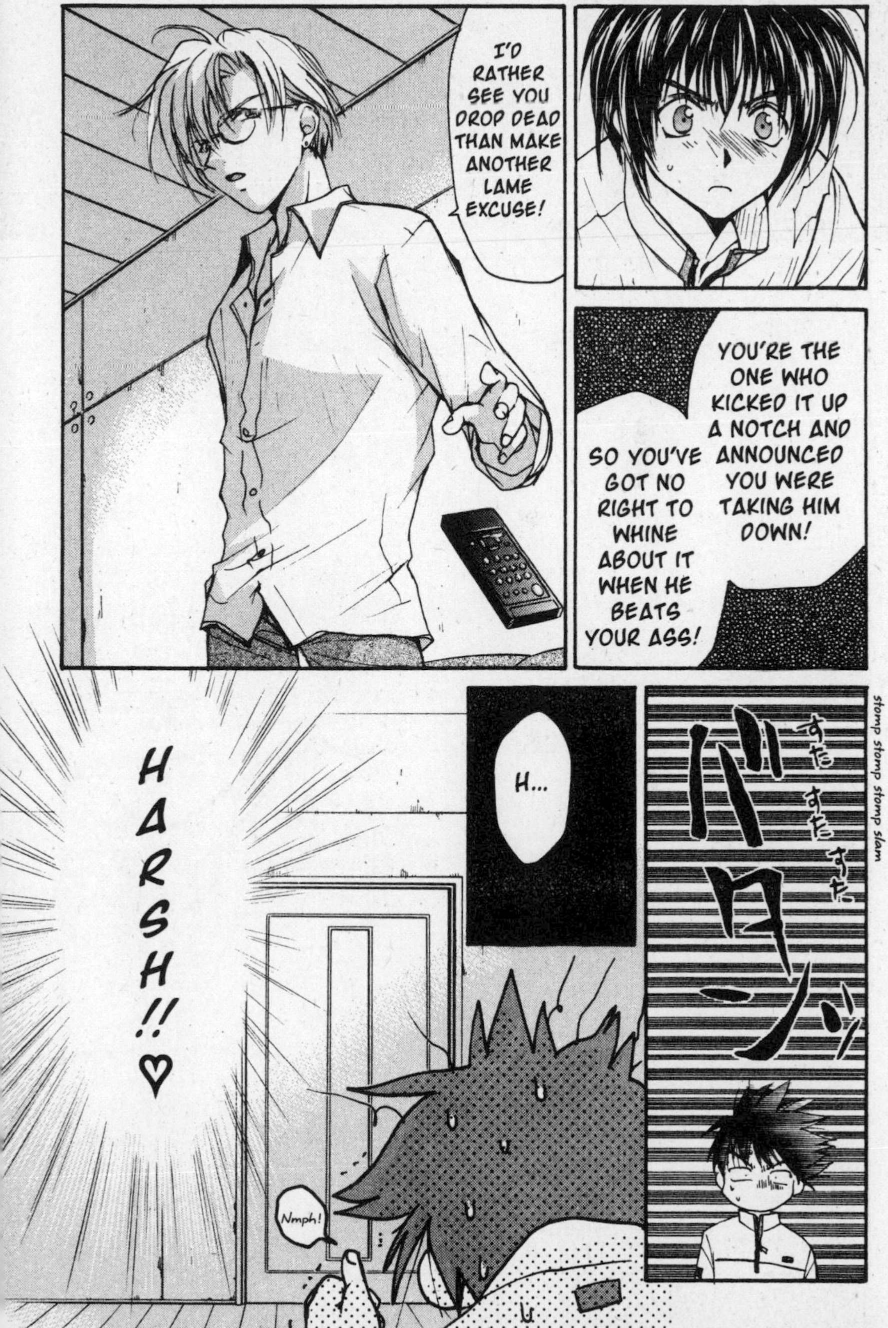

YOU'RE THE ONE WHO KICKED IT UP A NOTCH AND ANNOUNCED YOU WERE TAKING HIM DOWN!
SO YOU'VE GOT NO RIGHT TO WHINE ABOUT IT WHEN HE BEATS YOUR ASS!
I'D RATHER SEE YOU DROP DEAD THAN MAKE ANOTHER LAME EXCUSE!
すた すた すた
バタン
stomp stomp stomp slam
H...
HARSH!!♥
Nmph!

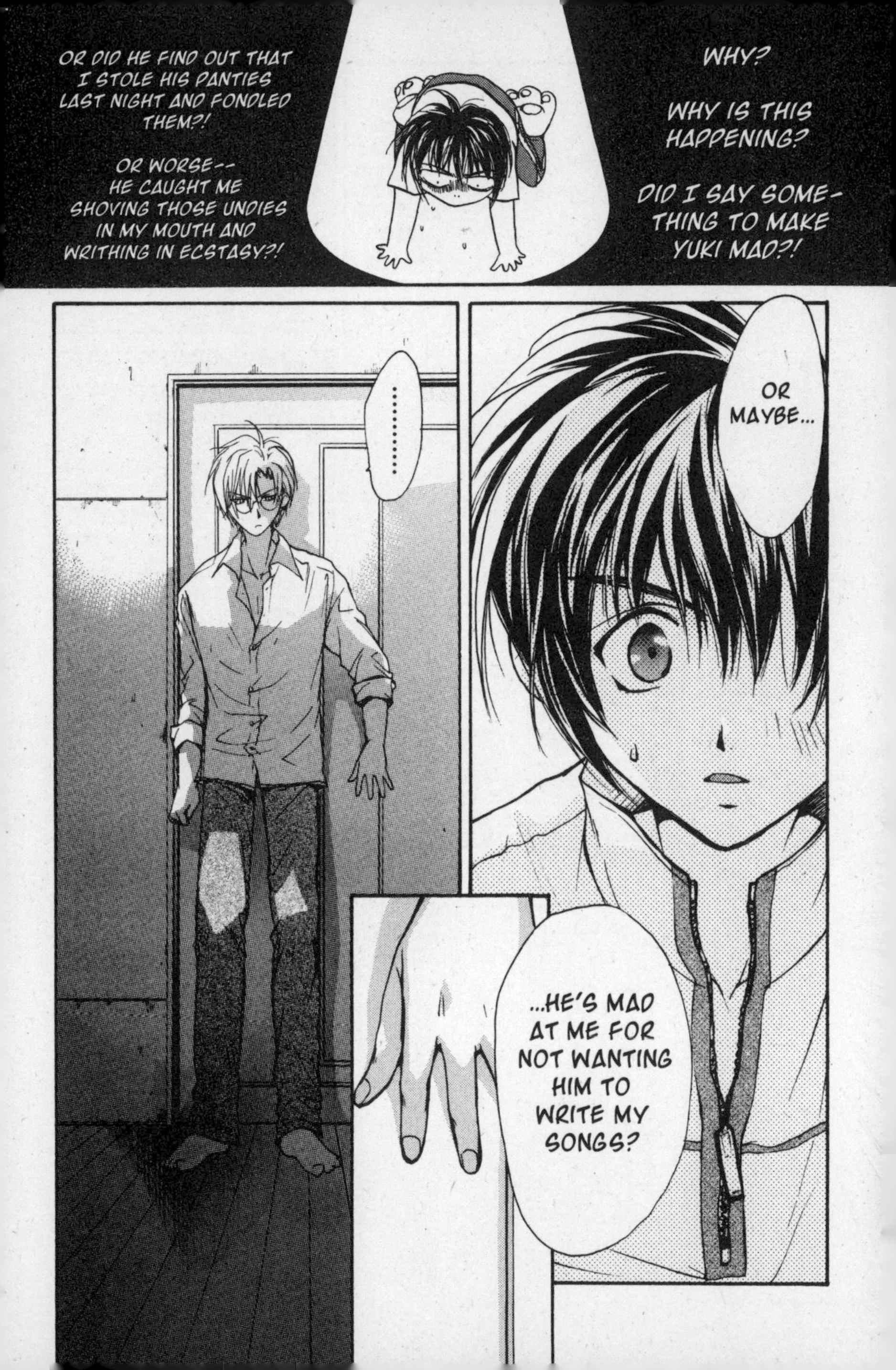
WHY?
WHY IS THIS HAPPENING?
DID I SAY SOME-THING TO MAKE YUKI MAD?!
OR DID HE FIND OUT THAT I STOLE HIS PANTIES LAST NIGHT AND FONDLED THEM?!
OR WORSE-- HE CAUGHT ME SHOVING THOSE UNDIES IN MY MOUTH AND WRITHING IN ECSTASY?!
OR MAYBE...
...HE'S MAD AT ME FOR NOT WANTING HIM TO WRITE MY SONGS?
......

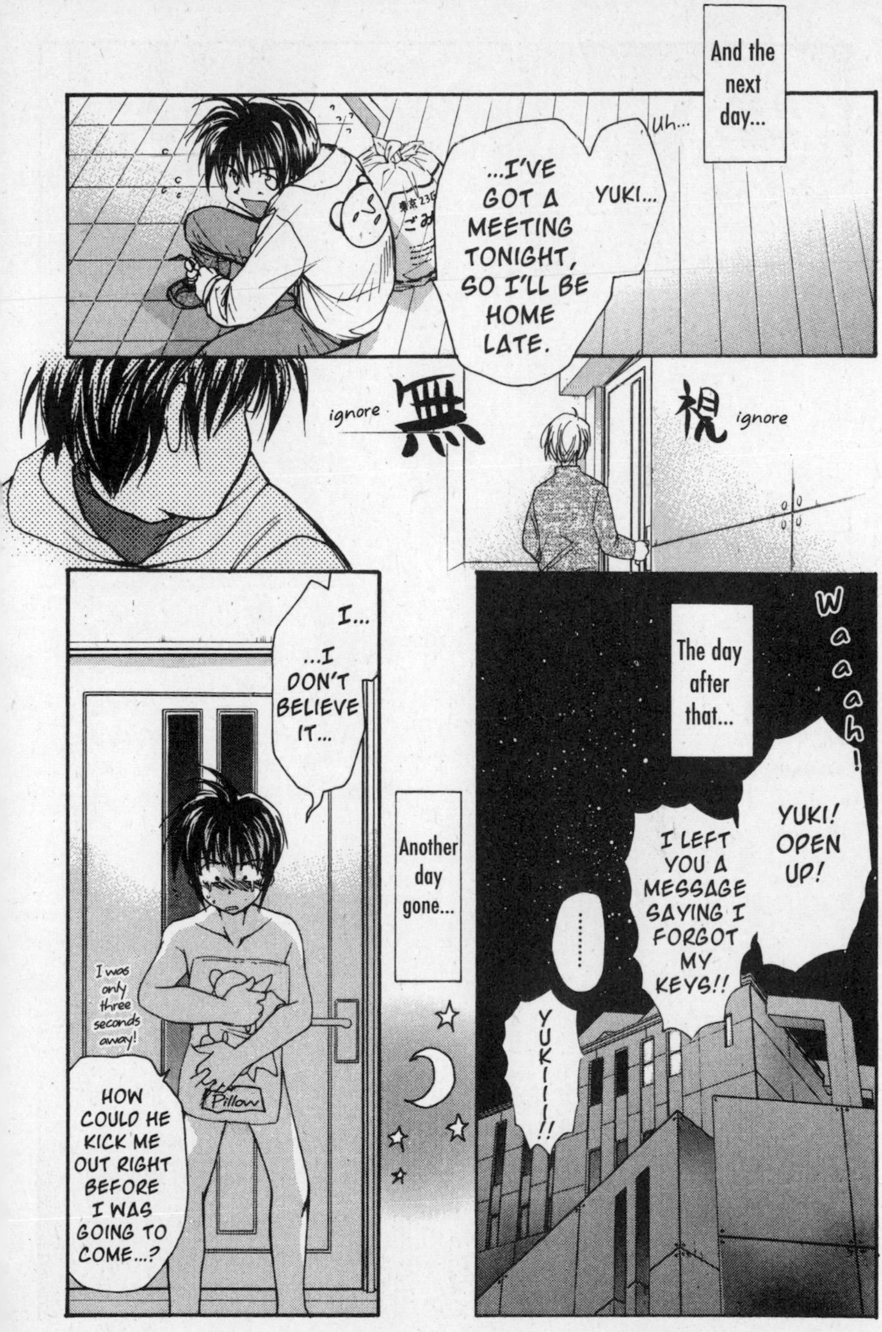
And the next day...
Uh...
YUKI...
...I'VE GOT A MEETING TONIGHT, SO I'LL BE HOME LATE.
ignore 無 視 ignore
The day after that...
Waaaah!
YUKI! OPEN UP!
I LEFT YOU A MESSAGE SAYING I FORGOT MY KEYS!!
........
YUKIIII!!
Another day gone...
I...
...I DON'T BELIEVE IT...
I was only three seconds away!
HOW COULD HE KICK ME OUT RIGHT BEFORE I WAS GOING TO COME...?
Pillow

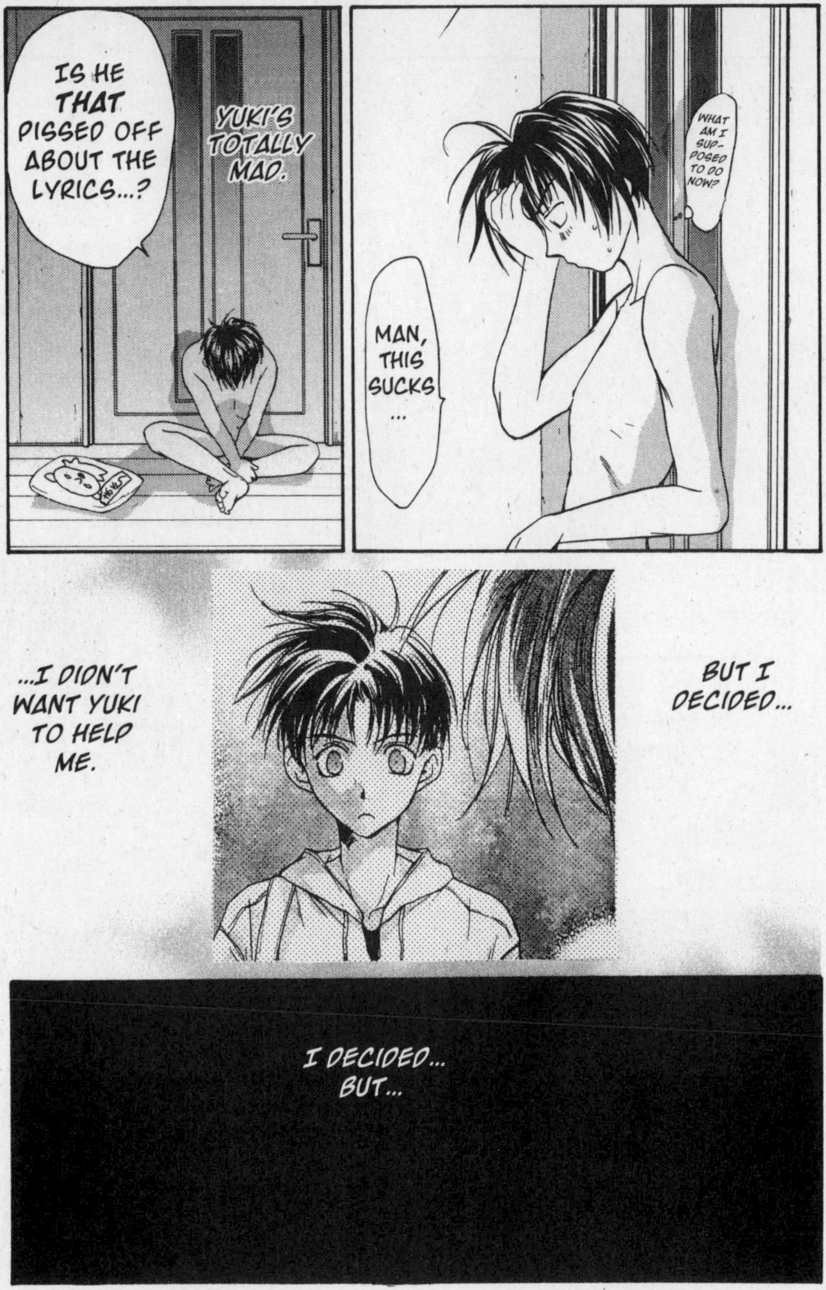
WHAT AM I SUPPOSED TO DO NOW?
MAN, THIS SUCKS ...
YUKI'S TOTALLY MAD.
IS HE **THAT** PISSED OFF ABOUT THE LYRICS...?
BUT I DECIDED...
...I DIDN'T WANT YUKI TO HELP ME.
I DECIDED... BUT...

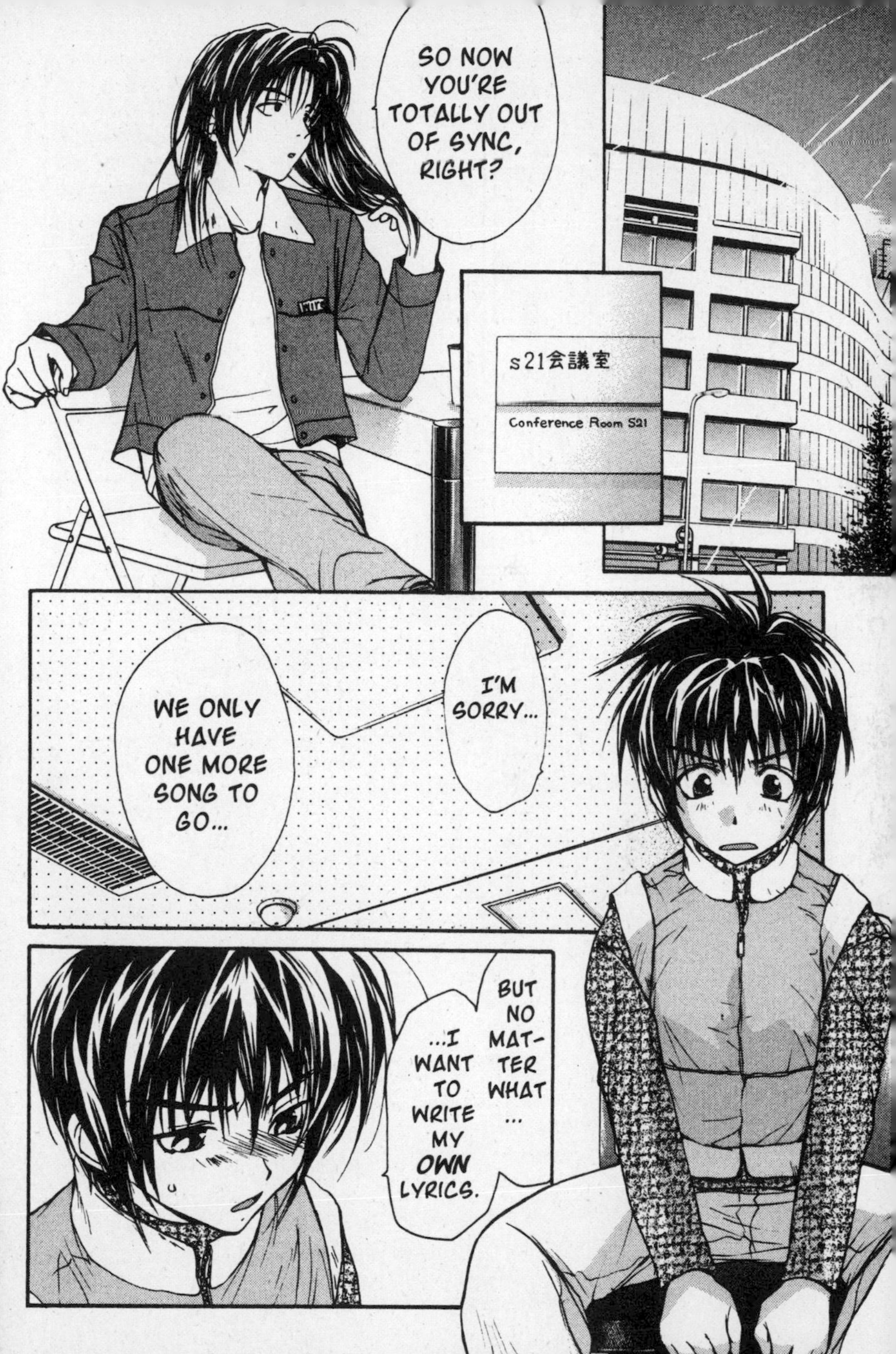
SO NOW YOU'RE TOTALLY OUT OF SYNC, RIGHT?
s21会議室
Conference Room S21
I'M SORRY...
WE ONLY HAVE ONE MORE SONG TO GO...
BUT NO MATTER WHAT ...
...I WANT TO WRITE MY OWN LYRICS.

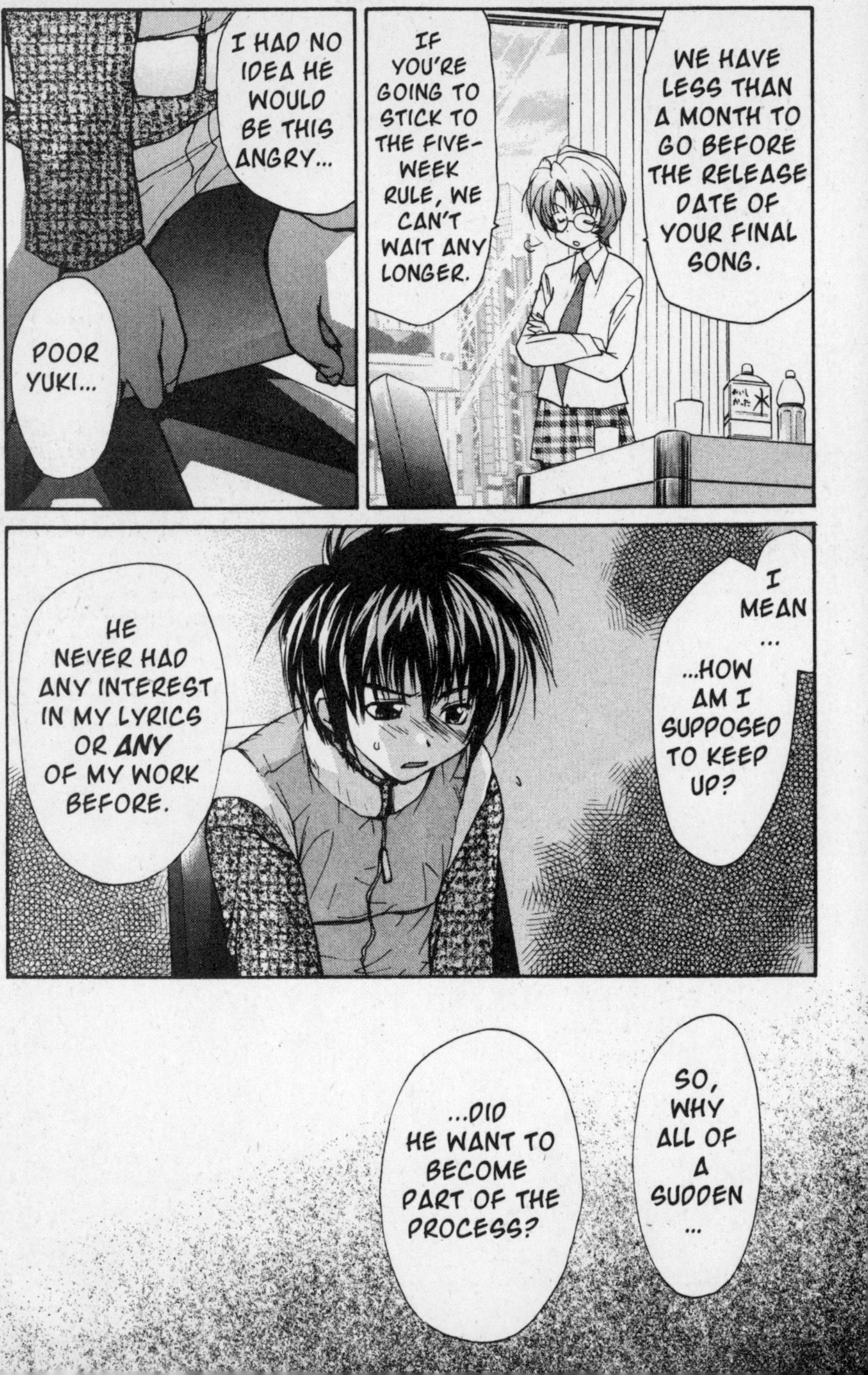
WE HAVE LESS THAN A MONTH TO GO BEFORE THE RELEASE DATE OF YOUR FINAL SONG.
IF YOU'RE GOING TO STICK TO THE FIVE-WEEK RULE, WE CAN'T WAIT ANY LONGER.
I HAD NO IDEA HE WOULD BE THIS ANGRY...
POOR YUKI...
I MEAN ...
...HOW AM I SUPPOSED TO KEEP UP?
HE NEVER HAD ANY INTEREST IN MY LYRICS OR ANY OF MY WORK BEFORE.
SO, WHY ALL OF A SUDDEN ...
...DID HE WANT TO BECOME PART OF THE PROCESS?

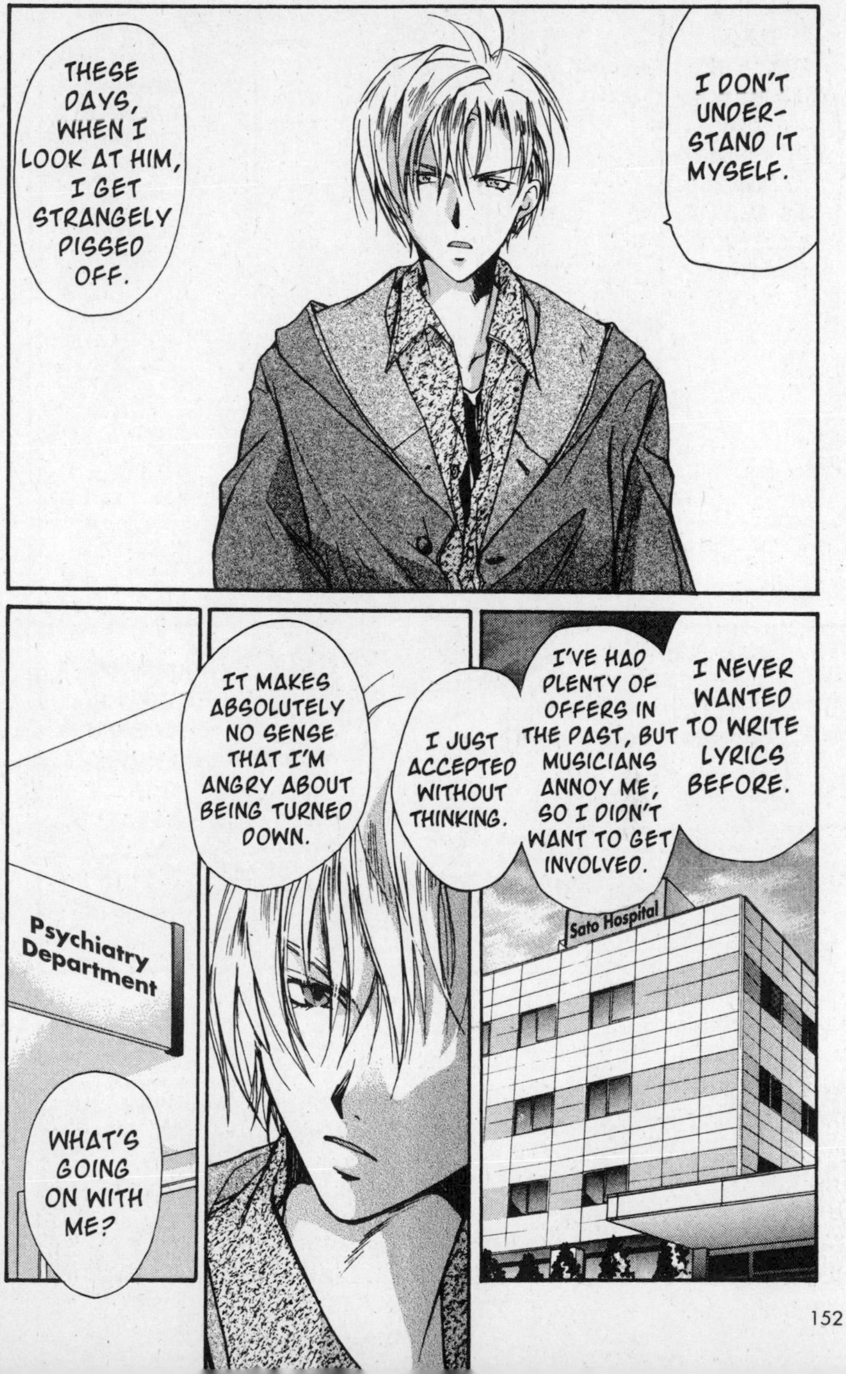
I DON'T UNDERSTAND IT MYSELF.
THESE DAYS, WHEN I LOOK AT HIM, I GET STRANGELY PISSED OFF.
I NEVER WANTED TO WRITE LYRICS BEFORE.
I'VE HAD PLENTY OF OFFERS IN THE PAST, BUT MUSICIANS ANNOY ME, SO I DIDN'T WANT TO GET INVOLVED.
Sato Hospital
I JUST ACCEPTED WITHOUT THINKING.
IT MAKES ABSOLUTELY NO SENSE THAT I'M ANGRY ABOUT BEING TURNED DOWN.
Psychiatry Department
WHAT'S GOING ON WITH ME?

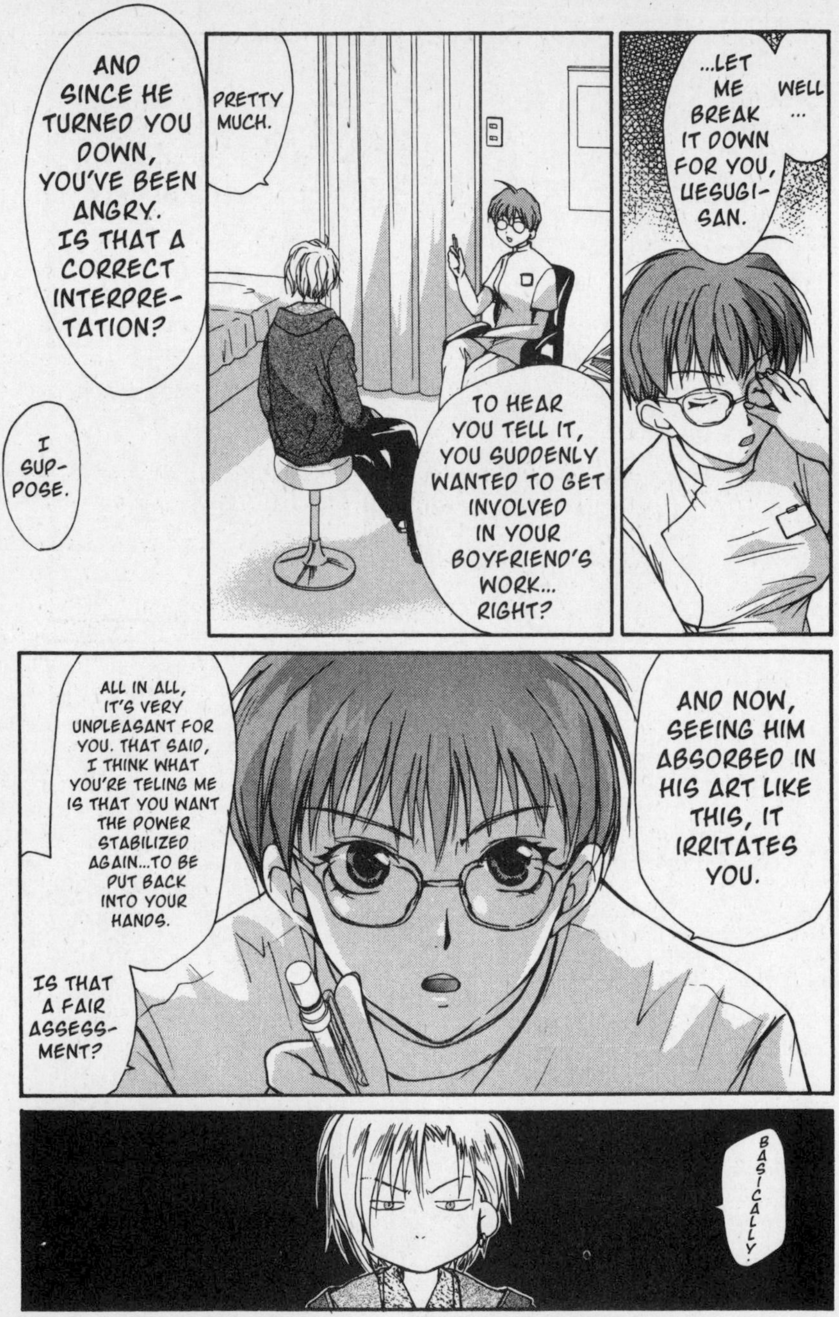
WELL ...
...LET ME BREAK IT DOWN FOR YOU, UESUGI-SAN.
TO HEAR YOU TELL IT, YOU SUDDENLY WANTED TO GET INVOLVED IN YOUR BOYFRIEND'S WORK... RIGHT?
PRETTY MUCH.
AND SINCE HE TURNED YOU DOWN, YOU'VE BEEN ANGRY. IS THAT A CORRECT INTERPRE-TATION?
I SUP-POSE.
AND NOW, SEEING HIM ABSORBED IN HIS ART LIKE THIS, IT IRRITATES YOU.
ALL IN ALL, IT'S VERY UNPLEASANT FOR YOU. THAT SAID, I THINK WHAT YOU'RE TELING ME IS THAT YOU WANT THE POWER STABILIZED AGAIN...TO BE PUT BACK INTO YOUR HANDS.
IS THAT A FAIR ASSESS-MENT?
BASICALLY.

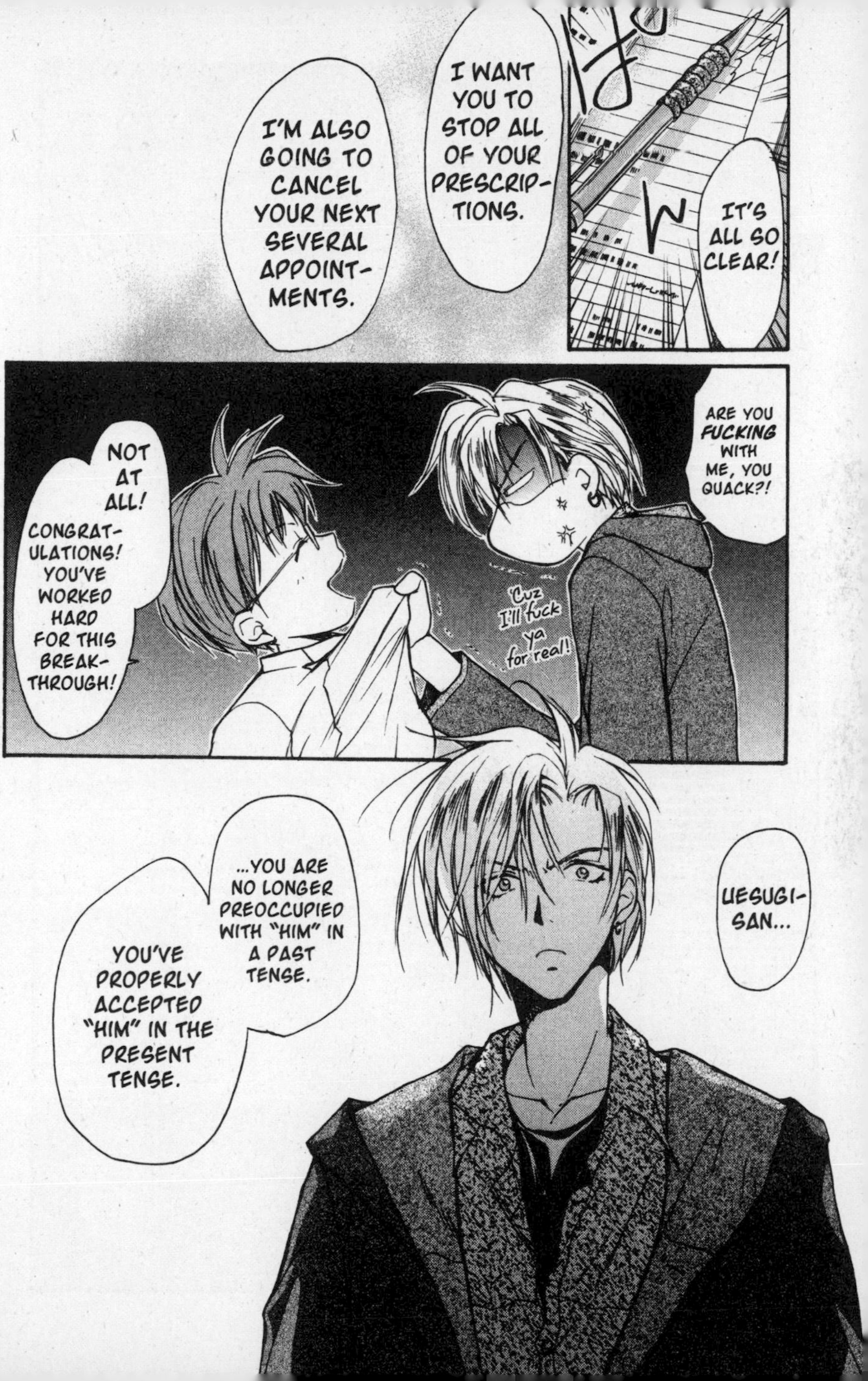

IT'S ALL SO CLEAR!
I WANT YOU TO STOP ALL OF YOUR PRESCRIP-TIONS.
I'M ALSO GOING TO CANCEL YOUR NEXT SEVERAL APPOINT-MENTS.
ARE YOU FUCKING WITH ME, YOU QUACK?!
'Cuz I'll fuck ya for real!
NOT AT ALL!
CONGRAT-ULATIONS! YOU'VE WORKED HARD FOR THIS BREAK-THROUGH!
UESUGI-SAN...
...YOU ARE NO LONGER PREOCCUPIED WITH "HIM" IN A PAST TENSE.
YOU'VE PROPERLY ACCEPTED "HIM" IN THE PRESENT TENSE.

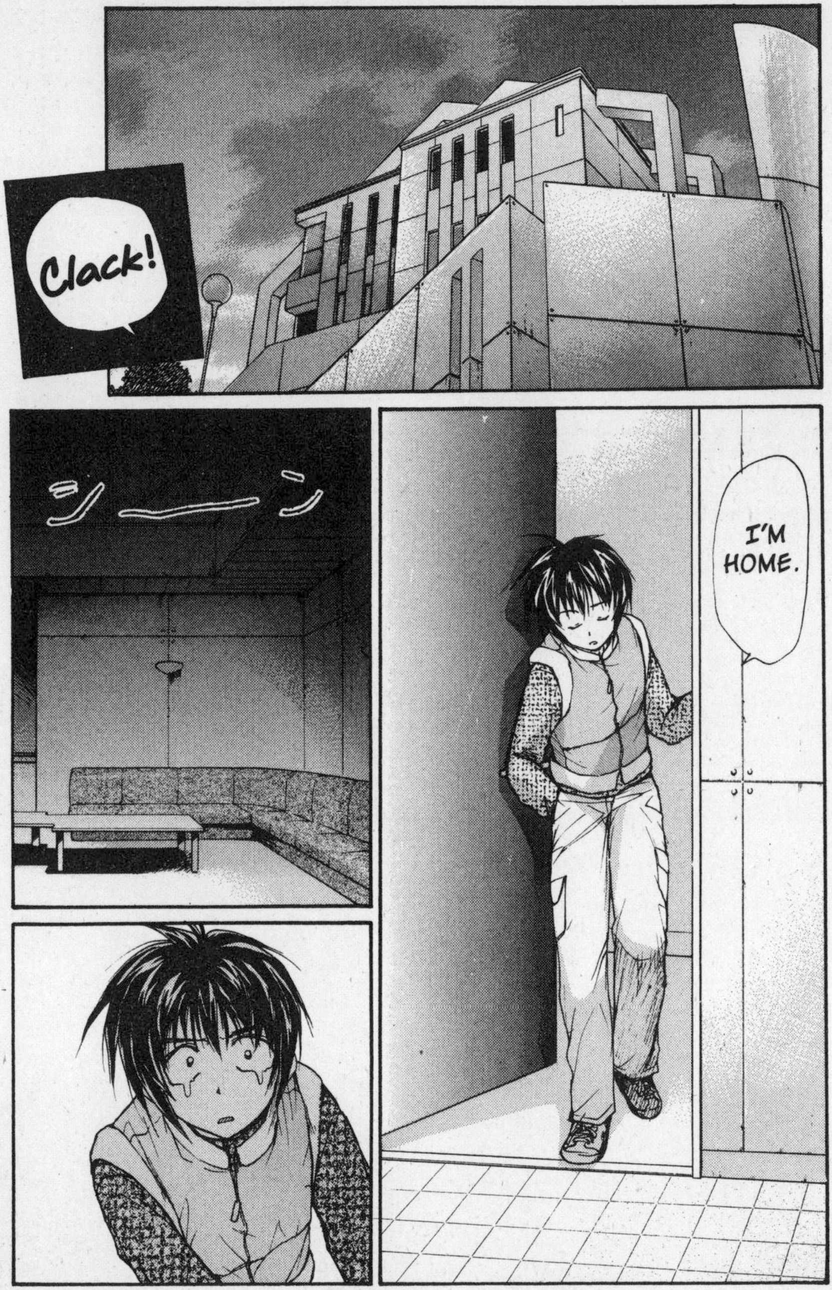
Clack!
I'M HOME.
シーーン

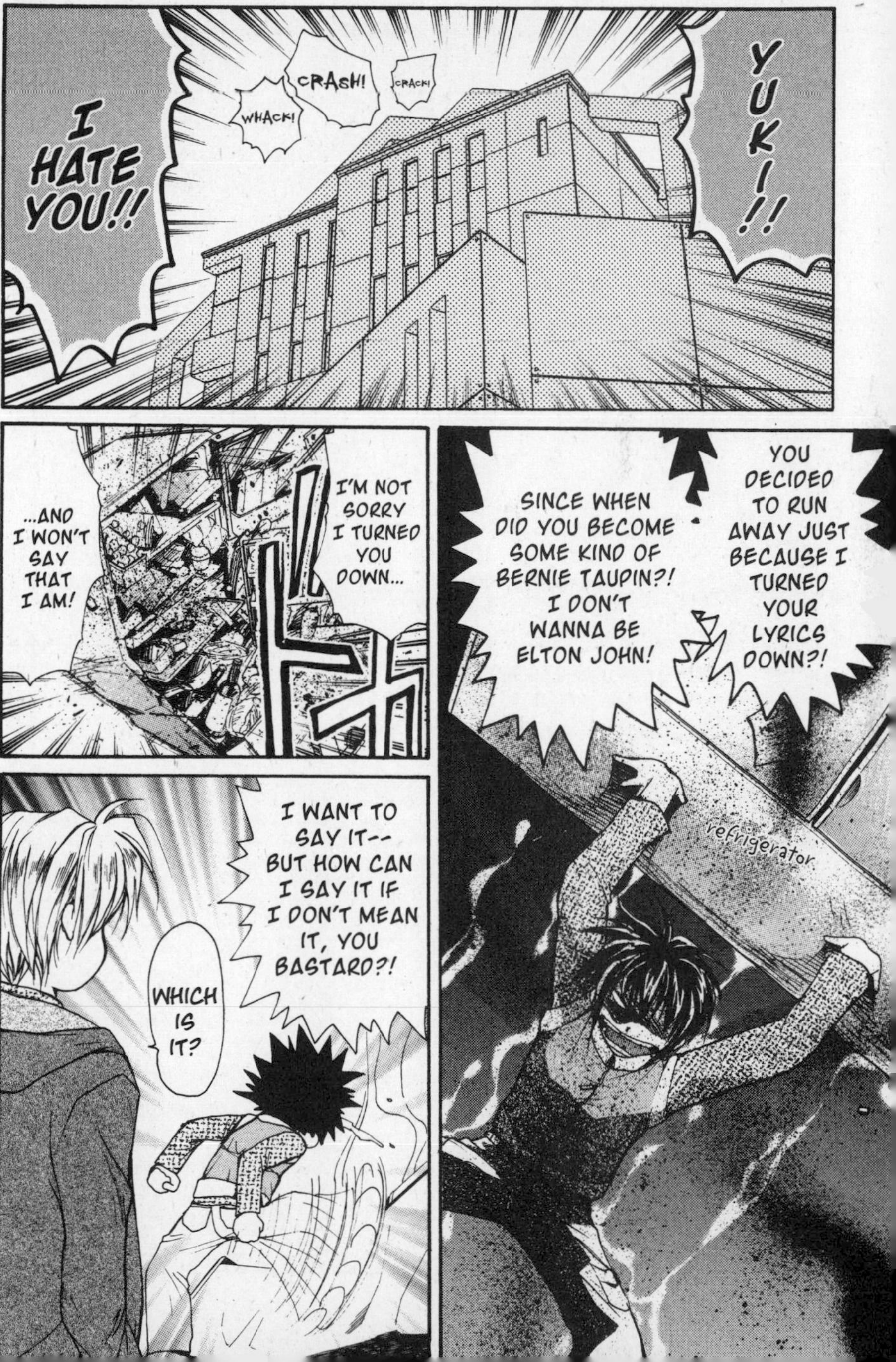
YUKI!!
CRACK!
CRASH!
WHACK!
I HATE YOU!!
YOU DECIDED TO RUN AWAY JUST BECAUSE I TURNED YOUR LYRICS DOWN?!
SINCE WHEN DID YOU BECOME SOME KIND OF BERNIE TAUPIN?! I DON'T WANNA BE ELTON JOHN!
refrigerator
I'M NOT SORRY I TURNED YOU DOWN...
...AND I WON'T SAY THAT I AM!
I WANT TO SAY IT-- BUT HOW CAN I SAY IT IF I DON'T MEAN IT, YOU BASTARD?!
WHICH IS IT?

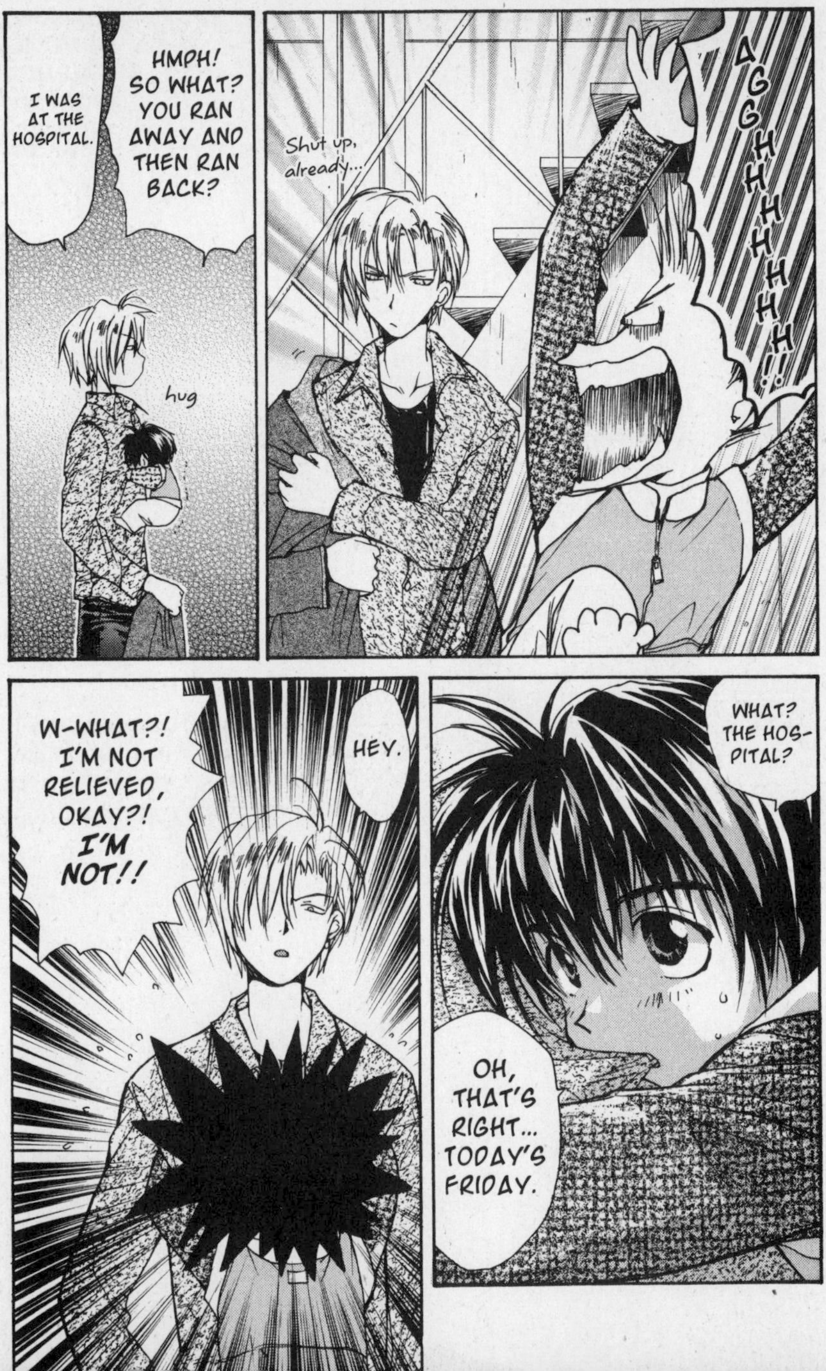
AGGHHHHHHHH!!
Shut up, already...
HMPH! SO WHAT? YOU RAN AWAY AND THEN RAN BACK?
I WAS AT THE HOSPITAL.
hug
WHAT? THE HOS-PITAL?
OH, THAT'S RIGHT... TODAY'S FRIDAY.
HEY.
W-WHAT?! I'M NOT RELIEVED, OKAY?! I'M NOT!!

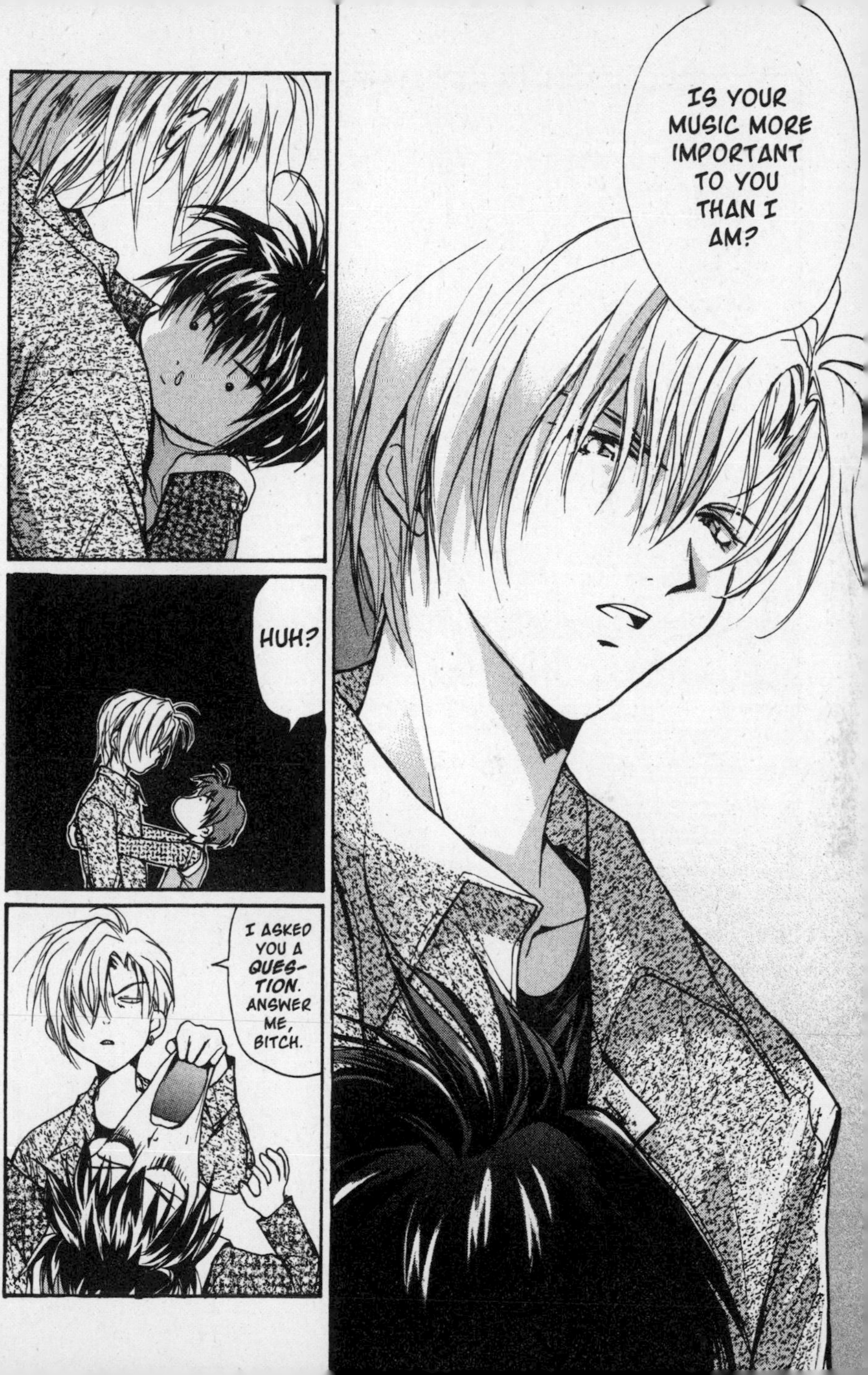
IS YOUR MUSIC MORE IMPORTANT TO YOU THAN I AM?
HUH?
I ASKED YOU A QUESTION. ANSWER ME, BITCH.

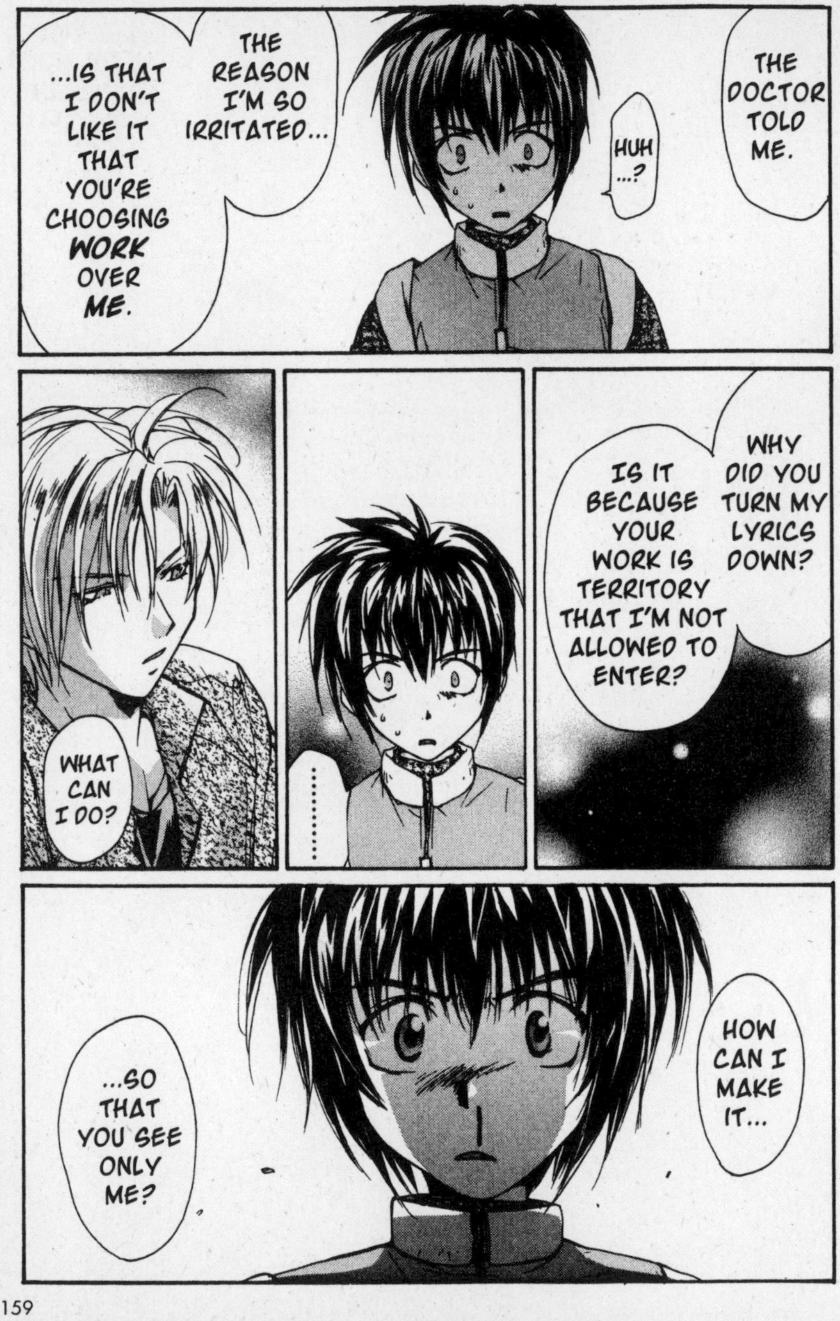
THE DOCTOR TOLD ME.
HUH ...?
THE REASON I'M SO IRRITATED...
...IS THAT I DON'T LIKE IT THAT YOU'RE CHOOSING WORK OVER ME.
WHY DID YOU TURN MY LYRICS DOWN?
IS IT BECAUSE YOUR WORK IS TERRITORY THAT I'M NOT ALLOWED TO ENTER?
......
WHAT CAN I DO?
HOW CAN I MAKE IT...
...SO THAT YOU SEE ONLY ME?

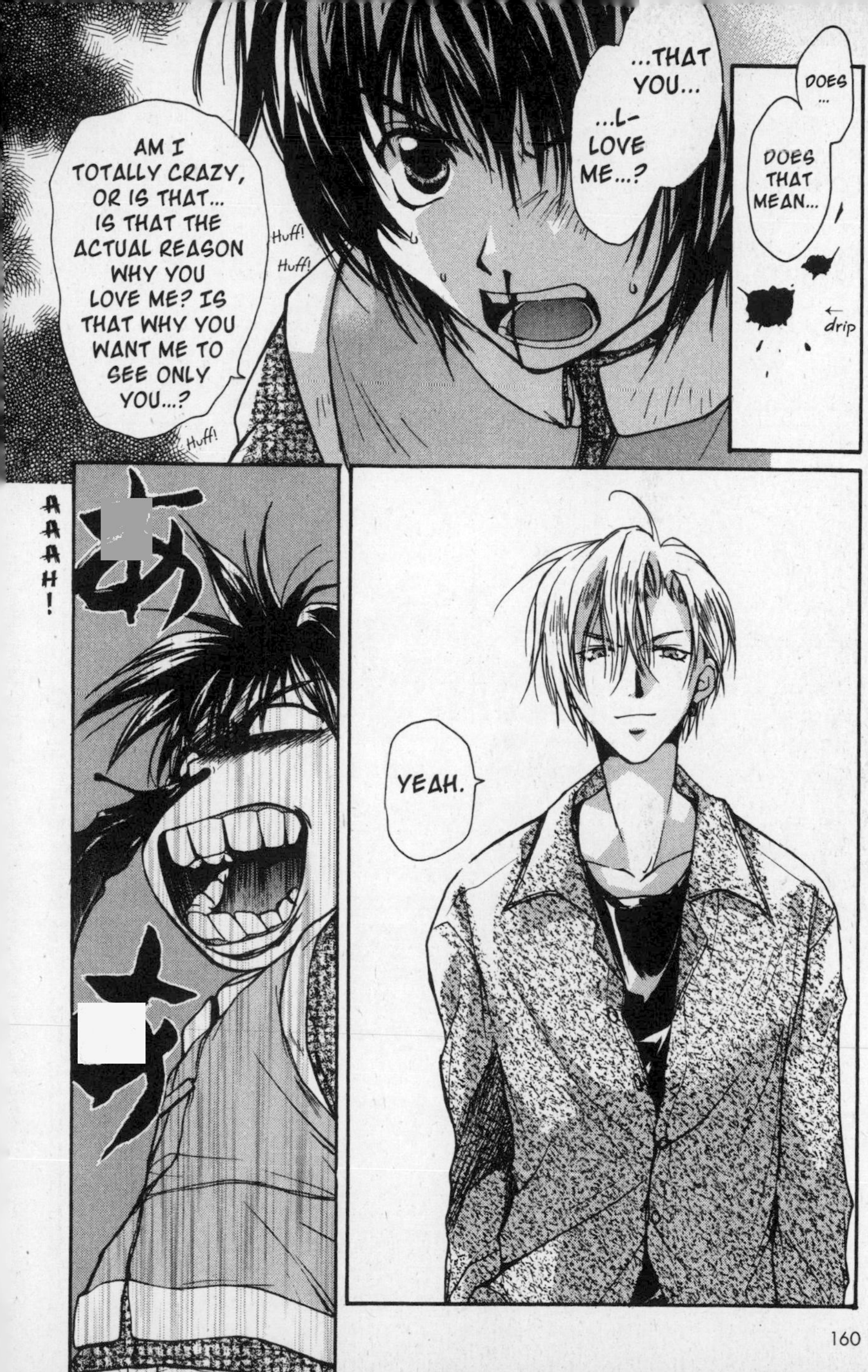
DOES...
DOES THAT MEAN...
drip
...THAT YOU...
...L-LOVE ME...?
AM I TOTALLY CRAZY, OR IS THAT... IS THAT THE ACTUAL REASON WHY YOU LOVE ME? IS THAT WHY YOU WANT ME TO SEE ONLY YOU...?
Huff!
Huff!
Huff!
YEAH.
AAAAH!

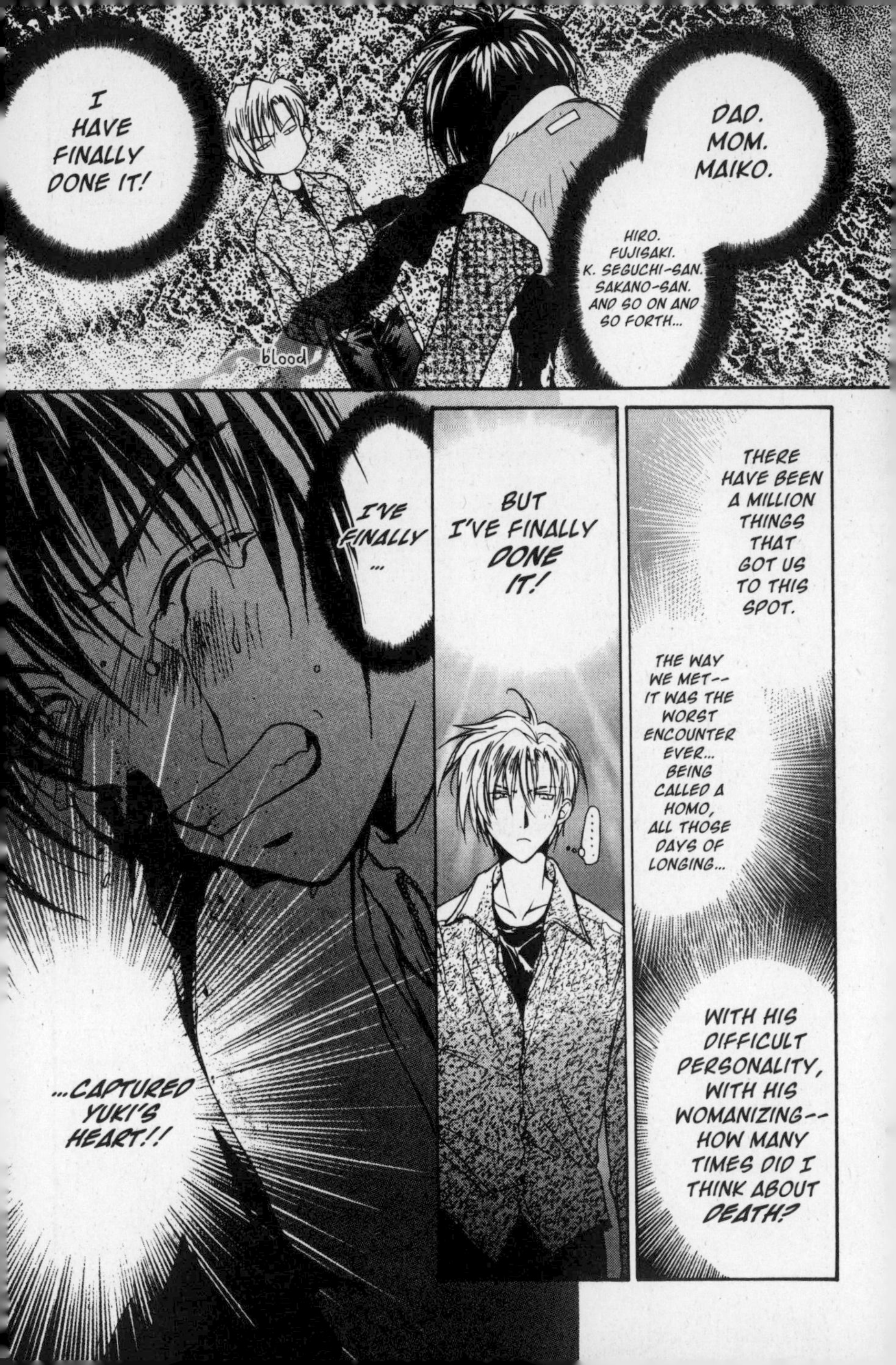
DAD. MOM. MAIKO.
HIRO. FUJISAKI. K. SEGUCHI-SAN. SAKANO-SAN. AND SO ON AND SO FORTH...
I HAVE FINALLY DONE IT!
blood
THERE HAVE BEEN A MILLION THINGS THAT GOT US TO THIS SPOT.
THE WAY WE MET-- IT WAS THE WORST ENCOUNTER EVER... BEING CALLED A HOMO, ALL THOSE DAYS OF LONGING...
WITH HIS DIFFICULT PERSONALITY, WITH HIS WOMANIZING-- HOW MANY TIMES DID I THINK ABOUT DEATH?
BUT I'VE FINALLY DONE IT!
I'VE FINALLY...
...CAPTURED YUKI'S HEART!!

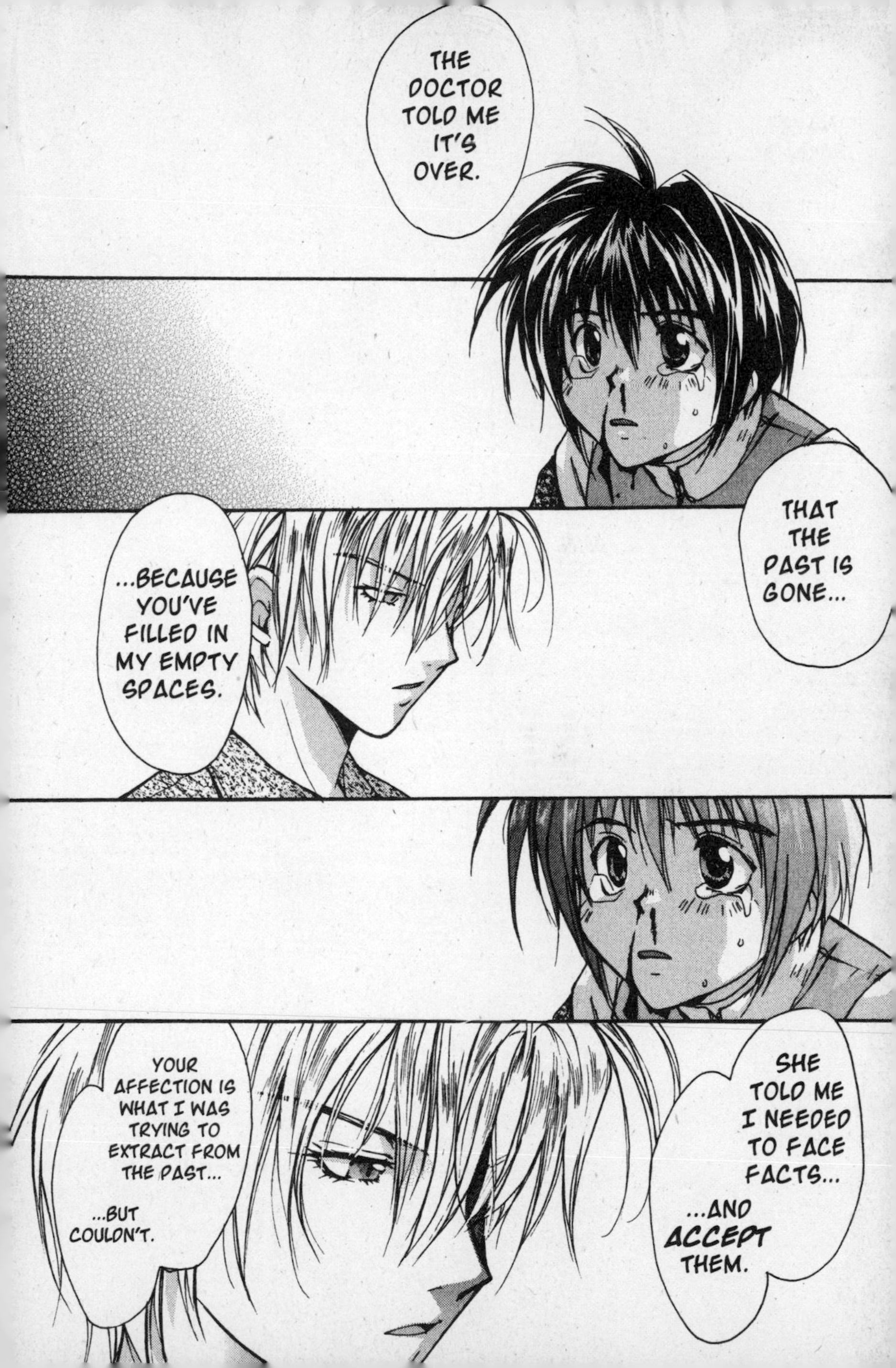
THE DOCTOR TOLD ME IT'S OVER.
THAT THE PAST IS GONE...
...BECAUSE YOU'VE FILLED IN MY EMPTY SPACES.
SHE TOLD ME I NEEDED TO FACE FACTS...
...AND ***ACCEPT*** THEM.
YOUR AFFECTION IS WHAT I WAS TRYING TO EXTRACT FROM THE PAST...
...BUT COULDN'T.

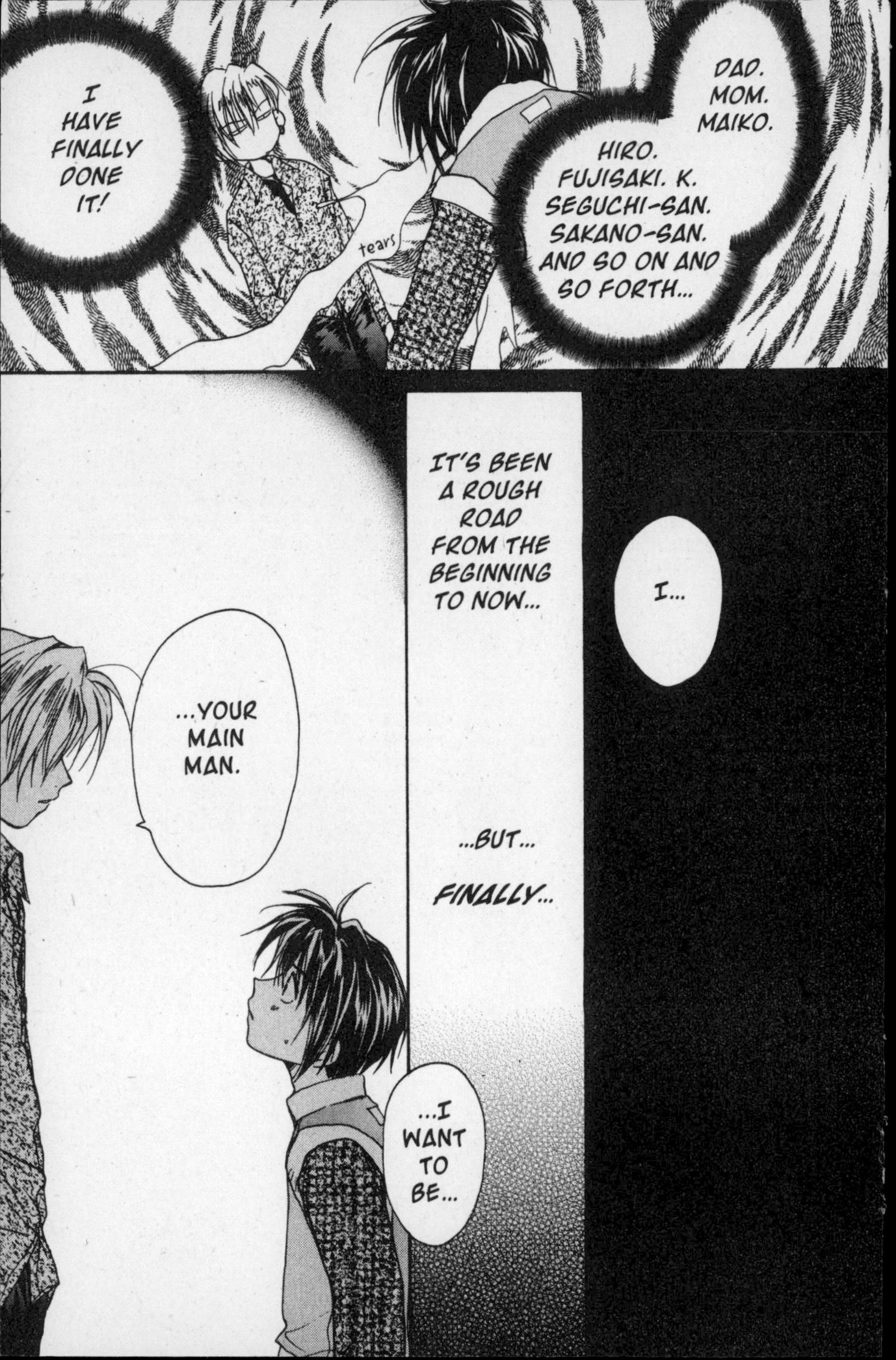
DAD. MOM. MAIKO.
HIRO. FUJISAKI. K. SEGUCHI-SAN. SAKANO-SAN. AND SO ON AND SO FORTH...
I HAVE FINALLY DONE IT!
tears
I...
IT'S BEEN A ROUGH ROAD FROM THE BEGINNING TO NOW...
...BUT...
FINALLY...
...I WANT TO BE...
...YOUR MAIN MAN.

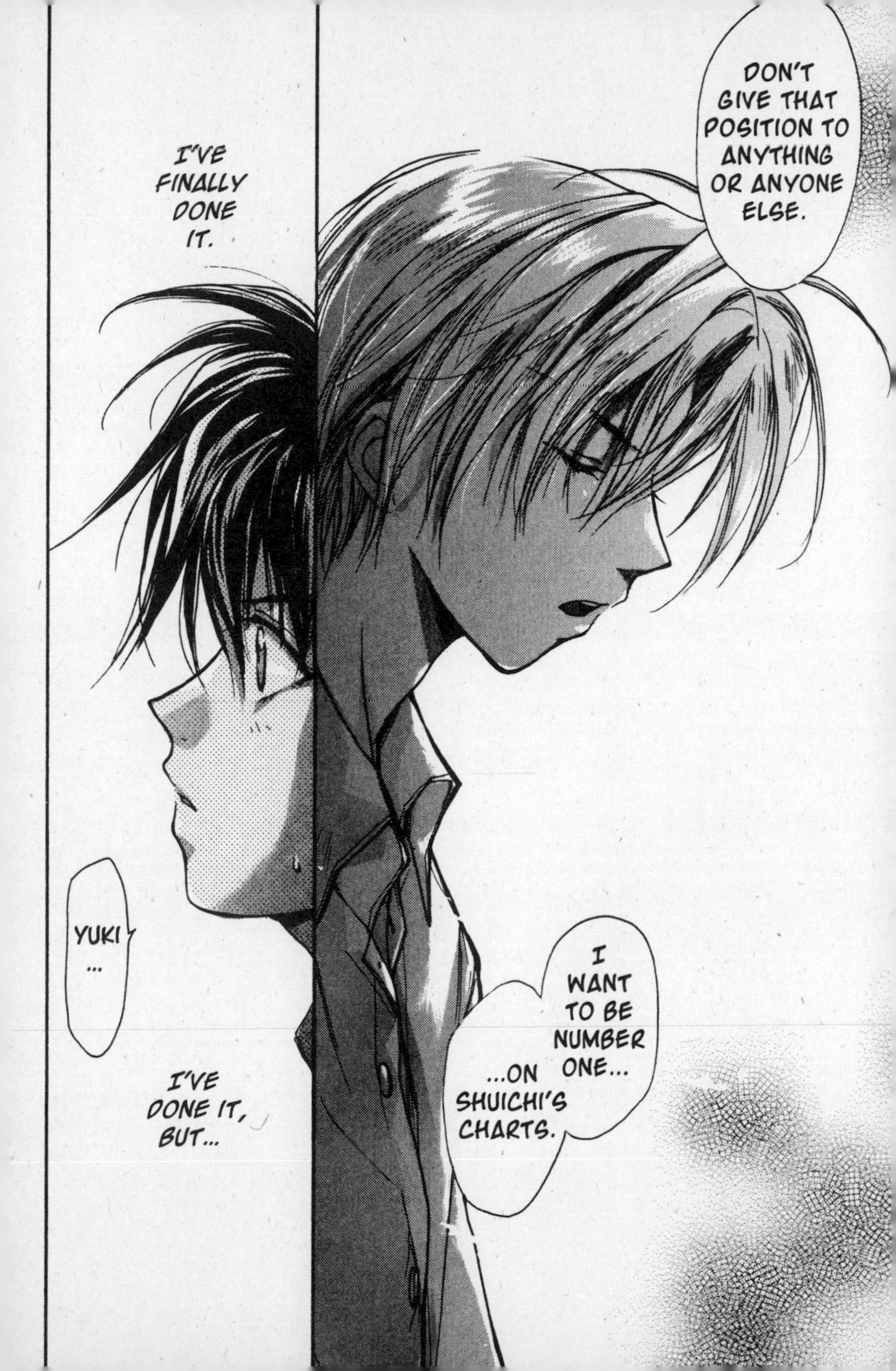

DON'T GIVE THAT POSITION TO ANYTHING OR ANYONE ELSE.
I WANT TO BE NUMBER ONE...
...ON SHUICHI'S CHARTS.
I'VE FINALLY DONE IT.
YUKI...
I'VE DONE IT, BUT...

...WHY CAN'T I STOP THINKING THAT THERE'S SOMETHING WRONG WITH ALL THIS?

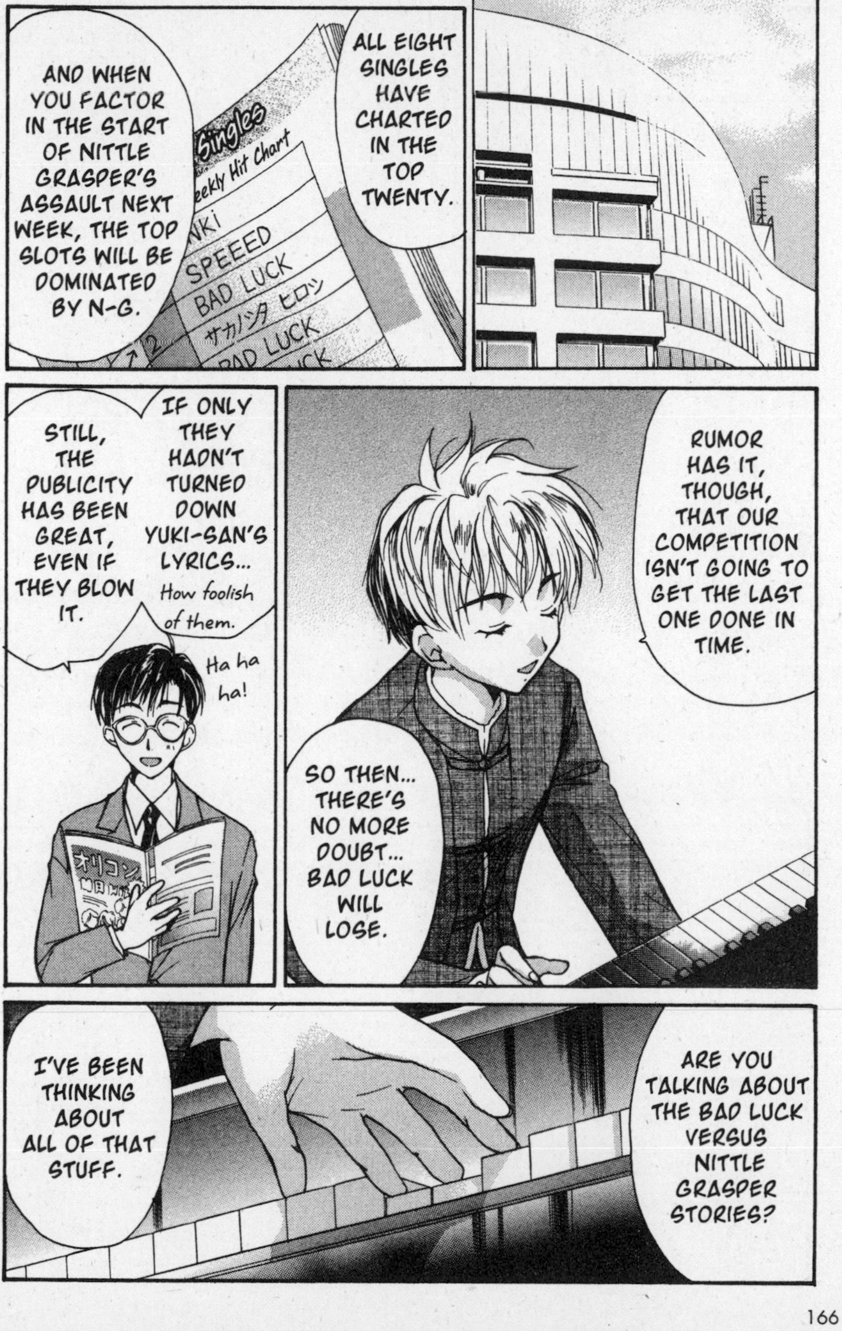
ALL EIGHT SINGLES HAVE CHARTED IN THE TOP TWENTY.
AND WHEN YOU FACTOR IN THE START OF NITTLE GRASPER'S ASSAULT NEXT WEEK, THE TOP SLOTS WILL BE DOMINATED BY N-G.
Singles
SPEEED
BAD LUCK
BAD LUCK
RUMOR HAS IT, THOUGH, THAT OUR COMPETITION ISN'T GOING TO GET THE LAST ONE DONE IN TIME.
SO THEN... THERE'S NO MORE DOUBT... BAD LUCK WILL LOSE.
IF ONLY THEY HADN'T TURNED DOWN YUKI-SAN'S LYRICS...
How foolish of them.
STILL, THE PUBLICITY HAS BEEN GREAT, EVEN IF THEY BLOW IT.
Ha ha ha!
ARE YOU TALKING ABOUT THE BAD LUCK VERSUS NITTLE GRASPER STORIES?
I'VE BEEN THINKING ABOUT ALL OF THAT STUFF.

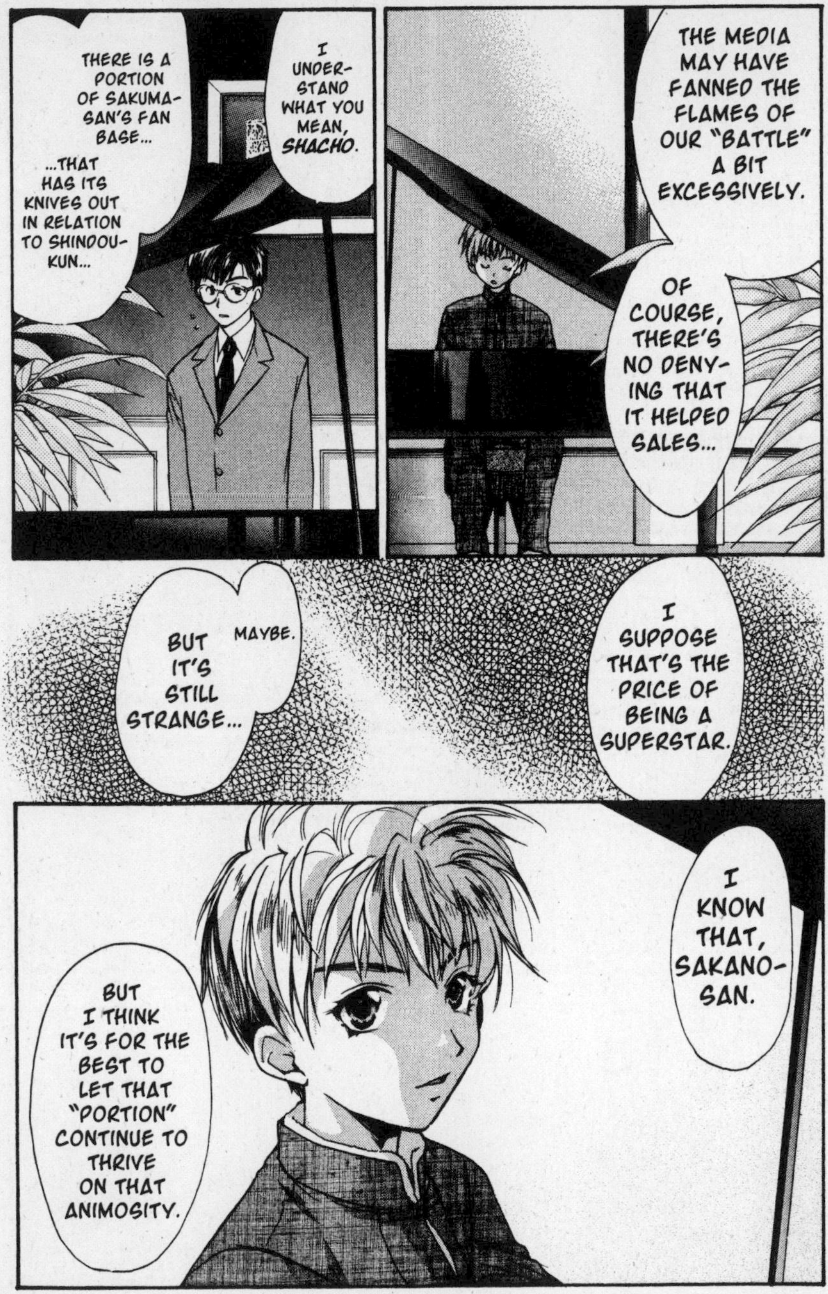
THE MEDIA MAY HAVE FANNED THE FLAMES OF OUR "BATTLE" A BIT EXCESSIVELY.
OF COURSE, THERE'S NO DENYING THAT IT HELPED SALES...
I UNDERSTAND WHAT YOU MEAN, SHACHO.
THERE IS A PORTION OF SAKUMA-SAN'S FAN BASE...
...THAT HAS ITS KNIVES OUT IN RELATION TO SHINDOU-KUN...
I SUPPOSE THAT'S THE PRICE OF BEING A SUPERSTAR.
MAYBE.
BUT IT'S STILL STRANGE...
I KNOW THAT, SAKANO-SAN.
BUT I THINK IT'S FOR THE BEST TO LET THAT "PORTION" CONTINUE TO THRIVE ON THAT ANIMOSITY.

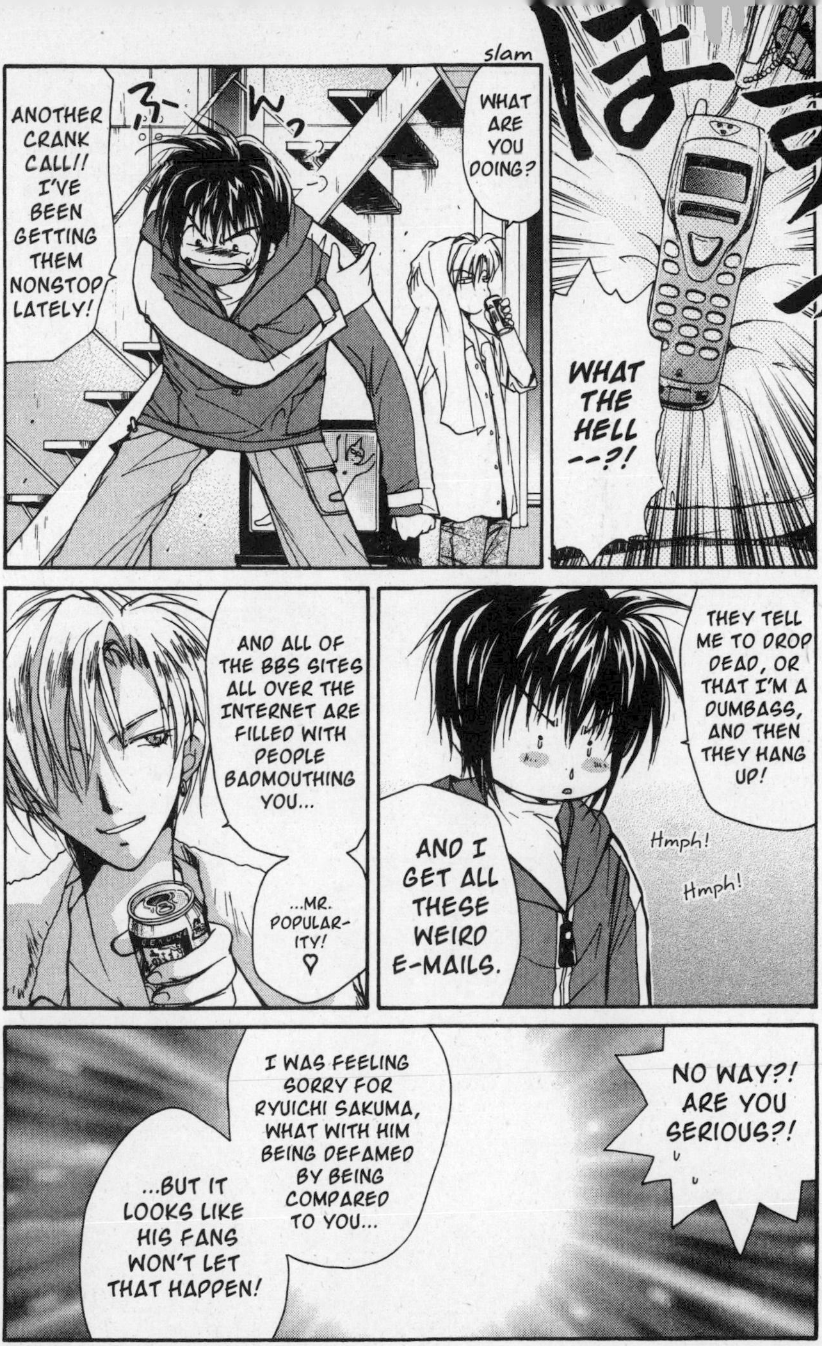
slam
ほすっ
WHAT THE HELL--?!
WHAT ARE YOU DOING?
ANOTHER CRANK CALL!! I'VE BEEN GETTING THEM NONSTOP LATELY!
THEY TELL ME TO DROP DEAD, OR THAT I'M A DUMBASS, AND THEN THEY HANG UP!
AND I GET ALL THESE WEIRD E-MAILS.
Hmph!
Hmph!
AND ALL OF THE BBS SITES ALL OVER THE INTERNET ARE FILLED WITH PEOPLE BADMOUTHING YOU...
...MR. POPULARITY! ♡
NO WAY?! ARE YOU SERIOUS?!
I WAS FEELING SORRY FOR RYUICHI SAKUMA, WHAT WITH HIM BEING DEFAMED BY BEING COMPARED TO YOU...
...BUT IT LOOKS LIKE HIS FANS WON'T LET THAT HAPPEN!

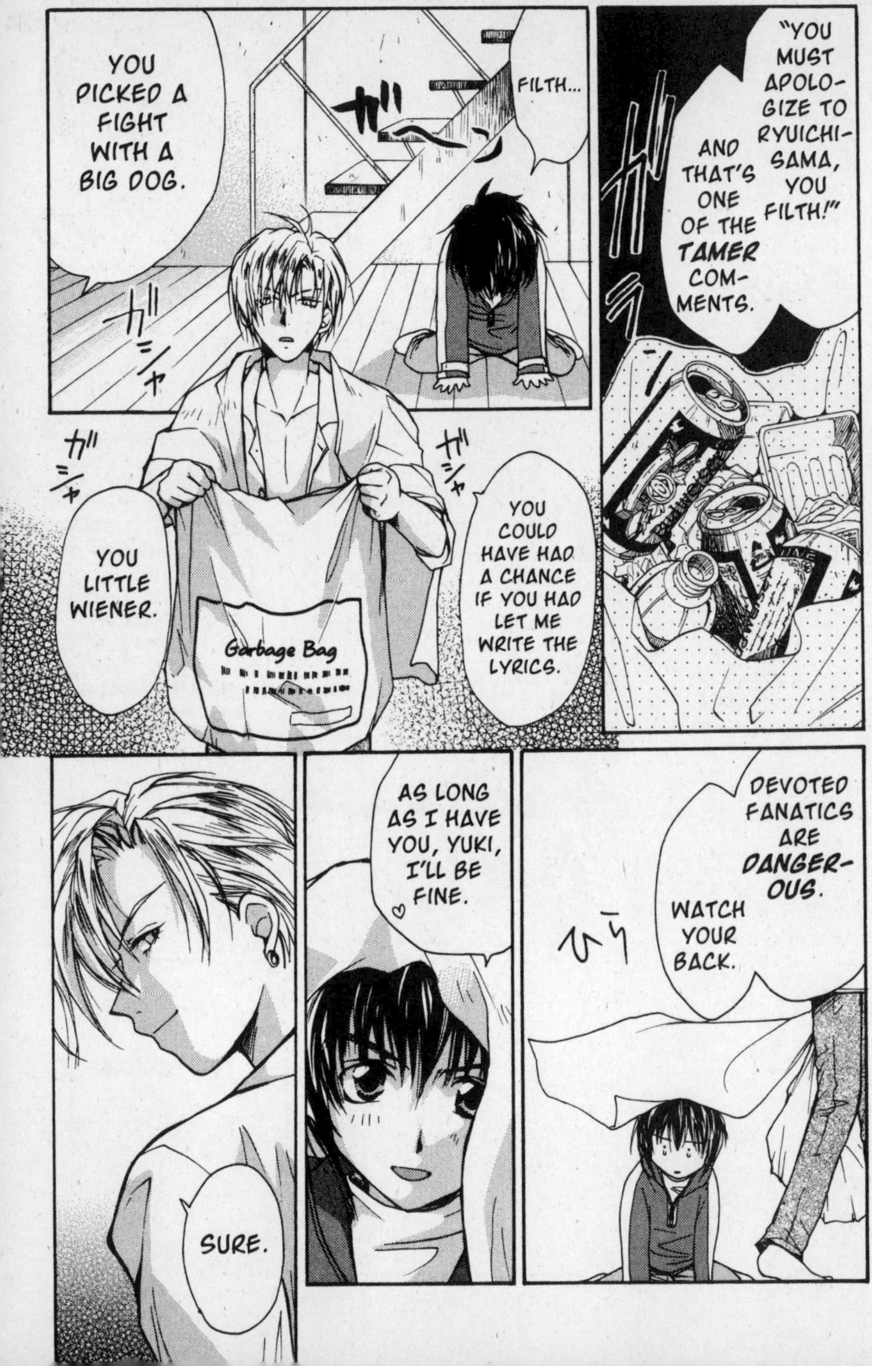
"YOU MUST APOLO-GIZE TO RYUICHI-SAMA, YOU FILTH!"
AND THAT'S ONE OF THE TAMER COM-MENTS.
FILTH...
YOU PICKED A FIGHT WITH A BIG DOG.
YOU COULD HAVE HAD A CHANCE IF YOU HAD LET ME WRITE THE LYRICS.
Garbage Bag
YOU LITTLE WIENER.
DEVOTED FANATICS ARE DANGER-OUS.
WATCH YOUR BACK.
AS LONG AS I HAVE YOU, YUKI, I'LL BE FINE. ♡
SURE.

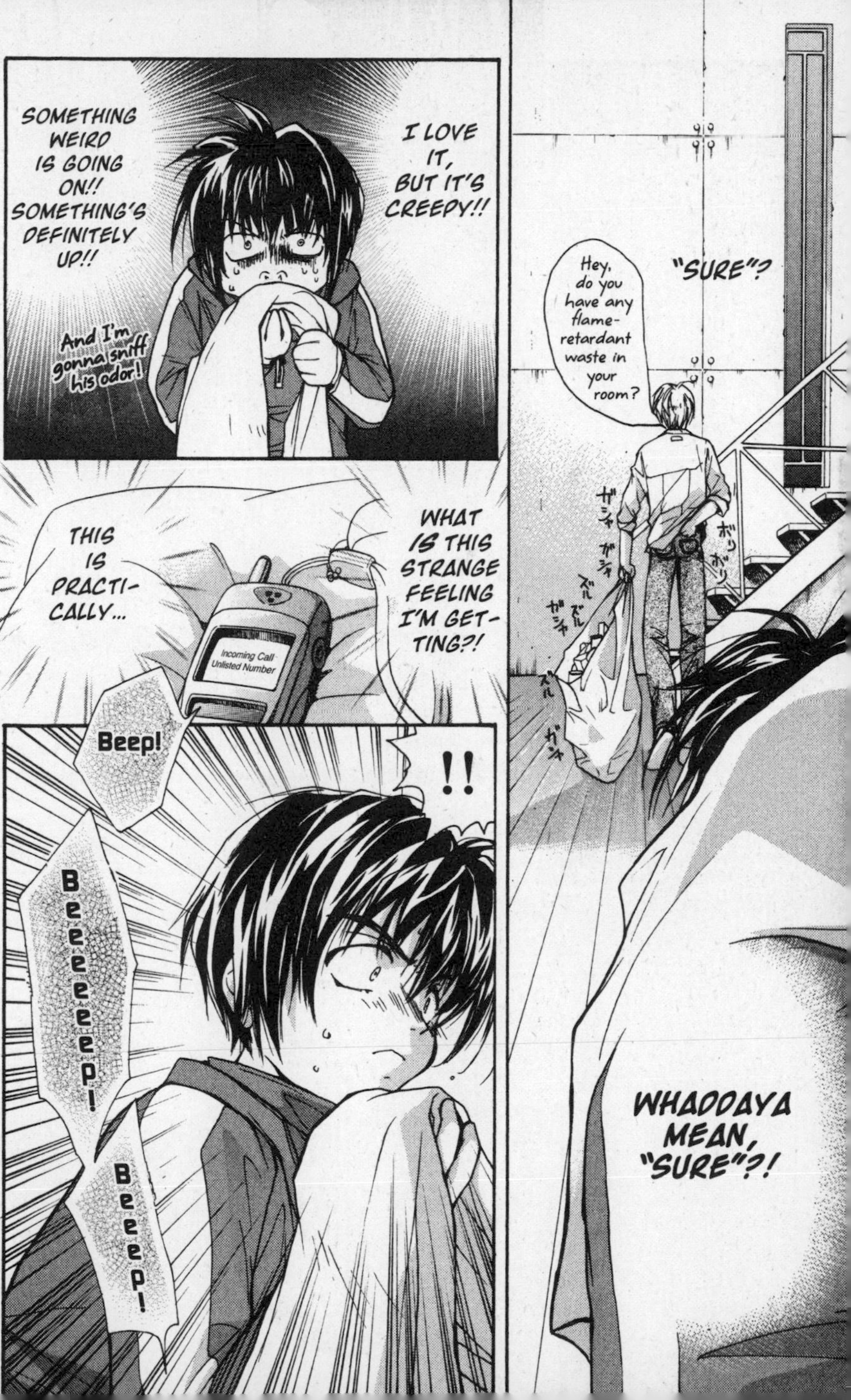
"SURE"?
Hey, do you have any flame-retardant waste in your room?
ガシャ ガシャ
ズル ズル
ガシャ
ズル
ガシャ
ボリ ボリ
WHADDAYA MEAN, "SURE"?!
I LOVE IT, BUT IT'S CREEPY!!
SOMETHING WEIRD IS GOING ON!! SOMETHING'S DEFINITELY UP!!
And I'm gonna sniff his odor!
WHAT IS THIS STRANGE FEELING I'M GETTING?!
THIS IS PRACTICALLY...
Incoming Call
Unlisted Number
!!
Beep!
Beeeeeeep!
Beeep!

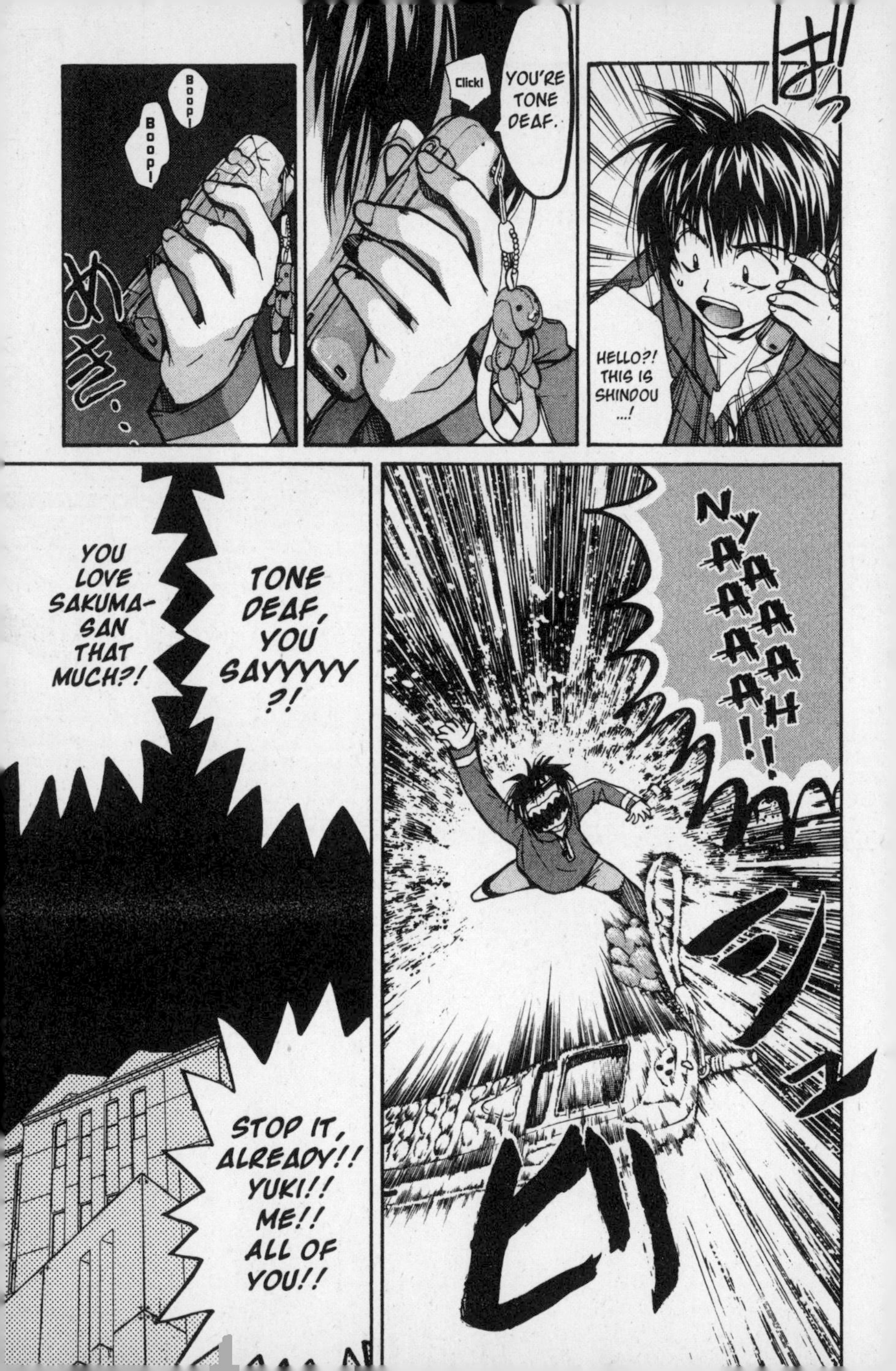
ぱっ
HELLO?! THIS IS SHINDOU ...!
YOU'RE TONE DEAF.
Click!
Boop!
Boop!
めきっ..
NyAAAAAAAAAH!!!
TONE DEAF, YOU SAYYYYY?!
YOU LOVE SAKUMA-SAN THAT MUCH?!
STOP IT, ALREADY!! YUKI!! ME!! ALL OF YOU!!

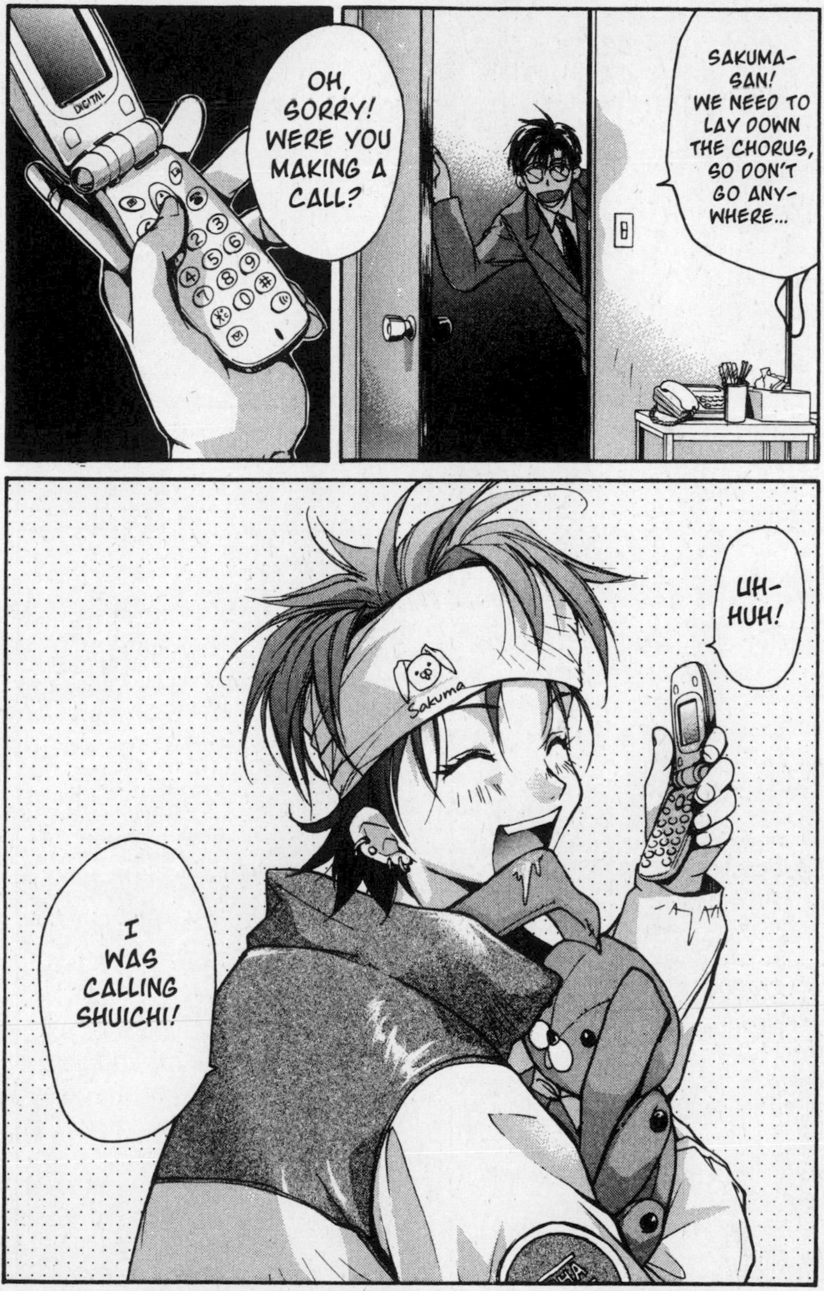
SAKUMA-SAN! WE NEED TO LAY DOWN THE CHORUS, SO DON'T GO ANY-WHERE...
DIGITAL
OH, SORRY! WERE YOU MAKING A CALL?
UH-HUH!
Sakuma
I WAS CALLING SHUICHI!

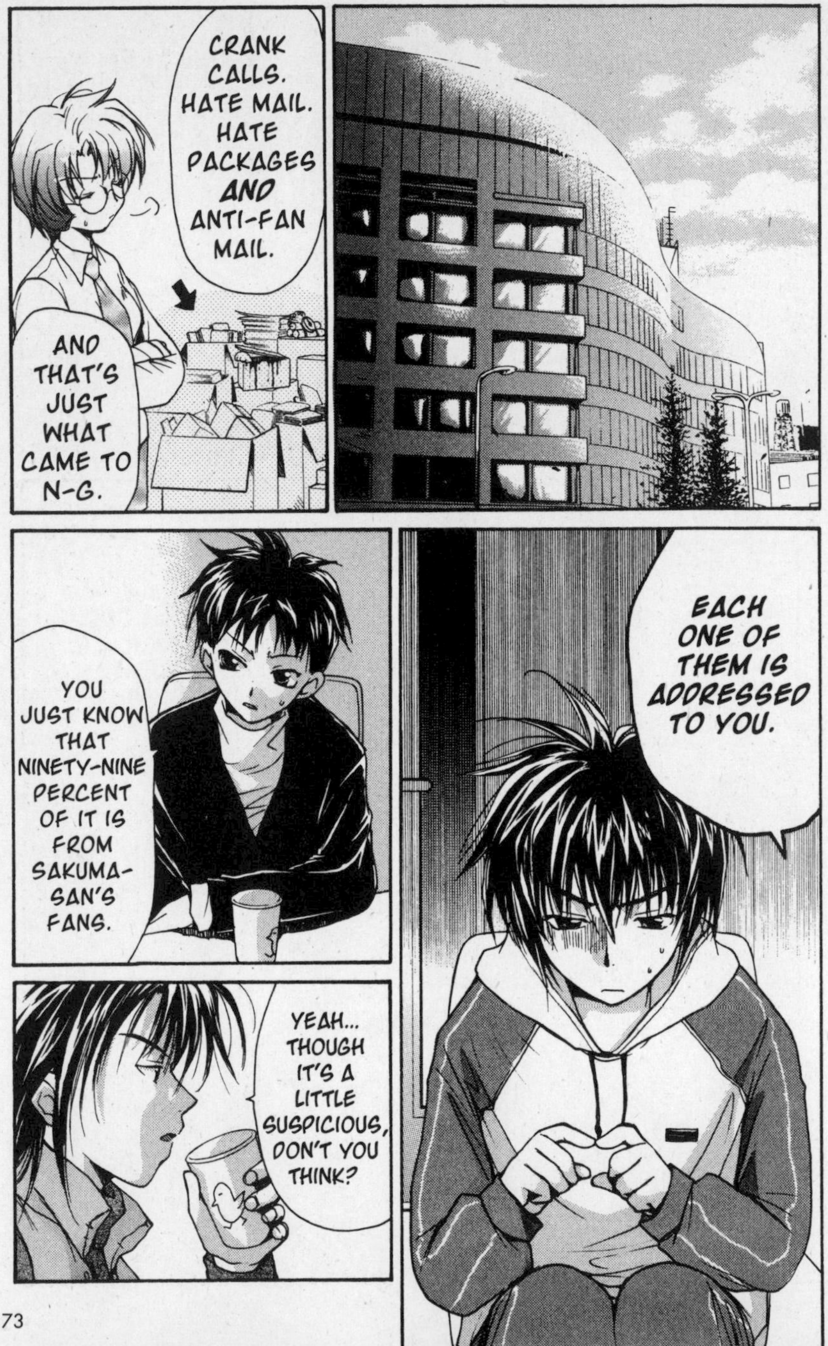
CRANK CALLS. HATE MAIL. HATE PACKAGES AND ANTI-FAN MAIL.
AND THAT'S JUST WHAT CAME TO N-G.
EACH ONE OF THEM IS ADDRESSED TO YOU.
YOU JUST KNOW THAT NINETY-NINE PERCENT OF IT IS FROM SAKUMA-SAN'S FANS.
YEAH... THOUGH IT'S A LITTLE SUSPICIOUS, DON'T YOU THINK?

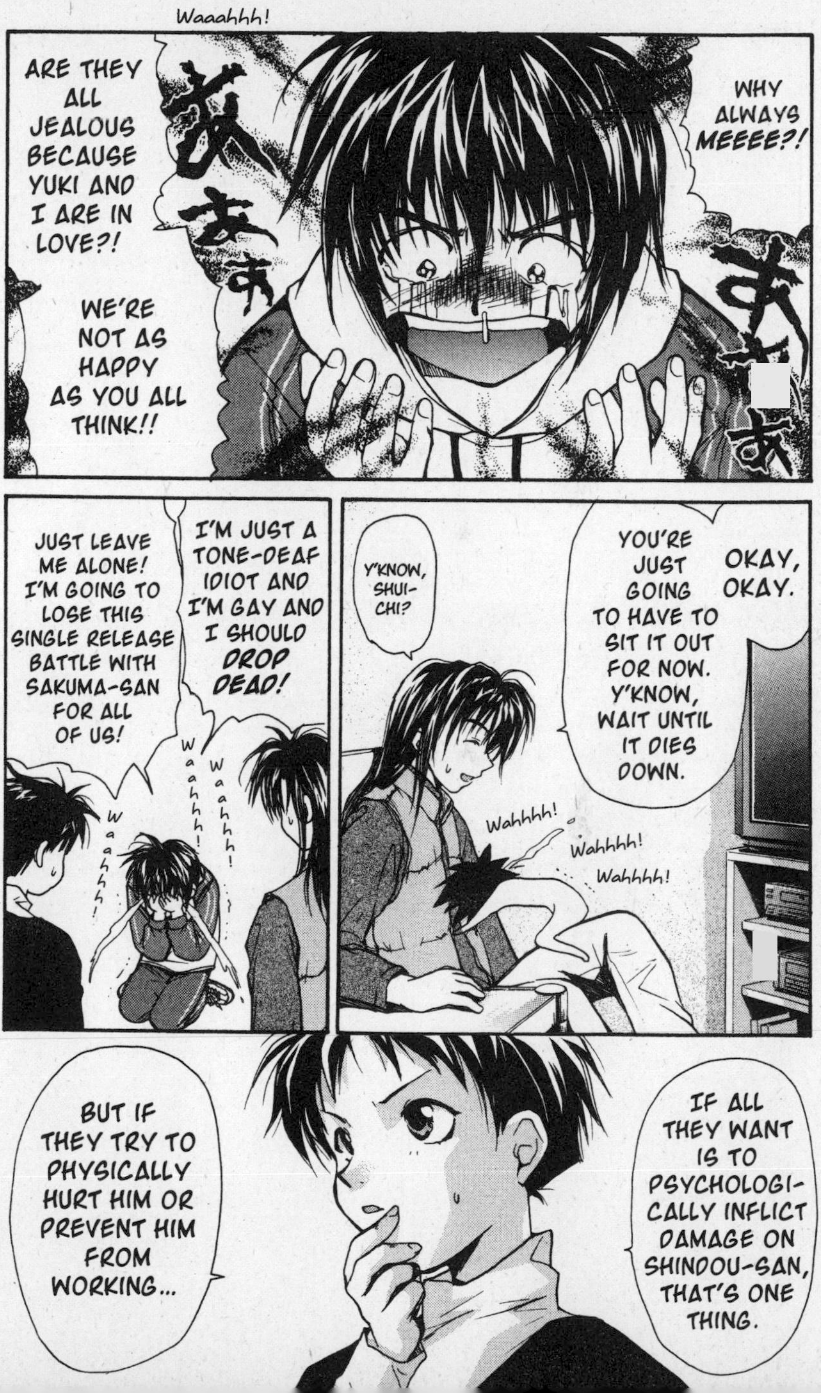
WHY ALWAYS MEEEE?!
Waaahhh!
ARE THEY ALL JEALOUS BECAUSE YUKI AND I ARE IN LOVE?!
WE'RE NOT AS HAPPY AS YOU ALL THINK!!
OKAY, OKAY.
YOU'RE JUST GOING TO HAVE TO SIT IT OUT FOR NOW. Y'KNOW, WAIT UNTIL IT DIES DOWN.
Y'KNOW, SHUI-CHI?
Wahhhh!
Wahhhh!
Wahhhh!
I'M JUST A TONE-DEAF IDIOT AND I'M GAY AND I SHOULD DROP DEAD!
JUST LEAVE ME ALONE! I'M GOING TO LOSE THIS SINGLE RELEASE BATTLE WITH SAKUMA-SAN FOR ALL OF US!
Waahhh!
Waahhh!
Waahhh!
IF ALL THEY WANT IS TO PSYCHOLOGICALLY INFLICT DAMAGE ON SHINDOU-SAN, THAT'S ONE THING.
BUT IF THEY TRY TO PHYSICALLY HURT HIM OR PREVENT HIM FROM WORKING...

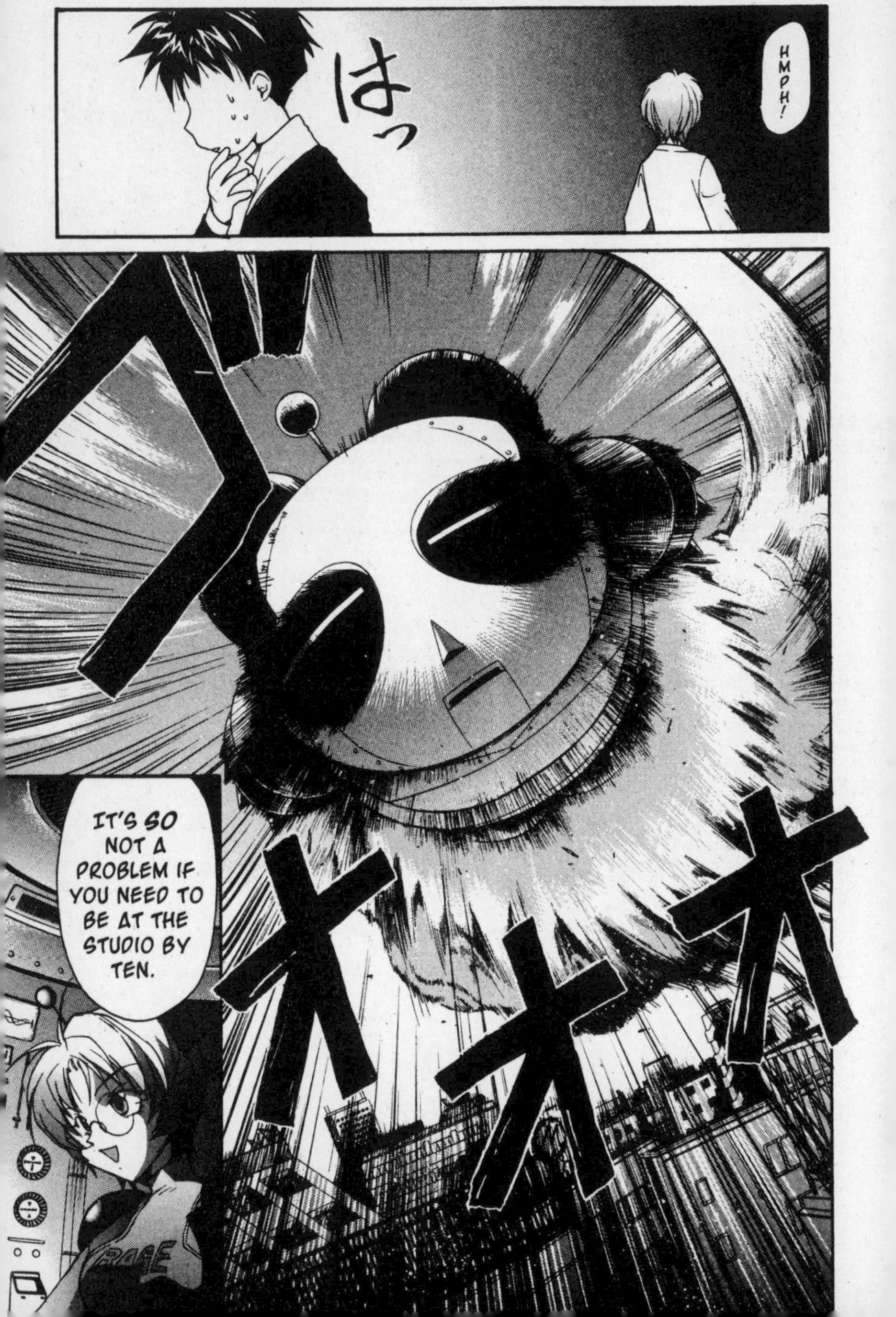
HMPH!
はっ
IT'S SO NOT A PROBLEM IF YOU NEED TO BE AT THE STUDIO BY TEN.
オォーォ

Ho ho ho ho ho ho ho!

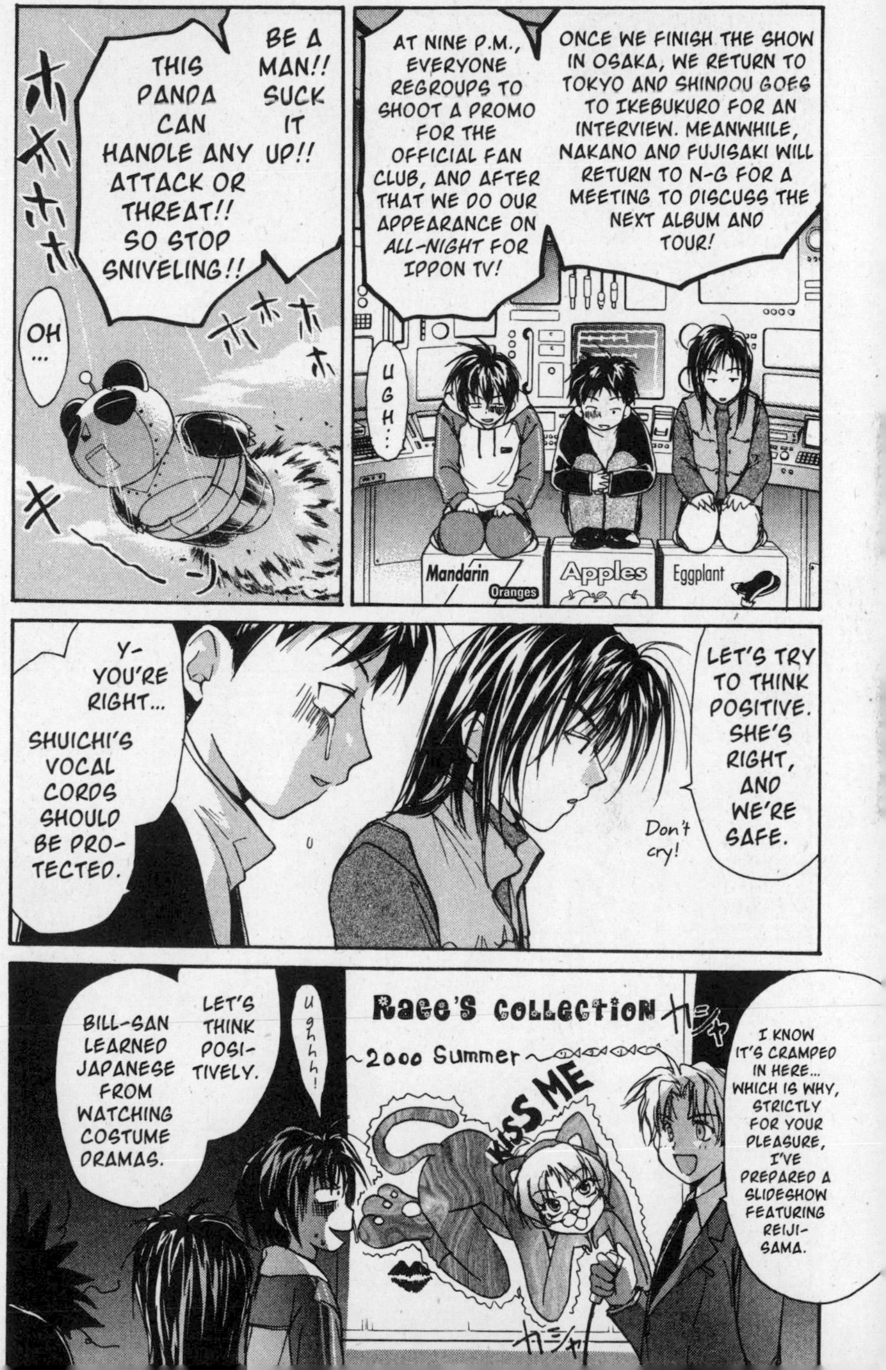

ONCE WE FINISH THE SHOW IN OSAKA, WE RETURN TO TOKYO AND SHINDOU GOES TO IKEBUKURO FOR AN INTERVIEW. MEANWHILE, NAKANO AND FUJISAKI WILL RETURN TO N-G FOR A MEETING TO DISCUSS THE NEXT ALBUM AND TOUR!
AT NINE P.M., EVERYONE REGROUPS TO SHOOT A PROMO FOR THE OFFICIAL FAN CLUB, AND AFTER THAT WE DO OUR APPEARANCE ON ALL-NIGHT FOR IPPON TV!
UGH...
Mandarin Oranges
Apples
Eggplant
BE A MAN!! SUCK IT UP!!
THIS PANDA CAN HANDLE ANY ATTACK OR THREAT!! SO STOP SNIVELING!!
OH...
LET'S TRY TO THINK POSITIVE. SHE'S RIGHT, AND WE'RE SAFE.
Don't cry!
Y-YOU'RE RIGHT...
SHUICHI'S VOCAL CORDS SHOULD BE PRO-TECTED.
I KNOW IT'S CRAMPED IN HERE... WHICH IS WHY, STRICTLY FOR YOUR PLEASURE, I'VE PREPARED A SLIDESHOW FEATURING REIJI-SAMA.
Race's Collection
~2000 Summer~
KISS ME
Ughhh!
LET'S THINK POSI-TIVELY.
BILL-SAN LEARNED JAPANESE FROM WATCHING COSTUME DRAMAS.

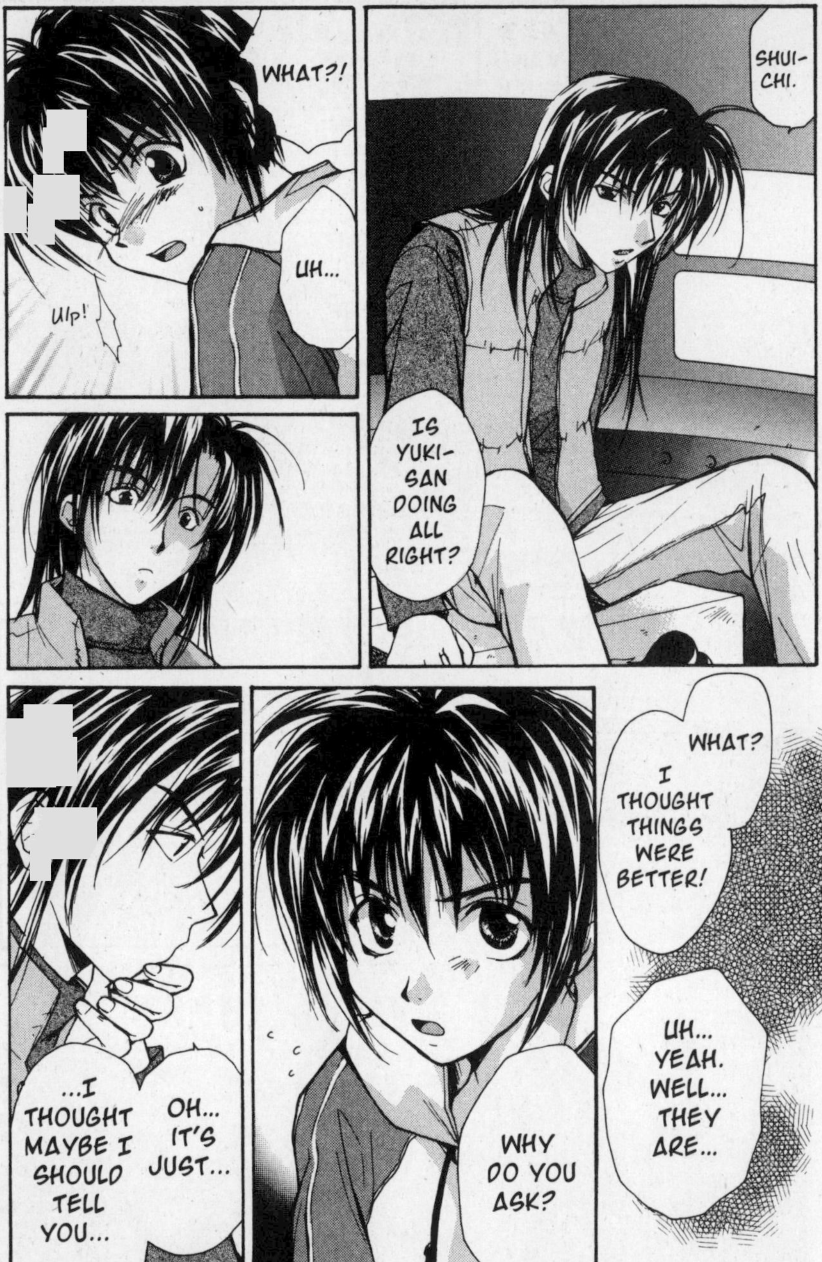
SHUI-CHI.
IS YUKI-SAN DOING ALL RIGHT?
WHAT?!
UH...
Ulp!
WHAT? I THOUGHT THINGS WERE BETTER!
UH... YEAH. WELL... THEY ARE...
WHY DO YOU ASK?
OH... IT'S JUST...
...I THOUGHT MAYBE I SHOULD TELL YOU...

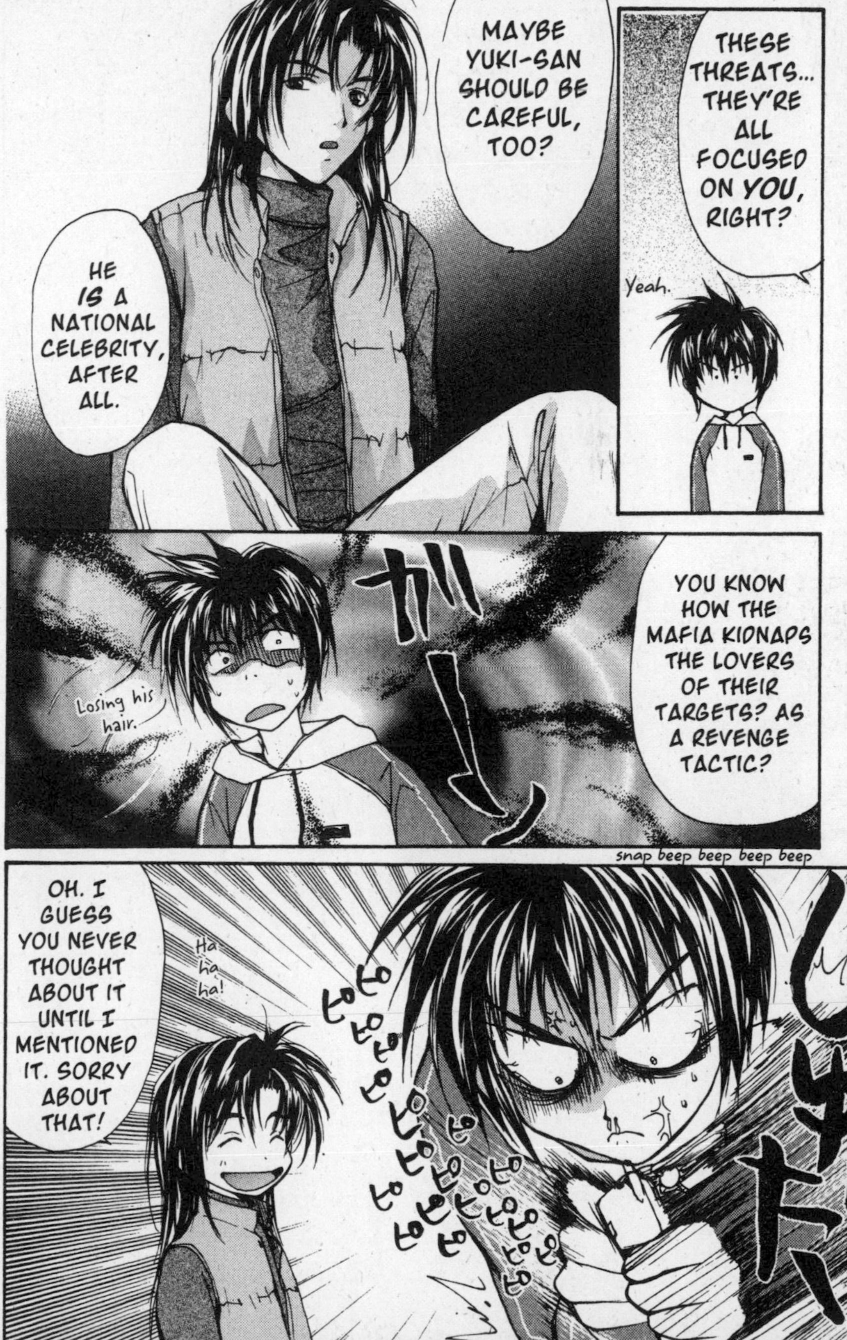
THESE THREATS... THEY'RE ALL FOCUSED ON *YOU*, RIGHT?
Yeah.
MAYBE YUKI-SAN SHOULD BE CAREFUL, TOO?
HE *IS* A NATIONAL CELEBRITY, AFTER ALL.
YOU KNOW HOW THE MAFIA KIDNAPS THE LOVERS OF THEIR TARGETS? AS A REVENGE TACTIC?
Losing his hair.
snap beep beep beep beep
OH. I GUESS YOU NEVER THOUGHT ABOUT IT UNTIL I MENTIONED IT. SORRY ABOUT THAT!
Ha ha ha!

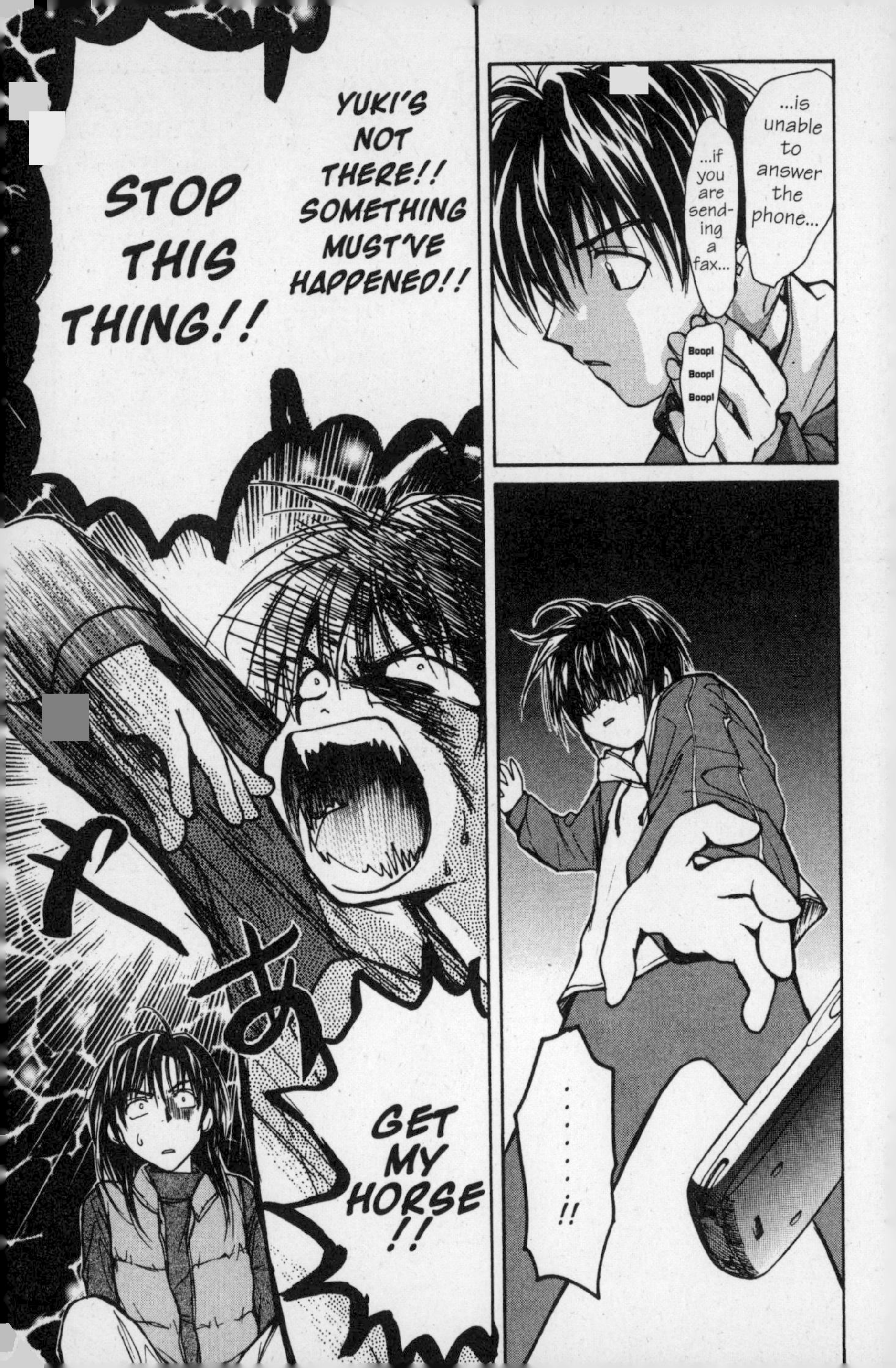
...is unable to answer the phone...
...if you are sending a fax...
Boop! Boop! Boop!
......!!
YUKI'S NOT THERE!! SOMETHING MUST'VE HAPPENED!!
STOP THIS THING!!
GET MY HORSE!!

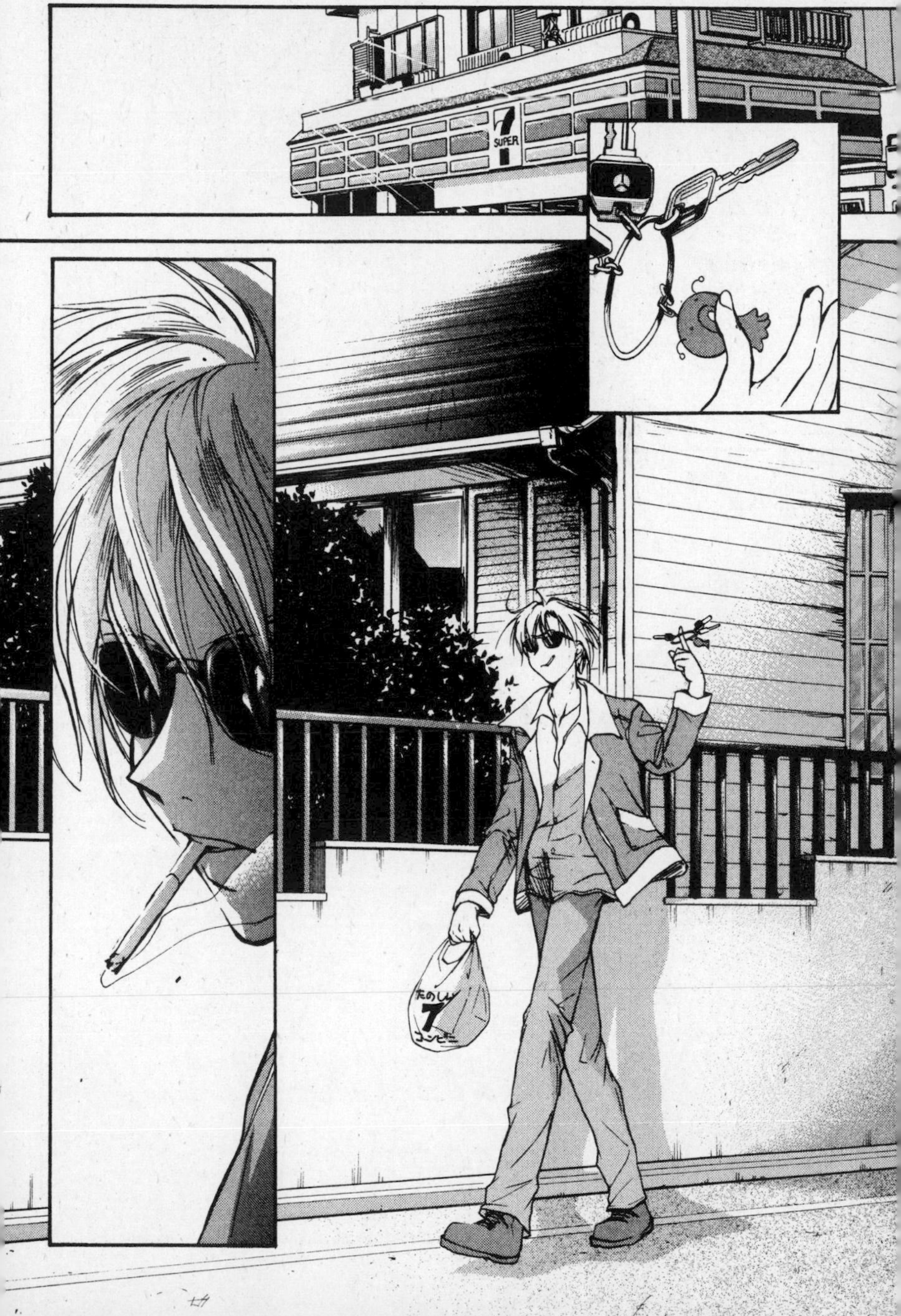
7
SUPER
たのし
7
コンビニ

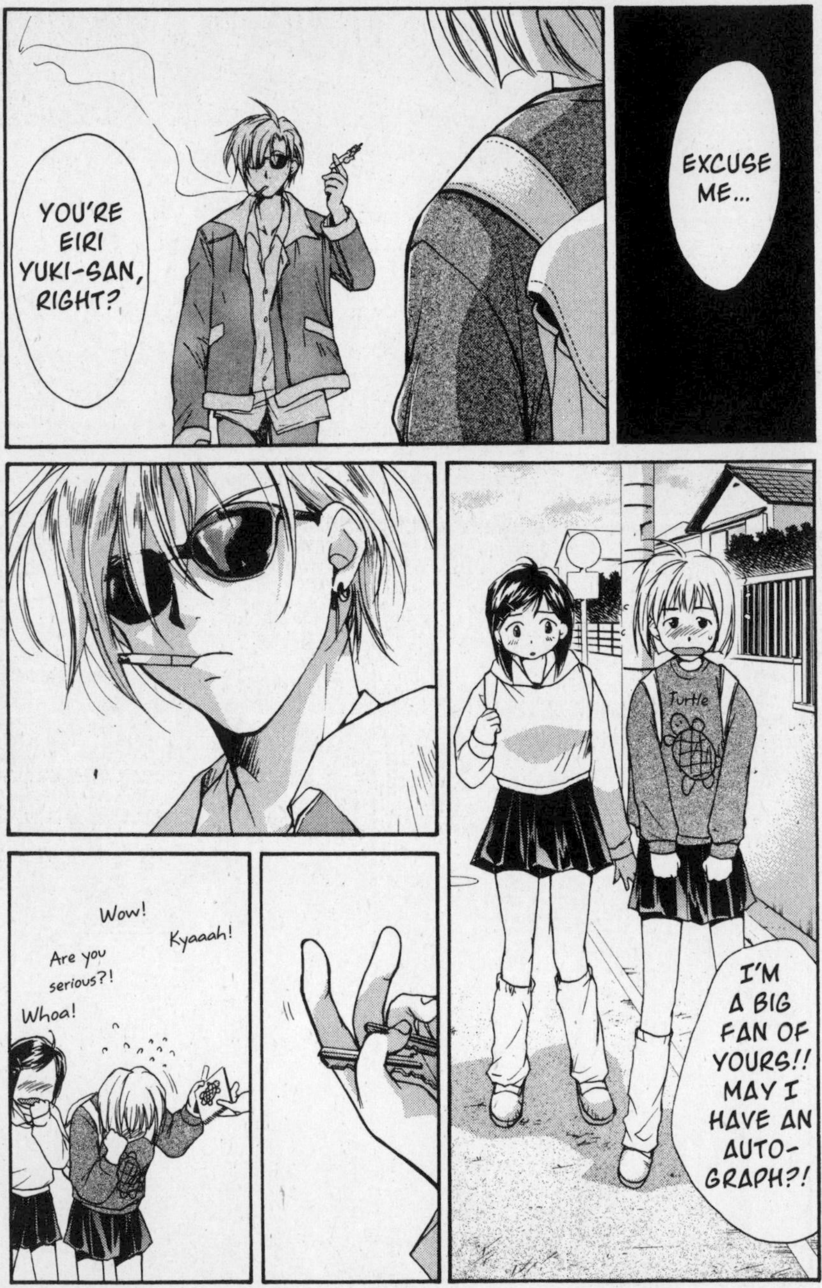
EXCUSE ME...
YOU'RE EIRI YUKI-SAN, RIGHT?
I'M A BIG FAN OF YOURS!! MAY I HAVE AN AUTO-GRAPH?!
Turtle
Wow!
Kyaaah!
Are you serious?!
Whoa!

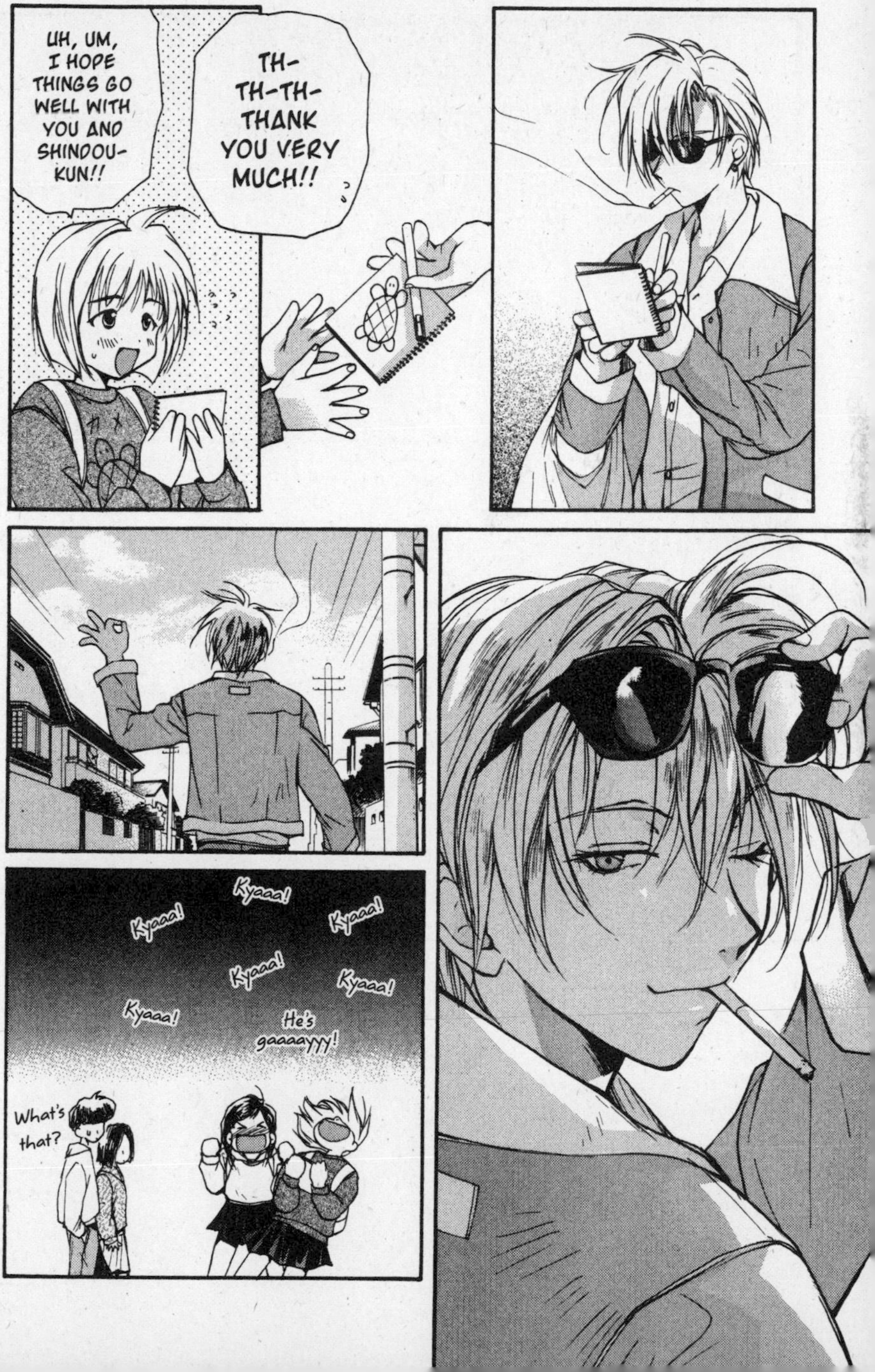
TH-TH-TH-THANK YOU VERY MUCH!!
UH, UM, I HOPE THINGS GO WELL WITH YOU AND SHINDOU-KUN!!
Kyaaa!
Kyaaa!
Kyaaa!
Kyaaa!
Kyaaa!
Kyaaa!
He's gaaaayyy!
What's that?

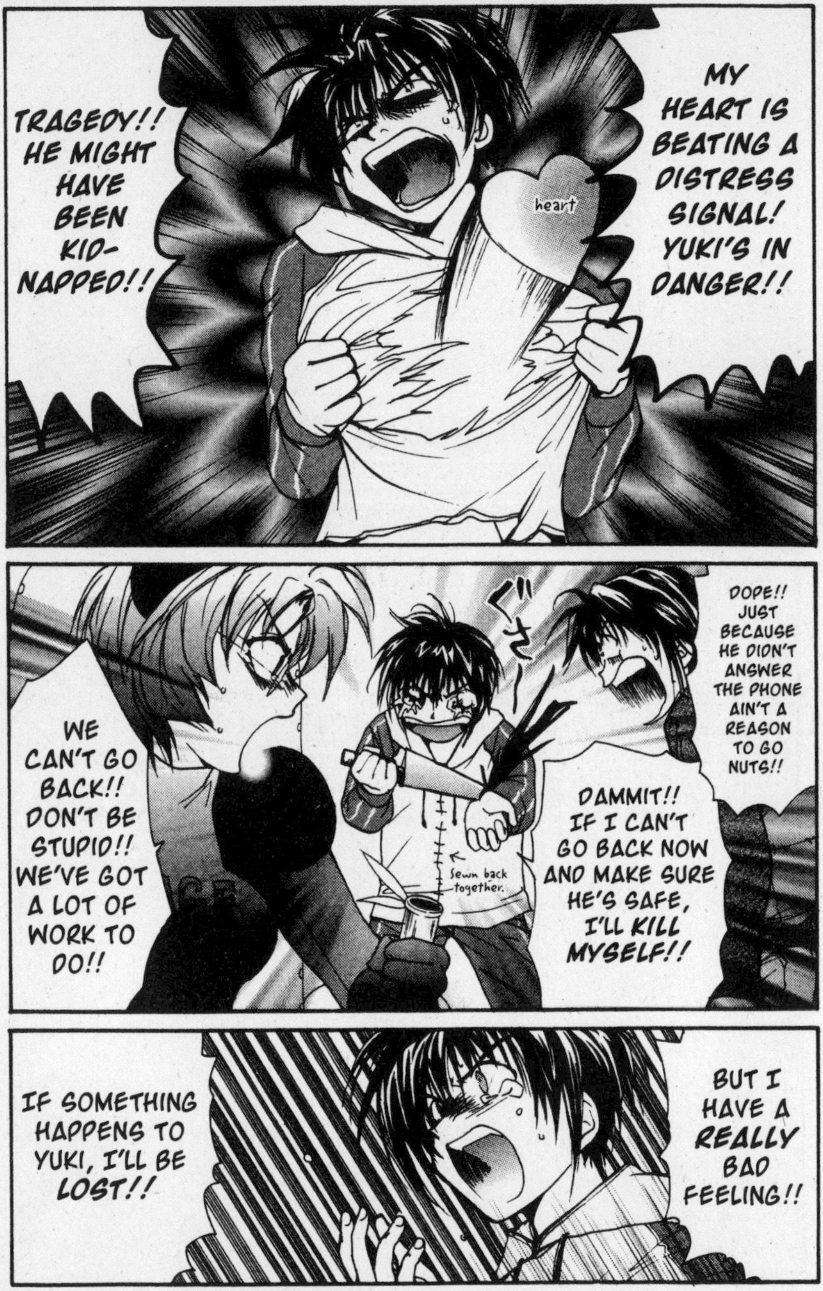

MY HEART IS BEATING A DISTRESS SIGNAL! YUKI'S IN DANGER!!
heart
TRAGEDY!! HE MIGHT HAVE BEEN KID-NAPPED!!
DOPE!! JUST BECAUSE HE DIDN'T ANSWER THE PHONE AIN'T A REASON TO GO NUTS!!
DAMMIT!! IF I CAN'T GO BACK NOW AND MAKE SURE HE'S SAFE, I'LL KILL MYSELF!!
Sewn back together.
WE CAN'T GO BACK!! DON'T BE STUPID!! WE'VE GOT A LOT OF WORK TO DO!!
BUT I HAVE A REALLY BAD FEELING!!
IF SOMETHING HAPPENS TO YUKI, I'LL BE LOST!!

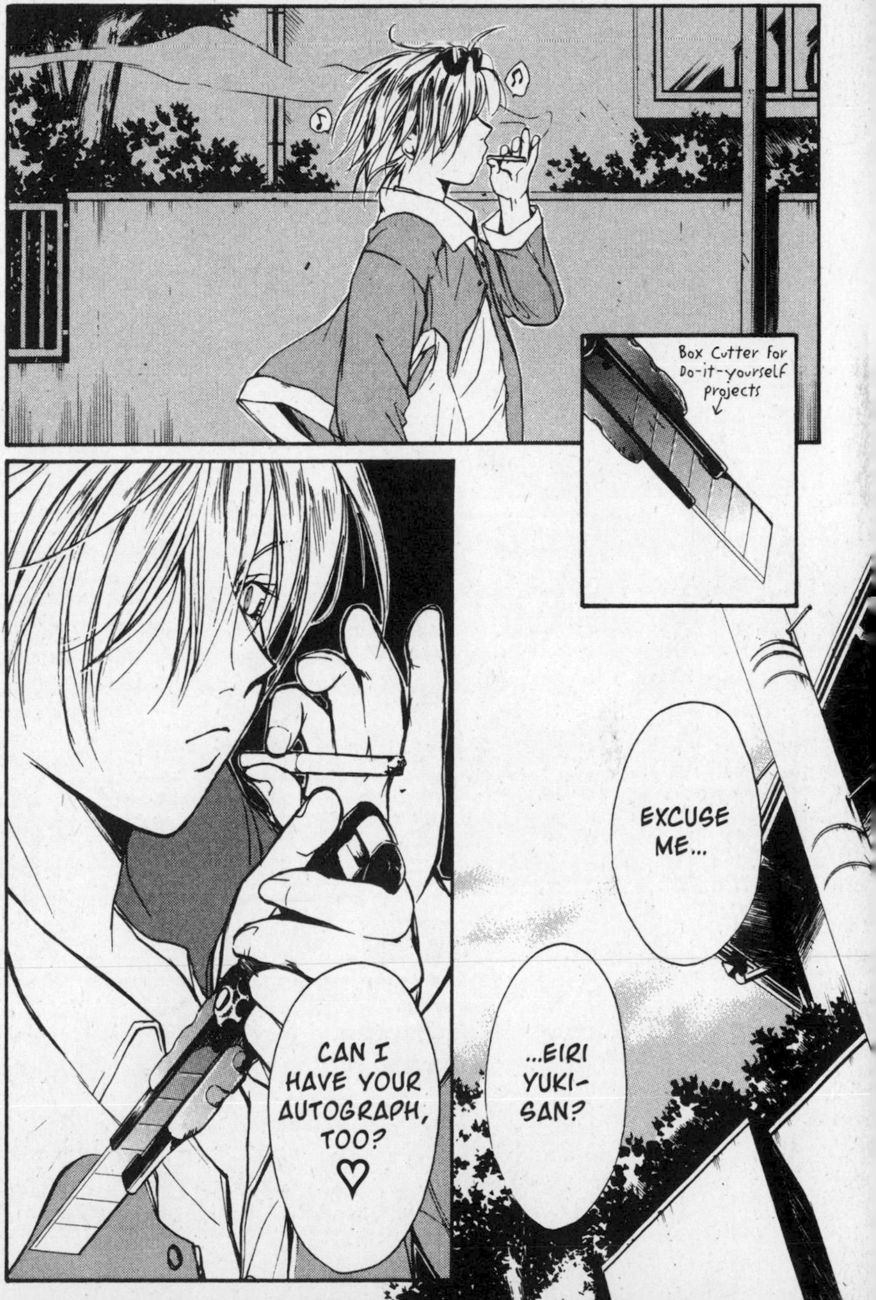
Box Cutter for Do-it-yourself projects
EXCUSE ME...
...EIRI YUKI-SAN?
CAN I HAVE YOUR AUTOGRAPH, TOO? ♡

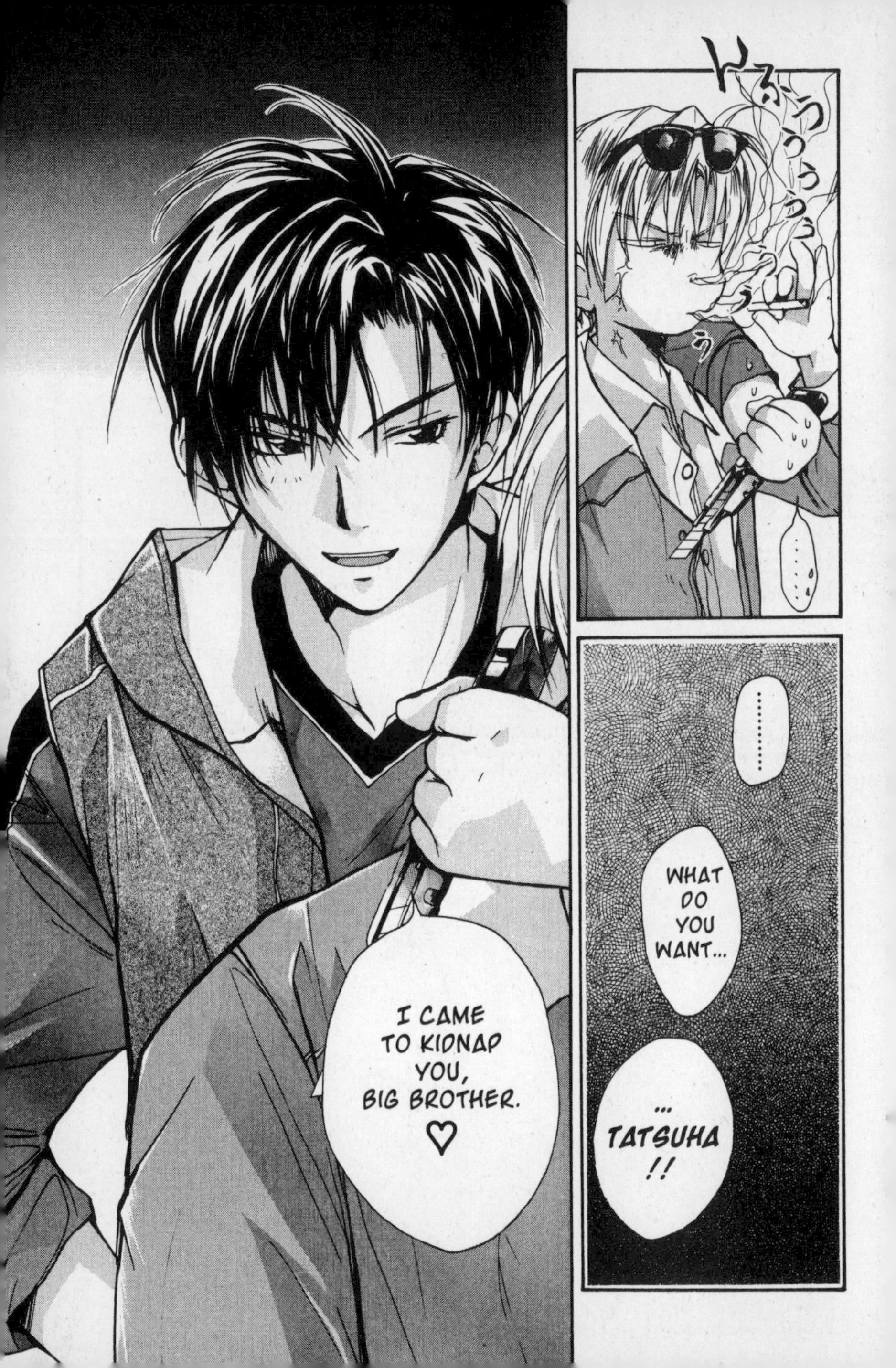
......
......
WHAT DO YOU WANT...
... TATSUHA !!
I CAME TO KIDNAP YOU, BIG BROTHER. ♥

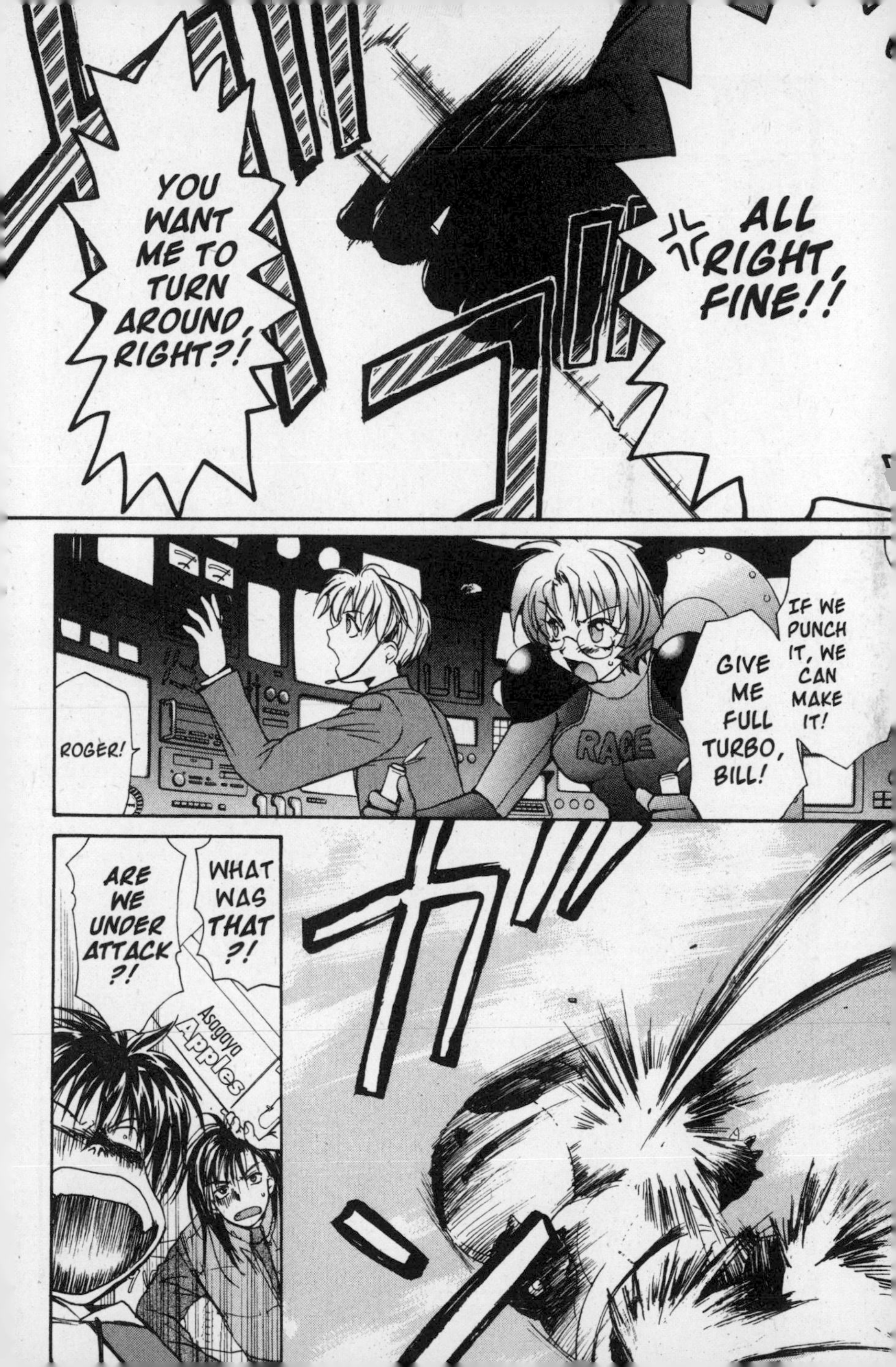
ALL RIGHT, FINE!!
YOU WANT ME TO TURN AROUND RIGHT?!
IF WE PUNCH IT, WE CAN MAKE IT!
GIVE ME FULL TURBO, BILL!
ROGER!
WHAT WAS THAT?!
ARE WE UNDER ATTACK?!
Asagaya Apples

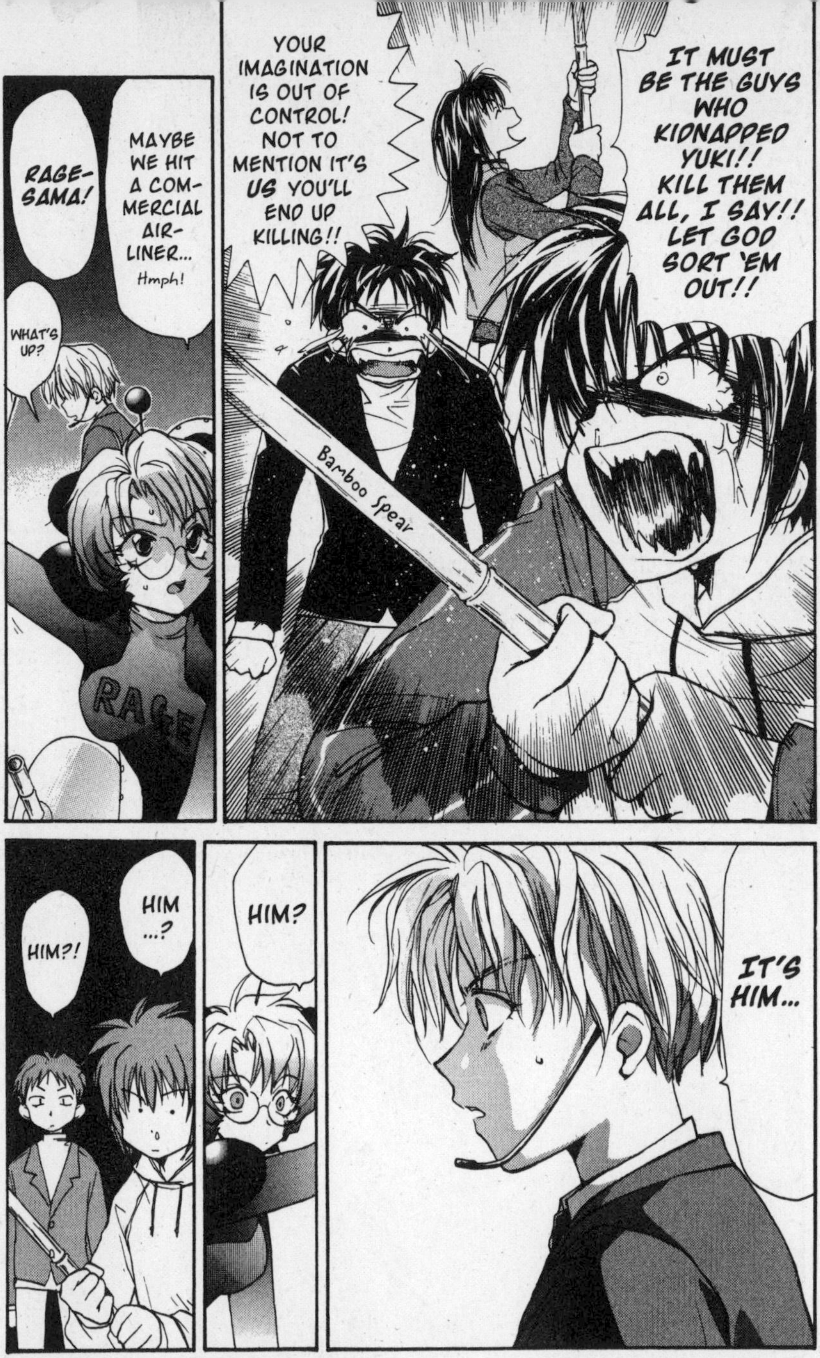

IT MUST BE THE GUYS WHO KIDNAPPED YUKI!! KILL THEM ALL, I SAY!! LET GOD SORT 'EM OUT!!
YOUR IMAGINATION IS OUT OF CONTROL! NOT TO MENTION IT'S US YOU'LL END UP KILLING!!
Bamboo Spear
MAYBE WE HIT A COM-MERCIAL AIR-LINER...
Hmph!
RAGE-SAMA!
WHAT'S UP?
RAGE
IT'S HIM...
HIM?
HIM...?
HIM?!

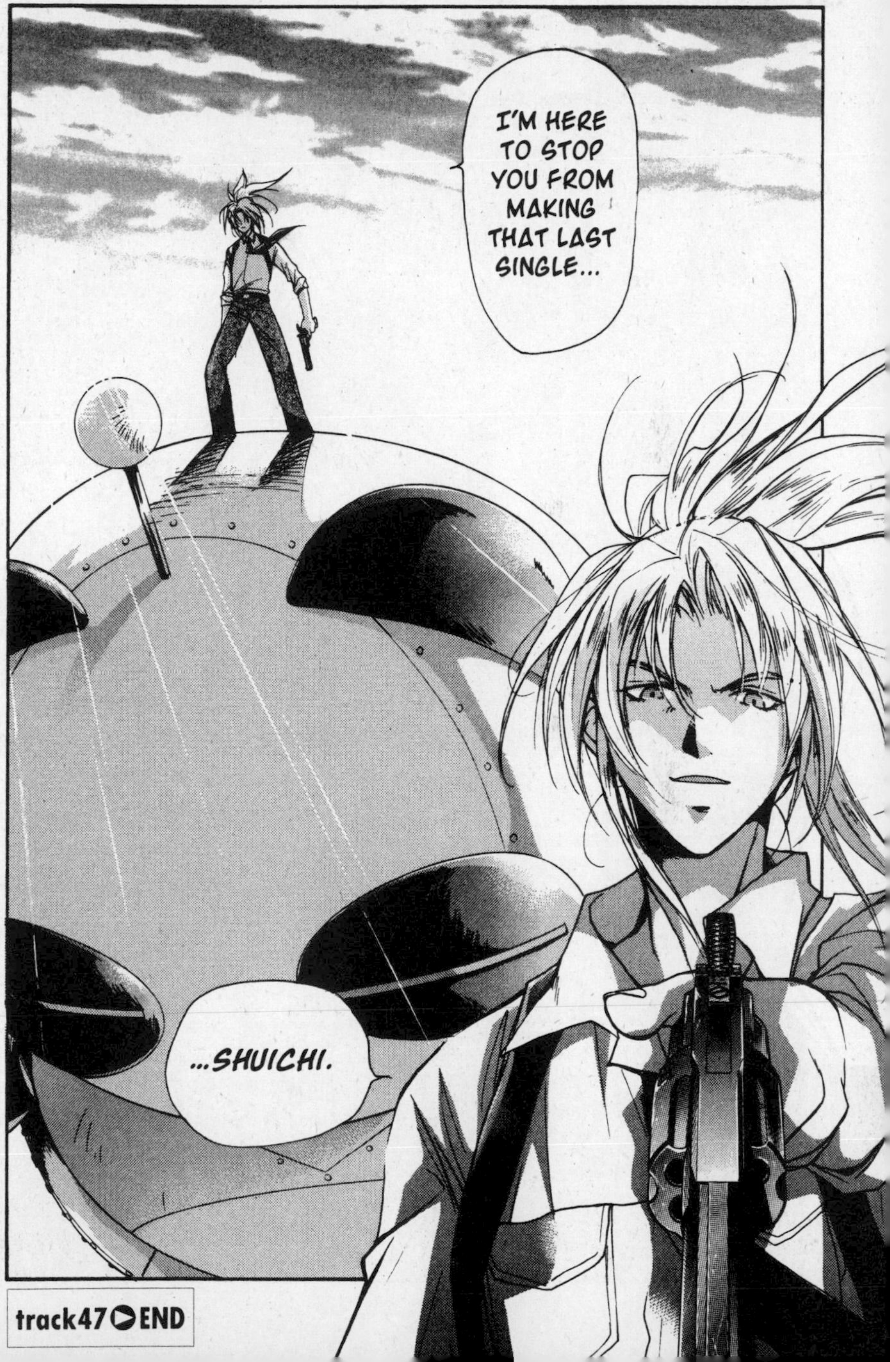
I'M HERE TO STOP YOU FROM MAKING THAT LAST SINGLE...
...SHUICHI.

track47 ▶ END

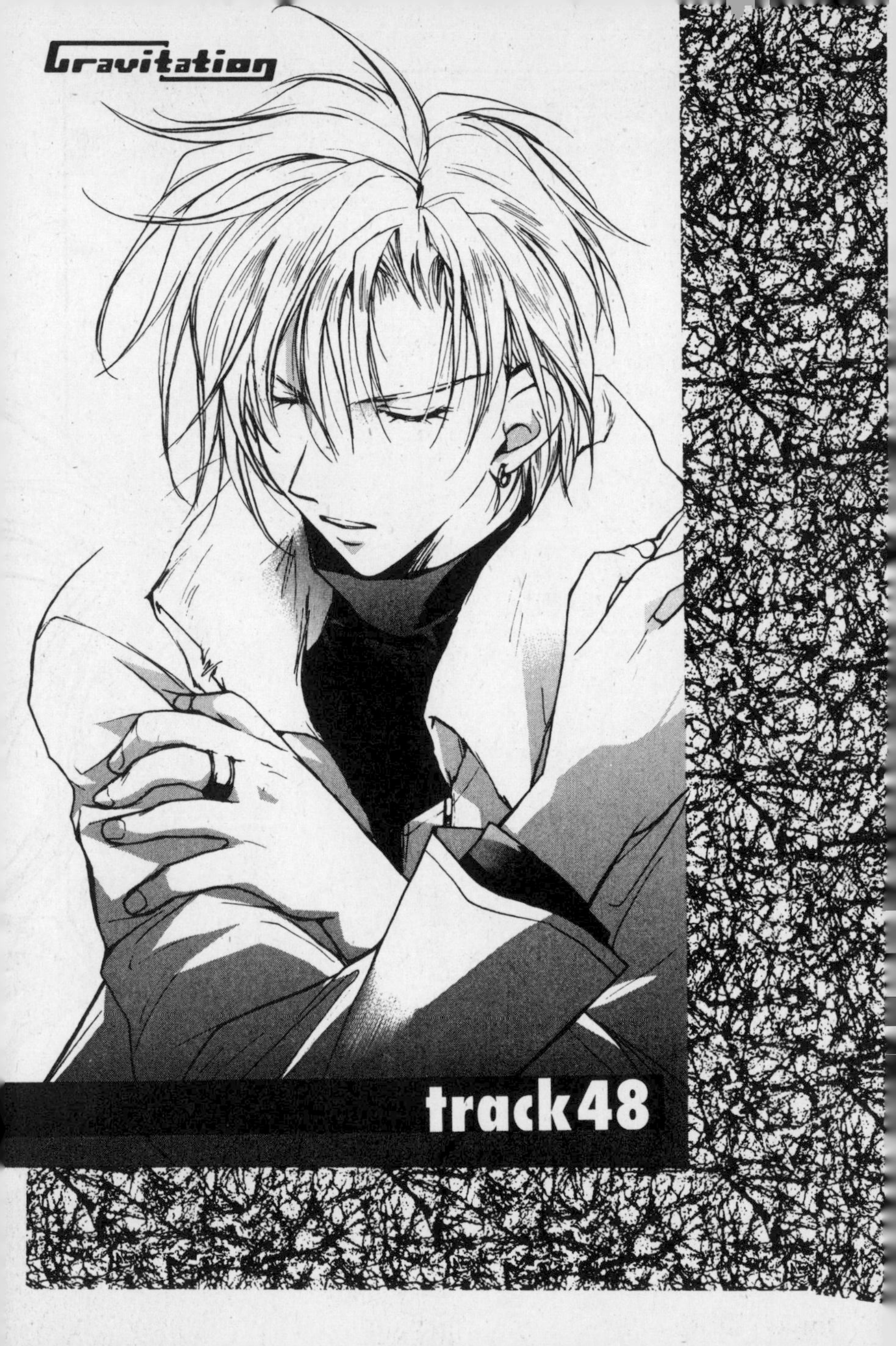
Gravitation
track 48

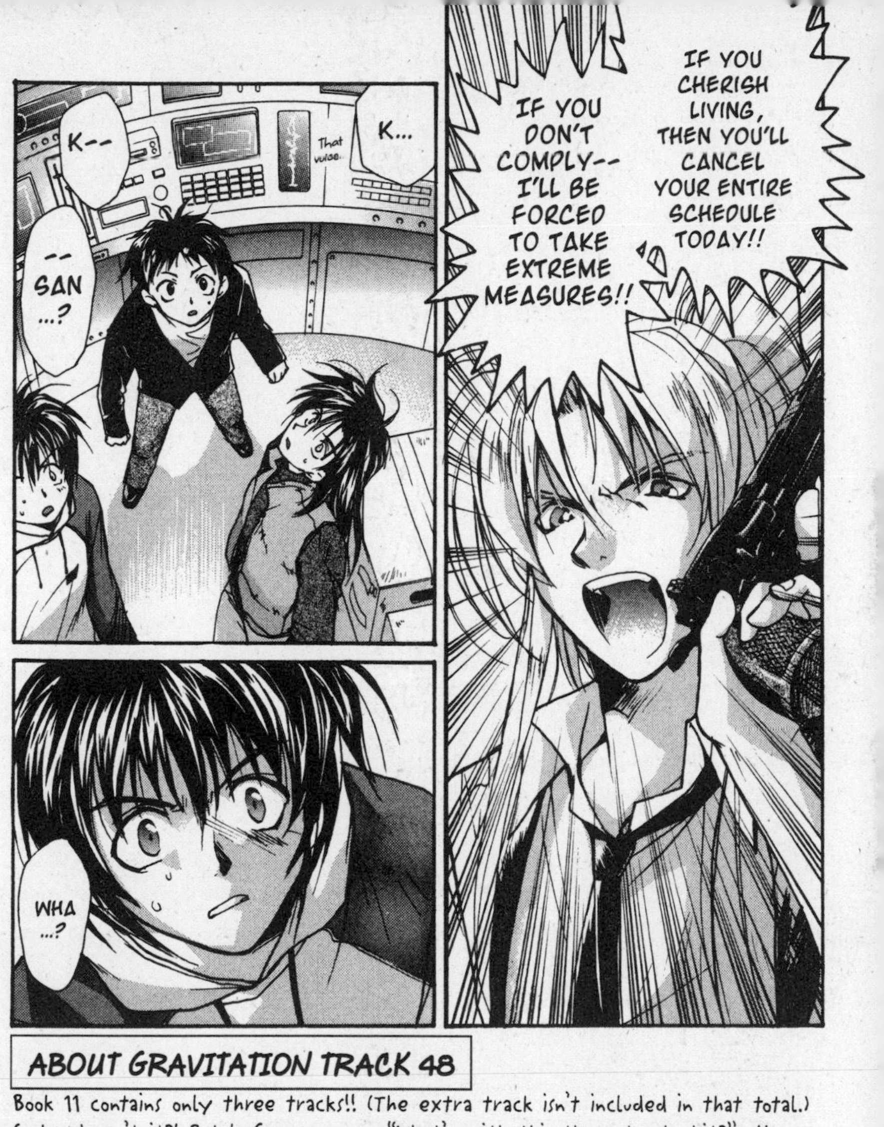
IF YOU CHERISH LIVING, THEN YOU'LL CANCEL YOUR ENTIRE SCHEDULE TODAY!!
IF YOU DON'T COMPLY-- I'LL BE FORCED TO TAKE EXTREME MEASURES!!
K...
That voice..
K--
--SAN ...?
WHA ...?

## ABOUT GRAVITATION TRACK 48

Book 11 contains only three tracks!! (The extra track isn't included in that total.) Sucks, doesn't it?! But before you say "What's with this three track shit?" allow me to explain!! It's not enough!! The second track is 80 pages, but compared to that, the third track is only 24 pages!! Somehow, I made it to 100 pages, so I think I can just squeak by!! I worked hard to draw these pages, so please read track 48 as well! I'm going to be causing trouble for a lot of people from here on out. So please, don't give up on me...! Ughhh...

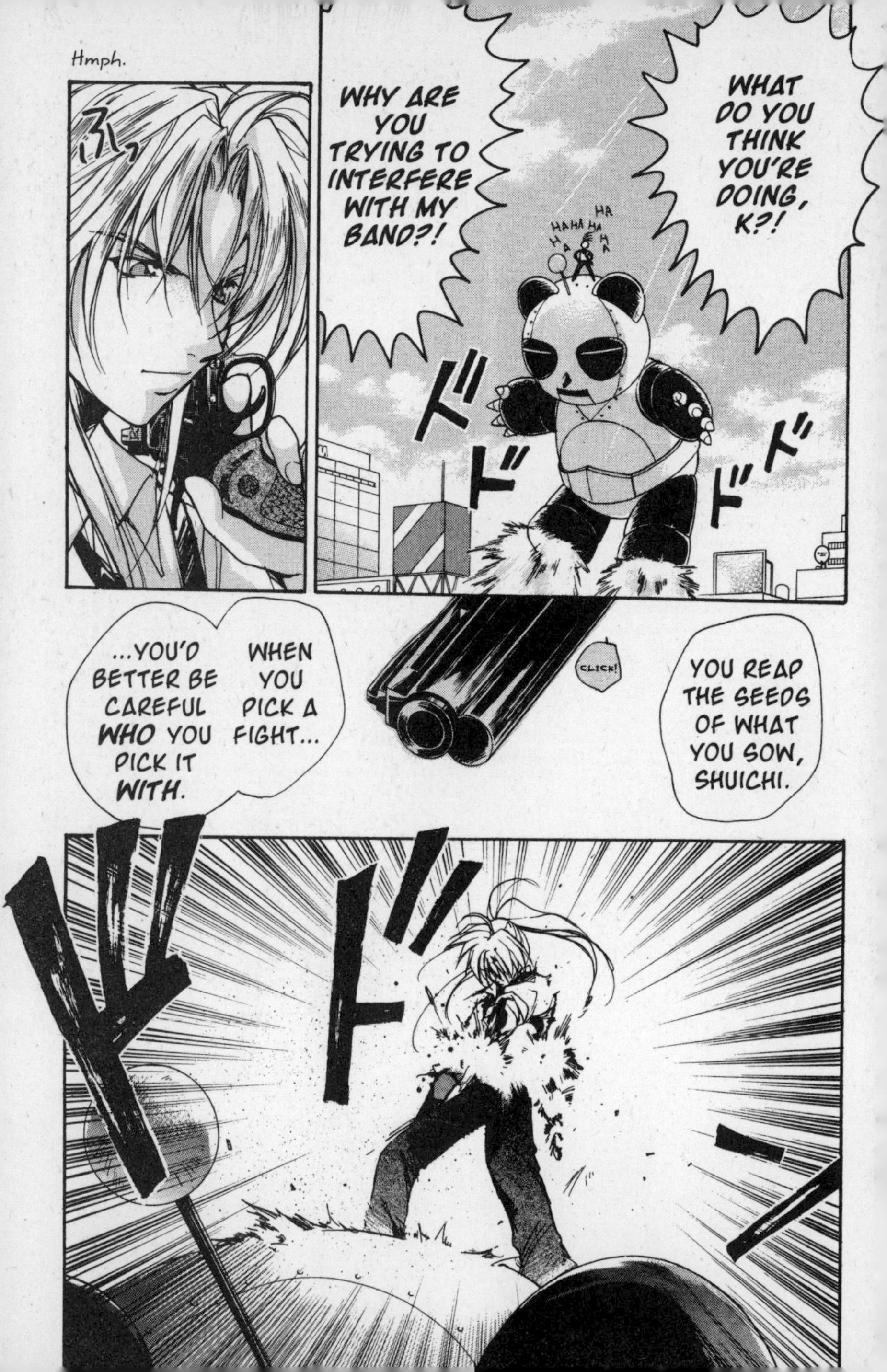
WHAT DO YOU THINK YOU'RE DOING, K?!
WHY ARE YOU TRYING TO INTERFERE WITH MY BAND?!
HA HAHA HA HA HA
Hmph.
YOU REAP THE SEEDS OF WHAT YOU SOW, SHUICHI.
CLICK!
WHEN YOU PICK A FIGHT...
...YOU'D BETTER BE CAREFUL WHO YOU PICK IT WITH.

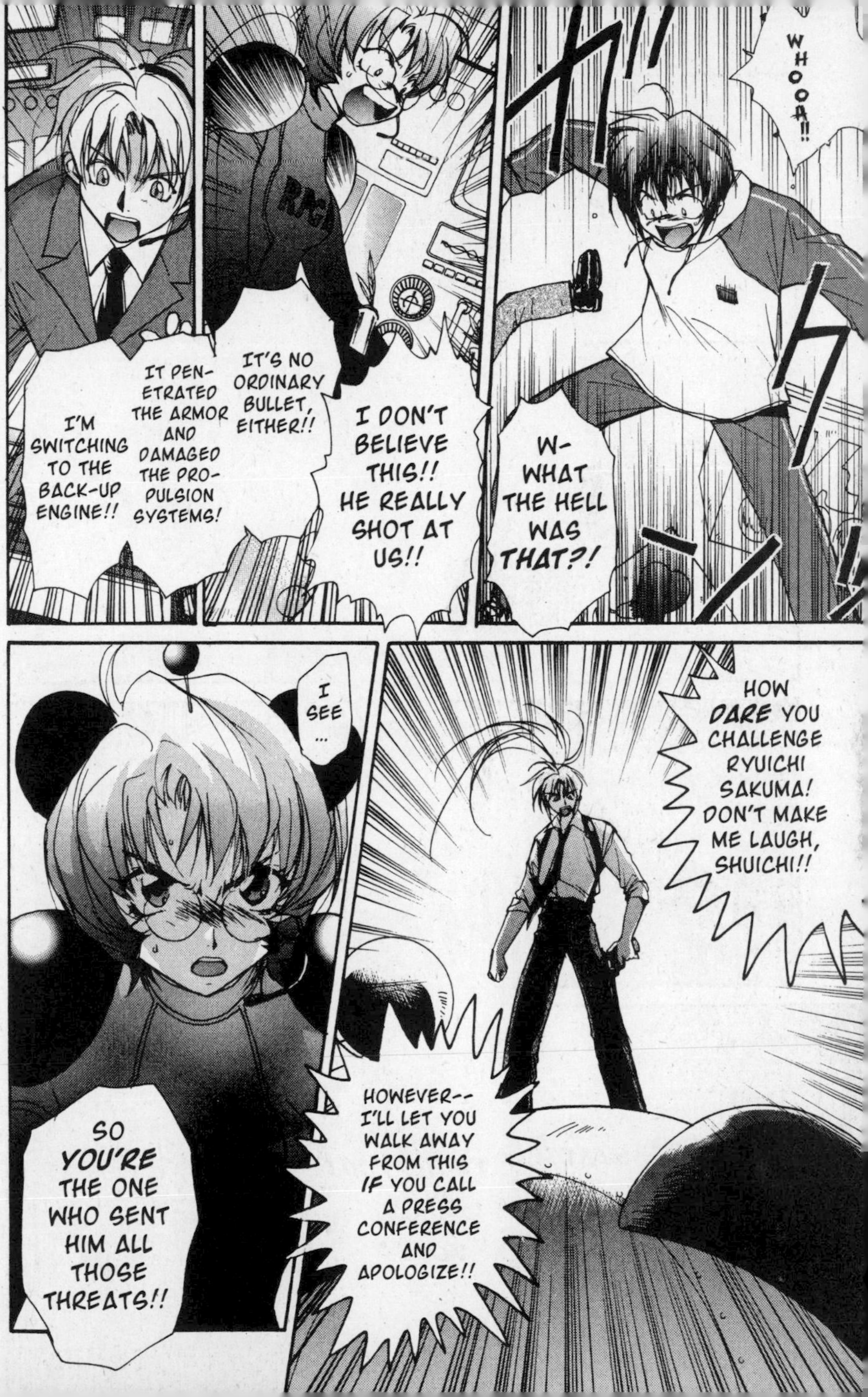
WHOOA!!
W- WHAT THE HELL WAS THAT?!
I DON'T BELIEVE THIS!! HE REALLY SHOT AT US!!
IT'S NO ORDINARY BULLET, EITHER!!
IT PENETRATED THE ARMOR AND DAMAGED THE PROPULSION SYSTEMS!
I'M SWITCHING TO THE BACK-UP ENGINE!!
HOW DARE YOU CHALLENGE RYUICHI SAKUMA! DON'T MAKE ME LAUGH, SHUICHI!!
HOWEVER-- I'LL LET YOU WALK AWAY FROM THIS IF YOU CALL A PRESS CONFERENCE AND APOLOGIZE!!
I SEE ...
SO YOU'RE THE ONE WHO SENT HIM ALL THOSE THREATS!!

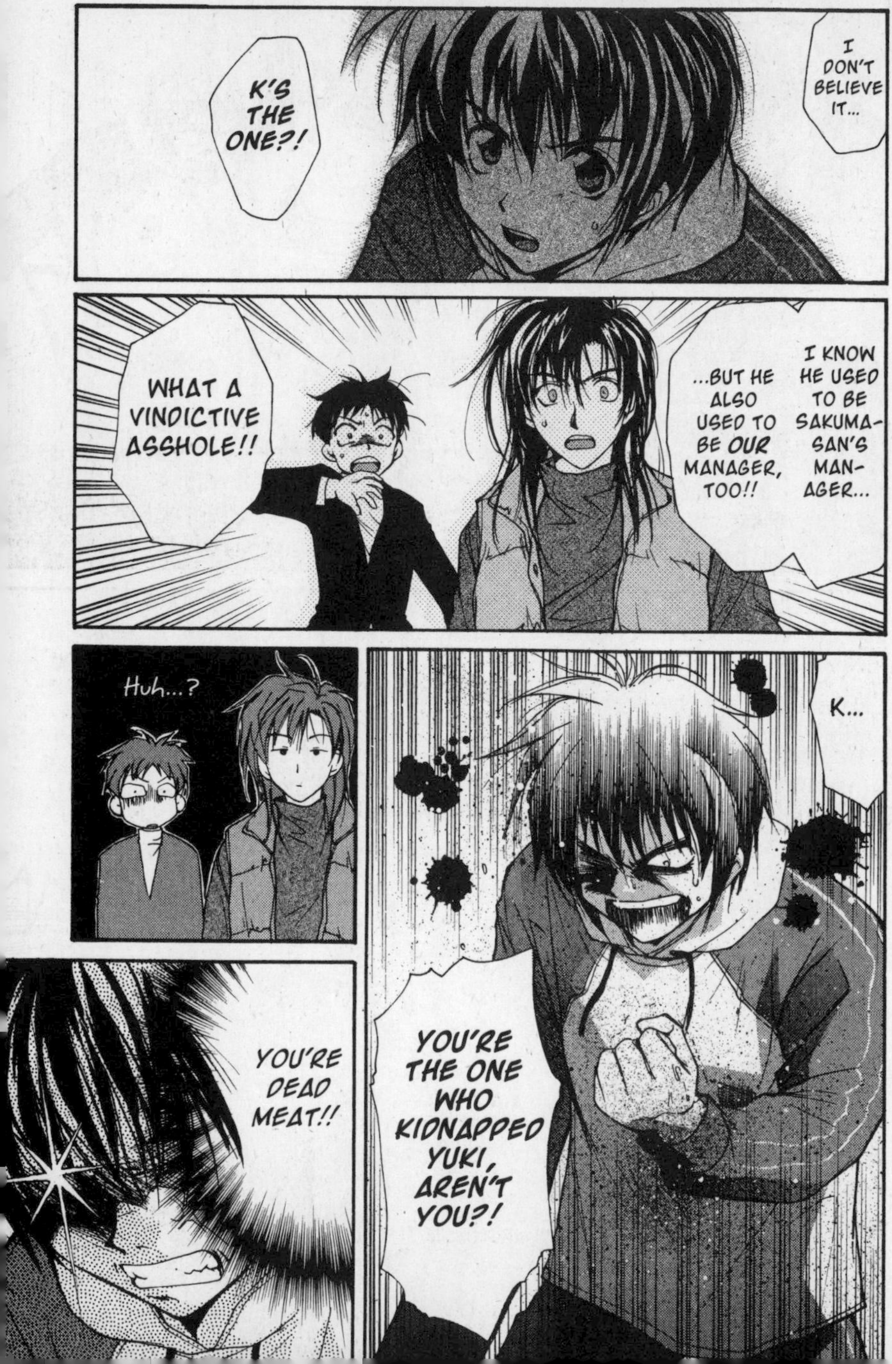
I DON'T BELIEVE IT...
K'S THE ONE?!
I KNOW HE USED TO BE SAKUMA-SAN'S MANAGER...
...BUT HE ALSO USED TO BE OUR MANAGER, TOO!!
WHAT A VINDICTIVE ASSHOLE!!
K...
YOU'RE THE ONE WHO KIDNAPPED YUKI, AREN'T YOU?!
Huh...?
YOU'RE DEAD MEAT!!

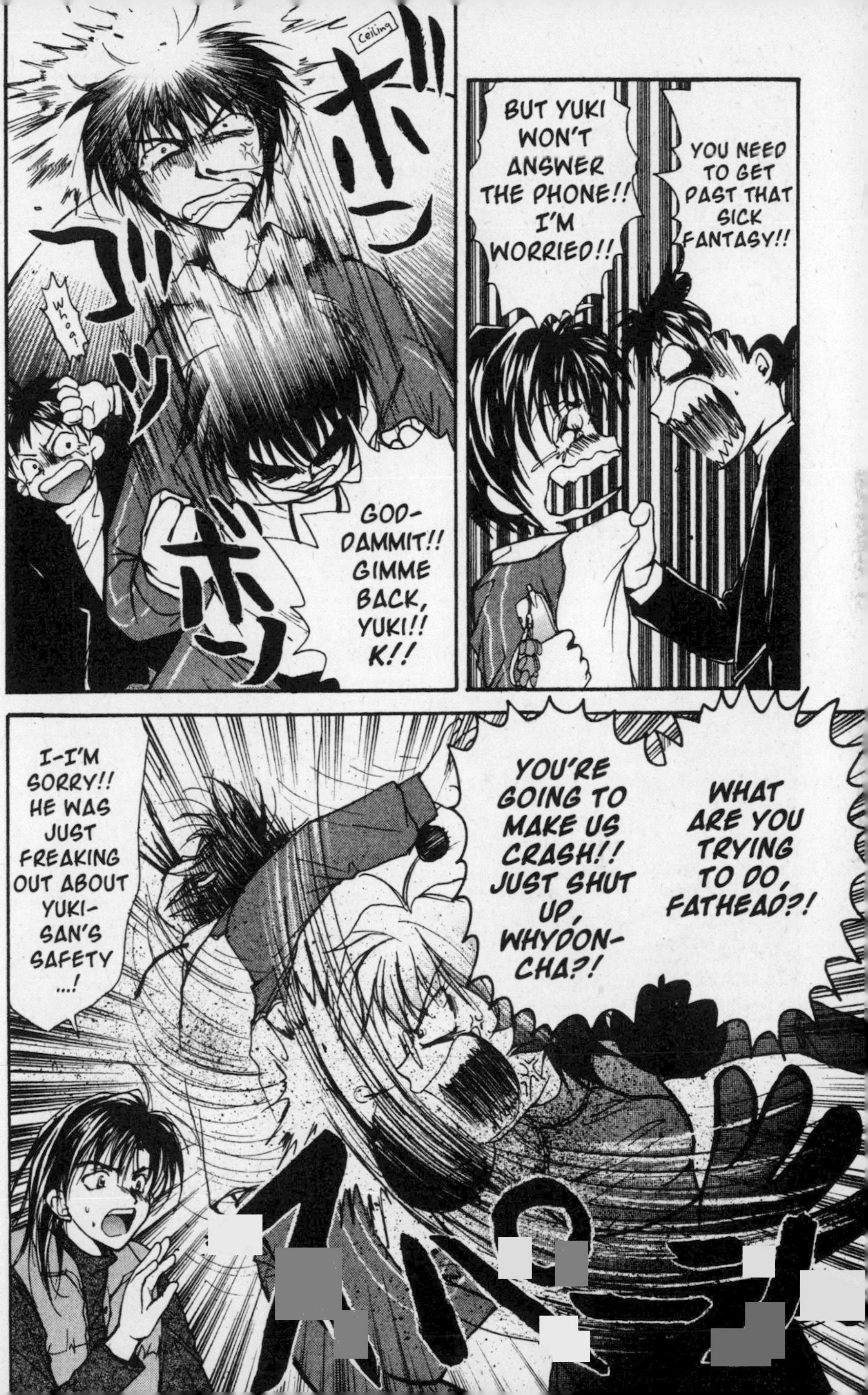
YOU NEED TO GET PAST THAT SICK FANTASY!!
BUT YUKI WON'T ANSWER THE PHONE!! I'M WORRIED!!
Ceiling
Whoa!
GOD-DAMMIT!! GIMME BACK, YUKI!! K!!
WHAT ARE YOU TRYING TO DO, FATHEAD?!
YOU'RE GOING TO MAKE US CRASH!! JUST SHUT UP, WHYDON-CHA?!
I-I'M SORRY!! HE WAS JUST FREAKING OUT ABOUT YUKI-SAN'S SAFETY ...!

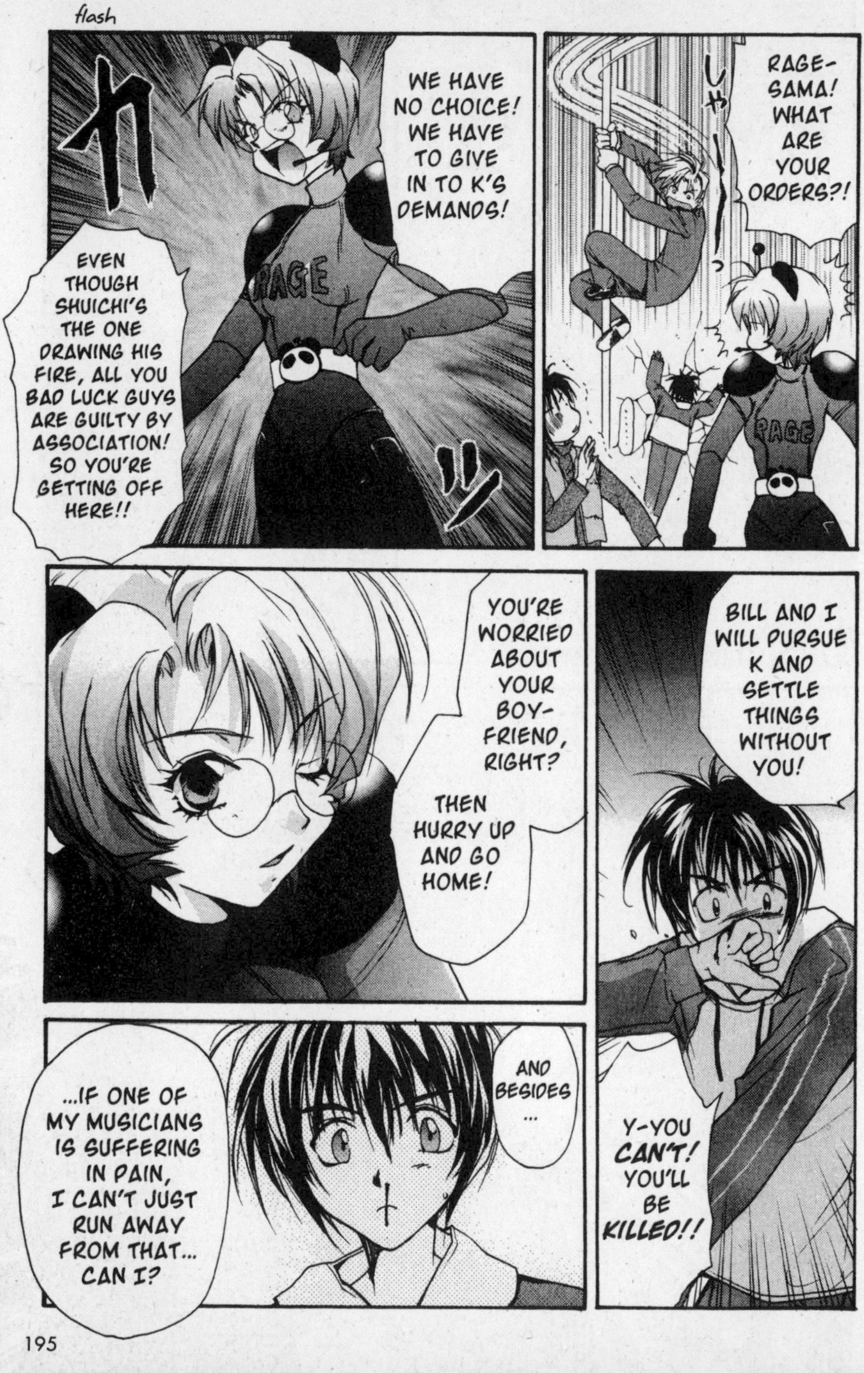
RAGE-SAMA! WHAT ARE YOUR ORDERS?!
flash
WE HAVE NO CHOICE! WE HAVE TO GIVE IN TO K'S DEMANDS!
EVEN THOUGH SHUICHI'S THE ONE DRAWING HIS FIRE, ALL YOU BAD LUCK GUYS ARE GUILTY BY ASSOCIATION! SO YOU'RE GETTING OFF HERE!!
BILL AND I WILL PURSUE K AND SETTLE THINGS WITHOUT YOU!
Y-YOU **CAN'T**! YOU'LL BE **KILLED**!!
YOU'RE WORRIED ABOUT YOUR BOY-FRIEND, RIGHT?
THEN HURRY UP AND GO HOME!
AND BESIDES...
...IF ONE OF MY MUSICIANS IS SUFFERING IN PAIN, I CAN'T JUST RUN AWAY FROM THAT... CAN I?

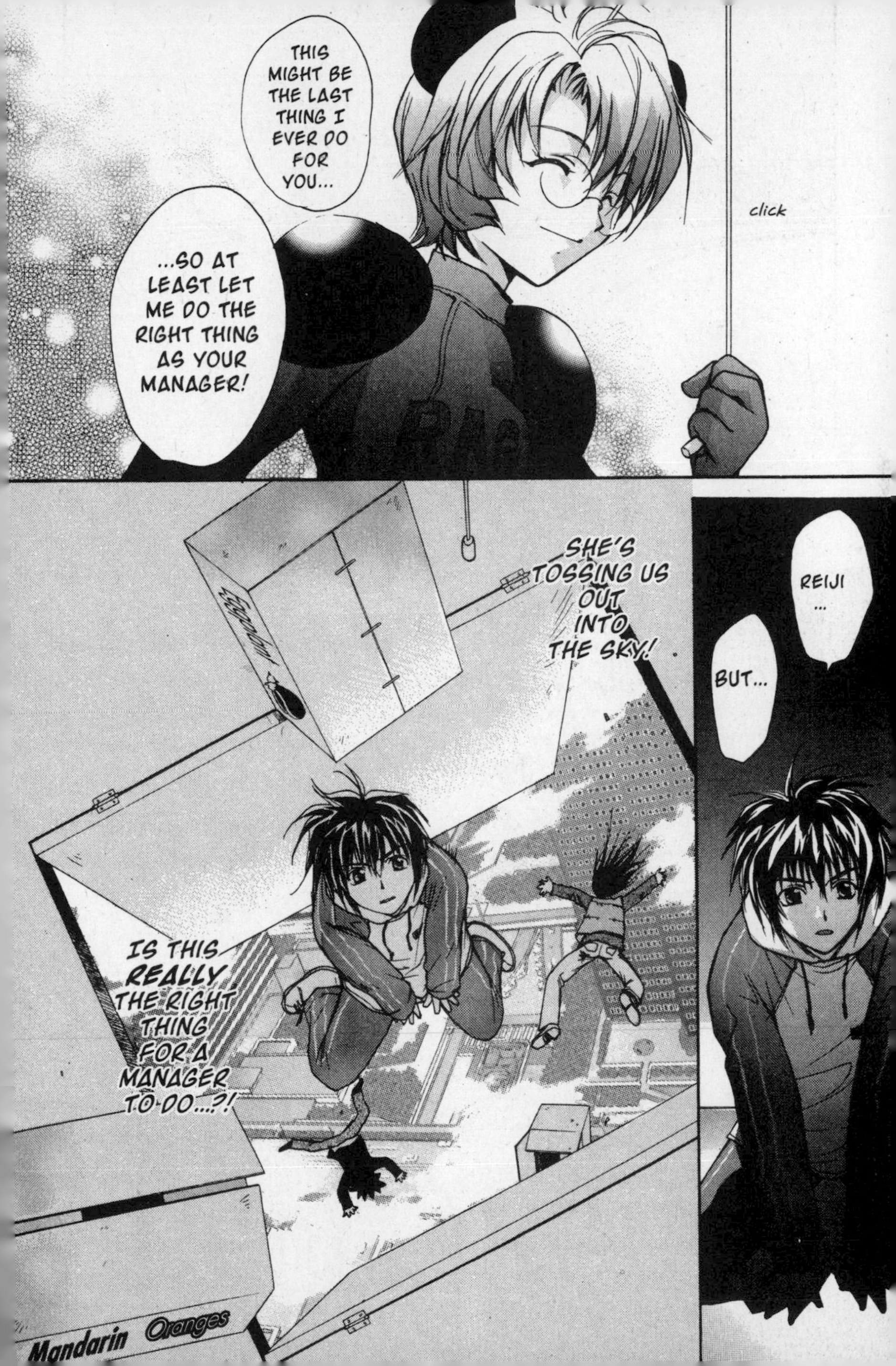
THIS MIGHT BE THE LAST THING I EVER DO FOR YOU...
...SO AT LEAST LET ME DO THE RIGHT THING AS YOUR MANAGER!
click
REIJI ...
BUT...
SHE'S TOSSING US OUT INTO THE SKY!
IS THIS REALLY THE RIGHT THING FOR A MANAGER TO DO...?!
Mandarin Oranges

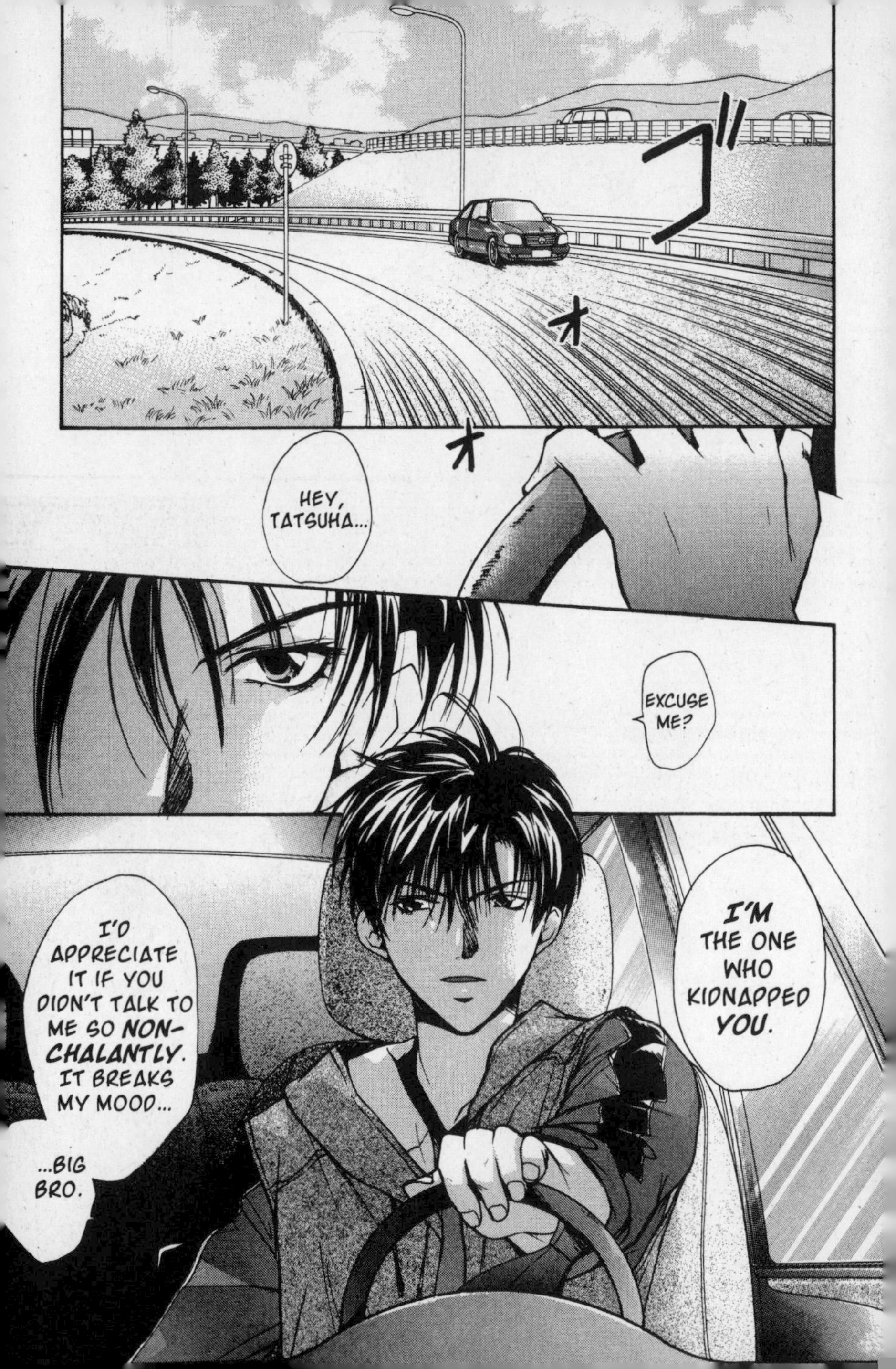
ゴ
HEY, TATSUHA...
EXCUSE ME?
I'M THE ONE WHO KIDNAPPED YOU.
I'D APPRECIATE IT IF YOU DIDN'T TALK TO ME SO NON-CHALANTLY. IT BREAKS MY MOOD...
...BIG BRO.

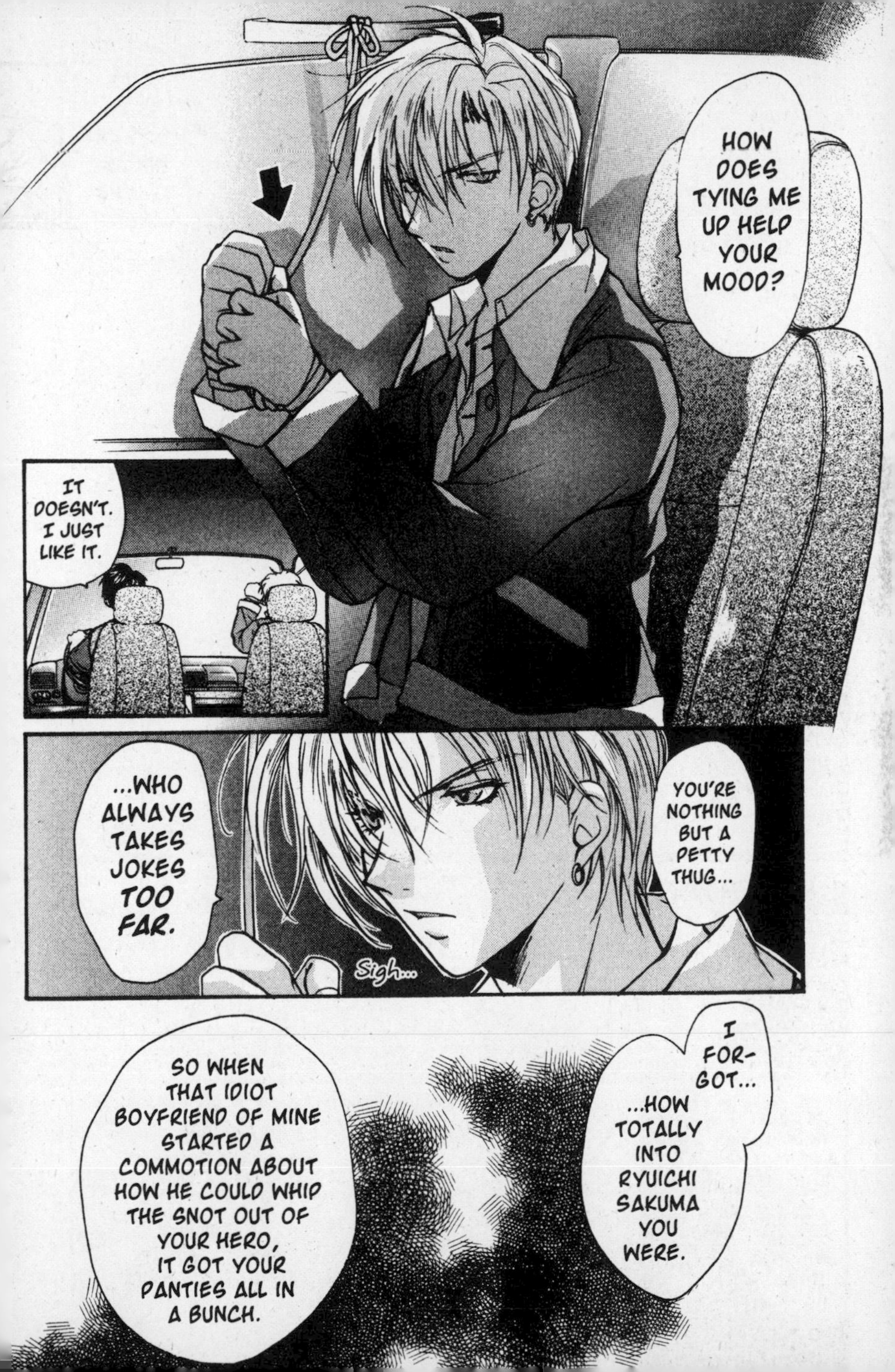
HOW DOES TYING ME UP HELP YOUR MOOD?
IT DOESN'T. I JUST LIKE IT.
YOU'RE NOTHING BUT A PETTY THUG...
...WHO ALWAYS TAKES JOKES TOO FAR.
Sigh...
I FOR-GOT...
...HOW TOTALLY INTO RYUICHI SAKUMA YOU WERE.
SO WHEN THAT IDIOT BOYFRIEND OF MINE STARTED A COMMOTION ABOUT HOW HE COULD WHIP THE SNOT OUT OF YOUR HERO, IT GOT YOUR PANTIES ALL IN A BUNCH.

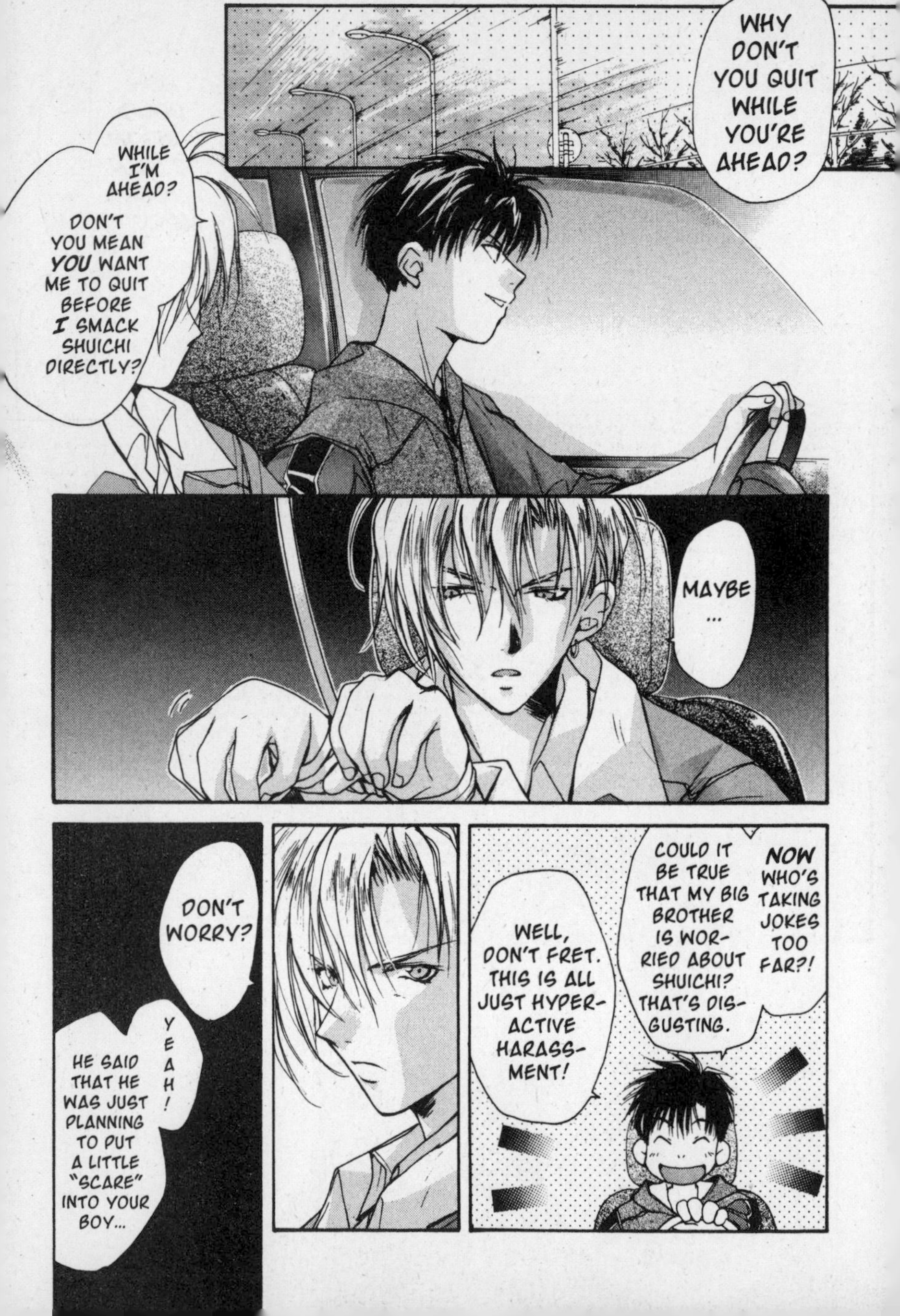
WHY DON'T YOU QUIT WHILE YOU'RE AHEAD?
WHILE I'M AHEAD?
DON'T YOU MEAN *YOU* WANT ME TO QUIT BEFORE *I* SMACK SHUICHI DIRECTLY?
MAYBE...
*NOW* WHO'S TAKING JOKES TOO FAR?!
COULD IT BE TRUE THAT MY BIG BROTHER IS WOR-RIED ABOUT SHUICHI? THAT'S DIS-GUSTING.
WELL, DON'T FRET. THIS IS ALL JUST HYPER-ACTIVE HARASS-MENT!
DON'T WORRY?
YEAH!
HE SAID THAT HE WAS JUST PLANNING TO PUT A LITTLE "SCARE" INTO YOUR BOY...

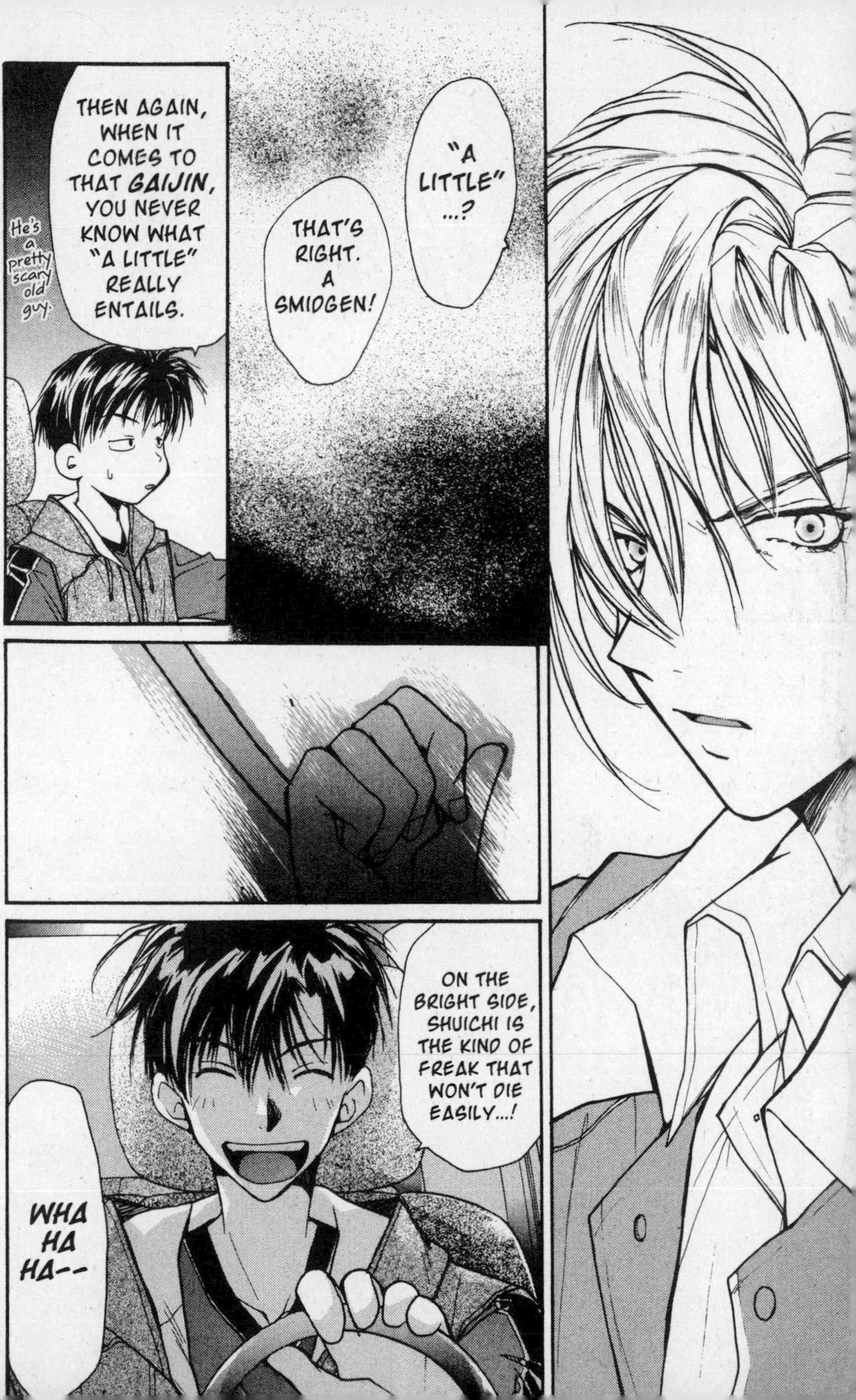
"A LITTLE" ...?
THAT'S RIGHT. A SMIDGEN!
THEN AGAIN, WHEN IT COMES TO THAT GAIJIN, YOU NEVER KNOW WHAT "A LITTLE" REALLY ENTAILS.
He's a pretty scary old guy.
ON THE BRIGHT SIDE, SHUICHI IS THE KIND OF FREAK THAT WON'T DIE EASILY...!
WHA HA HA--

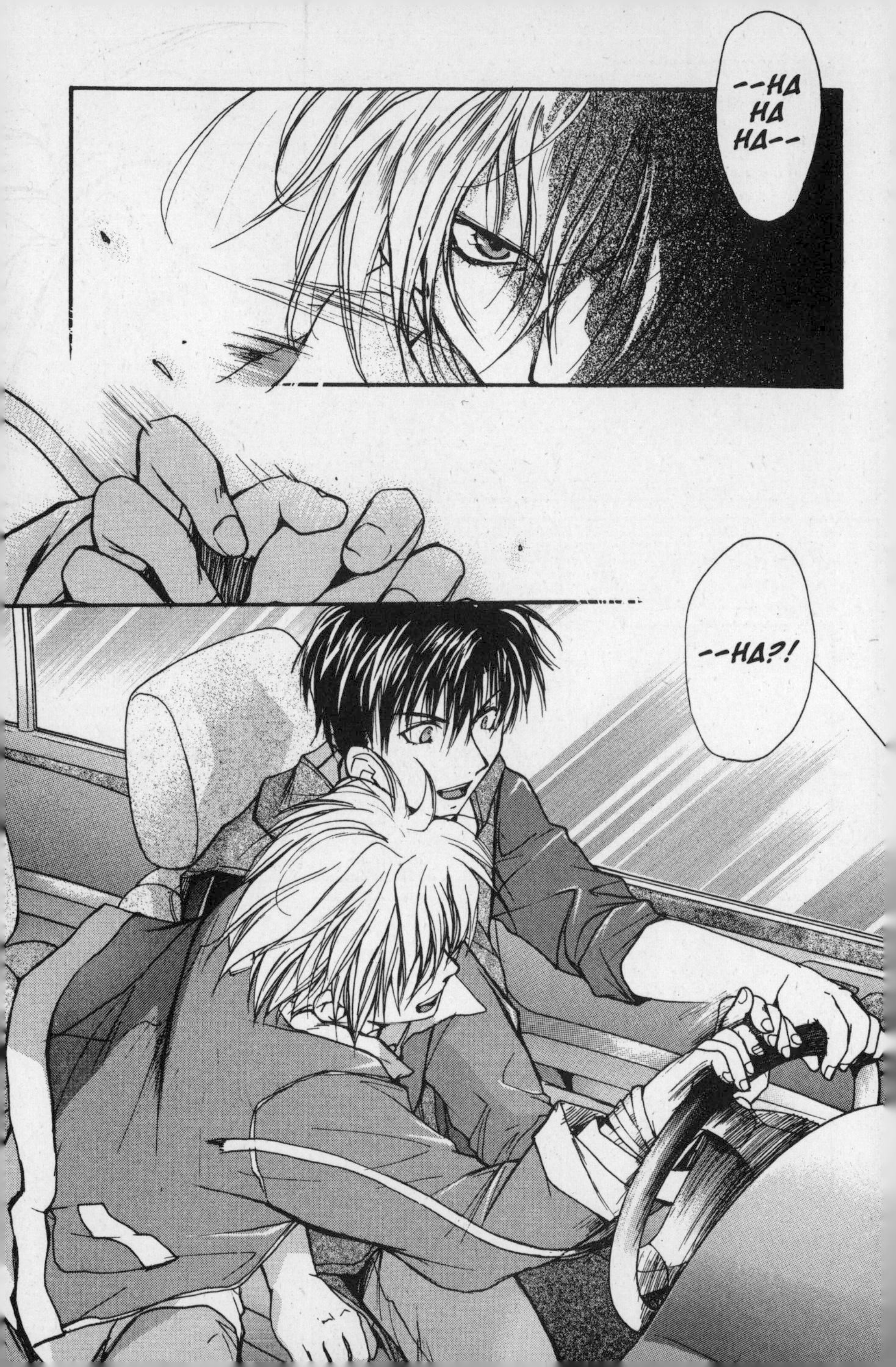
--HA HA HA--
--HA?!

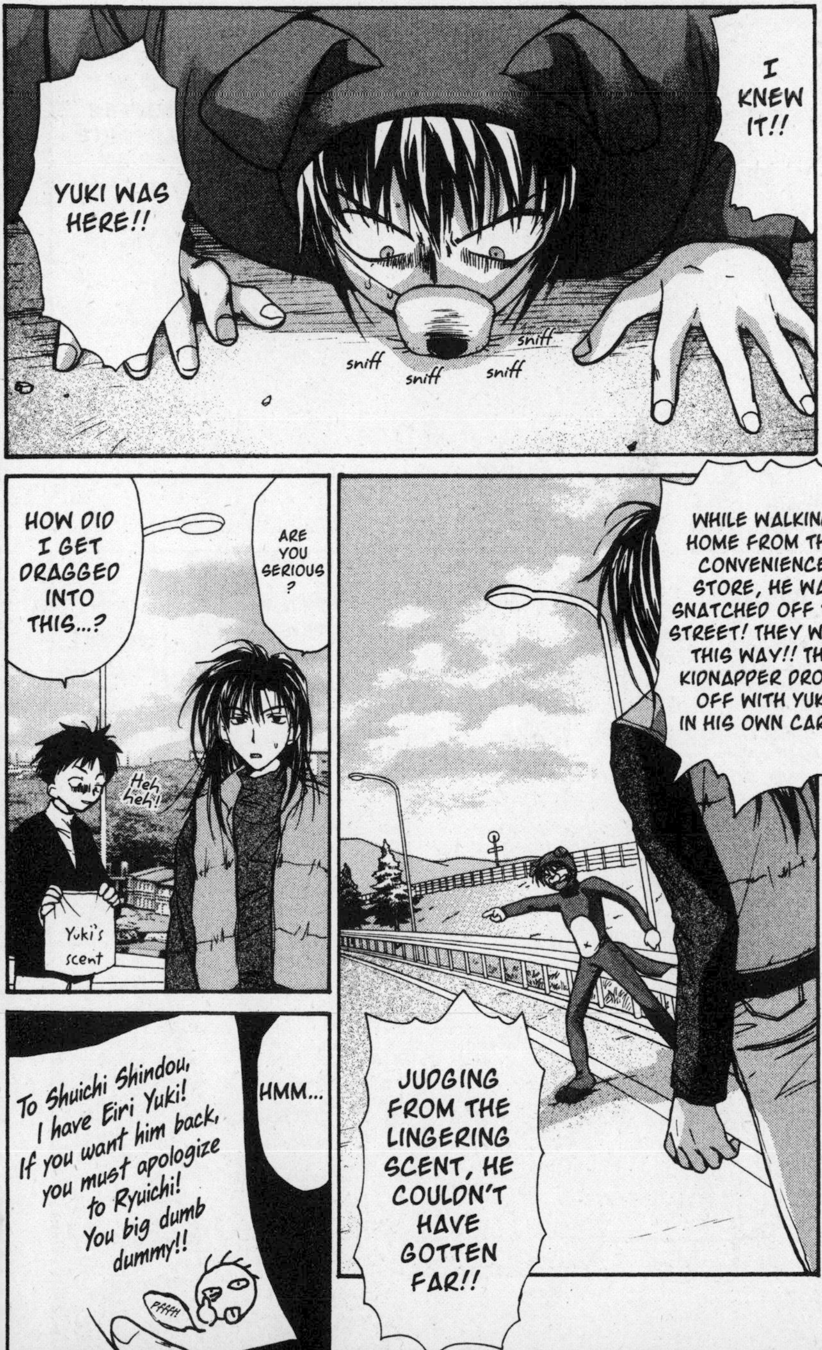
I KNEW IT!!
YUKI WAS HERE!!
sniff
sniff
sniff
sniff
WHILE WALKING HOME FROM THE CONVENIENCE STORE, HE WAS SNATCHED OFF THE STREET! THEY WENT THIS WAY!! THE KIDNAPPER DROVE OFF WITH YUKI IN HIS OWN CAR!!
JUDGING FROM THE LINGERING SCENT, HE COULDN'T HAVE GOTTEN FAR!!
ARE YOU SERIOUS?
HOW DID I GET DRAGGED INTO THIS...?
Heh heh!
Yuki's scent
HMM...
To Shuichi Shindou, I have Eiri Yuki! If you want him back, you must apologize to Ryuichi! You big dumb dummy!!

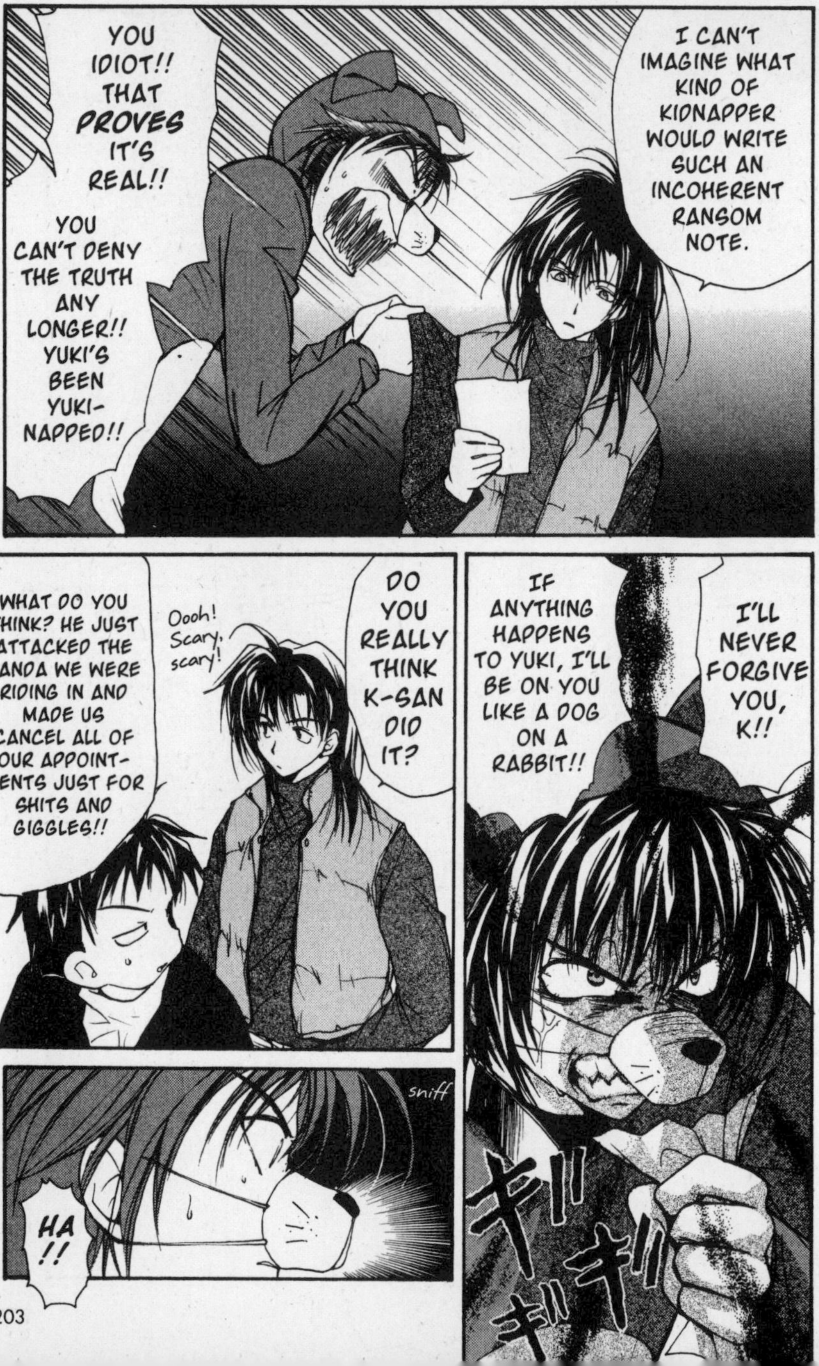
I CAN'T IMAGINE WHAT KIND OF KIDNAPPER WOULD WRITE SUCH AN INCOHERENT RANSOM NOTE.
YOU IDIOT!! THAT **PROVES** IT'S REAL!!
YOU CAN'T DENY THE TRUTH ANY LONGER!! YUKI'S BEEN YUKI-NAPPED!!
I'LL NEVER FORGIVE YOU, K!!
IF ANYTHING HAPPENS TO YUKI, I'LL BE ON YOU LIKE A DOG ON A RABBIT!!
ギリ
ギリ
ギリ
DO YOU REALLY THINK K-SAN DID IT?
Oooh! Scary, scary!
WHAT DO YOU THINK? HE JUST ATTACKED THE PANDA WE WERE RIDING IN AND MADE US CANCEL ALL OF OUR APPOINTMENTS JUST FOR SHITS AND GIGGLES!!
sniff
HA!!

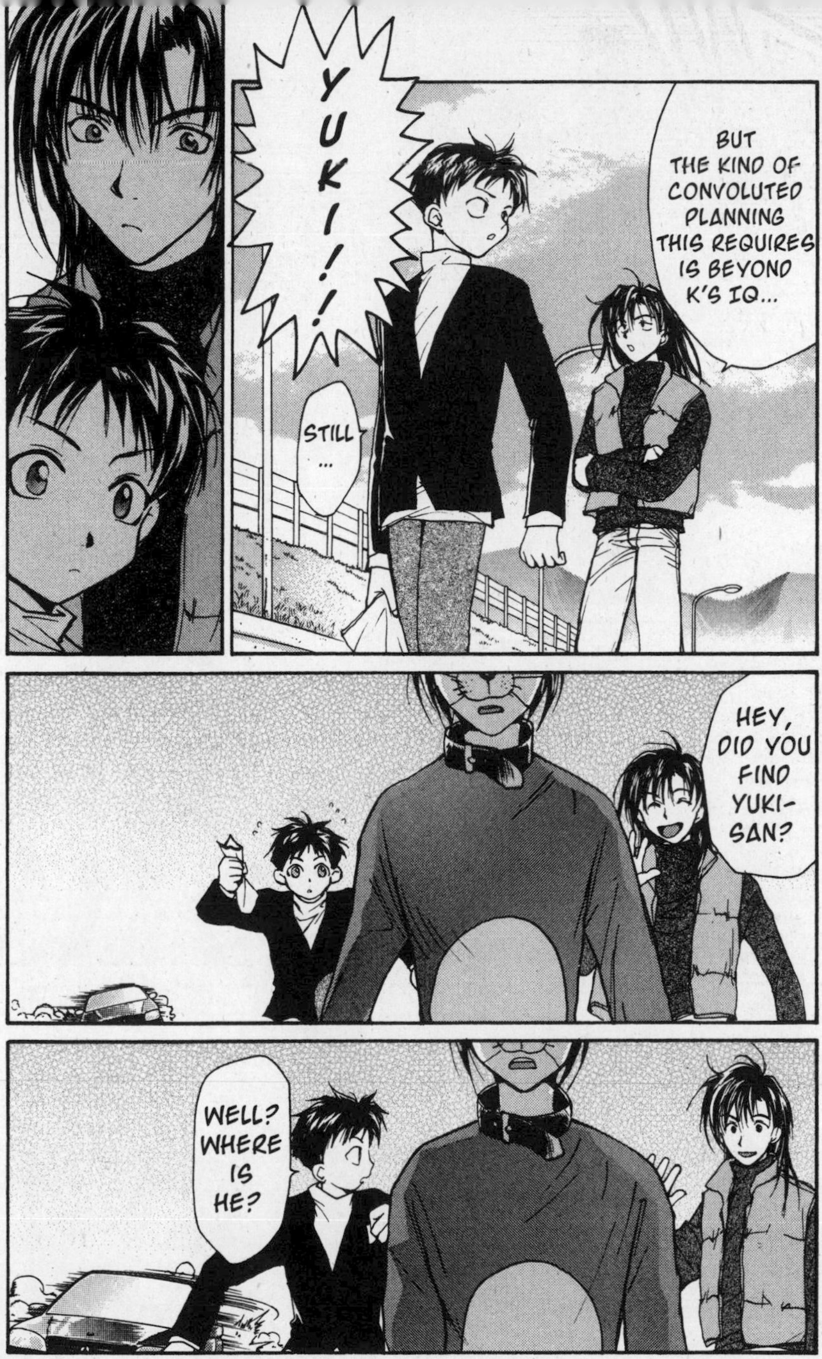
BUT THE KIND OF CONVOLUTED PLANNING THIS REQUIRES IS BEYOND K'S IQ...
YUKI!!!
STILL ...
HEY, DID YOU FIND YUKI-SAN?
WELL? WHERE IS HE?

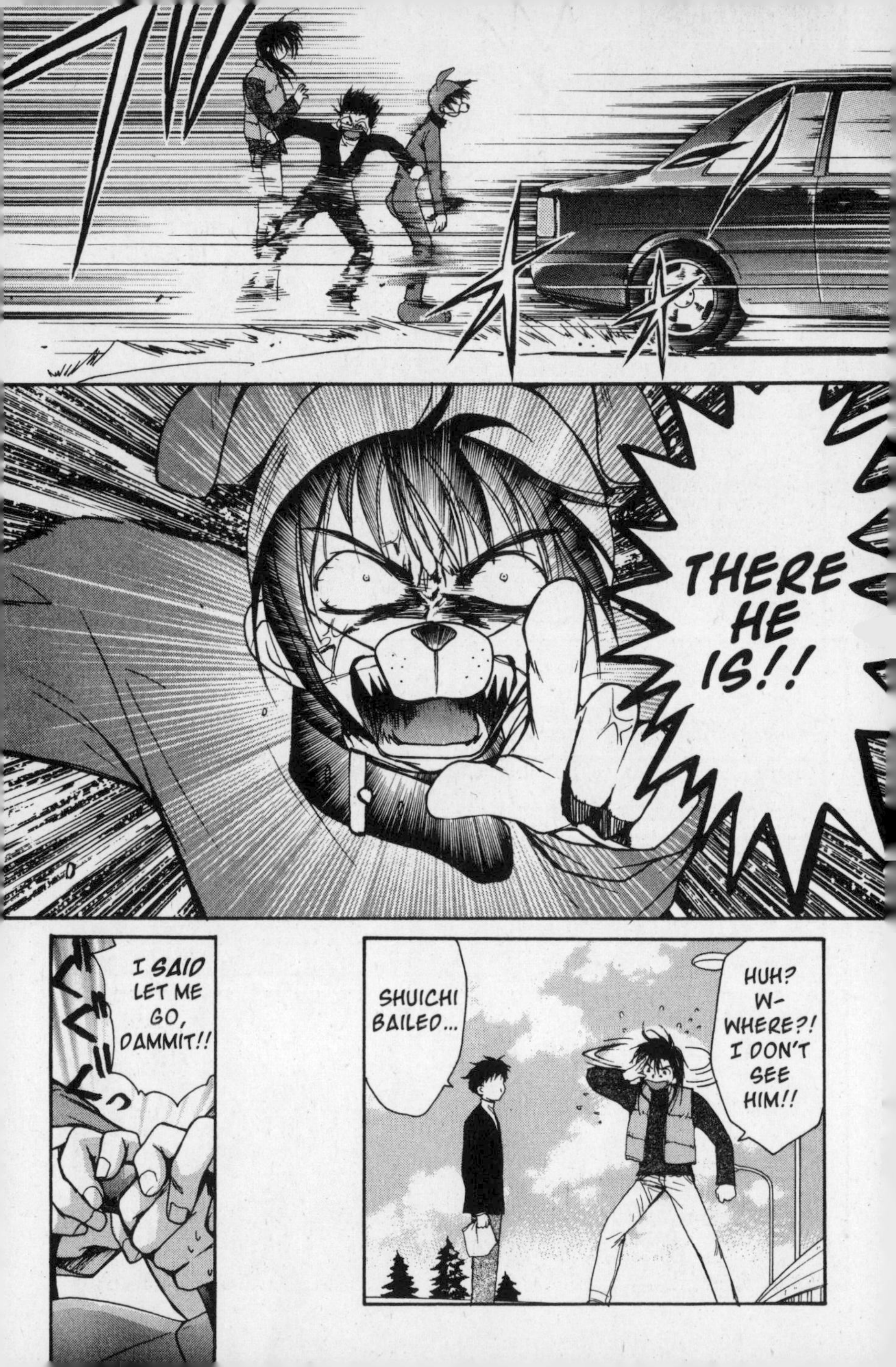
THERE HE IS!!
HUH? W-WHERE?! I DON'T SEE HIM!!
SHUICHI BAILED...
I SAID LET ME GO, DAMMIT!!

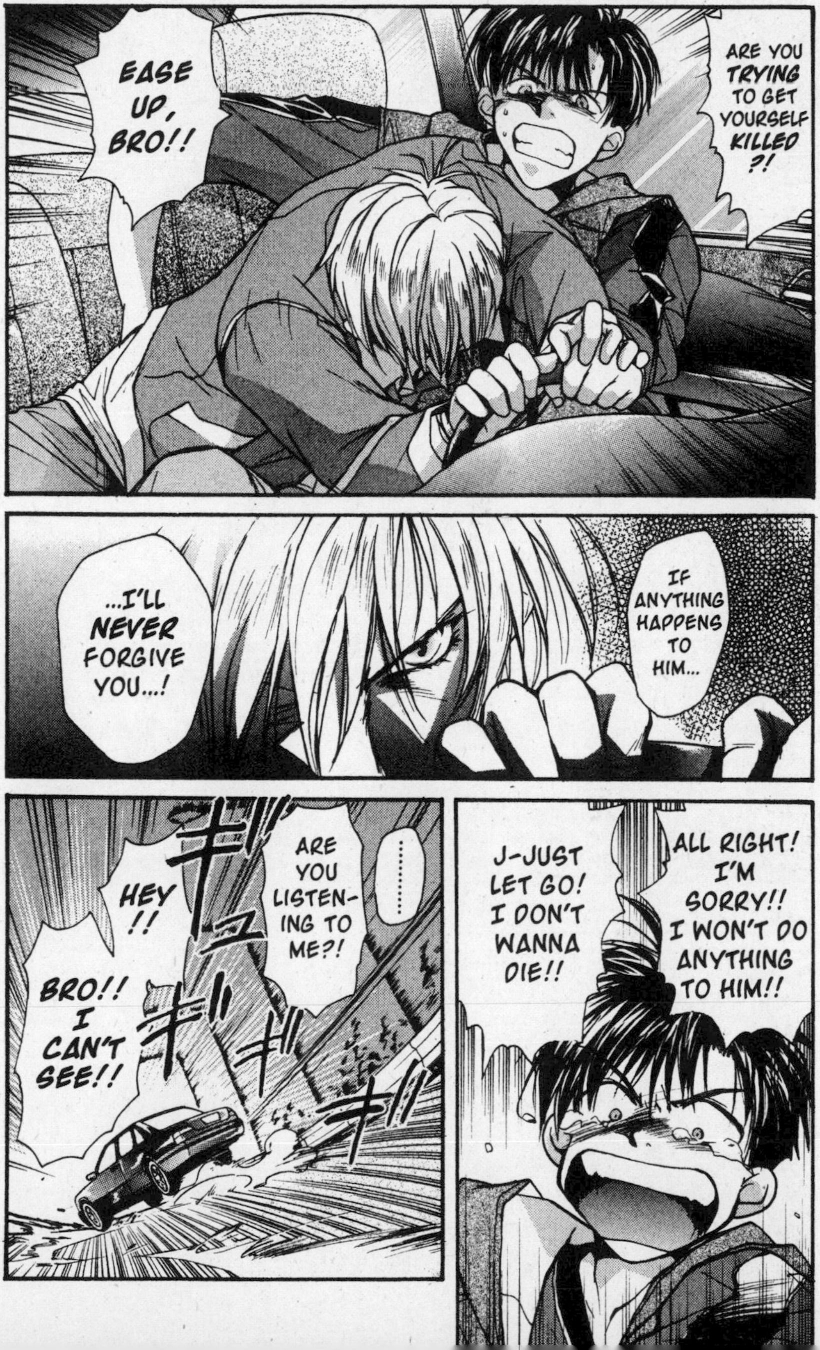
ARE YOU TRYING TO GET YOURSELF KILLED?!
EASE UP, BRO!!
IF ANYTHING HAPPENS TO HIM...
...I'LL NEVER FORGIVE YOU...!
ALL RIGHT! I'M SORRY!! I WON'T DO ANYTHING TO HIM!!
J-JUST LET GO! I DON'T WANNA DIE!!
......
ARE YOU LISTEN-ING TO ME?!
HEY!!
BRO!! I CAN'T SEE!!

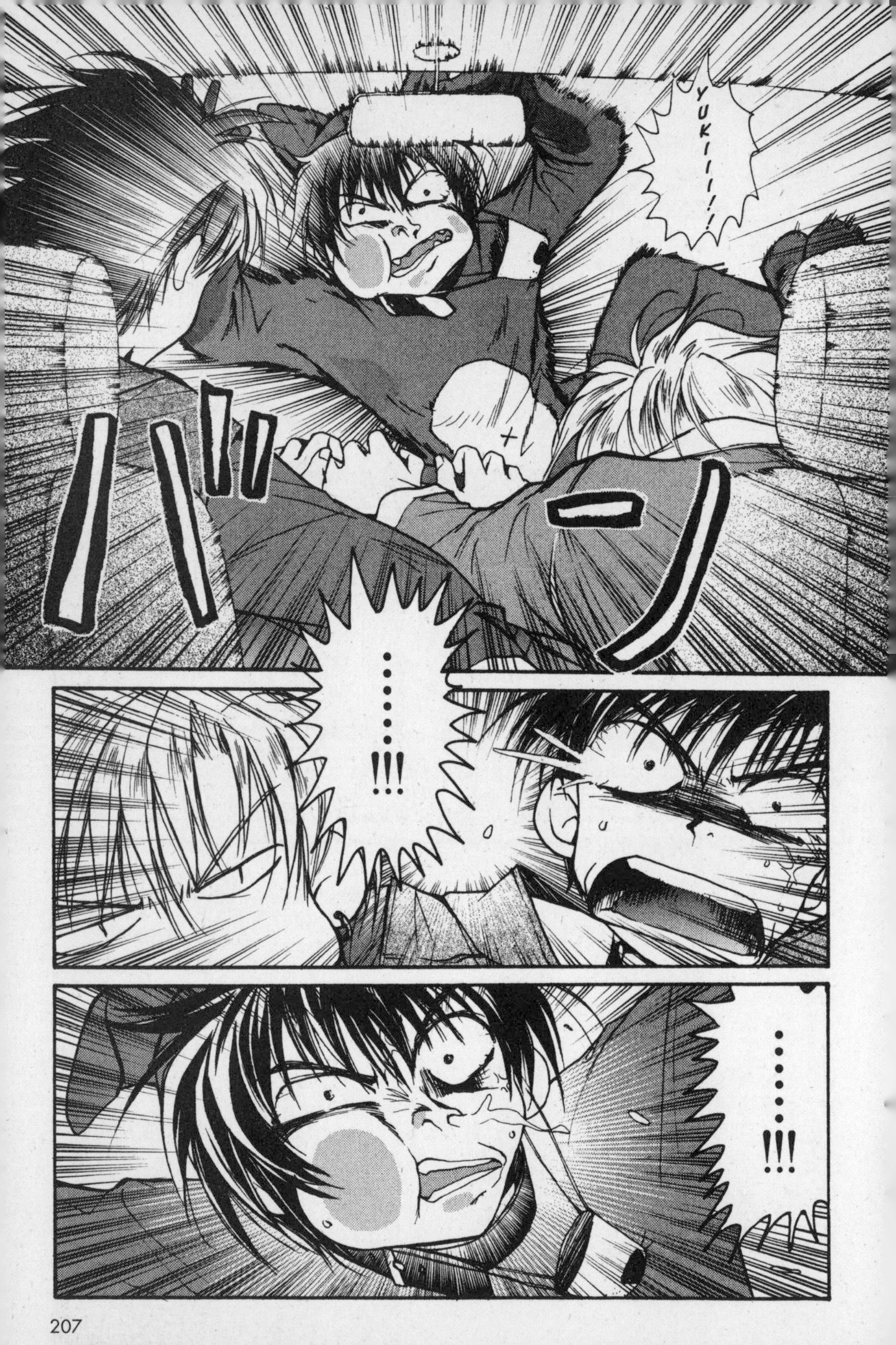
YUKI!!!!!
......!!!
......!!!

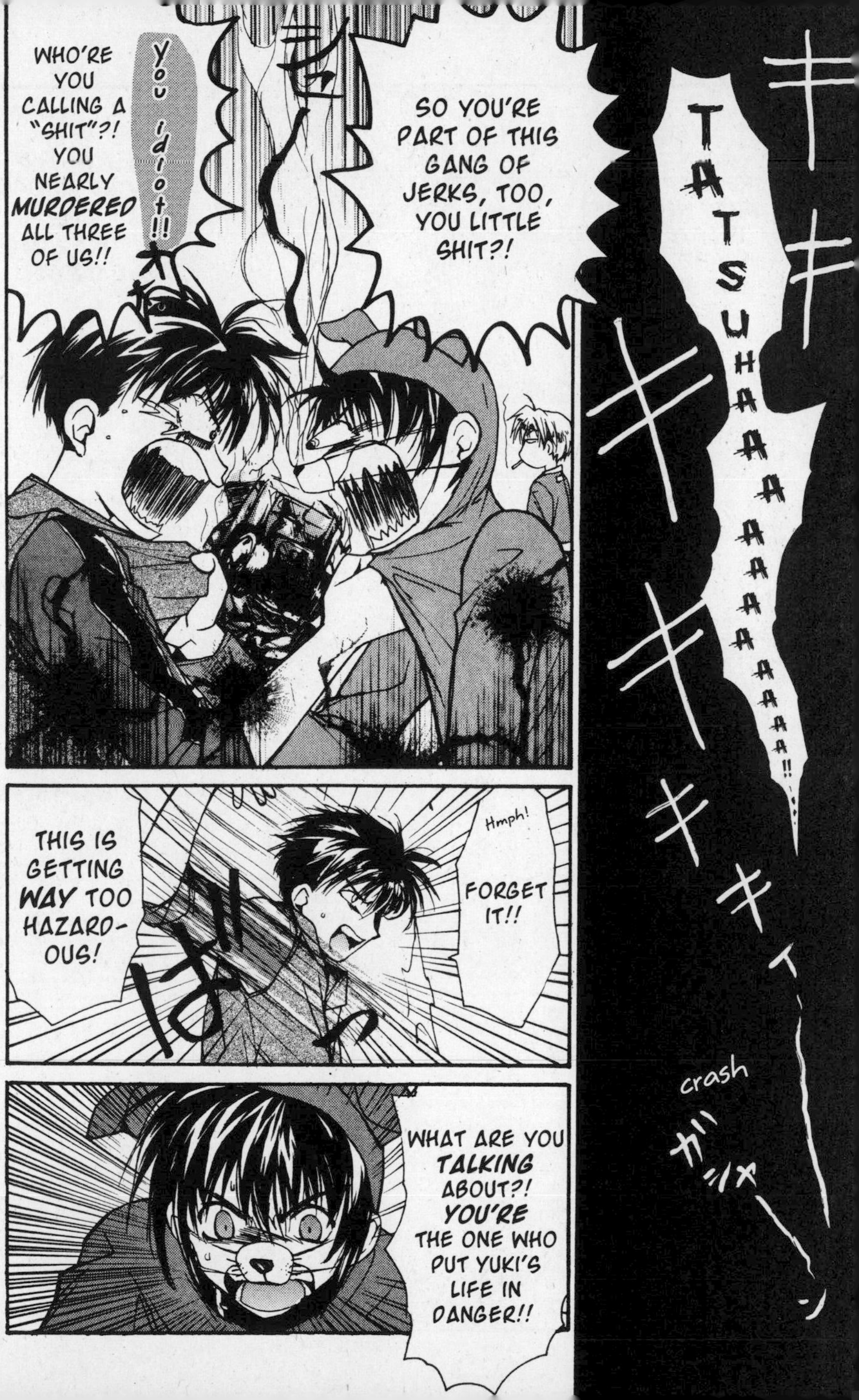
TATSUHAAAAAAAAAAAA!!
crash
SO YOU'RE PART OF THIS GANG OF JERKS, TOO, YOU LITTLE SHIT?!
You idiot!!
WHO'RE YOU CALLING A "SHIT"?! YOU NEARLY MURDERED ALL THREE OF US!!
Hmph!
FORGET IT!!
THIS IS GETTING WAY TOO HAZARDOUS!
WHAT ARE YOU TALKING ABOUT?! YOU'RE THE ONE WHO PUT YUKI'S LIFE IN DANGER!!

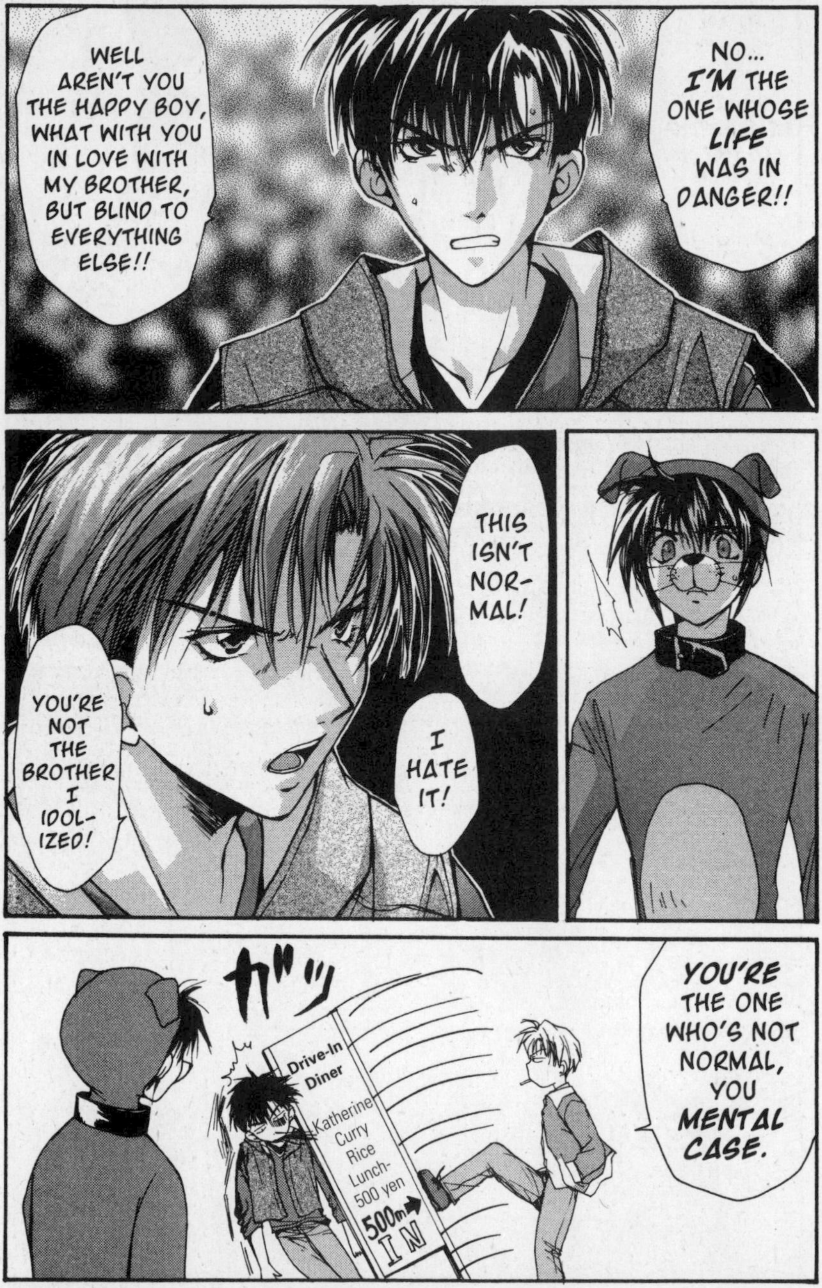
NO... ***I'M*** THE ONE WHOSE ***LIFE*** WAS IN DANGER!!
WELL AREN'T YOU THE HAPPY BOY, WHAT WITH YOU IN LOVE WITH MY BROTHER, BUT BLIND TO EVERYTHING ELSE!!
THIS ISN'T NOR-MAL!
I HATE IT!
YOU'RE NOT THE BROTHER I IDOL-IZED!
***YOU'RE*** THE ONE WHO'S NOT NORMAL, YOU ***MENTAL CASE.***
ガッ
Drive-In Diner
Katherine Curry Rice Lunch-500 yen
500m IN

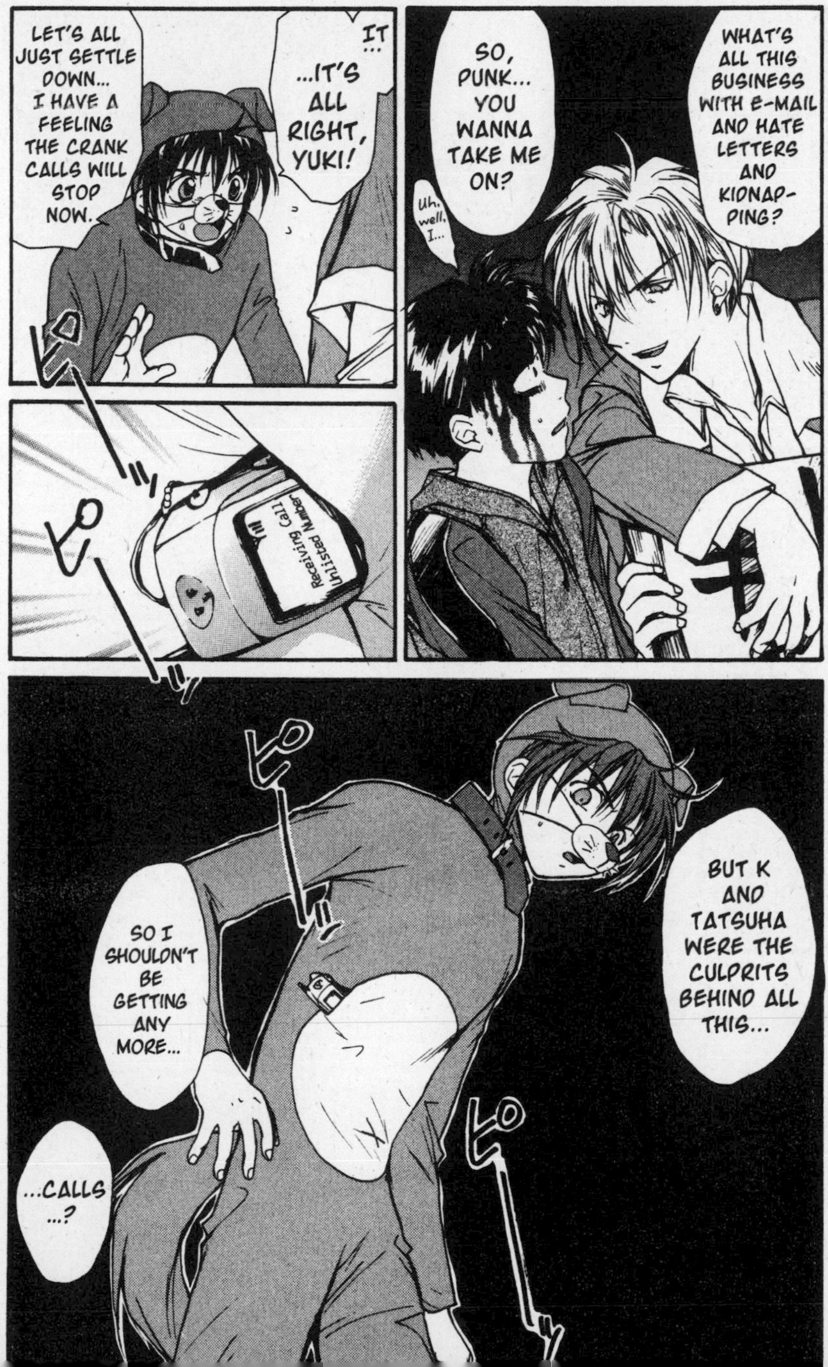
WHAT'S ALL THIS BUSINESS WITH E-MAIL AND HATE LETTERS AND KIDNAP-PING?
SO, PUNK... YOU WANNA TAKE ME ON?
Uh, well, I...
IT...
...IT'S ALL RIGHT, YUKI!
LET'S ALL JUST SETTLE DOWN... I HAVE A FEELING THE CRANK CALLS WILL STOP NOW.
Receiving Call
Unlisted Number
BUT K AND TATSUHA WERE THE CULPRITS BEHIND ALL THIS...
SO I SHOULDN'T BE GETTING ANY MORE...
...CALLS...?

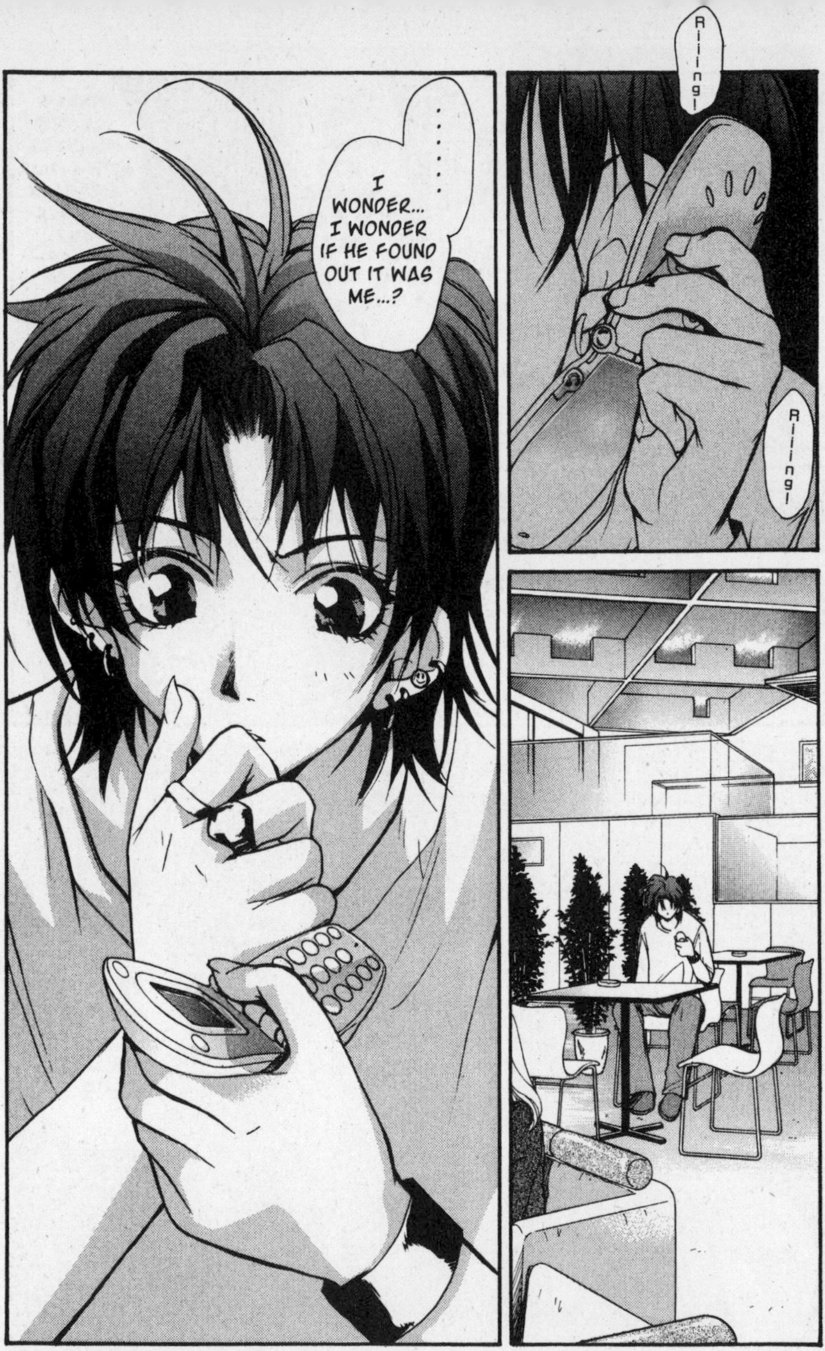
Riiing!
Riiing!
......
I WONDER... I WONDER IF HE FOUND OUT IT WAS ME...?

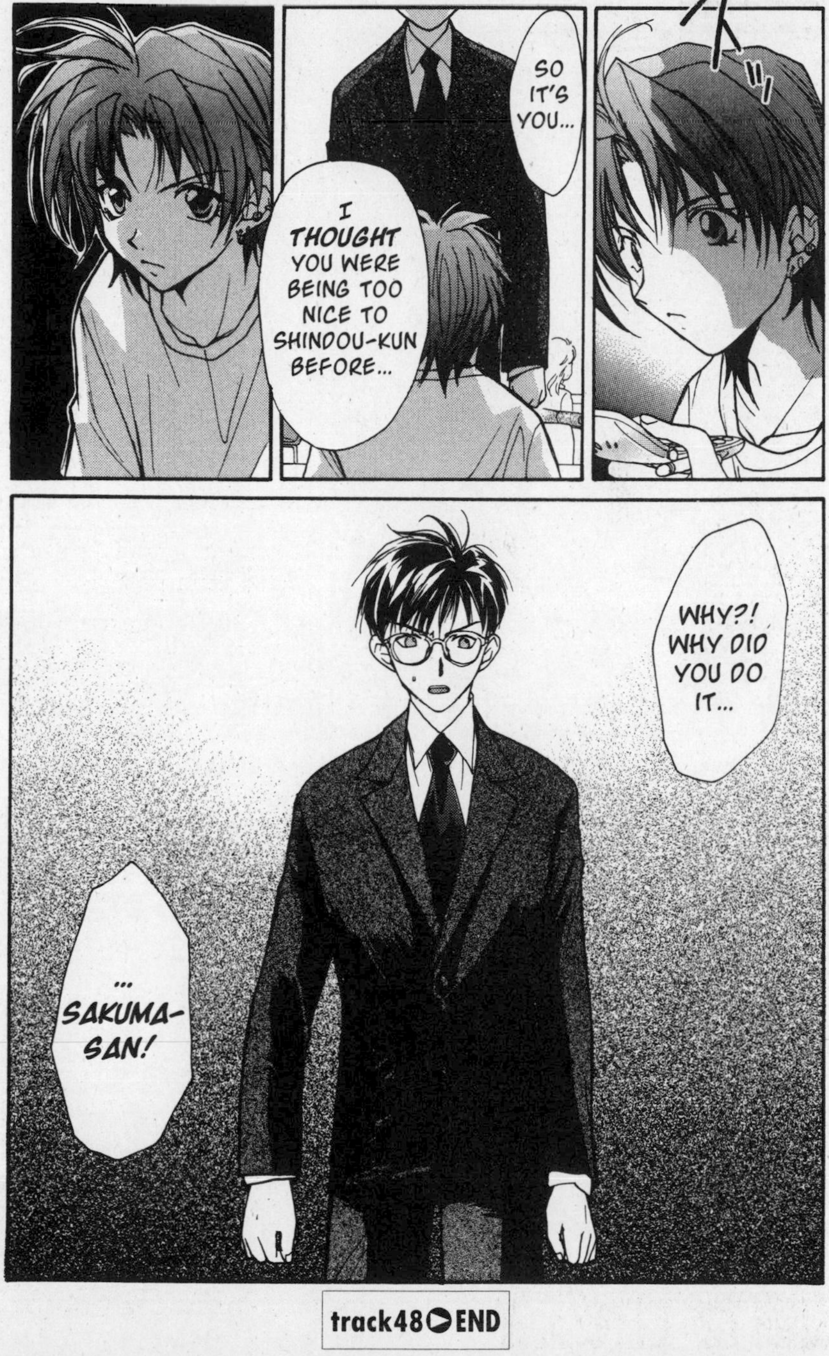
SO IT'S YOU...
I THOUGHT YOU WERE BEING TOO NICE TO SHINDOU-KUN BEFORE...
WHY?! WHY DID YOU DO IT...
... SAKUMA-SAN!

track48 ▶ END

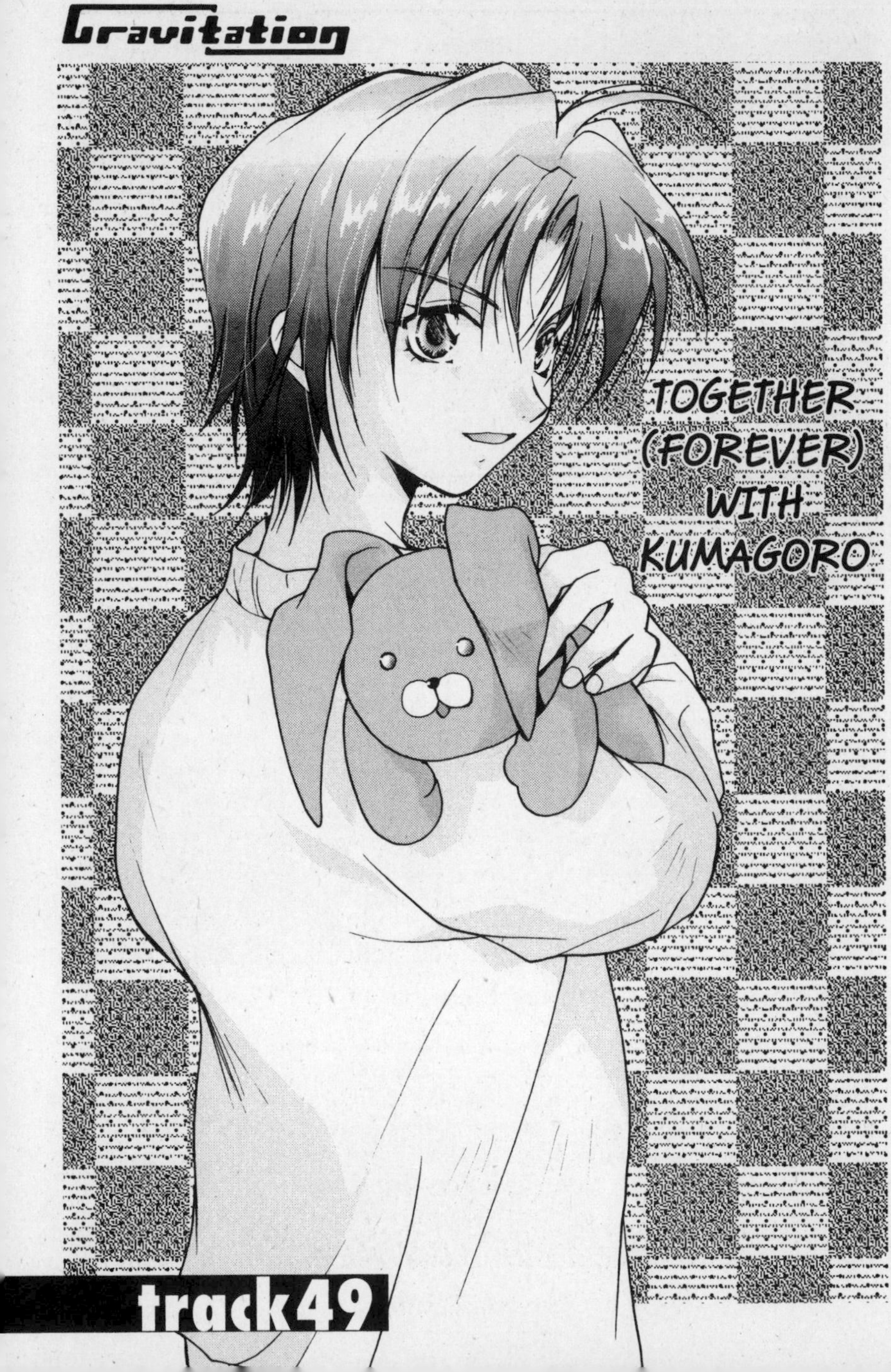
Gravitation
TOGETHER (FOREVER) WITH KUMAGORO
track 49

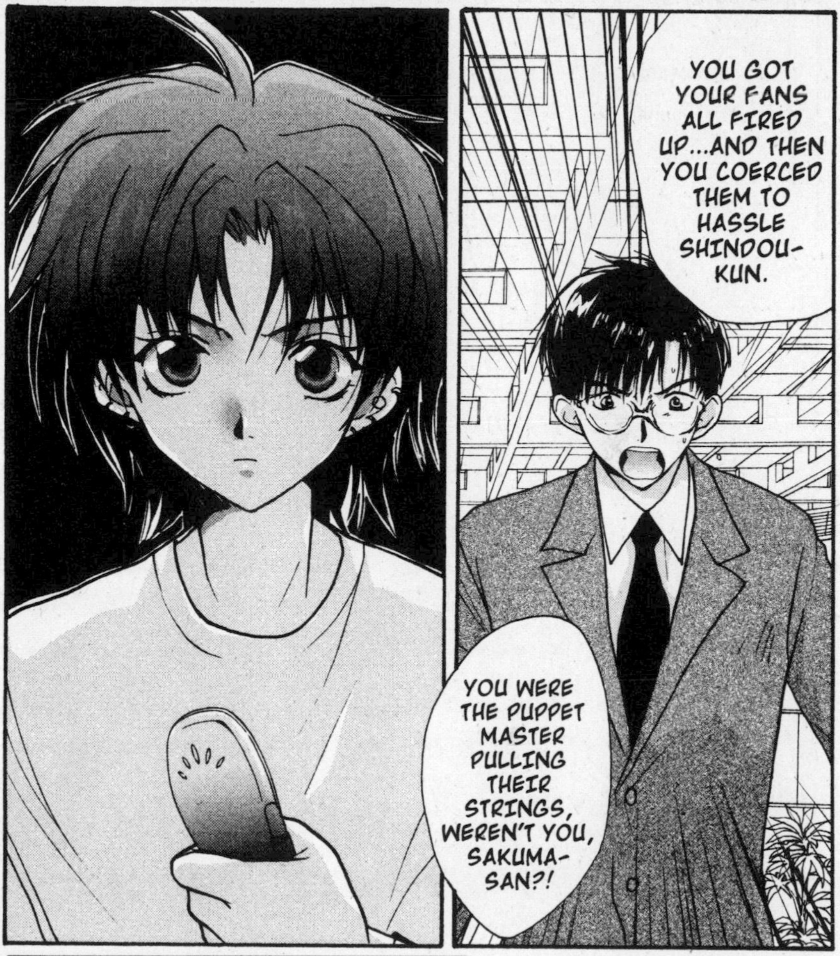
YOU GOT YOUR FANS ALL FIRED UP...AND THEN YOU COERCED THEM TO HASSLE SHINDOU-KUN.
YOU WERE THE PUPPET MASTER PULLING THEIR STRINGS, WEREN'T YOU, SAKUMA-SAN?!

## ABOUT GRAVITATION TRACK 49

It's been a long time. It's me, the scum of the human race, Murakami. Happily, *Gravitation* has finally reached its conclusion in this, its final volume. Its prolonged existence is all thanks to you readers. On this happy occasion, I decided to draw some nipples on Shindou as part of the front cover art. So...did they come through in the printing? Plus, I gave Yuki wings. Ain't I just too darn happy? I think this book's cover is exactly what all of my fans have been waiting for. I can just hear their shrieks now... (Shindou's nipples will do that to 'em!)

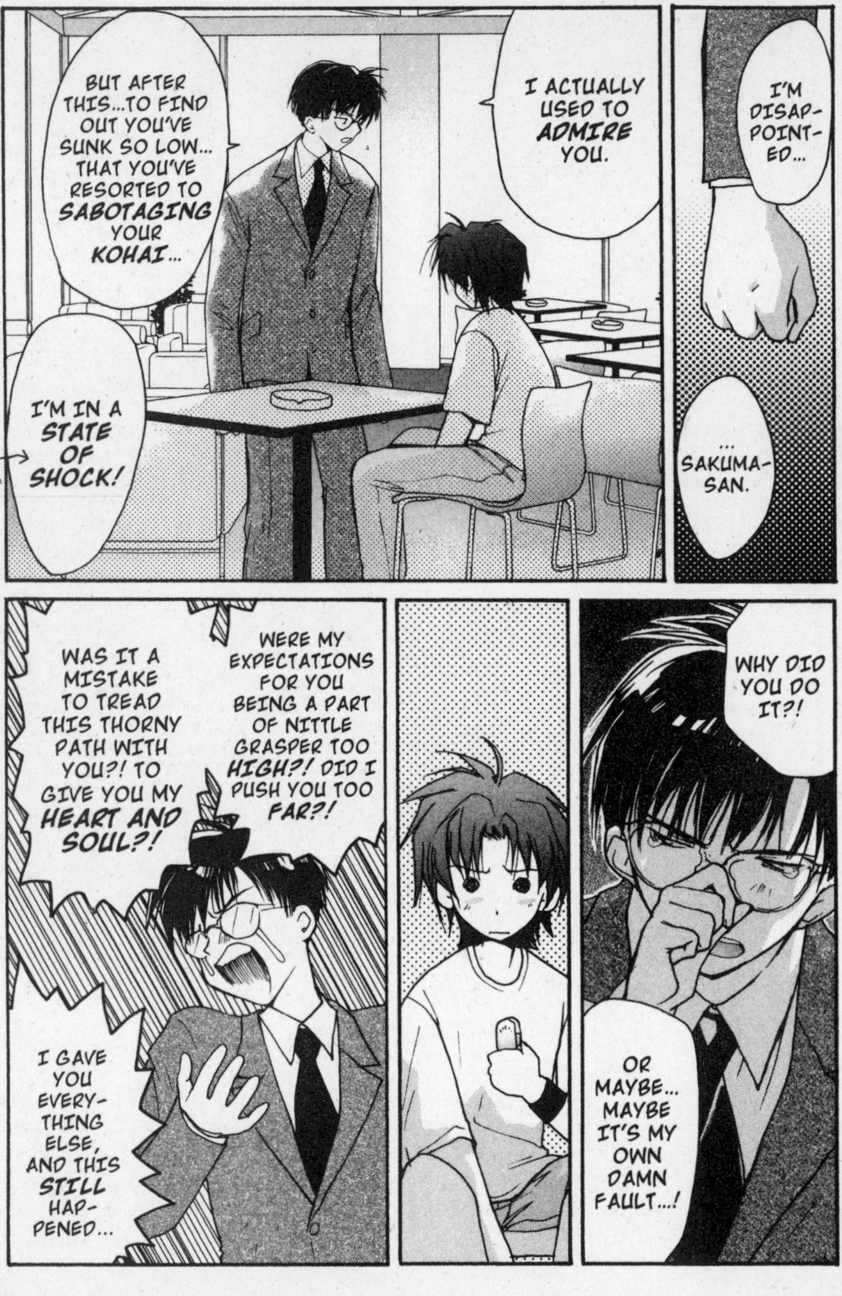
I'M DISAPPOINTED...
...SAKUMA-SAN.
I ACTUALLY USED TO ADMIRE YOU.
BUT AFTER THIS...TO FIND OUT YOU'VE SUNK SO LOW... THAT YOU'VE RESORTED TO SABOTAGING YOUR KOHAI...
I'M IN A STATE OF SHOCK!
Total Confusion
WHY DID YOU DO IT?!
OR MAYBE... MAYBE IT'S MY OWN DAMN FAULT...!
WERE MY EXPECTATIONS FOR YOU BEING A PART OF NITTLE GRASPER TOO HIGH?! DID I PUSH YOU TOO FAR?!
WAS IT A MISTAKE TO TREAD THIS THORNY PATH WITH YOU?! TO GIVE YOU MY HEART AND SOUL?!
I GAVE YOU EVERYTHING ELSE, AND THIS STILL HAPPENED...

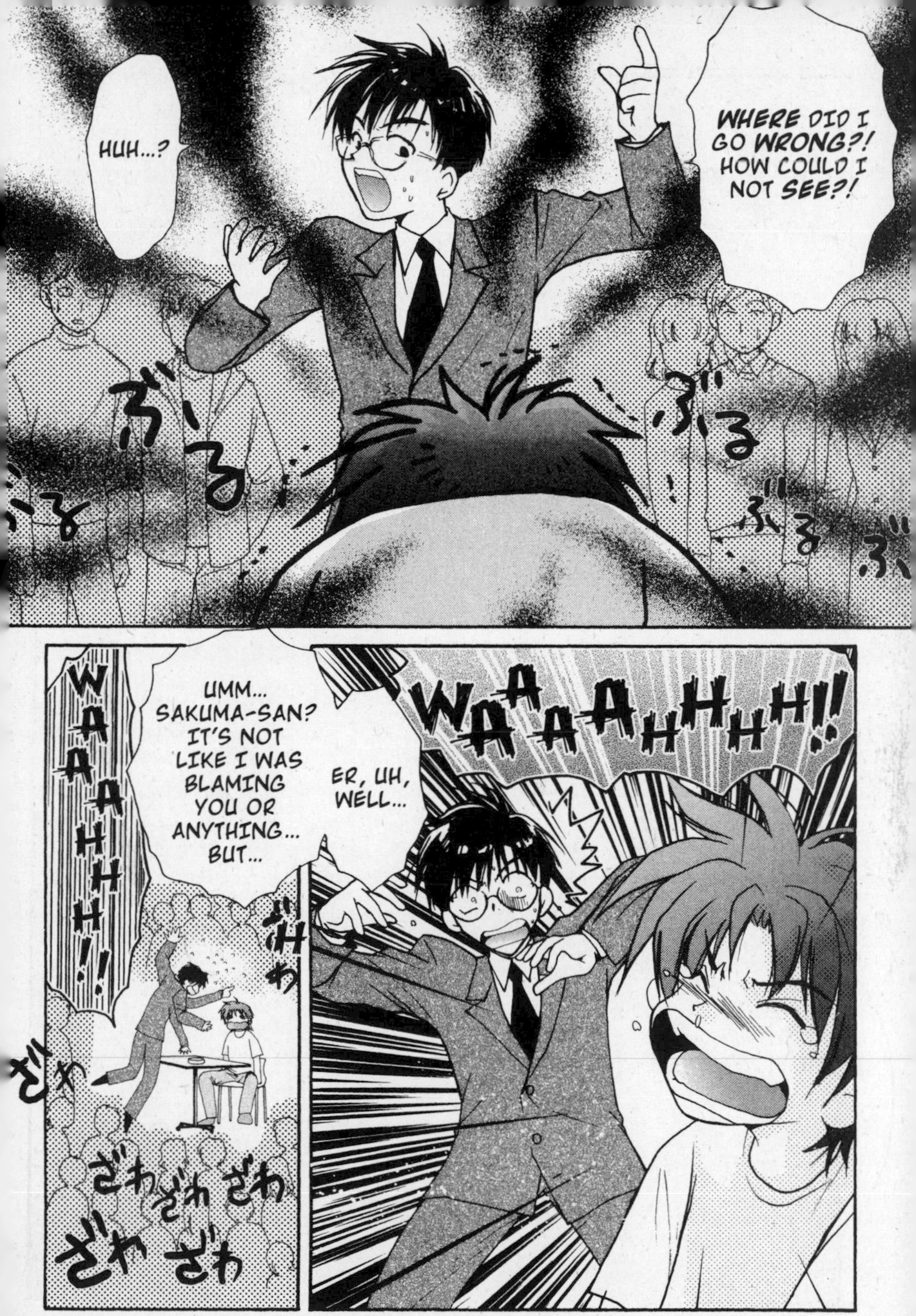
WHERE DID I GO WRONG?! HOW COULD I NOT SEE?!
HUH...?
ぶる
ぶる
ぶる
ぶる
ぶ
WAAAAAHHHHH!!
ER, UH, WELL...
UMM... SAKUMA-SAN? IT'S NOT LIKE I WAS BLAMING YOU OR ANYTHING... BUT...
WAAAAHHHHH!!
ざわ
ざわ
ざわ ざわ ざわ
ざわ ざわ

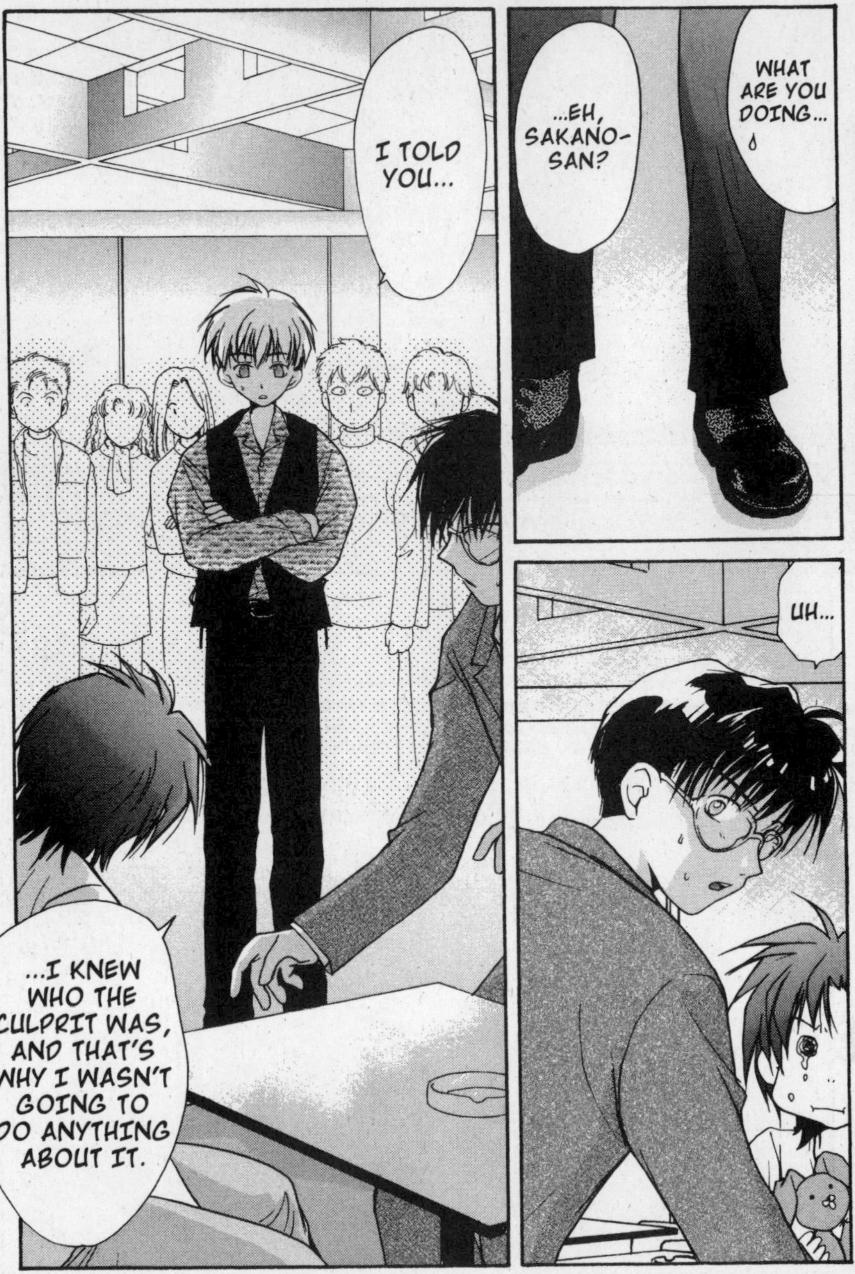
WHAT ARE YOU DOING...
...EH, SAKANO-SAN?
UH...
I TOLD YOU...
...I KNEW WHO THE CULPRIT WAS, AND THAT'S WHY I WASN'T GOING TO DO ANYTHING ABOUT IT.

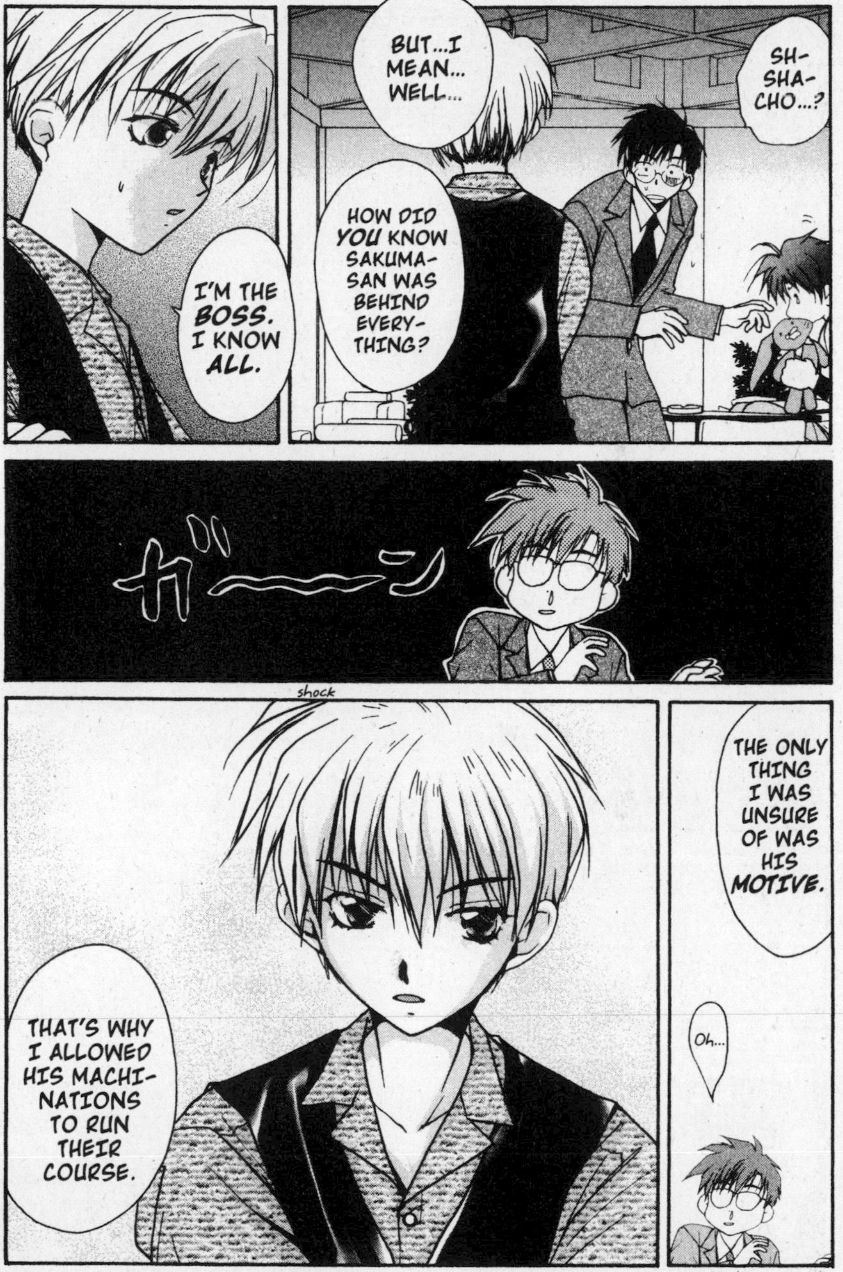
SH-SHA-CHO...?
BUT...I MEAN... WELL...
HOW DID YOU KNOW SAKUMA-SAN WAS BEHIND EVERY-THING?
I'M THE BOSS. I KNOW ALL.
ガーーーン
THE ONLY THING I WAS UNSURE OF WAS HIS MOTIVE.
Oh...
shock
THAT'S WHY I ALLOWED HIS MACHI-NATIONS TO RUN THEIR COURSE.

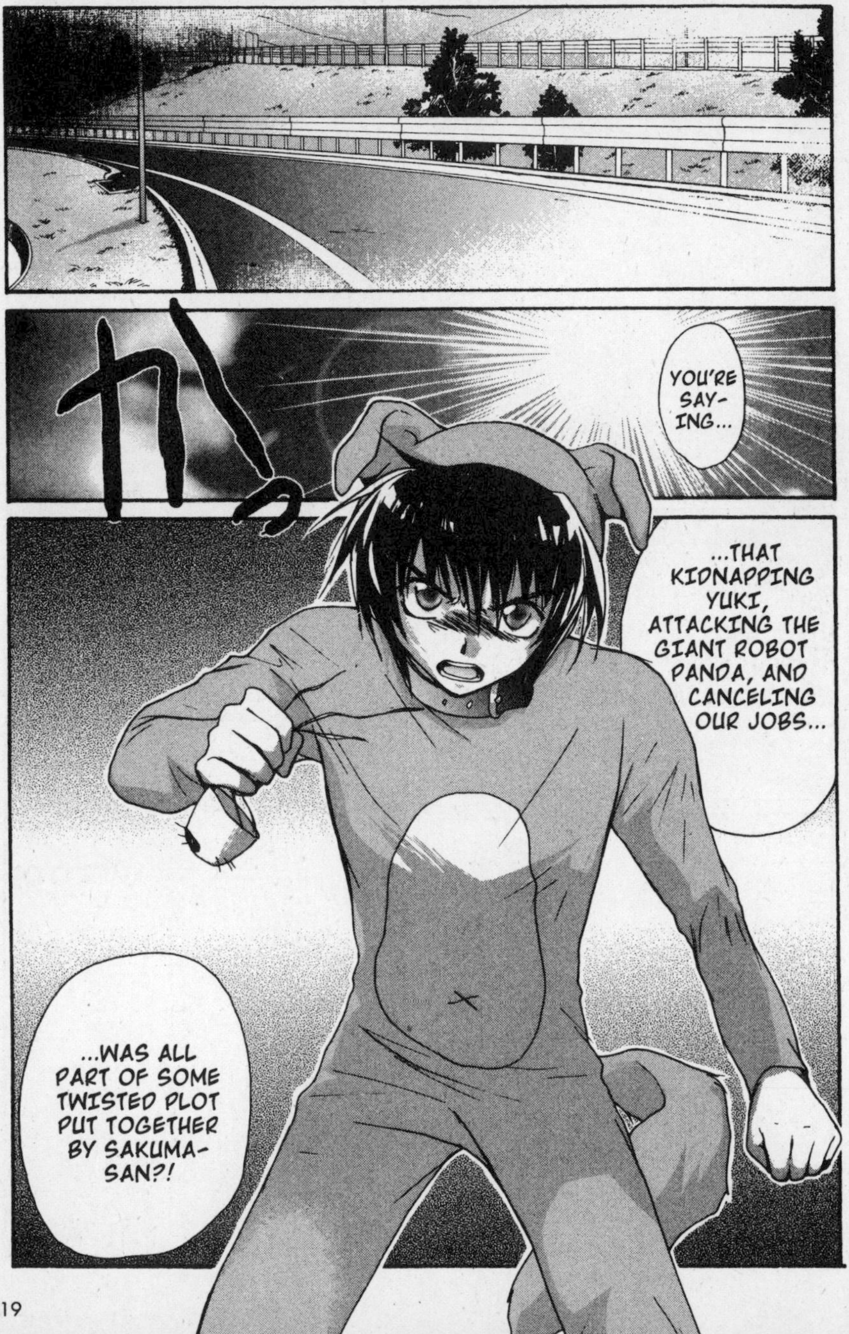
YOU'RE SAY-ING...
...THAT KIDNAPPING YUKI, ATTACKING THE GIANT ROBOT PANDA, AND CANCELING OUR JOBS...
...WAS ALL PART OF SOME TWISTED PLOT PUT TOGETHER BY SAKUMA-SAN?!

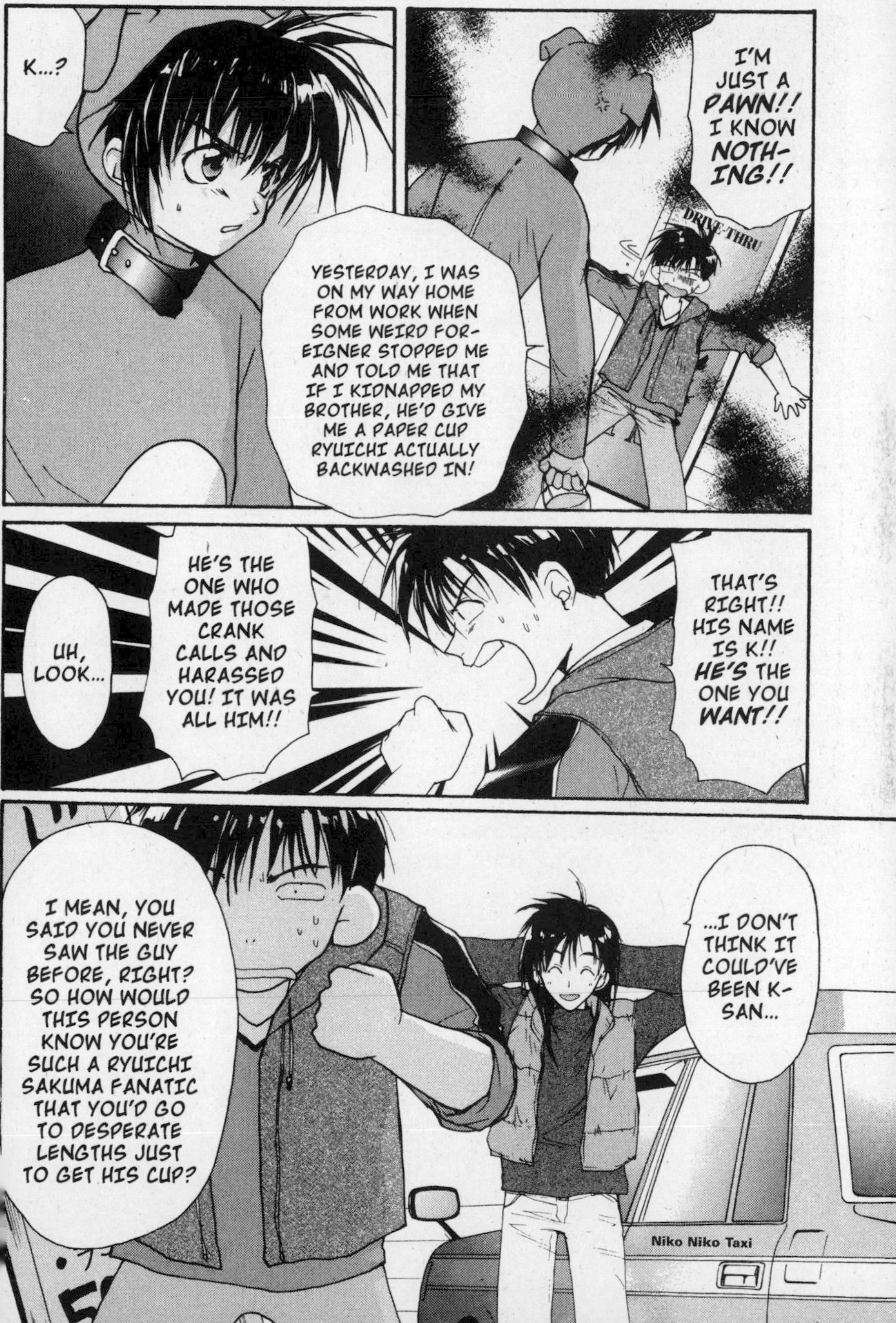
I'M JUST A PAWN!! I KNOW NOTHING!!
DRIVE-THRU
YESTERDAY, I WAS ON MY WAY HOME FROM WORK WHEN SOME WEIRD FOREIGNER STOPPED ME AND TOLD ME THAT IF I KIDNAPPED MY BROTHER, HE'D GIVE ME A PAPER CUP RYUICHI ACTUALLY BACKWASHED IN!
K...?
THAT'S RIGHT!! HIS NAME IS K!! HE'S THE ONE YOU WANT!!
HE'S THE ONE WHO MADE THOSE CRANK CALLS AND HARASSED YOU! IT WAS ALL HIM!!
UH, LOOK...
...I DON'T THINK IT COULD'VE BEEN K-SAN...
I MEAN, YOU SAID YOU NEVER SAW THE GUY BEFORE, RIGHT? SO HOW WOULD THIS PERSON KNOW YOU'RE SUCH A RYUICHI SAKUMA FANATIC THAT YOU'D GO TO DESPERATE LENGTHS JUST TO GET HIS CUP?
Niko Niko Taxi

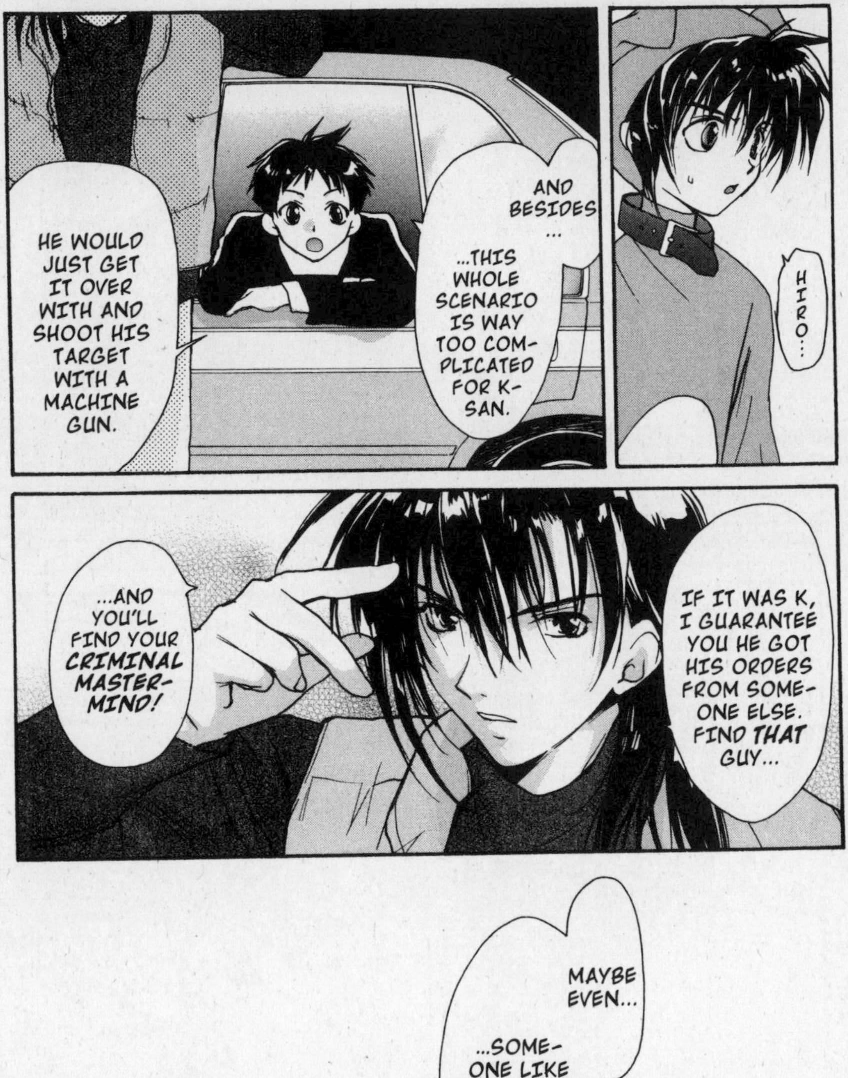
HIRO...
AND BESIDES...
...THIS WHOLE SCENARIO IS WAY TOO COMPLICATED FOR K-SAN.
HE WOULD JUST GET IT OVER WITH AND SHOOT HIS TARGET WITH A MACHINE GUN.
IF IT WAS K, I GUARANTEE YOU HE GOT HIS ORDERS FROM SOMEONE ELSE. FIND THAT GUY...
...AND YOU'LL FIND YOUR CRIMINAL MASTERMIND!
MAYBE EVEN...
...SOMEONE LIKE RYUICHI SAKUMA?

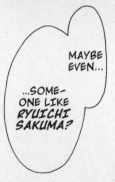

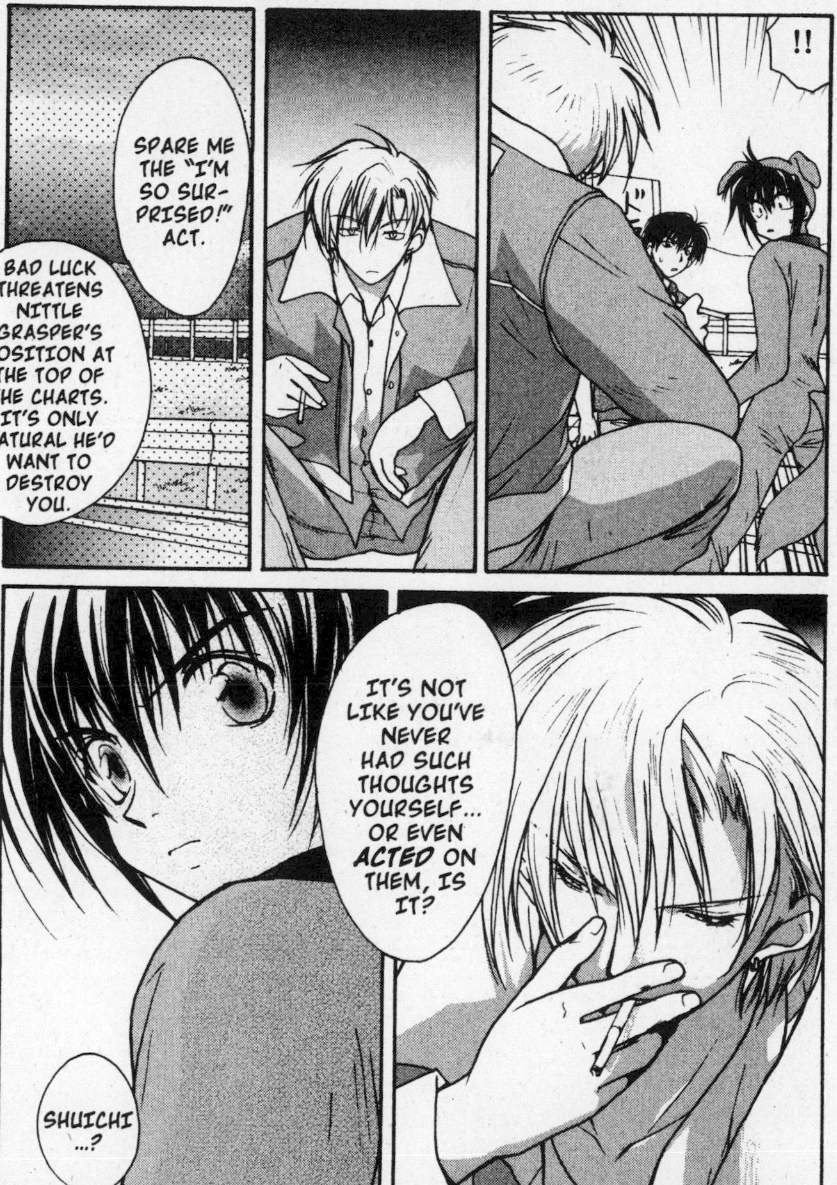
!!
SPARE ME THE "I'M SO SUR-PRISED!" ACT.
BAD LUCK THREATENS NITTLE GRASPER'S POSITION AT THE TOP OF THE CHARTS. IT'S ONLY NATURAL HE'D WANT TO DESTROY YOU.
IT'S NOT LIKE YOU'VE NEVER HAD SUCH THOUGHTS YOURSELF... OR EVEN ACTED ON THEM, IS IT?
SHUICHI ...?

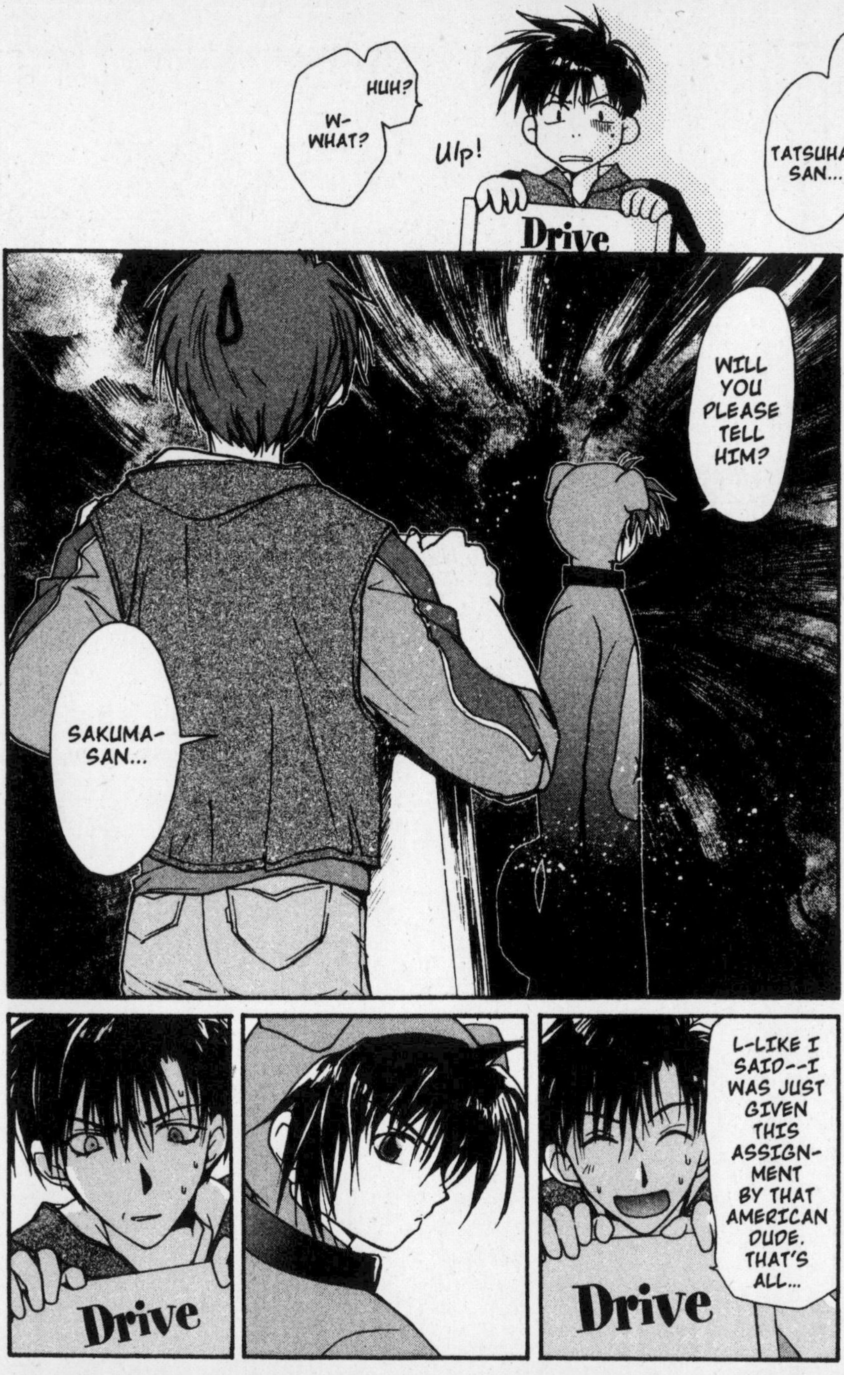

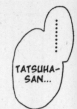

......... TATSUHA-SAN...
HUH? W-WHAT?
Ulp!
Drive
WILL YOU PLEASE TELL HIM?
SAKUMA-SAN...
L-LIKE I SAID--I WAS JUST GIVEN THIS ASSIGNMENT BY THAT AMERICAN DUDE. THAT'S ALL...
Drive
Drive

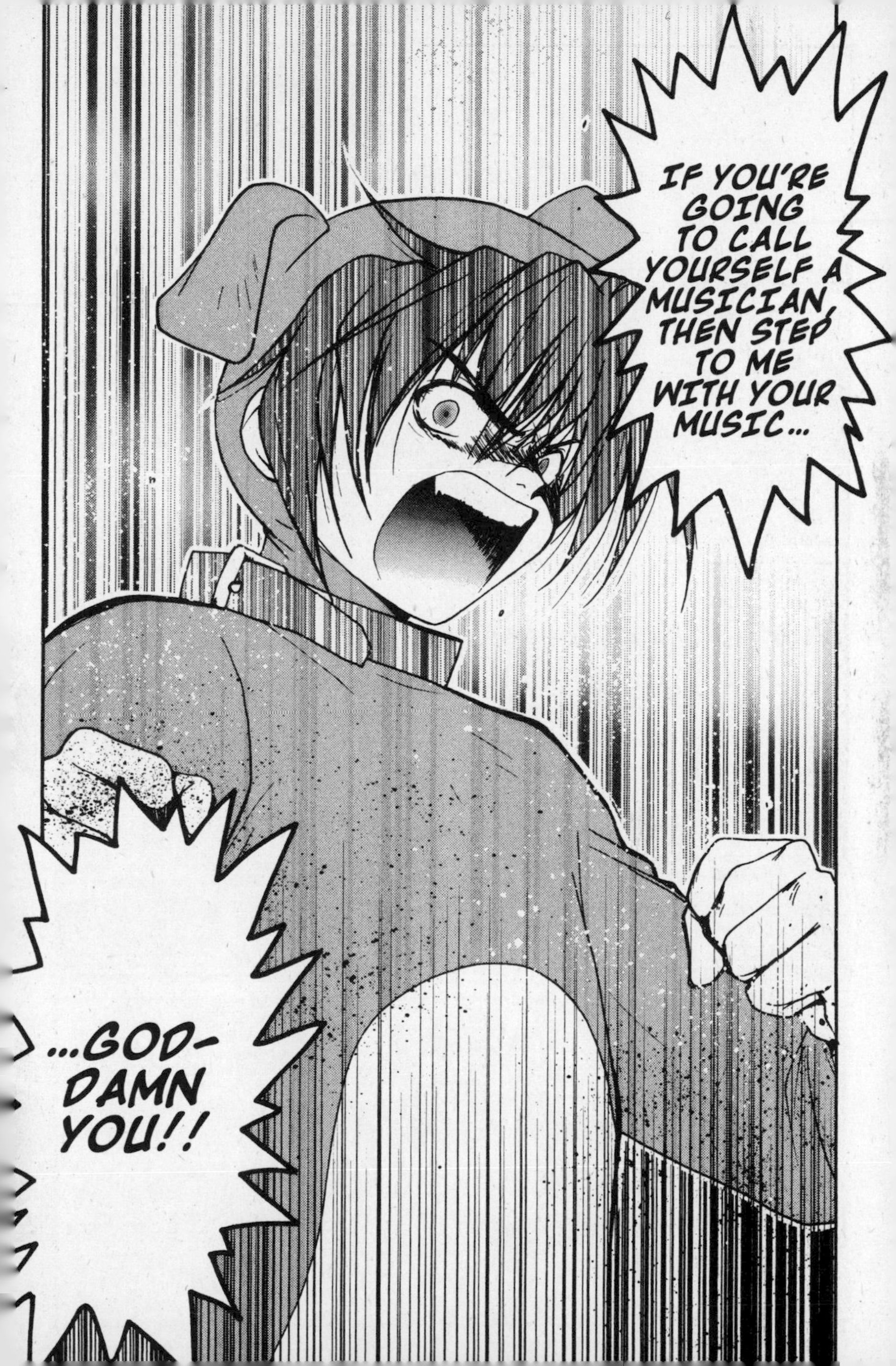
IF YOU'RE GOING TO CALL YOURSELF A MUSICIAN, THEN STEP TO ME WITH YOUR MUSIC...
...GOD-DAMN YOU!!

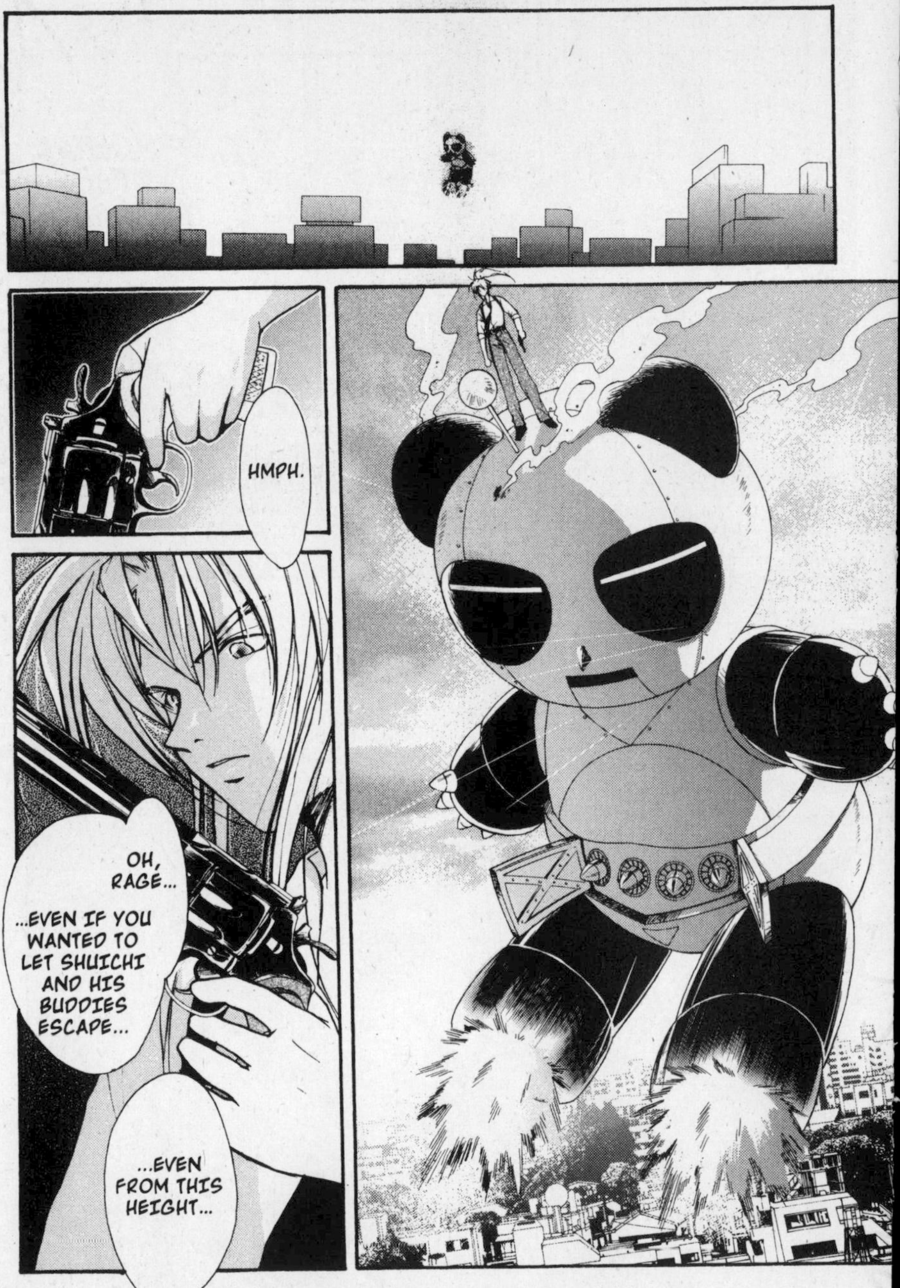
HMPH.
OH, RAGE...
...EVEN IF YOU WANTED TO LET SHUICHI AND HIS BUDDIES ESCAPE...
...EVEN FROM THIS HEIGHT...

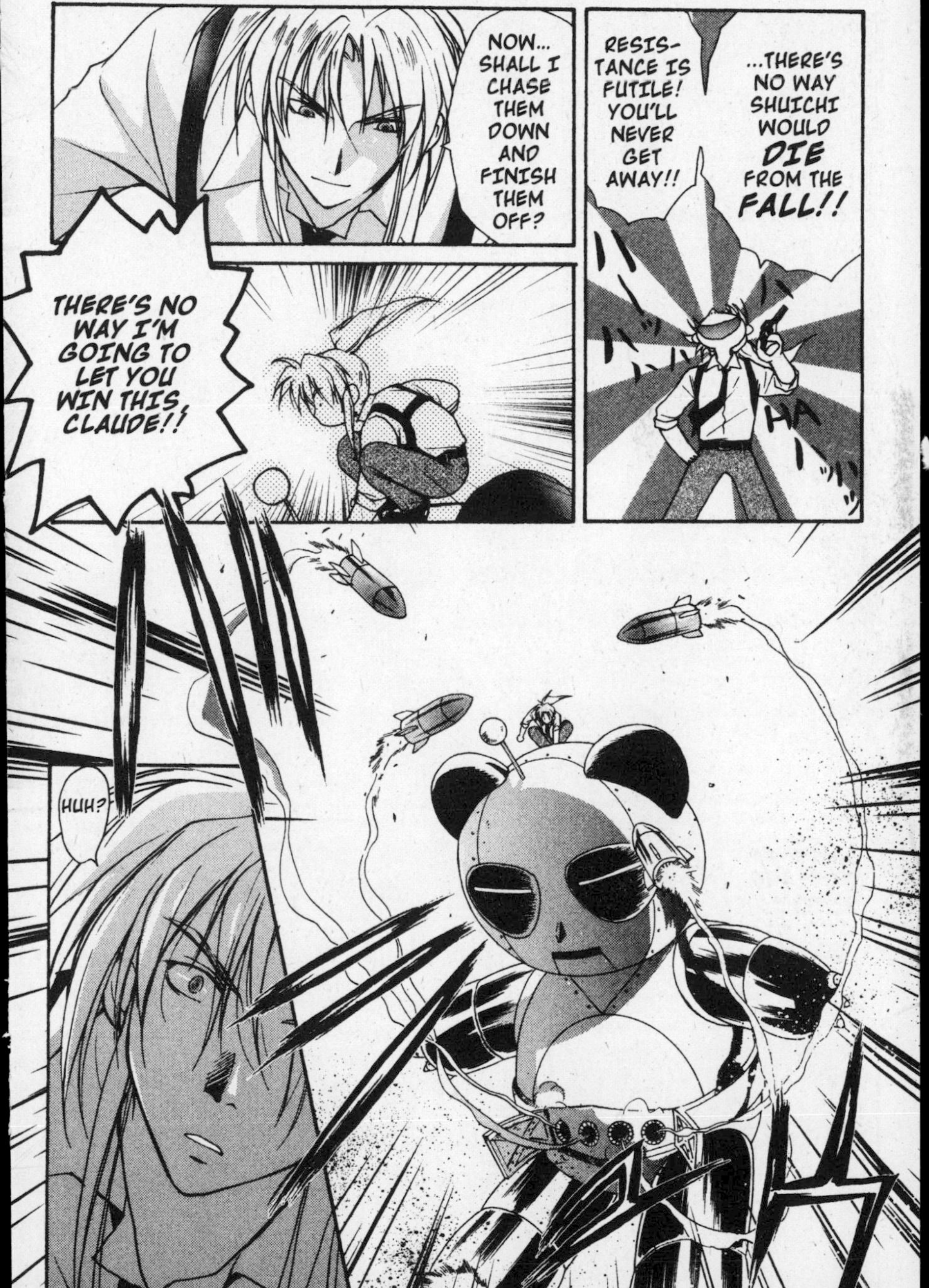
...THERE'S NO WAY SHUICHI WOULD DIE FROM THE FALL!!
RESISTANCE IS FUTILE! YOU'LL NEVER GET AWAY!!
HA
NOW... SHALL I CHASE THEM DOWN AND FINISH THEM OFF?
THERE'S NO WAY I'M GOING TO LET YOU WIN THIS, CLAUDE!!
HUH?

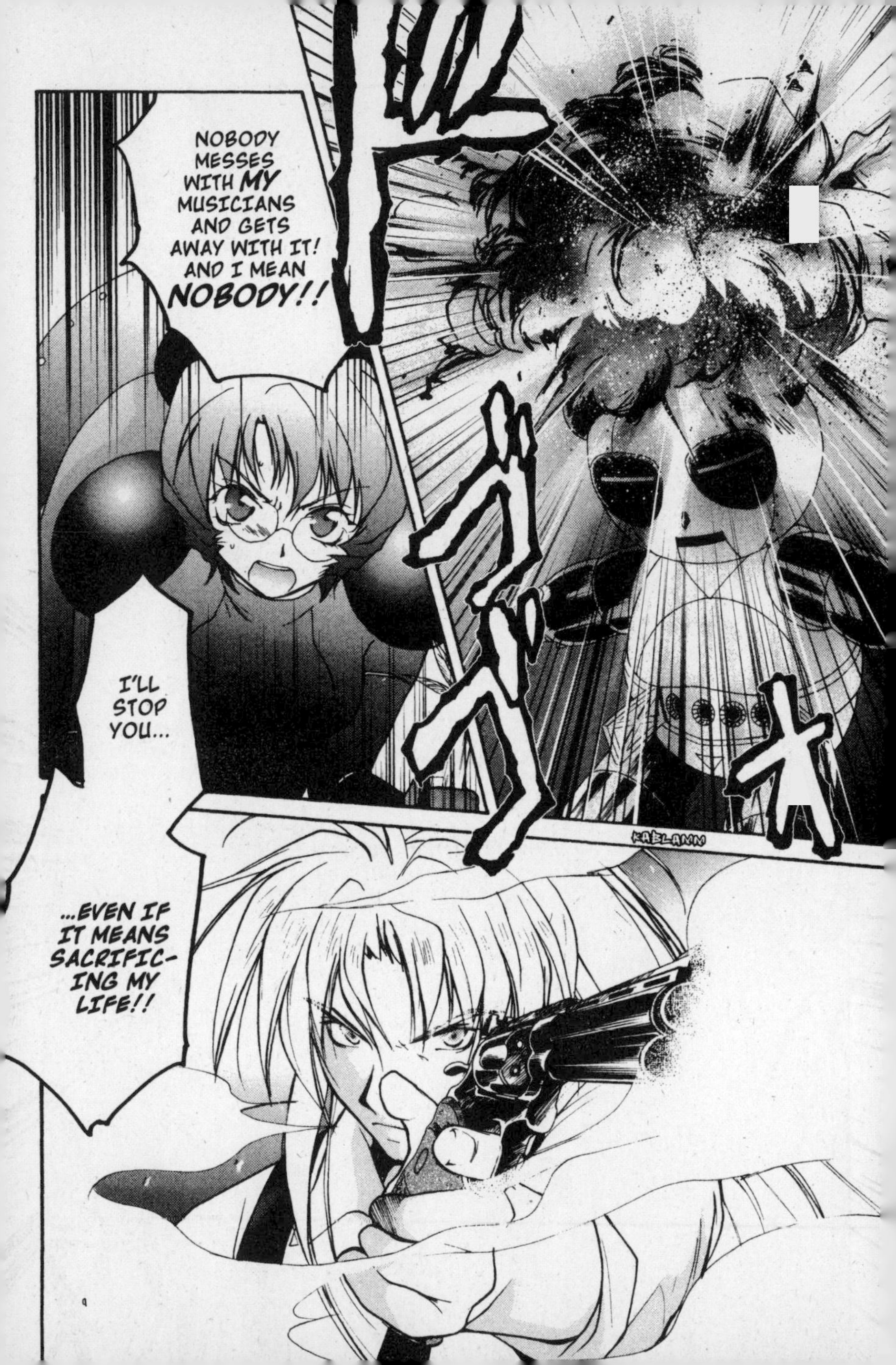
KABLAMM
NOBODY MESSES WITH MY MUSICIANS AND GETS AWAY WITH IT! AND I MEAN NOBODY!!
I'LL STOP YOU...
...EVEN IF IT MEANS SACRIFICING MY LIFE!!

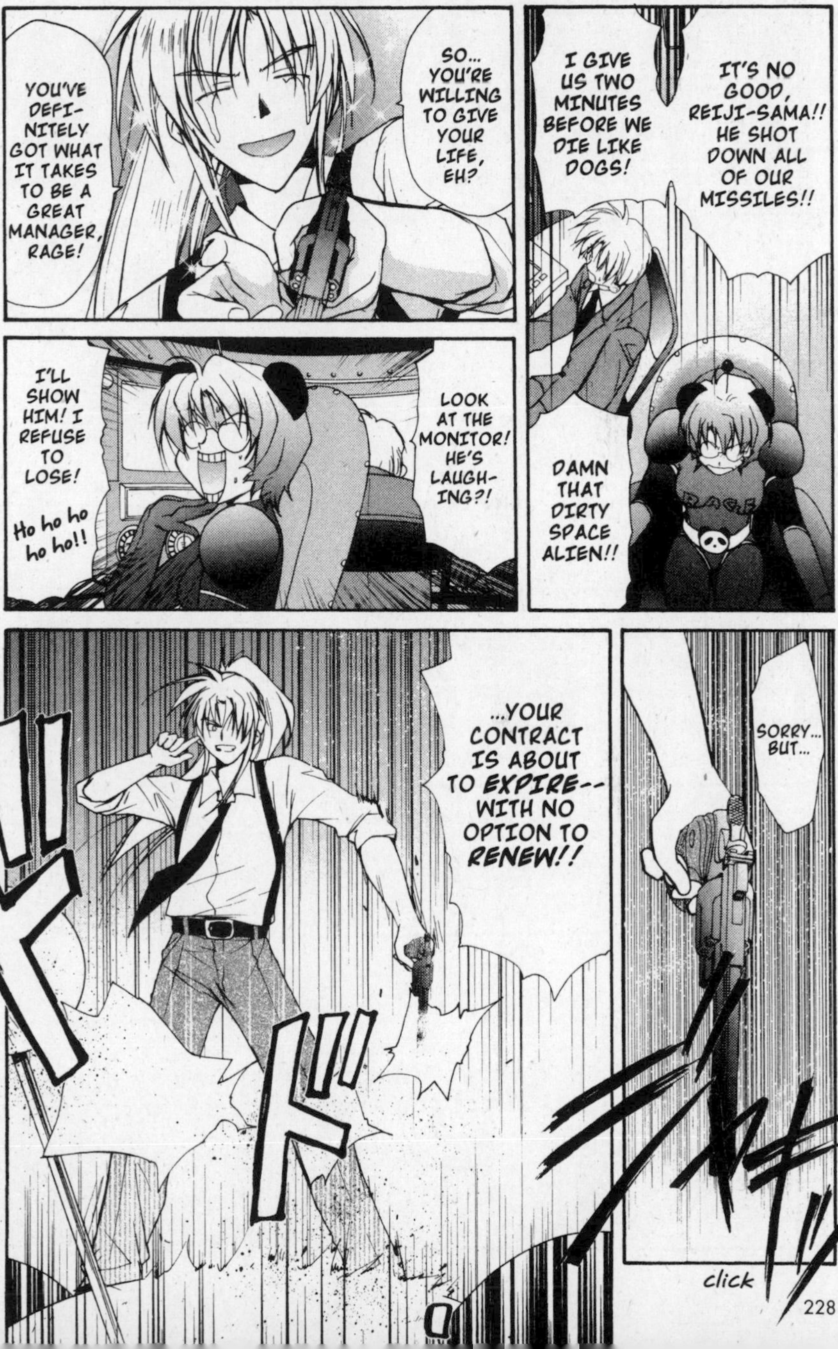
IT'S NO GOOD, REIJI-SAMA!! HE SHOT DOWN ALL OF OUR MISSILES!!
I GIVE US TWO MINUTES BEFORE WE DIE LIKE DOGS!
DAMN THAT DIRTY SPACE ALIEN!!
SO... YOU'RE WILLING TO GIVE YOUR LIFE, EH?
YOU'VE DEFINITELY GOT WHAT IT TAKES TO BE A GREAT MANAGER, RAGE!
LOOK AT THE MONITOR! HE'S LAUGHING?!
I'LL SHOW HIM! I REFUSE TO LOSE!
Ho ho ho ho ho!!
SORRY... BUT...
click
...YOUR CONTRACT IS ABOUT TO EXPIRE-- WITH NO OPTION TO RENEW!!

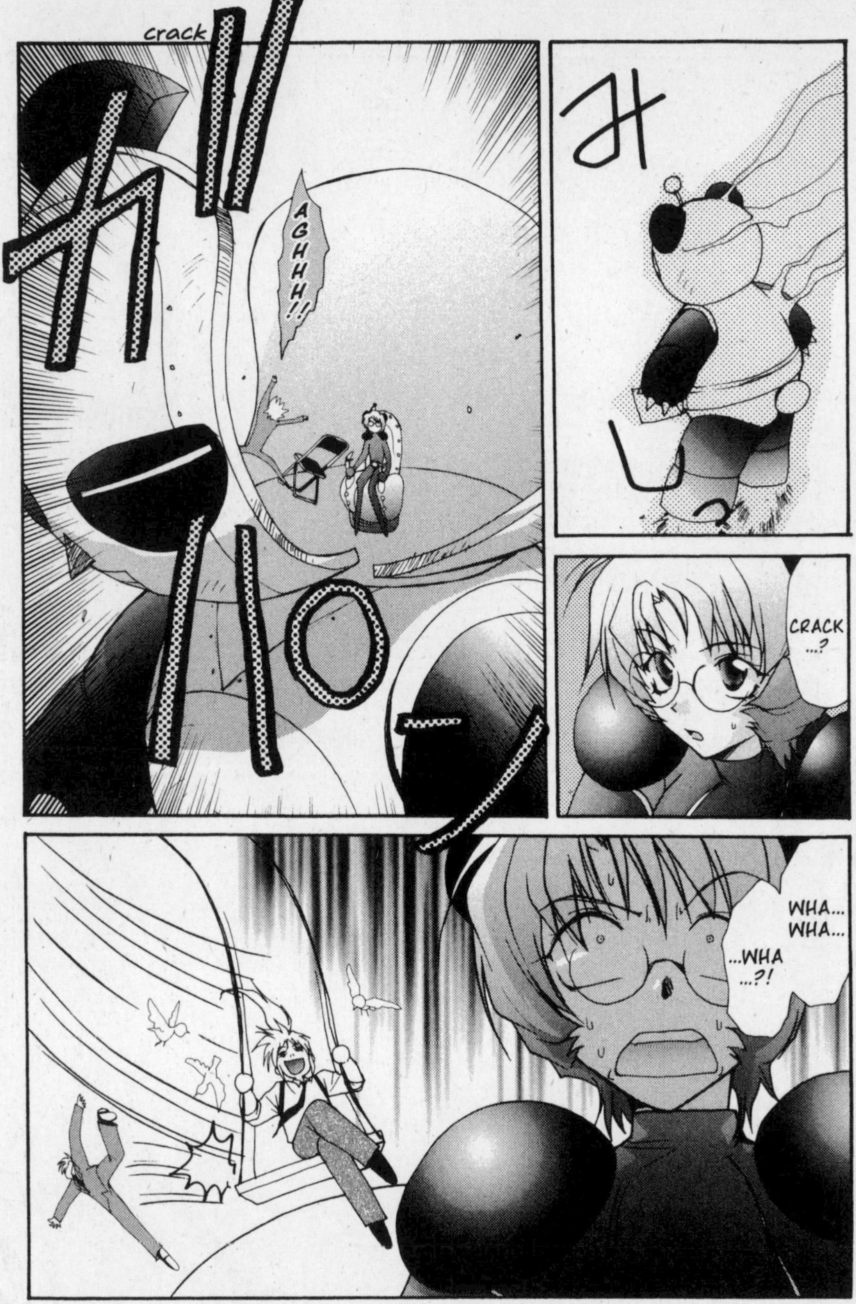
み
CRACK ...?
crack
AGHHH!!
WHA... WHA...
...WHA ...?!

0.7 seconds

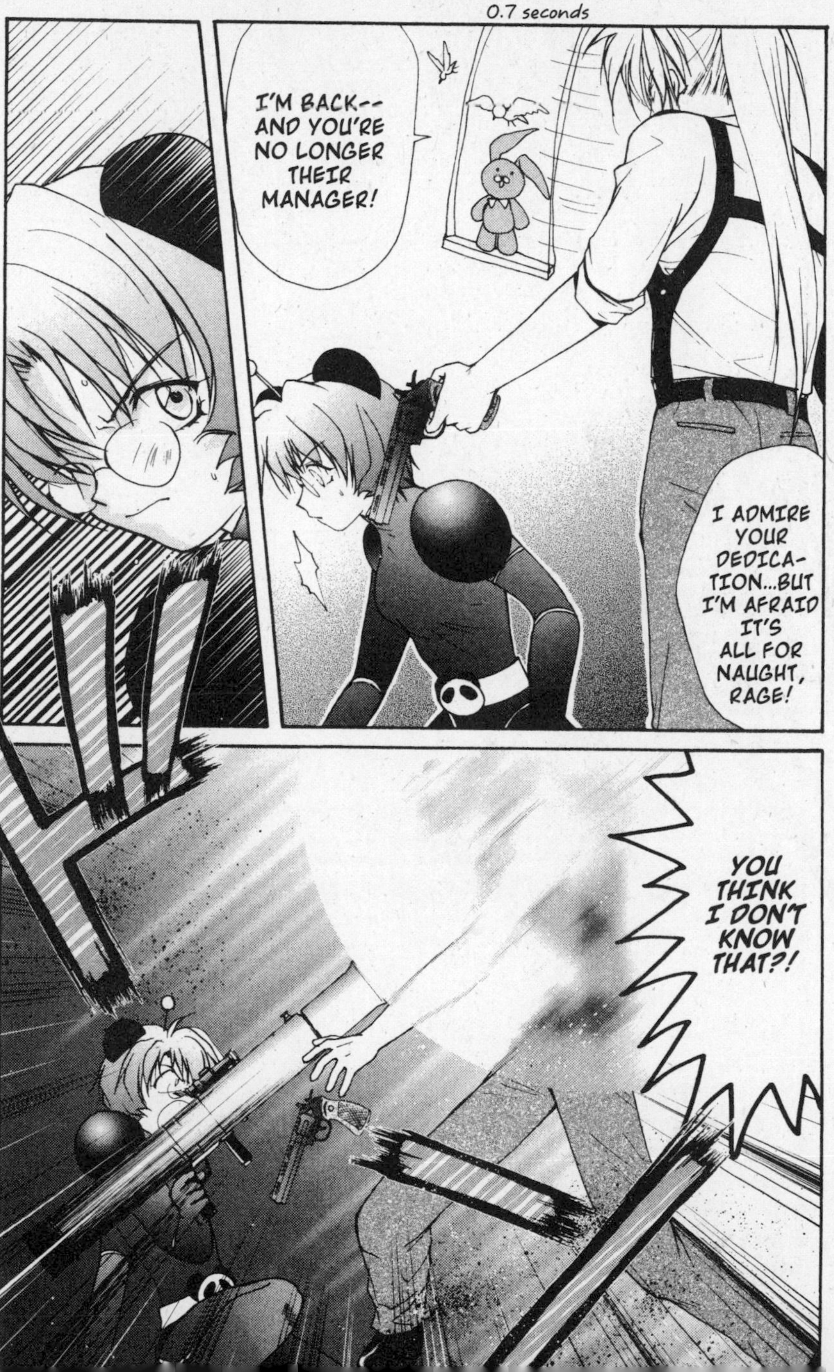
I'M BACK--AND YOU'RE NO LONGER THEIR MANAGER!
I ADMIRE YOUR DEDICATION...BUT I'M AFRAID IT'S ALL FOR NAUGHT, RAGE!
YOU THINK I DON'T KNOW THAT?!

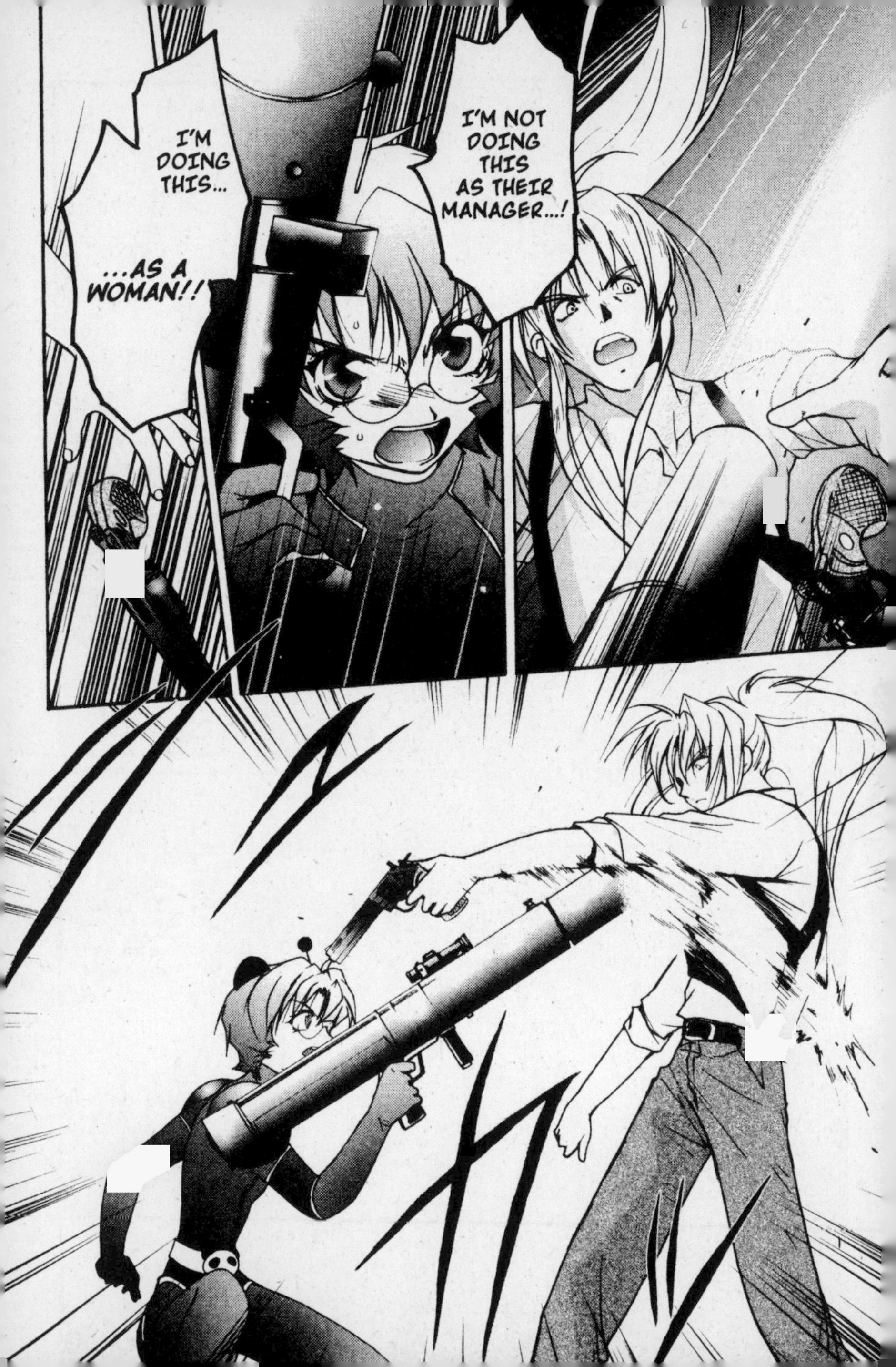
I'M NOT DOING THIS AS THEIR MANAGER...!
I'M DOING THIS...
...AS A WOMAN!!

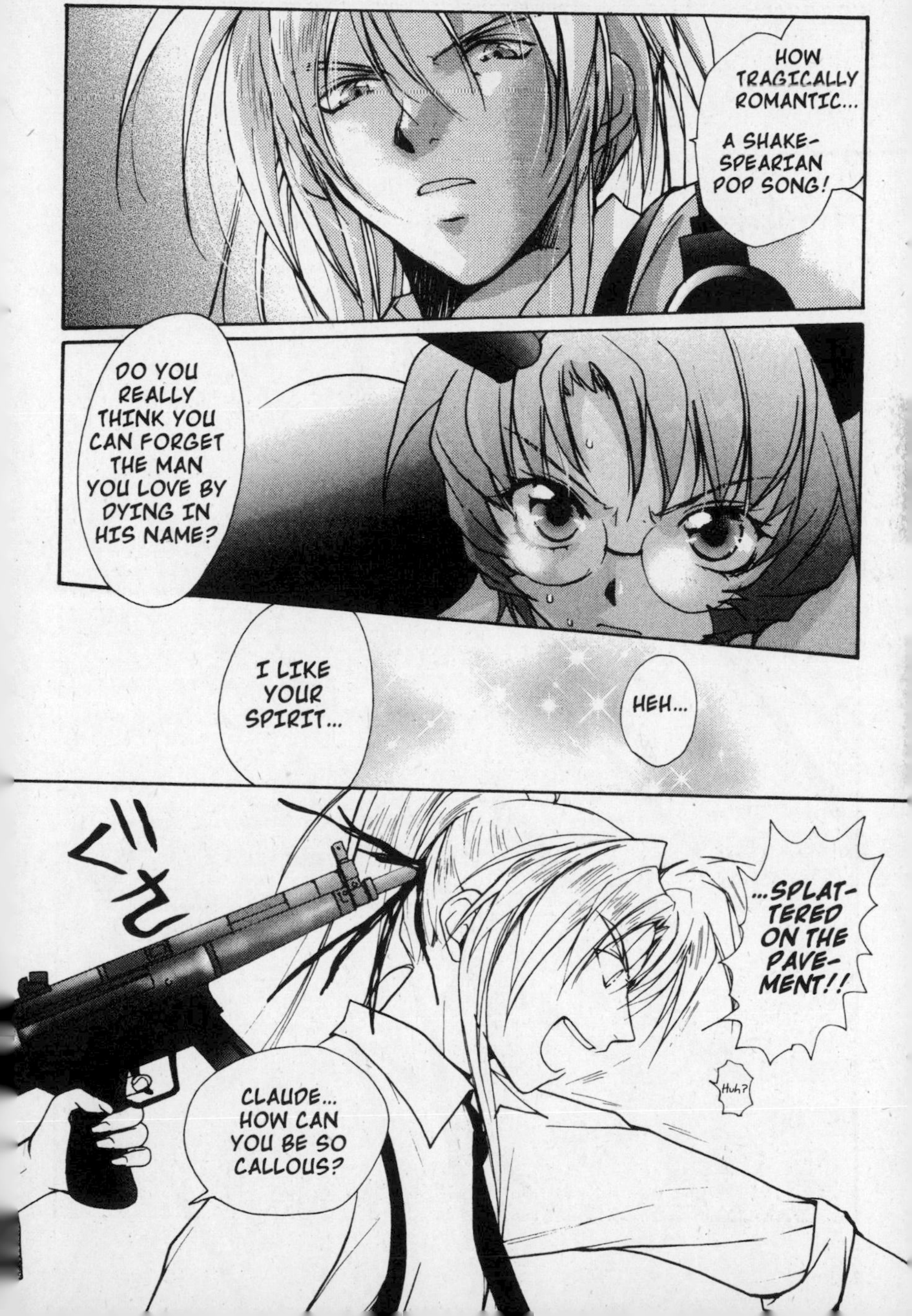
HOW TRAGICALLY ROMANTIC...
A SHAKE-SPEARIAN POP SONG!
DO YOU REALLY THINK YOU CAN FORGET THE MAN YOU LOVE BY DYING IN HIS NAME?
HEH...
I LIKE YOUR SPIRIT...
...SPLAT-TERED ON THE PAVE-MENT!!
Huh?
CLAUDE... HOW CAN YOU BE SO CALLOUS?

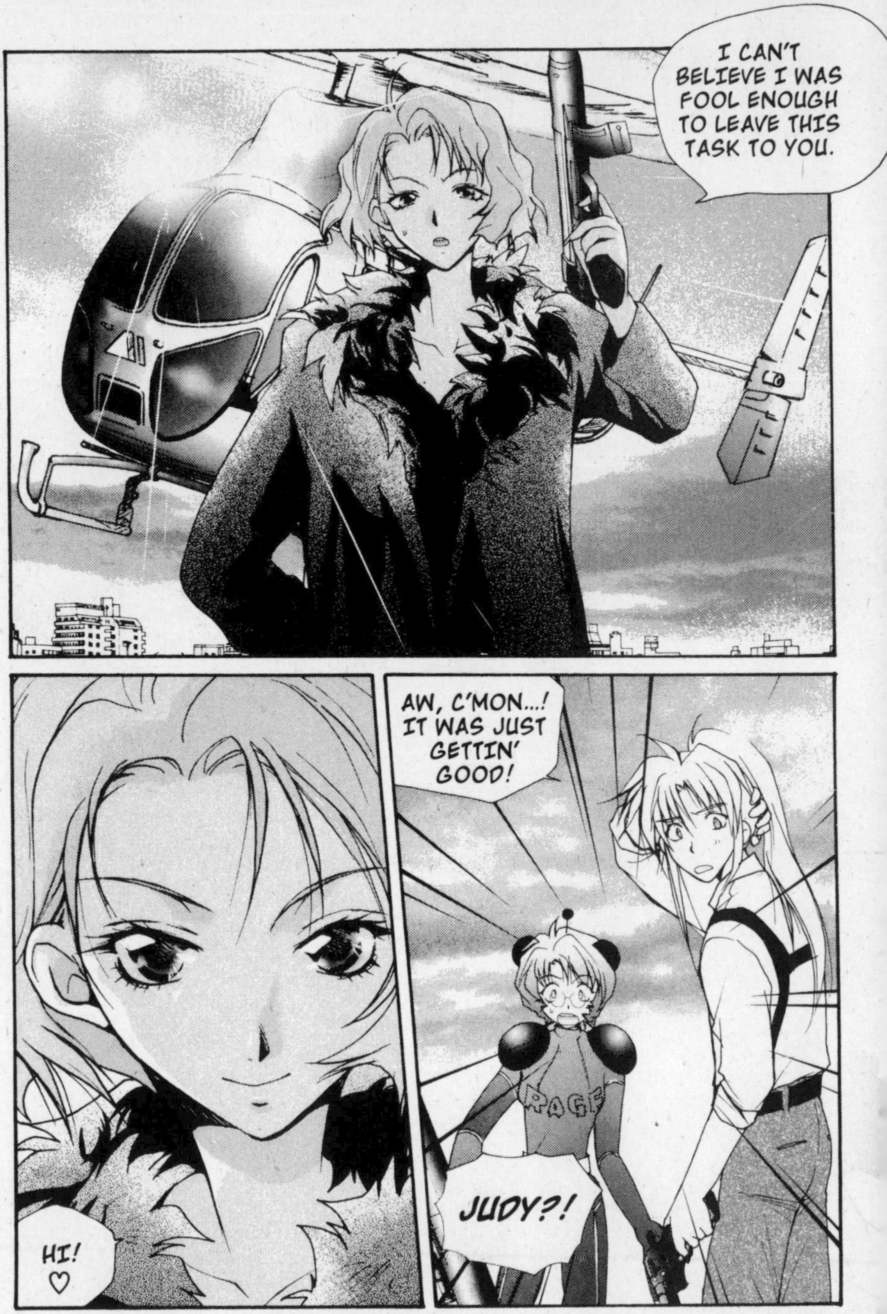
I CAN'T BELIEVE I WAS FOOL ENOUGH TO LEAVE THIS TASK TO YOU.
AW, C'MON...! IT WAS JUST GETTIN' GOOD!
JUDY?!
HI! ♡

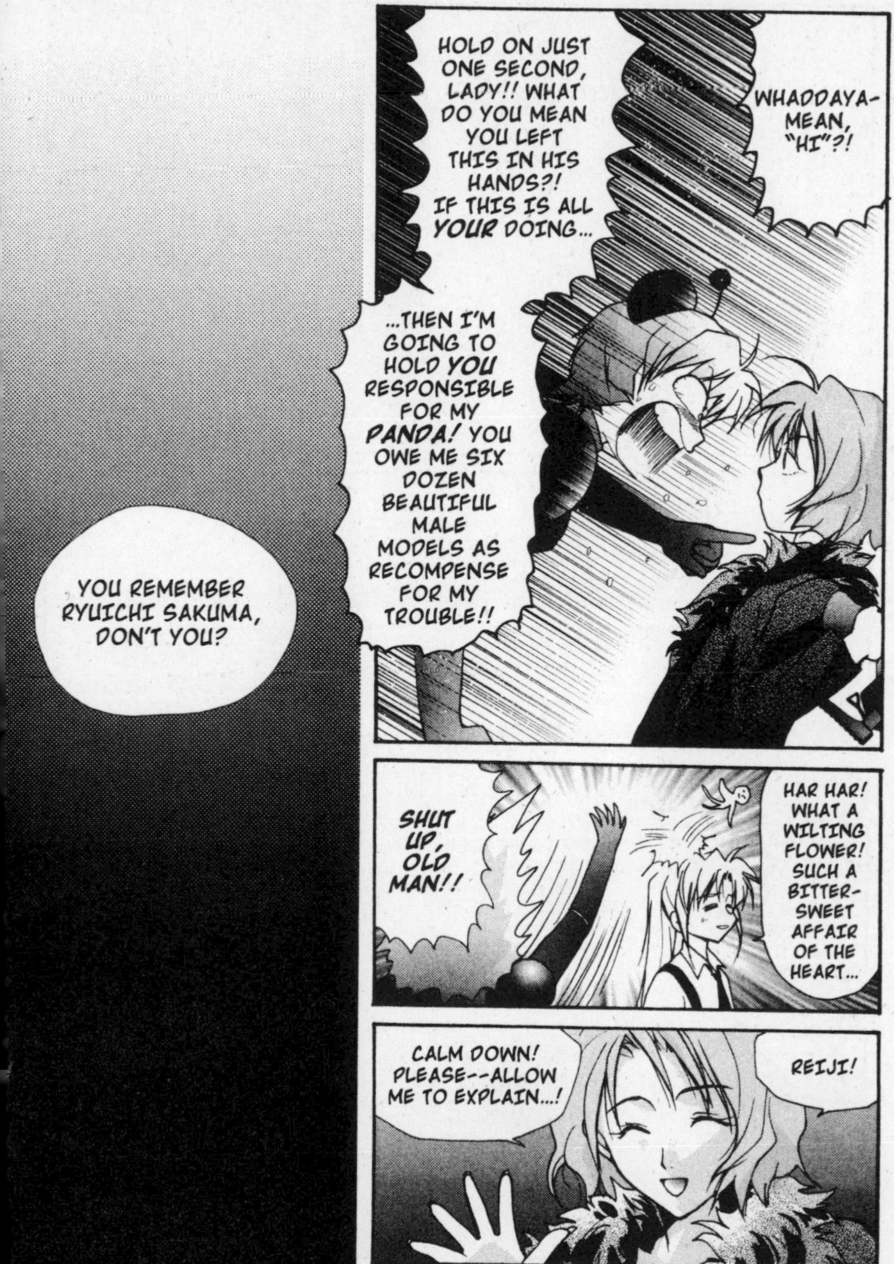
WHADDAYA-MEAN, "HI"?!
HOLD ON JUST ONE SECOND, LADY!! WHAT DO YOU MEAN YOU LEFT THIS IN HIS HANDS?! IF THIS IS ALL *YOUR* DOING...
...THEN I'M GOING TO HOLD *YOU* RESPONSIBLE FOR MY *PANDA!* YOU OWE ME SIX DOZEN BEAUTIFUL MALE MODELS AS RECOMPENSE FOR MY TROUBLE!!
HAR HAR! WHAT A WILTING FLOWER! SUCH A BITTER-SWEET AFFAIR OF THE HEART...
SHUT UP, OLD MAN!!
REIJI!
CALM DOWN! PLEASE--ALLOW ME TO EXPLAIN...!
YOU REMEMBER RYUICHI SAKUMA, DON'T YOU?

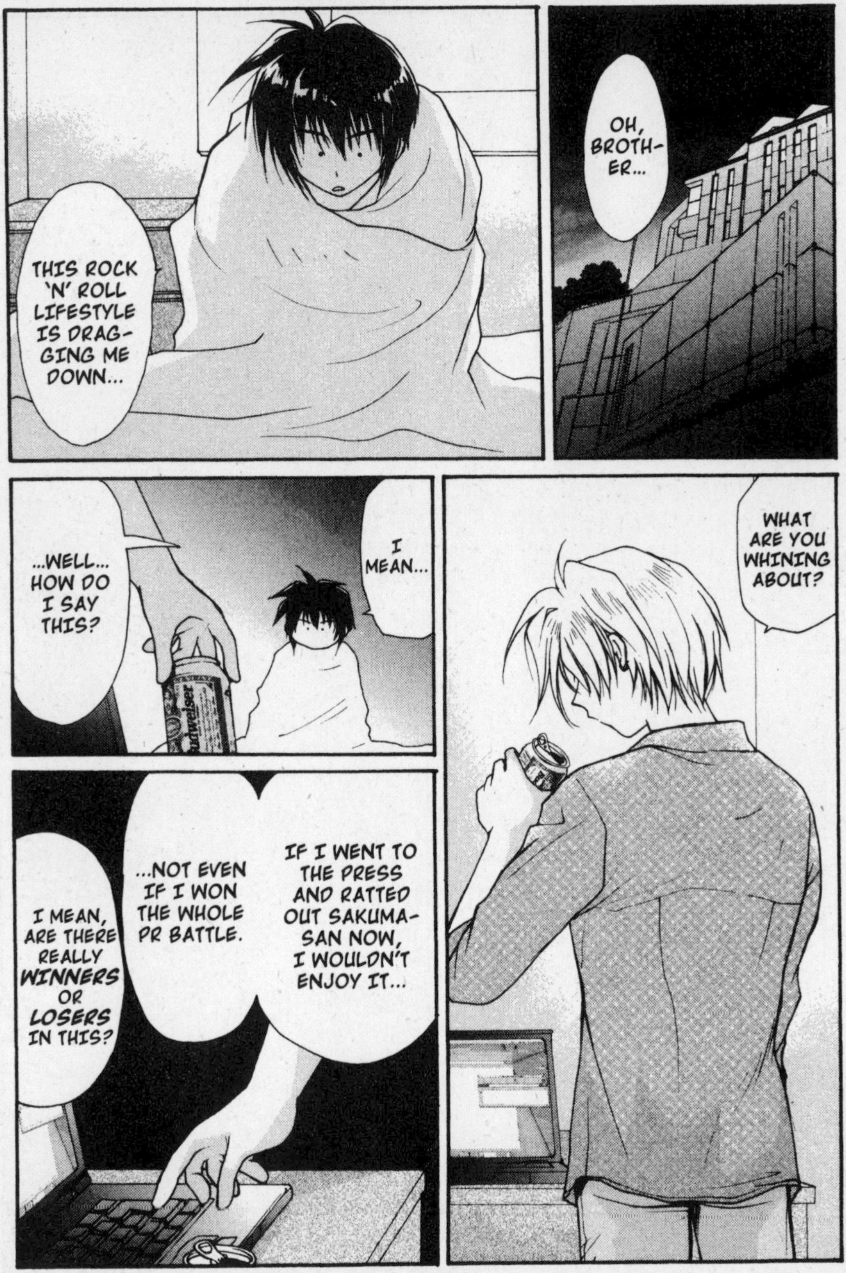
OH, BROTHER-ER...
THIS ROCK 'N' ROLL LIFESTYLE IS DRAGGING ME DOWN...
WHAT ARE YOU WHINING ABOUT?
I MEAN...
...WELL... HOW DO I SAY THIS?
IF I WENT TO THE PRESS AND RATTED OUT SAKUMA-SAN NOW, I WOULDN'T ENJOY IT...
...NOT EVEN IF I WON THE WHOLE PR BATTLE.
I MEAN, ARE THERE REALLY WINNERS OR LOSERS IN THIS?

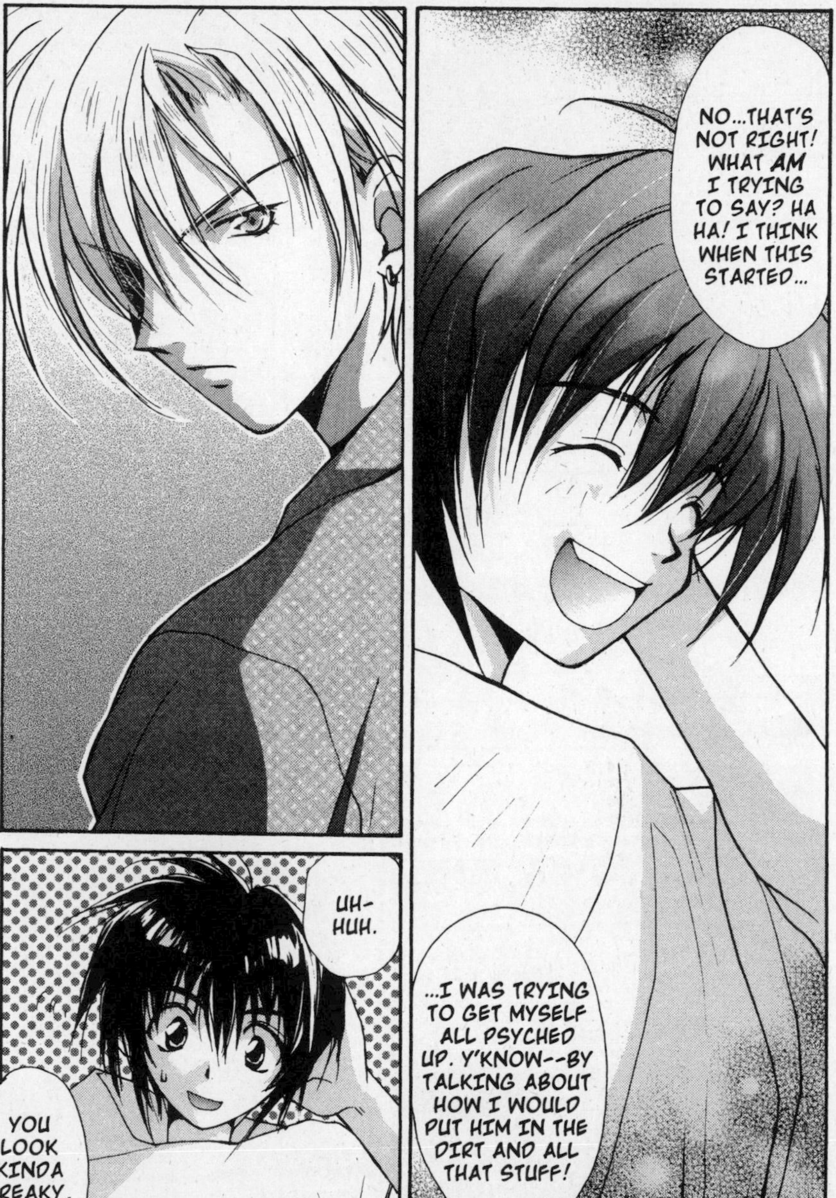
NO...THAT'S NOT RIGHT! WHAT AM I TRYING TO SAY? HA HA! I THINK WHEN THIS STARTED...
...I WAS TRYING TO GET MYSELF ALL PSYCHED UP. Y'KNOW--BY TALKING ABOUT HOW I WOULD PUT HIM IN THE DIRT AND ALL THAT STUFF!
UH-HUH.
YOU LOOK KINDA FREAKY, YUKI.

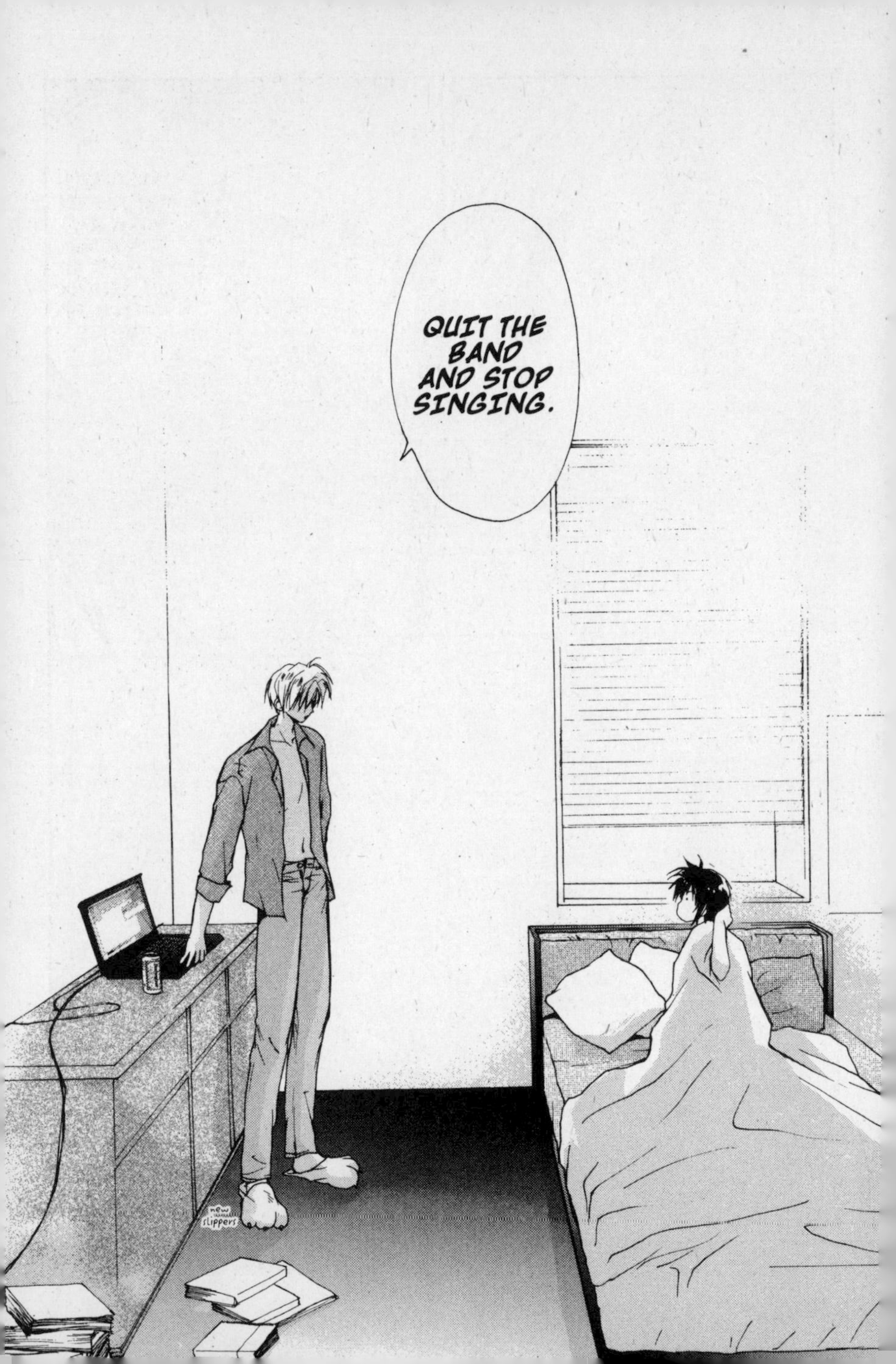
QUIT THE BAND AND STOP SINGING.
new slippers

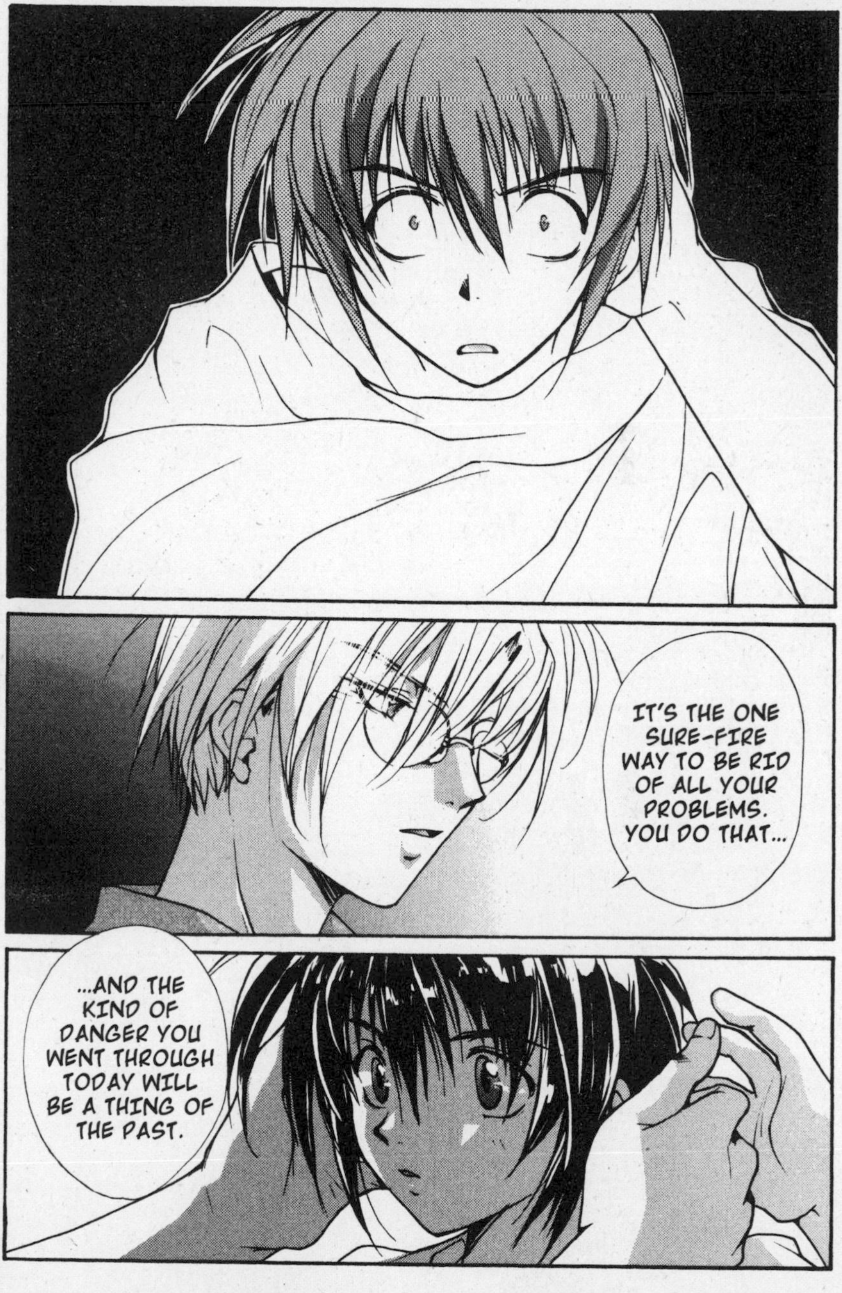
IT'S THE ONE SURE-FIRE WAY TO BE RID OF ALL YOUR PROBLEMS. YOU DO THAT...
...AND THE KIND OF DANGER YOU WENT THROUGH TODAY WILL BE A THING OF THE PAST.

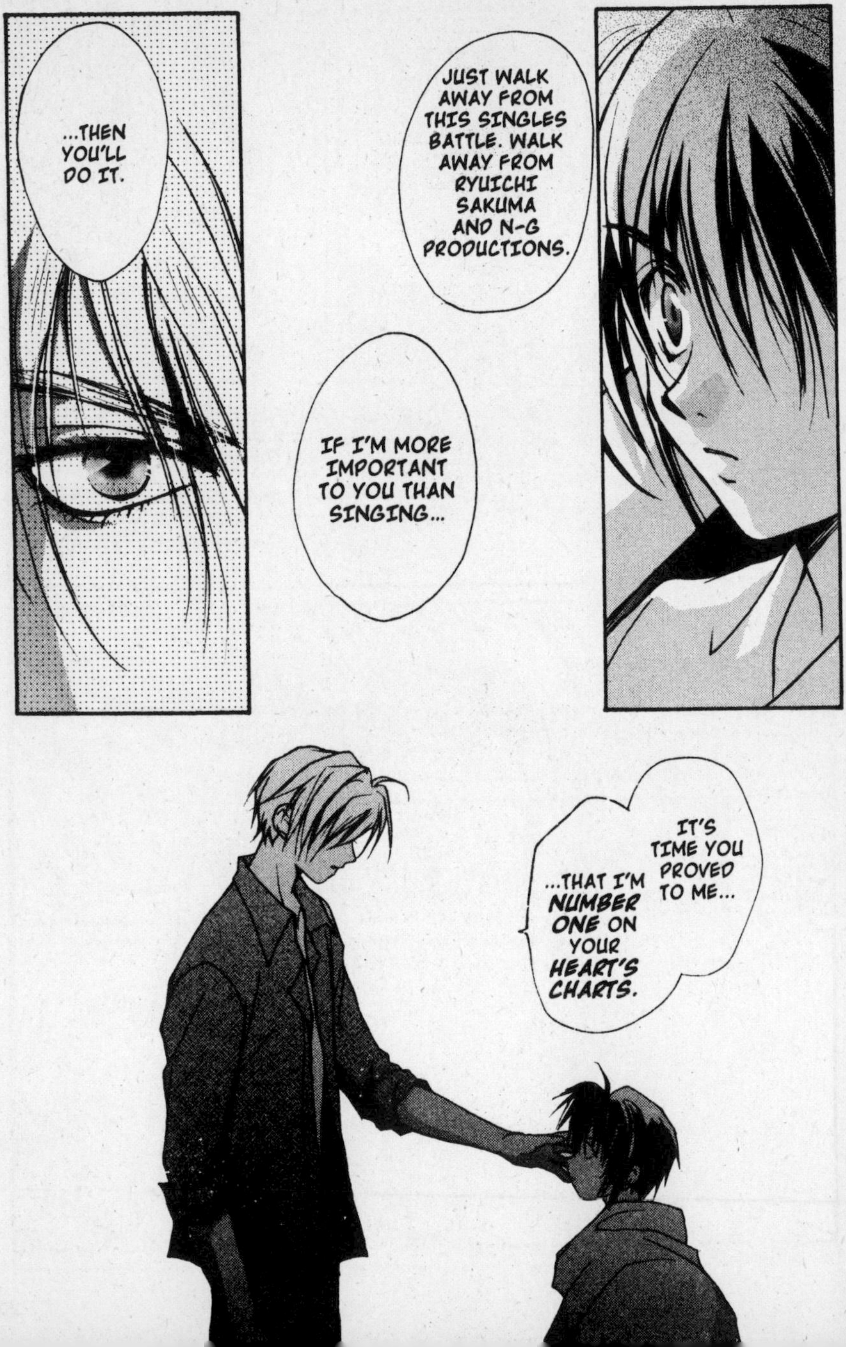
JUST WALK AWAY FROM THIS SINGLES BATTLE. WALK AWAY FROM RYUICHI SAKUMA AND N-G PRODUCTIONS.
IF I'M MORE IMPORTANT TO YOU THAN SINGING...
...THEN YOU'LL DO IT.
IT'S TIME YOU PROVED TO ME...
...THAT I'M NUMBER ONE ON YOUR HEART'S CHARTS.

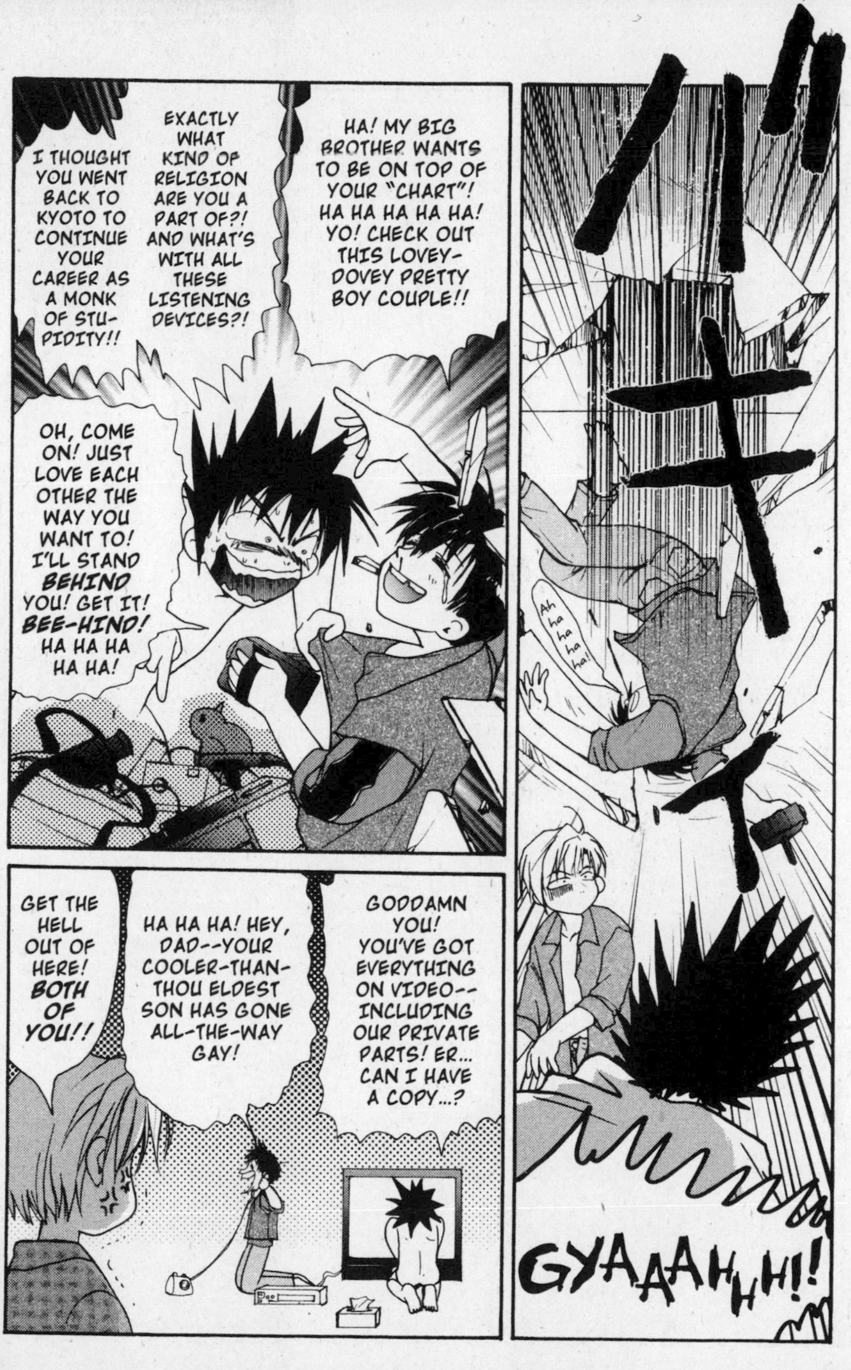
Ah ha ha ha ha!
GYAAAHHH!
EXACTLY WHAT KIND OF RELIGION ARE YOU A PART OF?! AND WHAT'S WITH ALL THESE LISTENING DEVICES?!
HA! MY BIG BROTHER WANTS TO BE ON TOP OF YOUR "CHART"! HA HA HA HA HA! YO! CHECK OUT THIS LOVEY-DOVEY PRETTY BOY COUPLE!!
I THOUGHT YOU WENT BACK TO KYOTO TO CONTINUE YOUR CAREER AS A MONK OF STU-PIDITY!!
OH, COME ON! JUST LOVE EACH OTHER THE WAY YOU WANT TO! I'LL STAND ***BEHIND*** YOU! GET IT! ***BEE-HIND!*** HA HA HA HA HA!
GODDAMN YOU! YOU'VE GOT EVERYTHING ON VIDEO--INCLUDING OUR PRIVATE PARTS! ER... CAN I HAVE A COPY...?
HA HA HA! HEY, DAD--YOUR COOLER-THAN-THOU ELDEST SON HAS GONE ALL-THE-WAY GAY!
GET THE HELL OUT OF HERE! ***BOTH OF YOU!!***

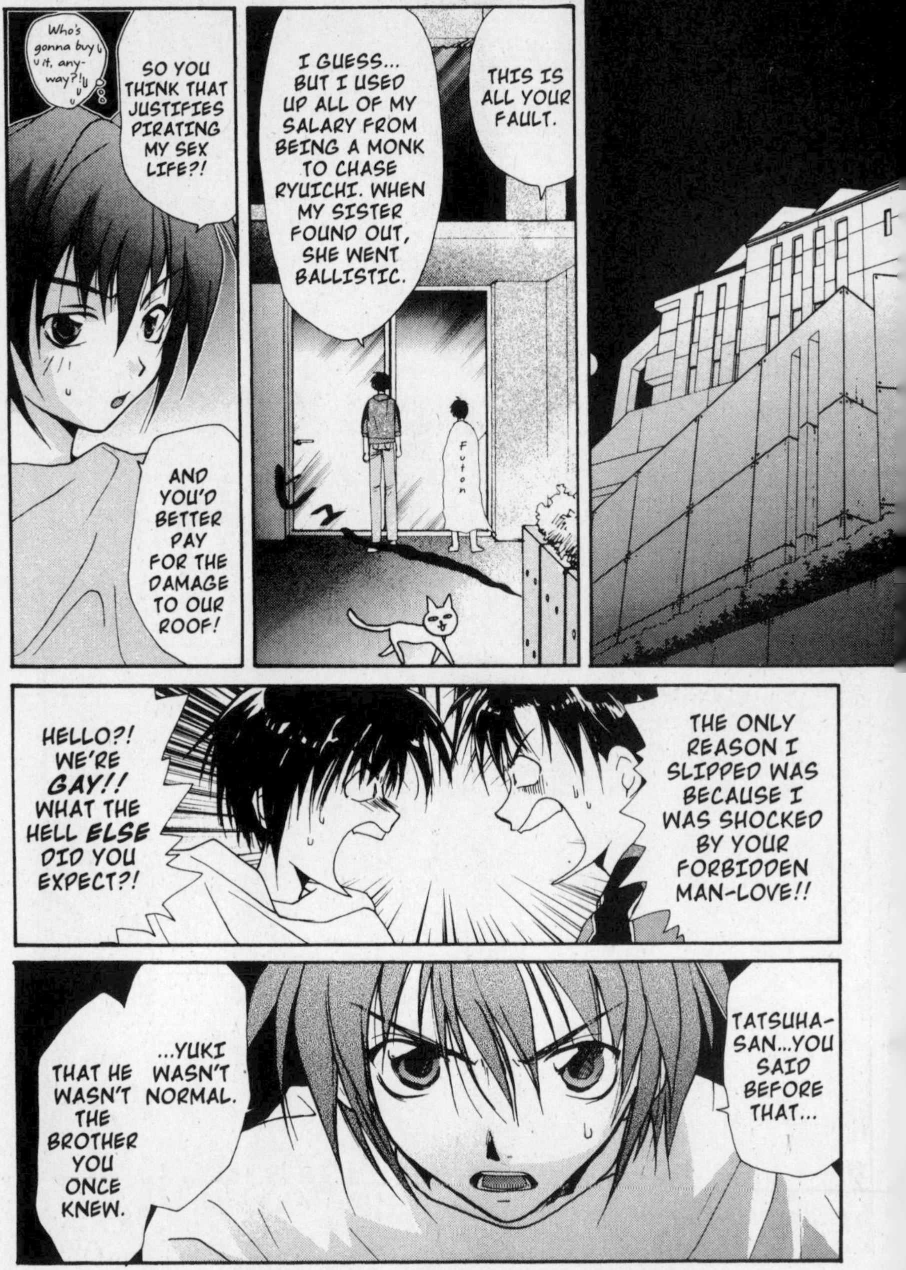
THIS IS ALL YOUR FAULT.
I GUESS... BUT I USED UP ALL OF MY SALARY FROM BEING A MONK TO CHASE RYUICHI. WHEN MY SISTER FOUND OUT, SHE WENT BALLISTIC.
Futon
SO YOU THINK THAT JUSTIFIES PIRATING MY SEX LIFE?!
Who's gonna buy it, anyway?!
AND YOU'D BETTER PAY FOR THE DAMAGE TO OUR ROOF!
THE ONLY REASON I SLIPPED WAS BECAUSE I WAS SHOCKED BY YOUR FORBIDDEN MAN-LOVE!!
HELLO?! WE'RE GAY!! WHAT THE HELL ELSE DID YOU EXPECT?!
TATSUHA-SAN...YOU SAID BEFORE THAT...
...YUKI WASN'T NORMAL.
THAT HE WASN'T THE BROTHER YOU ONCE KNEW.

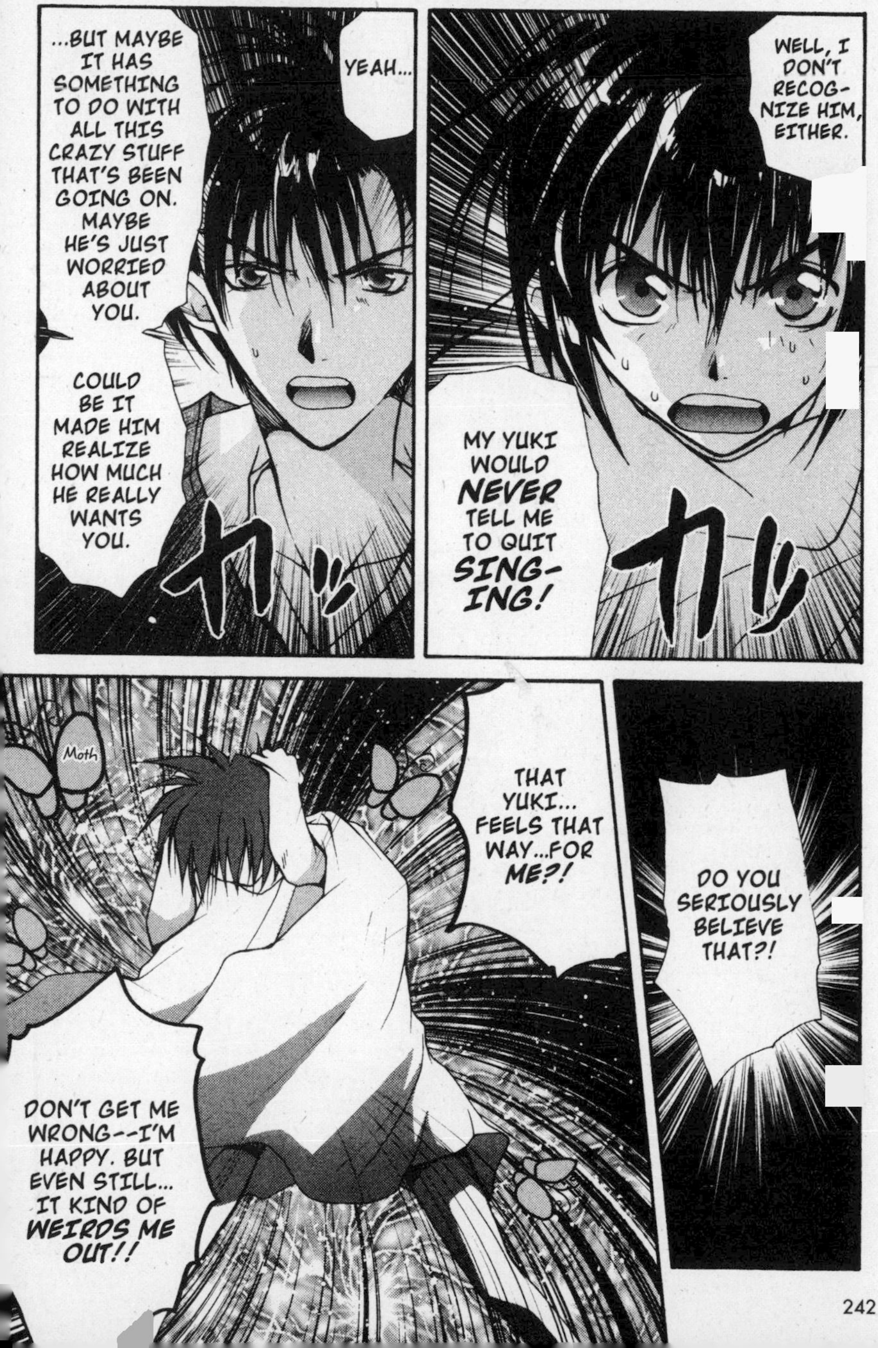
WELL, I DON'T RECOGNIZE HIM, EITHER.
MY YUKI WOULD NEVER TELL ME TO QUIT SINGING!
YEAH...
...BUT MAYBE IT HAS SOMETHING TO DO WITH ALL THIS CRAZY STUFF THAT'S BEEN GOING ON. MAYBE HE'S JUST WORRIED ABOUT YOU.
COULD BE IT MADE HIM REALIZE HOW MUCH HE REALLY WANTS YOU.
DO YOU SERIOUSLY BELIEVE THAT?!
THAT YUKI... FEELS THAT WAY...FOR ME?!
Moth
DON'T GET ME WRONG--I'M HAPPY. BUT EVEN STILL... IT KIND OF WEIRDS ME OUT!!

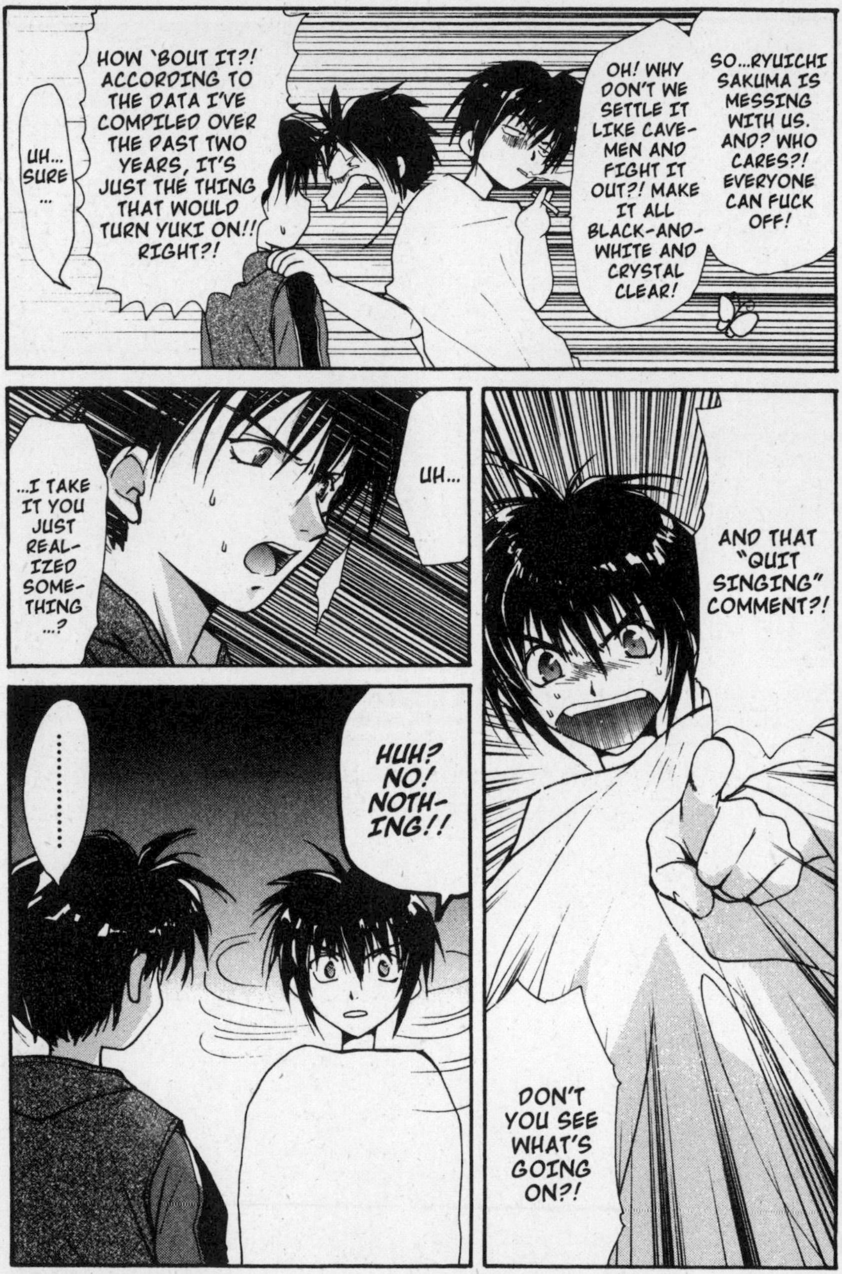
SO...RYUICHI SAKUMA IS MESSING WITH US. AND? WHO CARES?! EVERYONE CAN FUCK OFF!
OH! WHY DON'T WE SETTLE IT LIKE CAVE-MEN AND FIGHT IT OUT?! MAKE IT ALL BLACK-AND-WHITE AND CRYSTAL CLEAR!
HOW `BOUT IT?! ACCORDING TO THE DATA I'VE COMPILED OVER THE PAST TWO YEARS, IT'S JUST THE THING THAT WOULD TURN YUKI ON!! RIGHT?!
UH... SURE ...
AND THAT "QUIT SINGING" COMMENT?!
DON'T YOU SEE WHAT'S GOING ON?!
UH...
...I TAKE IT YOU JUST REAL-IZED SOME-THING ...?
HUH? NO! NOTH-ING!!
.........

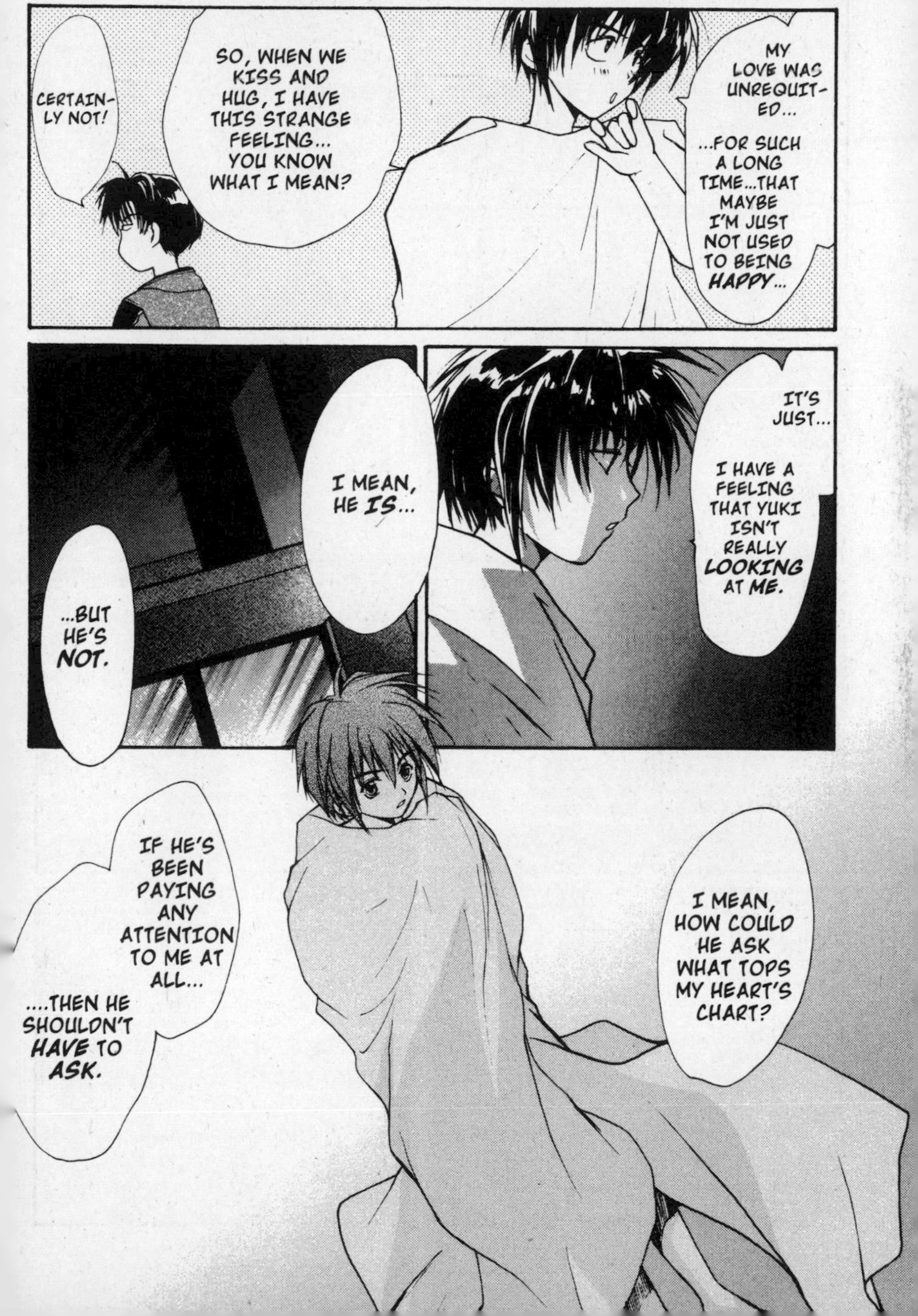
MY LOVE WAS UNREQUIT-ED...
...FOR SUCH A LONG TIME...THAT MAYBE I'M JUST NOT USED TO BEING **HAPPY**...
SO, WHEN WE KISS AND HUG, I HAVE THIS STRANGE FEELING... YOU KNOW WHAT I MEAN?
CERTAIN-LY NOT!
IT'S JUST...
I HAVE A FEELING THAT YUKI ISN'T REALLY **LOOKING** AT **ME**.
I MEAN, HE **IS**...
...BUT HE'S **NOT**.
I MEAN, HOW COULD HE ASK WHAT TOPS MY HEART'S CHART?
IF HE'S BEEN PAYING ANY ATTENTION TO ME AT ALL...
....THEN HE SHOULDN'T **HAVE** TO **ASK**.

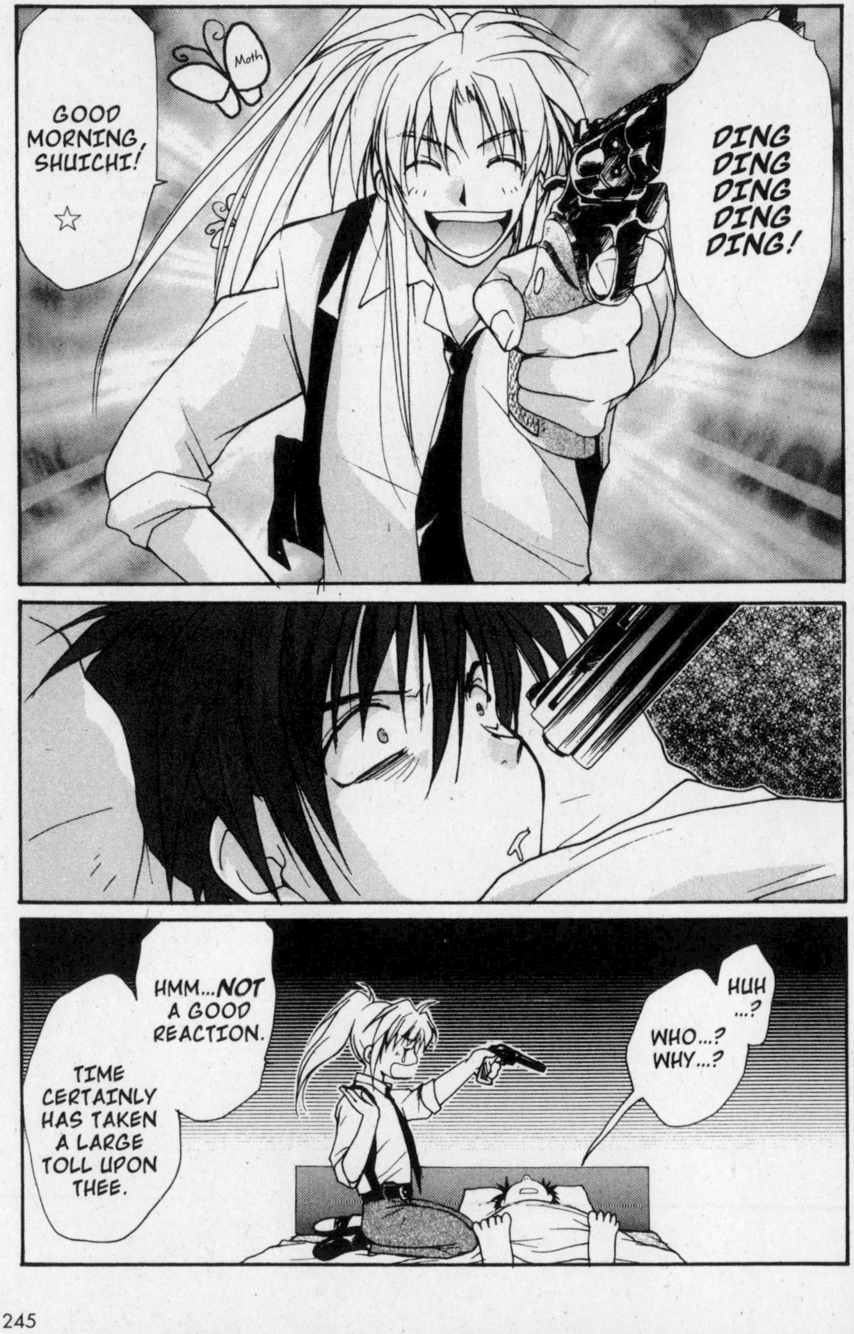
DING DING DING DING DING!
GOOD MORNING, SHUICHI! ☆
Moth
HUH ...?
WHO...? WHY...?
HMM...NOT A GOOD REACTION.
TIME CERTAINLY HAS TAKEN A LARGE TOLL UPON THEE.

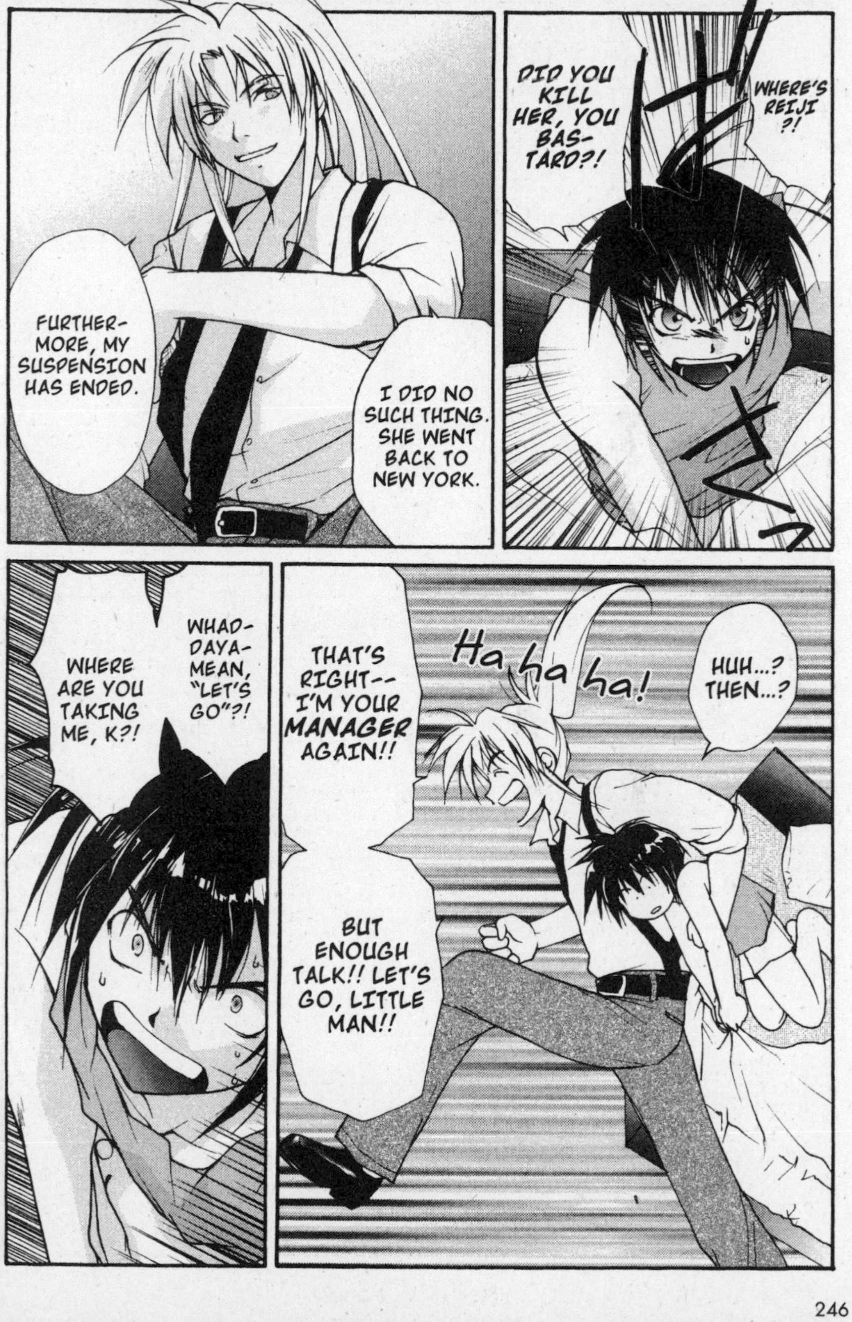

WHERE'S REIJI ?!
DID YOU KILL HER, YOU BASTARD?!
I DID NO SUCH THING. SHE WENT BACK TO NEW YORK.
FURTHERMORE, MY SUSPENSION HAS ENDED.
HUH...? THEN...?
Ha ha ha!
THAT'S RIGHT-- I'M YOUR **MANAGER** AGAIN!!
BUT ENOUGH TALK!! LET'S GO, LITTLE MAN!!
WHADDAYAMEAN, "LET'S GO"?!
WHERE ARE YOU TAKING ME, K?!

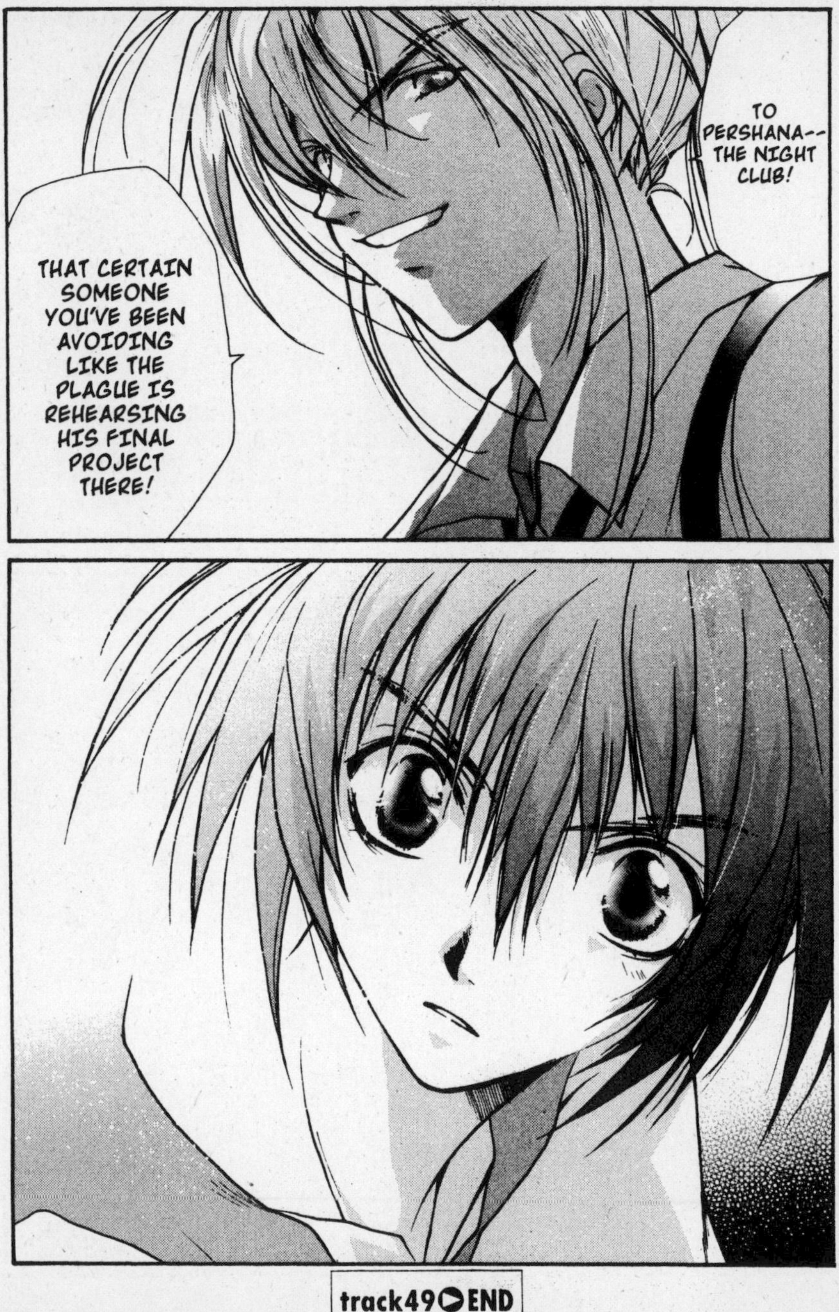
TO PERSHANA-- THE NIGHT CLUB!
THAT CERTAIN SOMEONE YOU'VE BEEN AVOIDING LIKE THE PLAGUE IS REHEARSING HIS FINAL PROJECT THERE!

track49 ▶ END

# Gravitation Volume 12 Special Bonus!!

## Costume Play

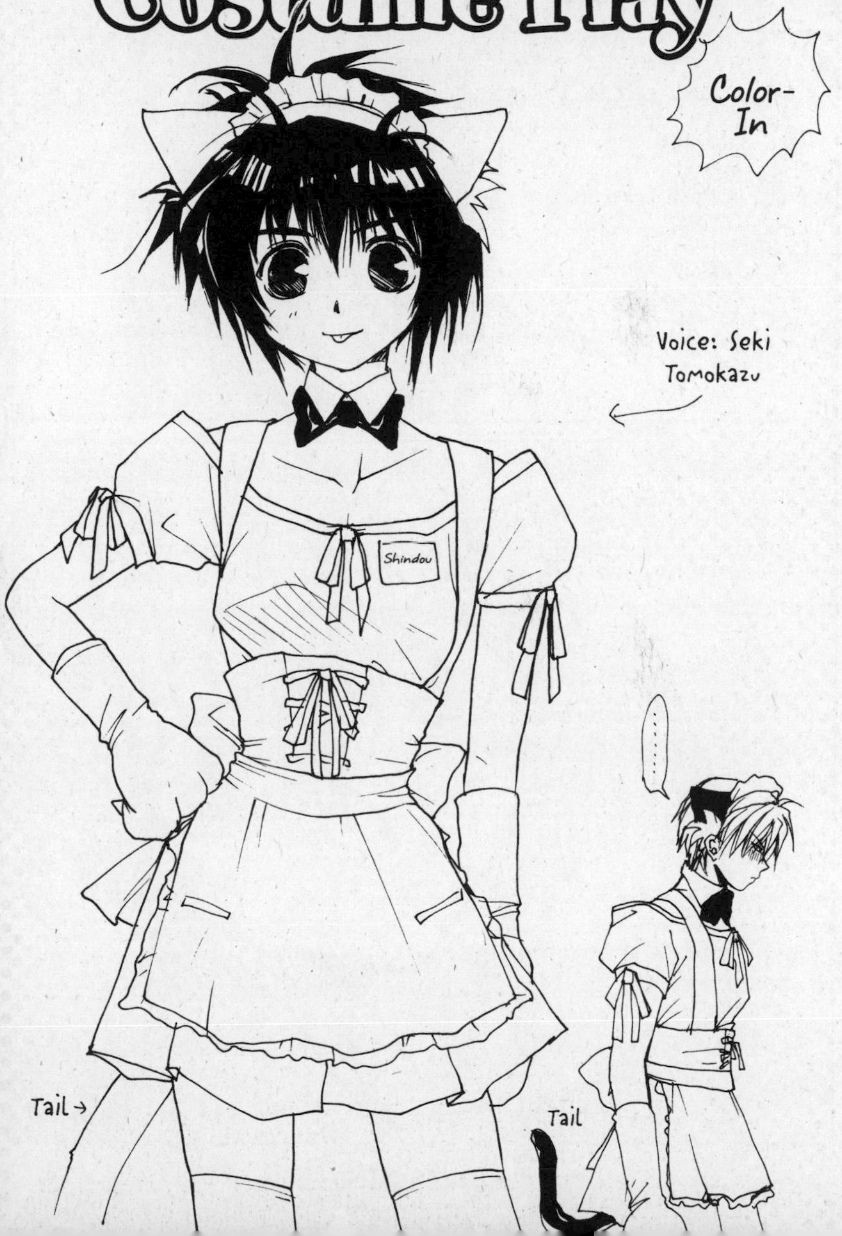
Color-In
Voice: Seki Tomokazu
Shindou
......
Tail→
Tail

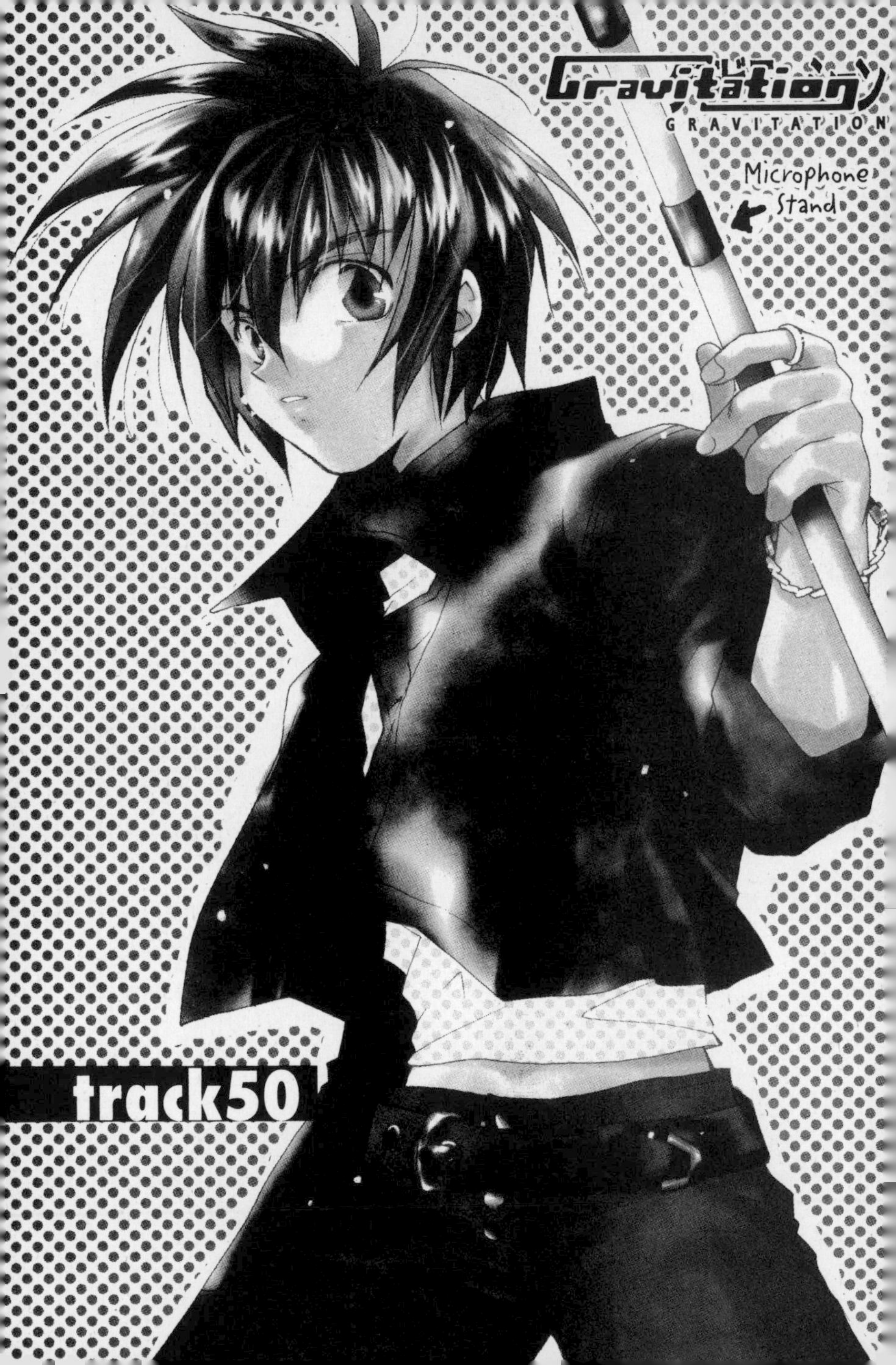
Gravitation
GRAVITATION
Microphone Stand
track50

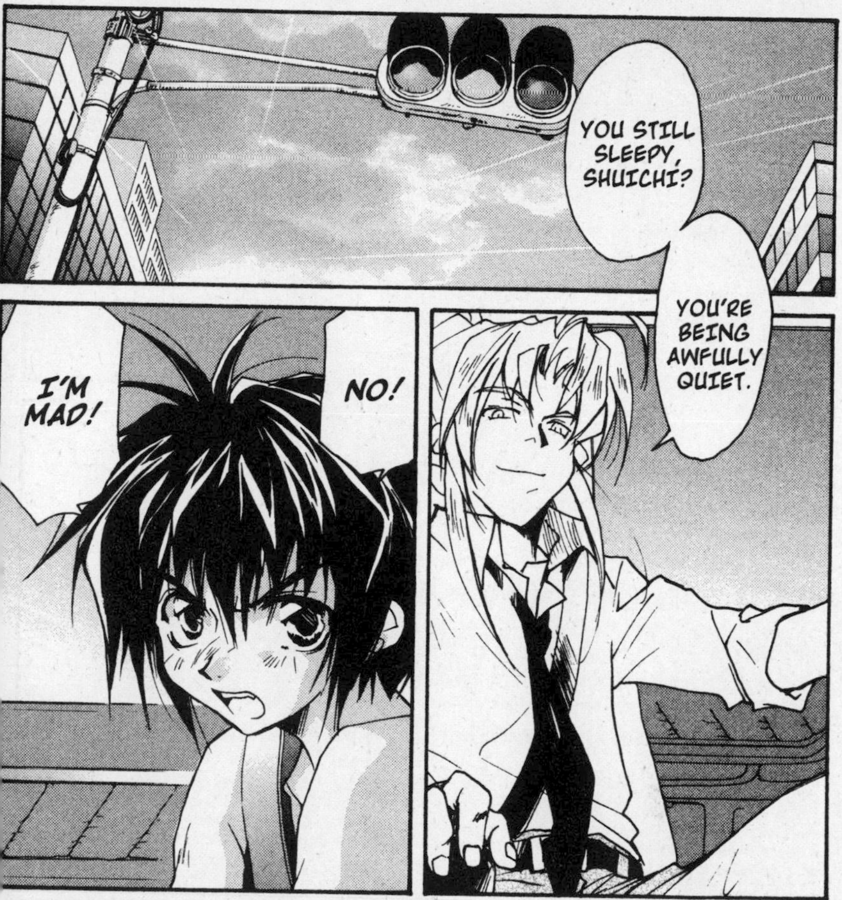
YOU STILL SLEEPY, SHUICHI?
YOU'RE BEING AWFULLY QUIET.
NO!
I'M MAD!

## ABOUT GRAVITATION TRACK 50

Although I know that nobody is looking at my drawings anymore, the illustrations in this chapter are very sloppy. My changing the way I inked the boys' hair is not an indication of me working hard to grow as an artist or anything positive like that. It's just that I forgot how I did it the last time...so I'm sorry. Ugh... At this point, my drawing has become very old lady-like, so I want to hurry up and fix that. Or maybe overall, I'm being redundant. I beg of you, please don't look at the drawings. I'm just no good. Usually, most artists get better at making comics the more they do it. Strangely though, I've become worse. Heh heh...oh boy...

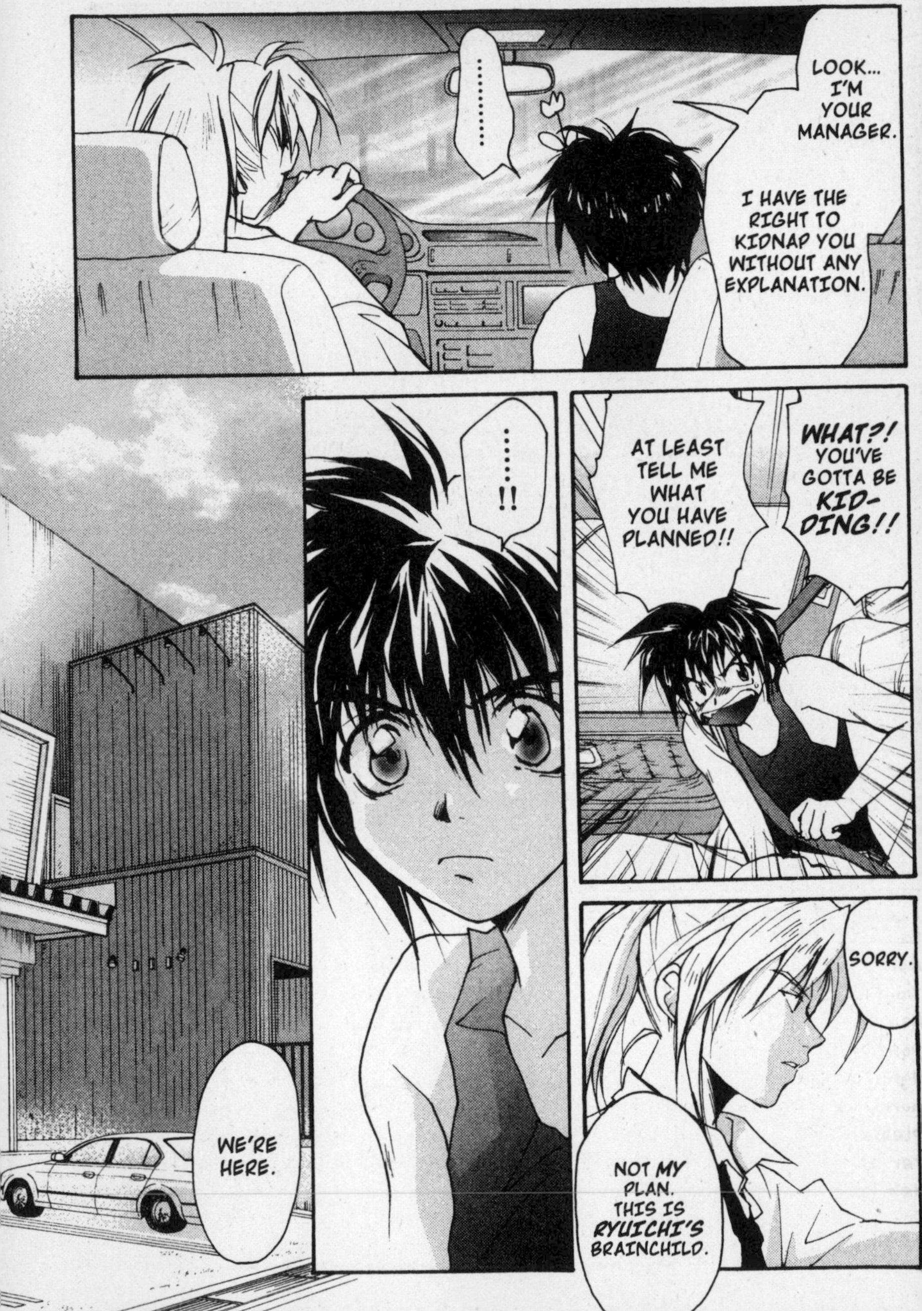
LOOK... I'M YOUR MANAGER.
I HAVE THE RIGHT TO KIDNAP YOU WITHOUT ANY EXPLANATION.
......
WHAT?! YOU'VE GOTTA BE KID-DING!!
AT LEAST TELL ME WHAT YOU HAVE PLANNED!!
SORRY.
NOT MY PLAN. THIS IS RYUICHI'S BRAINCHILD.
......!!
WE'RE HERE.

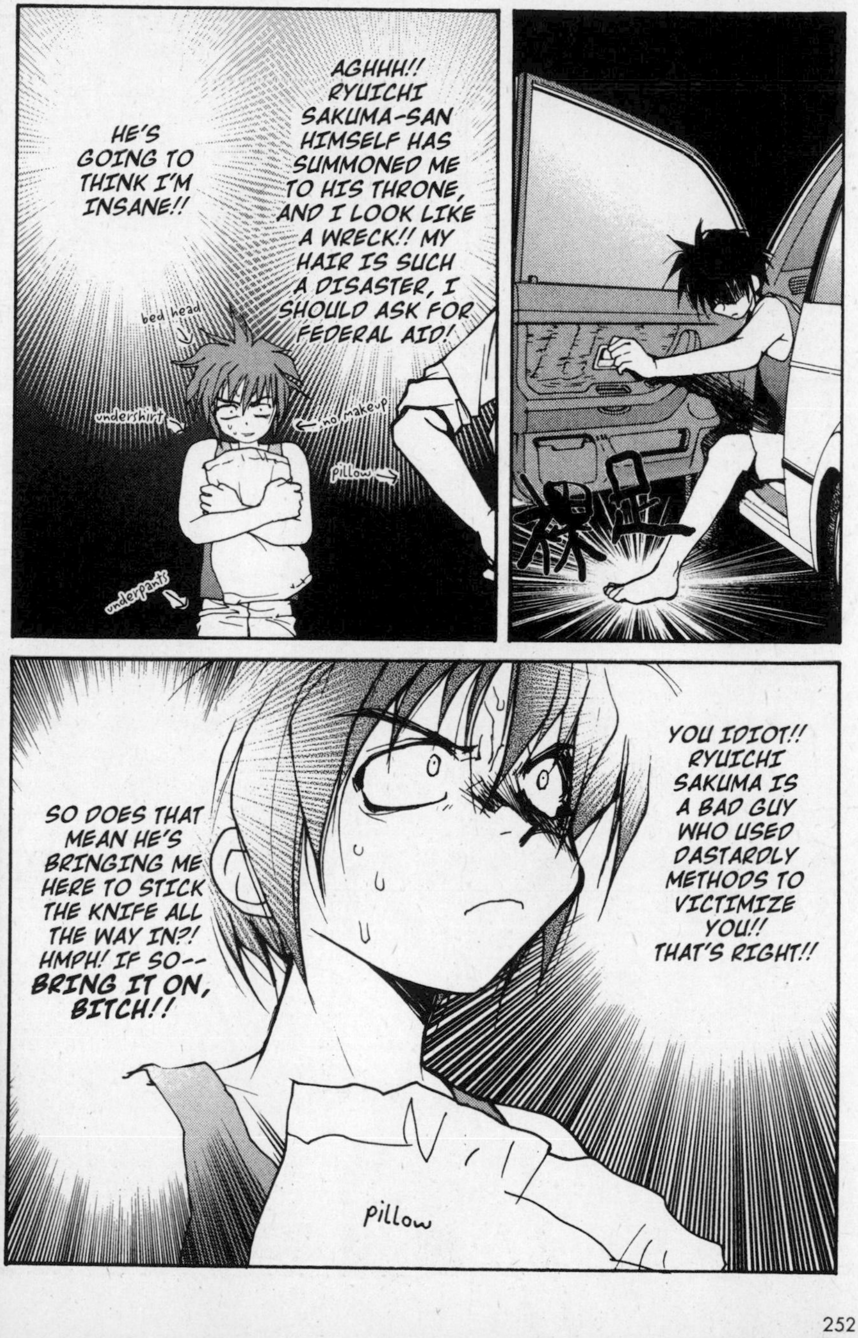
裸足
AGHHH!! RYUICHI SAKUMA-SAN HIMSELF HAS SUMMONED ME TO HIS THRONE, AND I LOOK LIKE A WRECK!! MY HAIR IS SUCH A DISASTER, I SHOULD ASK FOR FEDERAL AID!
HE'S GOING TO THINK I'M INSANE!!
bed head
no makeup
undershirt
pillow
underpants
YOU IDIOT!! RYUICHI SAKUMA IS A BAD GUY WHO USED DASTARDLY METHODS TO VICTIMIZE YOU!! THAT'S RIGHT!!
SO DOES THAT MEAN HE'S BRINGING ME HERE TO STICK THE KNIFE ALL THE WAY IN?! HMPH! IF SO-- BRING IT ON, BITCH!!
pillow

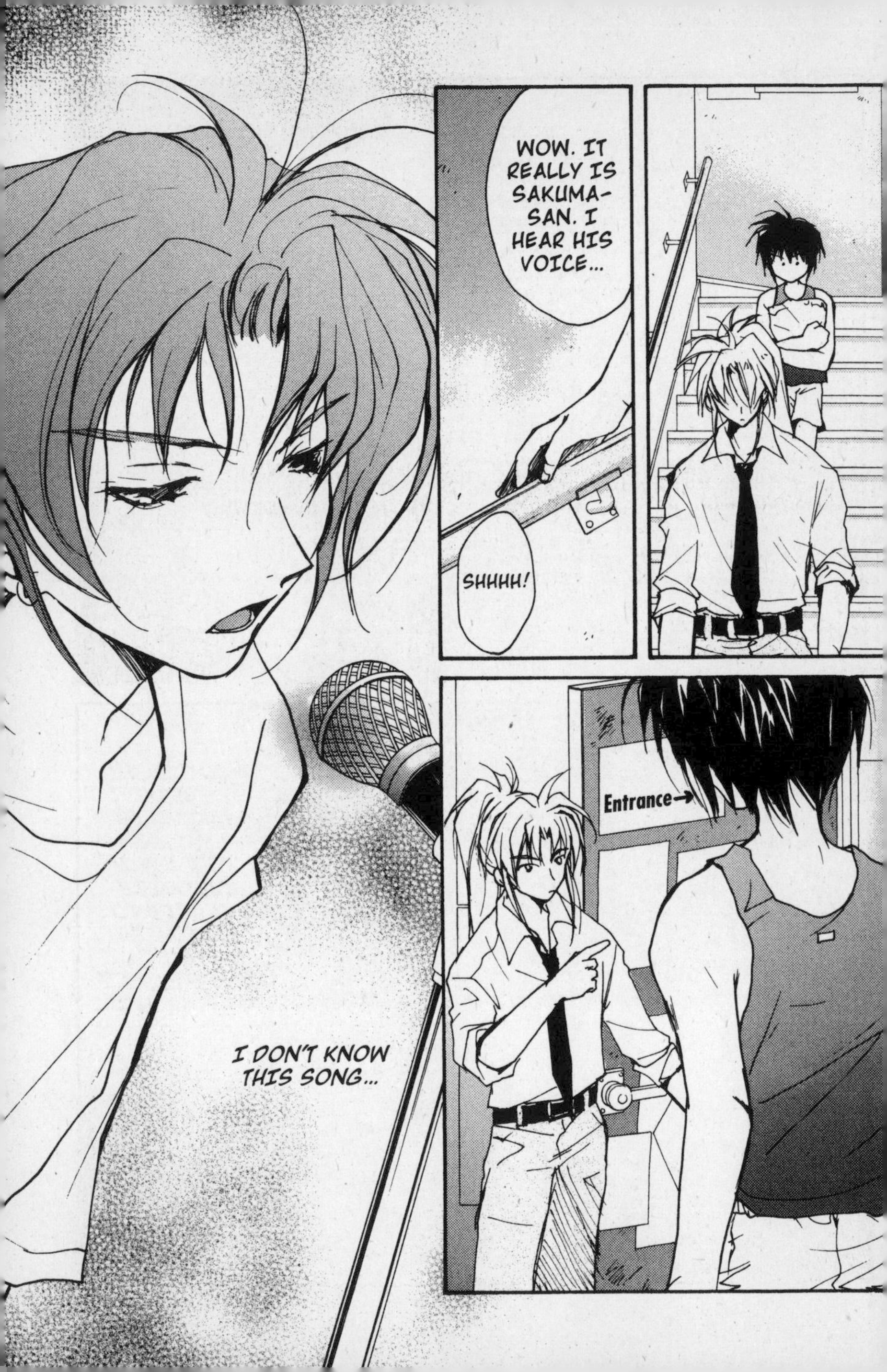
WOW. IT REALLY IS SAKUMA-SAN. I HEAR HIS VOICE...
SHHHH!
Entrance→
I DON'T KNOW THIS SONG...

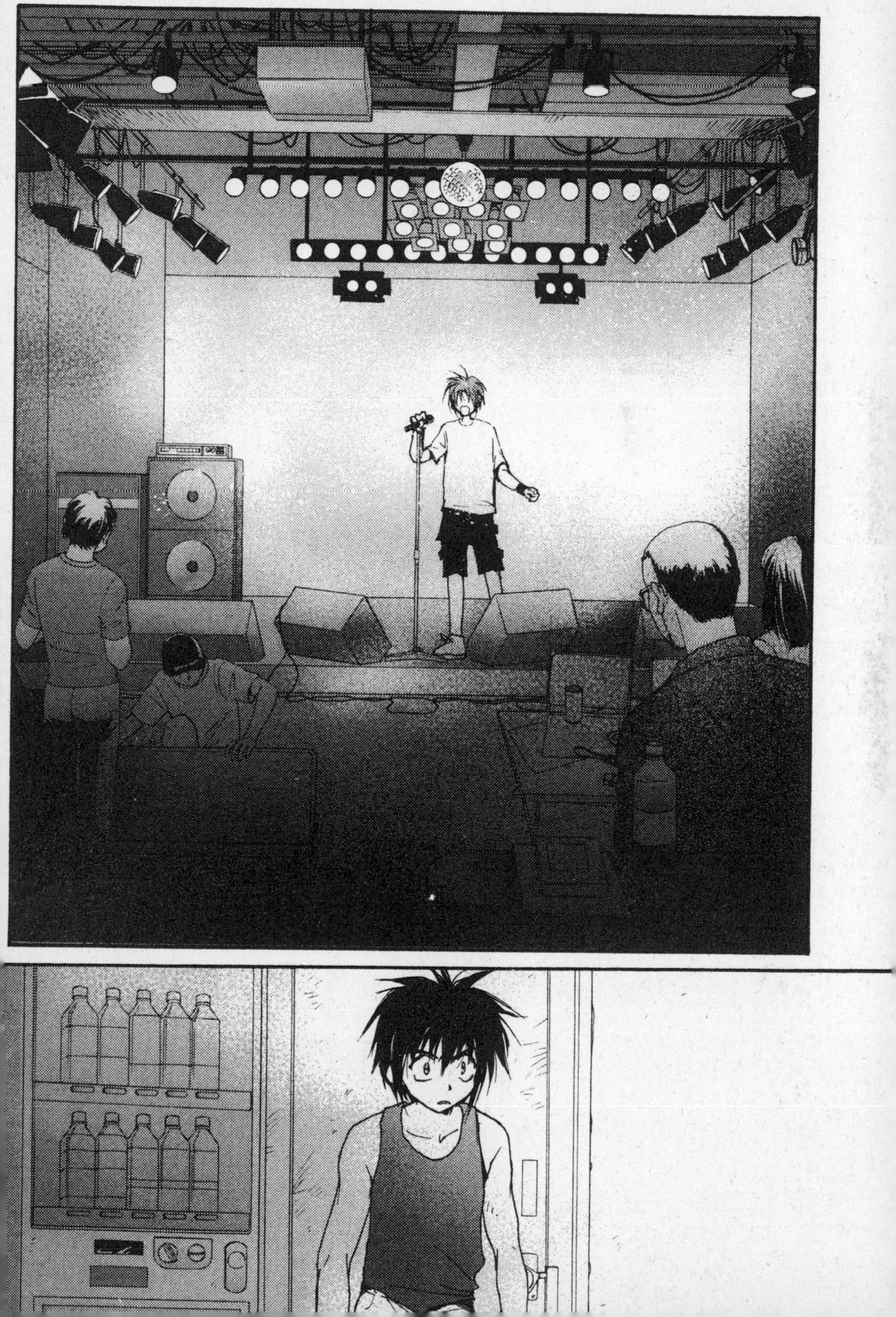

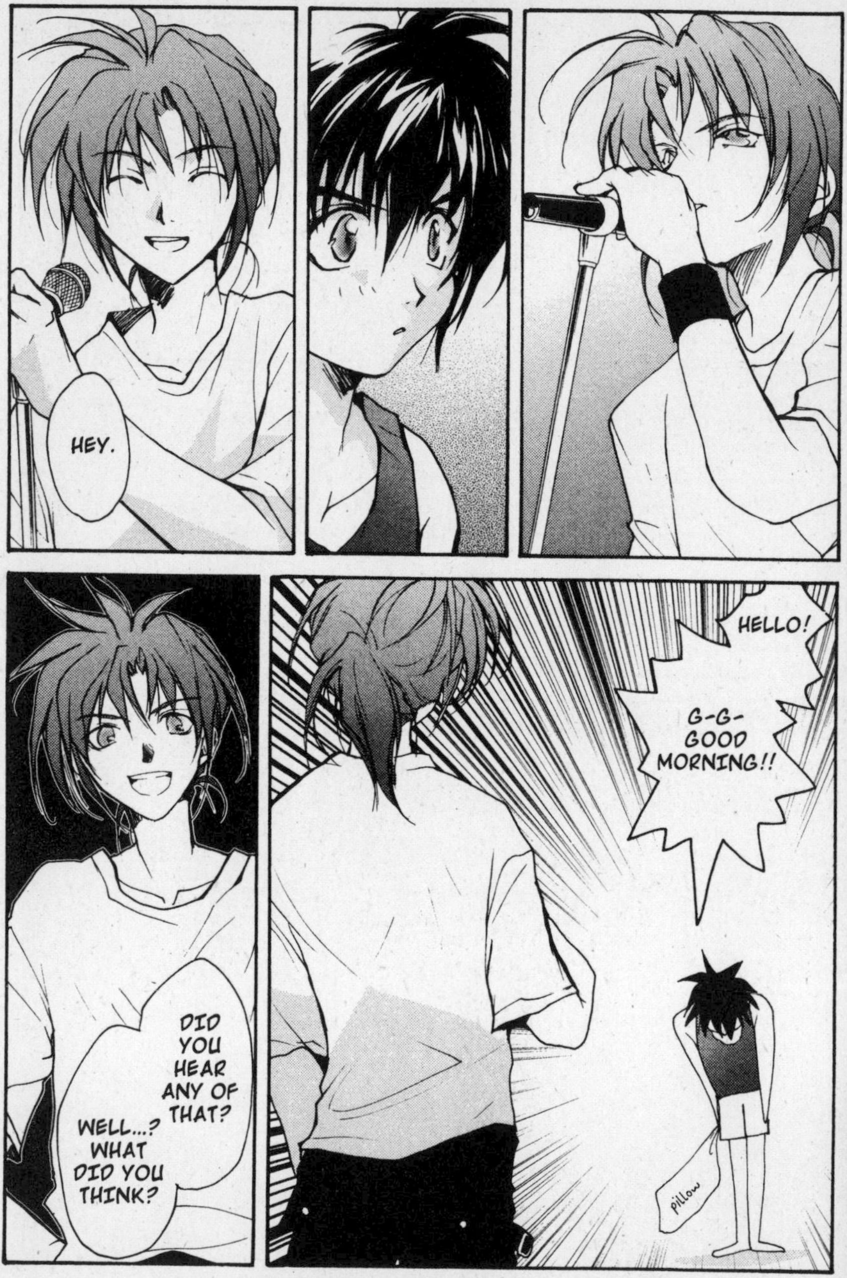
HEY.
HELLO!
G-G-GOOD MORNING!!
pillow
DID YOU HEAR ANY OF THAT?
WELL...? WHAT DID YOU THINK?

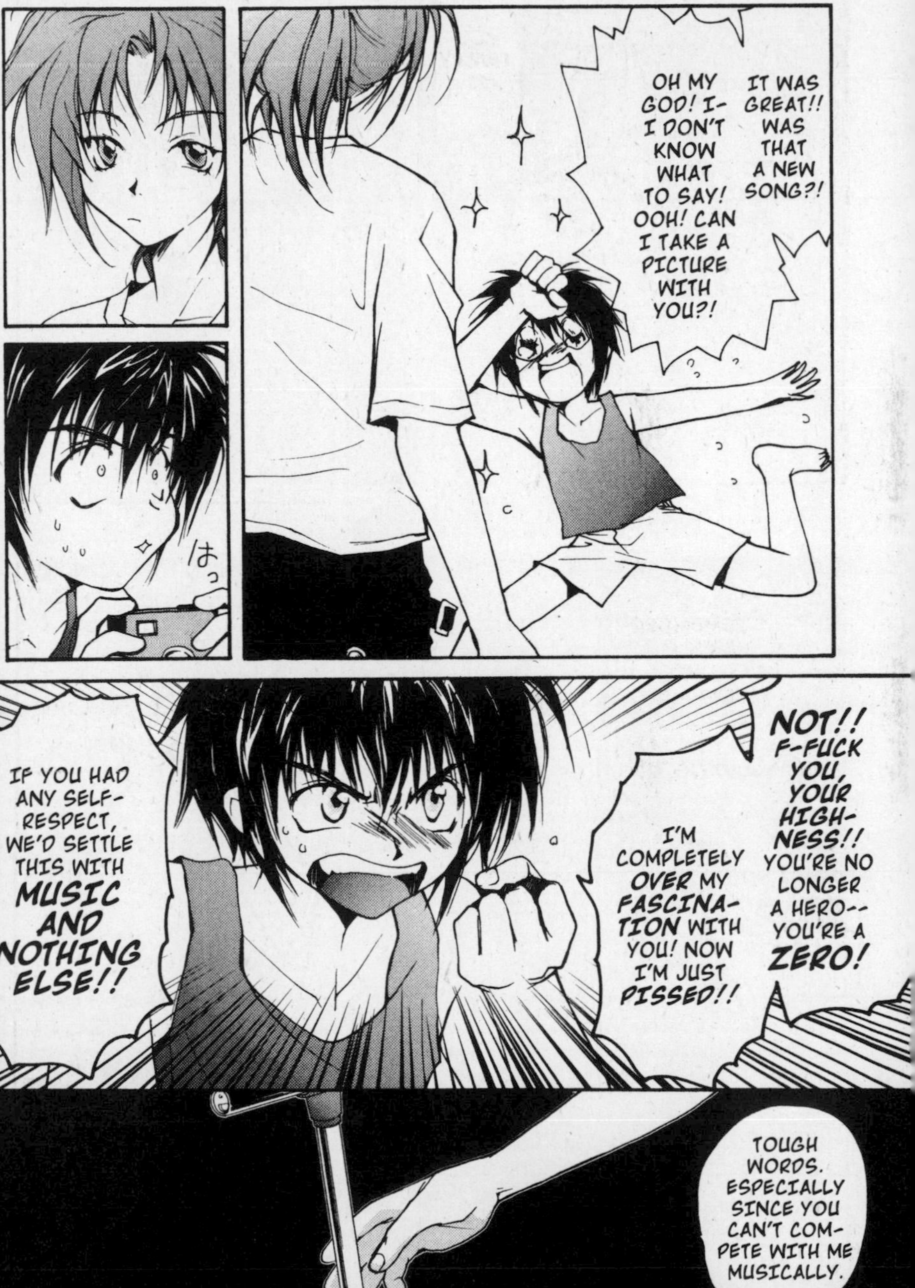
IT WAS GREAT!! WAS THAT A NEW SONG?!
OH MY GOD! I- I DON'T KNOW WHAT TO SAY! OOH! CAN I TAKE A PICTURE WITH YOU?!
はっ
NOT!! F-FUCK YOU, YOUR HIGHNESS!! YOU'RE NO LONGER A HERO-- YOU'RE A ZERO!
I'M COMPLETELY OVER MY FASCINATION WITH YOU! NOW I'M JUST PISSED!!
IF YOU HAD ANY SELF-RESPECT, WE'D SETTLE THIS WITH MUSIC AND NOTHING ELSE!!
TOUGH WORDS. ESPECIALLY SINCE YOU CAN'T COMPETE WITH ME MUSICALLY.

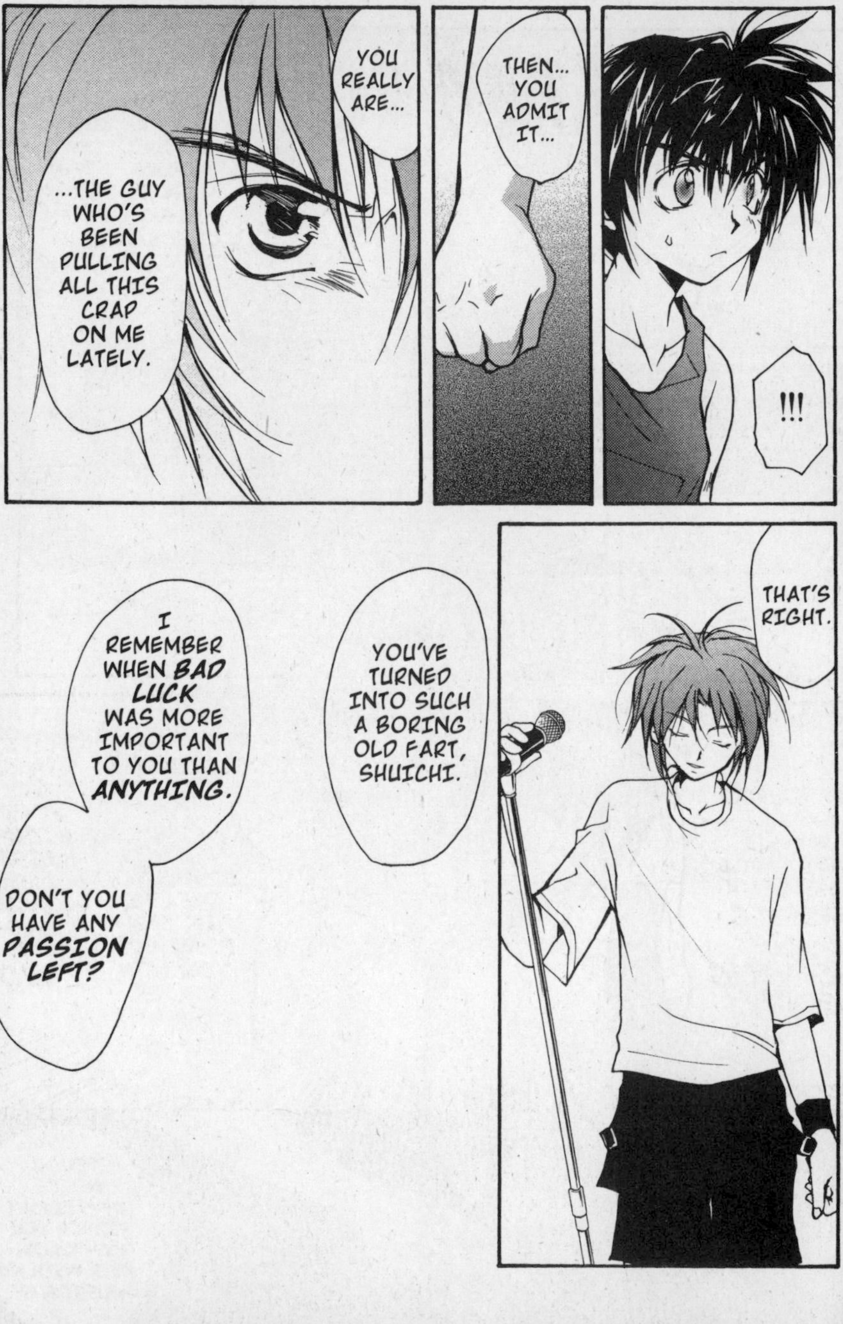
!!!
THEN... YOU ADMIT IT...
YOU REALLY ARE...
...THE GUY WHO'S BEEN PULLING ALL THIS CRAP ON ME LATELY.
THAT'S RIGHT.
YOU'VE TURNED INTO SUCH A BORING OLD FART, SHUICHI.
I REMEMBER WHEN BAD LUCK WAS MORE IMPORTANT TO YOU THAN ANYTHING.
DON'T YOU HAVE ANY PASSION LEFT?

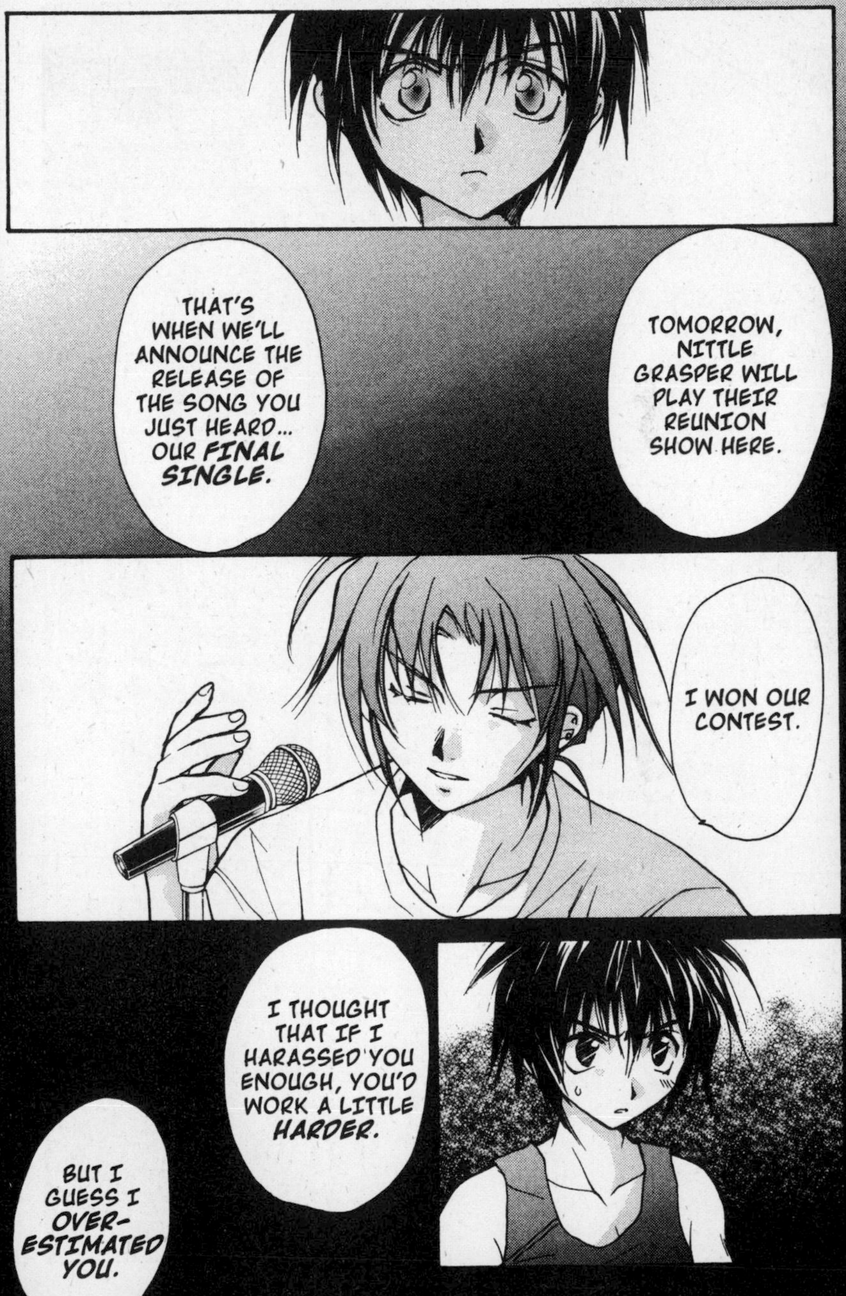
TOMORROW, NITTLE GRASPER WILL PLAY THEIR REUNION SHOW HERE.
THAT'S WHEN WE'LL ANNOUNCE THE RELEASE OF THE SONG YOU JUST HEARD... OUR FINAL SINGLE.
I WON OUR CONTEST.
I THOUGHT THAT IF I HARASSED YOU ENOUGH, YOU'D WORK A LITTLE HARDER.
BUT I GUESS I OVER-ESTIMATED YOU.

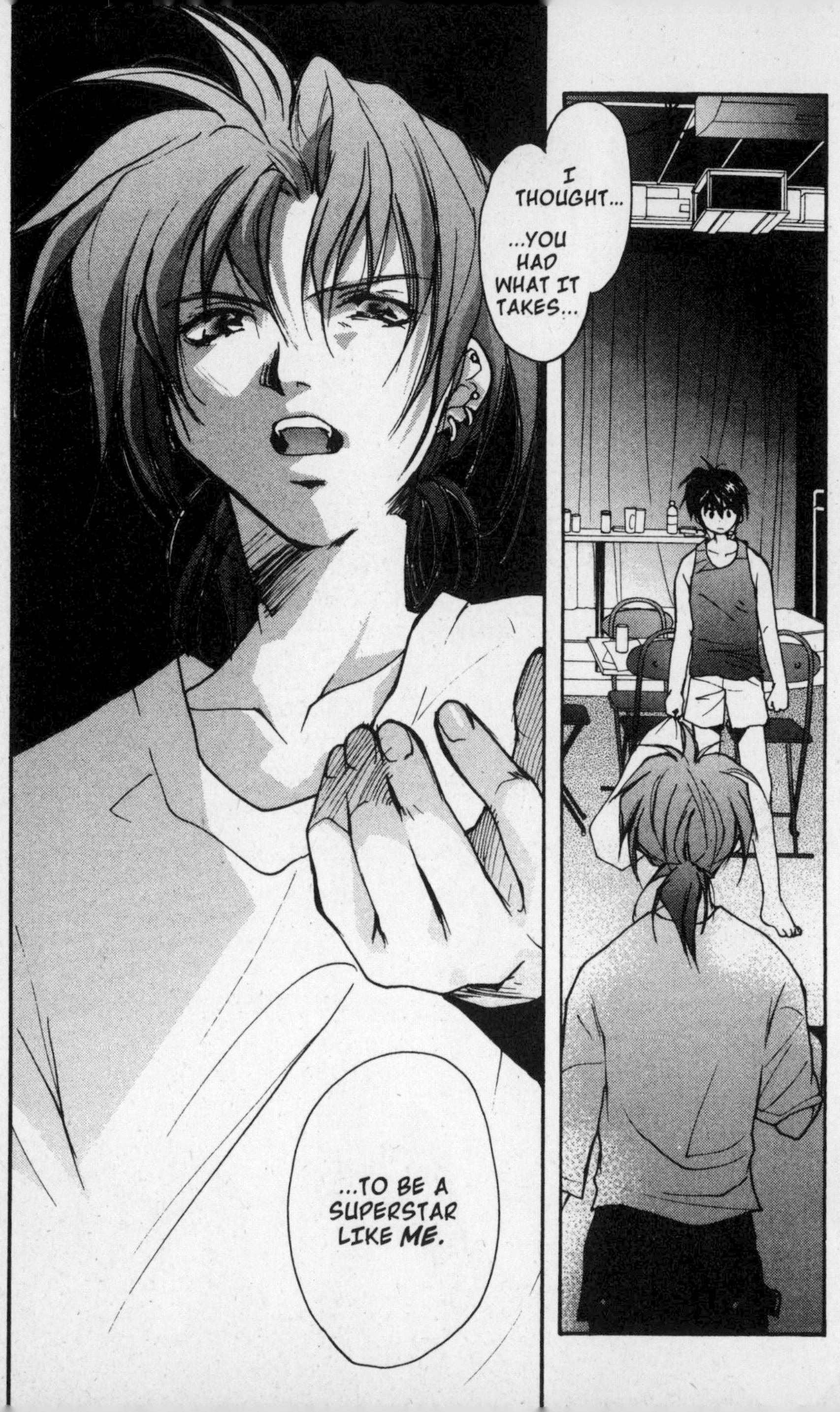
I THOUGHT...
...YOU HAD WHAT IT TAKES...
...TO BE A SUPERSTAR LIKE *ME*.

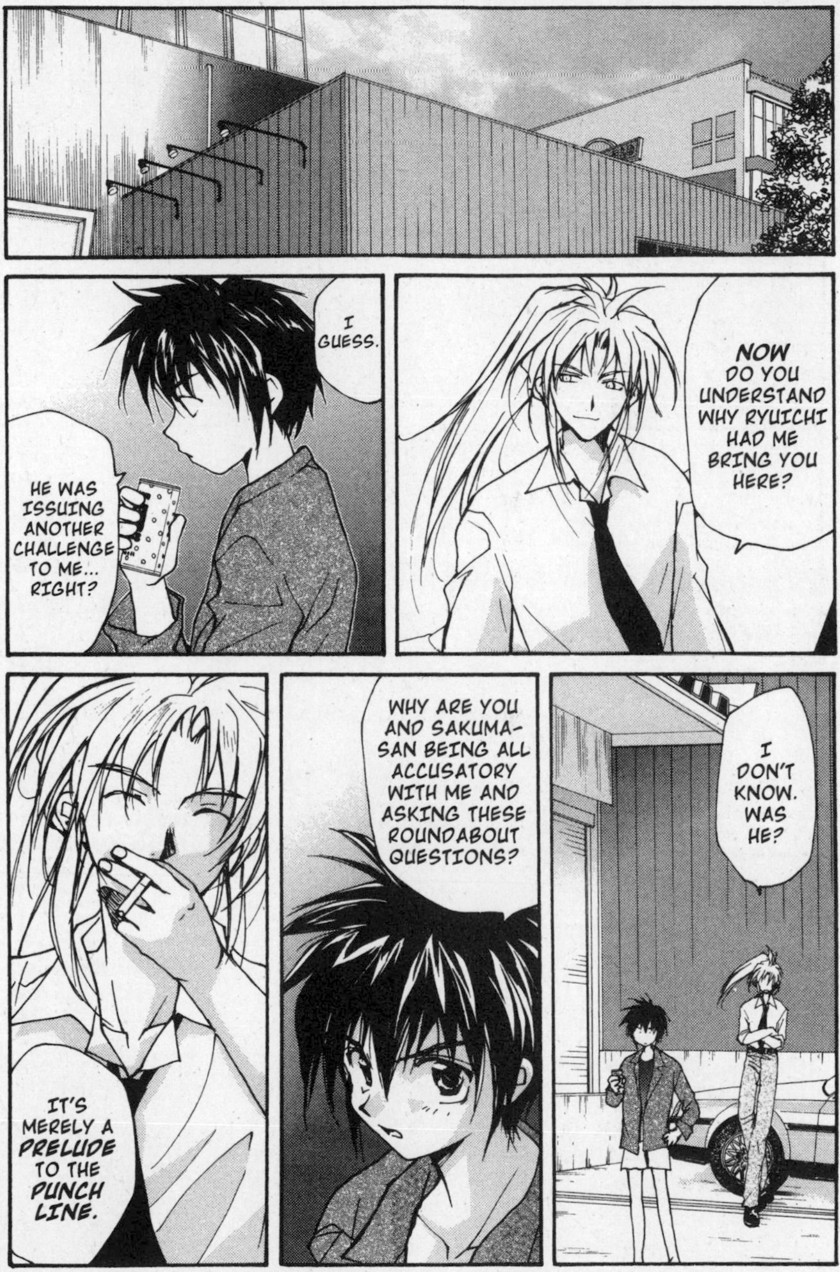
NOW DO YOU UNDERSTAND WHY RYUICHI HAD ME BRING YOU HERE?
I GUESS.
HE WAS ISSUING ANOTHER CHALLENGE TO ME... RIGHT?
I DON'T KNOW. WAS HE?
WHY ARE YOU AND SAKUMA-SAN BEING ALL ACCUSATORY WITH ME AND ASKING THESE ROUNDABOUT QUESTIONS?
IT'S MERELY A PRELUDE TO THE PUNCH LINE.

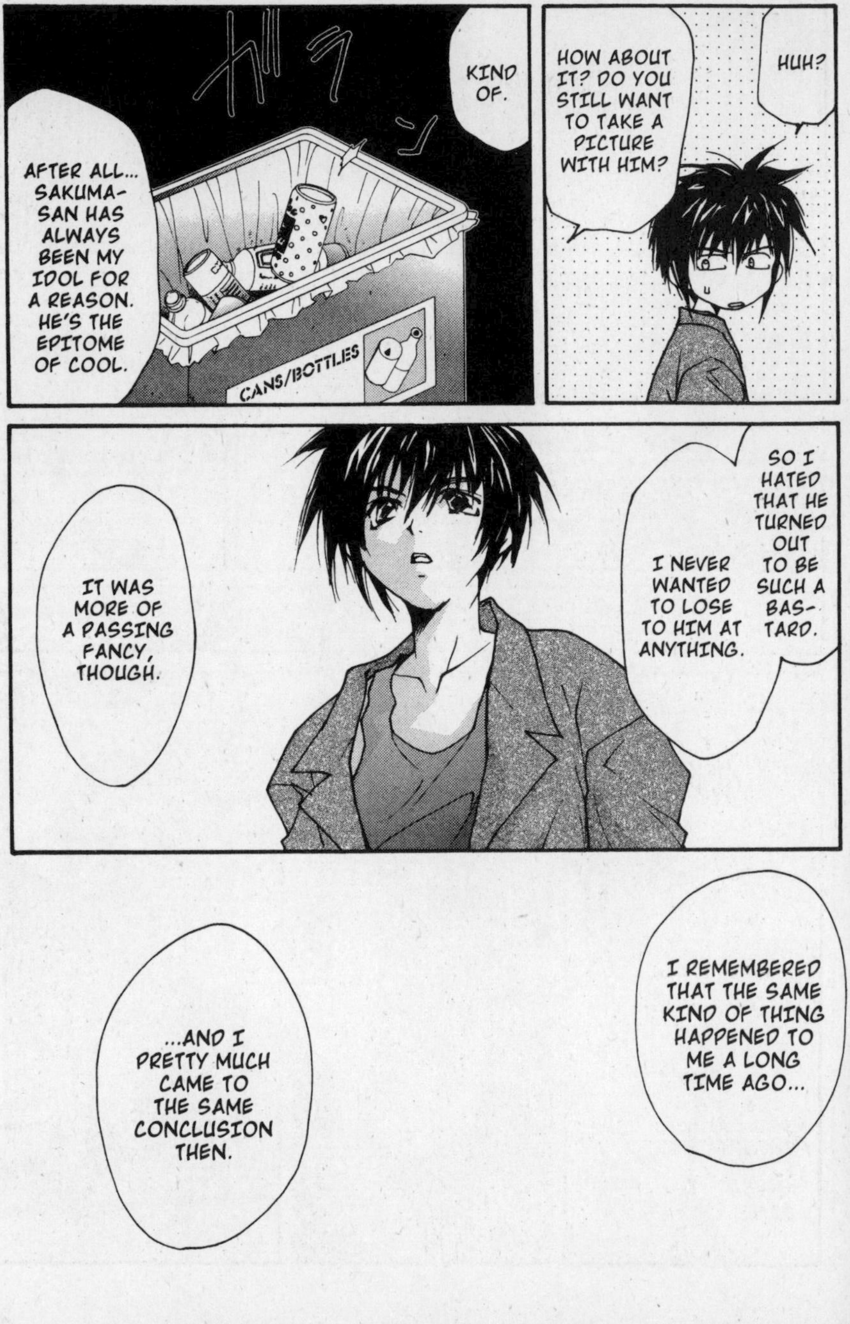
HUH?
HOW ABOUT IT? DO YOU STILL WANT TO TAKE A PICTURE WITH HIM?
KIND OF.
AFTER ALL... SAKUMA-SAN HAS ALWAYS BEEN MY IDOL FOR A REASON. HE'S THE EPITOME OF COOL.
CANS/BOTTLES
SO I HATED THAT HE TURNED OUT TO BE SUCH A BAS-TARD.
I NEVER WANTED TO LOSE TO HIM AT ANYTHING.
IT WAS MORE OF A PASSING FANCY, THOUGH.
I REMEMBERED THAT THE SAME KIND OF THING HAPPENED TO ME A LONG TIME AGO...
...AND I PRETTY MUCH CAME TO THE SAME CONCLUSION THEN.

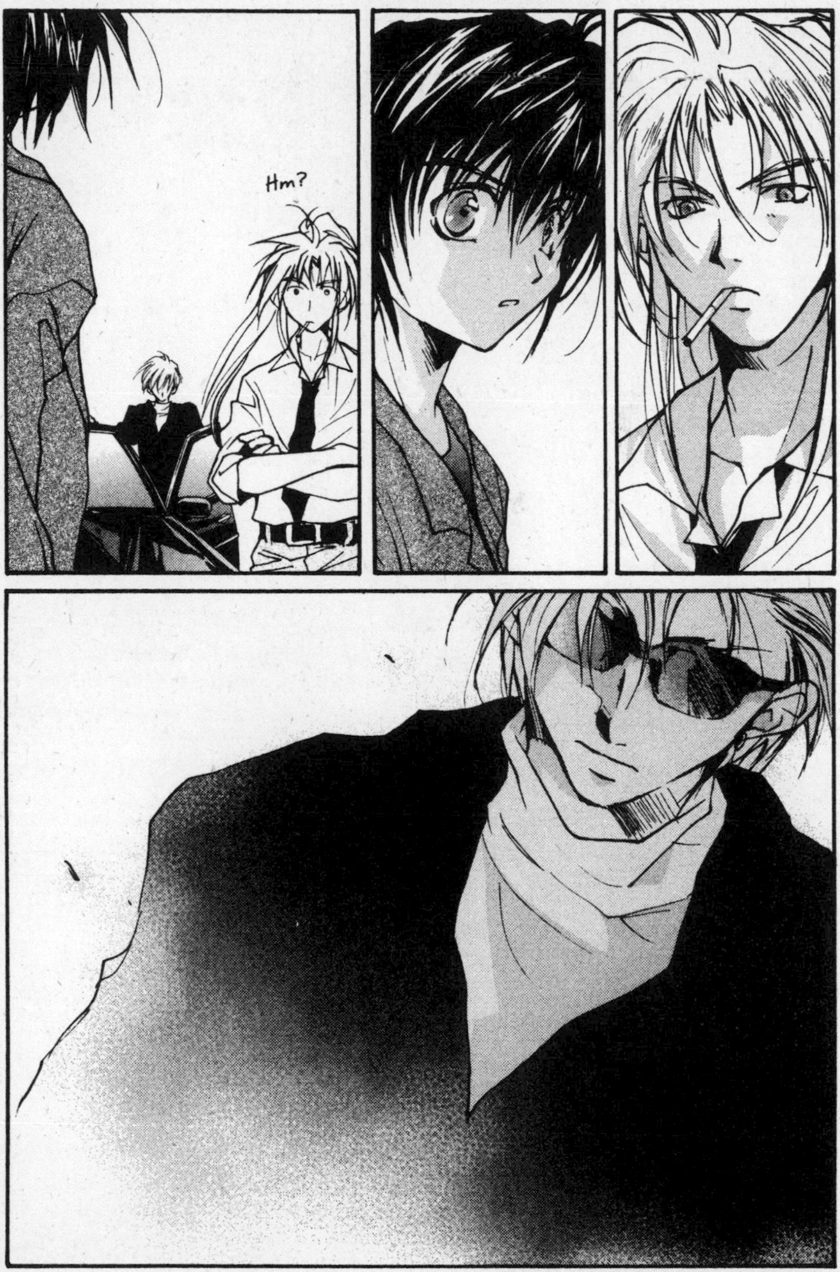
Hm?

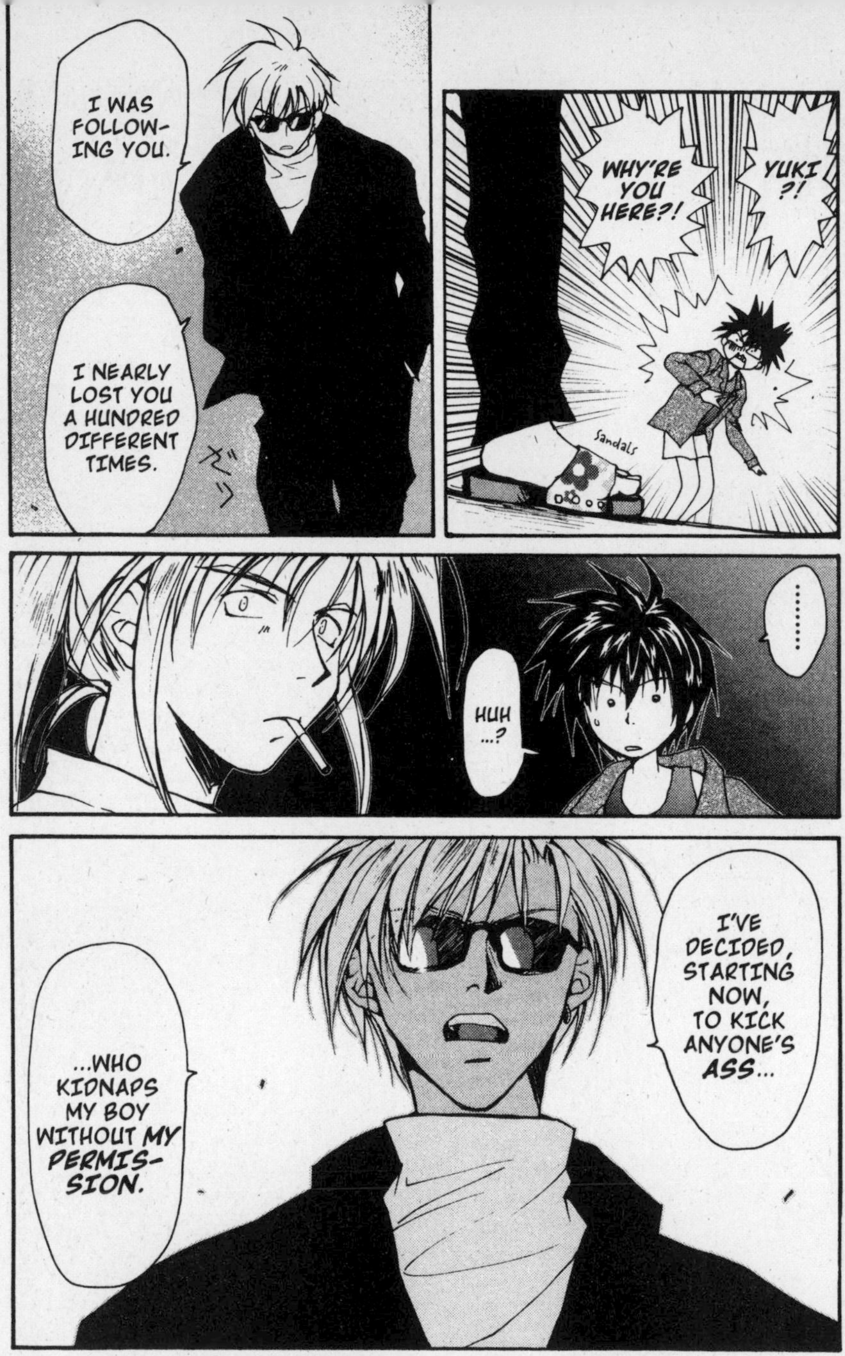
YUKI ?!
WHY'RE YOU HERE?!
Sandals
I WAS FOLLOW-ING YOU.
I NEARLY LOST YOU A HUNDRED DIFFERENT TIMES.
......
HUH ...?
I'VE DECIDED, STARTING NOW, TO KICK ANYONE'S ASS...
...WHO KIDNAPS MY BOY WITHOUT MY PERMIS-SION.

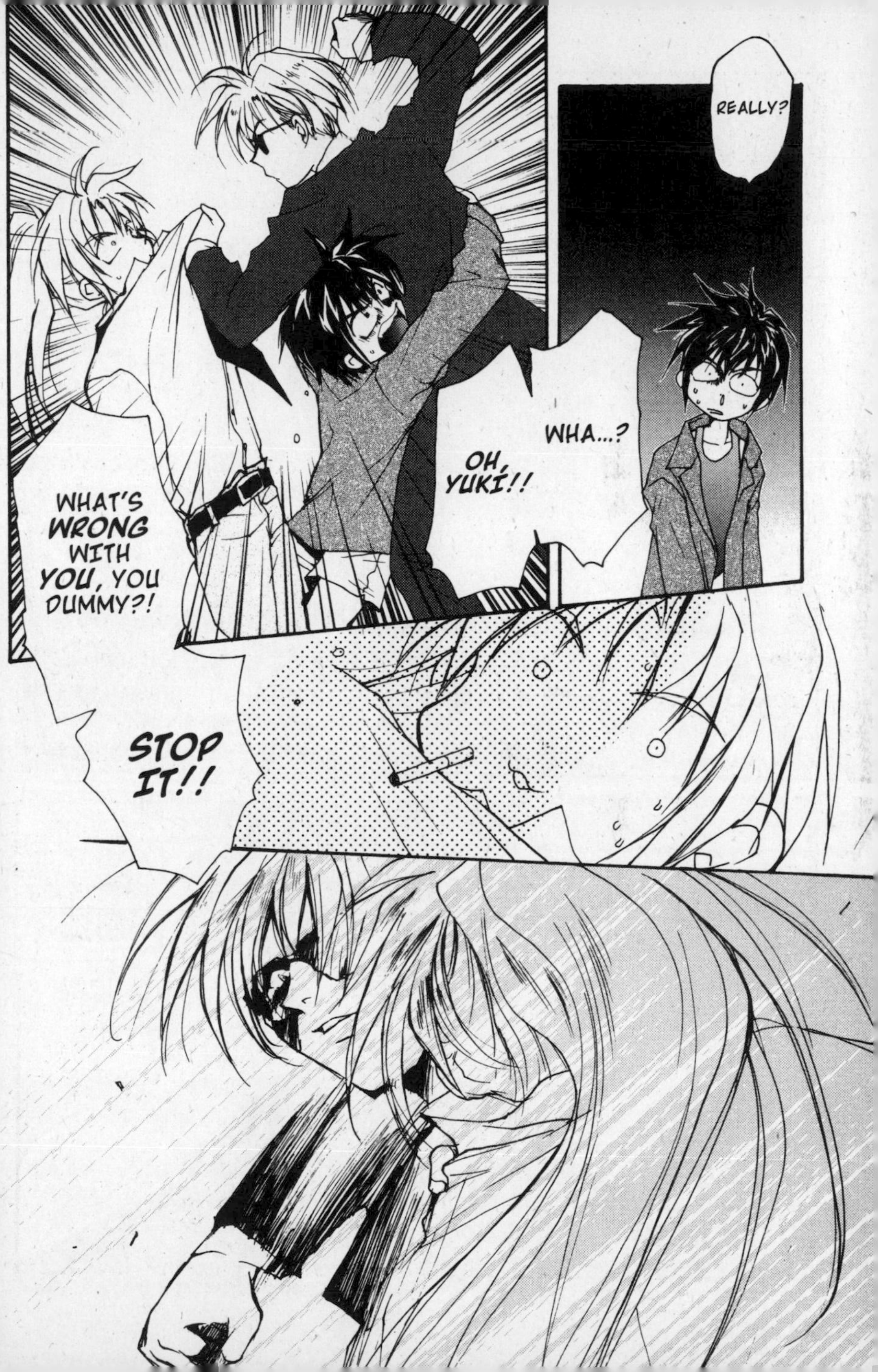

REALLY?
WHA...?
OH, YUKI!!
WHAT'S WRONG WITH YOU, YOU DUMMY?!
STOP IT!!

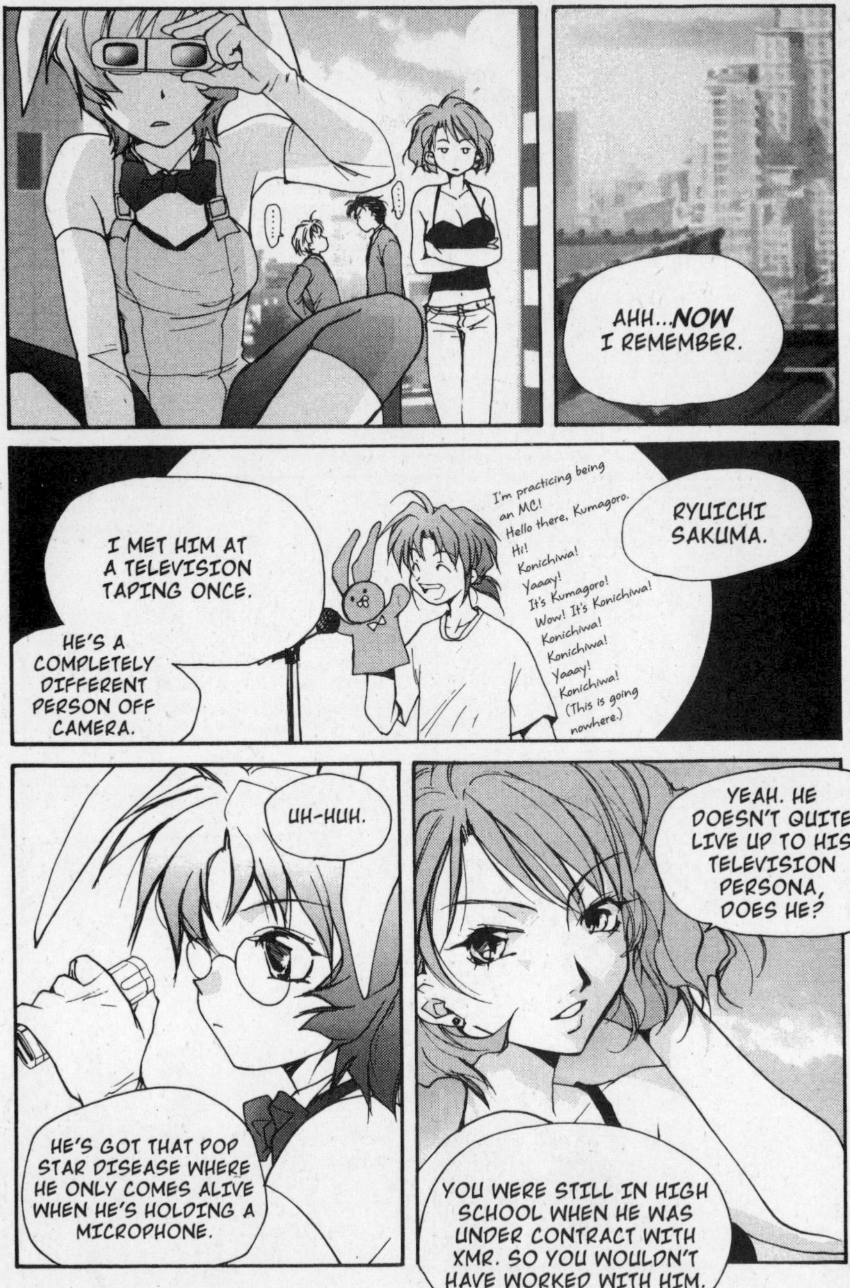

AHH...NOW I REMEMBER.
RYUICHI SAKUMA.
I'm practicing being an MC! Hello there, Kumagoro. Hi! Konichiwa! Yaaay! It's Kumagoro! Wow! It's Konichiwa! Konichiwa! Konichiwa! Yaaay! Konichiwa! (This is going nowhere.)
I MET HIM AT A TELEVISION TAPING ONCE.
HE'S A COMPLETELY DIFFERENT PERSON OFF CAMERA.
YEAH. HE DOESN'T QUITE LIVE UP TO HIS TELEVISION PERSONA, DOES HE?
YOU WERE STILL IN HIGH SCHOOL WHEN HE WAS UNDER CONTRACT WITH XMR. SO YOU WOULDN'T HAVE WORKED WITH HIM.
UH-HUH.
HE'S GOT THAT POP STAR DISEASE WHERE HE ONLY COMES ALIVE WHEN HE'S HOLDING A MICROPHONE.

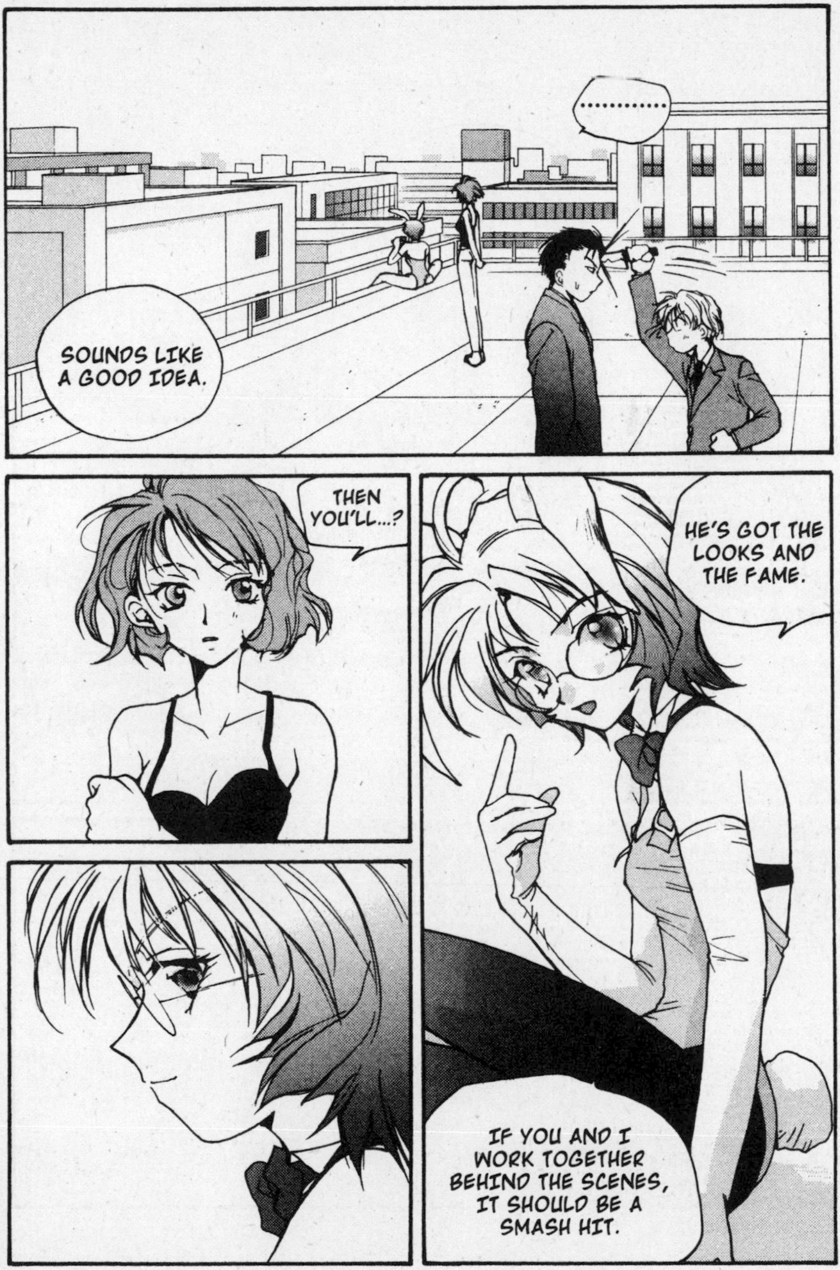
..........
SOUNDS LIKE A GOOD IDEA.
HE'S GOT THE LOOKS AND THE FAME.
IF YOU AND I WORK TOGETHER BEHIND THE SCENES, IT SHOULD BE A SMASH HIT.
THEN YOU'LL...?

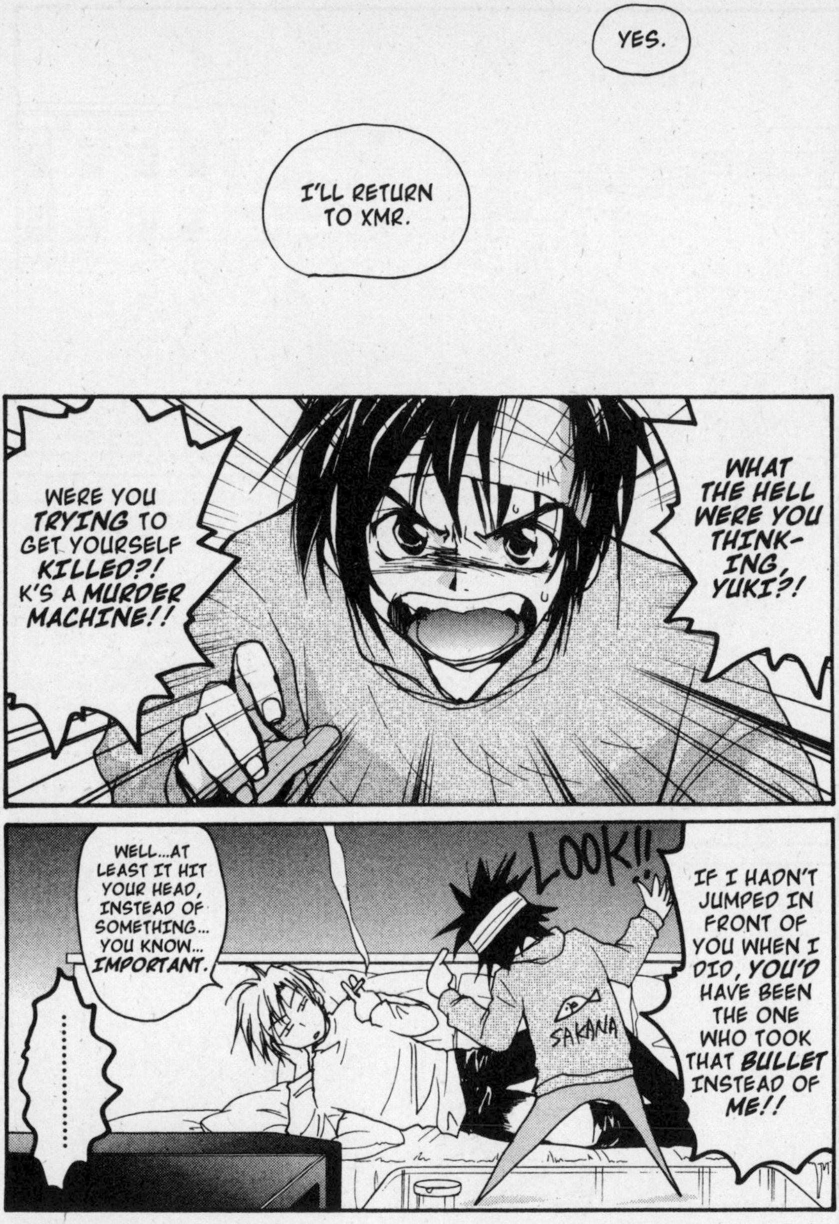
YES.
I'LL RETURN TO XMR.
WHAT THE HELL WERE YOU THINKING, YUKI?!
WERE YOU TRYING TO GET YOURSELF KILLED?! K'S A MURDER MACHINE!!
LOOK!!
IF I HADN'T JUMPED IN FRONT OF YOU WHEN I DID, YOU'D HAVE BEEN THE ONE WHO TOOK THAT BULLET INSTEAD OF ME!!
SAKANA
WELL...AT LEAST IT HIT YOUR HEAD, INSTEAD OF SOMETHING... YOU KNOW... IMPORTANT.
..........

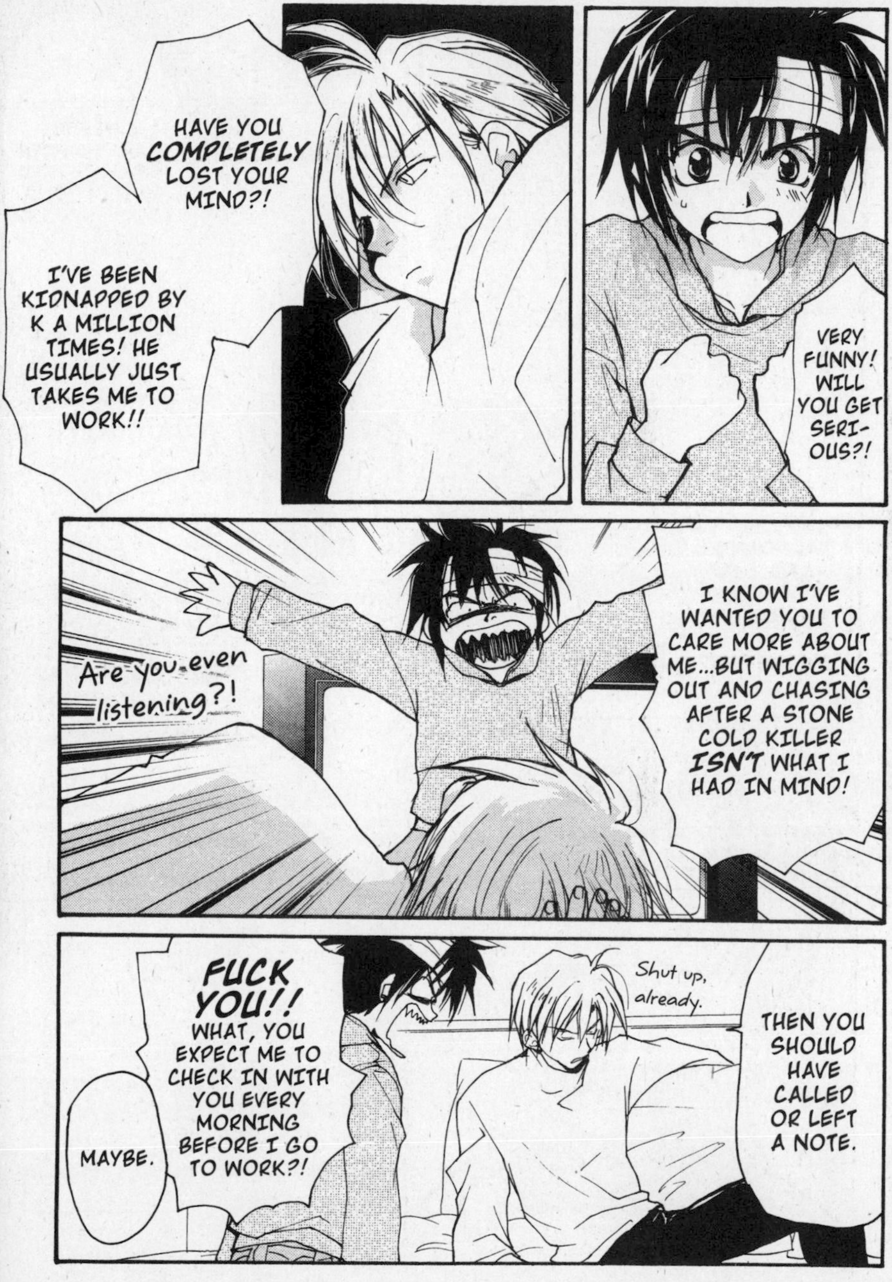
VERY FUNNY! WILL YOU GET SERI-OUS?!
HAVE YOU COMPLETELY LOST YOUR MIND?!
I'VE BEEN KIDNAPPED BY K A MILLION TIMES! HE USUALLY JUST TAKES ME TO WORK!!
I KNOW I'VE WANTED YOU TO CARE MORE ABOUT ME...BUT WIGGING OUT AND CHASING AFTER A STONE COLD KILLER ISN'T WHAT I HAD IN MIND!
Are you even listening?!
THEN YOU SHOULD HAVE CALLED OR LEFT A NOTE.
Shut up, already.
FUCK YOU!! WHAT, YOU EXPECT ME TO CHECK IN WITH YOU EVERY MORNING BEFORE I GO TO WORK?!
MAYBE.

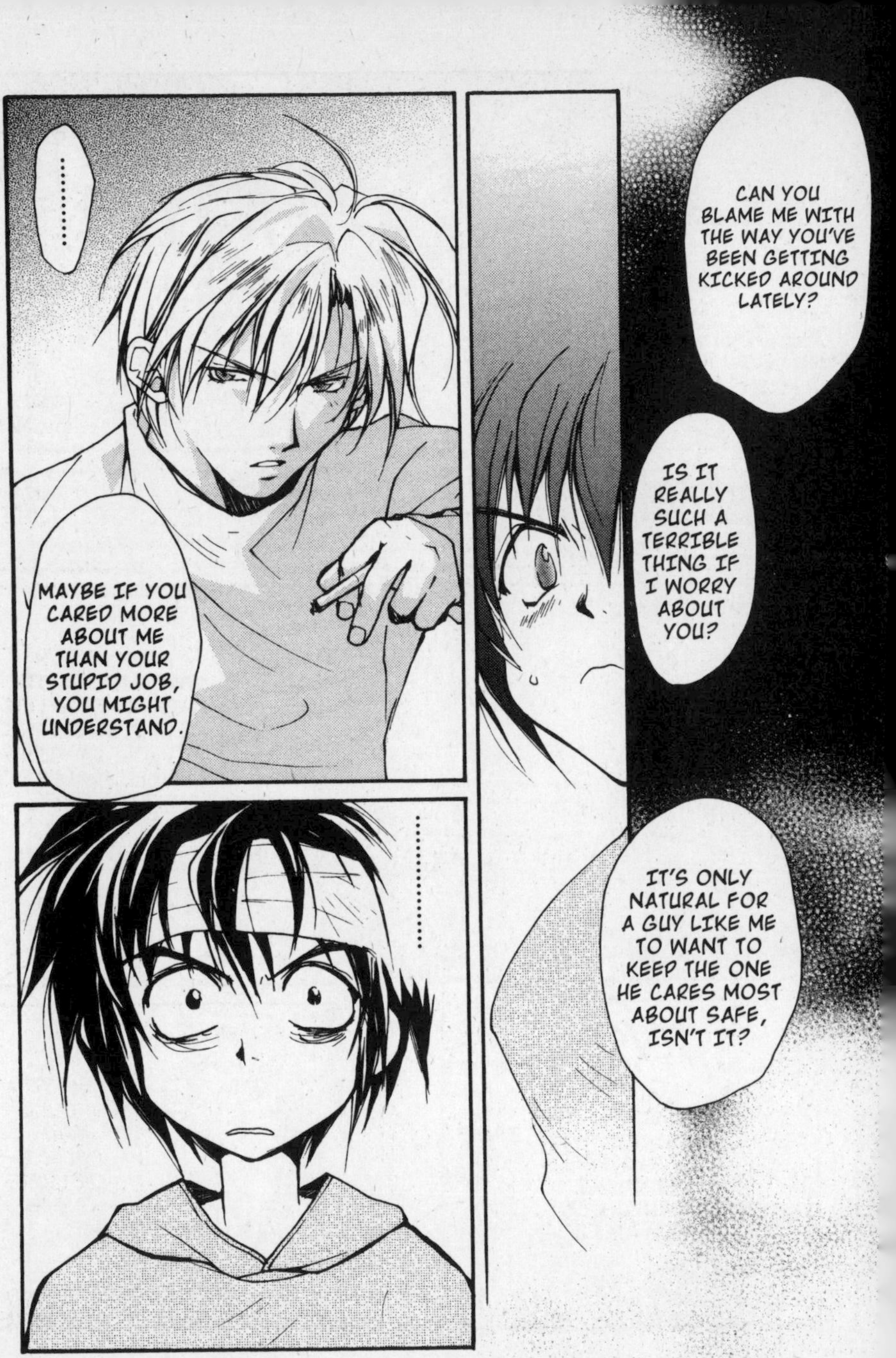
CAN YOU BLAME ME WITH THE WAY YOU'VE BEEN GETTING KICKED AROUND LATELY?
IS IT REALLY SUCH A TERRIBLE THING IF I WORRY ABOUT YOU?
IT'S ONLY NATURAL FOR A GUY LIKE ME TO WANT TO KEEP THE ONE HE CARES MOST ABOUT SAFE, ISN'T IT?
......
MAYBE IF YOU CARED MORE ABOUT ME THAN YOUR STUPID JOB, YOU MIGHT UNDERSTAND.
......

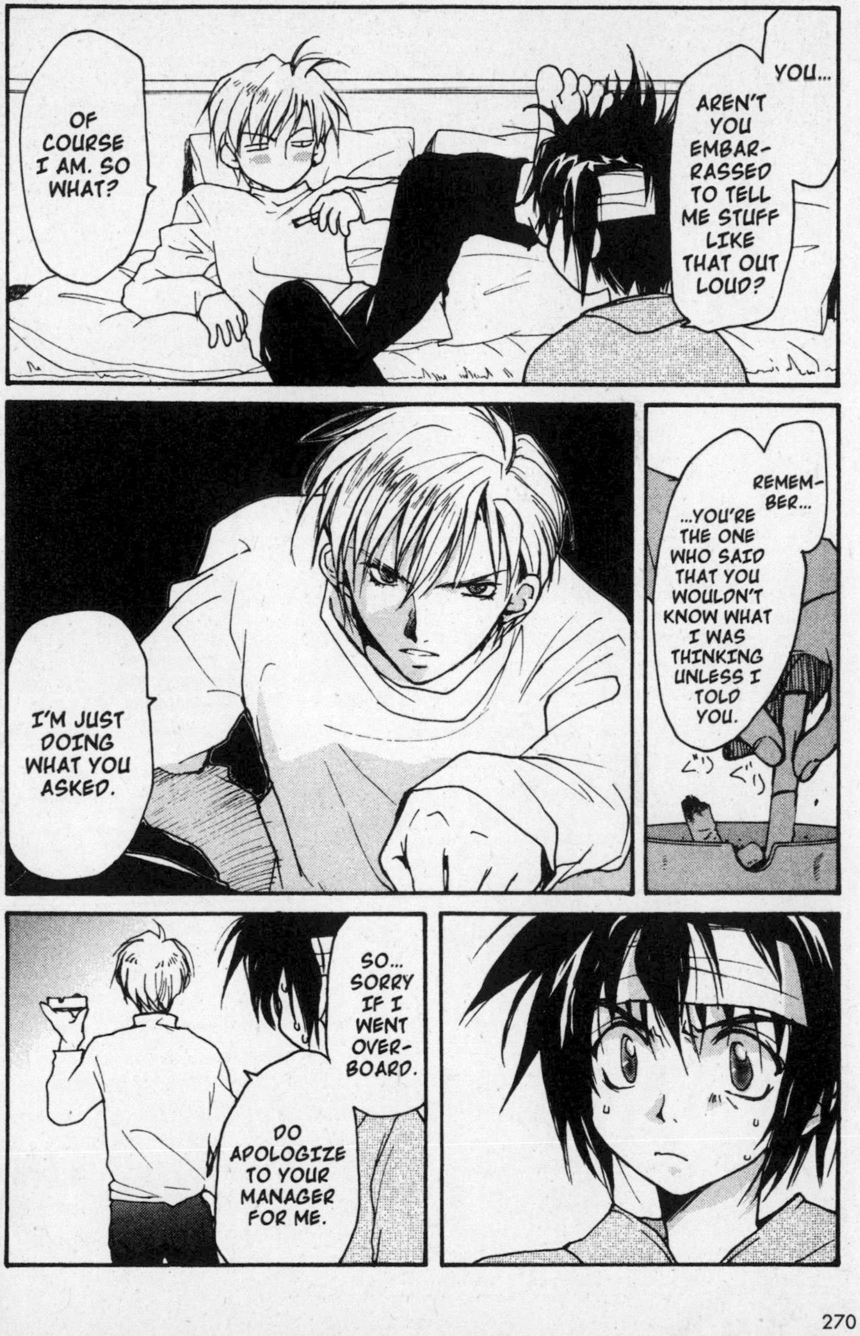
YOU...
AREN'T YOU EMBARRASSED TO TELL ME STUFF LIKE THAT OUT LOUD?
OF COURSE I AM. SO WHAT?
REMEMBER...
...YOU'RE THE ONE WHO SAID THAT YOU WOULDN'T KNOW WHAT I WAS THINKING UNLESS I TOLD YOU.
I'M JUST DOING WHAT YOU ASKED.
SO... SORRY IF I WENT OVERBOARD.
DO APOLOGIZE TO YOUR MANAGER FOR ME.

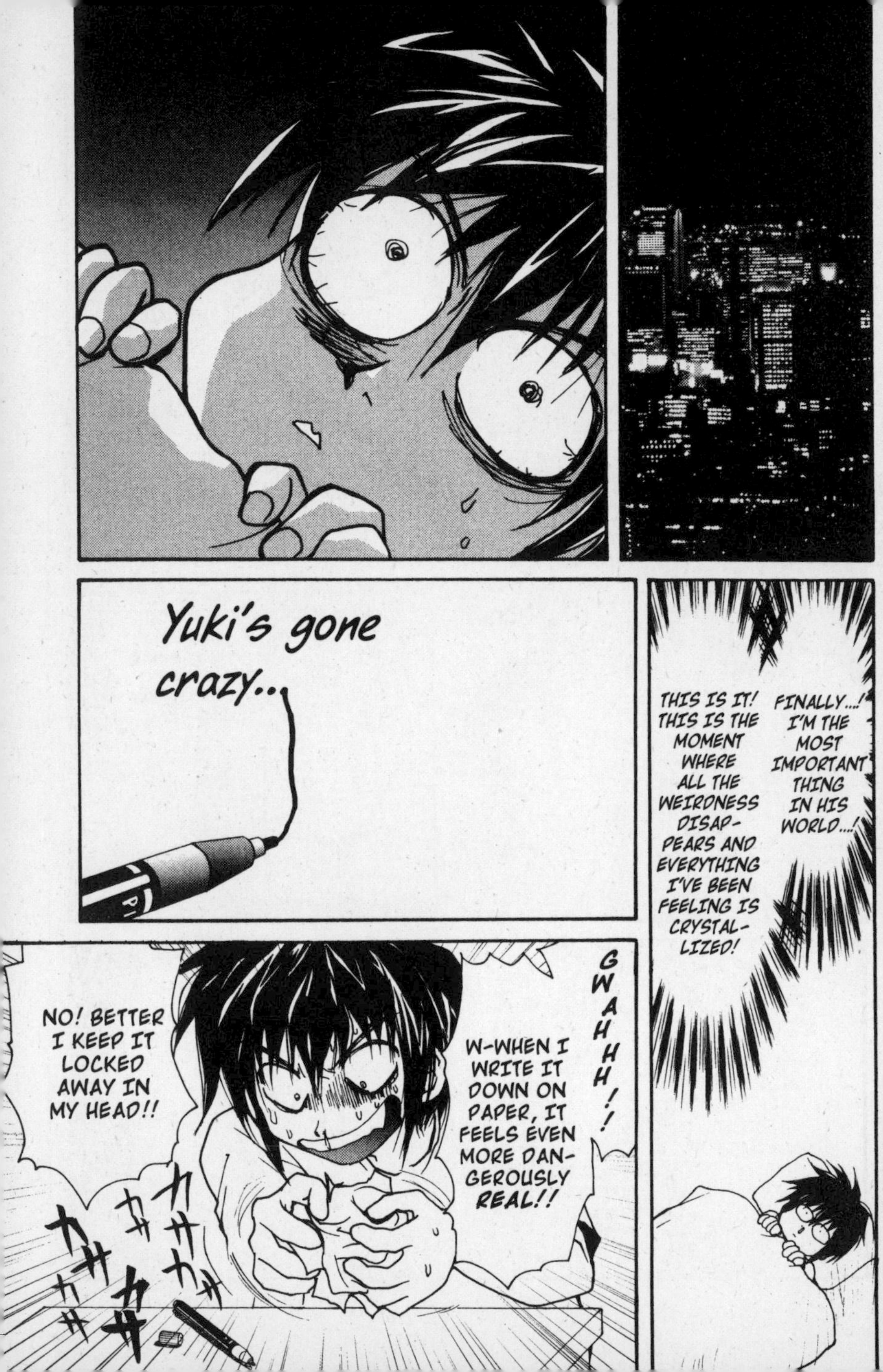
FINALLY...! I'M THE MOST IMPORTANT THING IN HIS WORLD...!
THIS IS IT! THIS IS THE MOMENT WHERE ALL THE WEIRDNESS DISAP-PEARS AND EVERYTHING I'VE BEEN FEELING IS CRYSTAL-LIZED!
Yuki's gone crazy...
GWAHHH!!
W-WHEN I WRITE IT DOWN ON PAPER, IT FEELS EVEN MORE DAN-GEROUSLY REAL!!
NO! BETTER I KEEP IT LOCKED AWAY IN MY HEAD!!

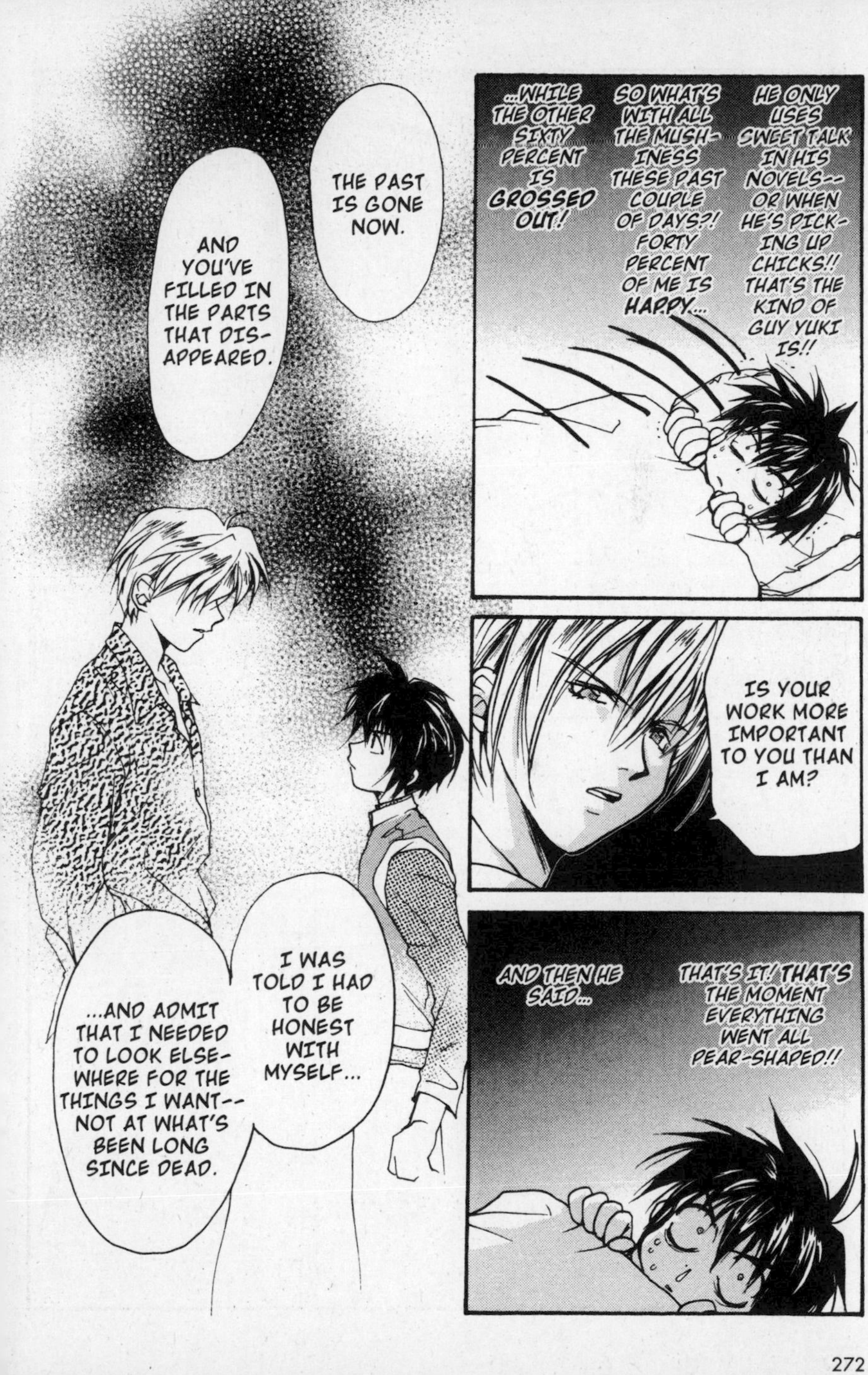
HE ONLY USES SWEET TALK IN HIS NOVELS--OR WHEN HE'S PICKING UP CHICKS!! THAT'S THE KIND OF GUY YUKI IS!!
SO WHAT'S WITH ALL THE MUSHINESS THESE PAST COUPLE OF DAYS?! FORTY PERCENT OF ME IS HAPPY...
...WHILE THE OTHER SIXTY PERCENT IS GROSSED OUT!
IS YOUR WORK MORE IMPORTANT TO YOU THAN I AM?
THAT'S IT! THAT'S THE MOMENT EVERYTHING WENT ALL PEAR-SHAPED!!
AND THEN HE SAID...
THE PAST IS GONE NOW.
AND YOU'VE FILLED IN THE PARTS THAT DISAPPEARED.
I WAS TOLD I HAD TO BE HONEST WITH MYSELF...
...AND ADMIT THAT I NEEDED TO LOOK ELSEWHERE FOR THE THINGS I WANT--NOT AT WHAT'S BEEN LONG SINCE DEAD.

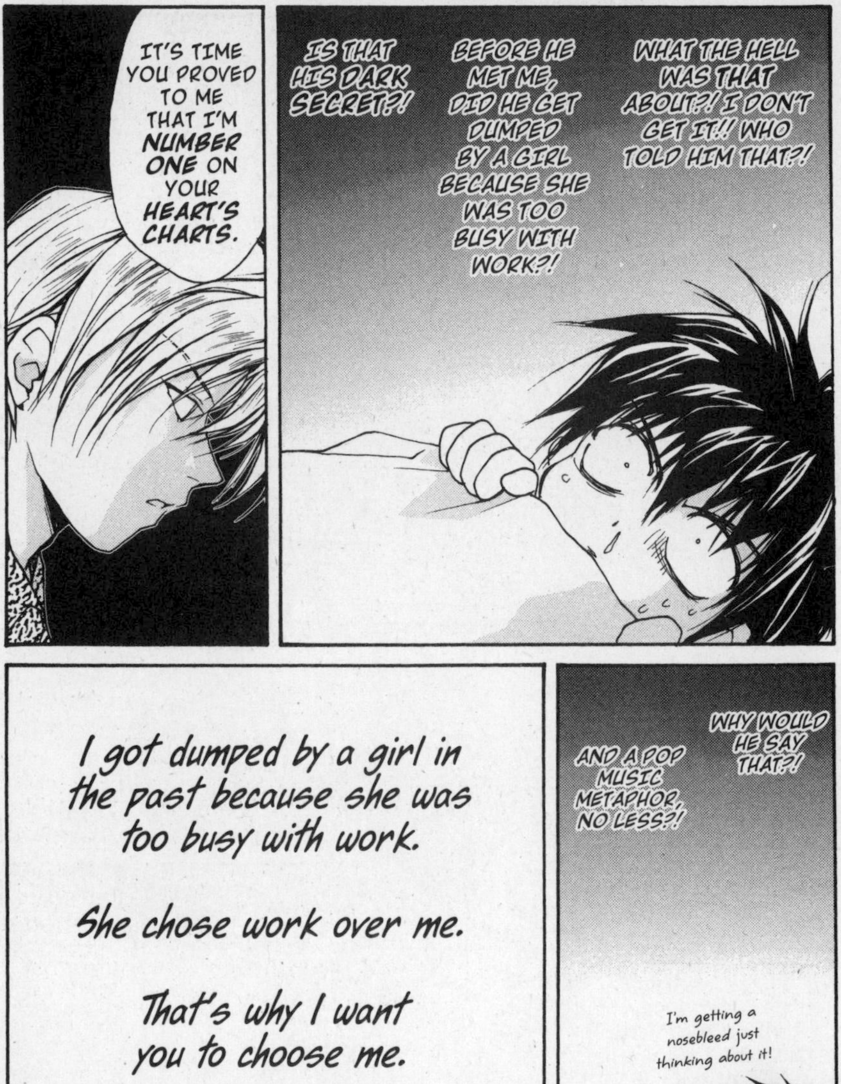
WHAT THE HELL WAS THAT ABOUT?! I DON'T GET IT!! WHO TOLD HIM THAT?!
BEFORE HE MET ME, DID HE GET DUMPED BY A GIRL BECAUSE SHE WAS TOO BUSY WITH WORK?!
IS THAT HIS DARK SECRET?!
IT'S TIME YOU PROVED TO ME THAT I'M **NUMBER ONE** ON YOUR **HEART'S CHARTS.**
WHY WOULD HE SAY THAT?!
AND A POP MUSIC METAPHOR, NO LESS?!
I'm getting a nosebleed just thinking about it!
I got dumped by a girl in the past because she was too busy with work.
She chose work over me.
That's why I want you to choose me.
Make me your number one priority!!

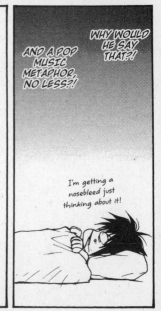

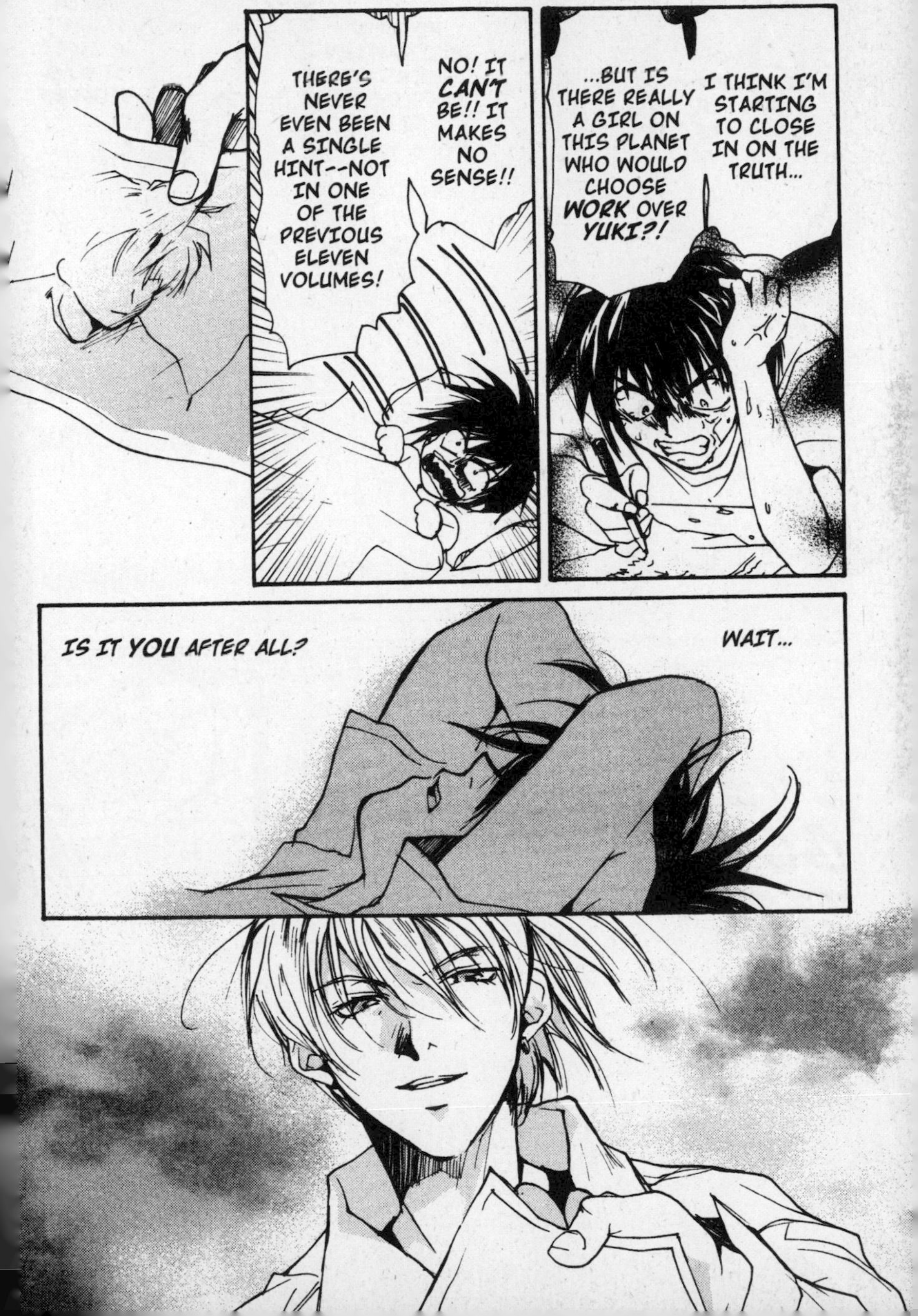
I THINK I'M STARTING TO CLOSE IN ON THE TRUTH...
...BUT IS THERE REALLY A GIRL ON THIS PLANET WHO WOULD CHOOSE WORK OVER YUKI?!
NO! IT CAN'T BE!! IT MAKES NO SENSE!!
THERE'S NEVER EVEN BEEN A SINGLE HINT--NOT IN ONE OF THE PREVIOUS ELEVEN VOLUMES!
WAIT...
IS IT YOU AFTER ALL?

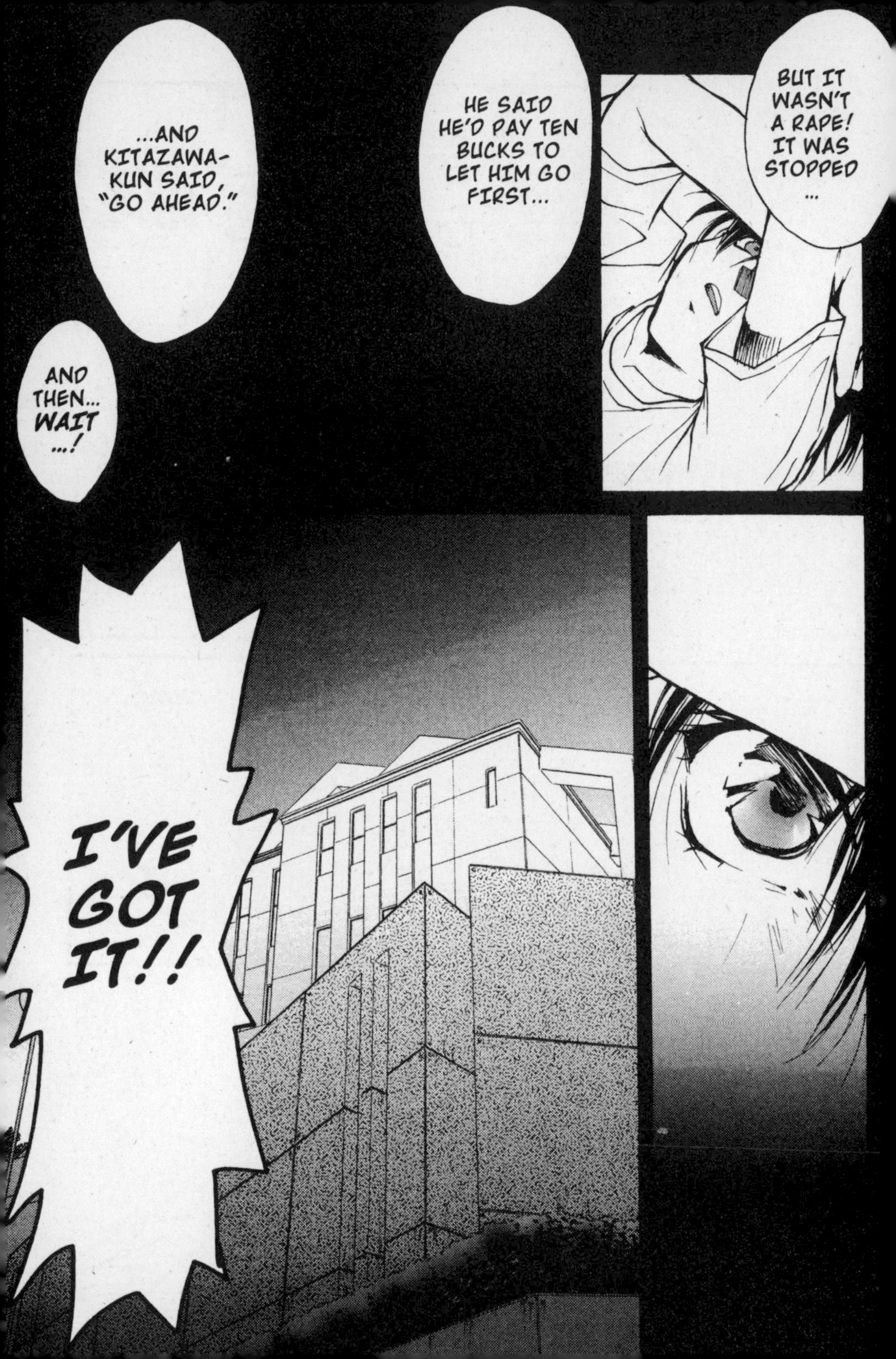
BUT IT WASN'T A RAPE! IT WAS STOPPED ...
HE SAID HE'D PAY TEN BUCKS TO LET HIM GO FIRST...
...AND KITAZAWA-KUN SAID, "GO AHEAD."
AND THEN... WAIT ...!
I'VE GOT IT!!

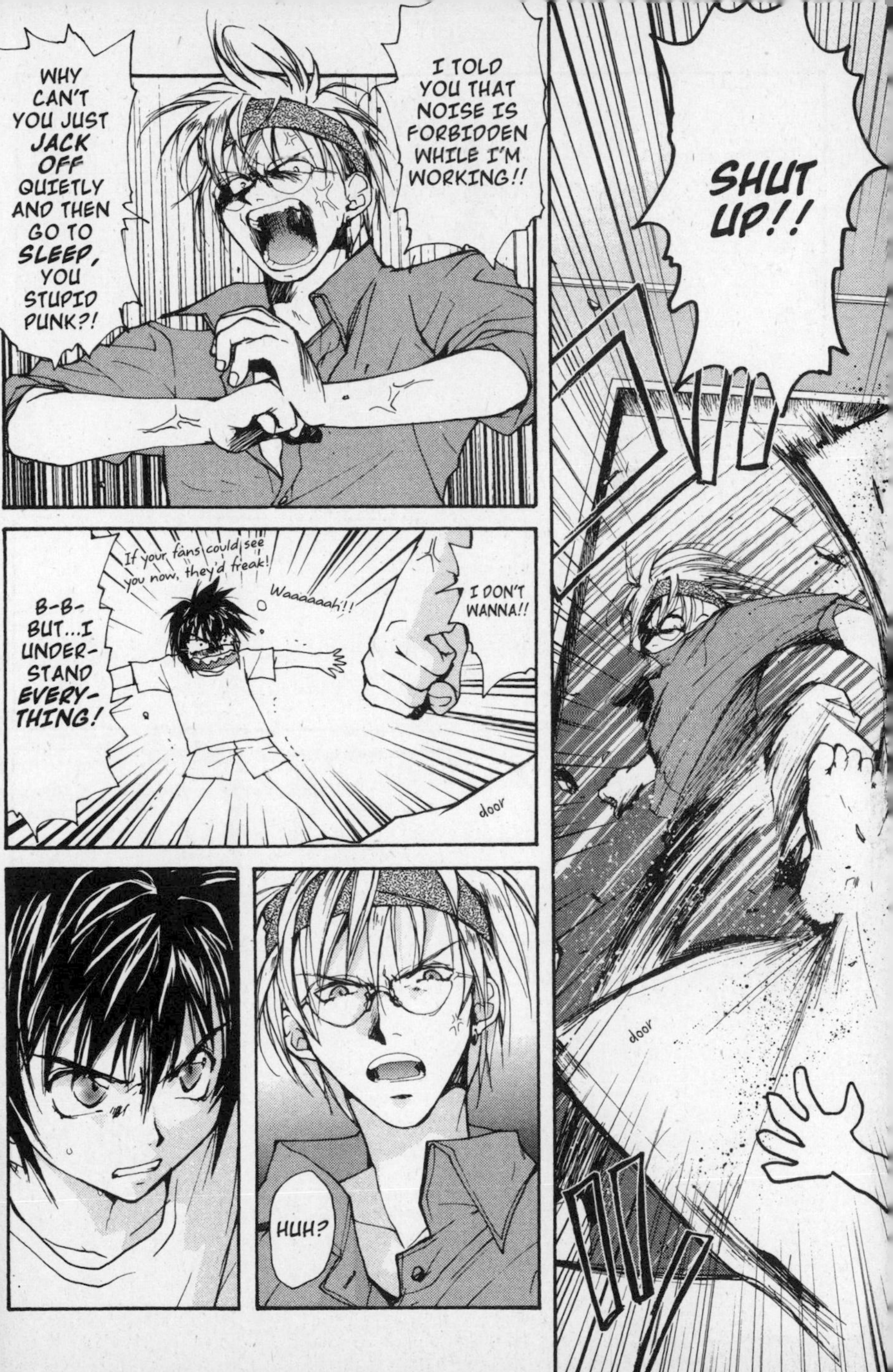
SHUT UP!!
door
I TOLD YOU THAT NOISE IS FORBIDDEN WHILE I'M WORKING!!
WHY CAN'T YOU JUST JACK OFF QUIETLY AND THEN GO TO SLEEP, YOU STUPID PUNK?!
I DON'T WANNA!!
Waaaaaah!!
If your fans could see you now, they'd freak!
B-B-BUT...I UNDER-STAND EVERY-THING!
door
HUH?

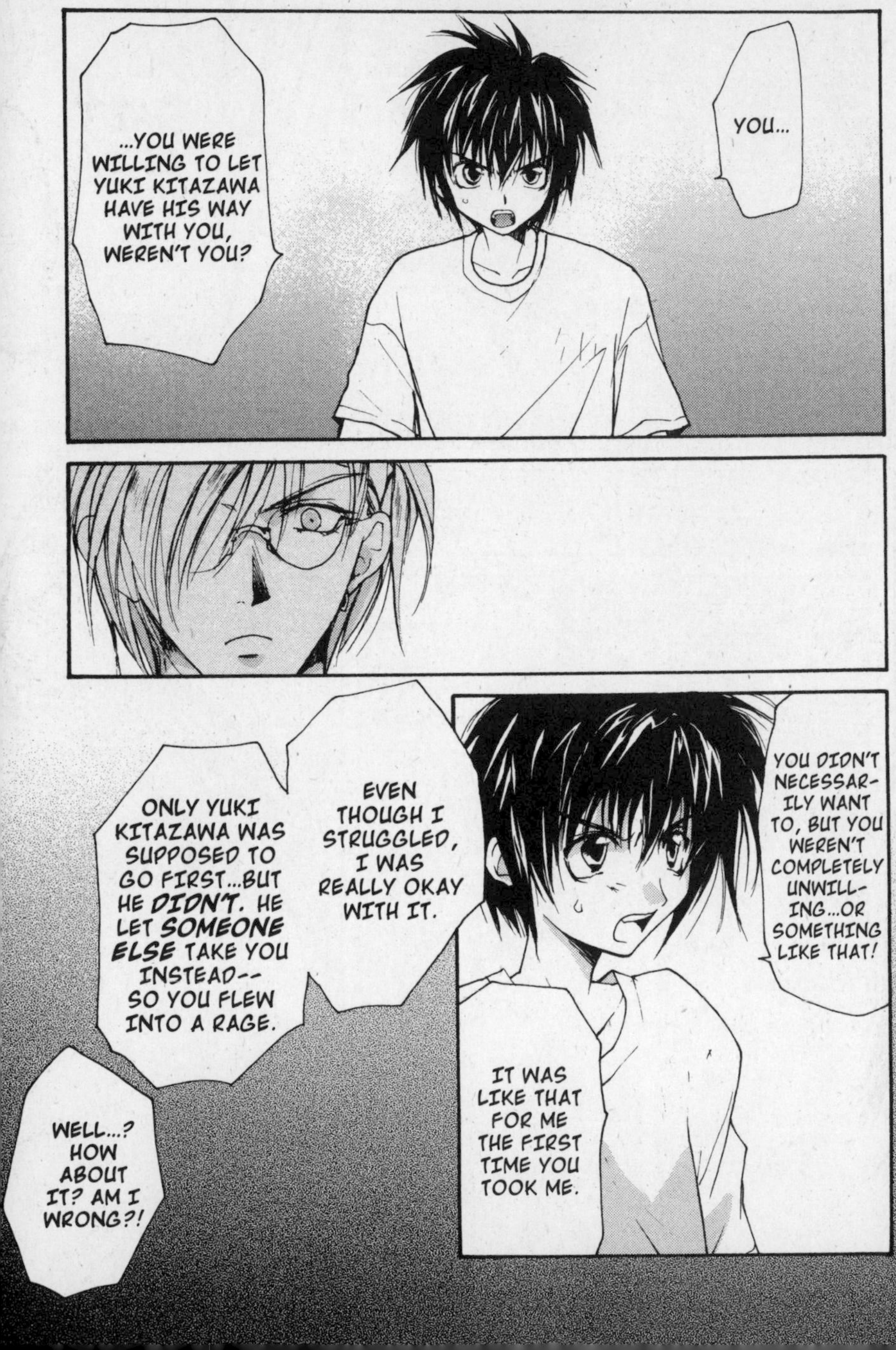
YOU...
...YOU WERE WILLING TO LET YUKI KITAZAWA HAVE HIS WAY WITH YOU, WEREN'T YOU?
YOU DIDN'T NECESSAR-ILY WANT TO, BUT YOU WEREN'T COMPLETELY UNWILL-ING...OR SOMETHING LIKE THAT!
IT WAS LIKE THAT FOR ME THE FIRST TIME YOU TOOK ME.
EVEN THOUGH I STRUGGLED, I WAS REALLY OKAY WITH IT.
ONLY YUKI KITAZAWA WAS SUPPOSED TO GO FIRST...BUT HE ***DIDN'T***. HE LET ***SOMEONE ELSE*** TAKE YOU INSTEAD-- SO YOU FLEW INTO A RAGE.
WELL...? HOW ABOUT IT? AM I WRONG?!

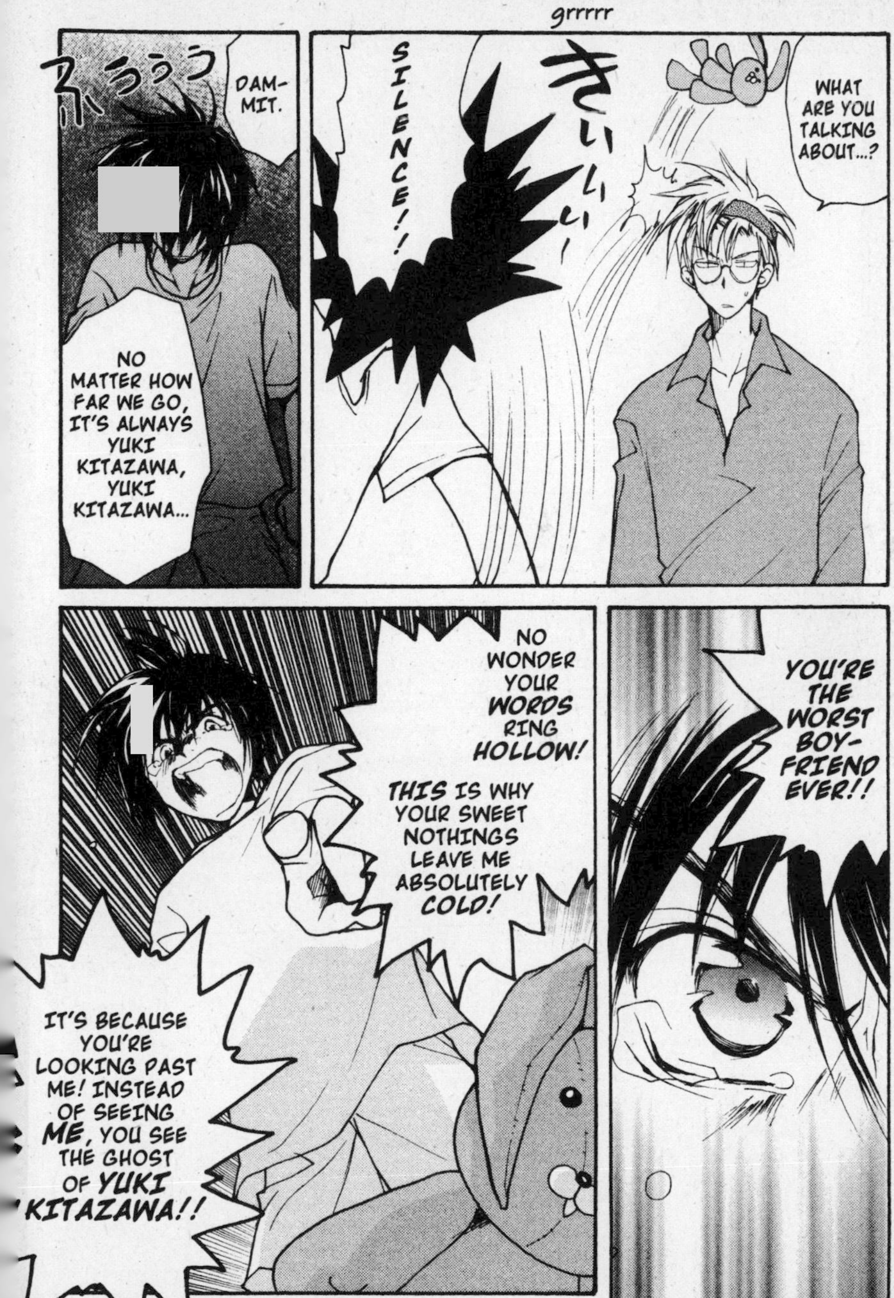
WHAT ARE YOU TALKING ABOUT...?
grrrrr
SILENCE!!
DAM-MIT.
NO MATTER HOW FAR WE GO, IT'S ALWAYS YUKI KITAZAWA, YUKI KITAZAWA...
YOU'RE THE WORST BOY-FRIEND EVER!!
NO WONDER YOUR WORDS RING HOLLOW!
THIS IS WHY YOUR SWEET NOTHINGS LEAVE ME ABSOLUTELY COLD!
IT'S BECAUSE YOU'RE LOOKING PAST ME! INSTEAD OF SEEING ME, YOU SEE THE GHOST OF YUKI KITAZAWA!!

track50▶END

# Gravitation

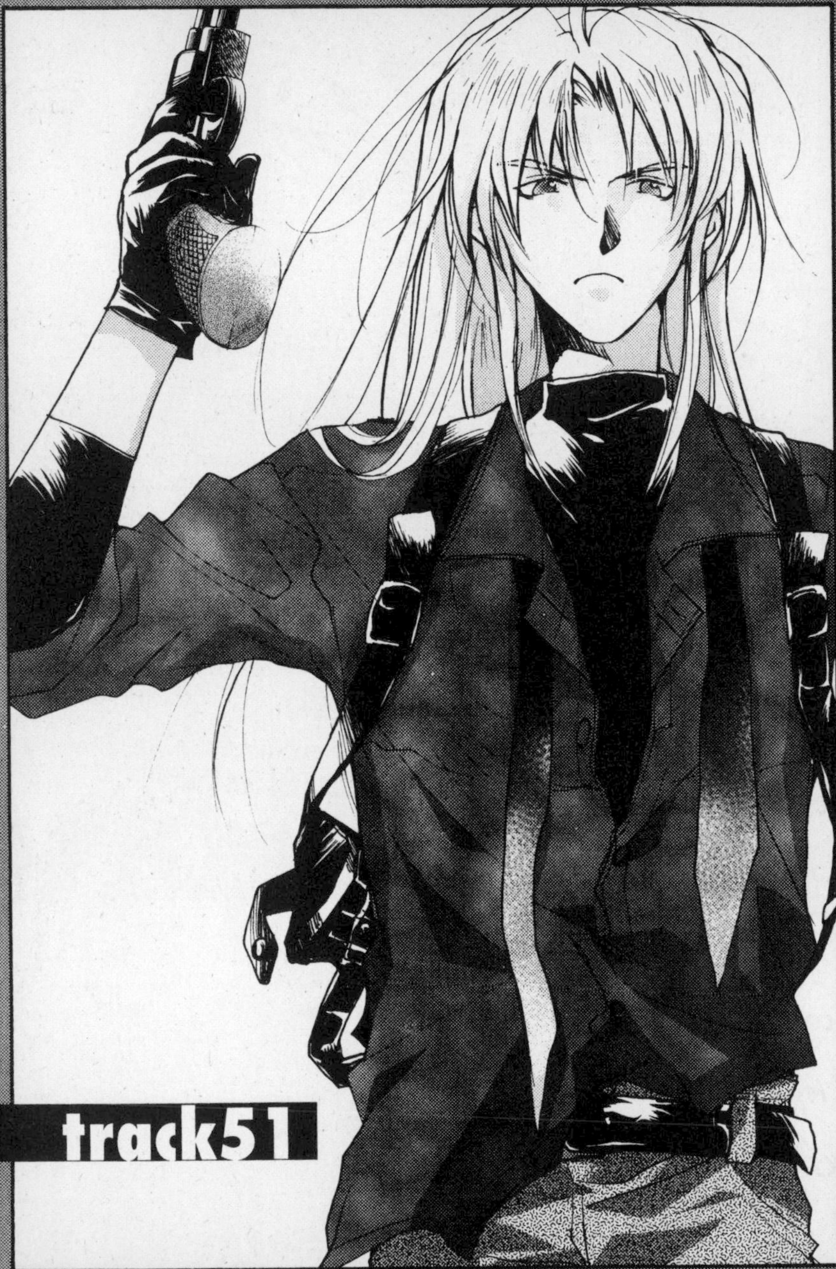

## track51

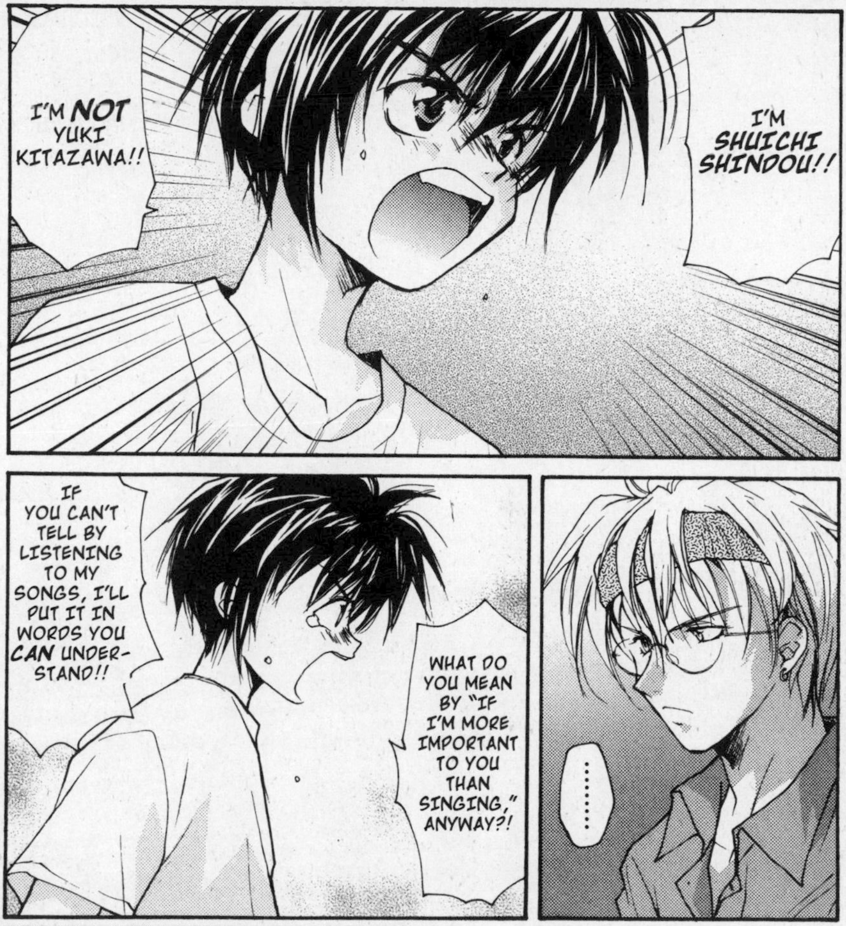
I'M SHUICHI SHINDOU!!
I'M NOT YUKI KITAZAWA!!
……
WHAT DO YOU MEAN BY "IF I'M MORE IMPORTANT TO YOU THAN SINGING," ANYWAY?!
IF YOU CAN'T TELL BY LISTENING TO MY SONGS, I'LL PUT IT IN WORDS YOU CAN UNDERSTAND!!

## ABOUT GRAVITATION TRACK 51

This one is short, so I'll just get to the point. Point 1: Tohma's fish apron. Point 2: Go home, baldy. That's it. Search for them. Lately, since my magazine has been publishing every few months, I keep forgetting to come up with a story. Needless to say, the story writing process ended up being a painful one. So, this last book will probably end up being published long after volume 11 comes out. I heard the delay might be as long as a year...

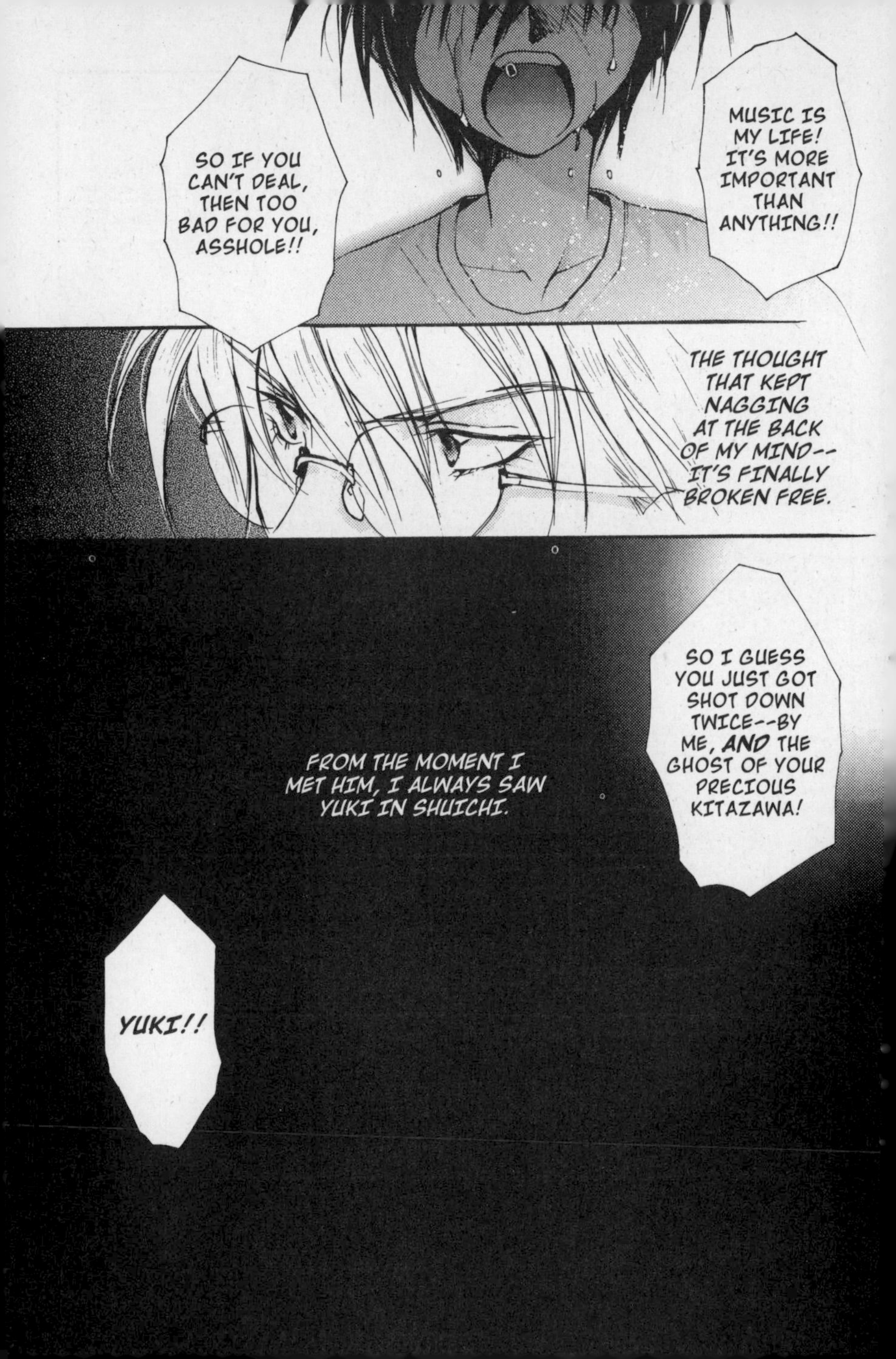
MUSIC IS MY LIFE! IT'S MORE IMPORTANT THAN ANYTHING!!
SO IF YOU CAN'T DEAL, THEN TOO BAD FOR YOU, ASSHOLE!!
THE THOUGHT THAT KEPT NAGGING AT THE BACK OF MY MIND-- IT'S FINALLY BROKEN FREE.
SO I GUESS YOU JUST GOT SHOT DOWN TWICE--BY ME, AND THE GHOST OF YOUR PRECIOUS KITAZAWA!
FROM THE MOMENT I MET HIM, I ALWAYS SAW YUKI IN SHUICHI.
YUKI!!

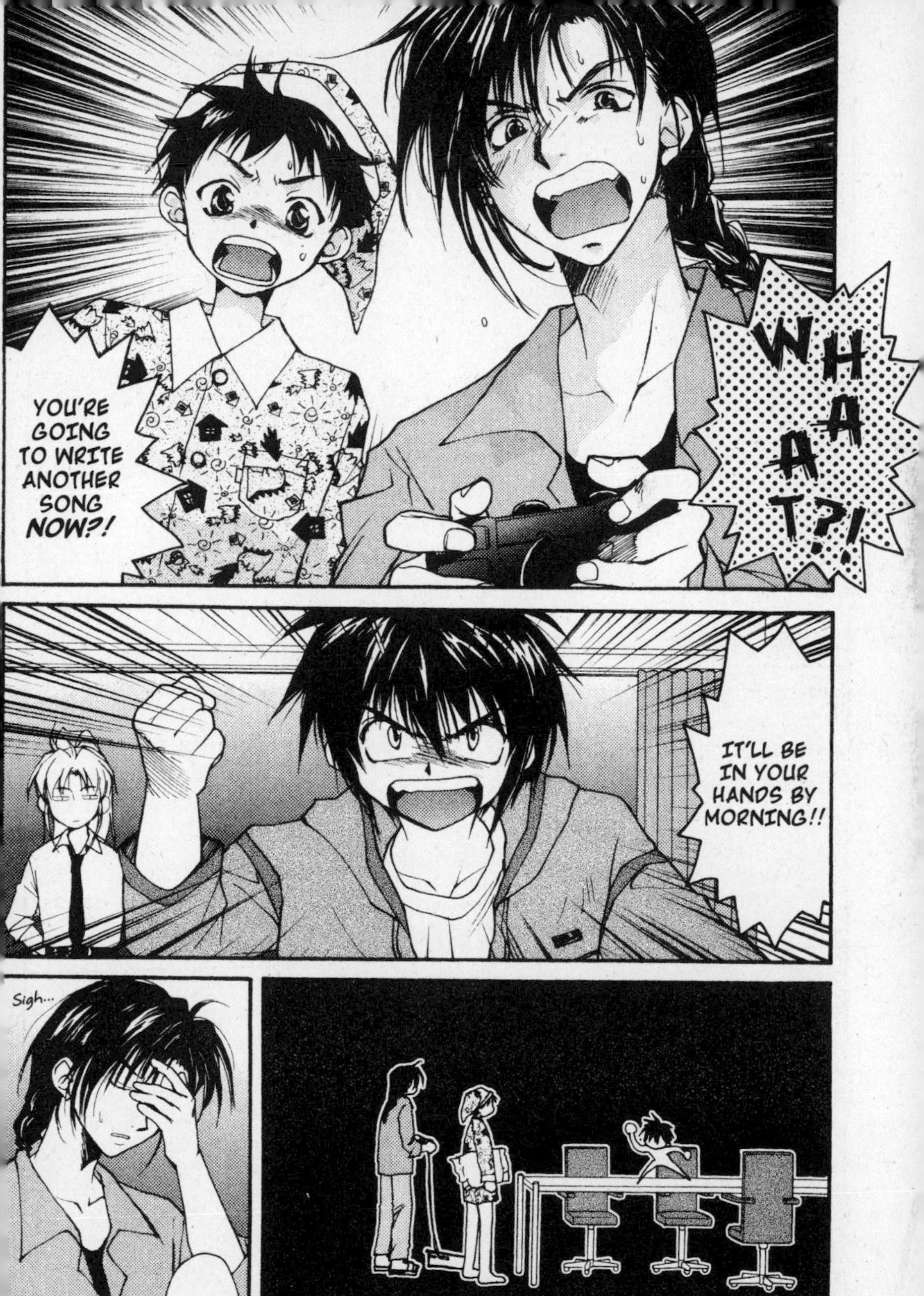
WHAAT?!
YOU'RE GOING TO WRITE ANOTHER SONG NOW?!
IT'LL BE IN YOUR HANDS BY MORNING!!
Sigh...
LOOK...

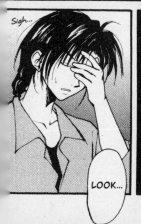

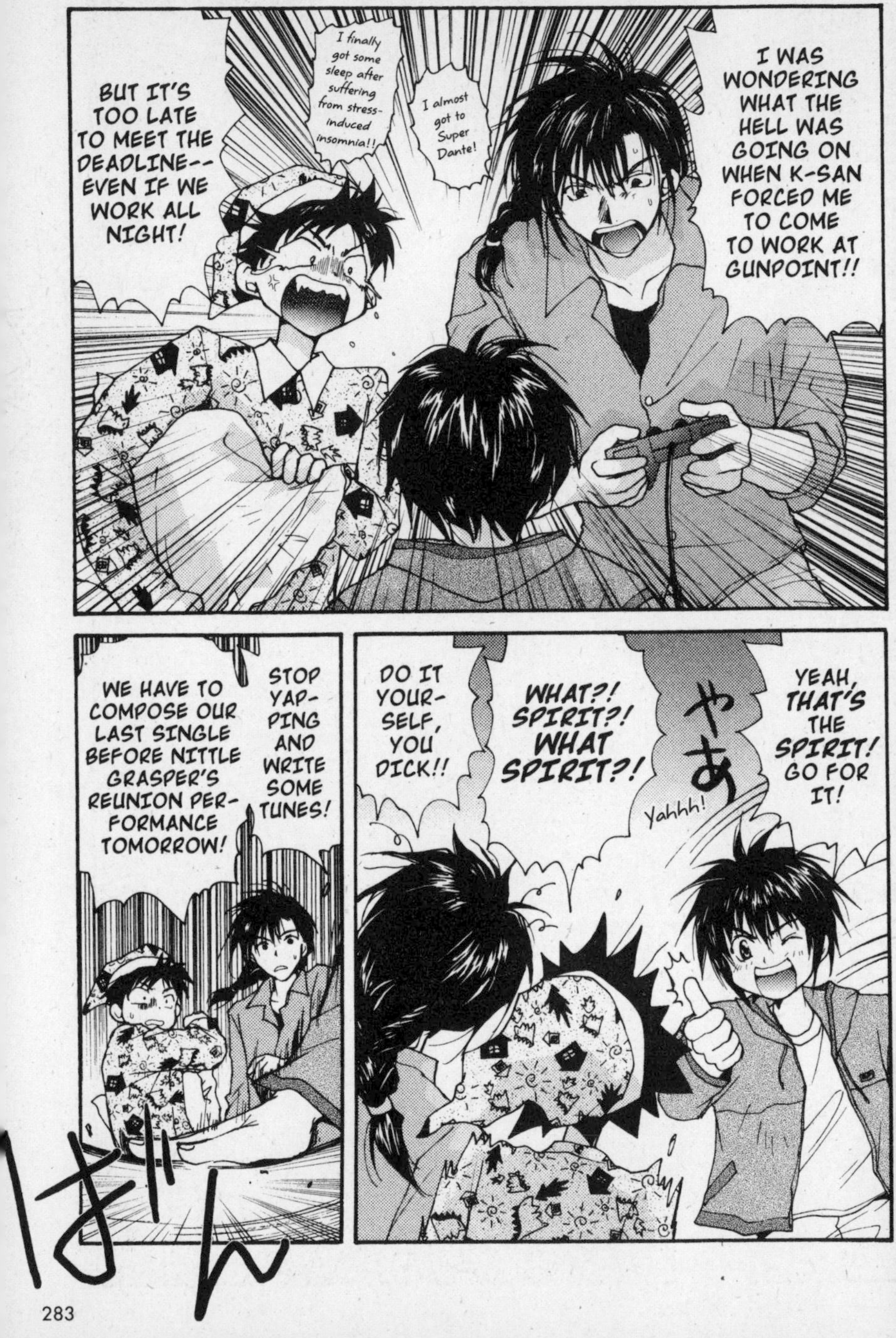
I WAS WONDERING WHAT THE HELL WAS GOING ON WHEN K-SAN FORCED ME TO COME TO WORK AT GUNPOINT!!
I almost got to Super Dante!
I finally got some sleep after suffering from stress-induced insomnia!!
BUT IT'S TOO LATE TO MEET THE DEADLINE--EVEN IF WE WORK ALL NIGHT!
YEAH, THAT'S THE SPIRIT! GO FOR IT!
やあ
Yahhh!
WHAT?! SPIRIT?! WHAT SPIRIT?!
DO IT YOURSELF, YOU DICK!!
STOP YAPPING AND WRITE SOME TUNES!
WE HAVE TO COMPOSE OUR LAST SINGLE BEFORE NITTLE GRASPER'S REUNION PERFORMANCE TOMORROW!
ばん

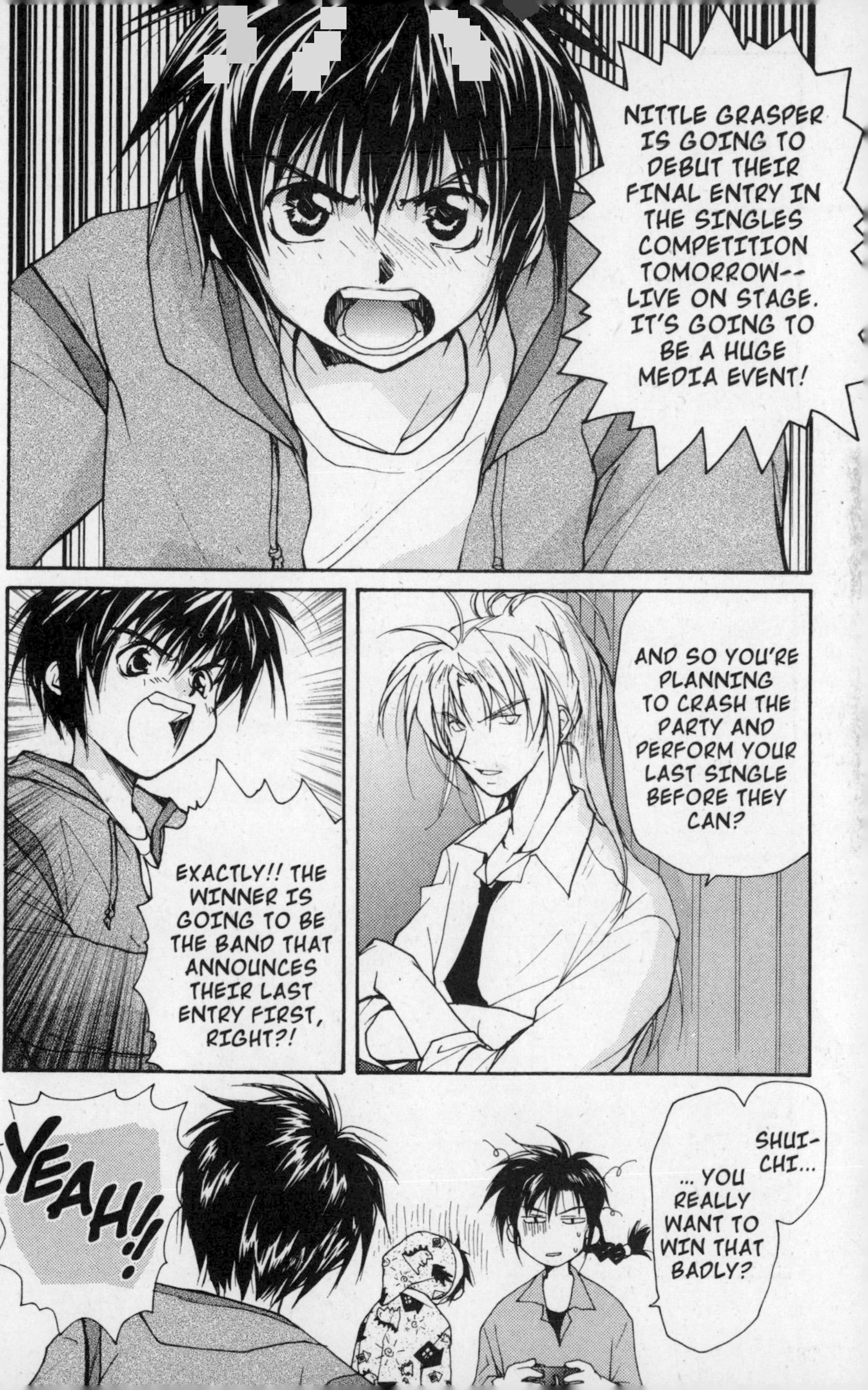
NITTLE GRASPER IS GOING TO DEBUT THEIR FINAL ENTRY IN THE SINGLES COMPETITION TOMORROW-- LIVE ON STAGE. IT'S GOING TO BE A HUGE MEDIA EVENT!
AND SO YOU'RE PLANNING TO CRASH THE PARTY AND PERFORM YOUR LAST SINGLE BEFORE THEY CAN?
EXACTLY!! THE WINNER IS GOING TO BE THE BAND THAT ANNOUNCES THEIR LAST ENTRY FIRST, RIGHT?!
SHUI-CHI...
... YOU REALLY WANT TO WIN THAT BADLY?
YEAH!!

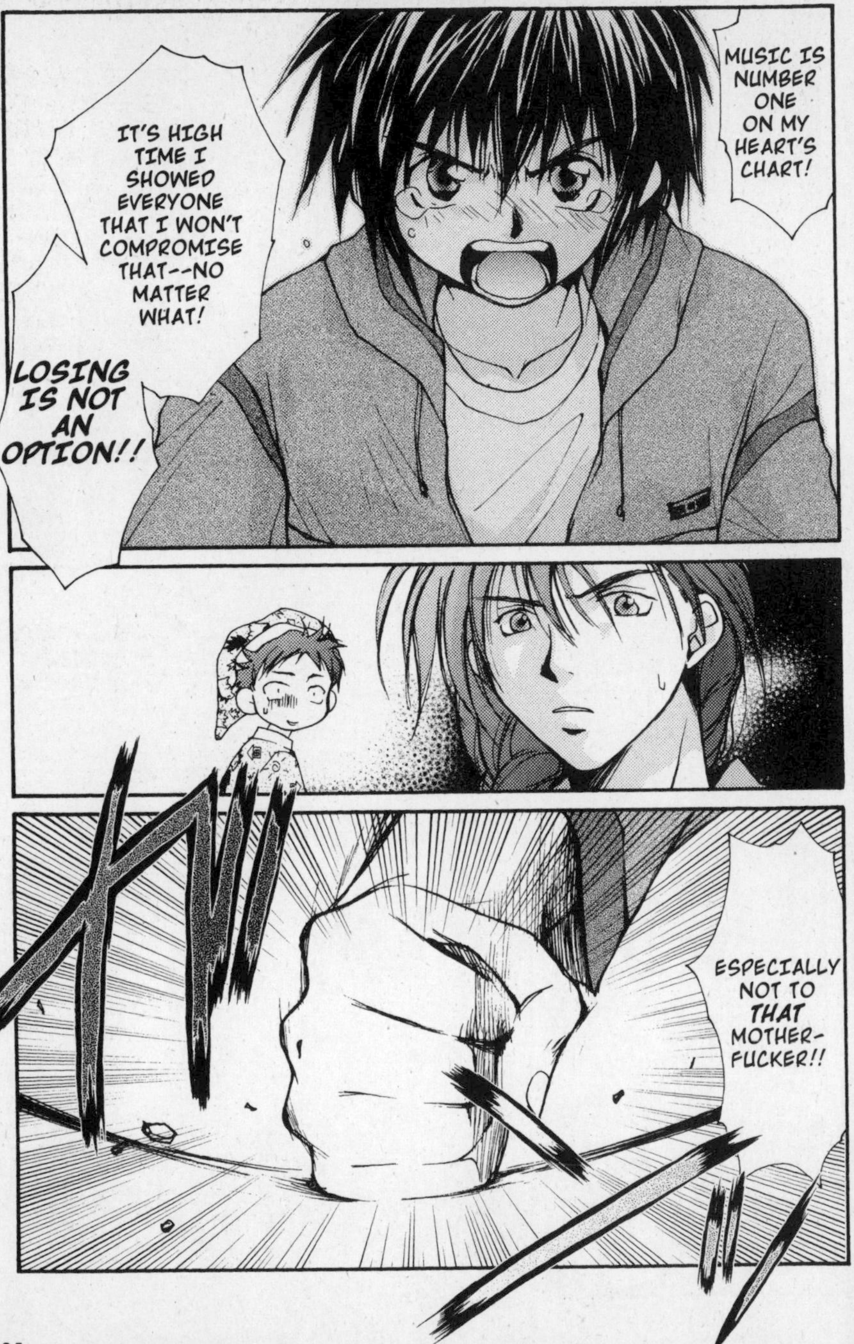
MUSIC IS NUMBER ONE ON MY HEART'S CHART!
IT'S HIGH TIME I SHOWED EVERYONE THAT I WON'T COMPROMISE THAT--NO MATTER WHAT!
LOSING IS NOT AN OPTION!!
ESPECIALLY NOT TO *THAT* MOTHER-FUCKER!!

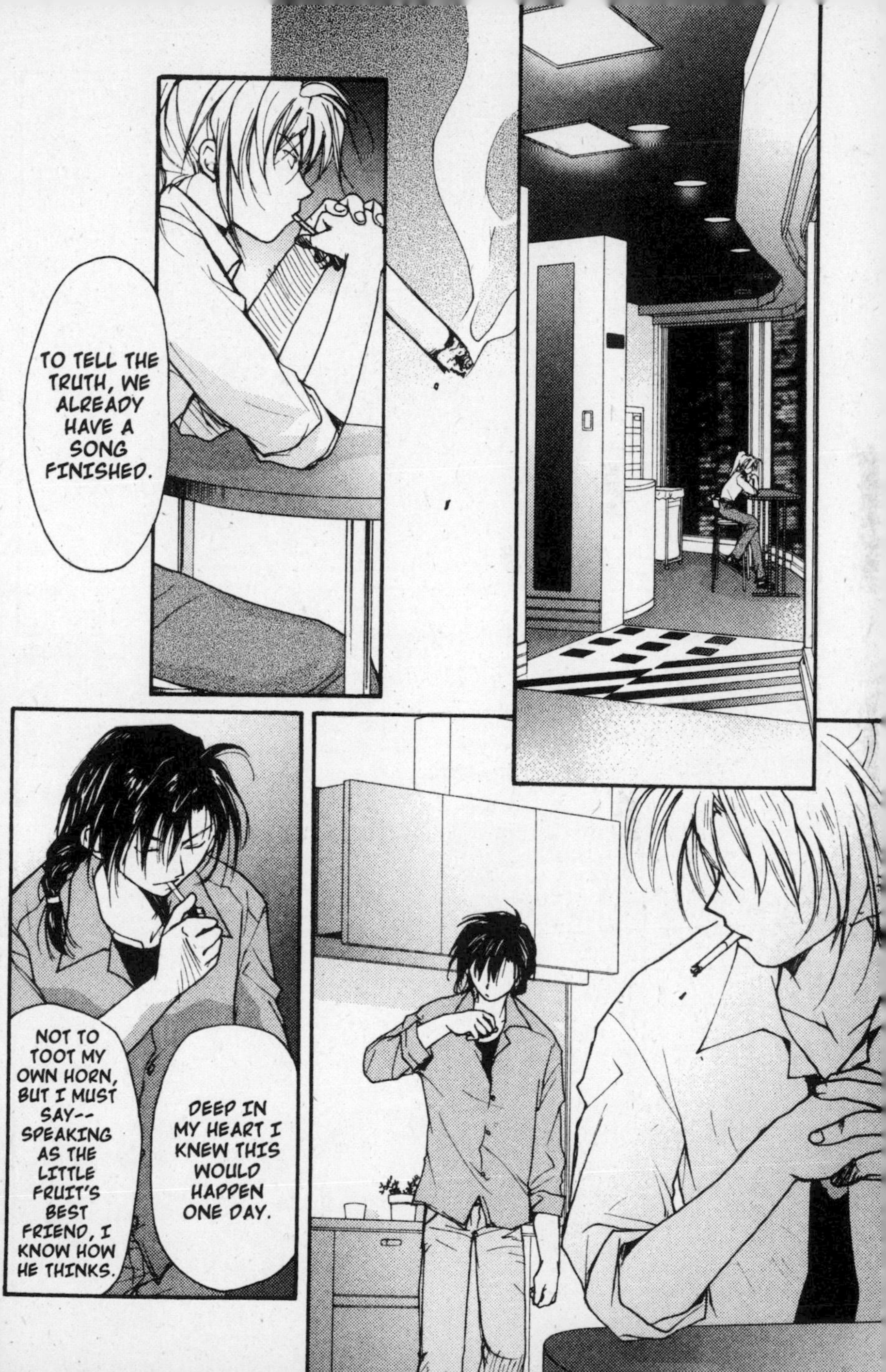
TO TELL THE TRUTH, WE ALREADY HAVE A SONG FINISHED.
DEEP IN MY HEART I KNEW THIS WOULD HAPPEN ONE DAY.
NOT TO TOOT MY OWN HORN, BUT I MUST SAY-- SPEAKING AS THE LITTLE FRUIT'S BEST FRIEND, I KNOW HOW HE THINKS.

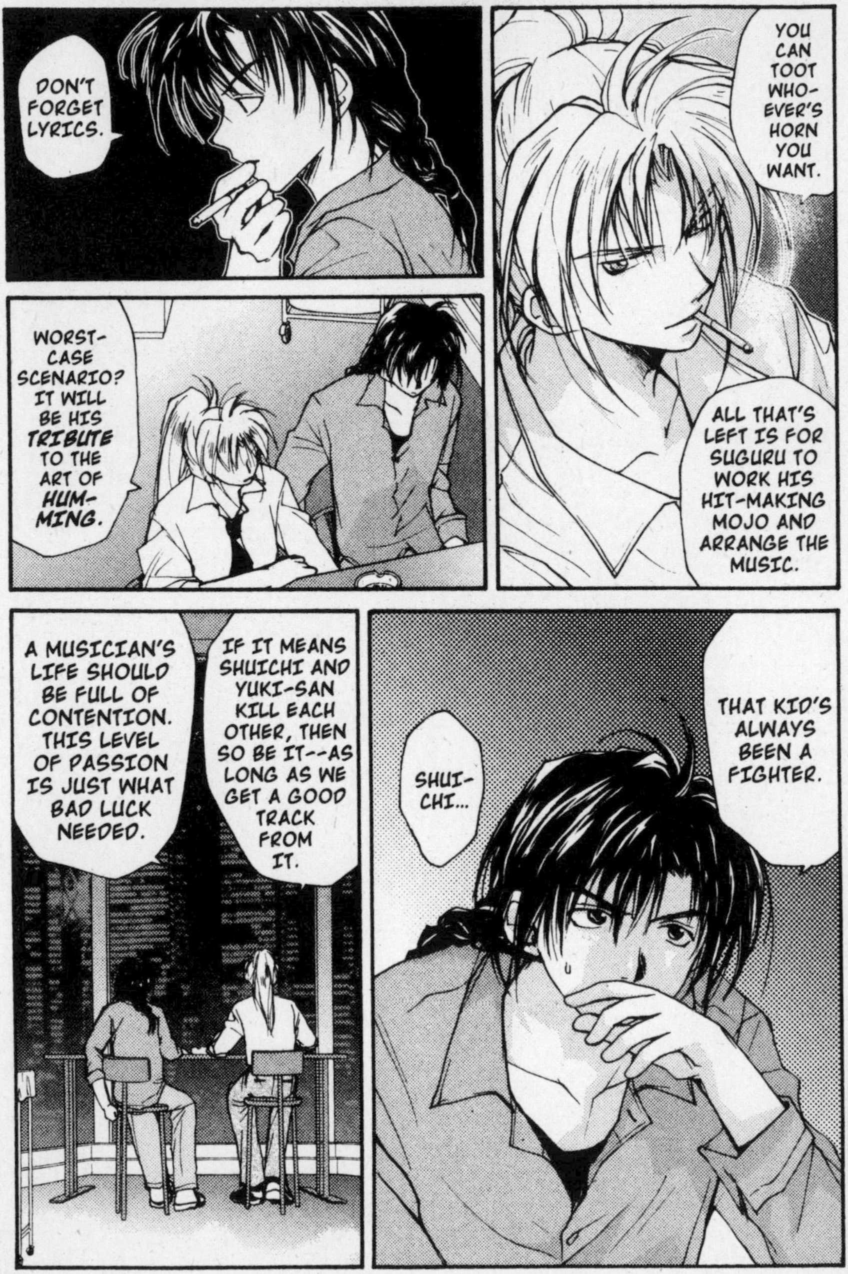
YOU CAN TOOT WHOEVER'S HORN YOU WANT.
ALL THAT'S LEFT IS FOR SUGURU TO WORK HIS HIT-MAKING MOJO AND ARRANGE THE MUSIC.
DON'T FORGET LYRICS.
WORST-CASE SCENARIO? IT WILL BE HIS TRIBUTE TO THE ART OF HUMMING.
THAT KID'S ALWAYS BEEN A FIGHTER.
SHUICHI...
IF IT MEANS SHUICHI AND YUKI-SAN KILL EACH OTHER, THEN SO BE IT--AS LONG AS WE GET A GOOD TRACK FROM IT.
A MUSICIAN'S LIFE SHOULD BE FULL OF CONTENTION. THIS LEVEL OF PASSION IS JUST WHAT BAD LUCK NEEDED.

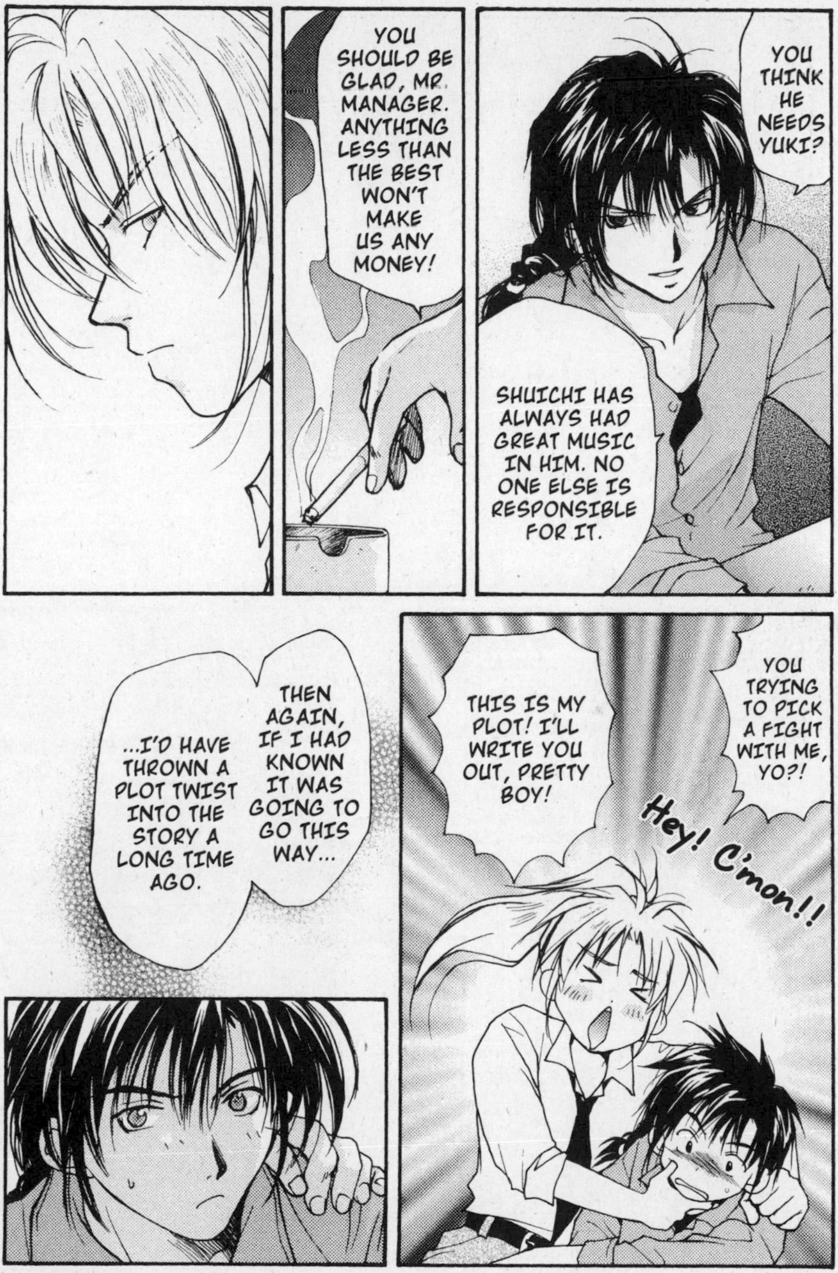
YOU THINK HE NEEDS YUKI?
SHUICHI HAS ALWAYS HAD GREAT MUSIC IN HIM. NO ONE ELSE IS RESPONSIBLE FOR IT.
YOU SHOULD BE GLAD, MR. MANAGER. ANYTHING LESS THAN THE BEST WON'T MAKE US ANY MONEY!
YOU TRYING TO PICK A FIGHT WITH ME, YO?!
THIS IS MY PLOT! I'LL WRITE YOU OUT, PRETTY BOY!
Hey! C'mon!!
THEN AGAIN, IF I HAD KNOWN IT WAS GOING TO GO THIS WAY...
...I'D HAVE THROWN A PLOT TWIST INTO THE STORY A LONG TIME AGO.

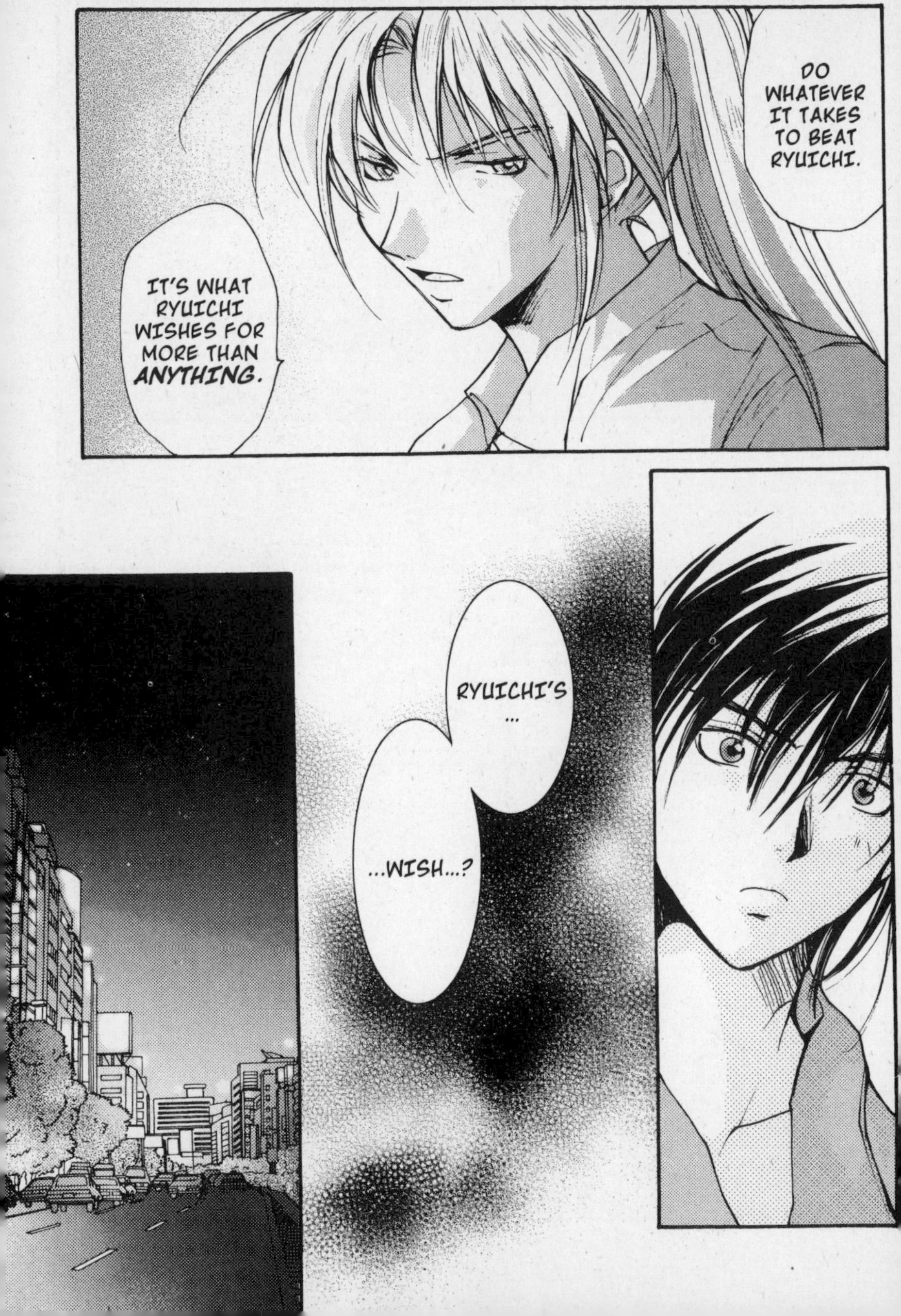
DO WHATEVER IT TAKES TO BEAT RYUICHI.
IT'S WHAT RYUICHI WISHES FOR MORE THAN ANYTHING.
RYUICHI'S ...
...WISH...?

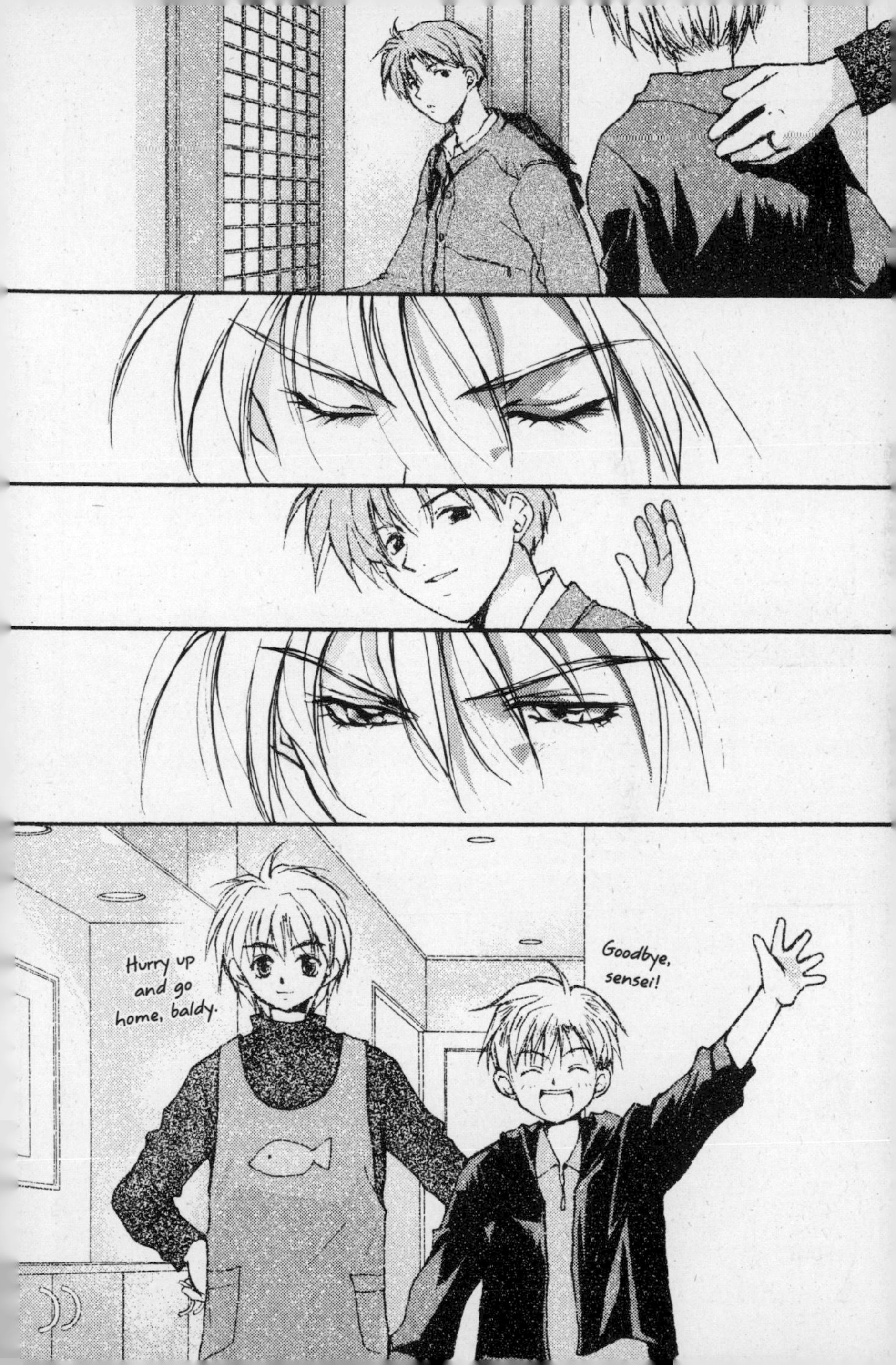
Goodbye, sensei!
Hurry up and go home, baldy.

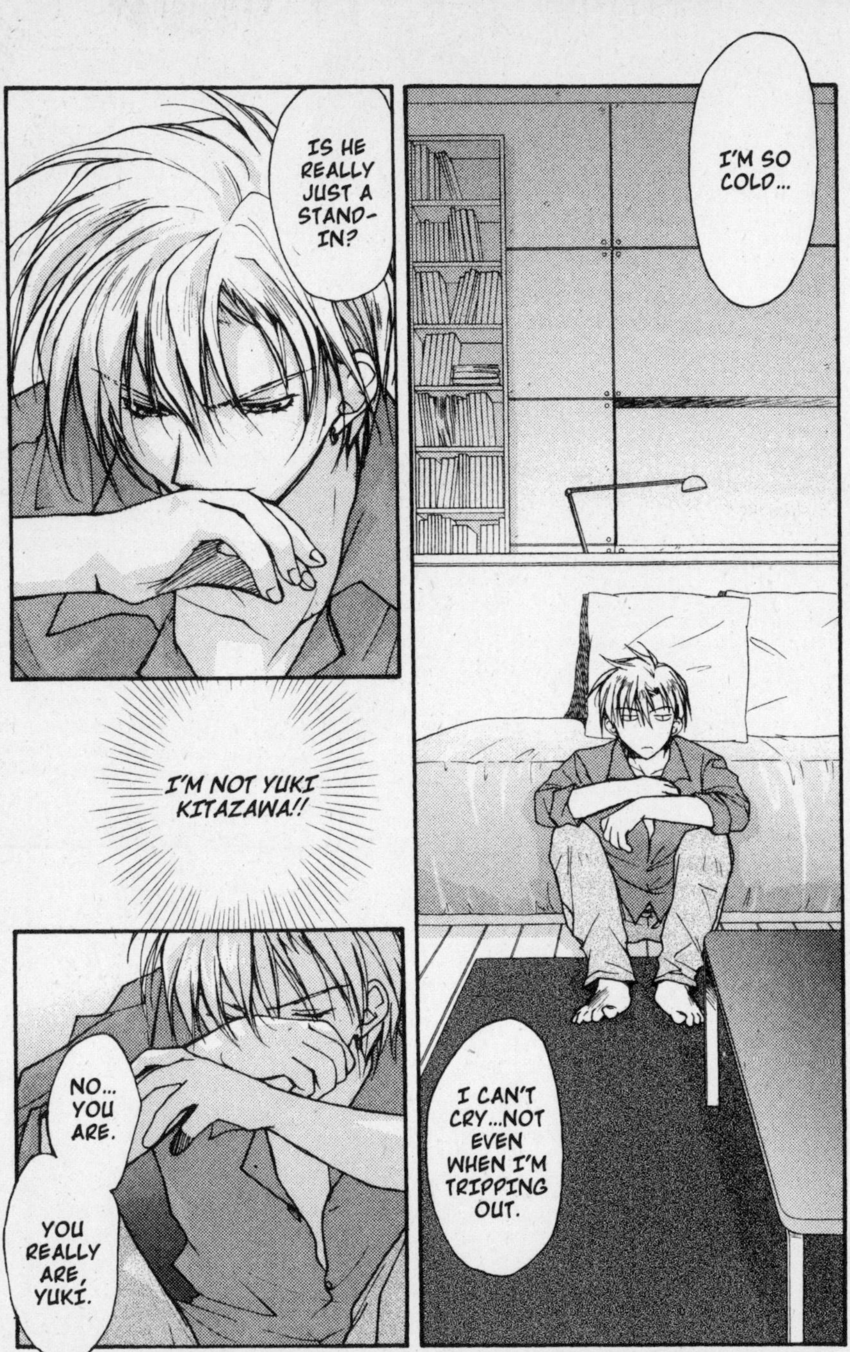
I'M SO COLD...
I CAN'T CRY...NOT EVEN WHEN I'M TRIPPING OUT.
IS HE REALLY JUST A STAND-IN?
I'M NOT YUKI KITAZAWA!!
NO... YOU ARE.
YOU REALLY ARE, YUKI.

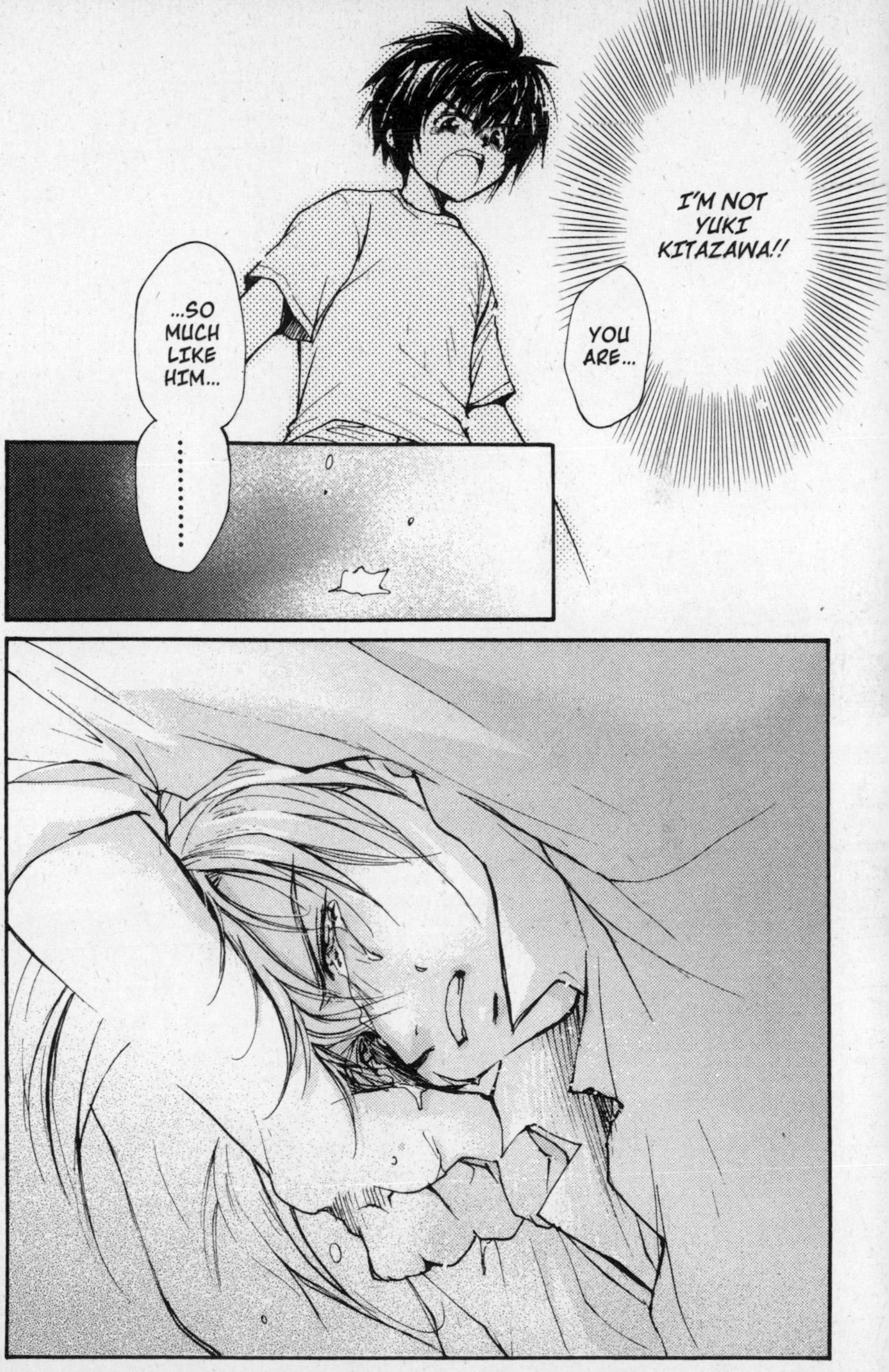
I'M NOT YUKI KITAZAWA!!
YOU ARE...
...SO MUCH LIKE HIM...
......

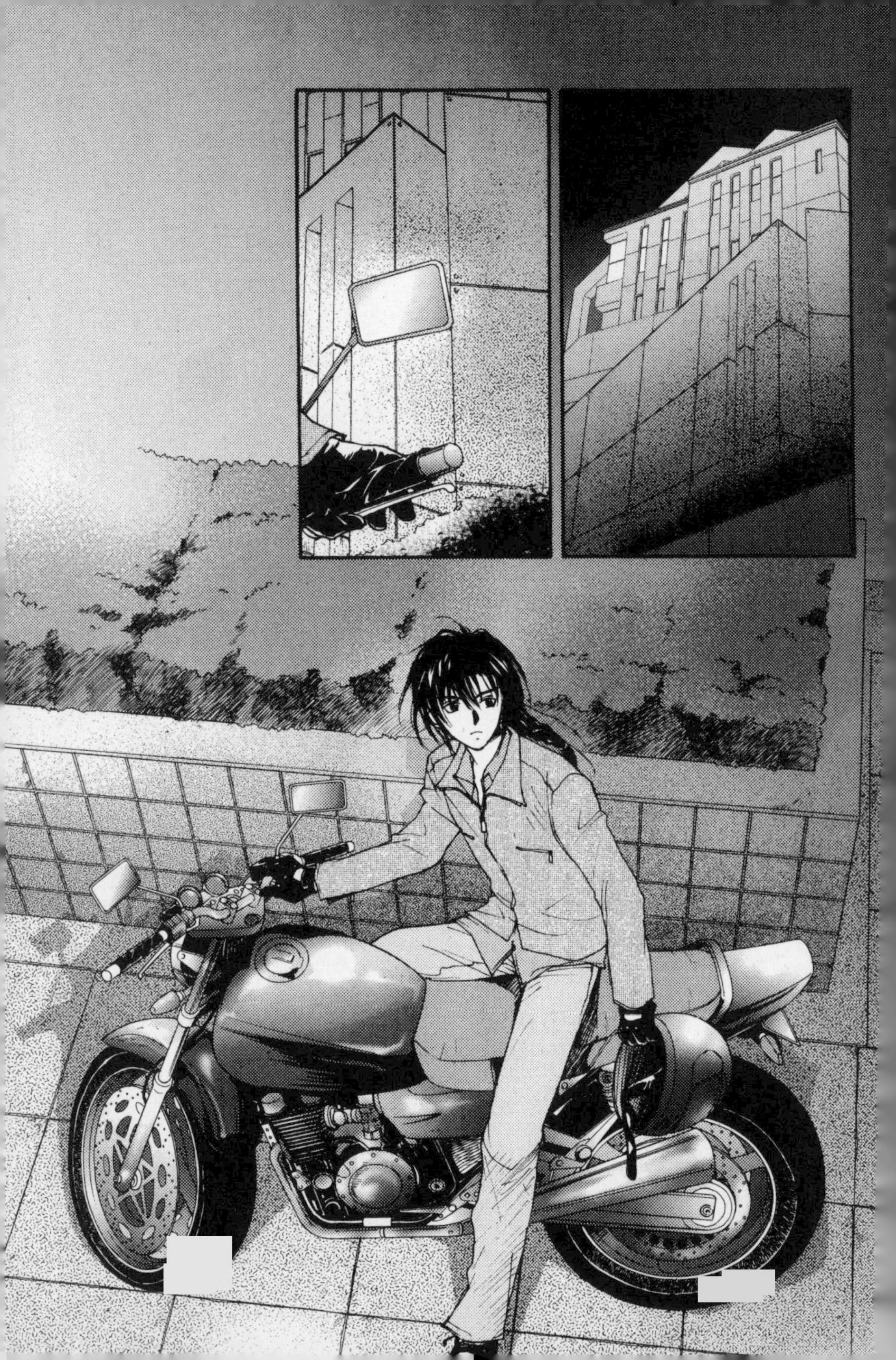

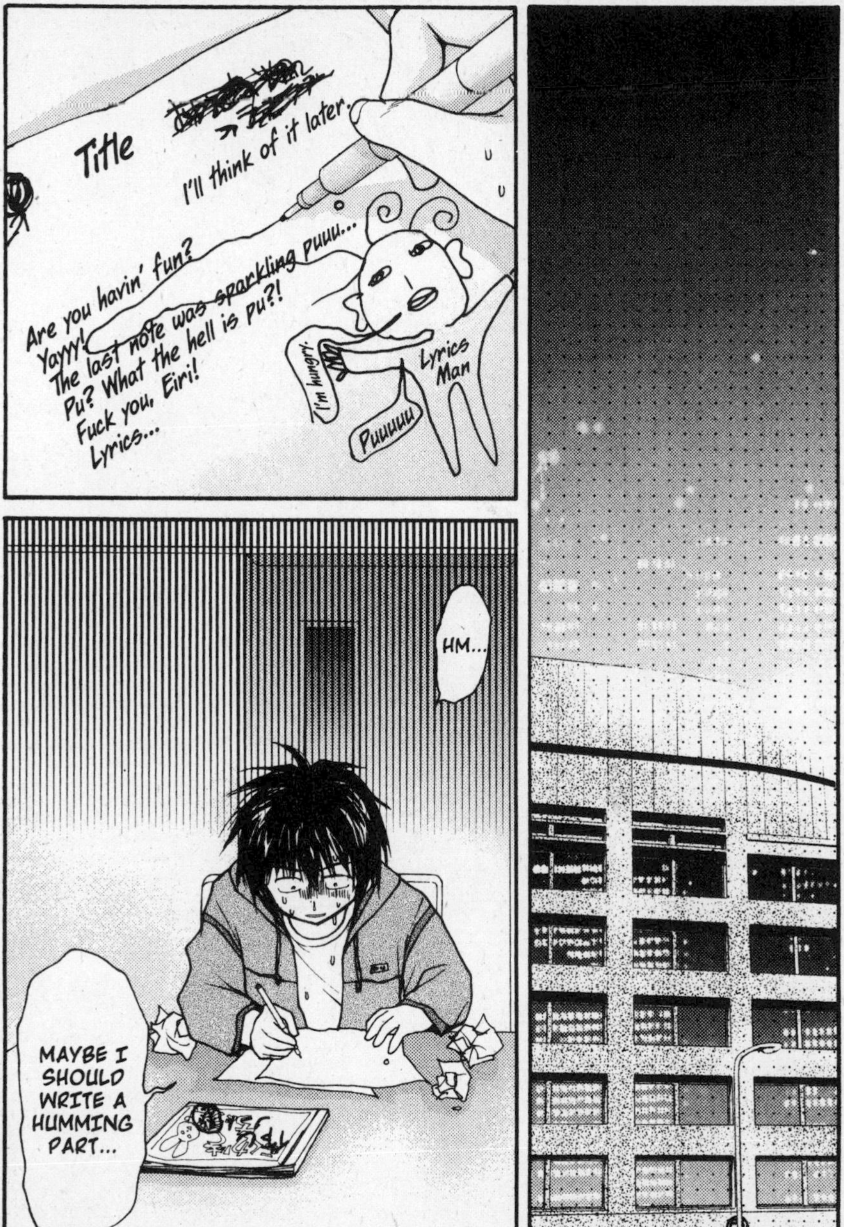
Title
I'll think of it later.
Are you havin' fun?
Yayyy!
The last note was sparkling puuu...
Pu? What the hell is pu?!
Fuck you, Eiri!
Lyrics...
Lyrics Man
I'm hungry.
Puuuuu
HM...
MAYBE I SHOULD WRITE A HUMMING PART...

track51 ▶ END

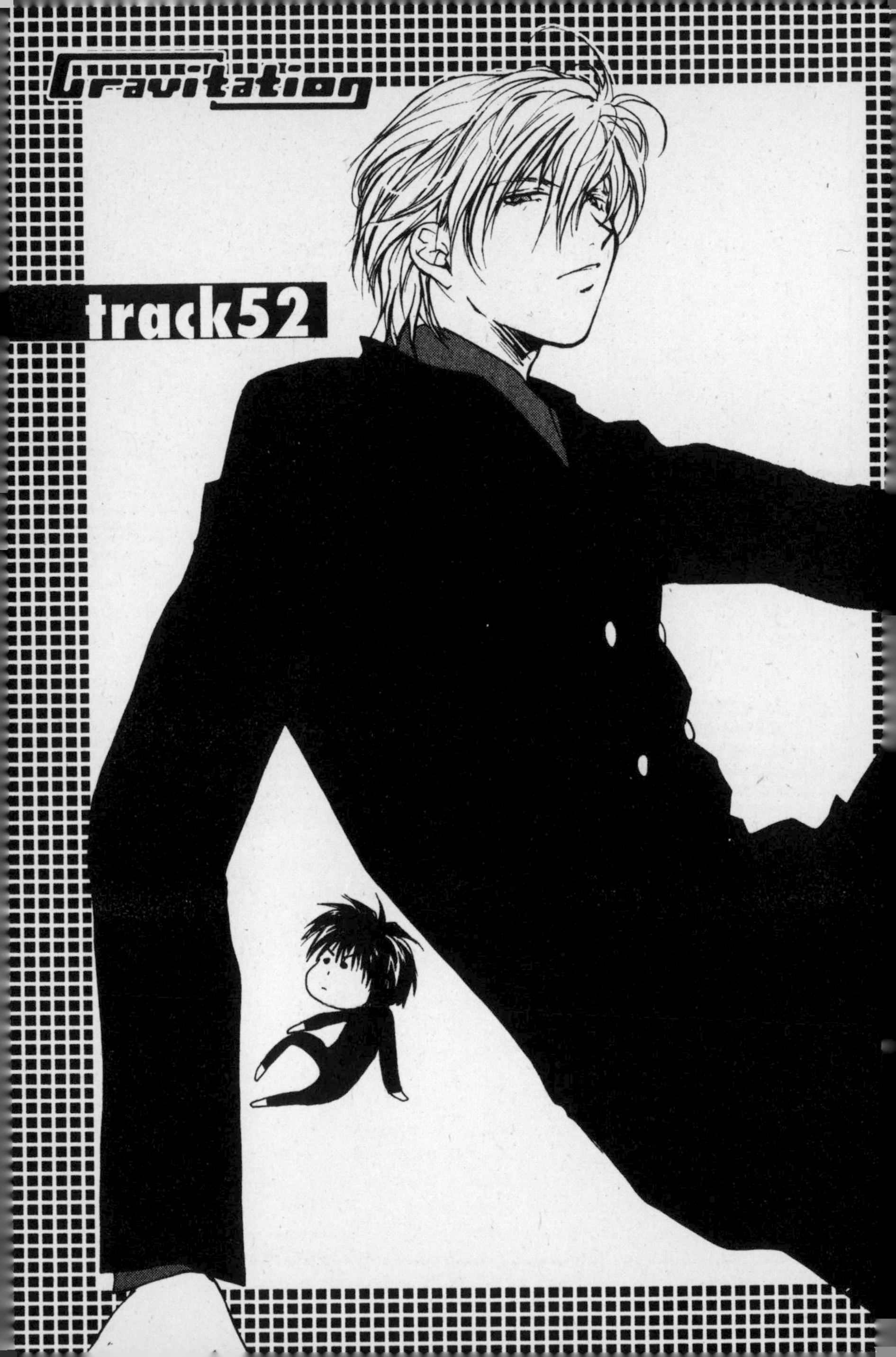

Gravitation
track52

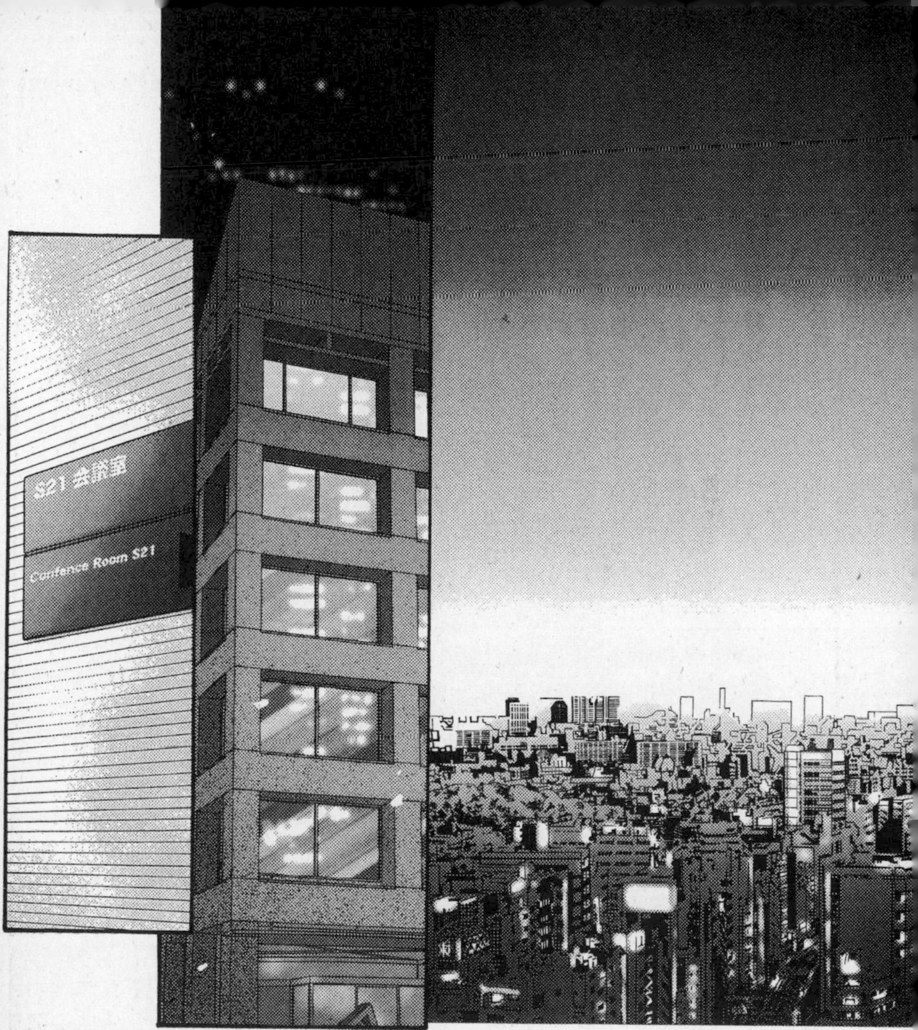
S21 会議室
Confence Room S21

## ABOUT GRAVITATION TRACK 52

This episode is about outrageous people in outrageous outfits doing outrageous things! Outrageous, eh?! Since Yuki didn't show up much in the last episode, I decided to draw him big on the front cover page as penance. That seemed to please the fans and the critics, which in turn makes me happy, as well. And don't you worry--that little bug Shindou is also alive and well. This episode is like emerging from a long, long, long, long tunnel and dashing towards the goal!! It's a refreshing, yet desperate, kind of story. (And yes, I know there aren't any tunnels on sports fields.) As far as how I'd rate it (on the top/middle/bottom scale) I'd say this one is the top level--of the bottom ranking.

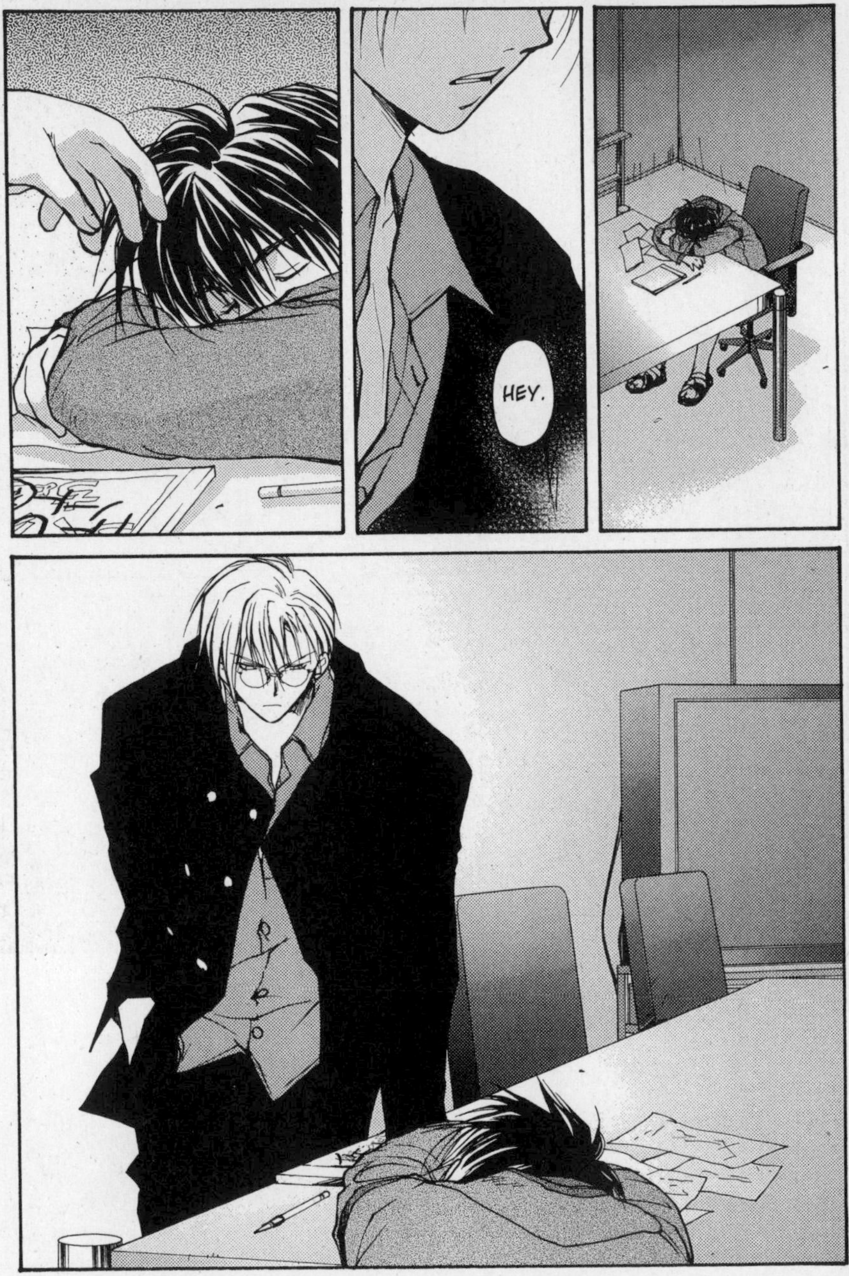
HEY.

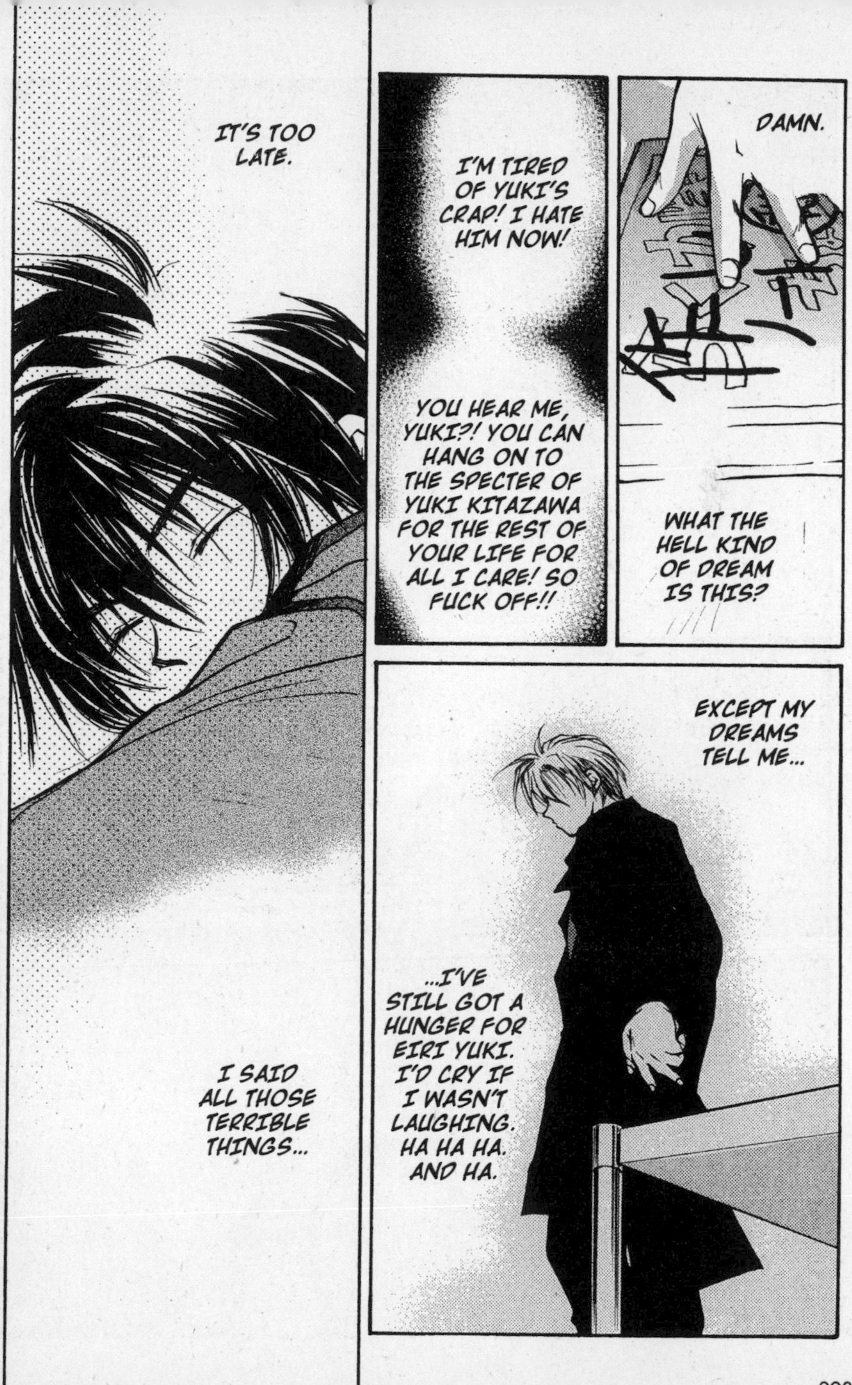
DAMN.
WHAT THE HELL KIND OF DREAM IS THIS?
I'M TIRED OF YUKI'S CRAP! I HATE HIM NOW!
YOU HEAR ME, YUKI?! YOU CAN HANG ON TO THE SPECTER OF YUKI KITAZAWA FOR THE REST OF YOUR LIFE FOR ALL I CARE! SO FUCK OFF!!
EXCEPT MY DREAMS TELL ME...
...I'VE STILL GOT A HUNGER FOR EIRI YUKI. I'D CRY IF I WASN'T LAUGHING. HA HA HA. AND HA.
IT'S TOO LATE.
I SAID ALL THOSE TERRIBLE THINGS...

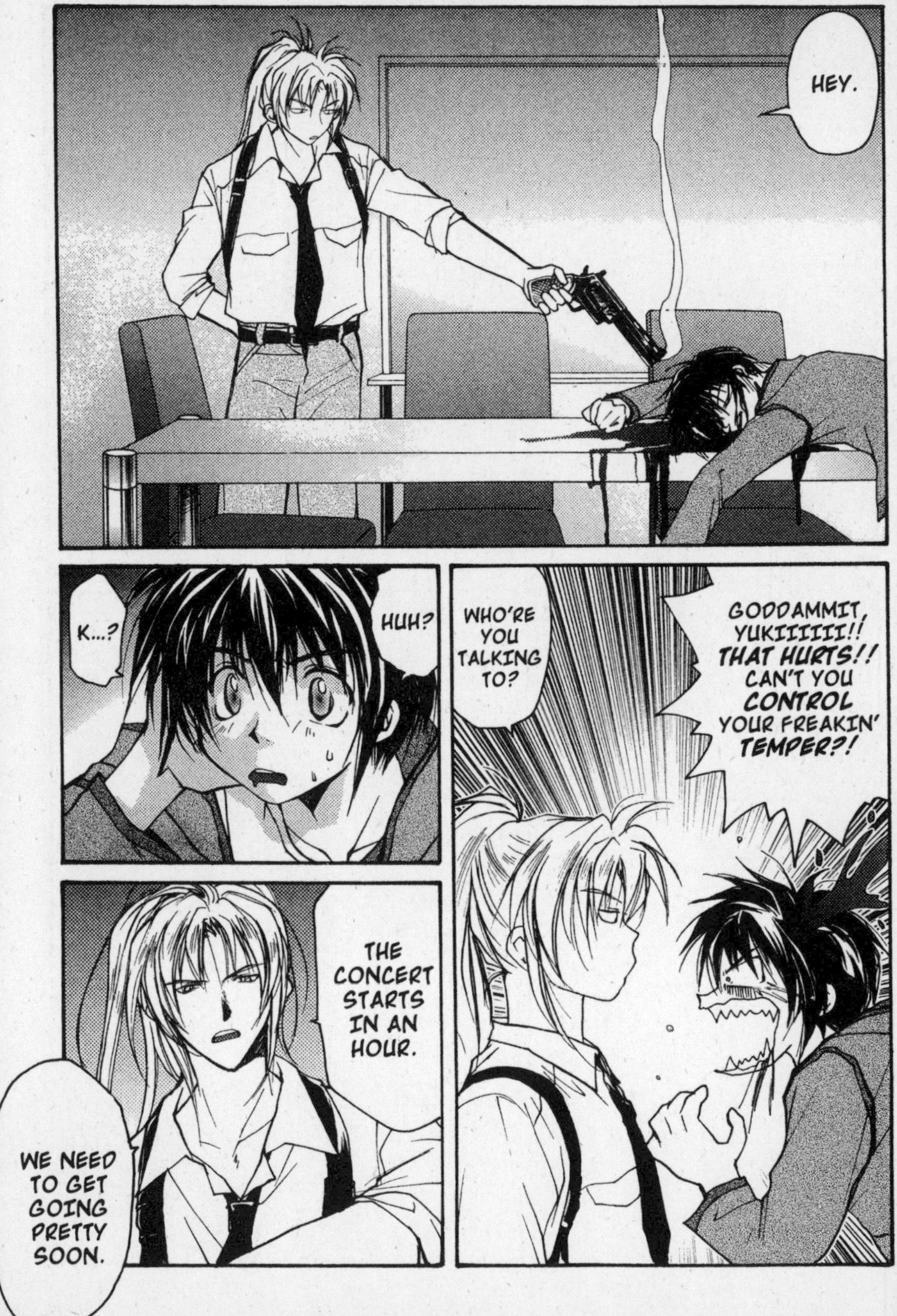
HEY.
GODDAMMIT, YUKIIIIII!! **THAT HURTS!!** CAN'T YOU **CONTROL** YOUR FREAKIN' **TEMPER?!**
WHO'RE YOU TALKING TO?
HUH?
K...?
THE CONCERT STARTS IN AN HOUR.
WE NEED TO GET GOING PRETTY SOON.

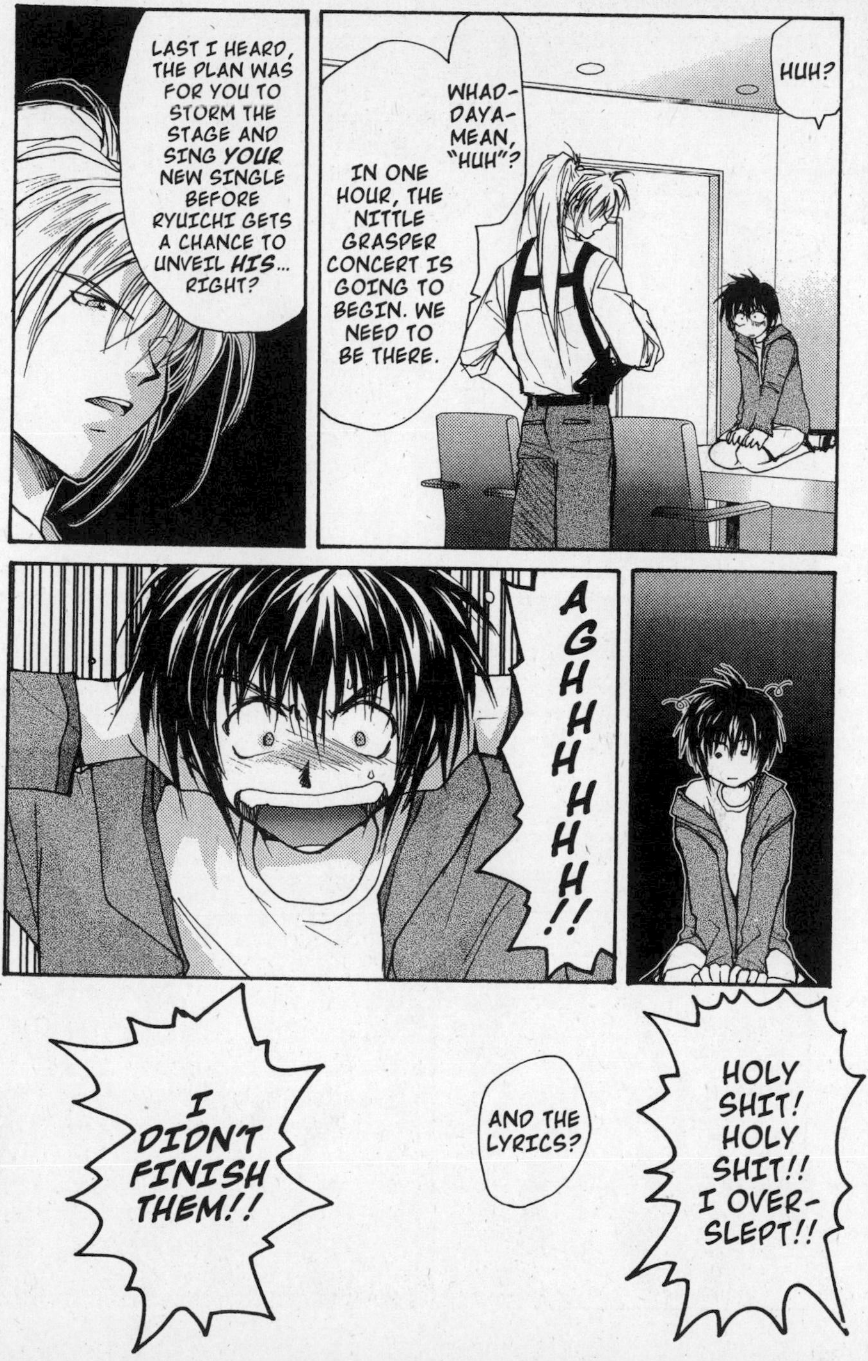
HUH?
WHAD-DAYA-MEAN, "HUH"?
IN ONE HOUR, THE NITTLE GRASPER CONCERT IS GOING TO BEGIN. WE NEED TO BE THERE.
LAST I HEARD, THE PLAN WAS FOR YOU TO STORM THE STAGE AND SING *YOUR* NEW SINGLE BEFORE RYUICHI GETS A CHANCE TO UNVEIL *HIS*... RIGHT?
AGHHHHHH!!
HOLY SHIT! HOLY SHIT!! I OVER-SLEPT!!
AND THE LYRICS?
I DIDN'T FINISH THEM!!

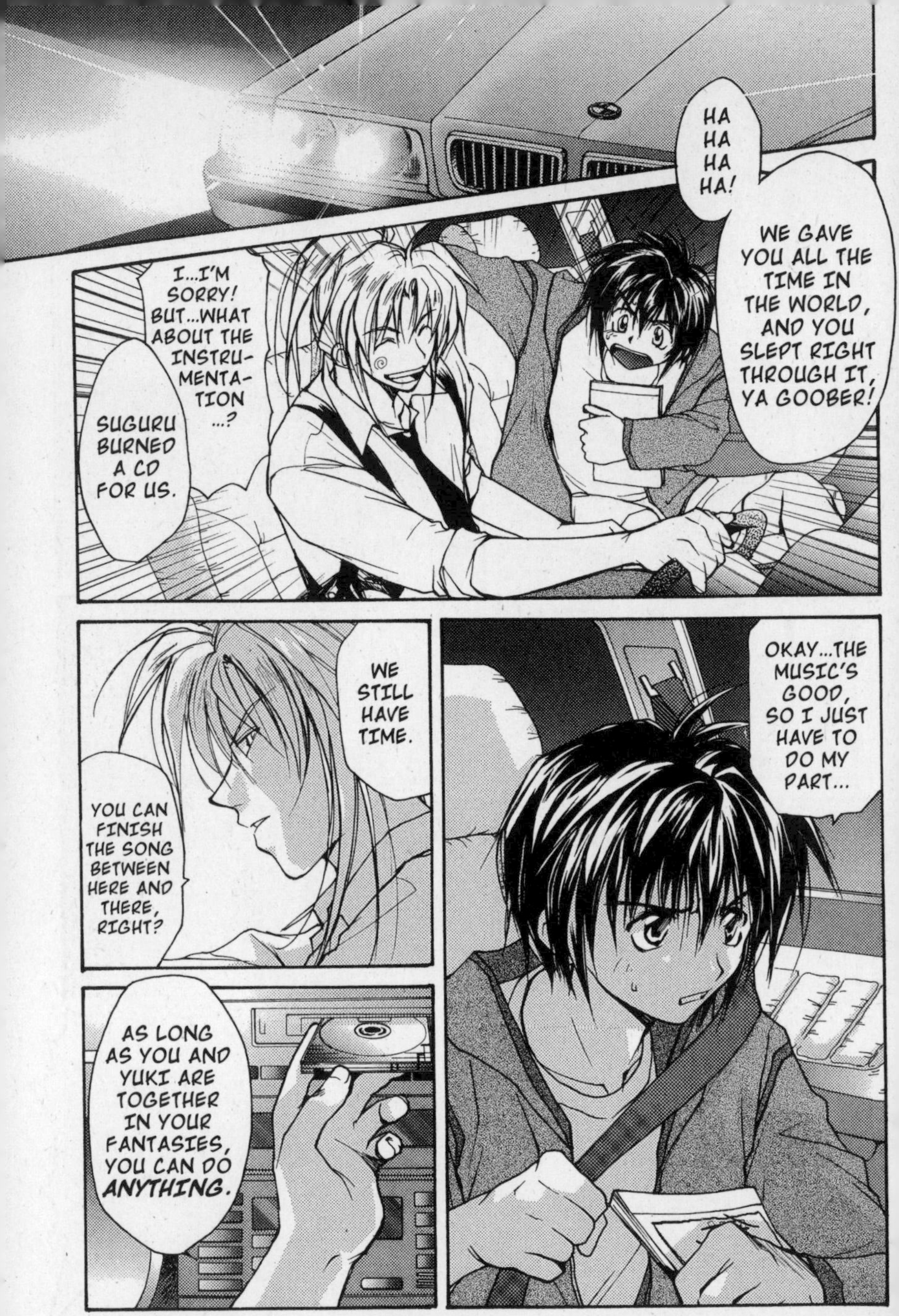
HA HA HA HA!
WE GAVE YOU ALL THE TIME IN THE WORLD, AND YOU SLEPT RIGHT THROUGH IT, YA GOOBER!
I...I'M SORRY! BUT...WHAT ABOUT THE INSTRU- MENTA- TION ...?
SUGURU BURNED A CD FOR US.
OKAY...THE MUSIC'S GOOD, SO I JUST HAVE TO DO MY PART...
WE STILL HAVE TIME.
YOU CAN FINISH THE SONG BETWEEN HERE AND THERE, RIGHT?
AS LONG AS YOU AND YUKI ARE TOGETHER IN YOUR FANTASIES, YOU CAN DO ***ANYTHING***.

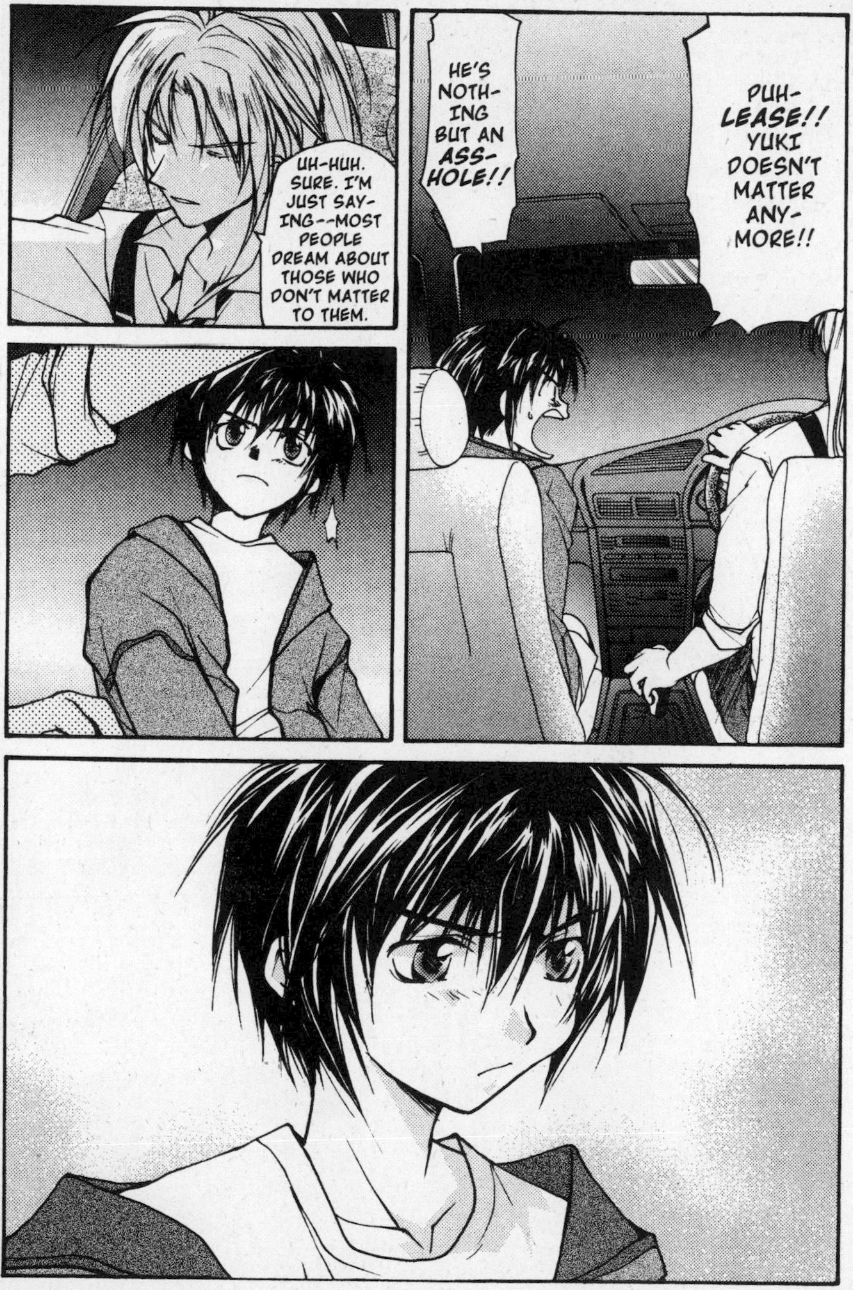
PUH-LEASE!! YUKI DOESN'T MATTER ANY-MORE!!
HE'S NOTH-ING BUT AN ASS-HOLE!!
UH-HUH. SURE. I'M JUST SAY-ING--MOST PEOPLE DREAM ABOUT THOSE WHO DON'T MATTER TO THEM.

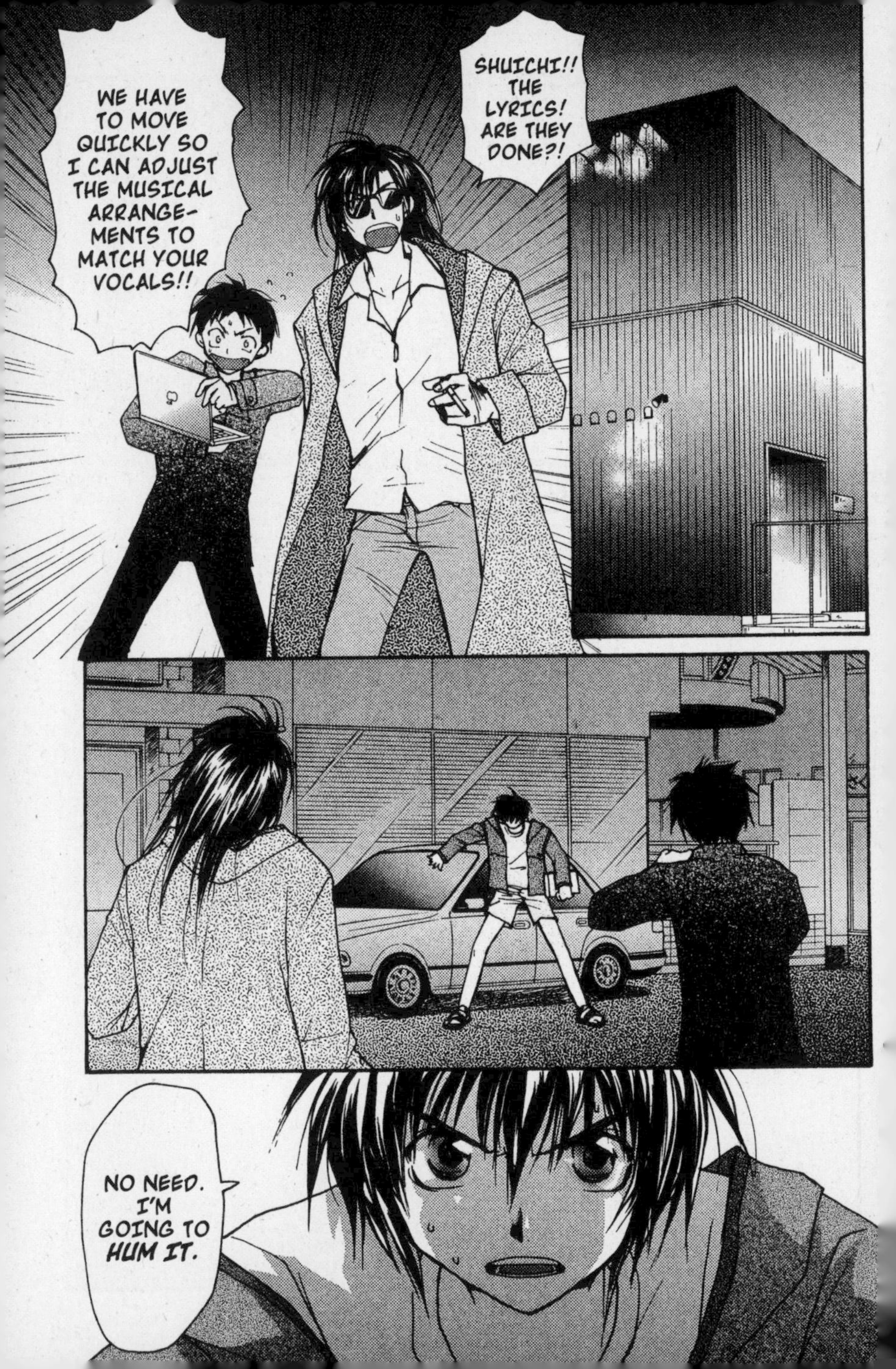
SHUICHI!! THE LYRICS! ARE THEY DONE?!
WE HAVE TO MOVE QUICKLY SO I CAN ADJUST THE MUSICAL ARRANGE-MENTS TO MATCH YOUR VOCALS!!
NO NEED. I'M GOING TO **HUM IT.**

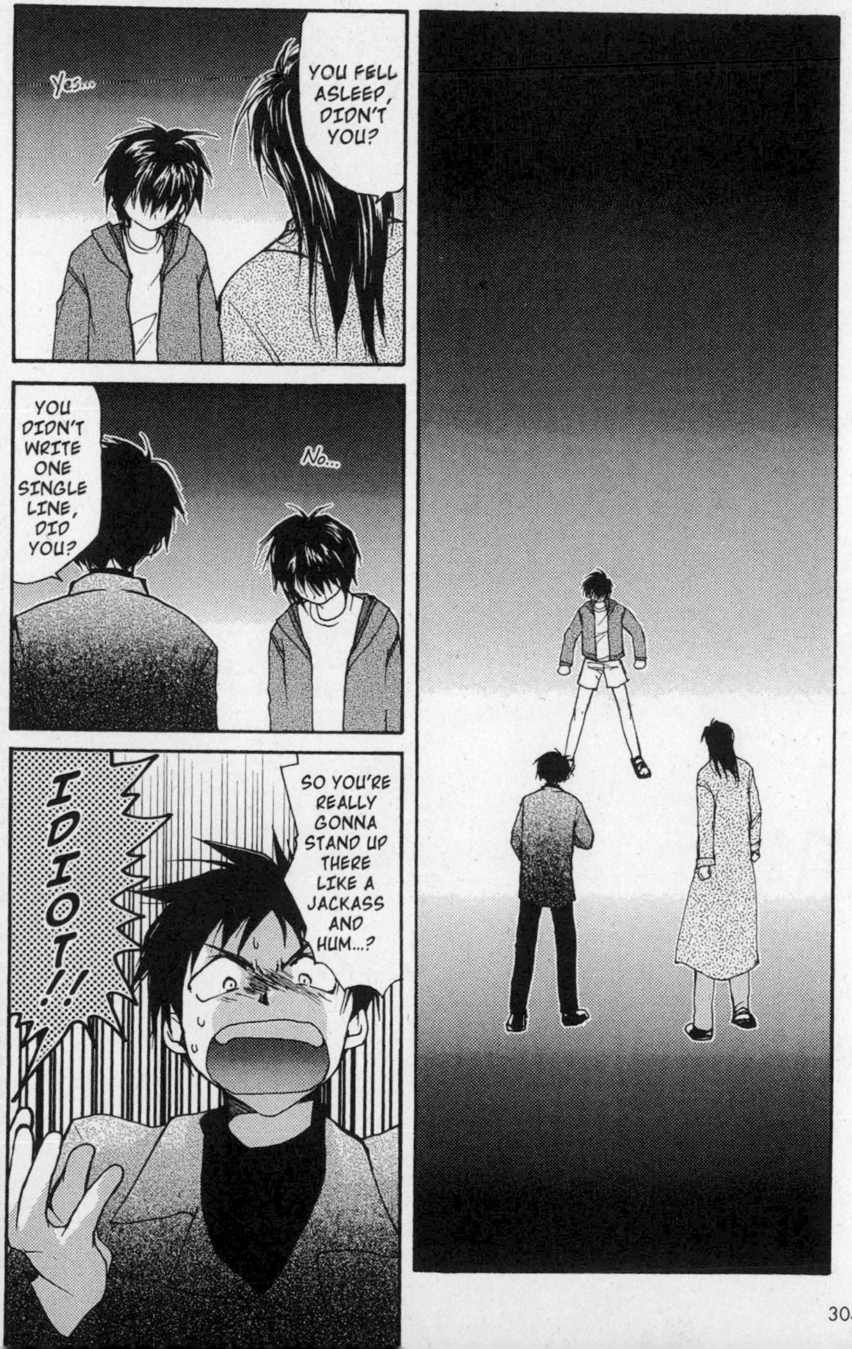
YOU FELL ASLEEP, DIDN'T YOU?
Yes...
No...
YOU DIDN'T WRITE ONE SINGLE LINE, DID YOU?
SO YOU'RE REALLY GONNA STAND UP THERE LIKE A JACKASS AND HUM...?
IDIOT!!

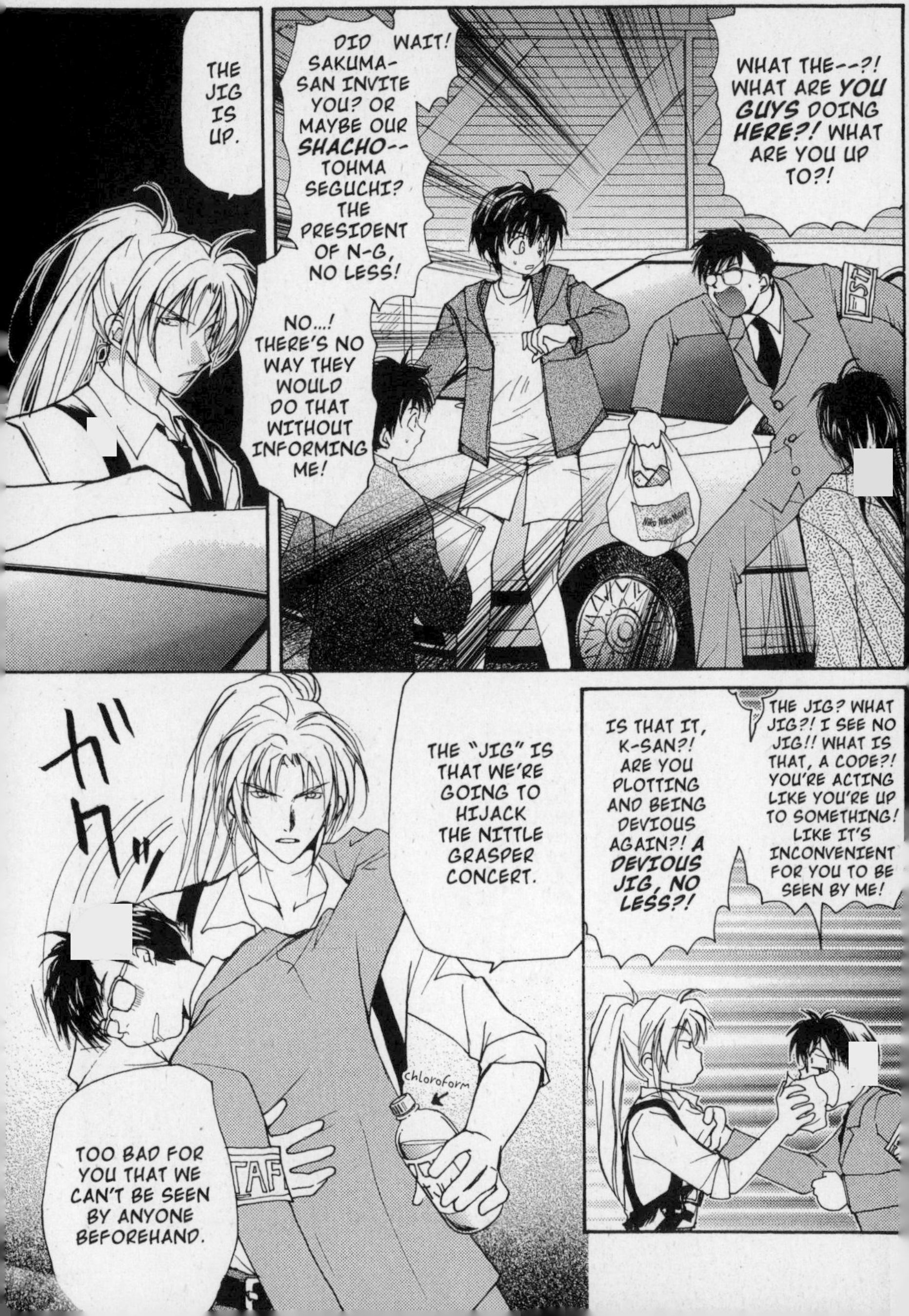
WHAT THE--?! WHAT ARE *YOU GUYS* DOING *HERE?!* WHAT ARE YOU UP TO?!
WAIT! DID SAKUMA-SAN INVITE YOU? OR MAYBE OUR *SHACHO*-- TOHMA SEGUCHI? THE PRESIDENT OF N-G, NO LESS!
NO...! THERE'S NO WAY THEY WOULD DO THAT WITHOUT INFORMING ME!
THE JIG IS UP.
THE JIG? WHAT JIG?! I SEE NO JIG!! WHAT IS THAT, A CODE?! YOU'RE ACTING LIKE YOU'RE UP TO SOMETHING! LIKE IT'S INCONVENIENT FOR YOU TO BE SEEN BY ME!
IS THAT IT, K-SAN?! ARE YOU PLOTTING AND BEING DEVIOUS AGAIN?! A *DEVIOUS JIG, NO LESS?!*
THE "JIG" IS THAT WE'RE GOING TO HIJACK THE NITTLE GRASPER CONCERT.
ガクッ
chloroform
TOO BAD FOR YOU THAT WE CAN'T BE SEEN BY ANYONE BEFOREHAND.

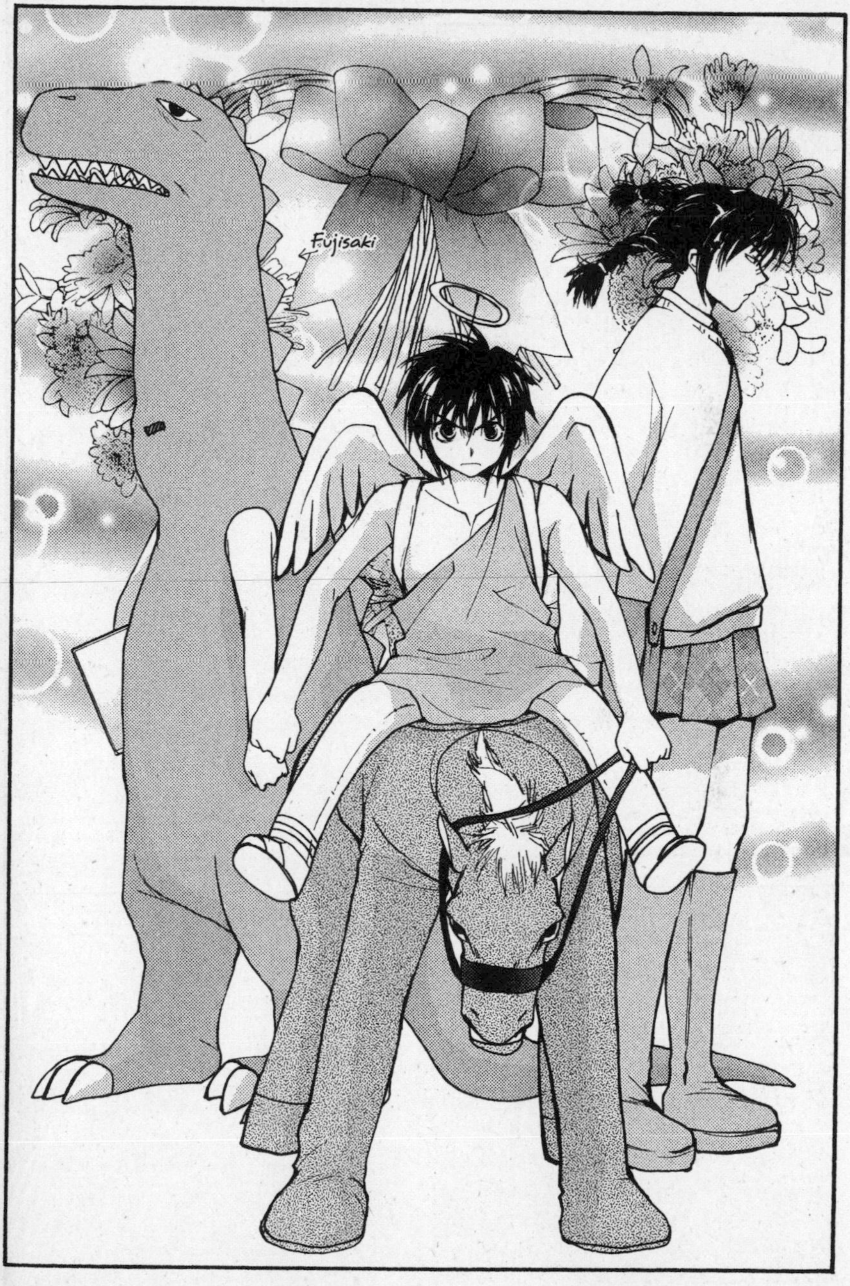
Fujisaki

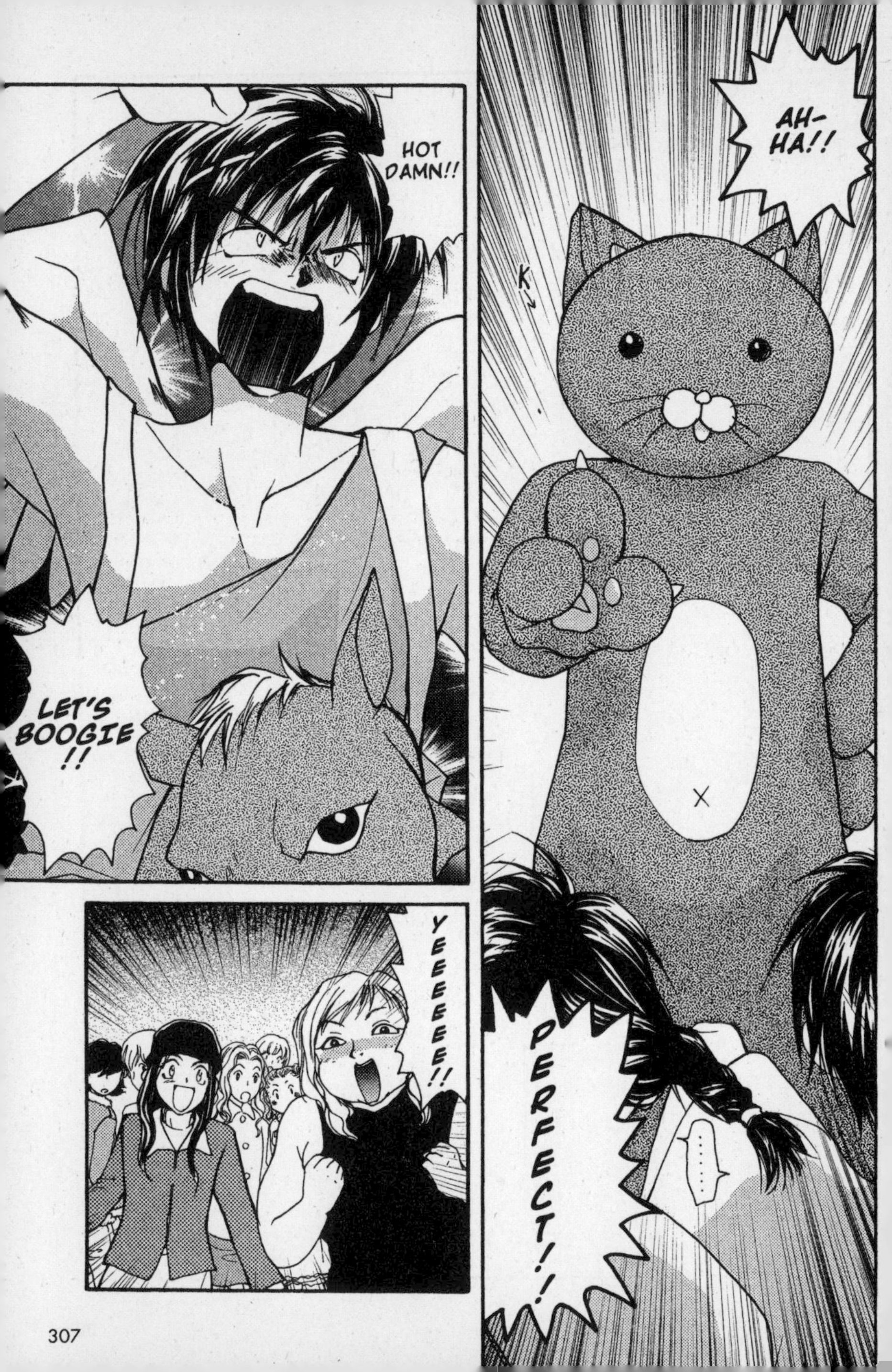
AH-HA!!
K
PERFECT!!
......
HOT DAMN!!
LET'S BOOGIE!!
YEEEEEE!!

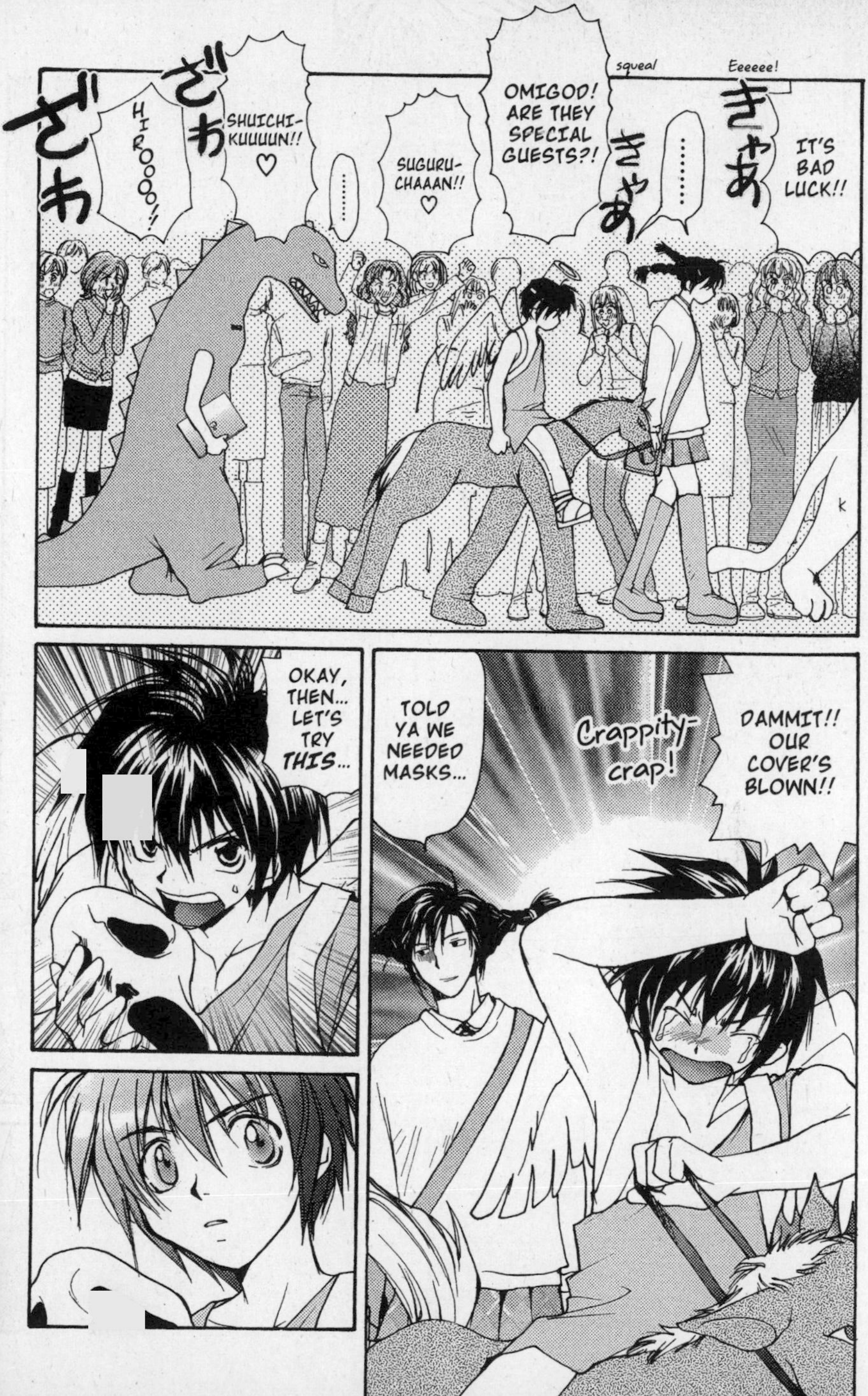
Eeeeee!
きゃあ
squeal
きゃあ
IT'S BAD LUCK!!
......
OMIGOD! ARE THEY SPECIAL GUESTS?!
SUGURU-CHAAAN!! ♡
......
SHUICHI-KUUUUN!! ♡
HIROOOO!!
ざわ
ざわ
DAMMIT!! OUR COVER'S BLOWN!!
Crappity-crap!
TOLD YA WE NEEDED MASKS...
OKAY, THEN... LET'S TRY THIS...

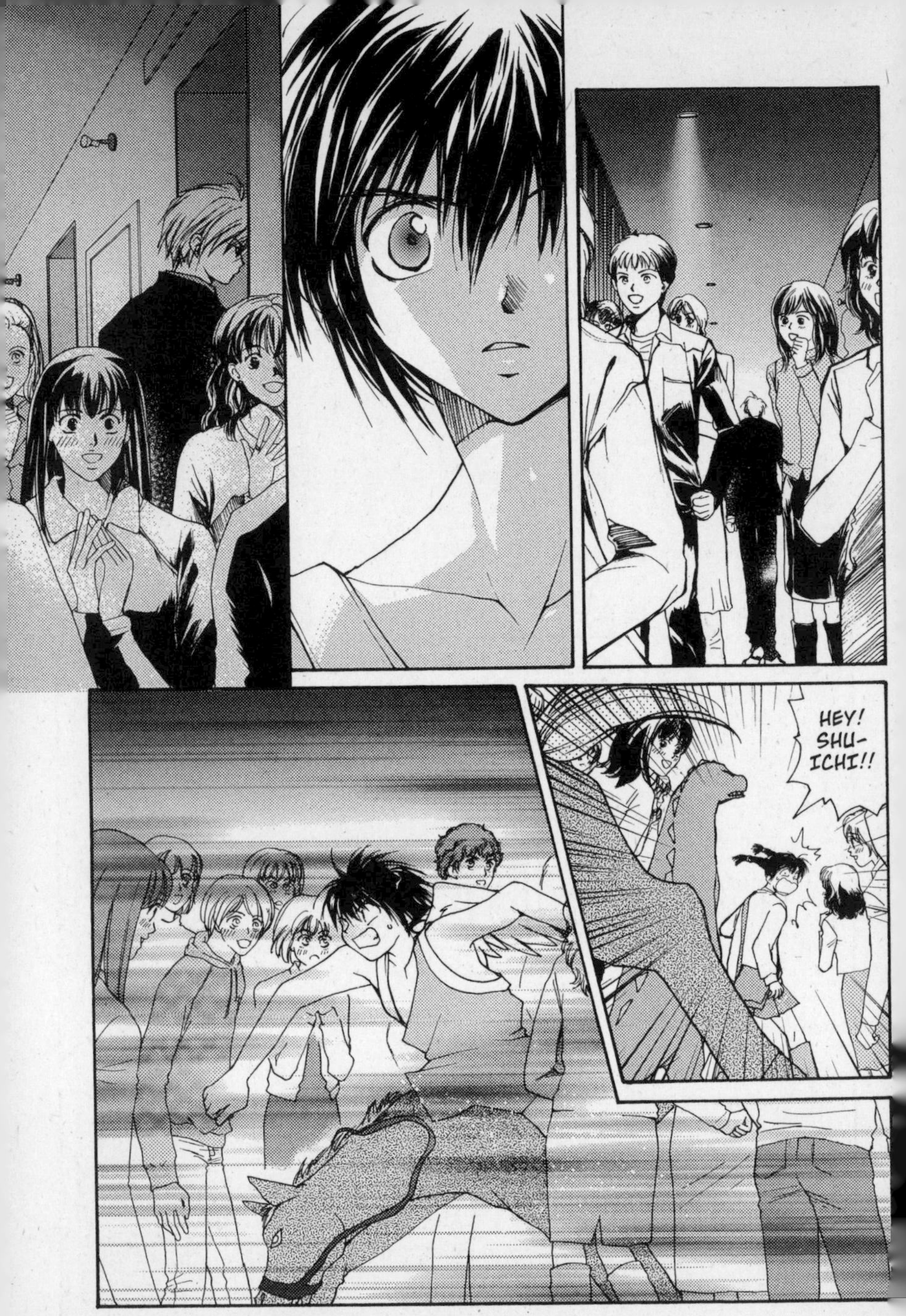
HEY! SHUICHI!!

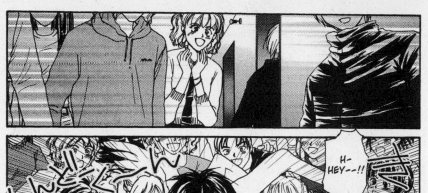

H-HEY--!!

W-WAIT--!!

Waaaaaaah!

Shindou-kuun!

SHINDOU-SAN...?

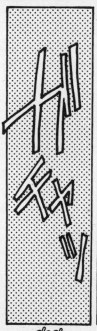

clack

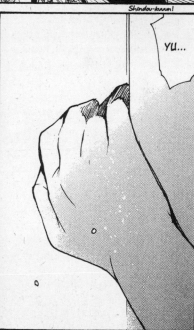

YU...

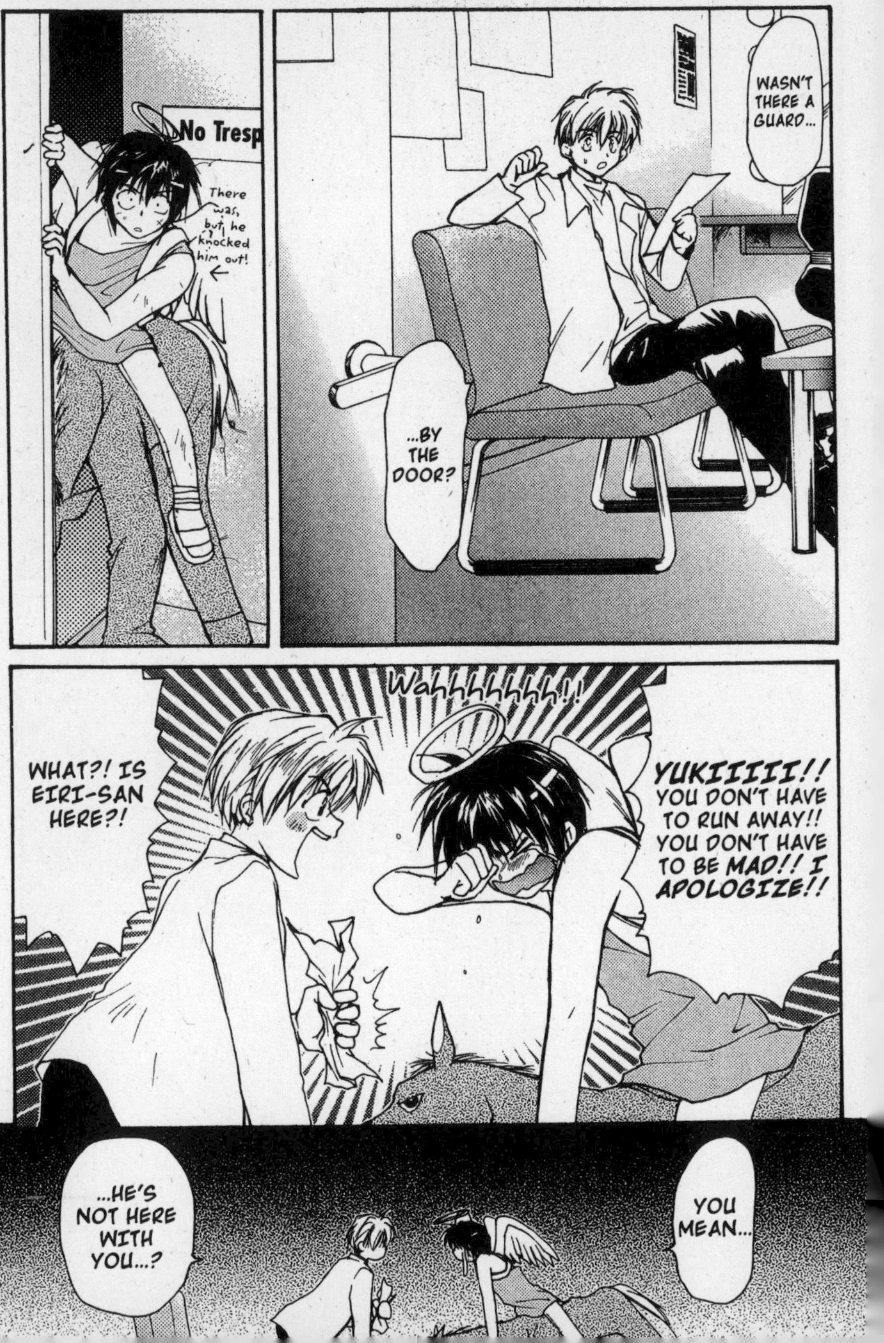
WASN'T THERE A GUARD...
...BY THE DOOR?
No Tresp
There was, but he knocked him out!
Wahhhhhhhh!!
YUKIIIII!! YOU DON'T HAVE TO RUN AWAY!! YOU DON'T HAVE TO BE MAD!! I APOLOGIZE!!
WHAT?! IS EIRI-SAN HERE?!
YOU MEAN...
...HE'S NOT HERE WITH YOU...?

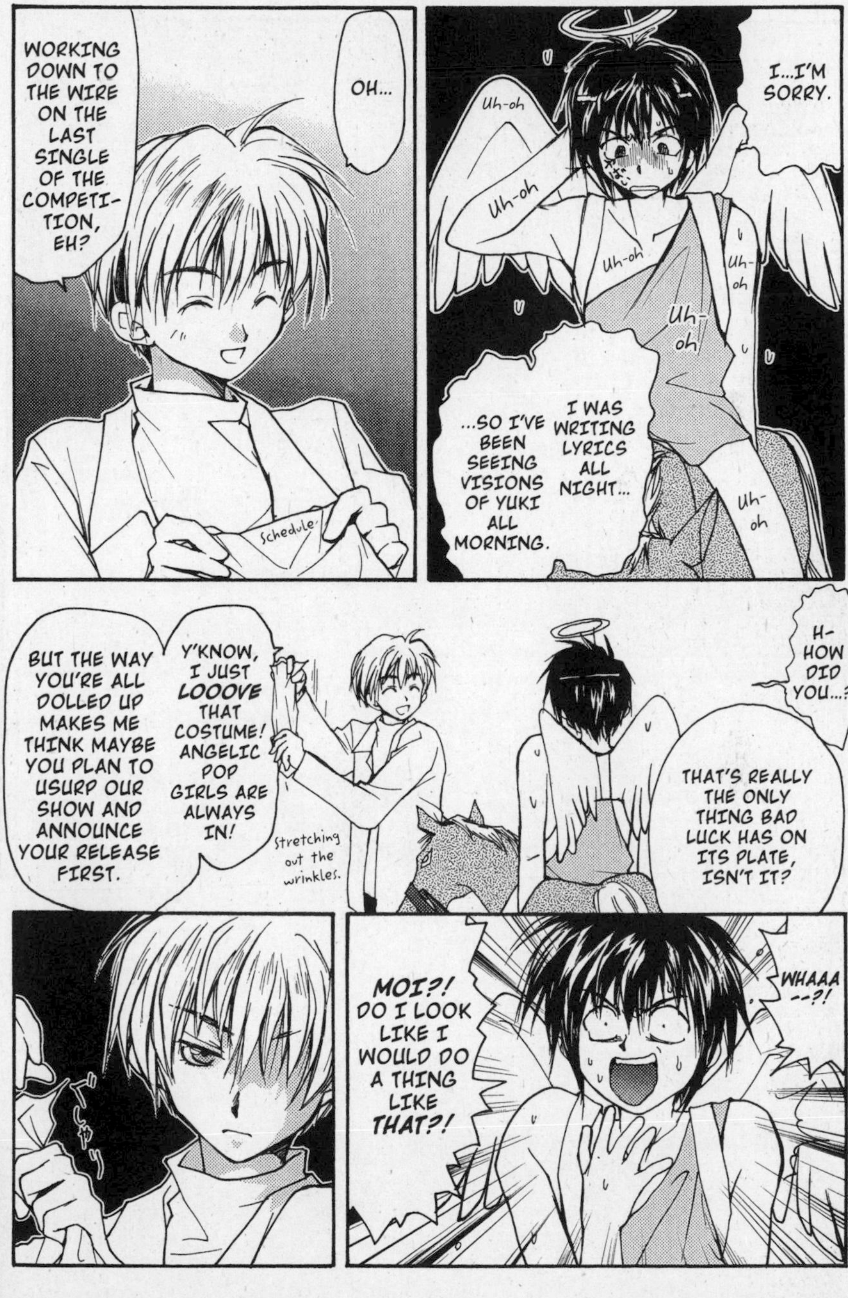
I...I'M SORRY.
Uh-oh
Uh-oh
Uh-oh
Uh-oh
Uh-oh
Uh-oh
I WAS WRITING LYRICS ALL NIGHT...
...SO I'VE BEEN SEEING VISIONS OF YUKI ALL MORNING.
OH...
WORKING DOWN TO THE WIRE ON THE LAST SINGLE OF THE COMPETITION, EH?
Schedule
H-HOW DID YOU...?
THAT'S REALLY THE ONLY THING BAD LUCK HAS ON ITS PLATE, ISN'T IT?
Y'KNOW, I JUST LOOOVE THAT COSTUME! ANGELIC POP GIRLS ARE ALWAYS IN!
Stretching out the wrinkles.
BUT THE WAY YOU'RE ALL DOLLED UP MAKES ME THINK MAYBE YOU PLAN TO USURP OUR SHOW AND ANNOUNCE YOUR RELEASE FIRST.
WHAAA--?!
MOI?! DO I LOOK LIKE I WOULD DO A THING LIKE THAT?!

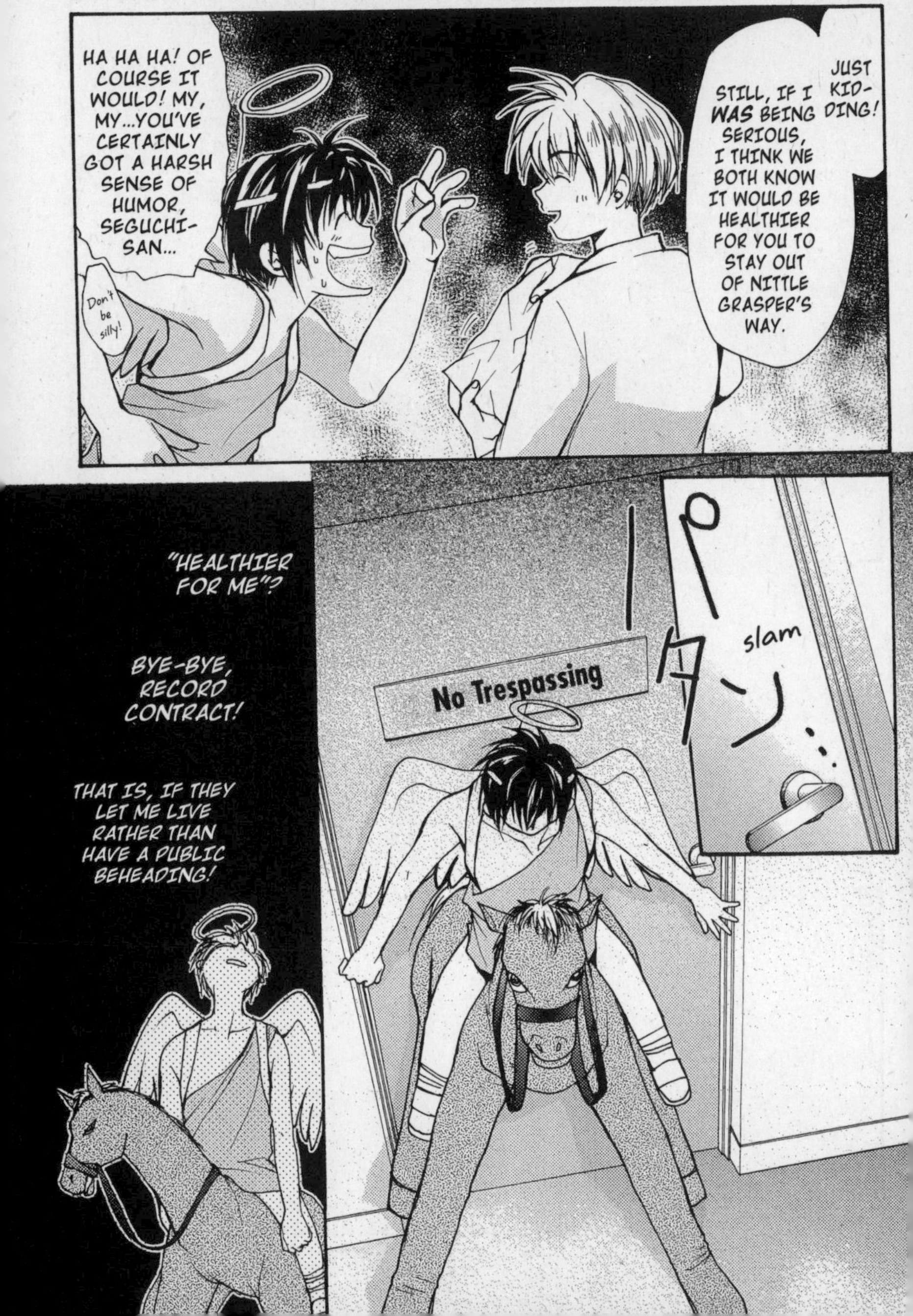
JUST KIDDING!
STILL, IF I WAS BEING SERIOUS, I THINK WE BOTH KNOW IT WOULD BE HEALTHIER FOR YOU TO STAY OUT OF NITTLE GRASPER'S WAY.
HA HA HA! OF COURSE IT WOULD! MY, MY...YOU'VE CERTAINLY GOT A HARSH SENSE OF HUMOR, SEGUCHI-SAN...
Don't be silly!
パタン
slam
No Trespassing
"HEALTHIER FOR ME"?
BYE-BYE, RECORD CONTRACT!
THAT IS, IF THEY LET ME LIVE RATHER THAN HAVE A PUBLIC BEHEADING!

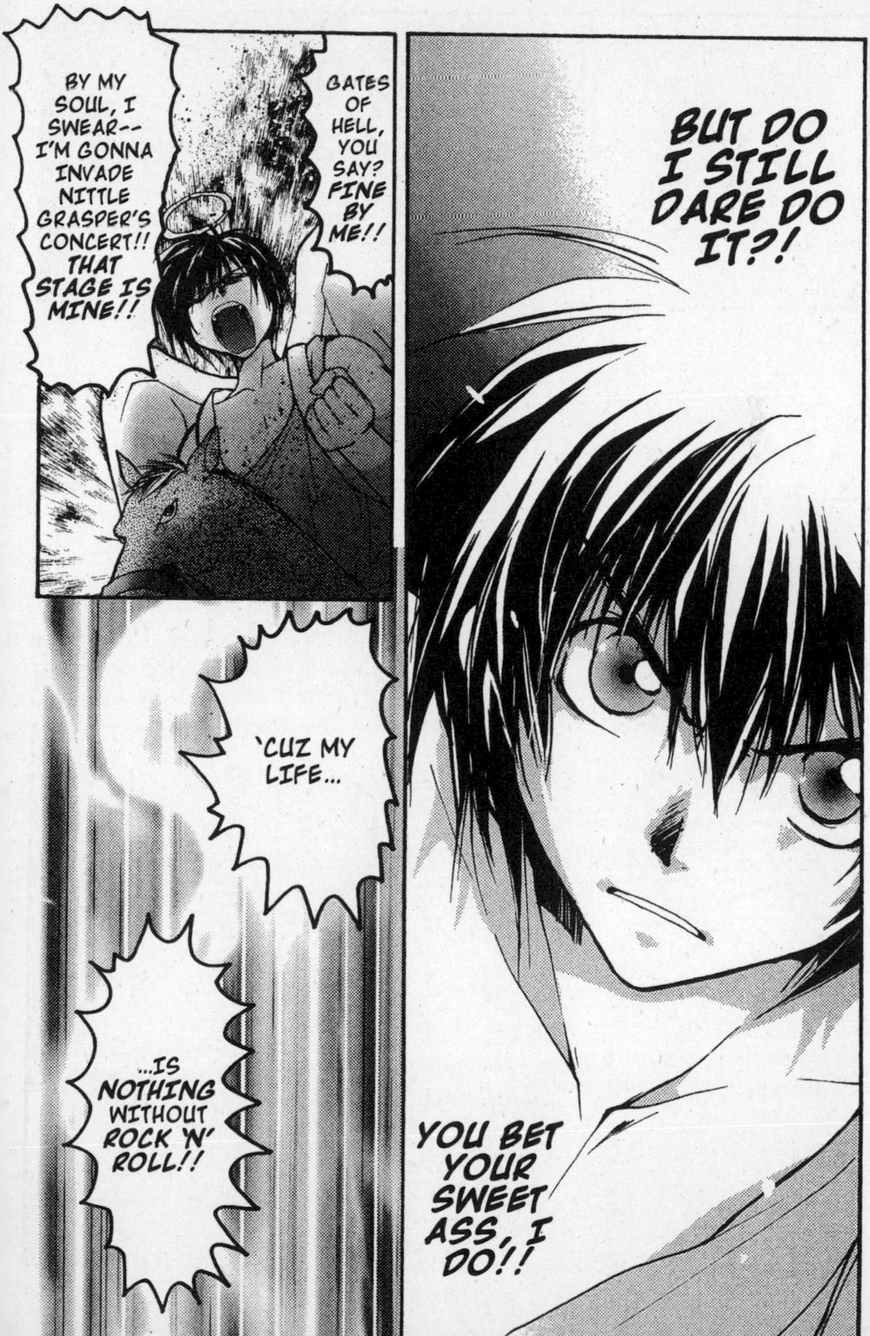
BUT DO I STILL DARE DO IT?!
YOU BET YOUR SWEET ASS, I DO!!
GATES OF HELL, YOU SAY? FINE BY ME!!
BY MY SOUL, I SWEAR-- I'M GONNA INVADE NITTLE GRASPER'S CONCERT!! THAT STAGE IS MINE!!
`CUZ MY LIFE...
...IS NOTHING WITHOUT ROCK 'N' ROLL!!

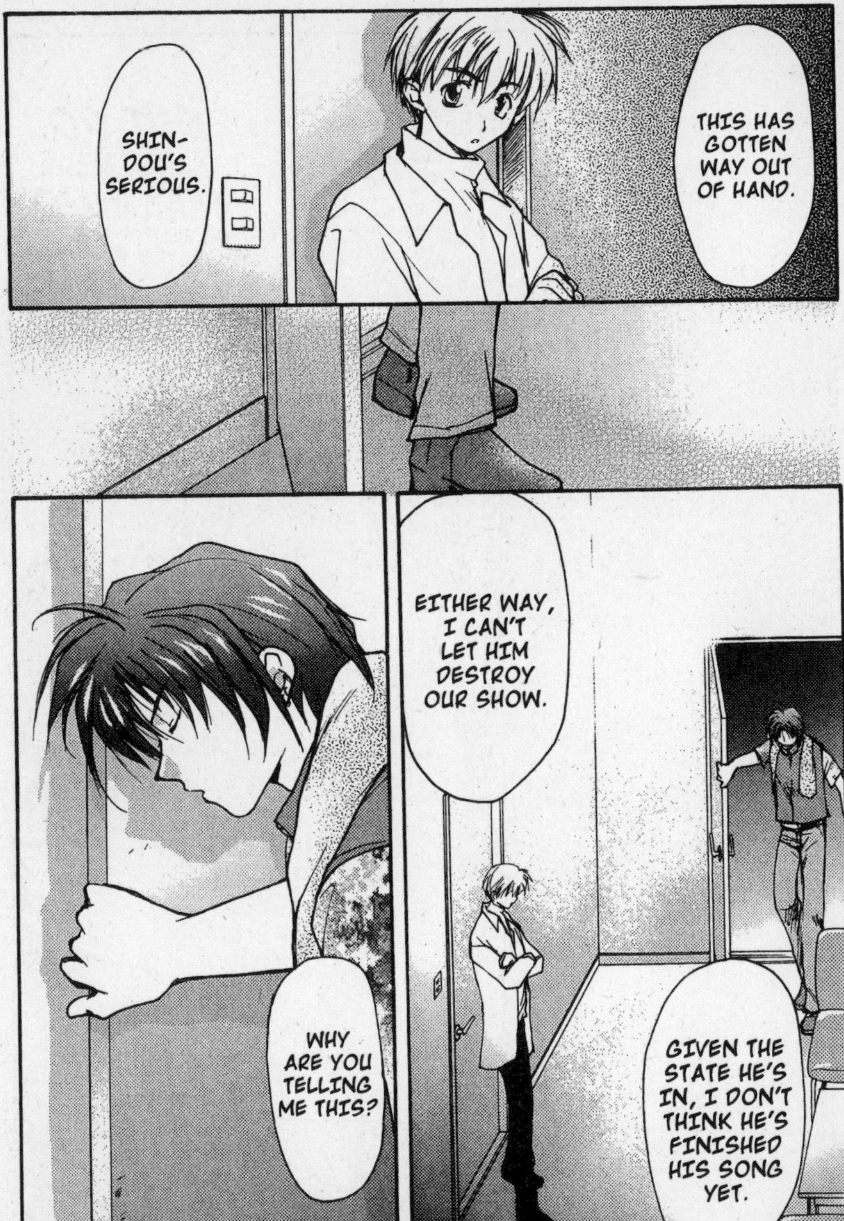
THIS HAS GOTTEN WAY OUT OF HAND.
SHIN-DOU'S SERIOUS.
EITHER WAY, I CAN'T LET HIM DESTROY OUR SHOW.
GIVEN THE STATE HE'S IN, I DON'T THINK HE'S FINISHED HIS SONG YET.
WHY ARE YOU TELLING ME THIS?

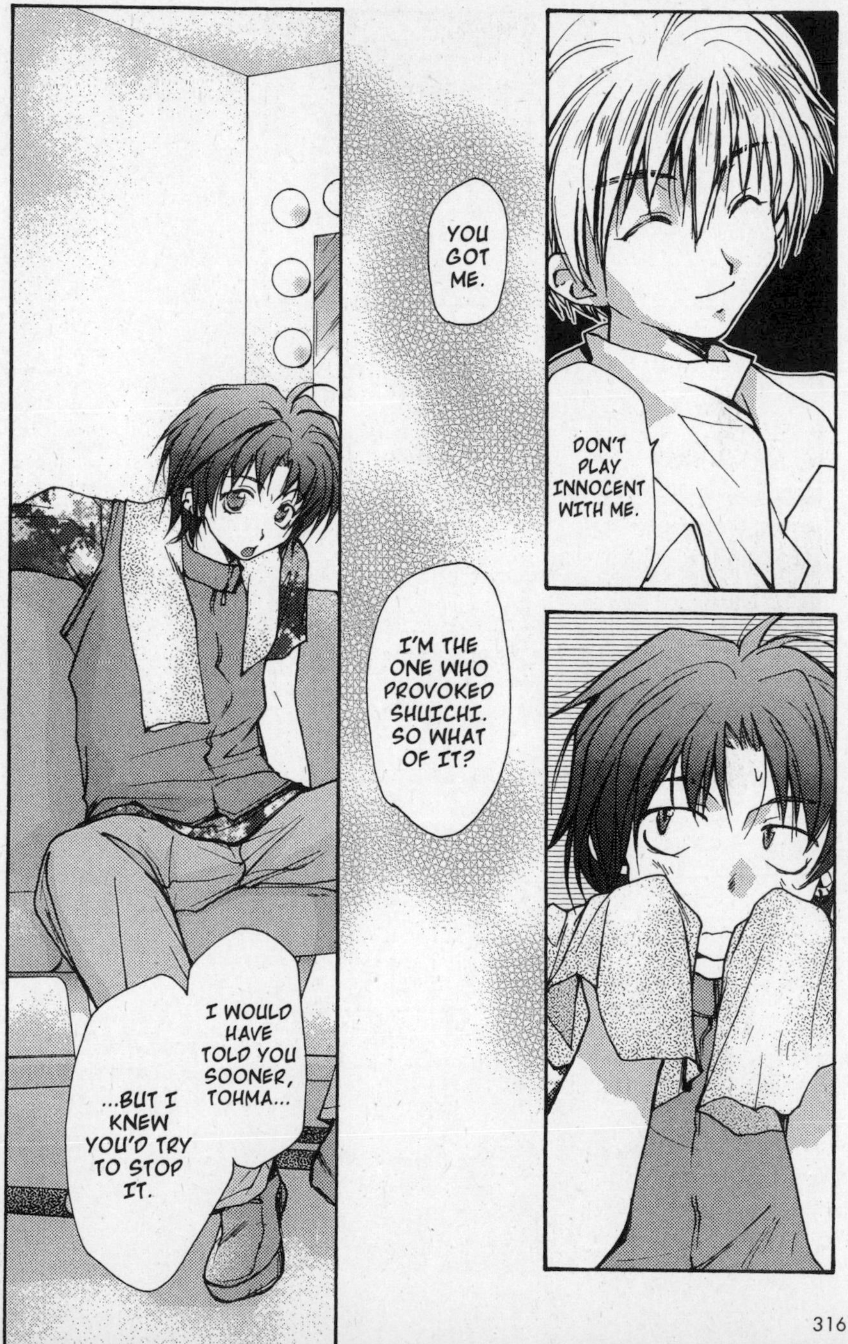
YOU GOT ME.
DON'T PLAY INNOCENT WITH ME.
I'M THE ONE WHO PROVOKED SHUICHI. SO WHAT OF IT?
I WOULD HAVE TOLD YOU SOONER, TOHMA...
...BUT I KNEW YOU'D TRY TO STOP IT.

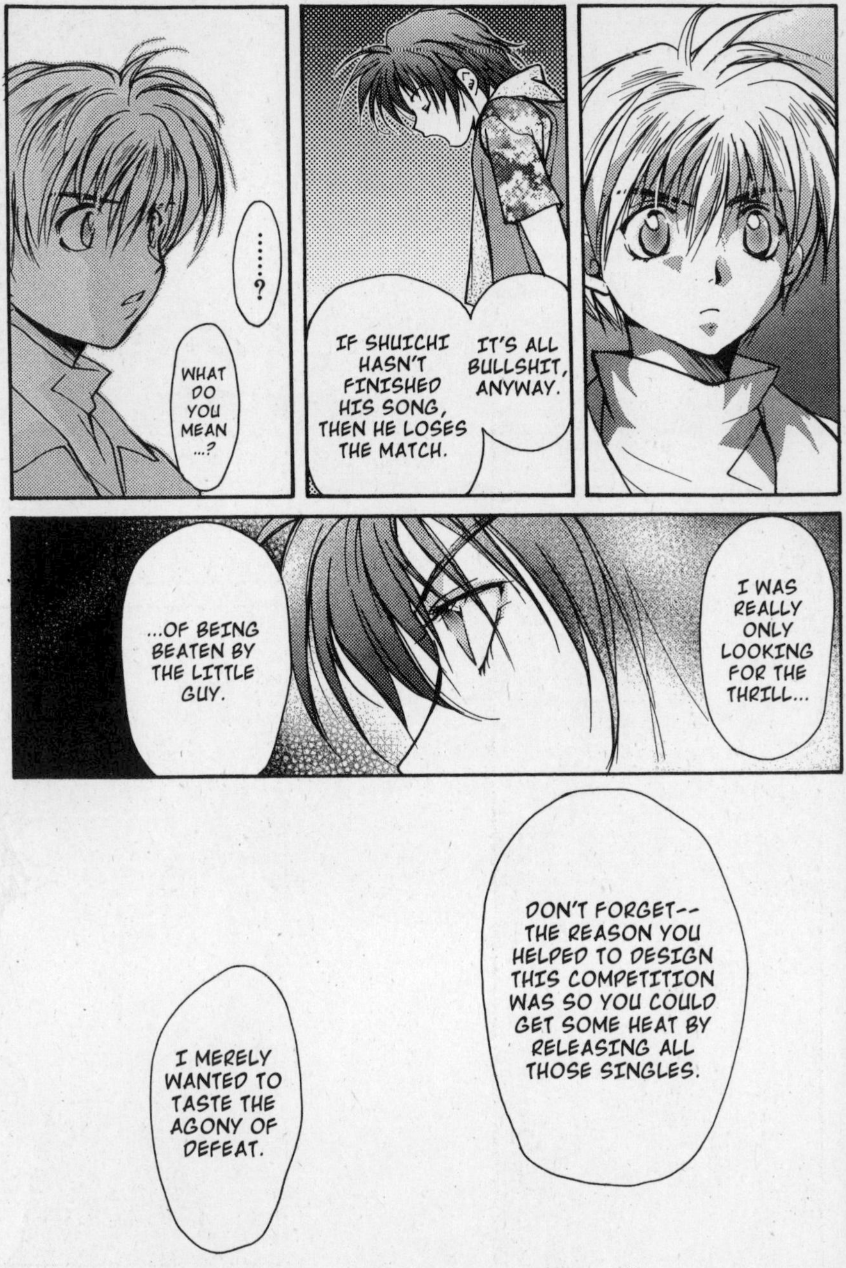
IT'S ALL BULLSHIT, ANYWAY.
IF SHUICHI HASN'T FINISHED HIS SONG, THEN HE LOSES THE MATCH.
......?
WHAT DO YOU MEAN ...?
I WAS REALLY ONLY LOOKING FOR THE THRILL...
...OF BEING BEATEN BY THE LITTLE GUY.
DON'T FORGET-- THE REASON YOU HELPED TO DESIGN THIS COMPETITION WAS SO YOU COULD GET SOME HEAT BY RELEASING ALL THOSE SINGLES.
I MERELY WANTED TO TASTE THE AGONY OF DEFEAT.

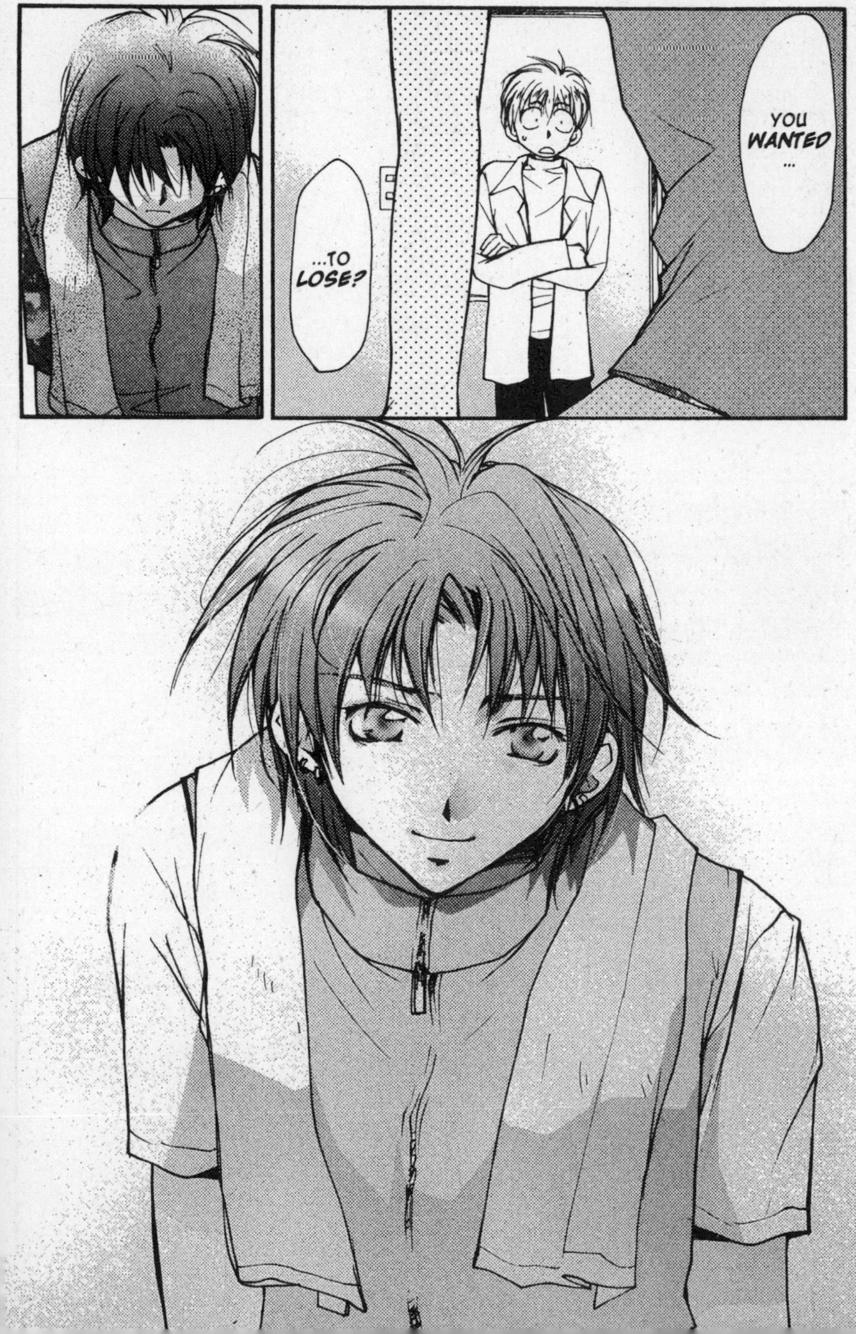
YOU WANTED ...
...TO LOSE?

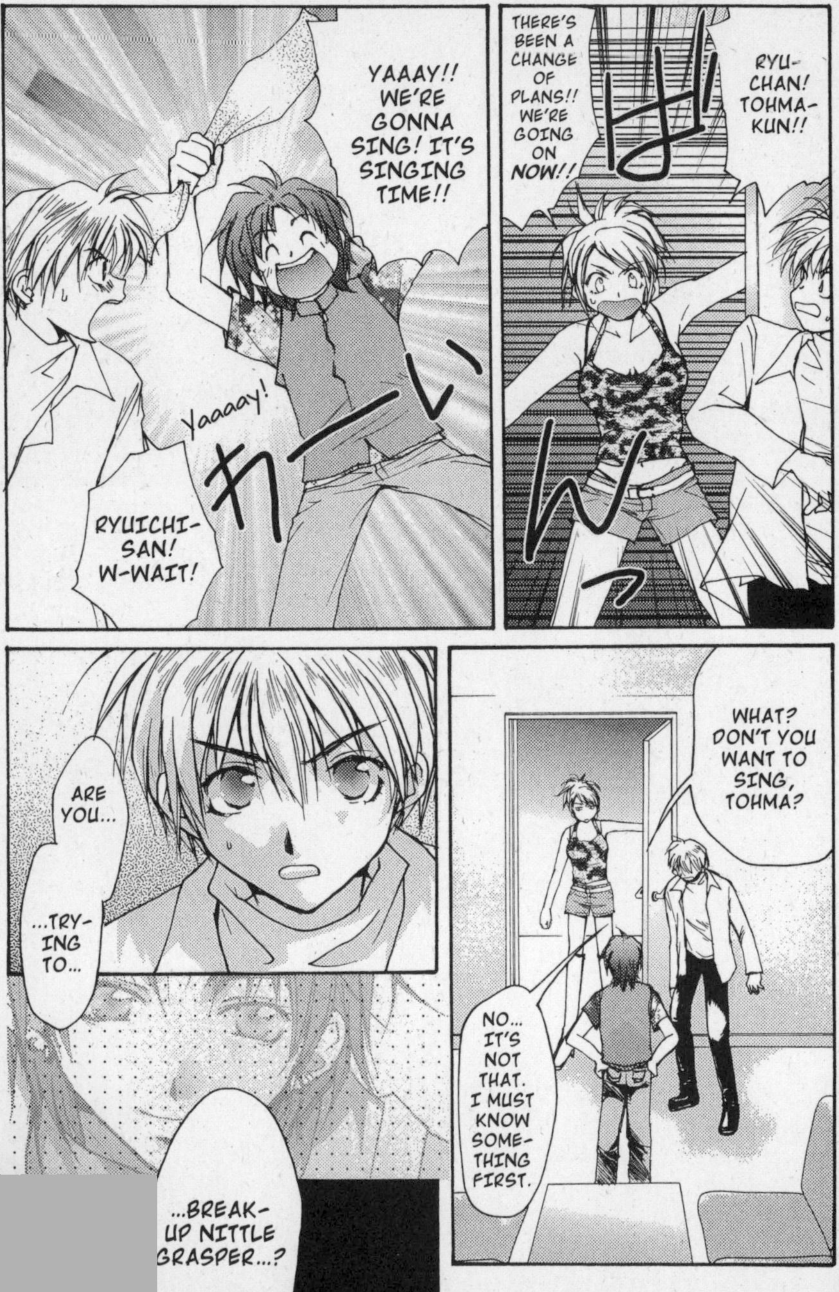
RYU-CHAN! TOHMA-KUN!!
THERE'S BEEN A CHANGE OF PLANS!! WE'RE GOING ON NOW!!
YAAAY!! WE'RE GONNA SING! IT'S SINGING TIME!!
Yaaaay!
RYUICHI-SAN! W-WAIT!
WHAT? DON'T YOU WANT TO SING, TOHMA?
NO... IT'S NOT THAT. I MUST KNOW SOMETHING FIRST.
ARE YOU...
...TRYING TO...
...BREAK-UP NITTLE GRASPER...?

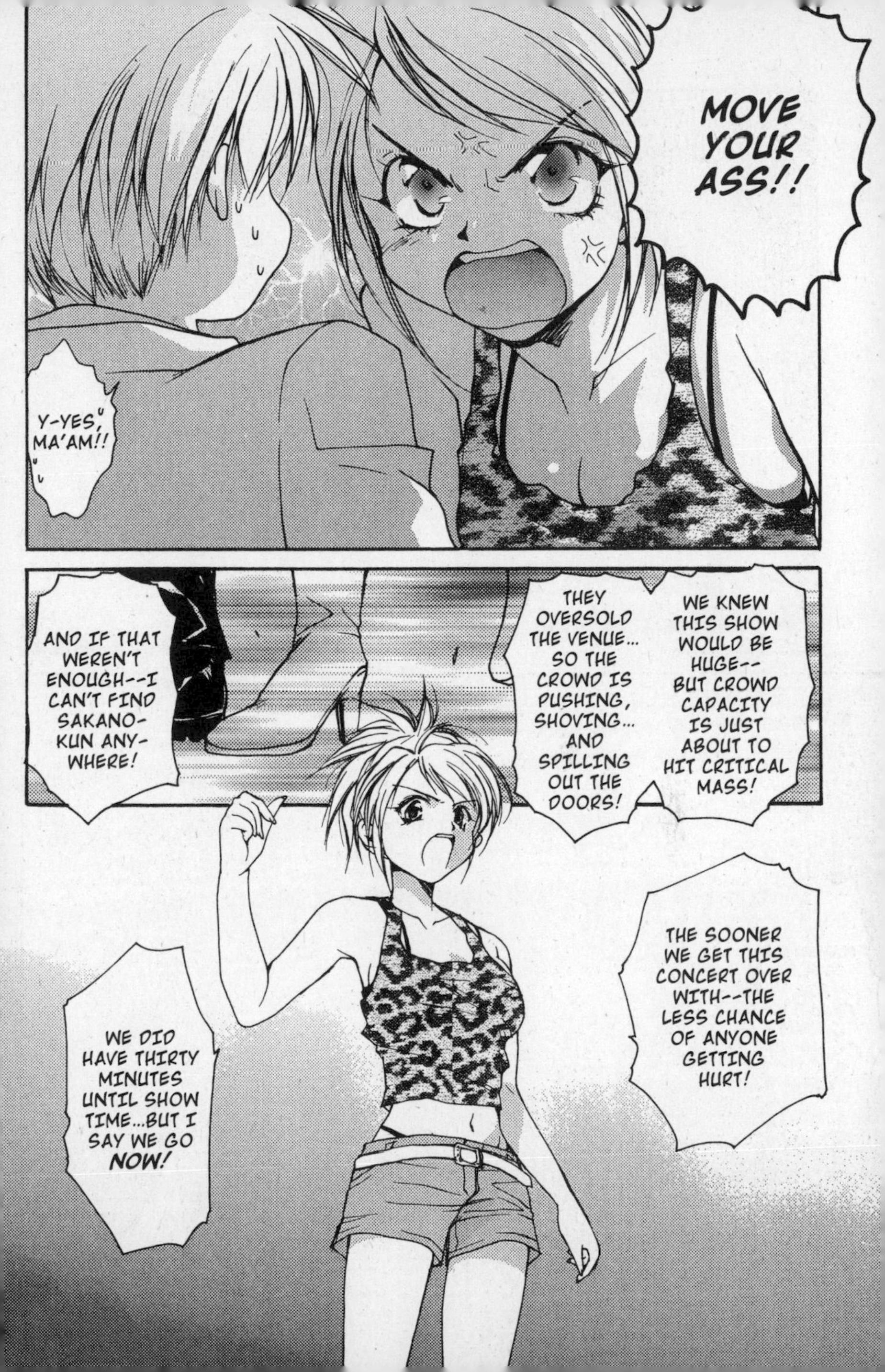
MOVE YOUR ASS!!
Y-YES, MA'AM!!
WE KNEW THIS SHOW WOULD BE HUGE-- BUT CROWD CAPACITY IS JUST ABOUT TO HIT CRITICAL MASS!
THEY OVERSOLD THE VENUE... SO THE CROWD IS PUSHING, SHOVING... AND SPILLING OUT THE DOORS!
AND IF THAT WEREN'T ENOUGH--I CAN'T FIND SAKANO-KUN ANYWHERE!
THE SOONER WE GET THIS CONCERT OVER WITH--THE LESS CHANCE OF ANYONE GETTING HURT!
WE DID HAVE THIRTY MINUTES UNTIL SHOW TIME...BUT I SAY WE GO NOW!

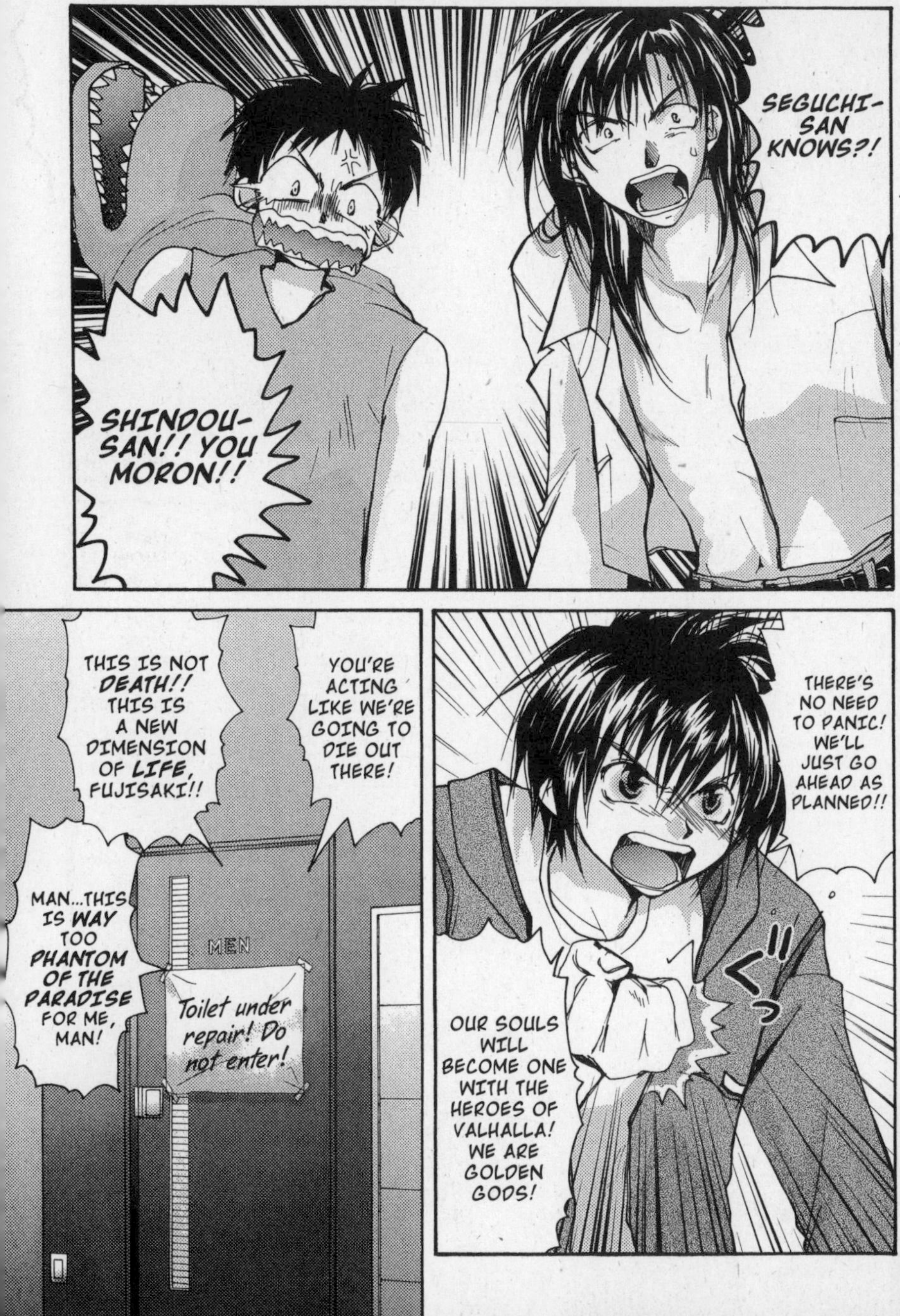
SEGUCHI-SAN KNOWS?!
SHINDOU-SAN!! YOU MORON!!
THERE'S NO NEED TO PANIC! WE'LL JUST GO AHEAD AS PLANNED!!
OUR SOULS WILL BECOME ONE WITH THE HEROES OF VALHALLA! WE ARE GOLDEN GODS!
YOU'RE ACTING LIKE WE'RE GOING TO DIE OUT THERE!
THIS IS NOT DEATH!! THIS IS A NEW DIMENSION OF LIFE, FUJISAKI!!
MAN...THIS IS WAY TOO PHANTOM OF THE PARADISE FOR ME, MAN!
MEN
Toilet under repair! Do not enter!

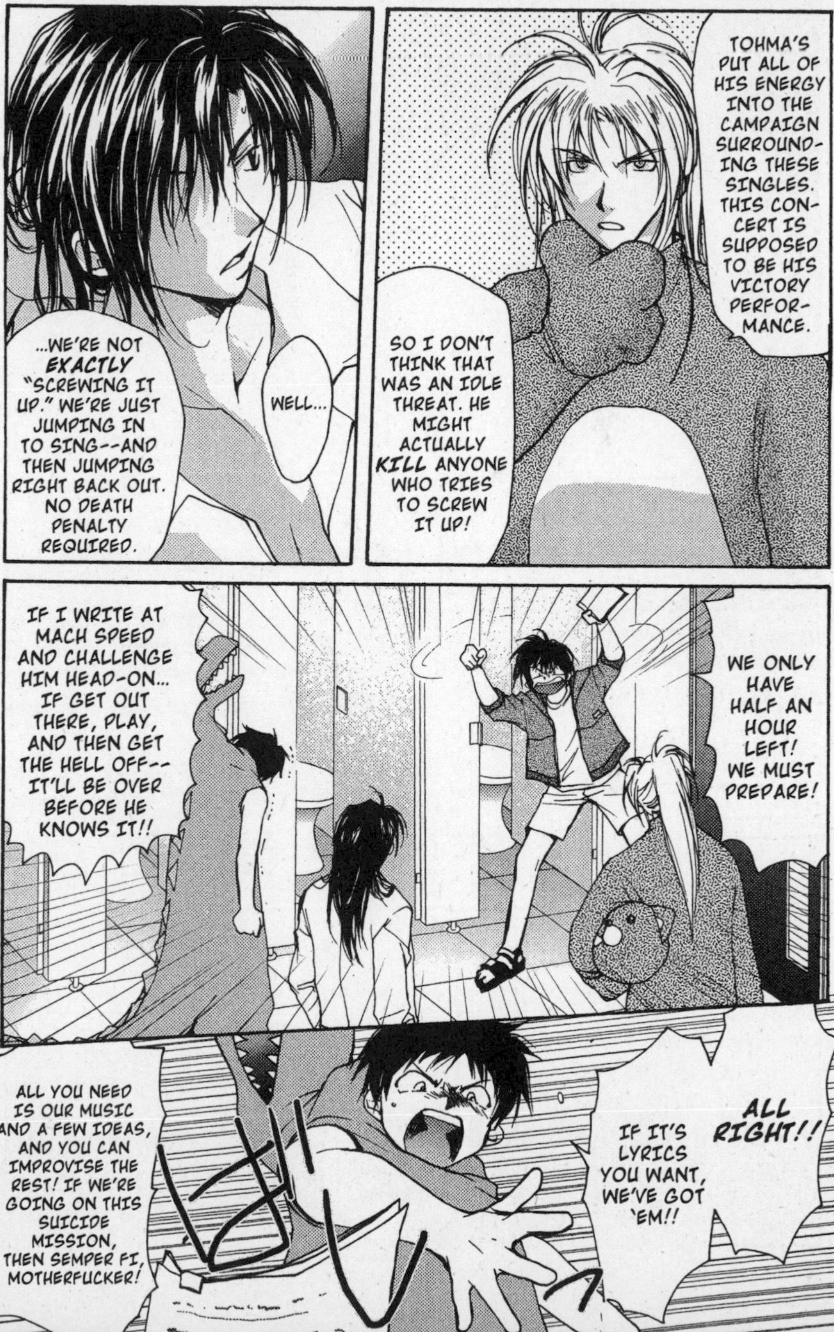
TOHMA'S PUT ALL OF HIS ENERGY INTO THE CAMPAIGN SURROUNDING THESE SINGLES. THIS CONCERT IS SUPPOSED TO BE HIS VICTORY PERFORMANCE.
SO I DON'T THINK THAT WAS AN IDLE THREAT. HE MIGHT ACTUALLY **KILL** ANYONE WHO TRIES TO SCREW IT UP!
WELL...
...WE'RE NOT ***EXACTLY*** "SCREWING IT UP." WE'RE JUST JUMPING IN TO SING--AND THEN JUMPING RIGHT BACK OUT. NO DEATH PENALTY REQUIRED.
WE ONLY HAVE HALF AN HOUR LEFT! WE MUST PREPARE!
IF I WRITE AT MACH SPEED AND CHALLENGE HIM HEAD-ON... IF GET OUT THERE, PLAY, AND THEN GET THE HELL OFF-- IT'LL BE OVER BEFORE HE KNOWS IT!!
**ALL RIGHT!!**
IF IT'S LYRICS YOU WANT, WE'VE GOT 'EM!!
ALL YOU NEED IS OUR MUSIC AND A FEW IDEAS, AND YOU CAN IMPROVISE THE REST! IF WE'RE GOING ON THIS SUICIDE MISSION, THEN SEMPER FI, MOTHERFUCKER!

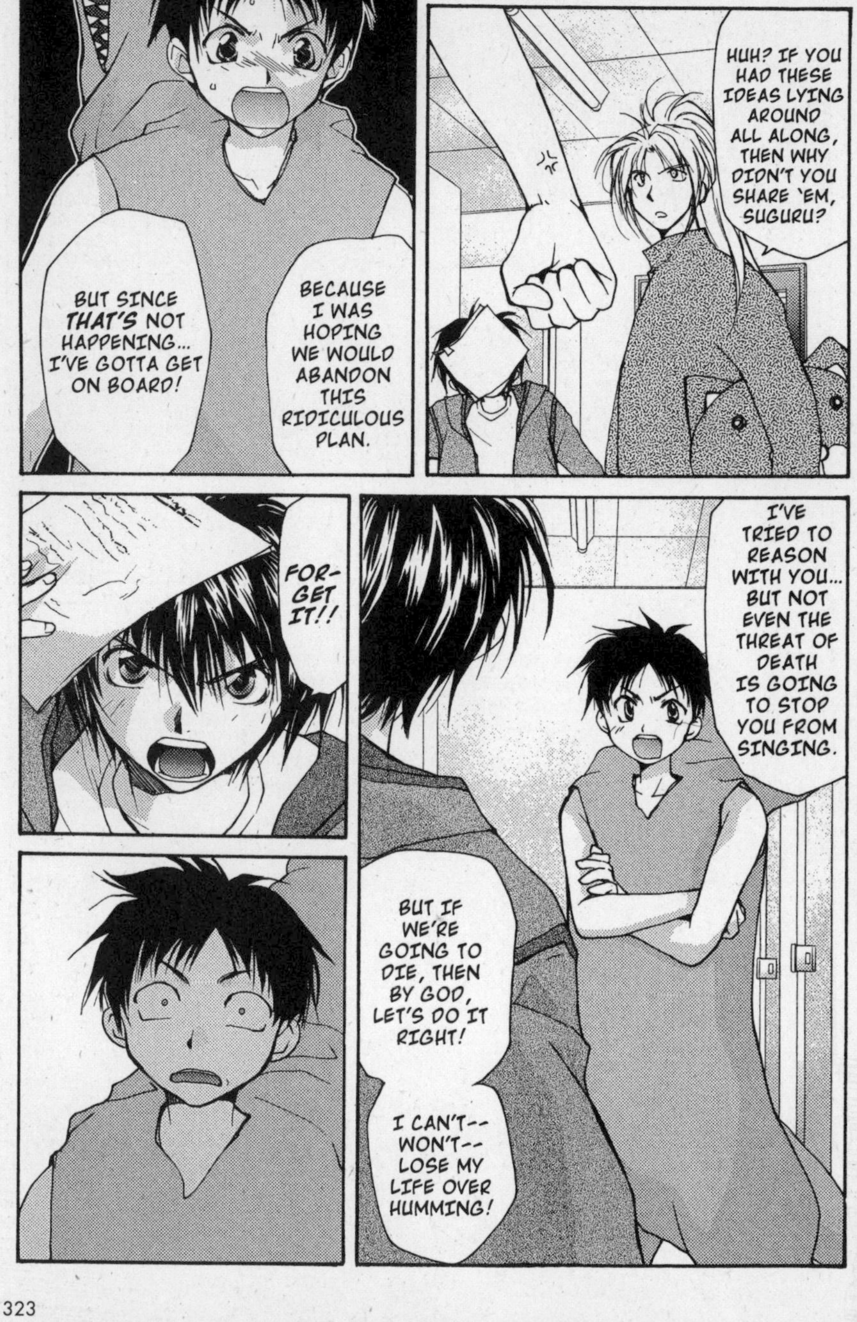
HUH? IF YOU HAD THESE IDEAS LYING AROUND ALL ALONG, THEN WHY DIDN'T YOU SHARE 'EM, SUGURU?
BECAUSE I WAS HOPING WE WOULD ABANDON THIS RIDICULOUS PLAN.
BUT SINCE *THAT'S* NOT HAPPENING... I'VE GOTTA GET ON BOARD!
I'VE TRIED TO REASON WITH YOU... BUT NOT EVEN THE THREAT OF DEATH IS GOING TO STOP YOU FROM SINGING.
BUT IF WE'RE GOING TO DIE, THEN BY GOD, LET'S DO IT RIGHT!
I CAN'T--WON'T--LOSE MY LIFE OVER HUMMING!
FOR-GET IT!!

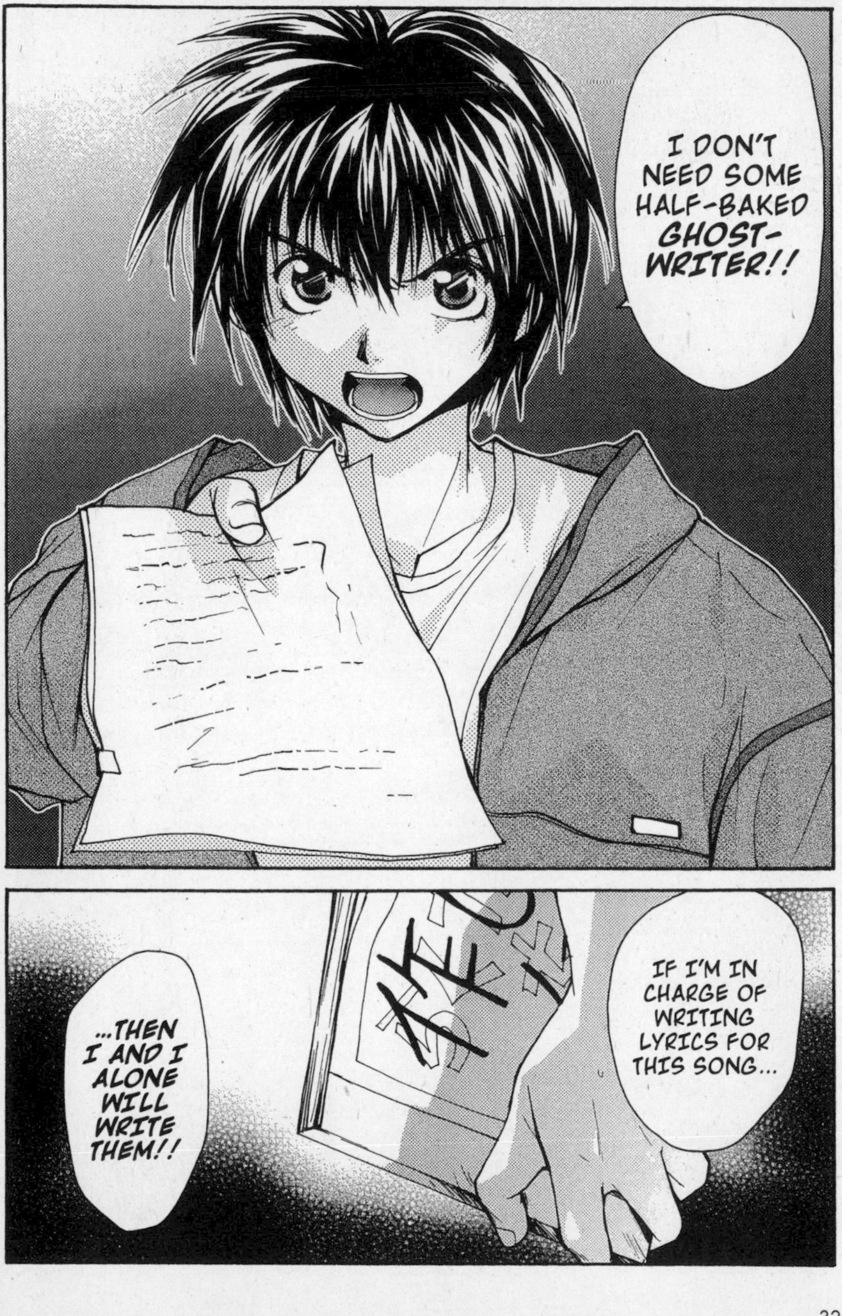
I DON'T NEED SOME HALF-BAKED GHOST-WRITER!!
IF I'M IN CHARGE OF WRITING LYRICS FOR THIS SONG...
...THEN I AND I ALONE WILL WRITE THEM!!

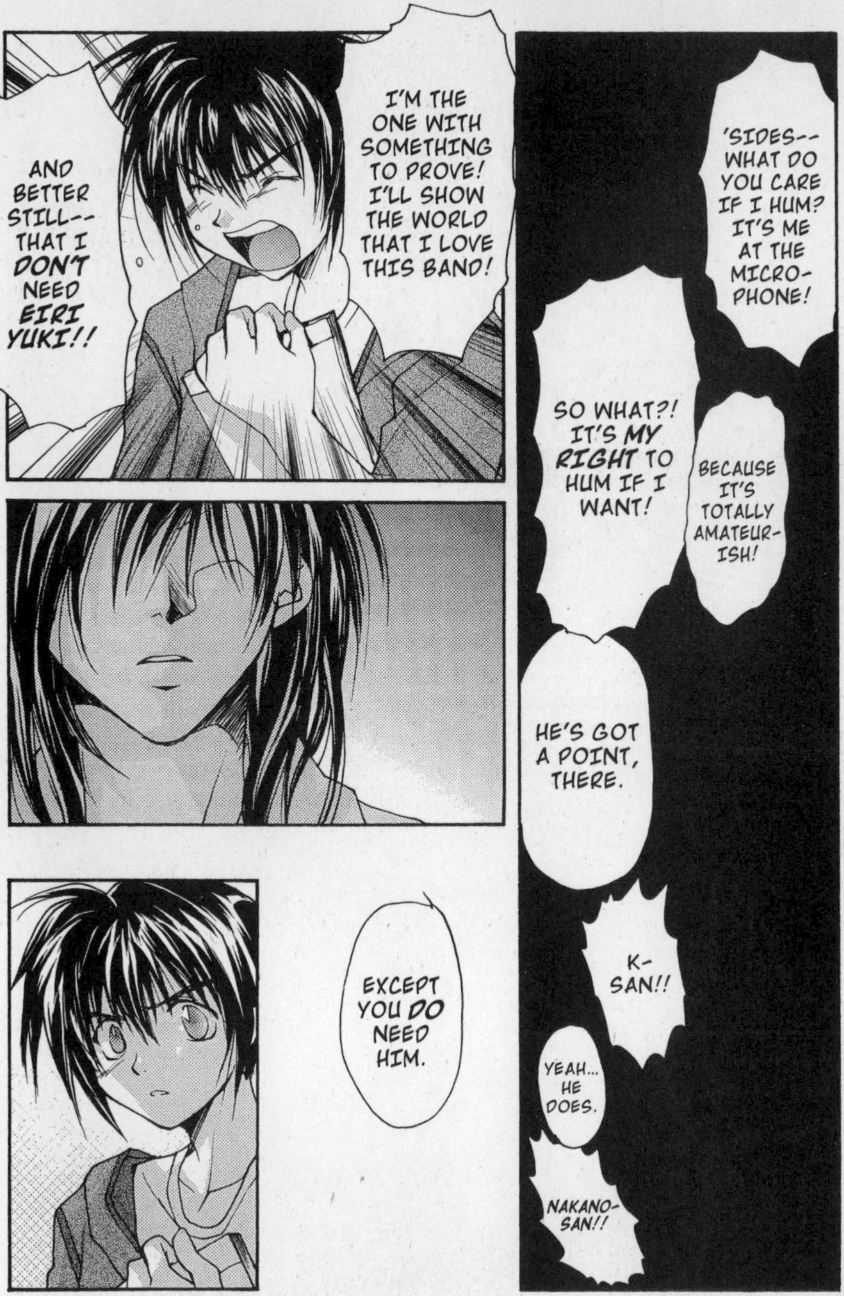
'SIDES--WHAT DO YOU CARE IF I HUM? IT'S ME AT THE MICRO-PHONE!
BECAUSE IT'S TOTALLY AMATEUR-ISH!
SO WHAT?! IT'S MY RIGHT TO HUM IF I WANT!
HE'S GOT A POINT, THERE.
K-SAN!!
YEAH... HE DOES.
NAKANO-SAN!!
I'M THE ONE WITH SOMETHING TO PROVE! I'LL SHOW THE WORLD THAT I LOVE THIS BAND!
AND BETTER STILL--THAT I DON'T NEED EIRI YUKI!!
EXCEPT YOU DO NEED HIM.

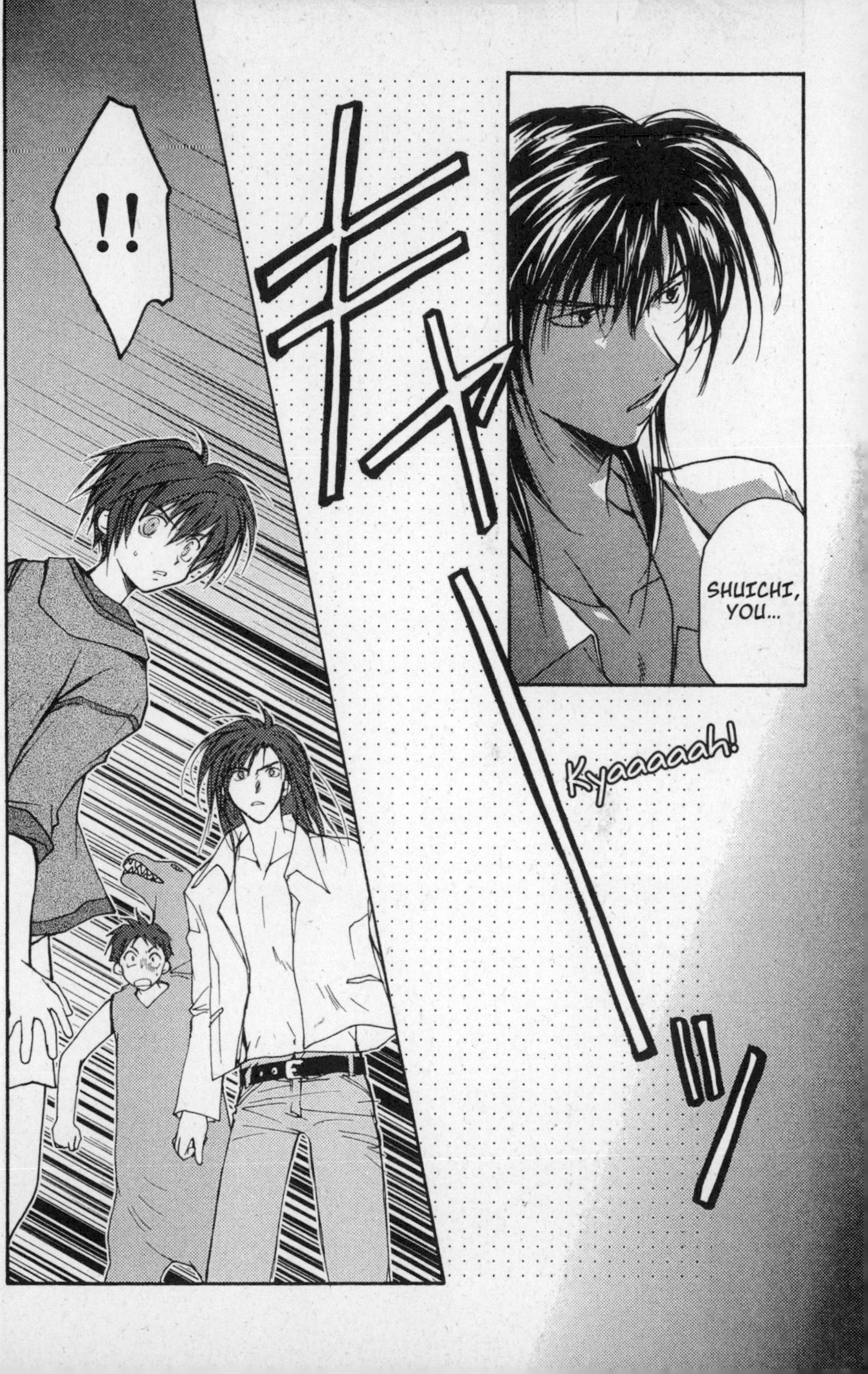
SHUICHI, YOU...
Kyaaaaah!
!!

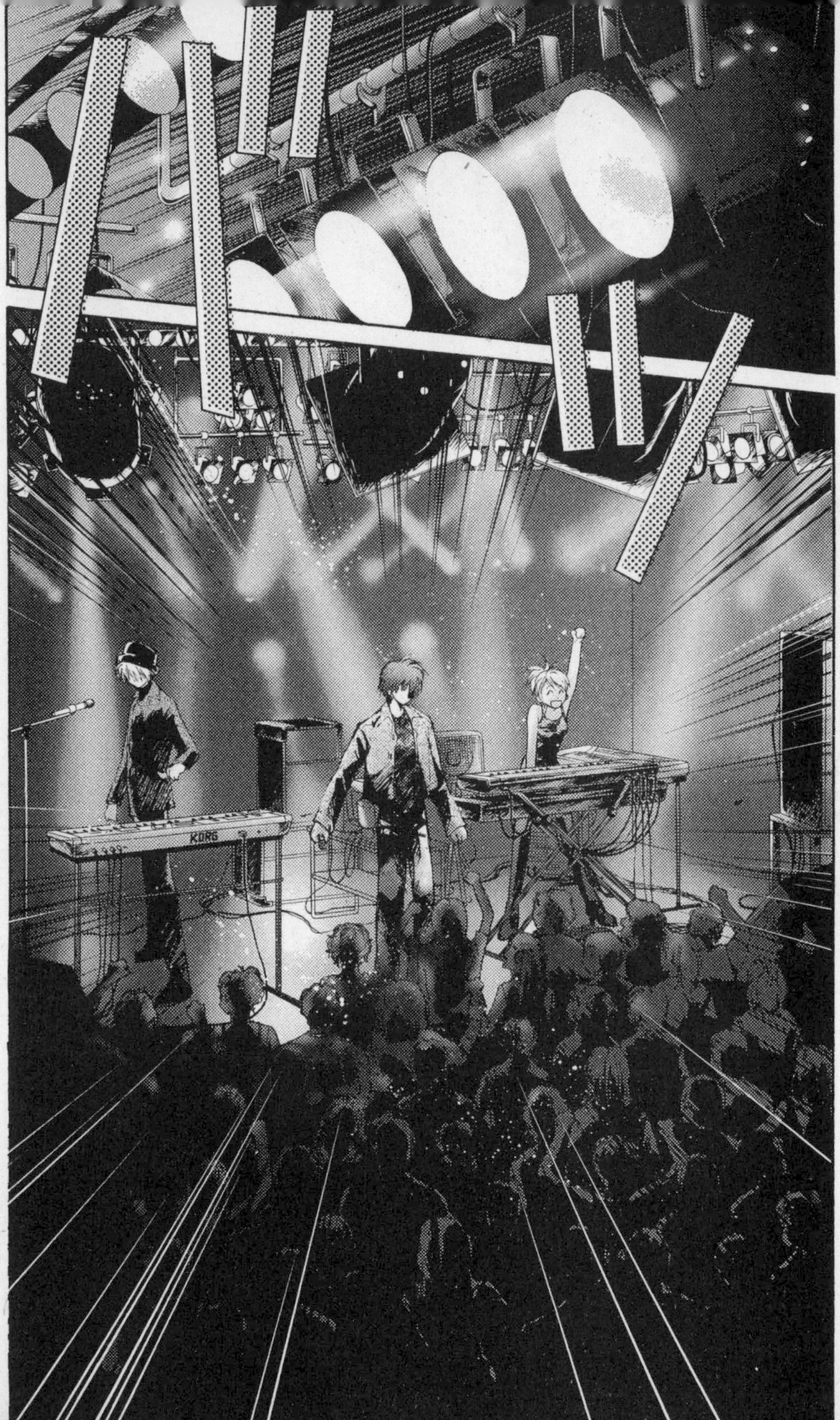
KORG

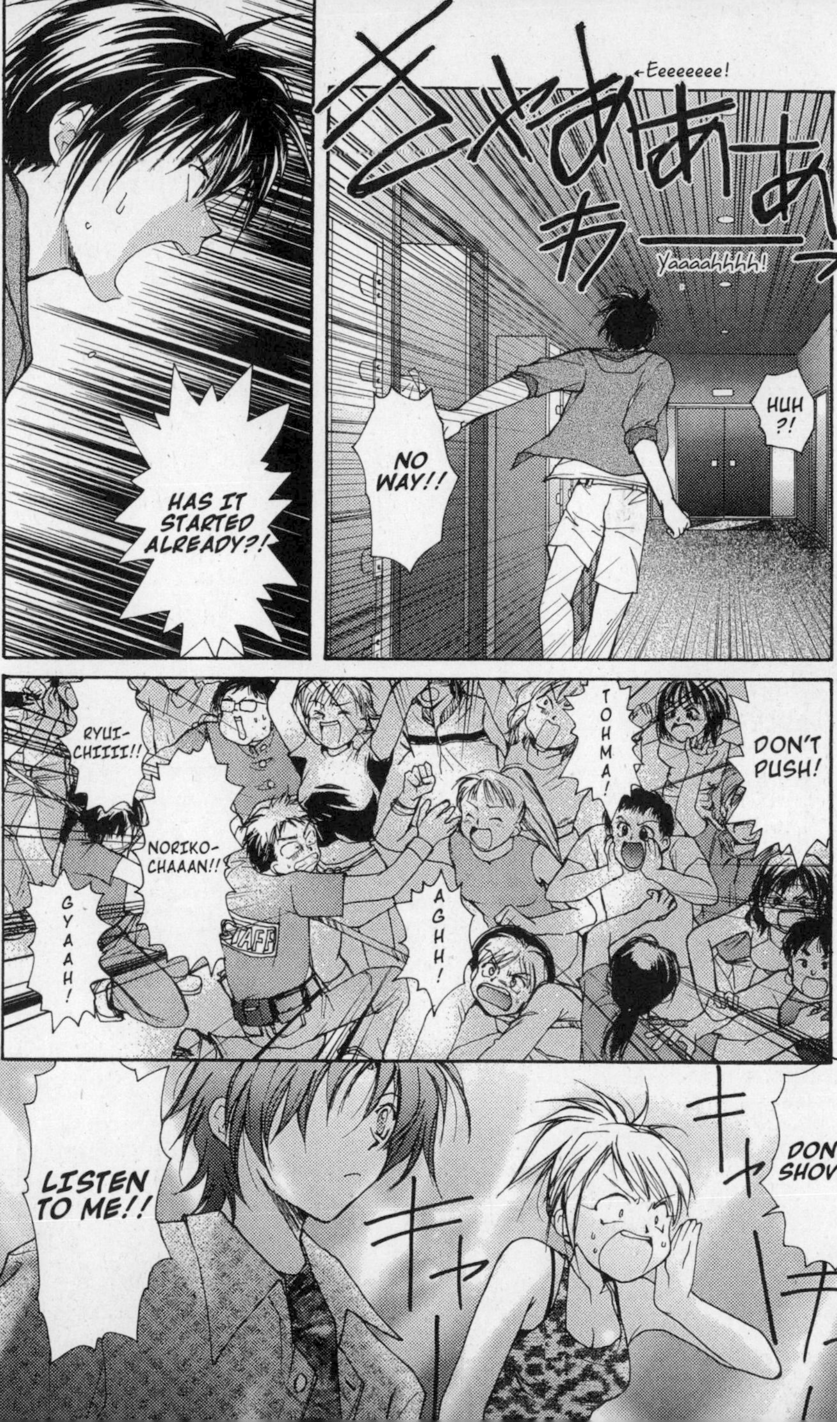

きゃあああー
Eeeeeeee!
Yaaaahhhh!
HUH?!
NO WAY!!
HAS IT STARTED ALREADY?!
DON'T PUSH!
TOHMA!
RYUI-CHIIIII!!
NORIKO-CHAAAN!!
AGHH!
GYAAH!
DON'T SHOVE!
キャーキャー
LISTEN TO ME!!

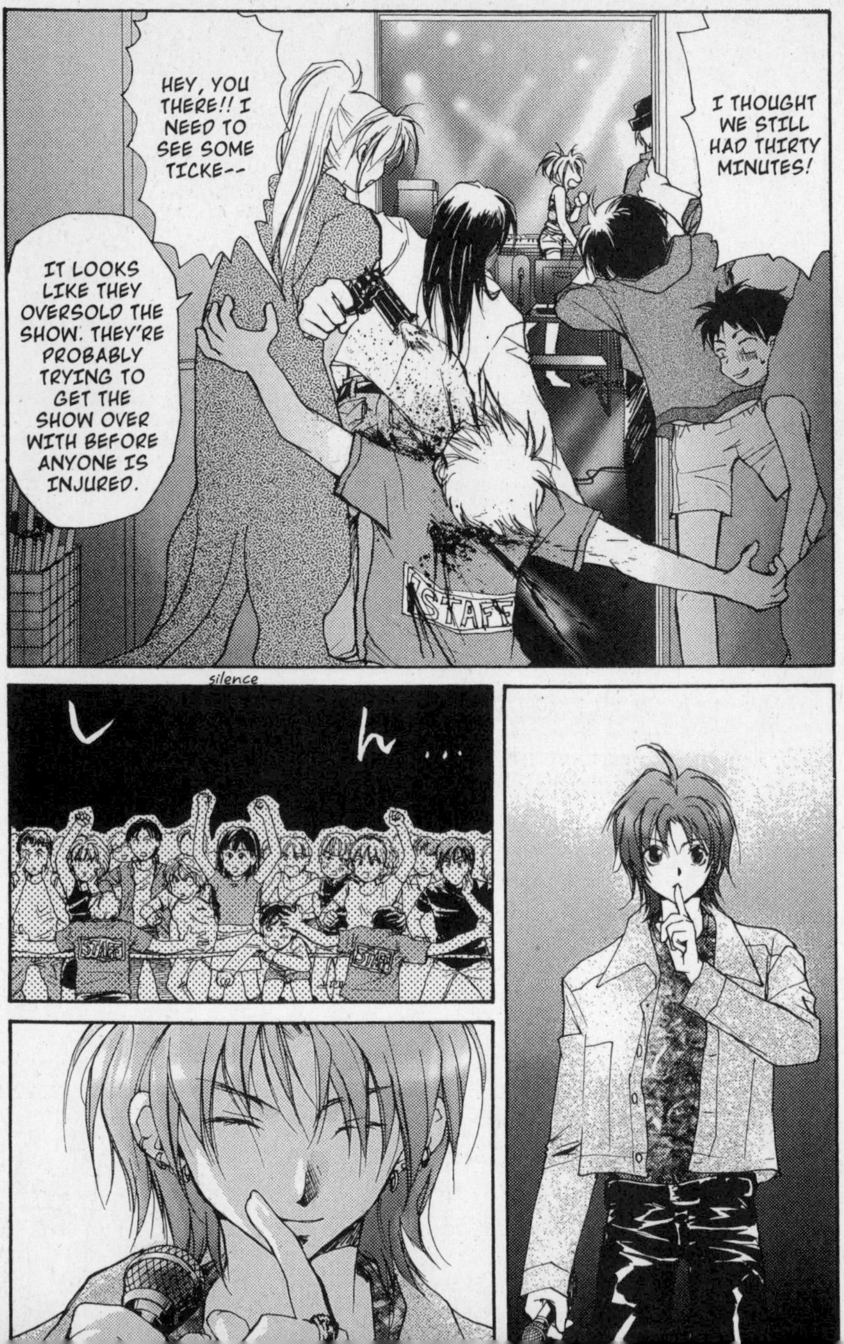
I THOUGHT WE STILL HAD THIRTY MINUTES!
HEY, YOU THERE!! I NEED TO SEE SOME TICKE--
IT LOOKS LIKE THEY OVERSOLD THE SHOW. THEY'RE PROBABLY TRYING TO GET THE SHOW OVER WITH BEFORE ANYONE IS INJURED.
silence
しん...

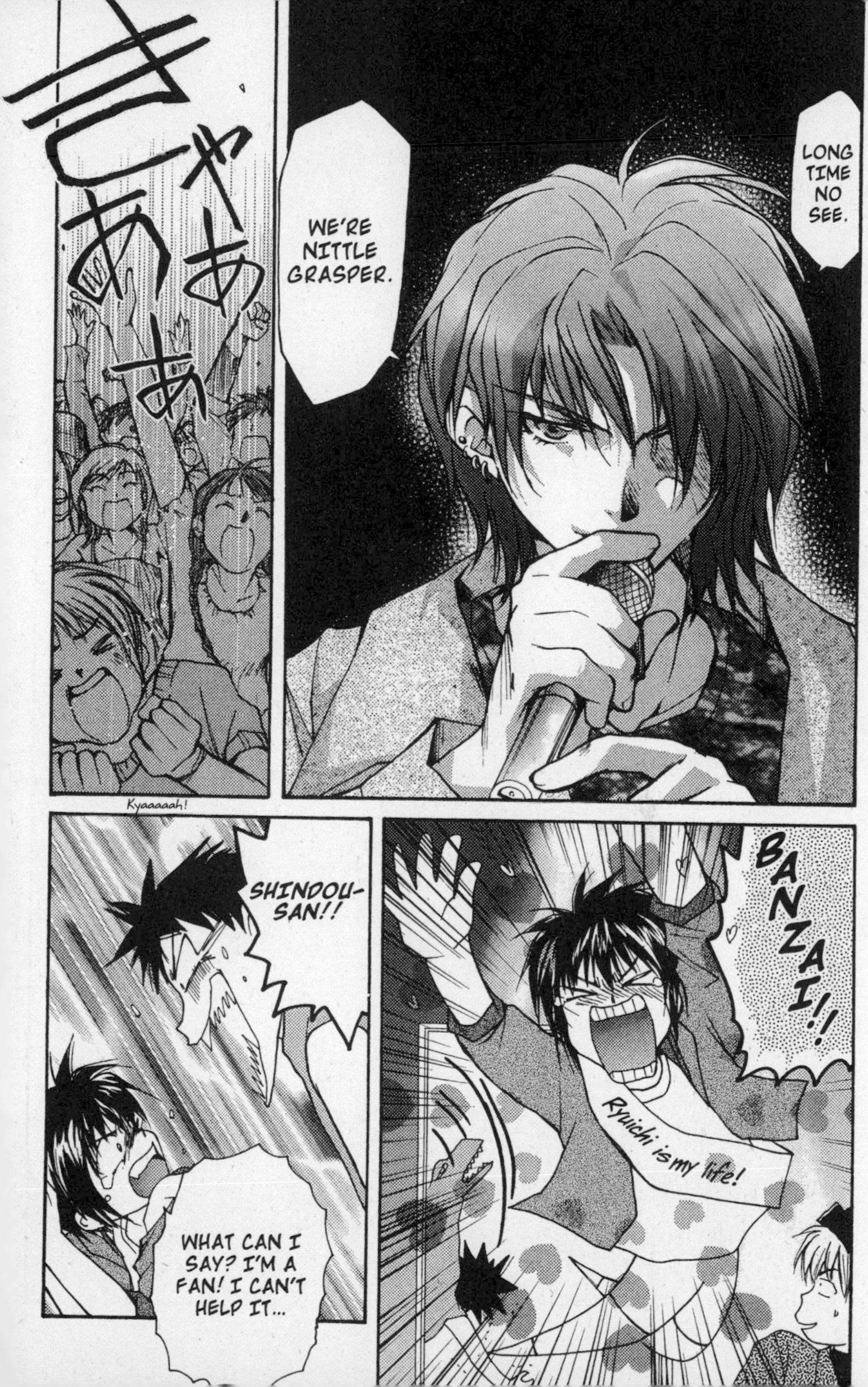
LONG TIME NO SEE.
WE'RE NITTLE GRASPER.
きゃあああ
Kyaaaaah!
BANZAI!!
Ryuichi is my life!
SHINDOU-SAN!!
WHAT CAN I SAY? I'M A FAN! I CAN'T HELP IT...

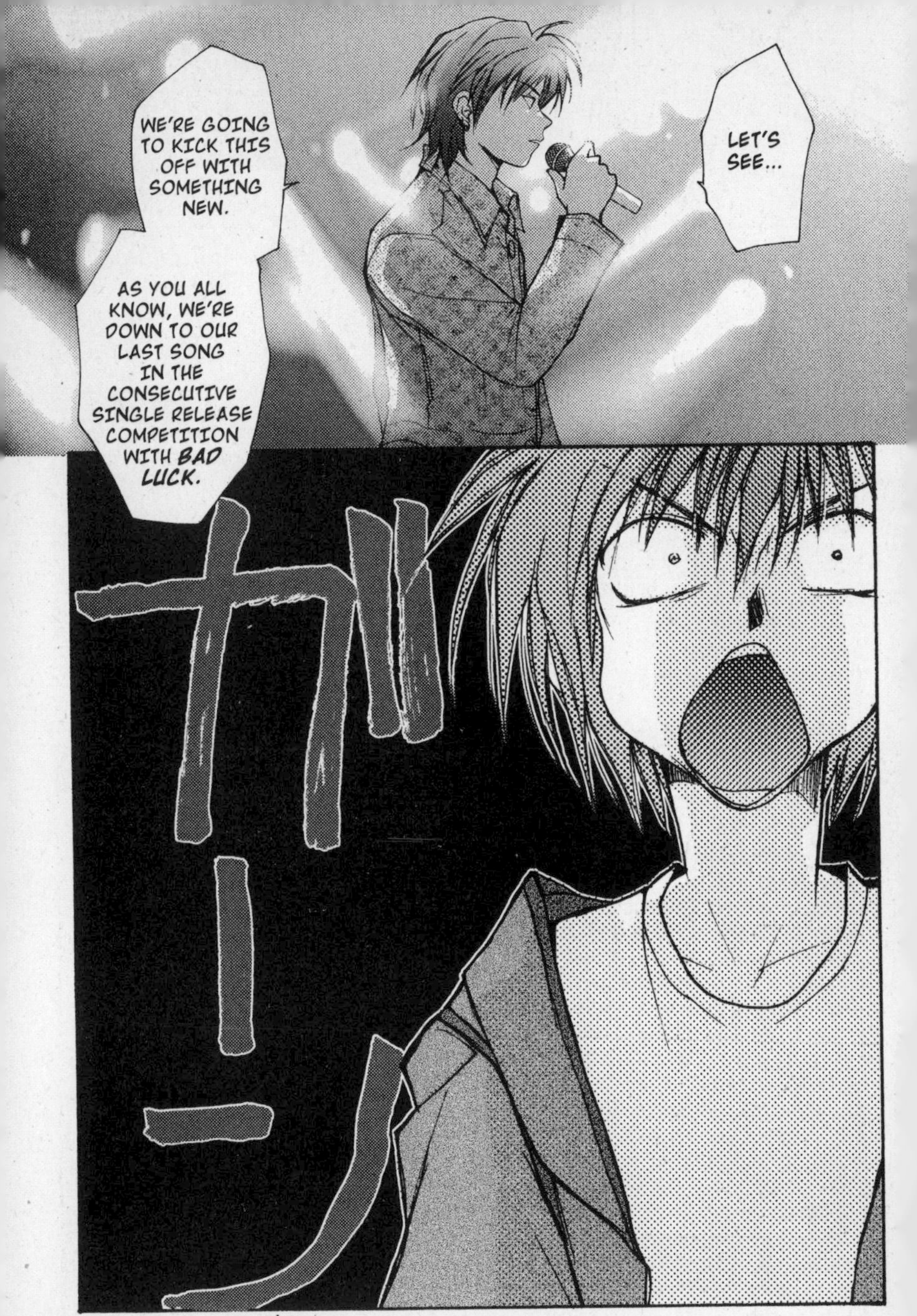
LET'S SEE...
WE'RE GOING TO KICK THIS OFF WITH SOMETHING NEW.
AS YOU ALL KNOW, WE'RE DOWN TO OUR LAST SONG IN THE CONSECUTIVE SINGLE RELEASE COMPETITION WITH *BAD LUCK*.
ガーン
shock

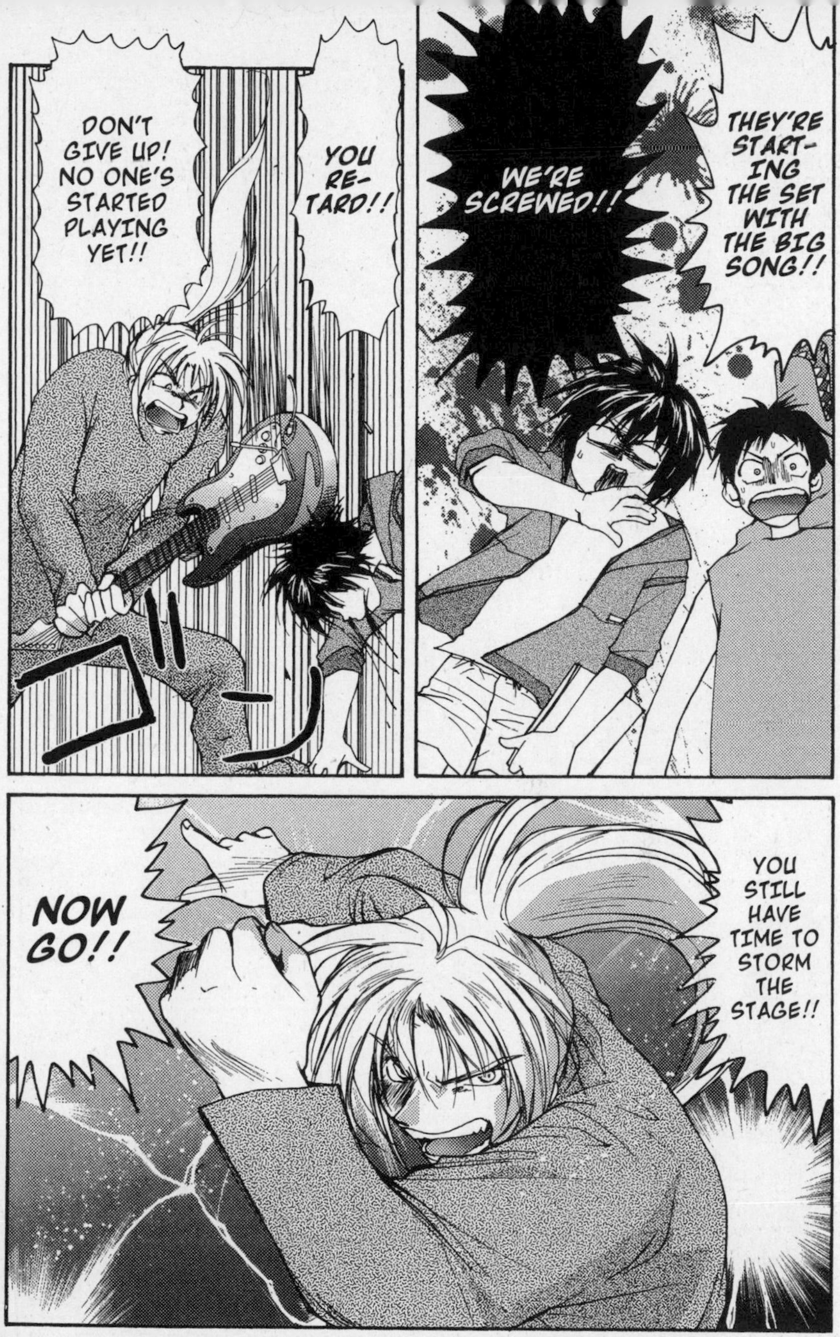
THEY'RE STARTING THE SET WITH THE BIG SONG!!
WE'RE SCREWED!!
YOU RE-TARD!!
DON'T GIVE UP! NO ONE'S STARTED PLAYING YET!!
YOU STILL HAVE TIME TO STORM THE STAGE!!
NOW GO!!

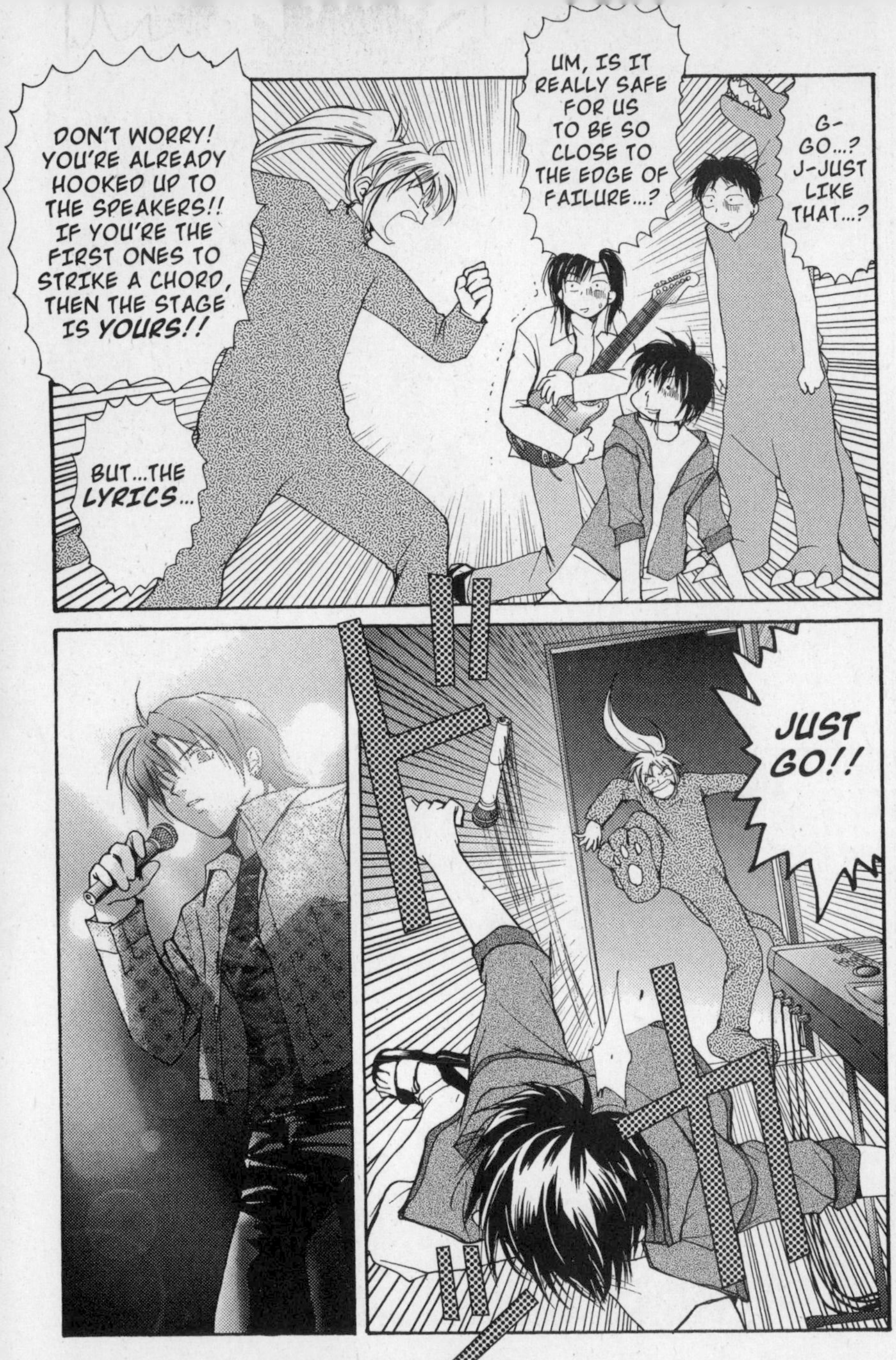
G-GO...? J-JUST LIKE THAT...?
UM, IS IT REALLY SAFE FOR US TO BE SO CLOSE TO THE EDGE OF FAILURE...?
DON'T WORRY! YOU'RE ALREADY HOOKED UP TO THE SPEAKERS!! IF YOU'RE THE FIRST ONES TO STRIKE A CHORD, THEN THE STAGE IS YOURS!!
BUT...THE LYRICS...
JUST GO!!

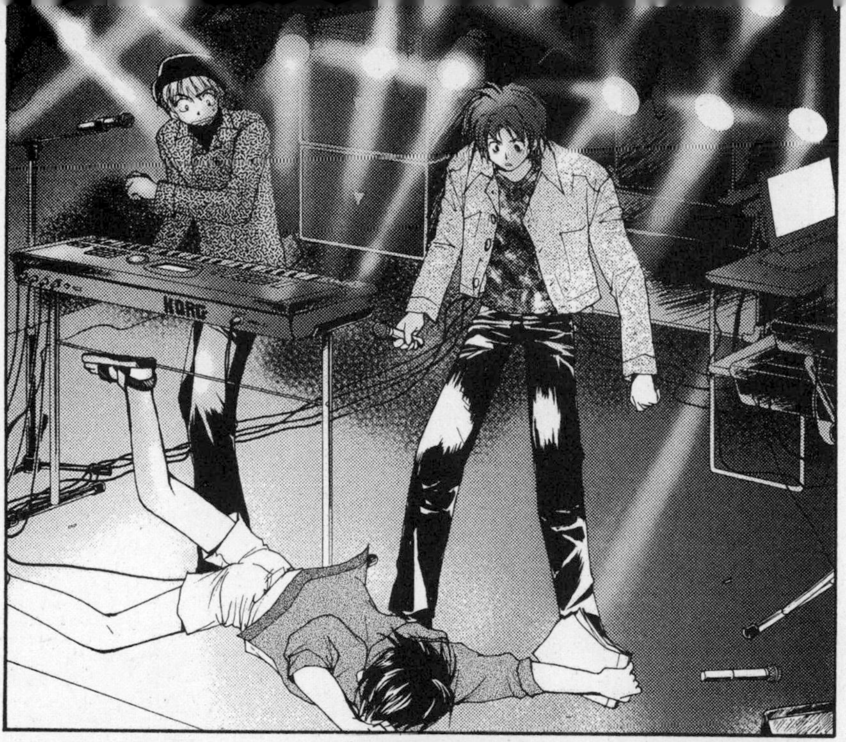

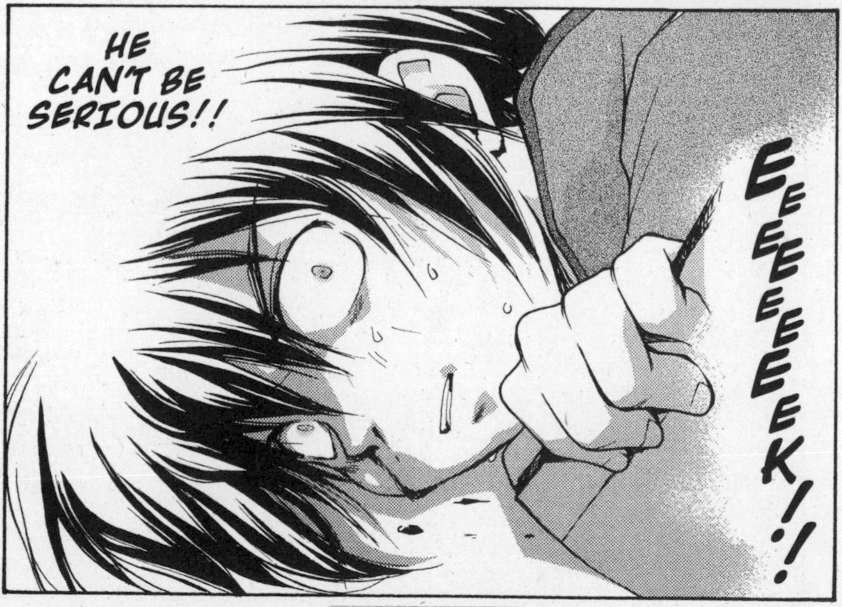
HE CAN'T BE SERIOUS!!
EEEEEEEEEK!!

track52 ▶ END

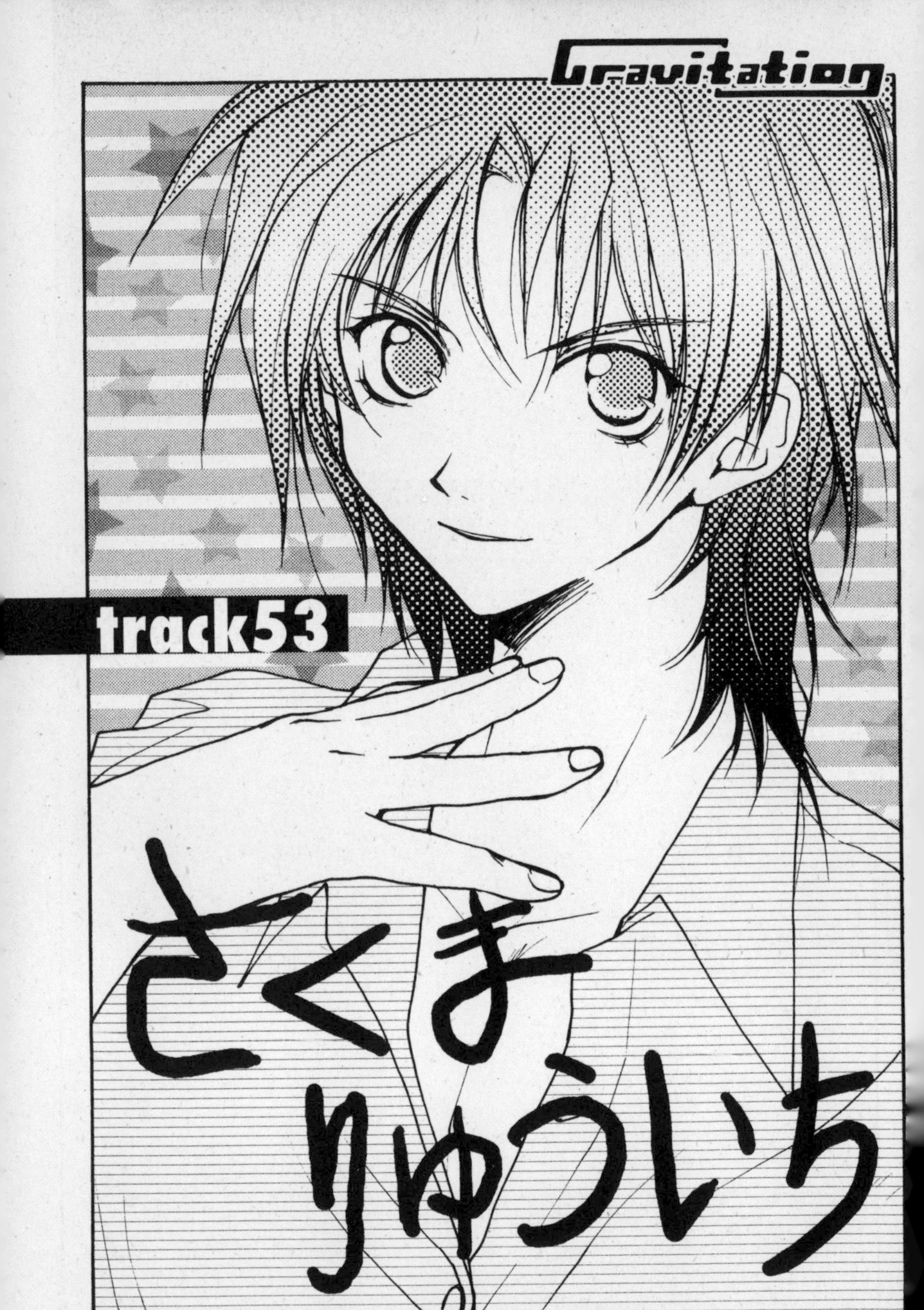
Gravitation
track53
さくまりゅういち
Ryuichi Sakuma

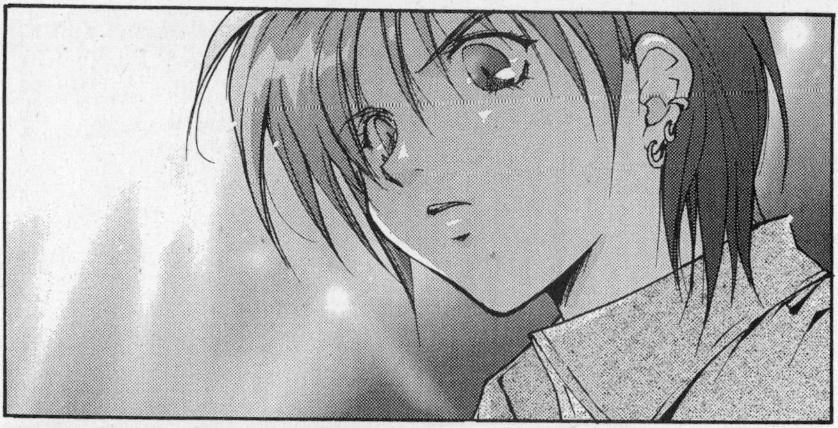

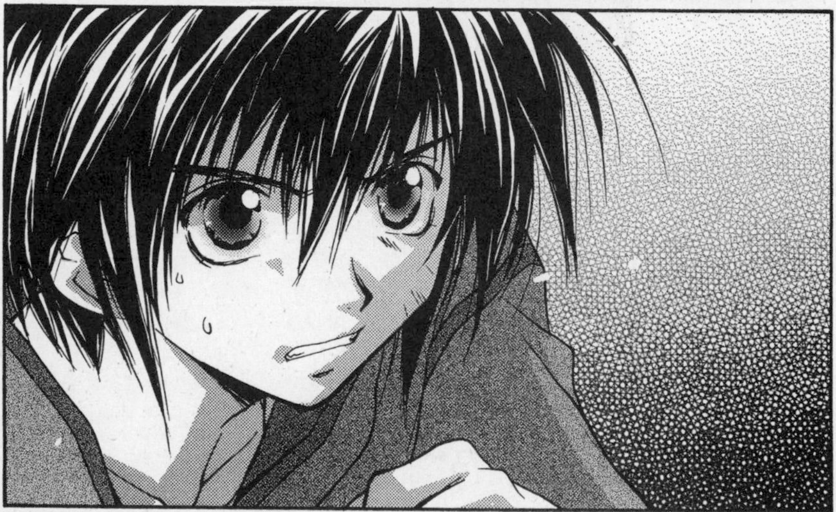

## ABOUT GRAVITATION TRACK 53

I want to make a confession...as of this moment, I don't have a copy of this episode at my disposal. I don't have the proofing sheets from the magazine, nor do I have the drafts, nor any script files. Perhaps if I didn't say it, nobody would know about it, but wouldn't you respect me more if I told you I can't fill this empty space with lies? And so, for the first time ever, I, Murakami, will be writing about some personal things. To tell the truth, I hardly ever read manga. I rarely ever watch anime, either. But I love video games, the internet, movies... and I'm such a shut-in that I can go an entire month without stepping a single foot outside (but yet still retain my sanity). I also love Z**RD (plastic model) and figurines (not of pretty boys). Z**RD is so cool!

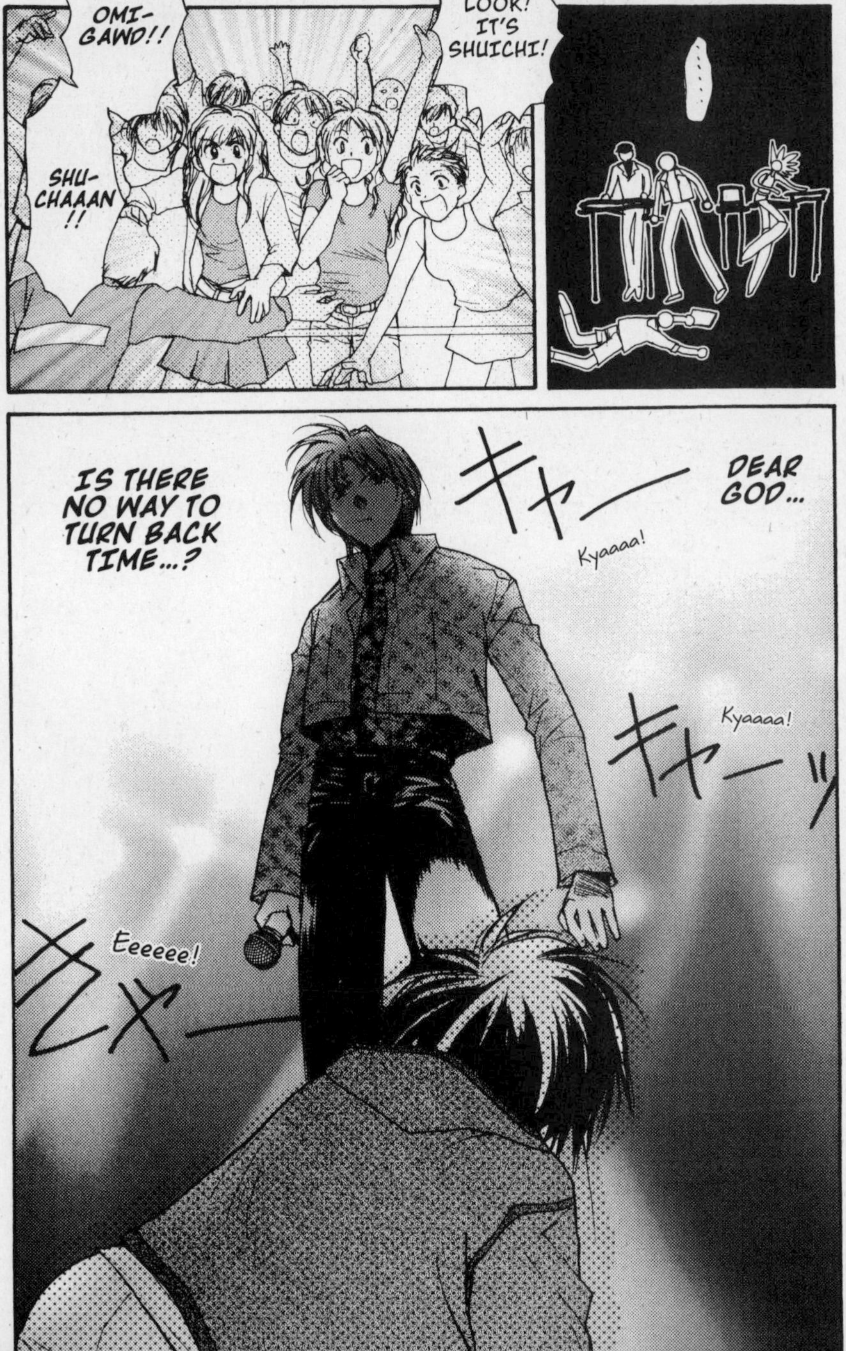
......
LOOK! IT'S SHUICHI!
OMI-GAWD!!
SHU-CHAAAN!!
DEAR GOD...
キャー
Kyaaaa!
IS THERE NO WAY TO TURN BACK TIME...?
キャーッ
Kyaaaa!
キャー
Eeeeee!

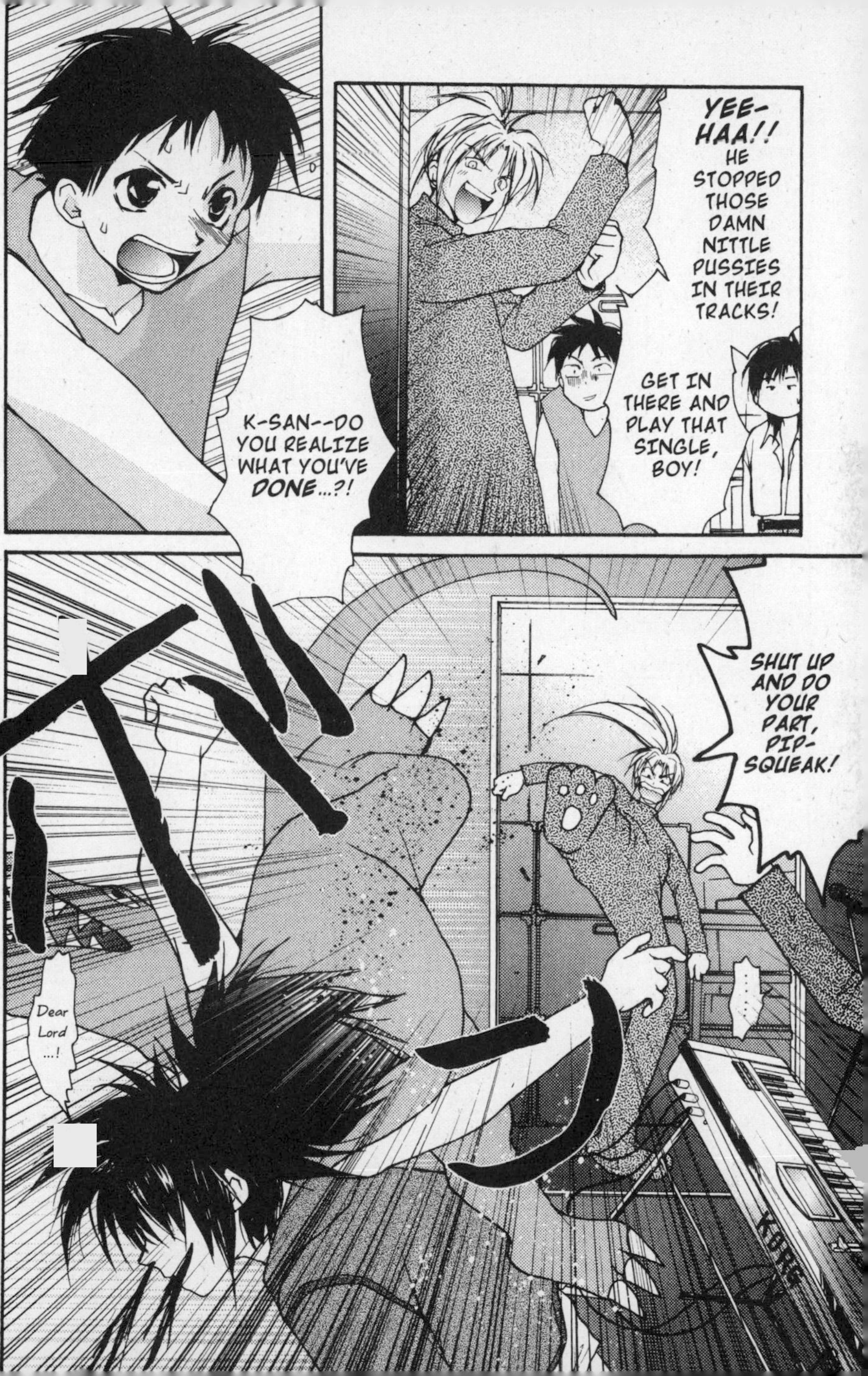
YEE-HAA!! HE STOPPED THOSE DAMN NITTLE PUSSIES IN THEIR TRACKS!
GET IN THERE AND PLAY THAT SINGLE, BOY!
K-SAN--DO YOU REALIZE WHAT YOU'VE DONE...?!
SHUT UP AND DO YOUR PART, PIP-SQUEAK!
...
Dear Lord ...!

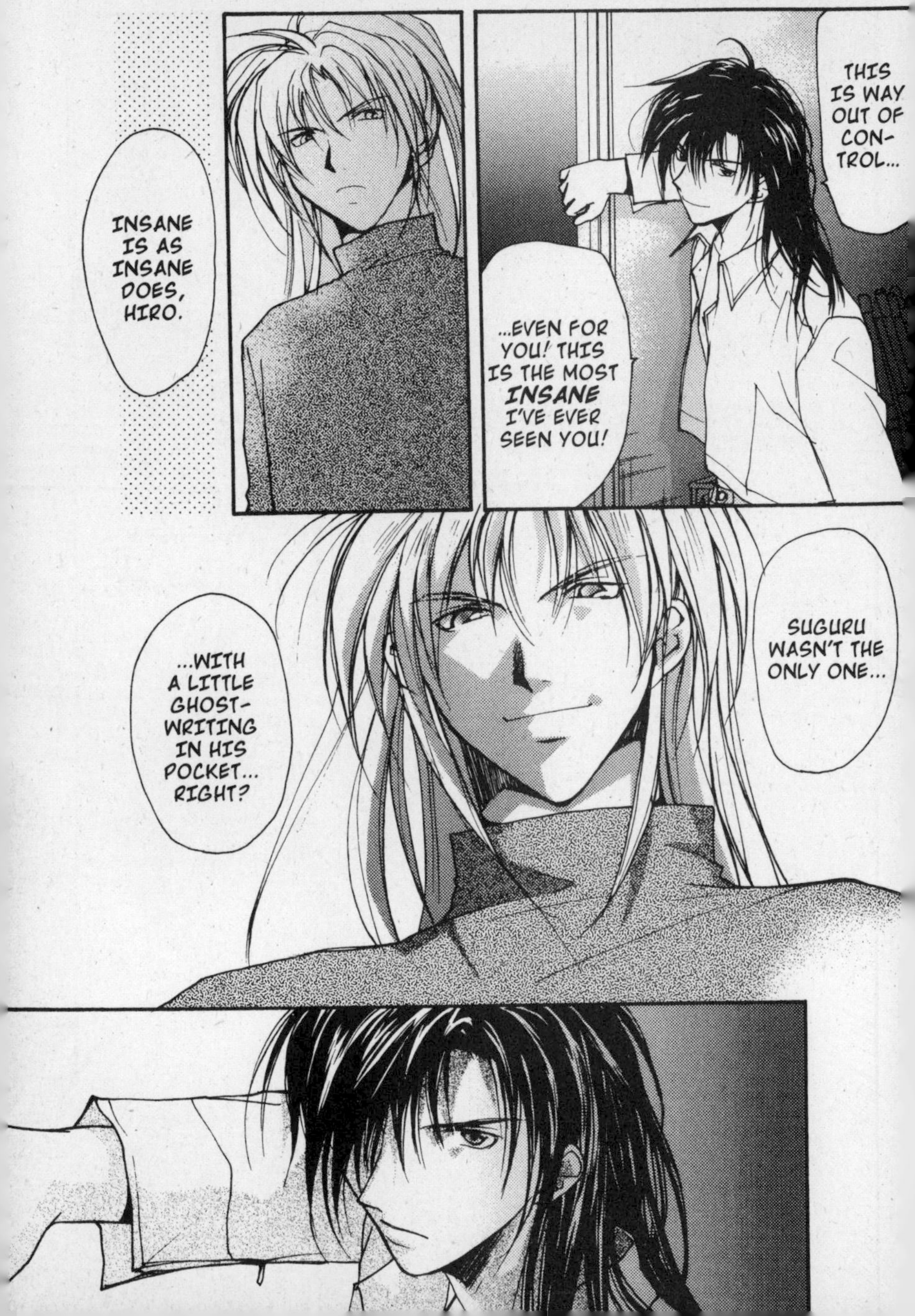
THIS IS WAY OUT OF CON-TROL...
...EVEN FOR YOU! THIS IS THE MOST *INSANE* I'VE EVER SEEN YOU!
INSANE IS AS INSANE DOES, HIRO.
SUGURU WASN'T THE ONLY ONE...
...WITH A LITTLE GHOST-WRITING IN HIS POCKET... RIGHT?

Kyaaa kyaaa kyaaa!

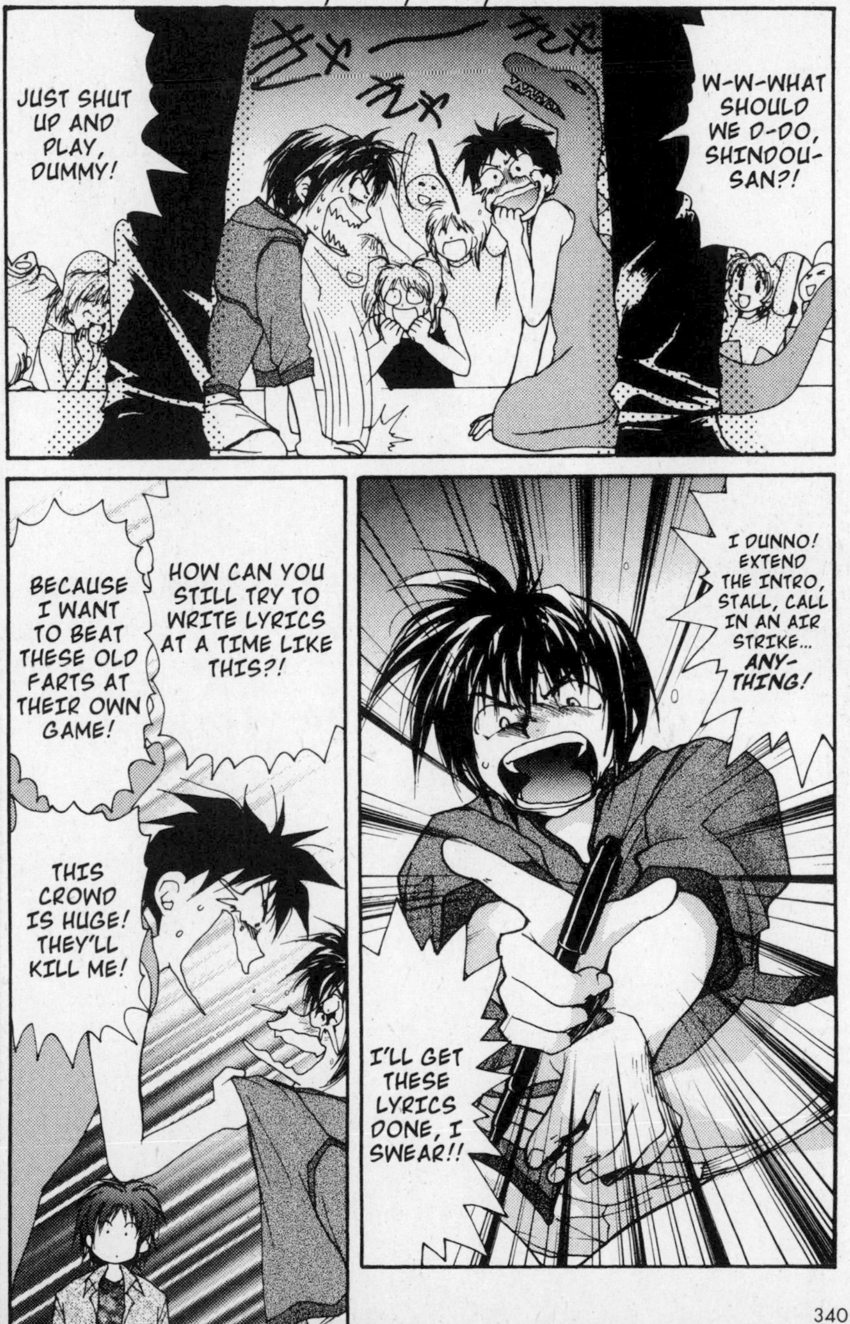

W-W-WHAT SHOULD WE D-DO, SHINDOU-SAN?!
JUST SHUT UP AND PLAY, DUMMY!
I DUNNO! EXTEND THE INTRO, STALL, CALL IN AN AIR STRIKE... ANY-THING!
I'LL GET THESE LYRICS DONE, I SWEAR!!
HOW CAN YOU STILL TRY TO WRITE LYRICS AT A TIME LIKE THIS?!
BECAUSE I WANT TO BEAT THESE OLD FARTS AT THEIR OWN GAME!
THIS CROWD IS HUGE! THEY'LL KILL ME!

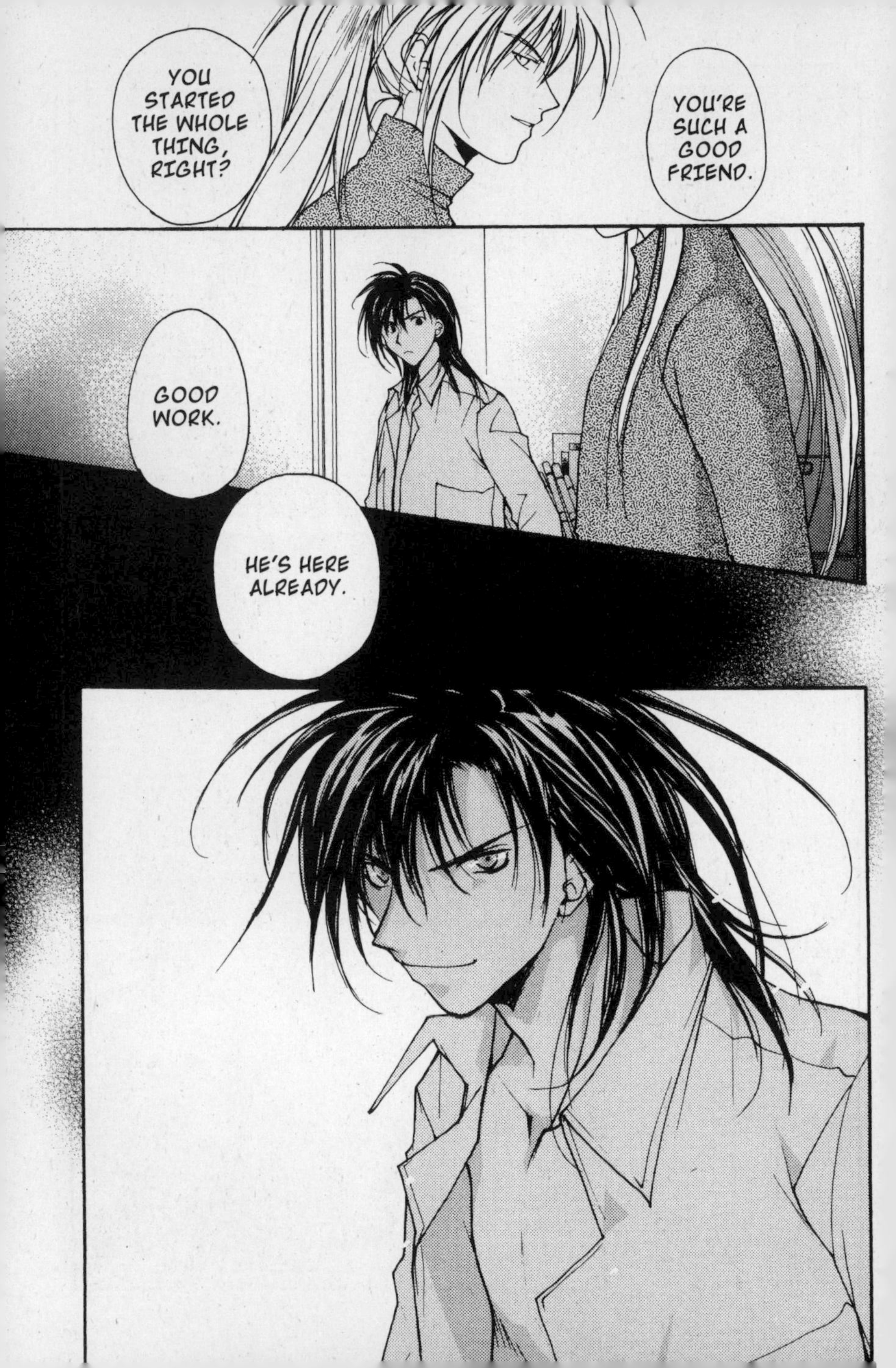
YOU'RE SUCH A GOOD FRIEND.
YOU STARTED THE WHOLE THING, RIGHT?
GOOD WORK.
HE'S HERE ALREADY.

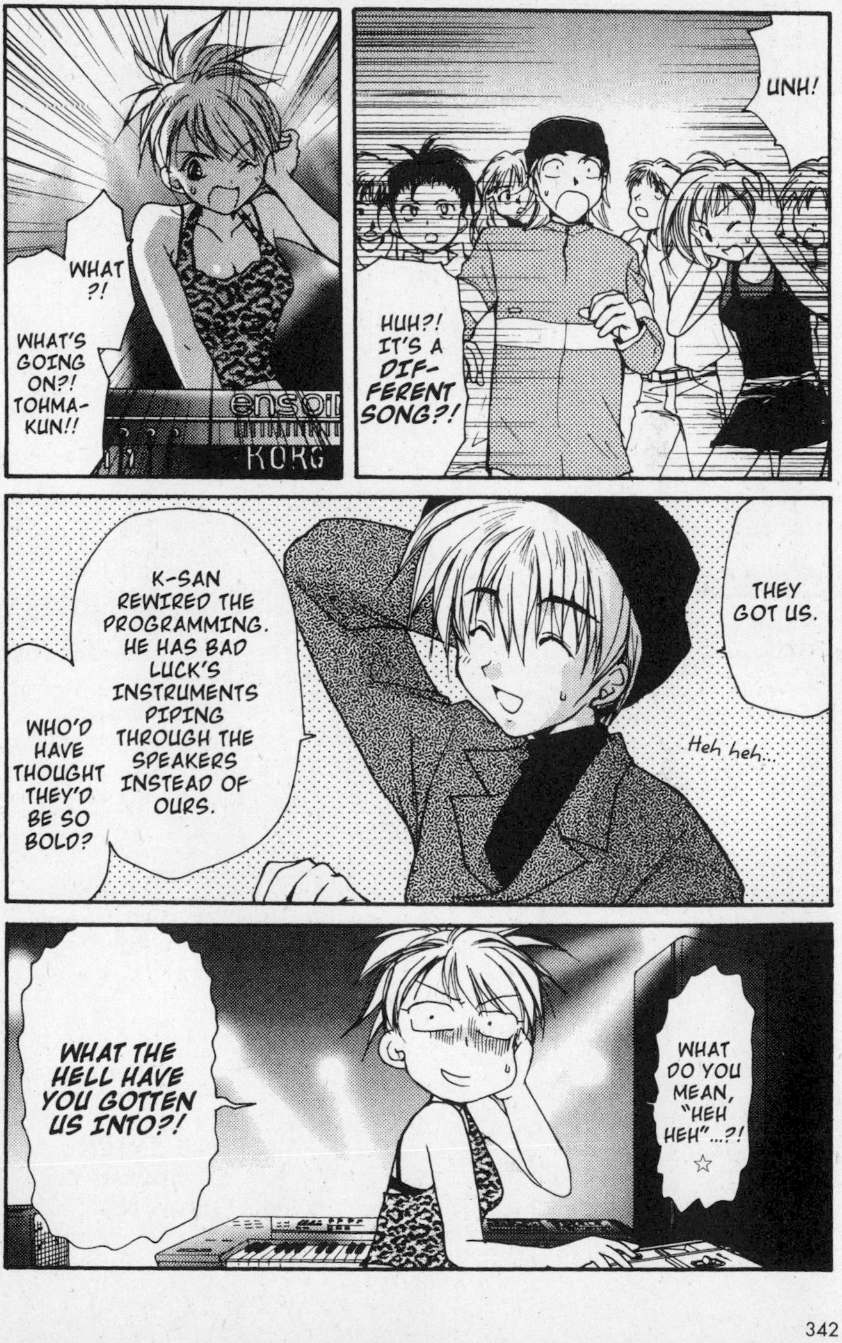
UNH!
HUH?! IT'S A DIF-FERENT SONG?!
WHAT ?!
WHAT'S GOING ON?! TOHMA-KUN!!
KORG
THEY GOT US.
Heh heh...
K-SAN REWIRED THE PROGRAMMING. HE HAS BAD LUCK'S INSTRUMENTS PIPING THROUGH THE SPEAKERS INSTEAD OF OURS.
WHO'D HAVE THOUGHT THEY'D BE SO BOLD?
WHAT DO YOU MEAN, "HEH HEH"...?! ☆
WHAT THE HELL HAVE YOU GOTTEN US INTO?!

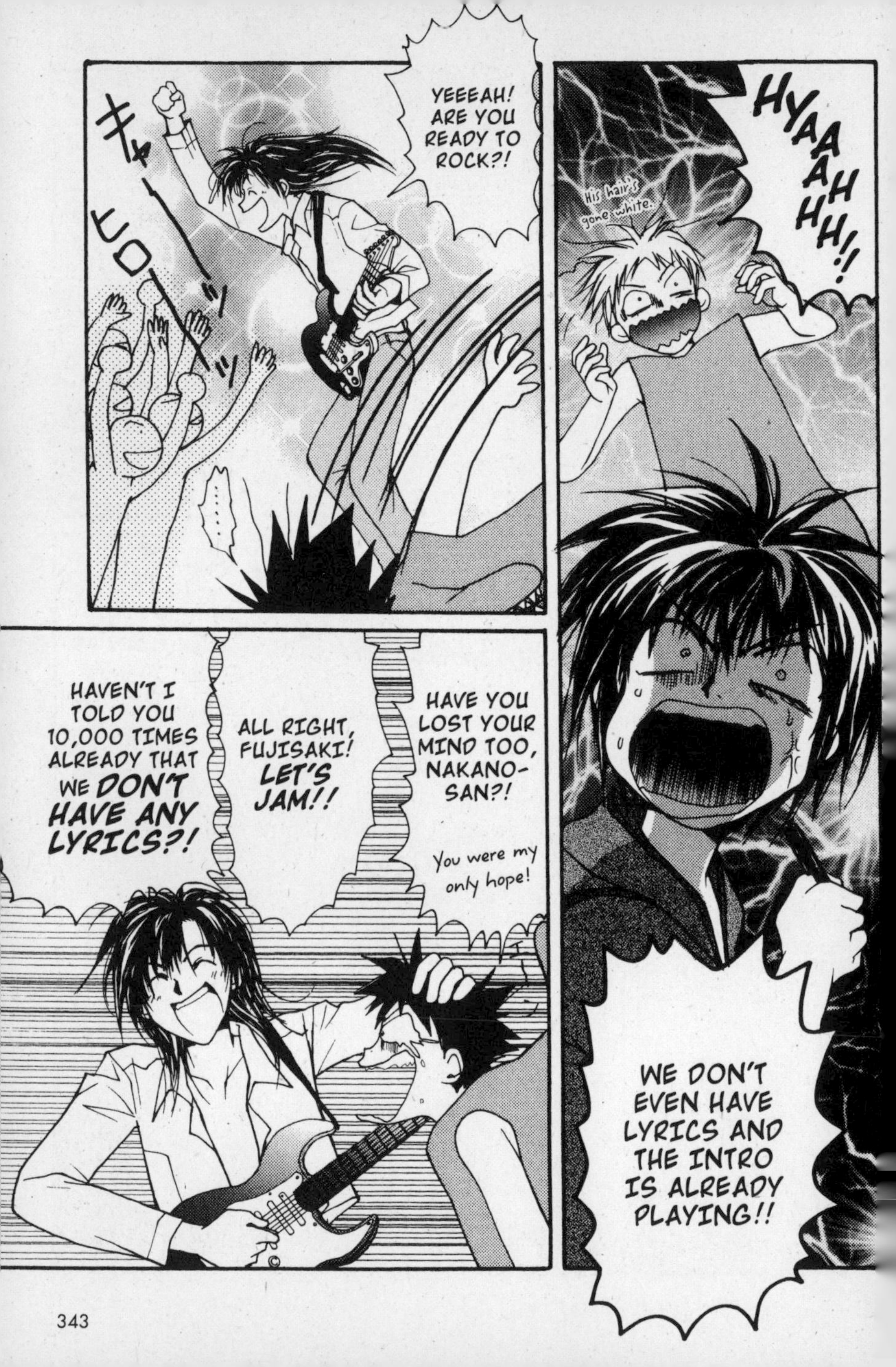
HYAAAHHH!!
His hair's gone white.
WE DON'T EVEN HAVE LYRICS AND THE INTRO IS ALREADY PLAYING!!
YEEEAH! ARE YOU READY TO ROCK?!
キャーヒローッ
......
HAVE YOU LOST YOUR MIND TOO, NAKANO-SAN?!
You were my only hope!
ALL RIGHT, FUJISAKI! LET'S JAM!!
HAVEN'T I TOLD YOU 10,000 TIMES ALREADY THAT WE DON'T HAVE ANY LYRICS?!

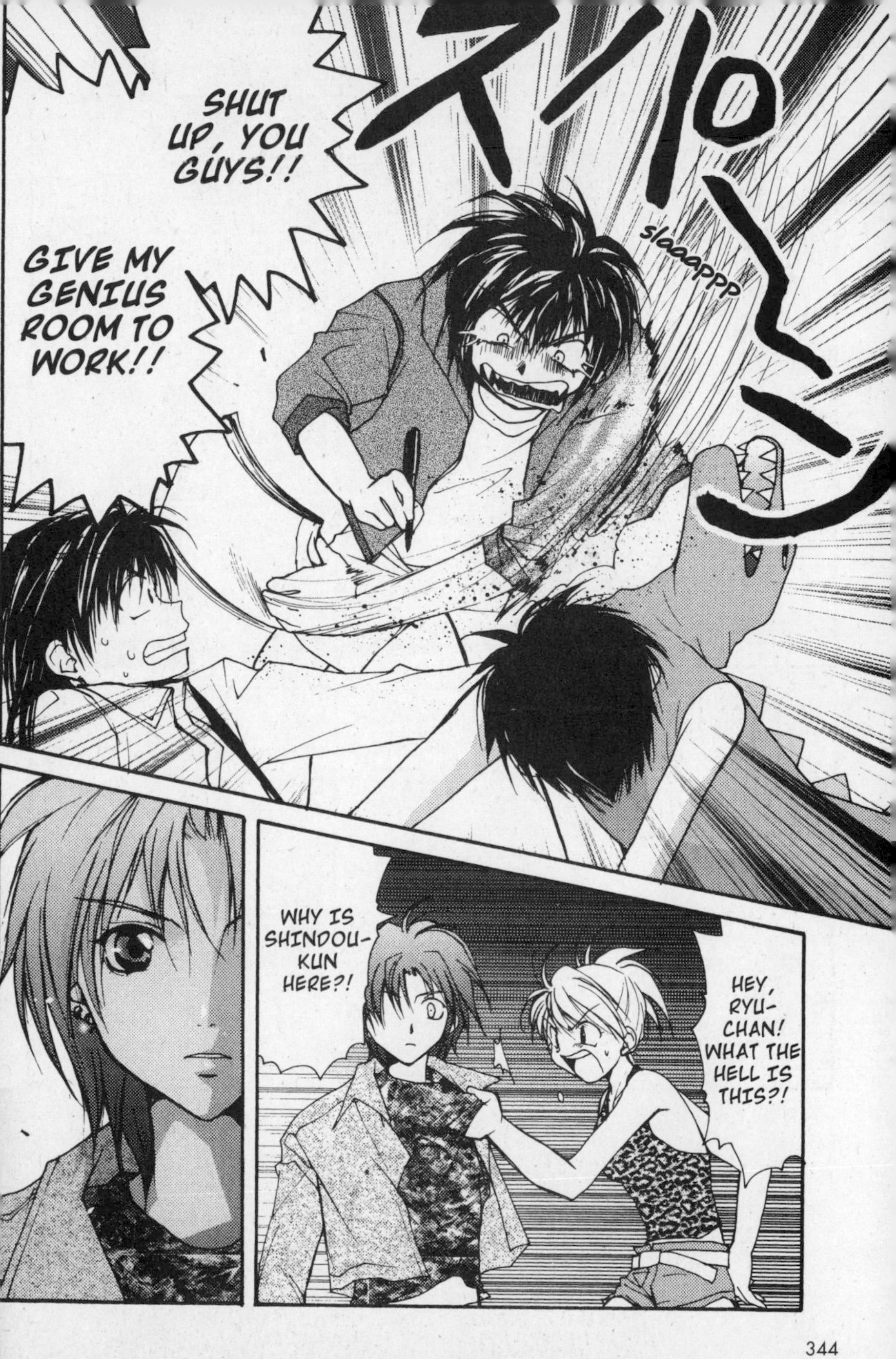
slaaaappp
SHUT UP, YOU GUYS!!
GIVE MY GENIUS ROOM TO WORK!!
HEY, RYU-CHAN! WHAT THE HELL IS THIS?!
WHY IS SHINDOU-KUN HERE?!

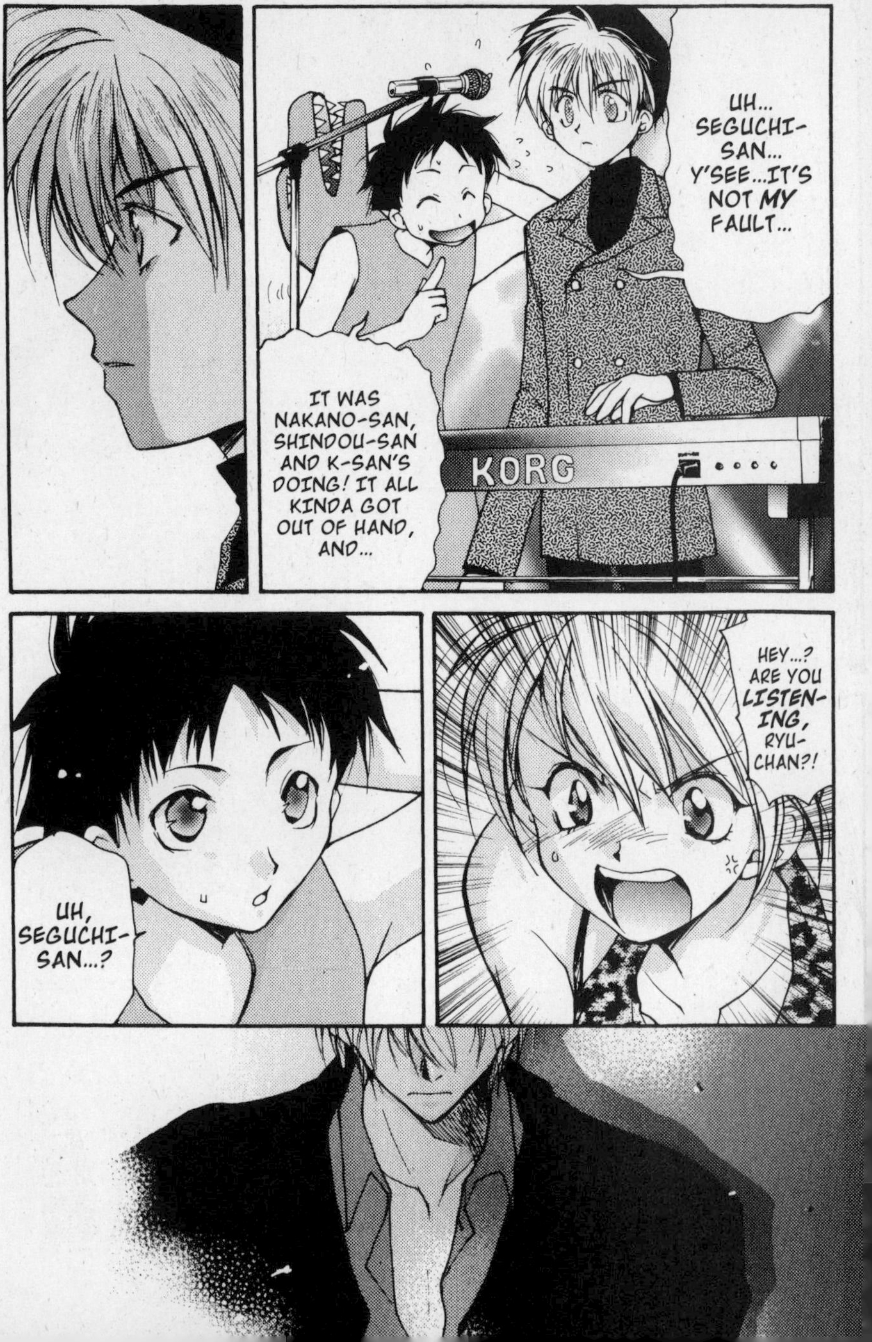
UH... SEGUCHI-SAN... Y'SEE...IT'S NOT *MY* FAULT...
IT WAS NAKANO-SAN, SHINDOU-SAN AND K-SAN'S DOING! IT ALL KINDA GOT OUT OF HAND, AND...
KORG
HEY...? ARE YOU *LISTENING*, RYU-CHAN?!
UH, SEGUCHI-SAN...?

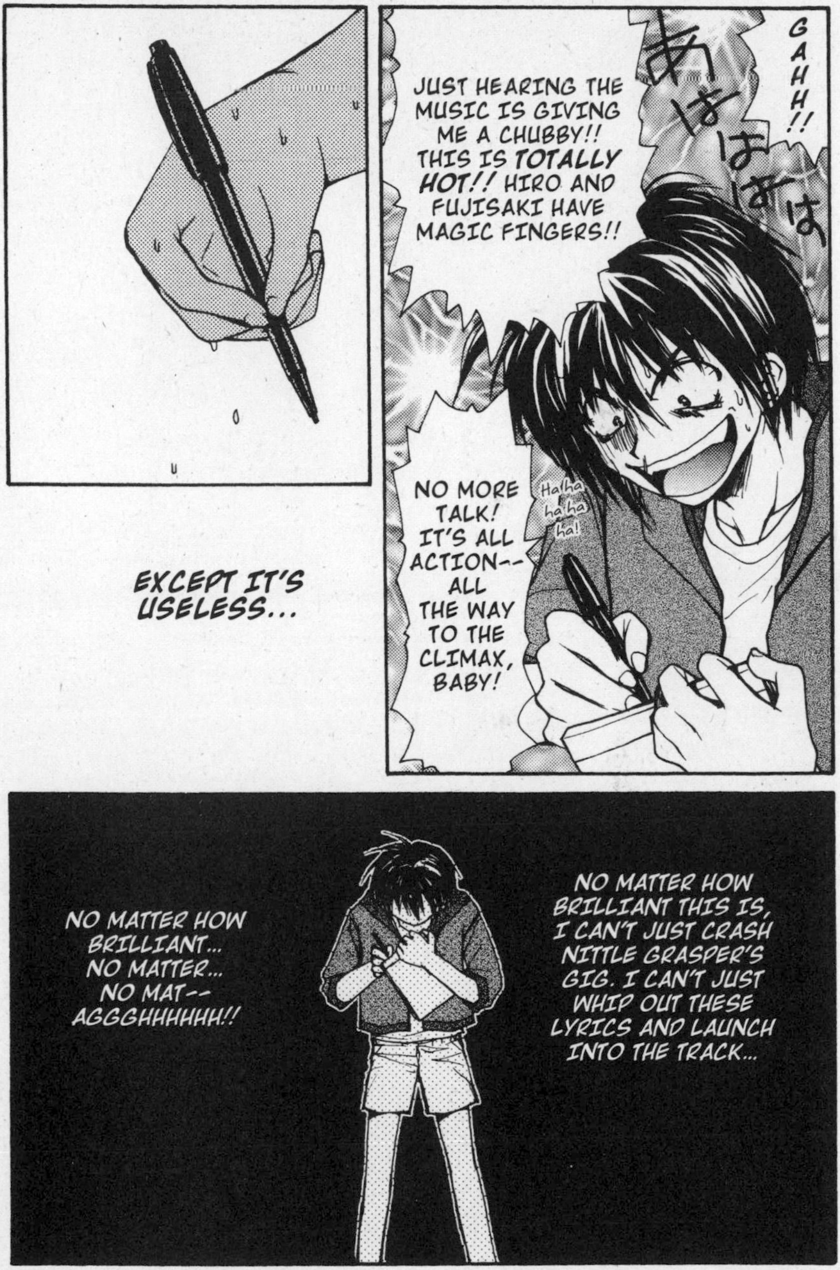
あははは
GAHH!!
JUST HEARING THE MUSIC IS GIVING ME A CHUBBY!! THIS IS *TOTALLY HOT!!* HIRO AND FUJISAKI HAVE MAGIC FINGERS!!
Ha ha ha ha ha!
NO MORE TALK! IT'S ALL ACTION--ALL THE WAY TO THE CLIMAX, BABY!
EXCEPT IT'S USELESS...
NO MATTER HOW BRILLIANT THIS IS, I CAN'T JUST CRASH NITTLE GRASPER'S GIG. I CAN'T JUST WHIP OUT THESE LYRICS AND LAUNCH INTO THE TRACK...
NO MATTER HOW BRILLIANT... NO MATTER... NO MAT--AGGGHHHHHH!!

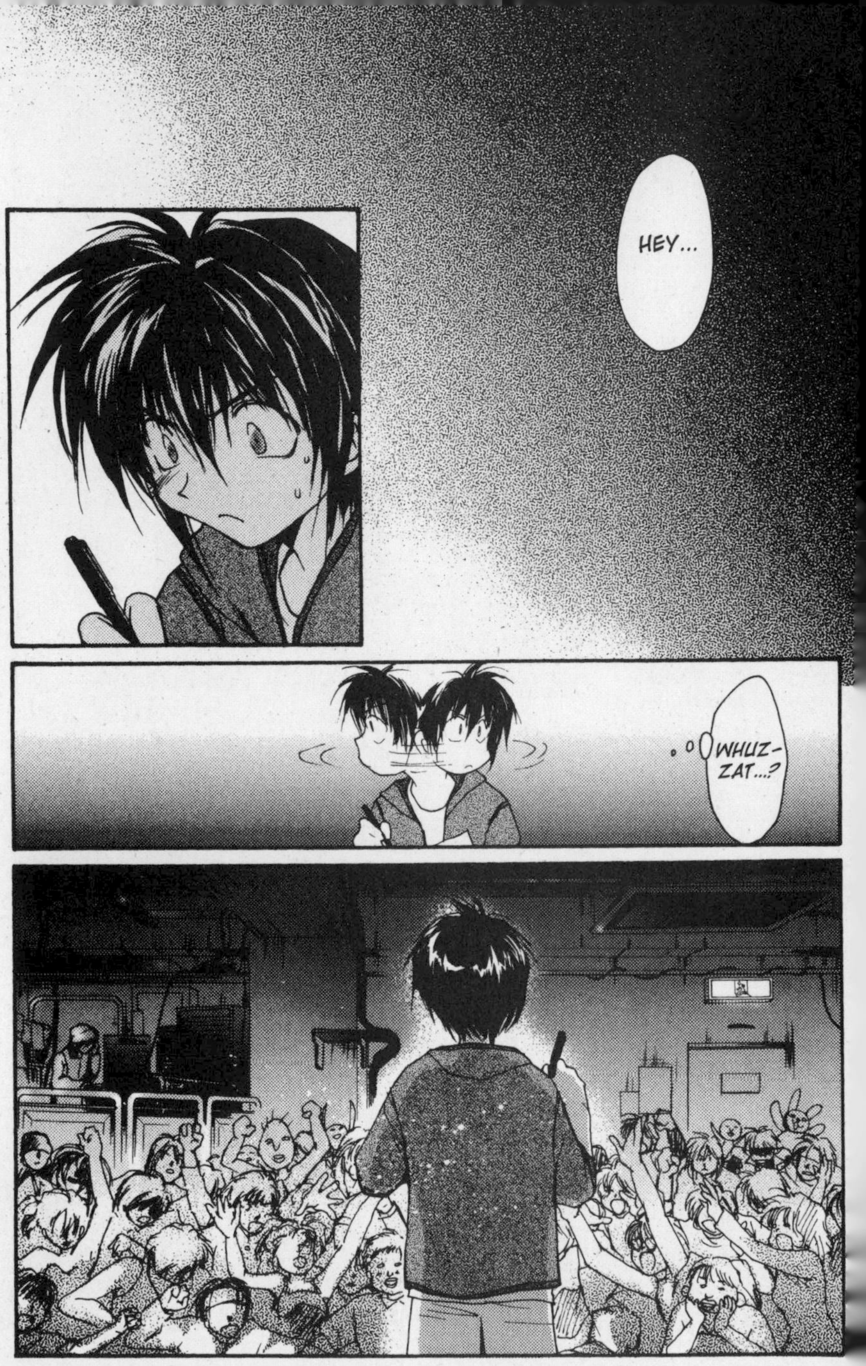
HEY...
WHUZ-ZAT...?

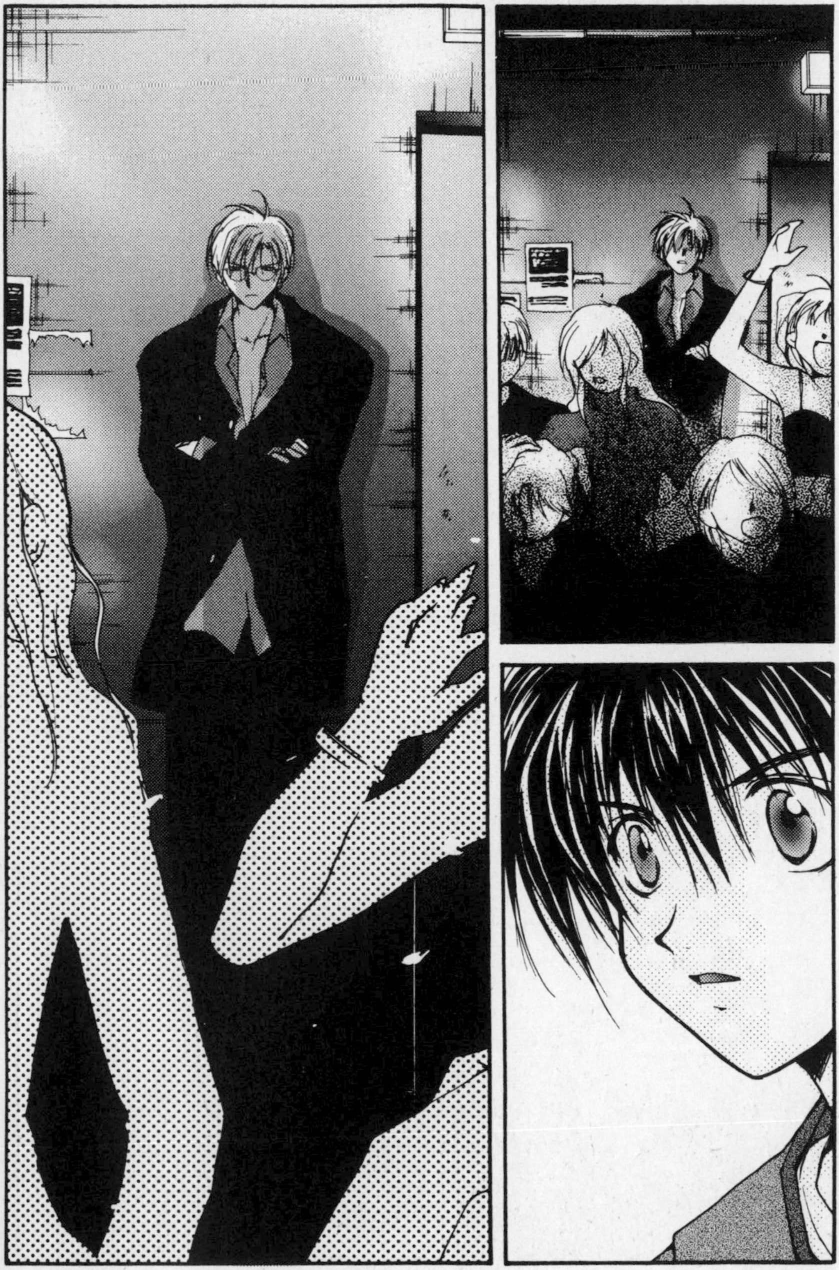

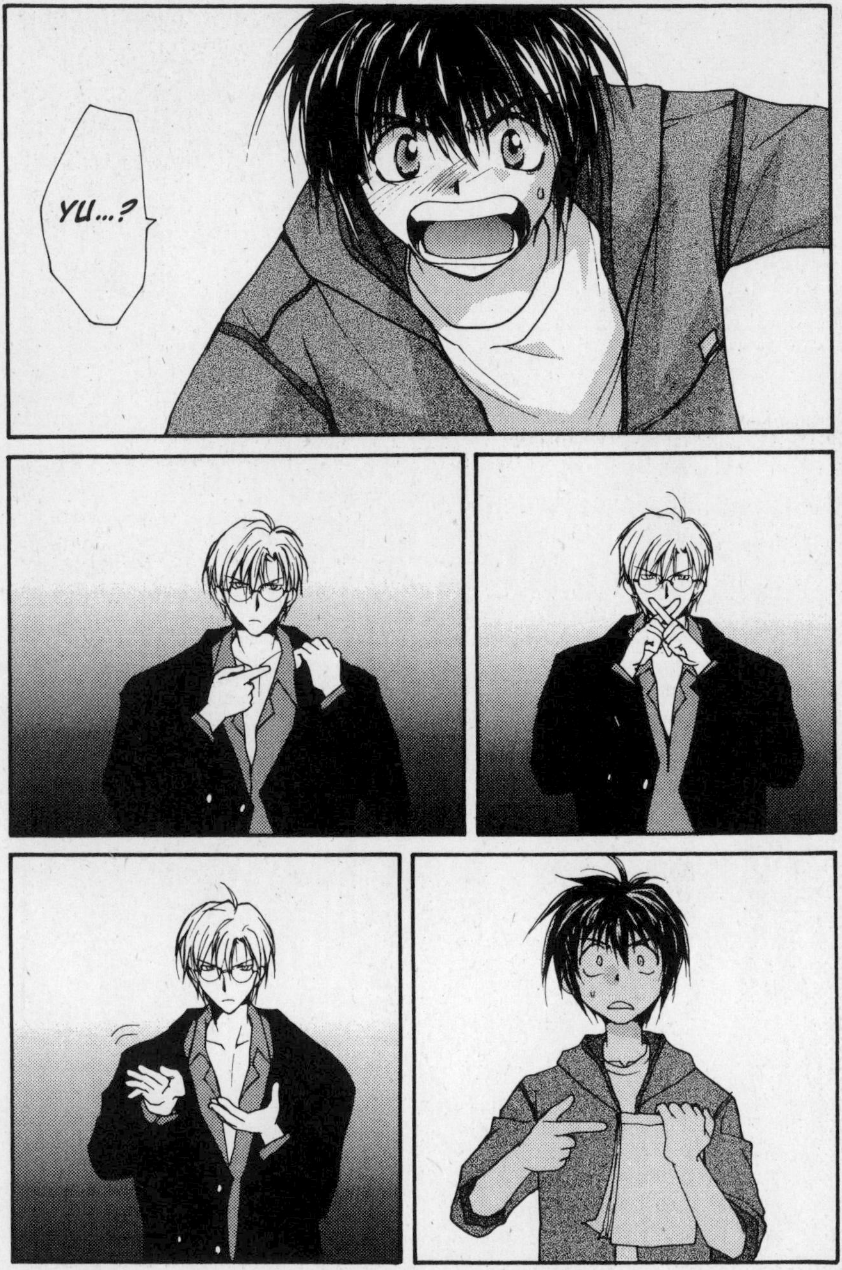
YU...?

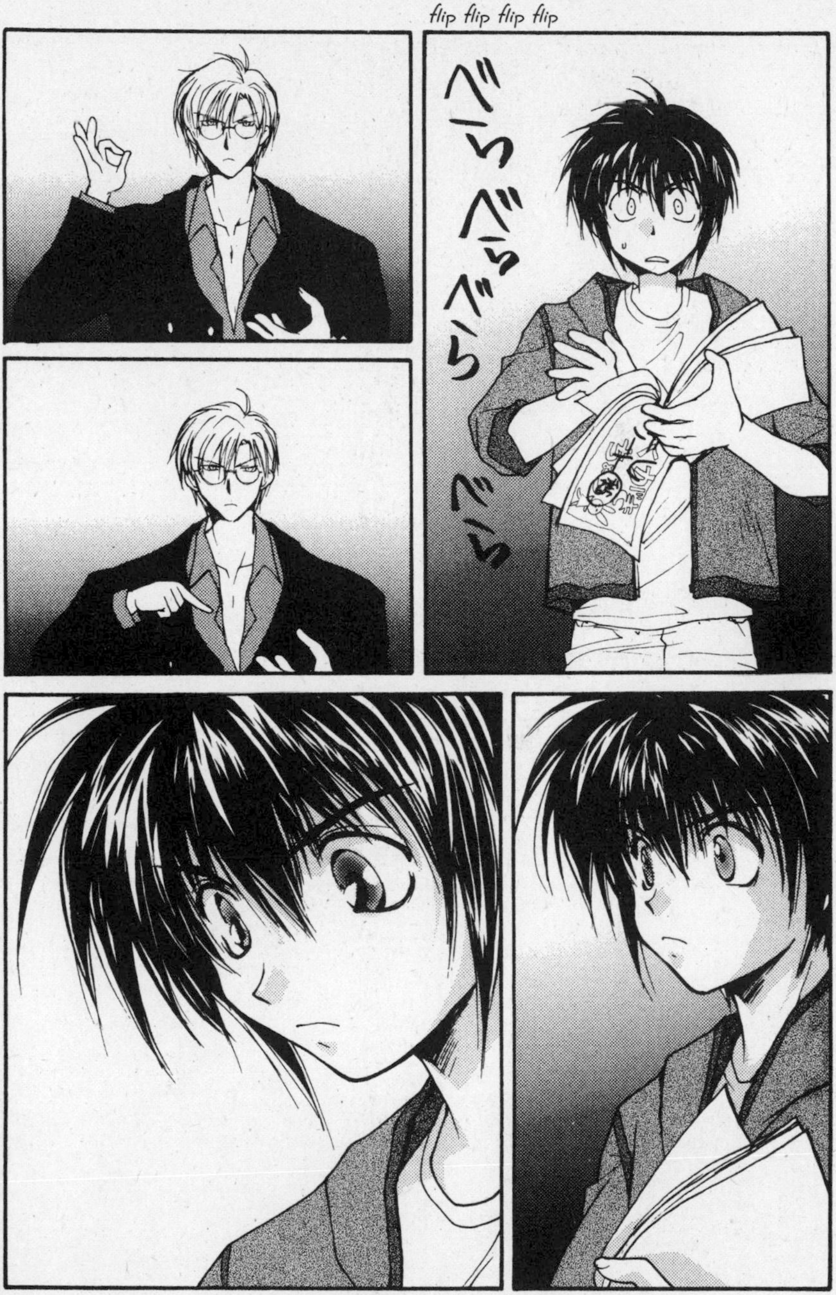
flip flip flip flip
ぺらぺらぺら
ぺら

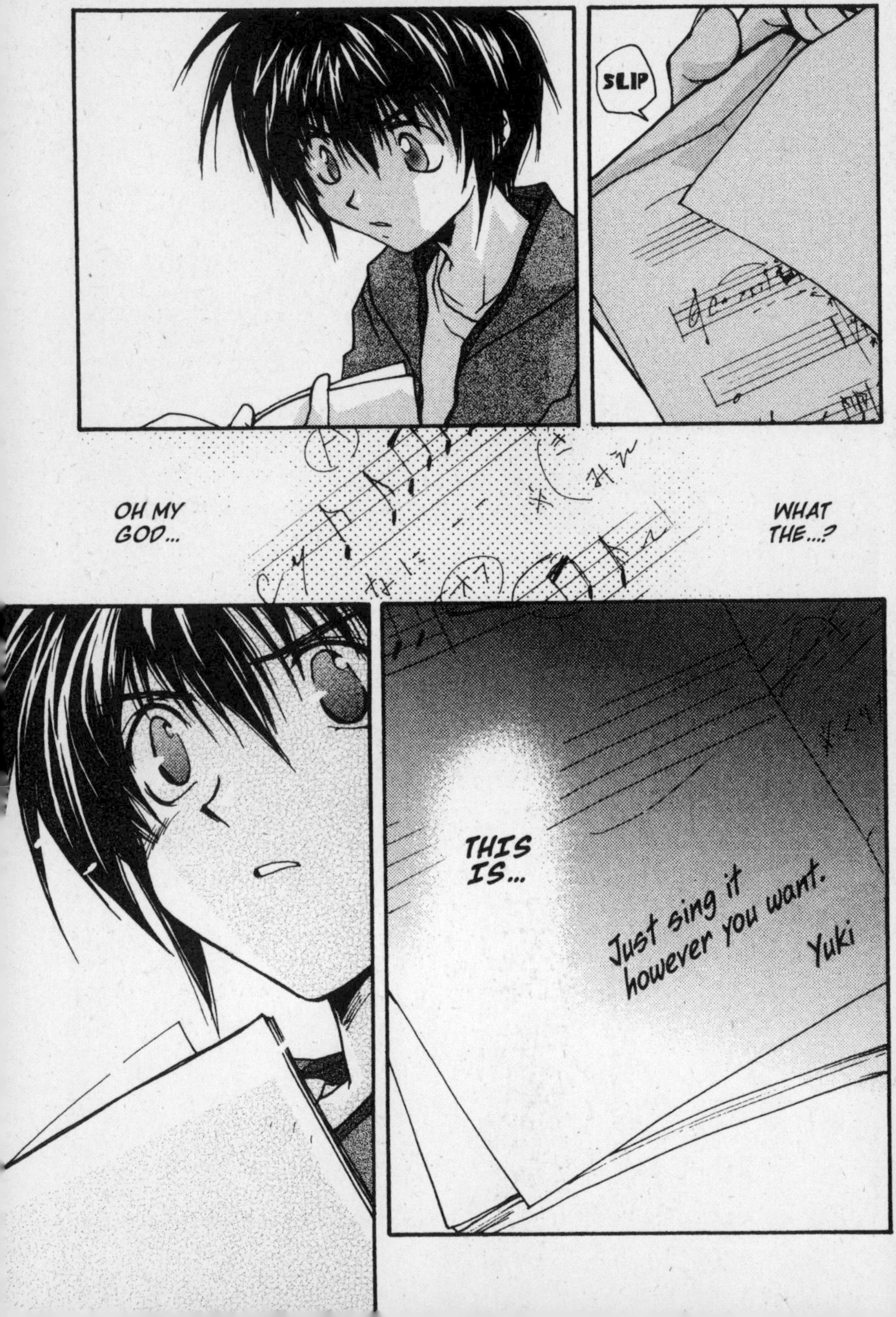
SLIP
WHAT THE...?
OH MY GOD...
THIS IS...
Just sing it however you want.
Yuki

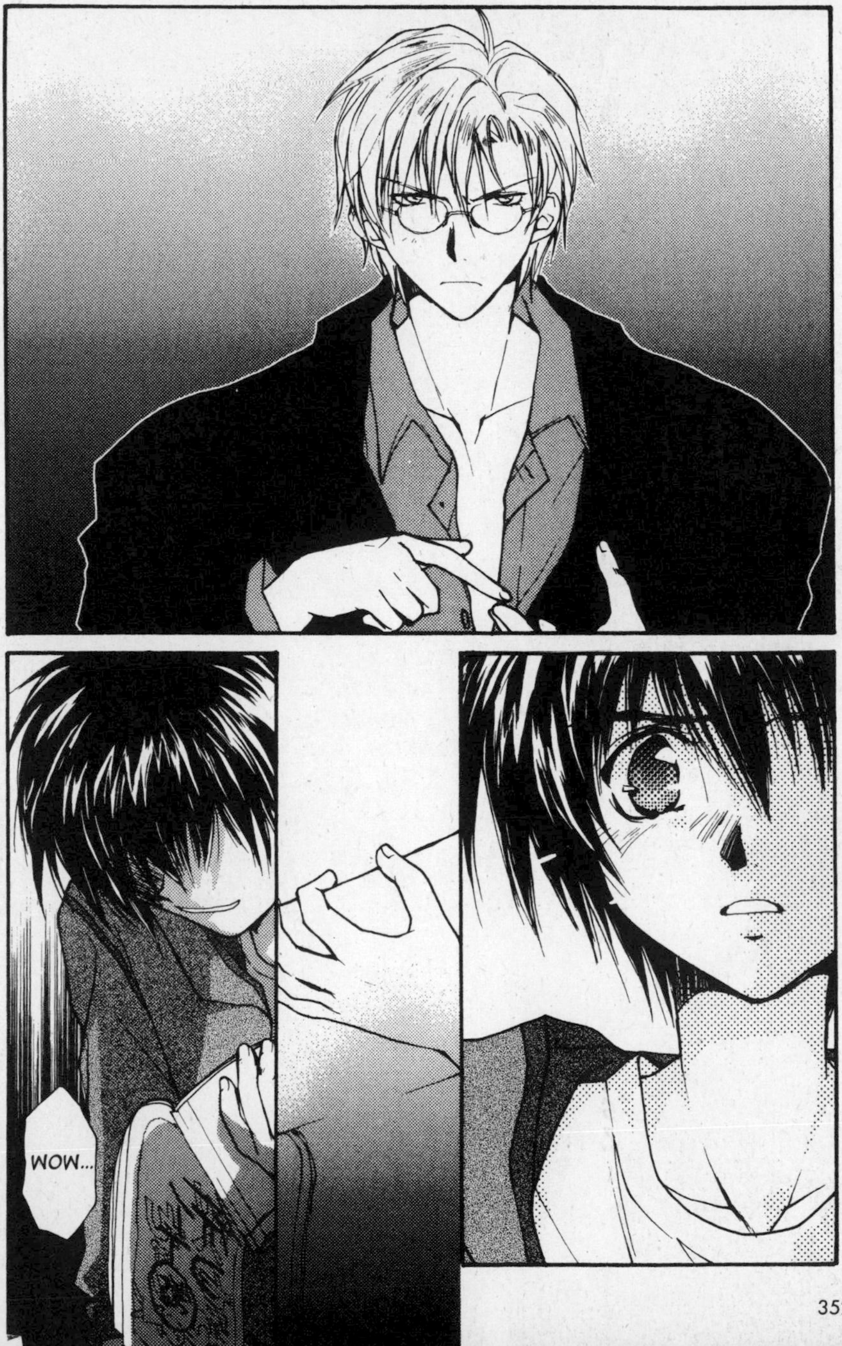
WOW...

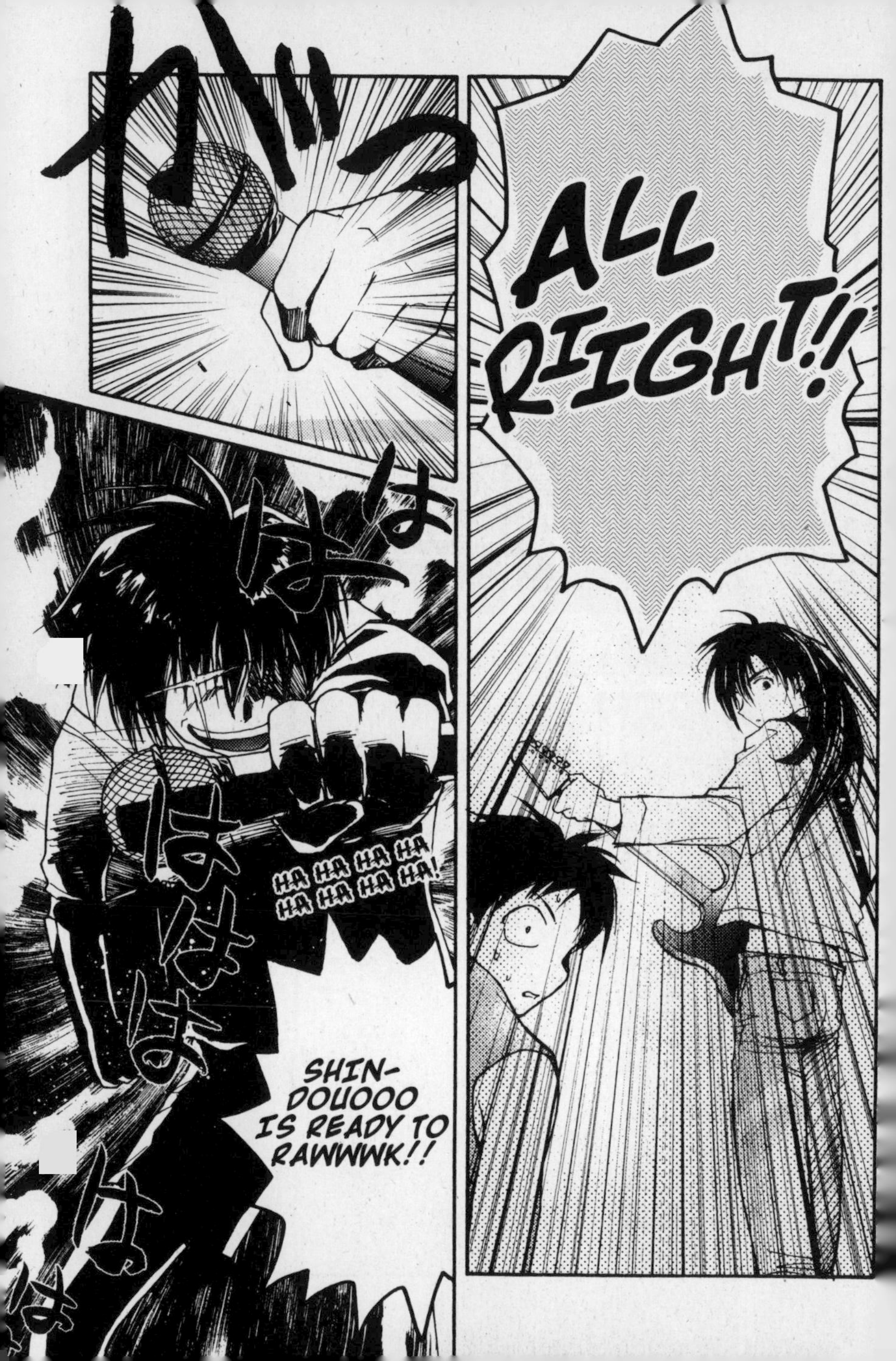
ALL RIIGHT!!
HA HA HA HA HA HA HA HA HA!
SHIN-DOUOOO IS READY TO RAWWWK!!

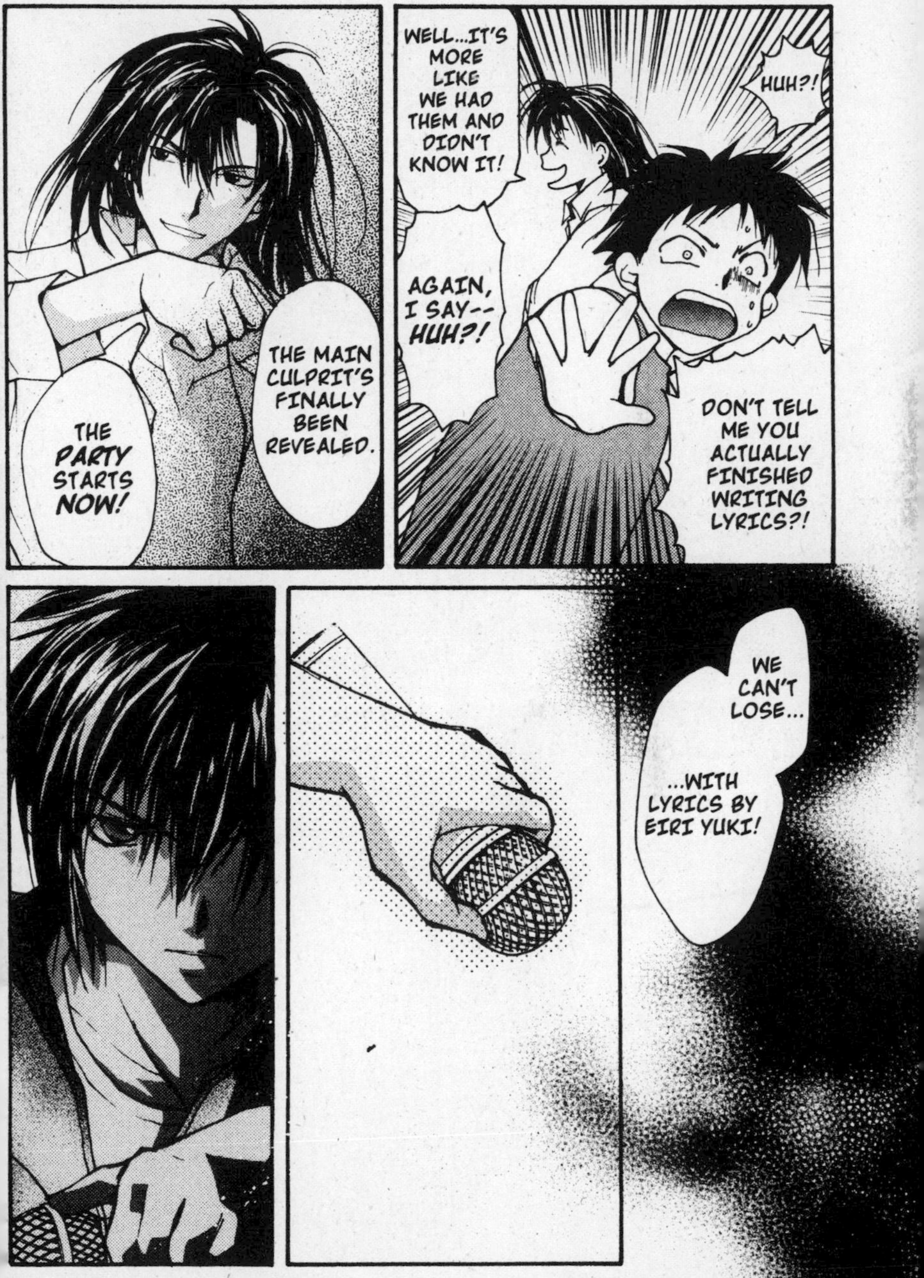
HUH?!
DON'T TELL ME YOU ACTUALLY FINISHED WRITING LYRICS?!
WELL...IT'S MORE LIKE WE HAD THEM AND DIDN'T KNOW IT!
AGAIN, I SAY--HUH?!
THE MAIN CULPRIT'S FINALLY BEEN REVEALED.
THE PARTY STARTS NOW!
WE CAN'T LOSE...
...WITH LYRICS BY EIRI YUKI!

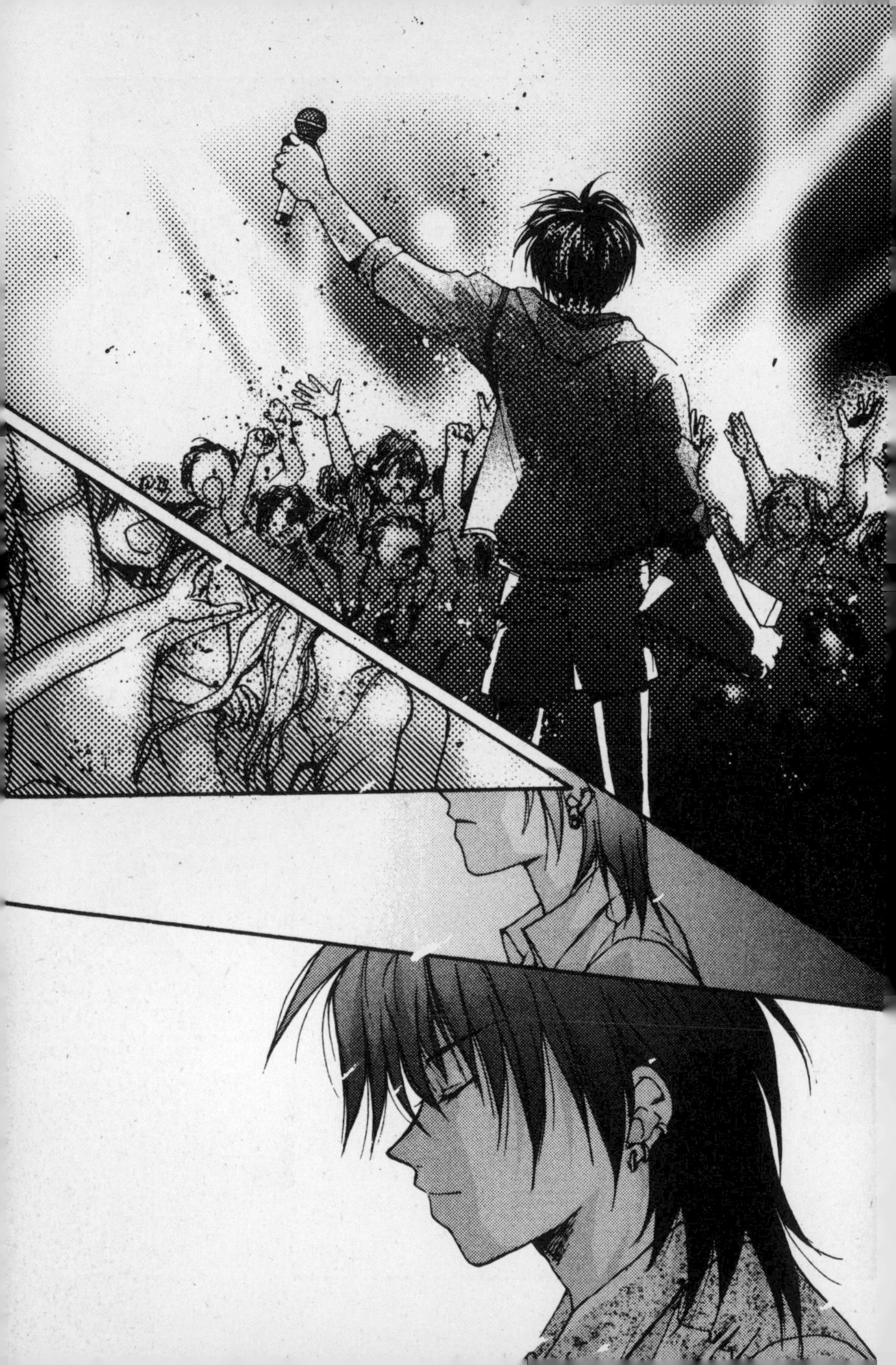

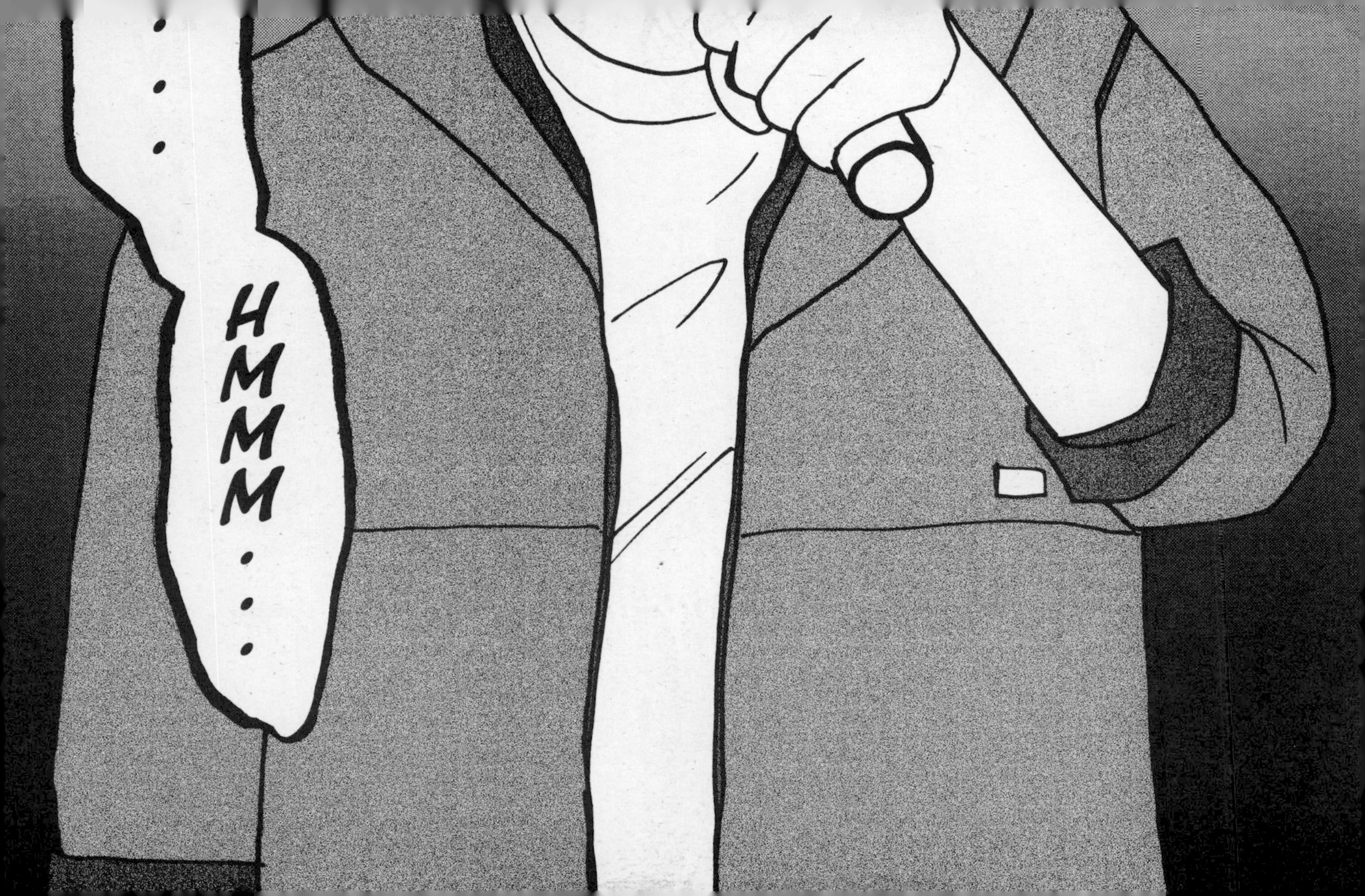
...
HMMM...

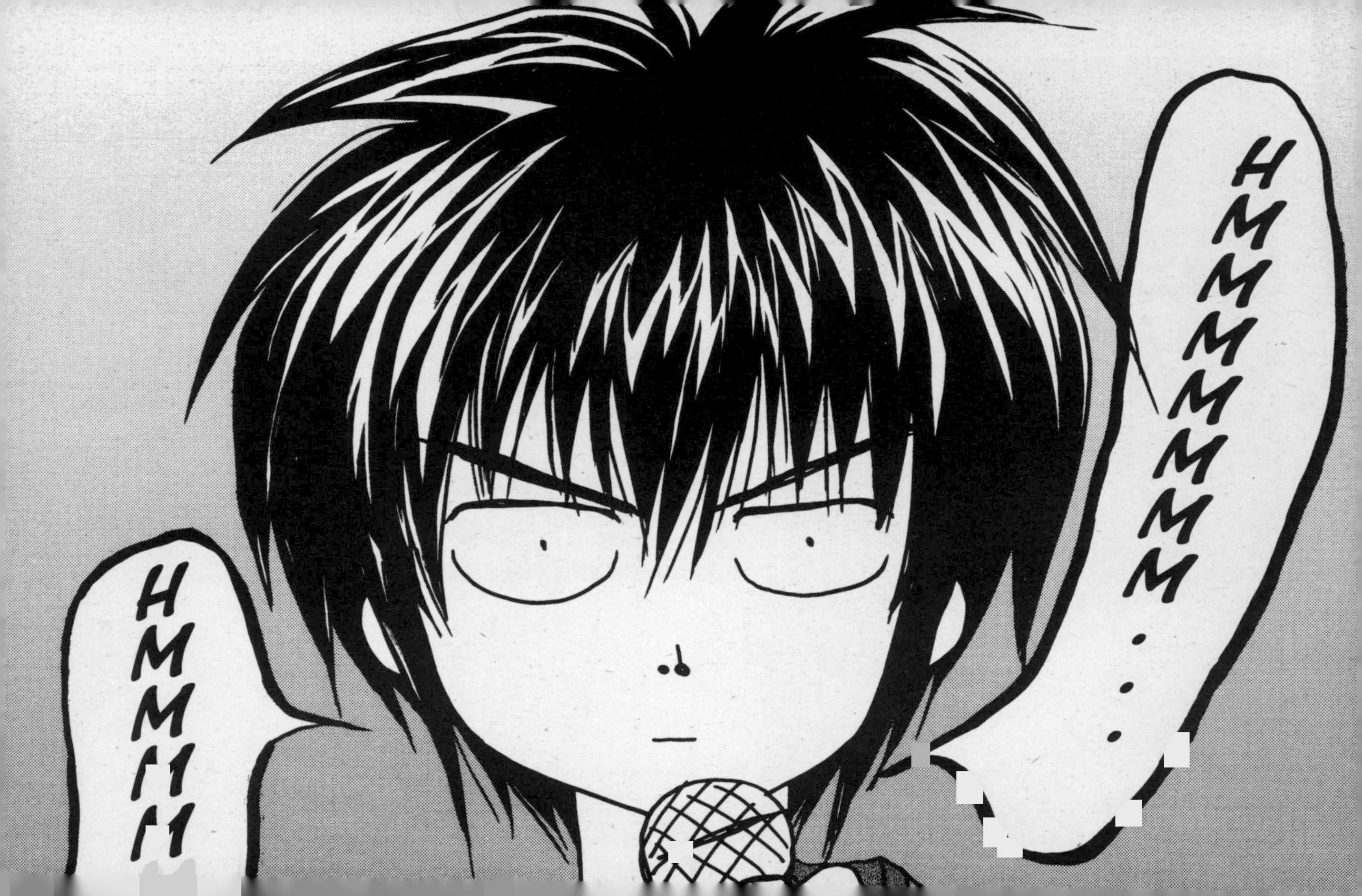
HMMMMMMM...
HMM!!

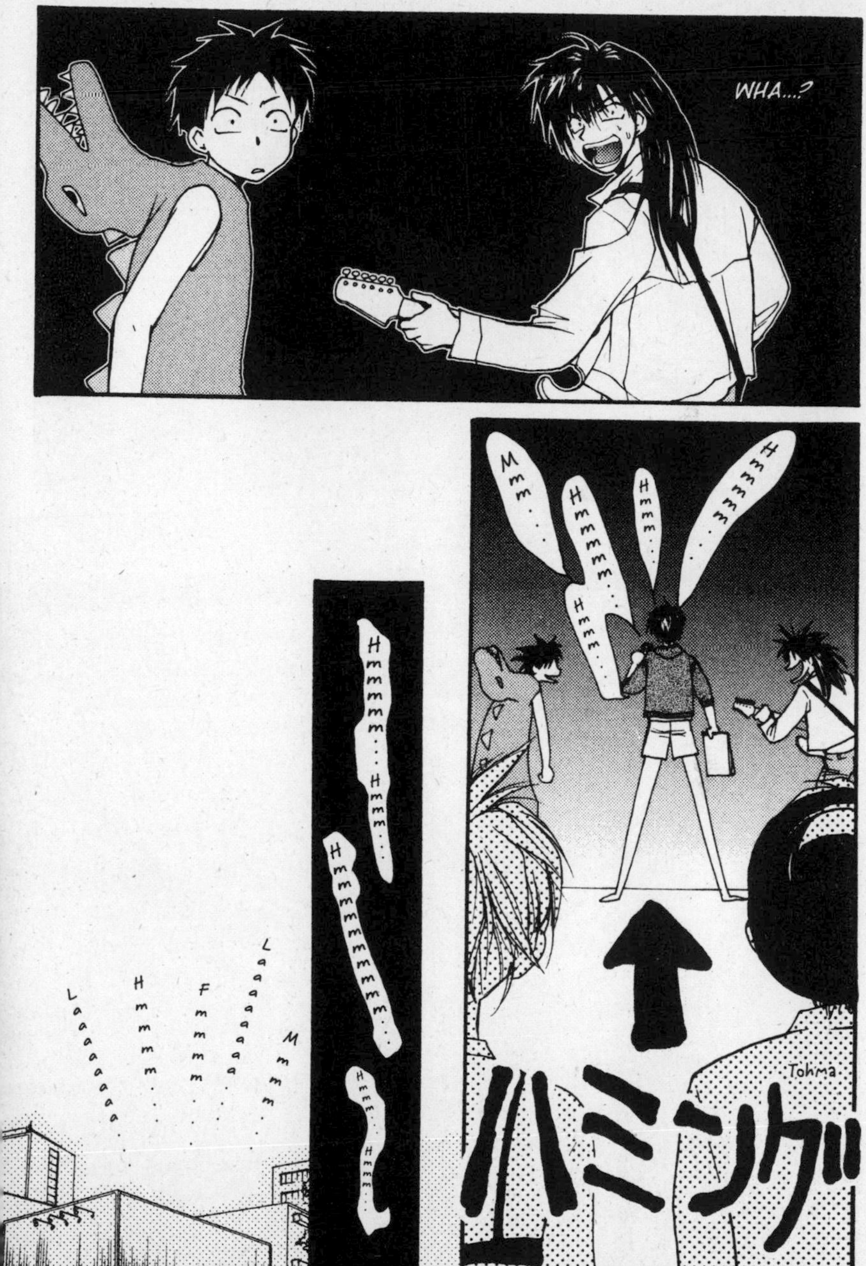
WHA...?
Hmmmmmm...
Hmmmm...
Hmmmmmm...
Hmmmm...
Mmm...
Tohma
ハミング
HUMMING
Hmmmmm... Hmmm...
Hmmmmmmmmmmm...
Hmmm... Hmmm...
Eiri
Mmmm...
Laaaaaaa...
Fmmmm...
Hmmmm...
Laaaaaaaa...

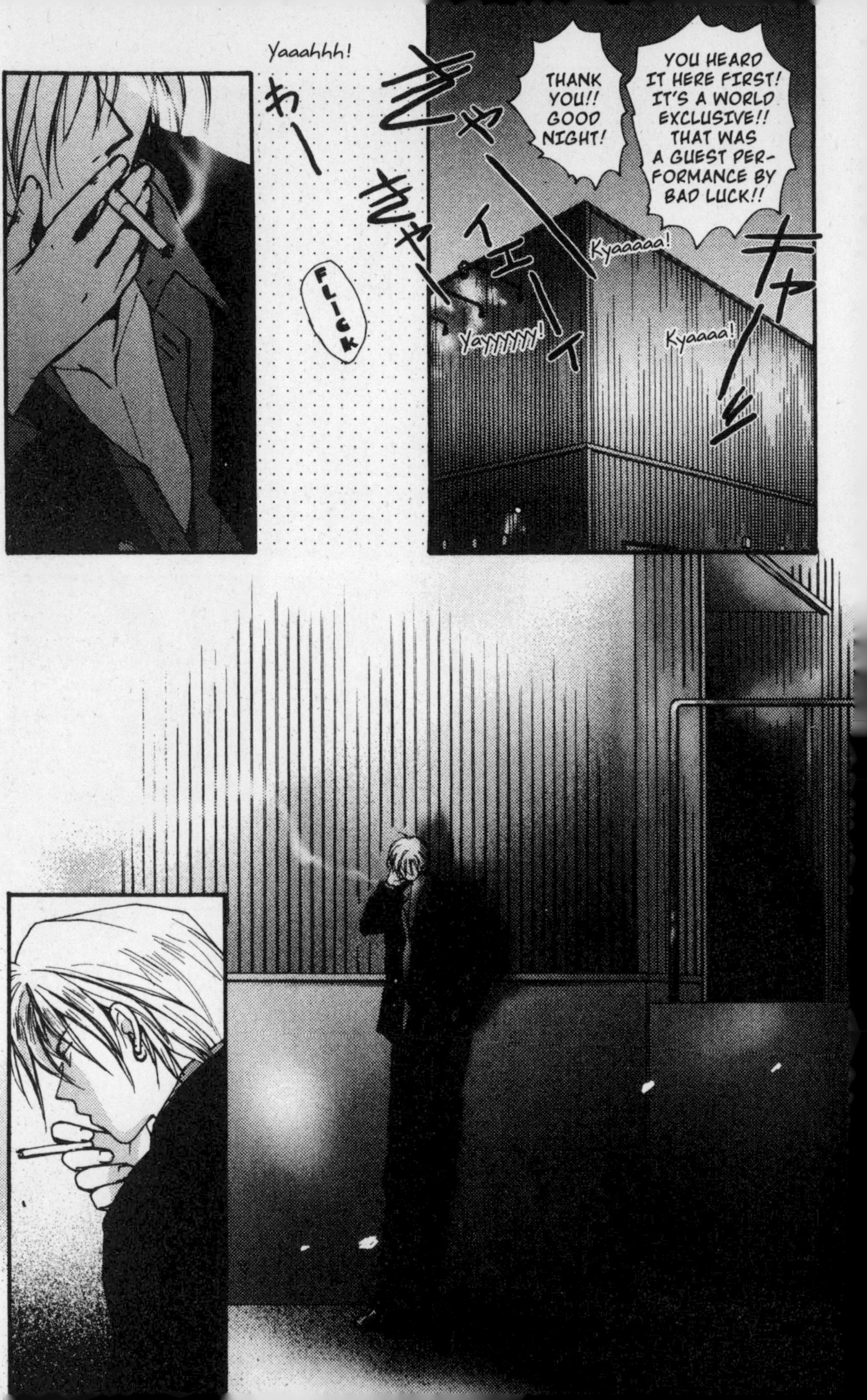
YOU HEARD IT HERE FIRST! IT'S A WORLD EXCLUSIVE!! THAT WAS A GUEST PERFORMANCE BY BAD LUCK!!
THANK YOU!! GOOD NIGHT!
Kyaaaaa!
Kyaaaa!
Yayyyyyy!
Yaaahhh!
FLICK

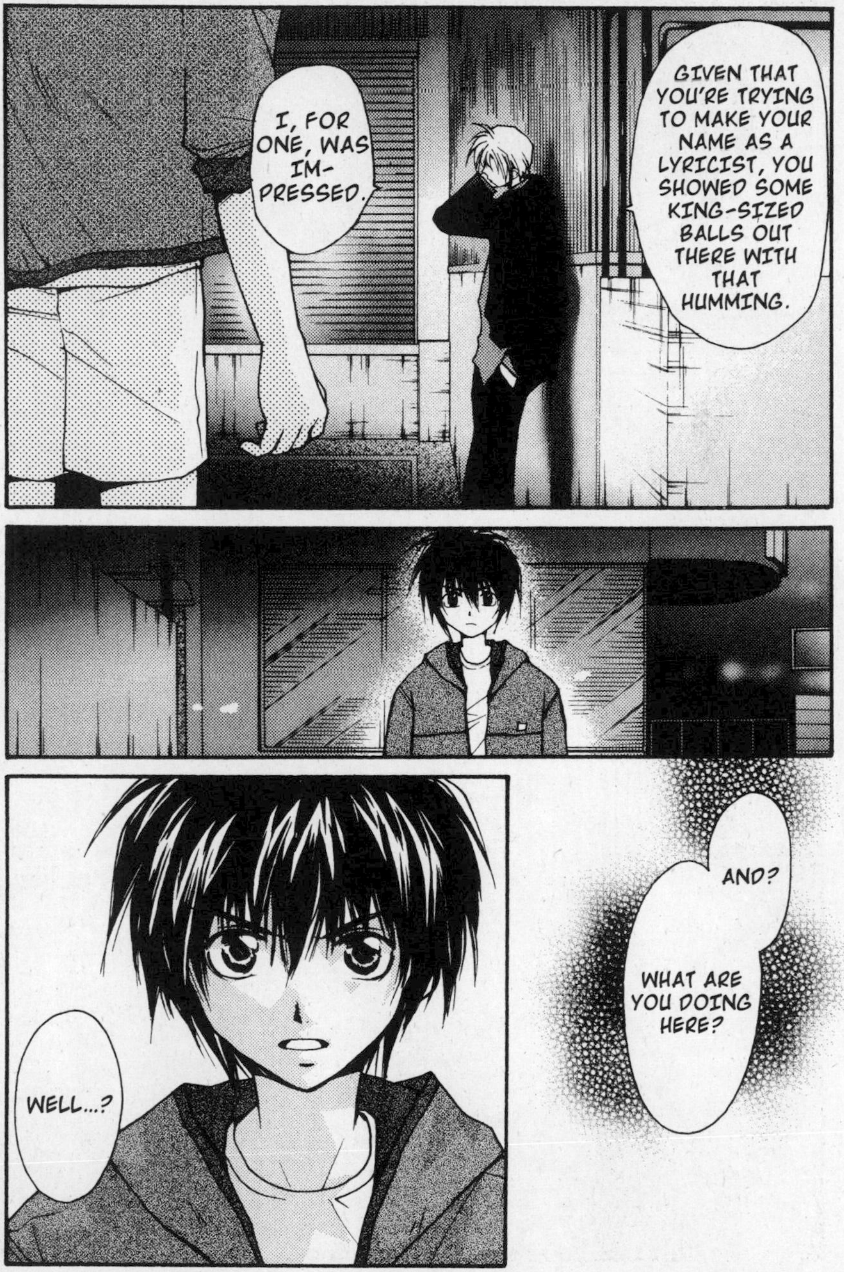
GIVEN THAT YOU'RE TRYING TO MAKE YOUR NAME AS A LYRICIST, YOU SHOWED SOME KING-SIZED BALLS OUT THERE WITH THAT HUMMING.
I, FOR ONE, WAS IM- PRESSED.
AND?
WHAT ARE YOU DOING HERE?
WELL...?

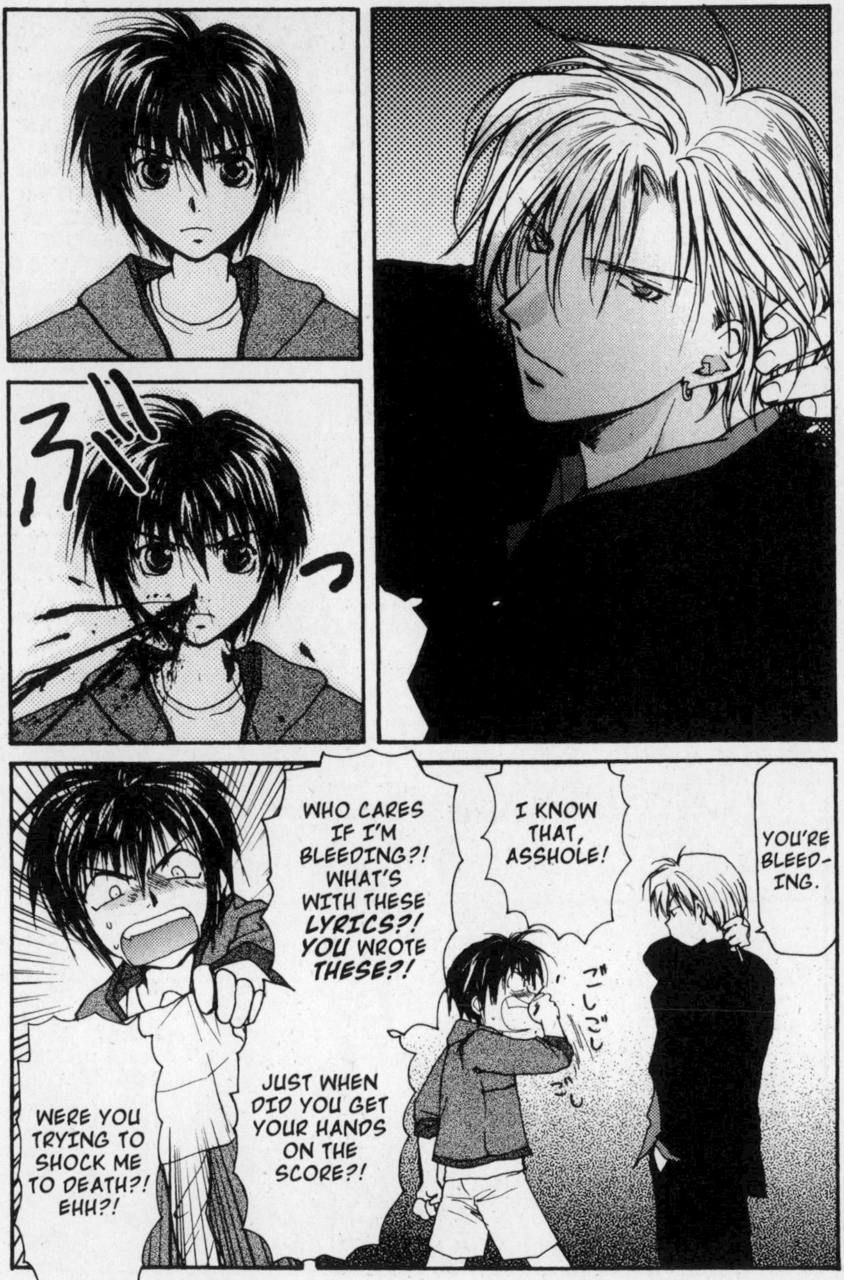
YOU'RE BLEED-ING.
I KNOW THAT, ASSHOLE!
ごしごし
ごし
WHO CARES IF I'M BLEEDING?! WHAT'S WITH THESE LYRICS?! YOU WROTE THESE?!
JUST WHEN DID YOU GET YOUR HANDS ON THE SCORE?!
WERE YOU TRYING TO SHOCK ME TO DEATH?! EHH?!

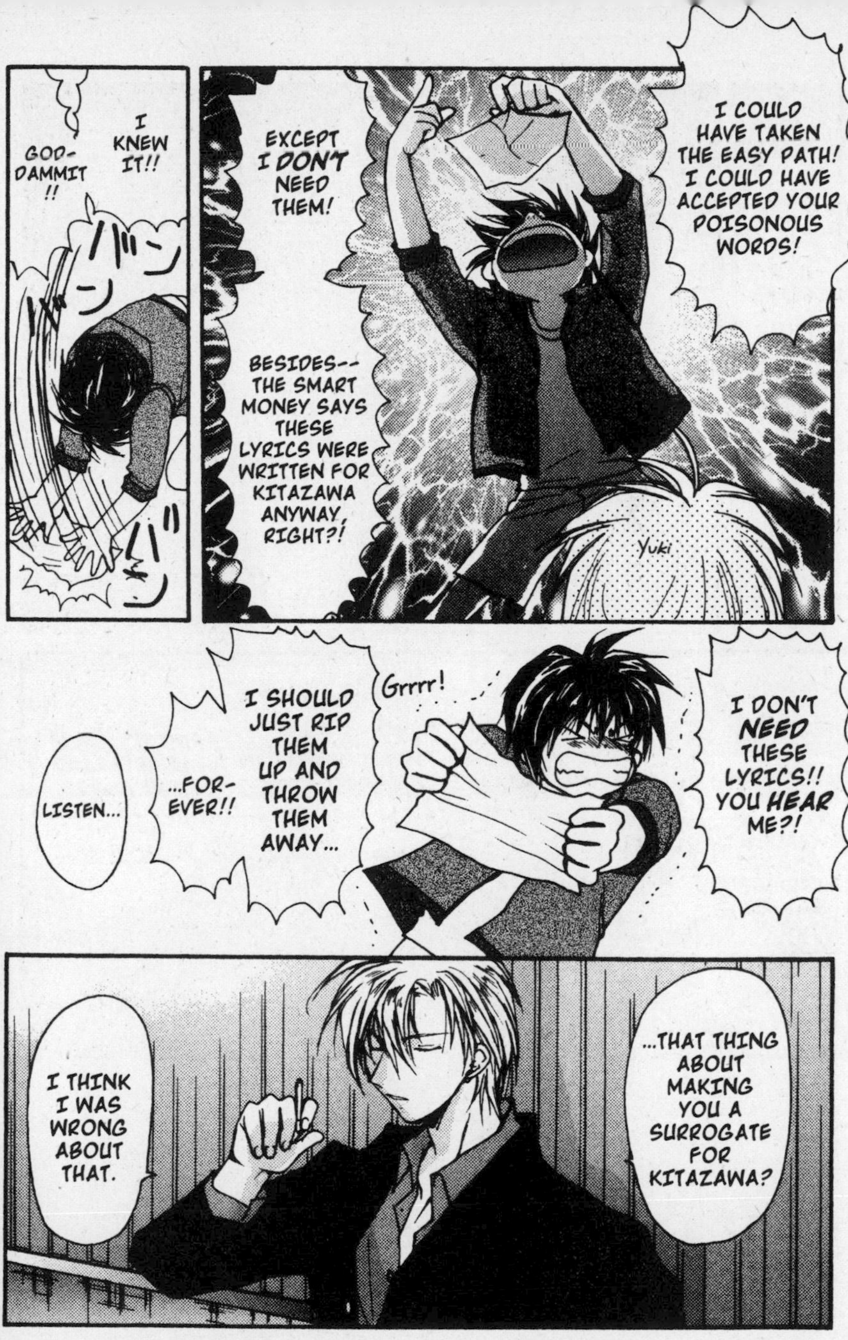
I COULD HAVE TAKEN THE EASY PATH! I COULD HAVE ACCEPTED YOUR POISONOUS WORDS!
EXCEPT I **DON'T** NEED THEM!
BESIDES-- THE SMART MONEY SAYS THESE LYRICS WERE WRITTEN FOR KITAZAWA ANYWAY, RIGHT?!
Yuki
I KNEW IT!!
GOD-DAMMIT!!
I DON'T **NEED** THESE LYRICS!! YOU **HEAR** ME?!
Grrrr!
I SHOULD JUST RIP THEM UP AND THROW THEM AWAY...
...FOR-EVER!!
LISTEN...
...THAT THING ABOUT MAKING YOU A SURROGATE FOR KITAZAWA?
I THINK I WAS WRONG ABOUT THAT.

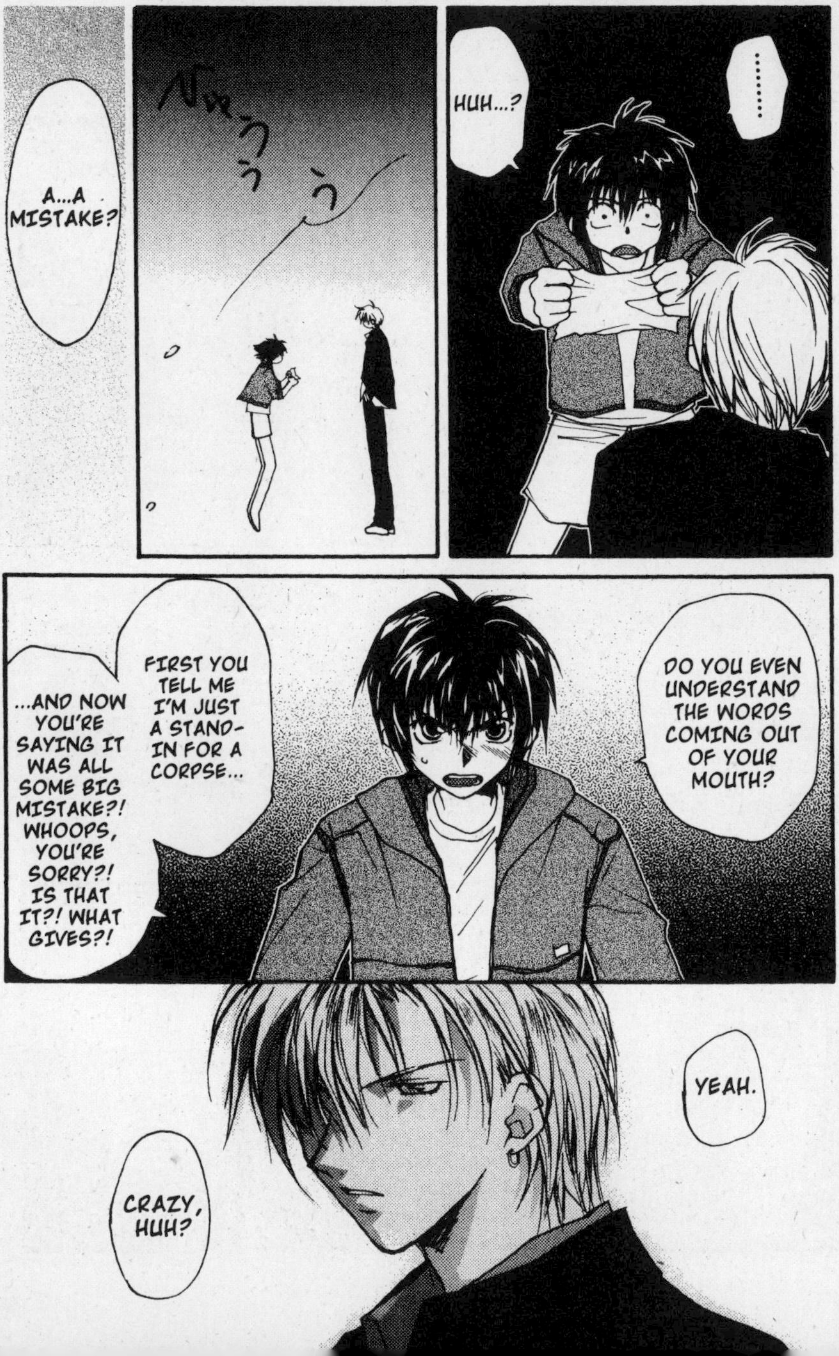
......
HUH...?
A...A MISTAKE?
DO YOU EVEN UNDERSTAND THE WORDS COMING OUT OF YOUR MOUTH?
FIRST YOU TELL ME I'M JUST A STAND-IN FOR A CORPSE...
...AND NOW YOU'RE SAYING IT WAS ALL SOME BIG MISTAKE?! WHOOPS, YOU'RE SORRY?! IS THAT IT?! WHAT GIVES?!
YEAH.
CRAZY, HUH?

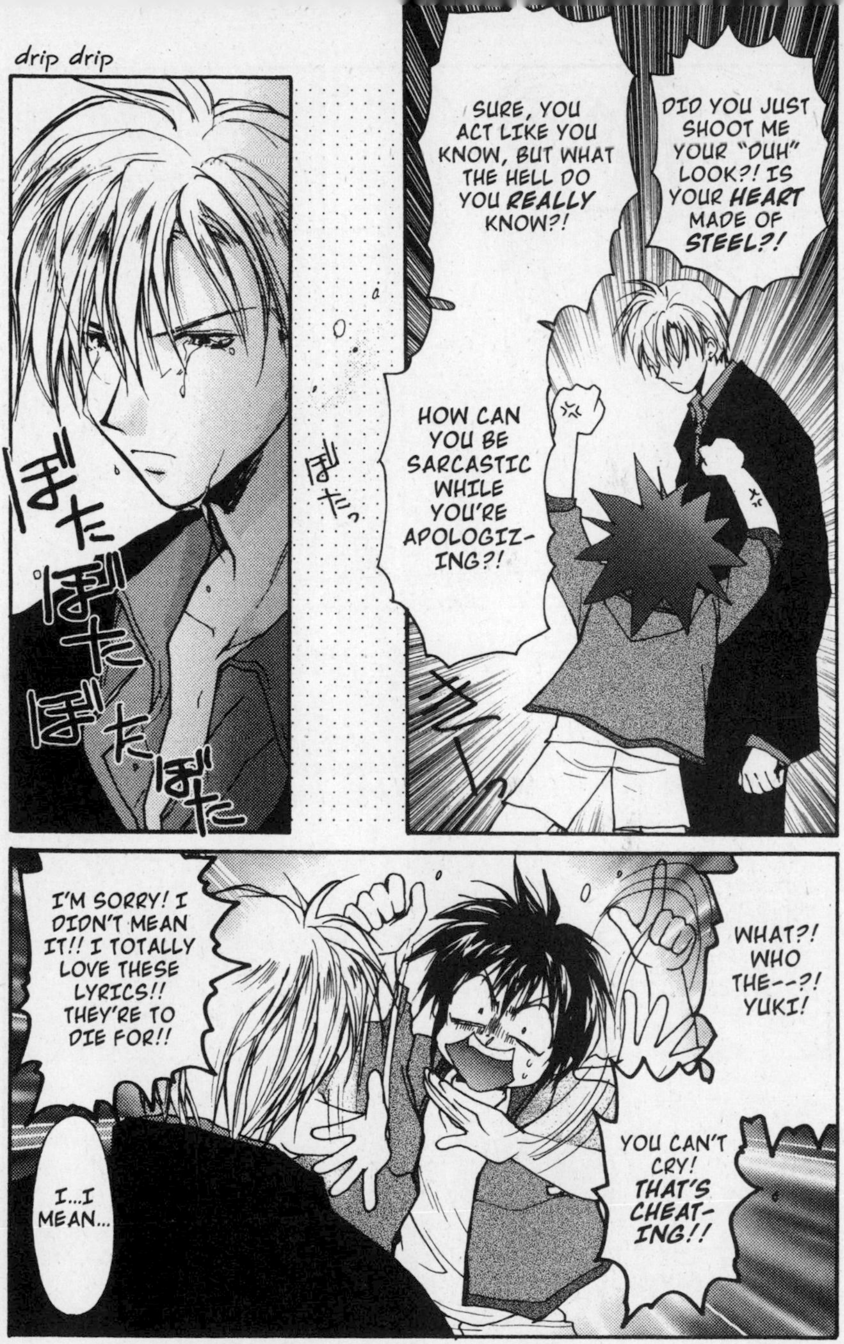
DID YOU JUST SHOOT ME YOUR "DUH" LOOK?! IS YOUR **HEART** MADE OF **STEEL?!**
SURE, YOU ACT LIKE YOU KNOW, BUT WHAT THE HELL DO YOU **REALLY** KNOW?!
HOW CAN YOU BE SARCASTIC WHILE YOU'RE APOLOGIZING?!
drip drip
WHAT?! WHO THE--?! YUKI!
YOU CAN'T CRY! **THAT'S CHEATING!!**
I'M SORRY! I DIDN'T MEAN IT!! I TOTALLY LOVE THESE LYRICS!! THEY'RE TO DIE FOR!!
I...I MEAN...

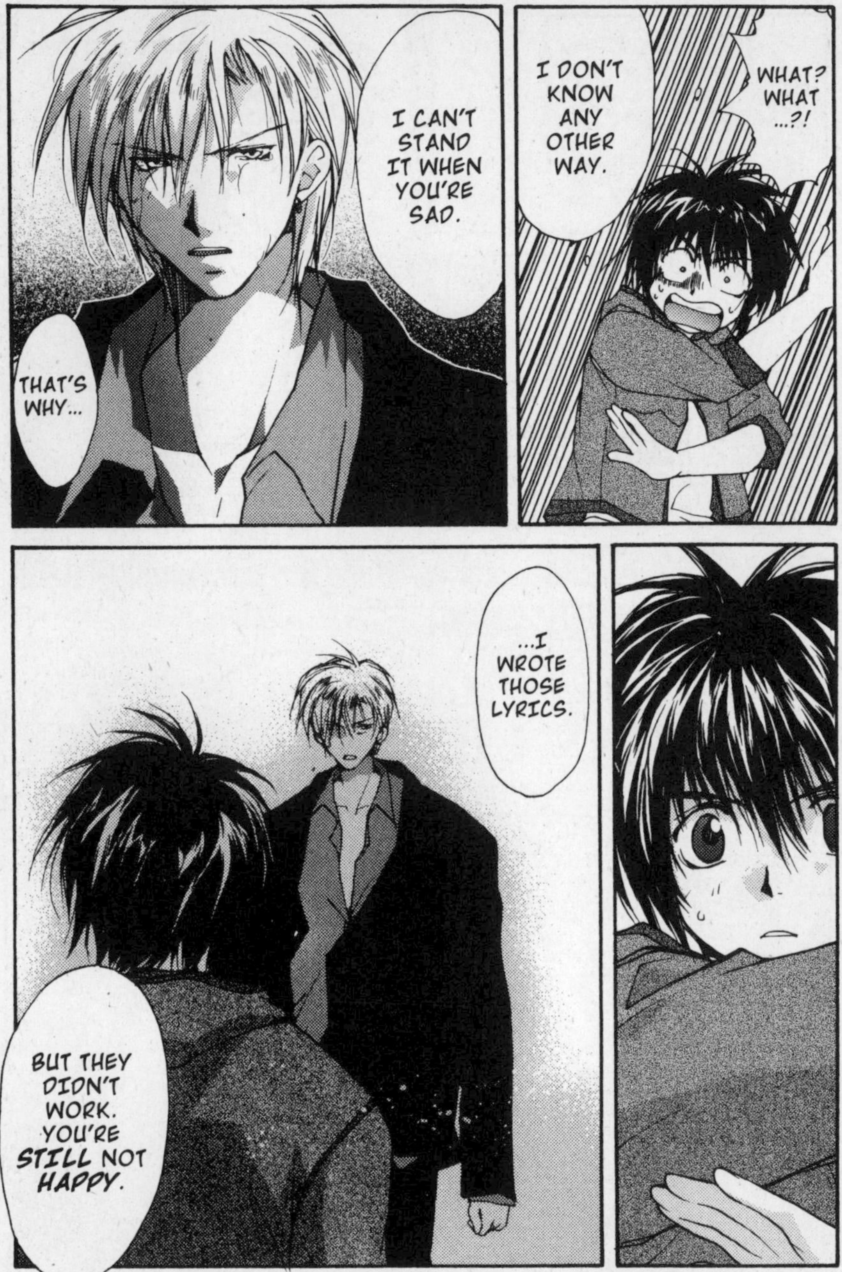
WHAT? WHAT ...?!
I DON'T KNOW ANY OTHER WAY.
I CAN'T STAND IT WHEN YOU'RE SAD.
THAT'S WHY...
...I WROTE THOSE LYRICS.
BUT THEY DIDN'T WORK. YOU'RE STILL NOT HAPPY.

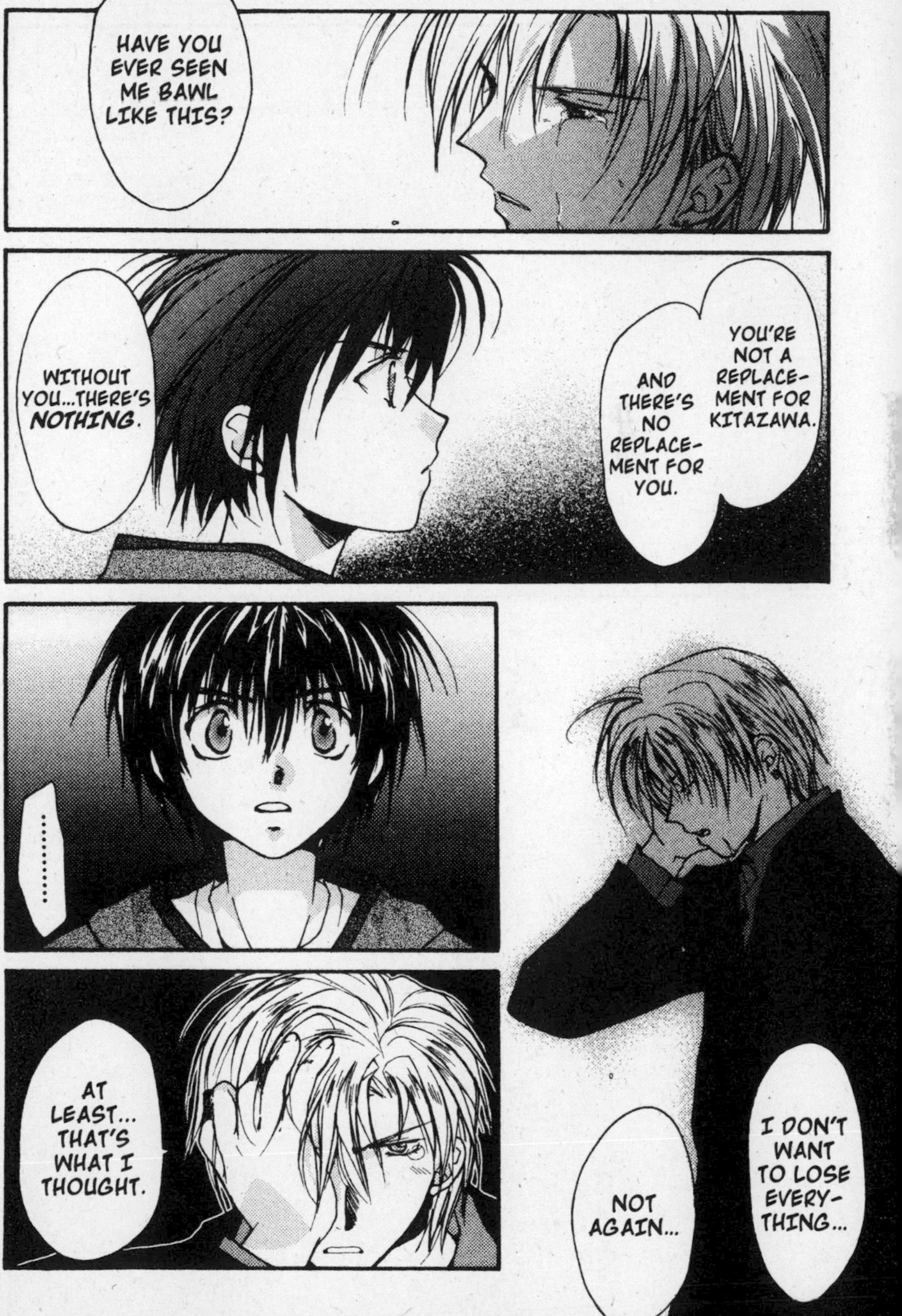
HAVE YOU EVER SEEN ME BAWL LIKE THIS?
YOU'RE NOT A REPLACEMENT FOR KITAZAWA.
AND THERE'S NO REPLACEMENT FOR YOU.
WITHOUT YOU...THERE'S NOTHING.
I DON'T WANT TO LOSE EVERYTHING...
NOT AGAIN...
......
AT LEAST... THAT'S WHAT I THOUGHT.

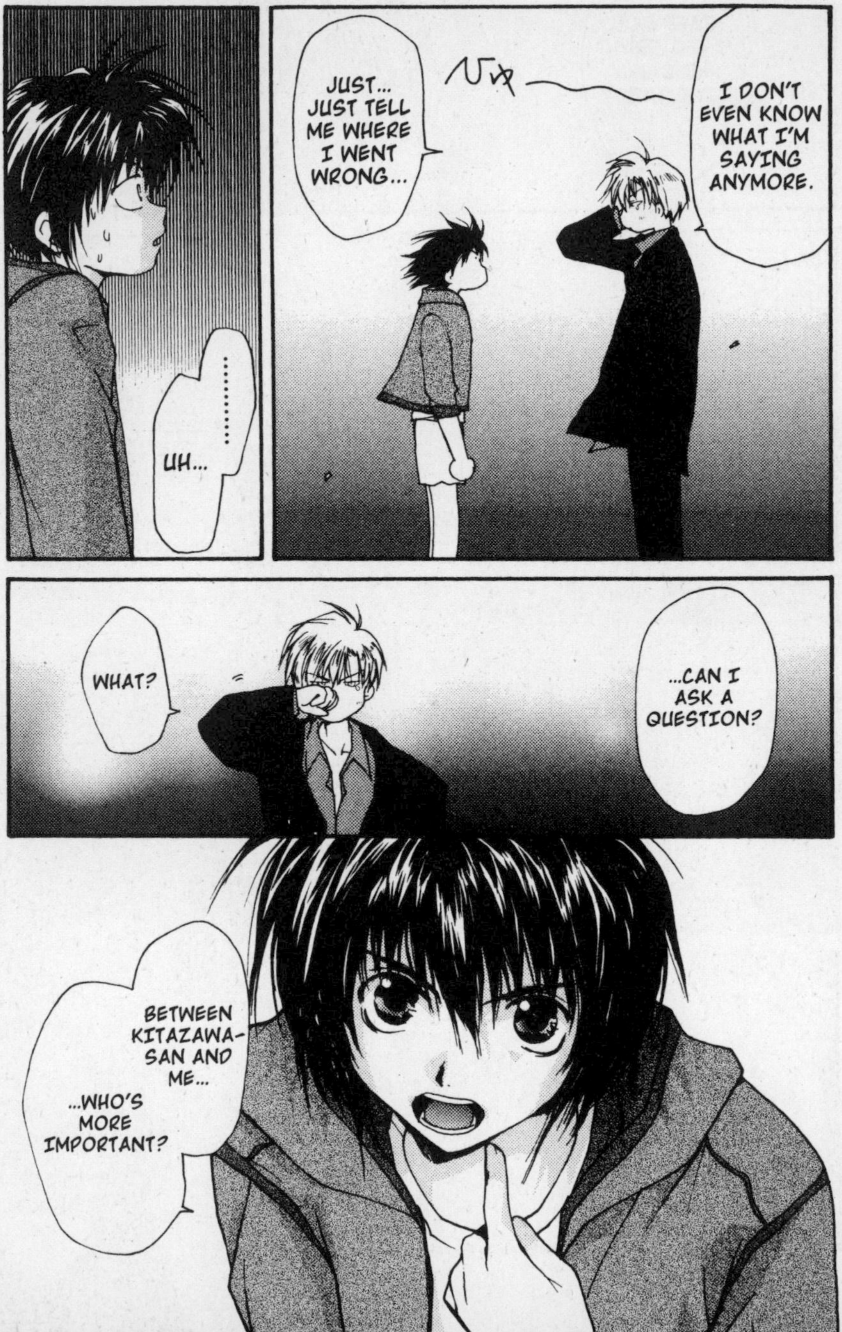
I DON'T EVEN KNOW WHAT I'M SAYING ANYMORE.
JUST... JUST TELL ME WHERE I WENT WRONG...
......
UH...
...CAN I ASK A QUESTION?
WHAT?
BETWEEN KITAZAWA-SAN AND ME...
...WHO'S MORE IMPORTANT?

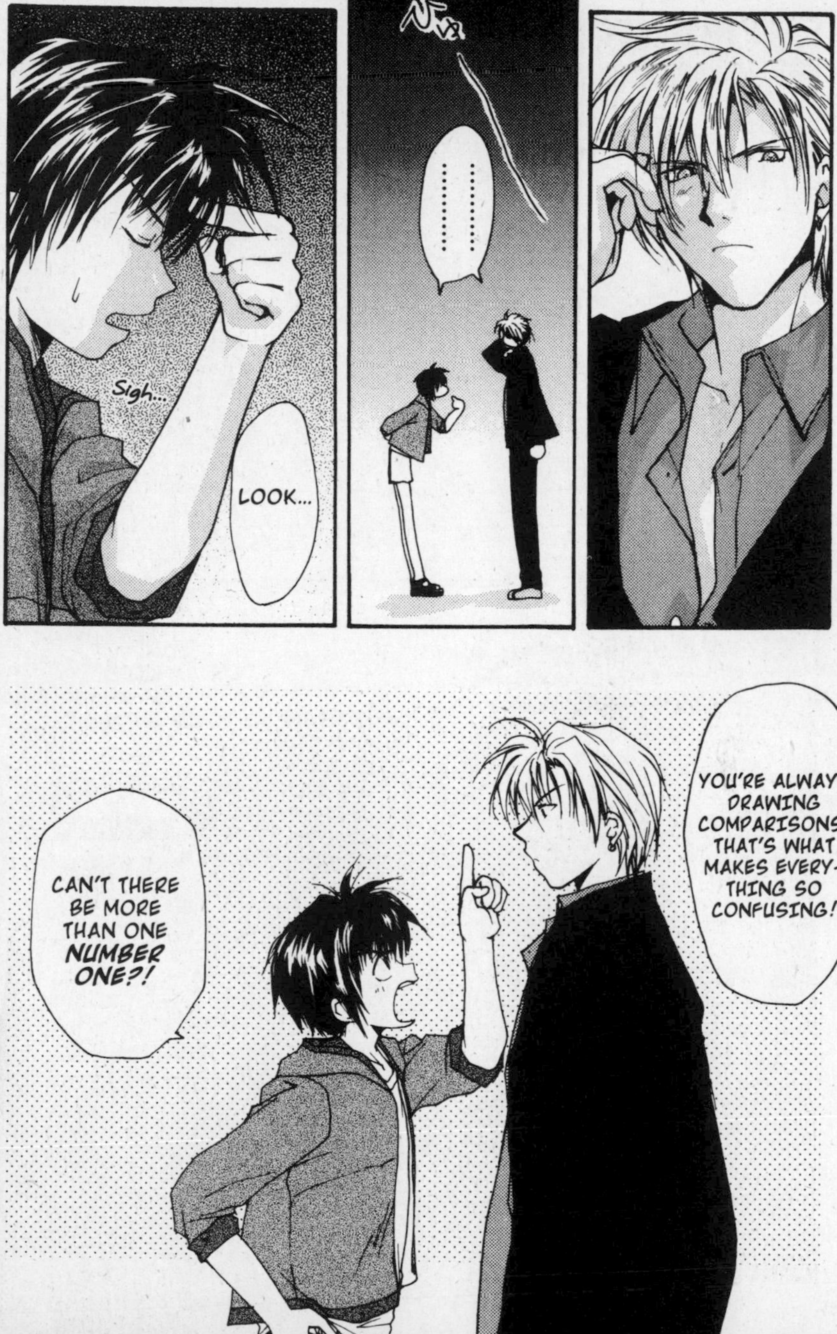
......
Sigh...
LOOK...
YOU'RE ALWAYS DRAWING COMPARISONS! THAT'S WHAT MAKES EVERY-THING SO CONFUSING!
CAN'T THERE BE MORE THAN ONE *NUMBER ONE?!*

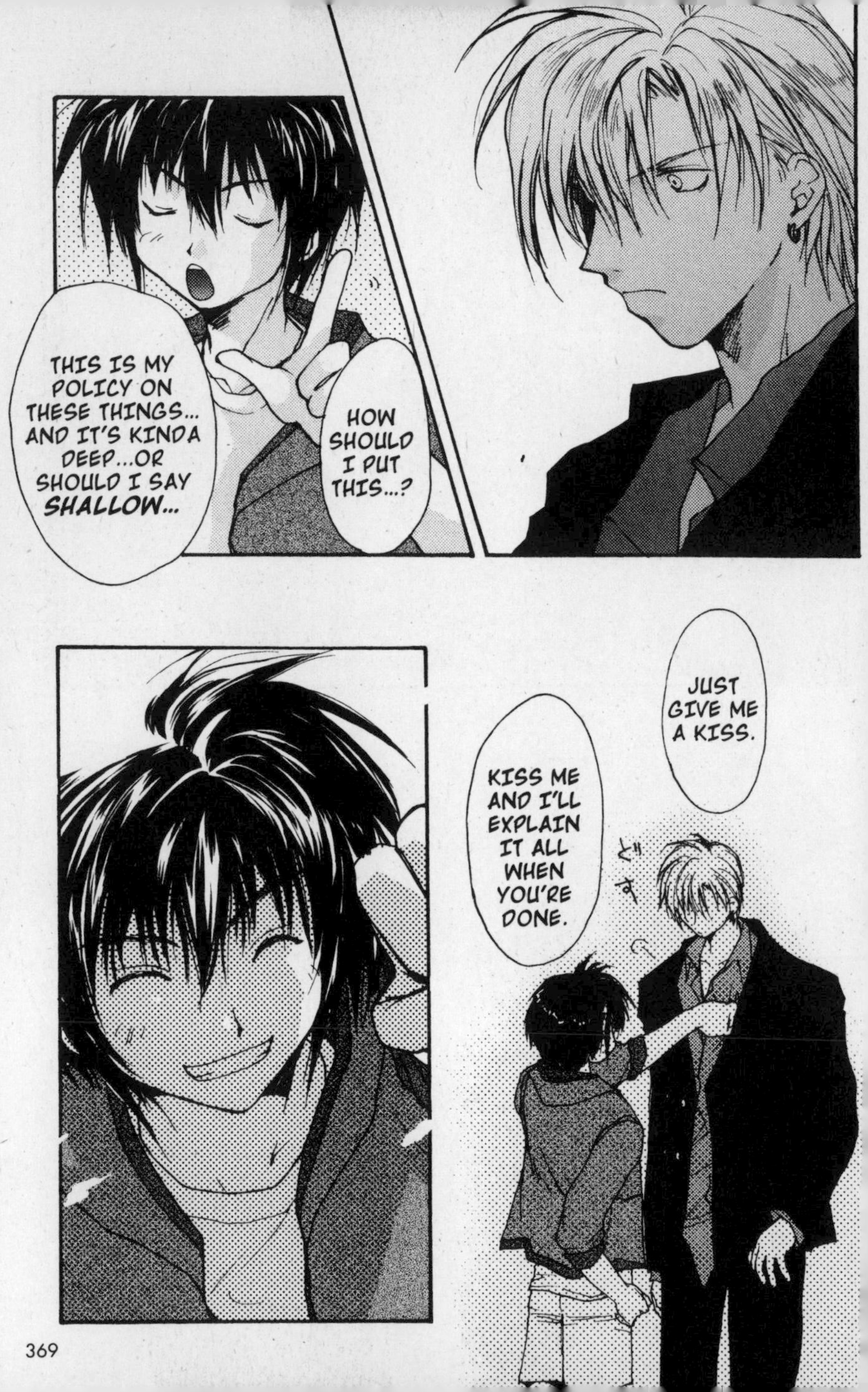
HOW SHOULD I PUT THIS...?
THIS IS MY POLICY ON THESE THINGS... AND IT'S KINDA DEEP...OR SHOULD I SAY **SHALLOW...**
JUST GIVE ME A KISS.
KISS ME AND I'LL EXPLAIN IT ALL WHEN YOU'RE DONE.

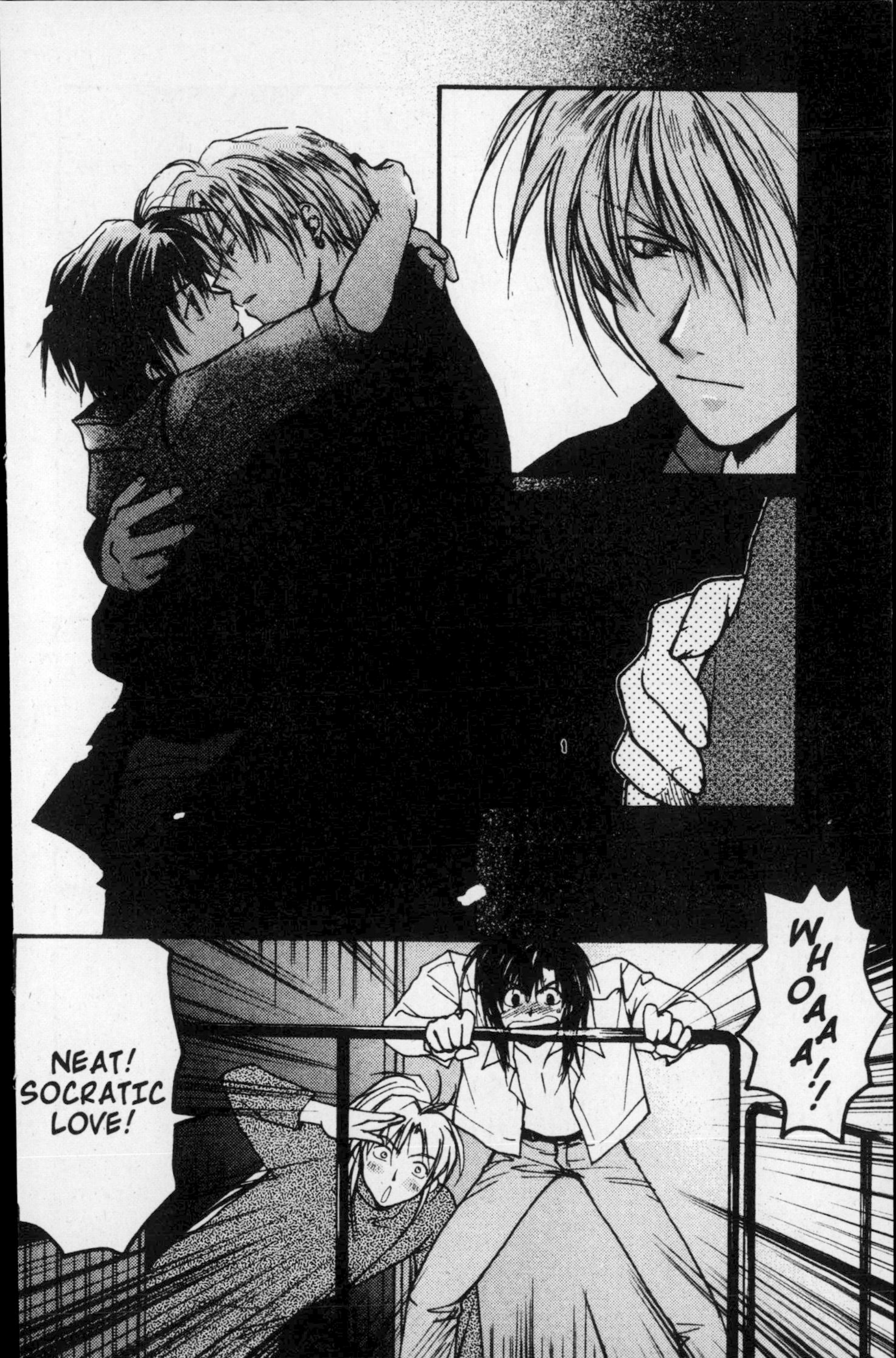
WHOAAA!!
NEAT! SOCRATIC LOVE!

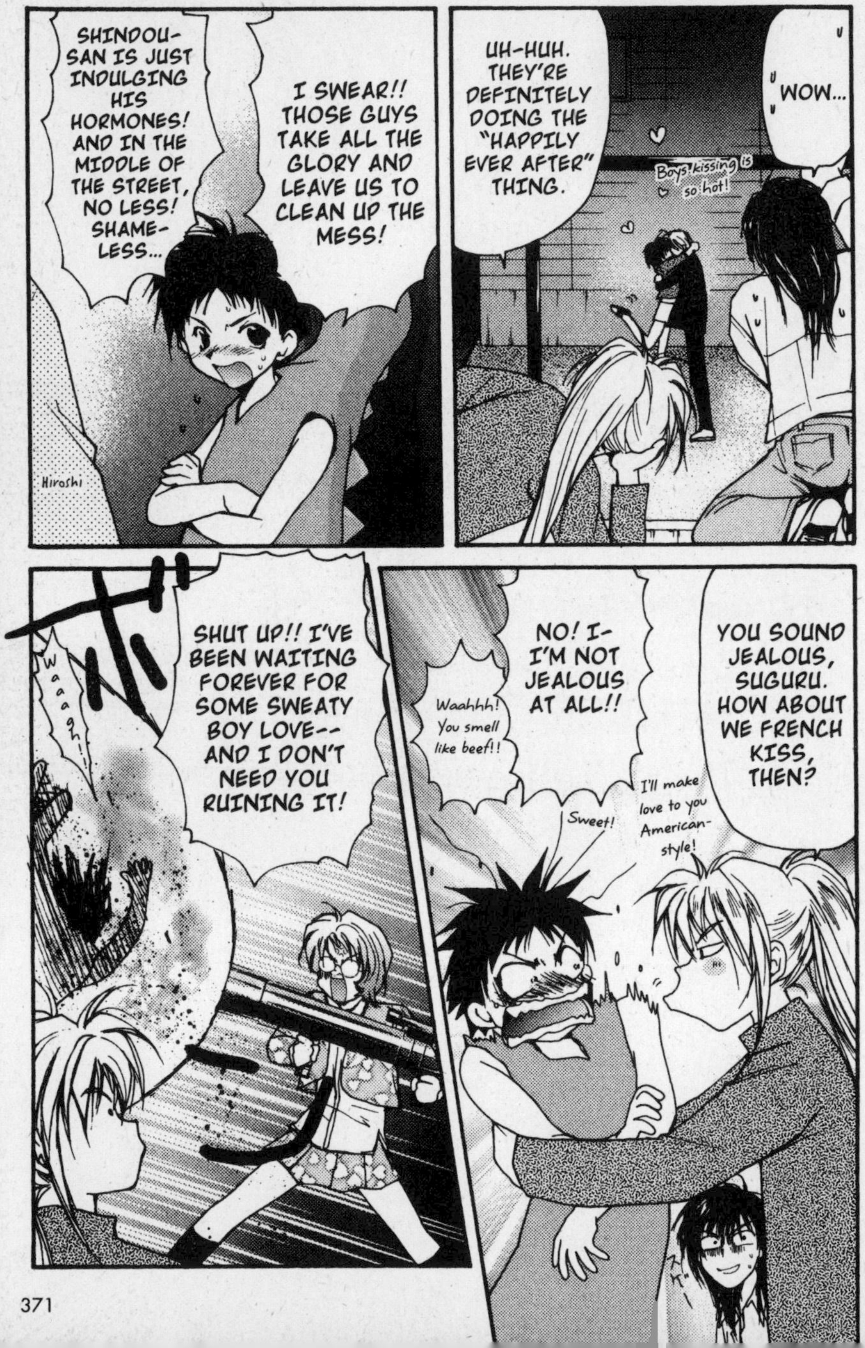
WOW...
UH-HUH. THEY'RE DEFINITELY DOING THE "HAPPILY EVER AFTER" THING.
Boys' kissing is so hot!
I SWEAR!! THOSE GUYS TAKE ALL THE GLORY AND LEAVE US TO CLEAN UP THE MESS!
SHINDOU-SAN IS JUST INDULGING HIS HORMONES! AND IN THE MIDDLE OF THE STREET, NO LESS! SHAME-LESS...
Hiroshi
YOU SOUND JEALOUS, SUGURU. HOW ABOUT WE FRENCH KISS, THEN?
I'll make love to you American-style!
NO! I- I'M NOT JEALOUS AT ALL!!
Sweet!
Waahhh! You smell like beef!!
SHUT UP!! I'VE BEEN WAITING FOREVER FOR SOME SWEATY BOY LOVE-- AND I DON'T NEED YOU RUINING IT!
Waaagh!!

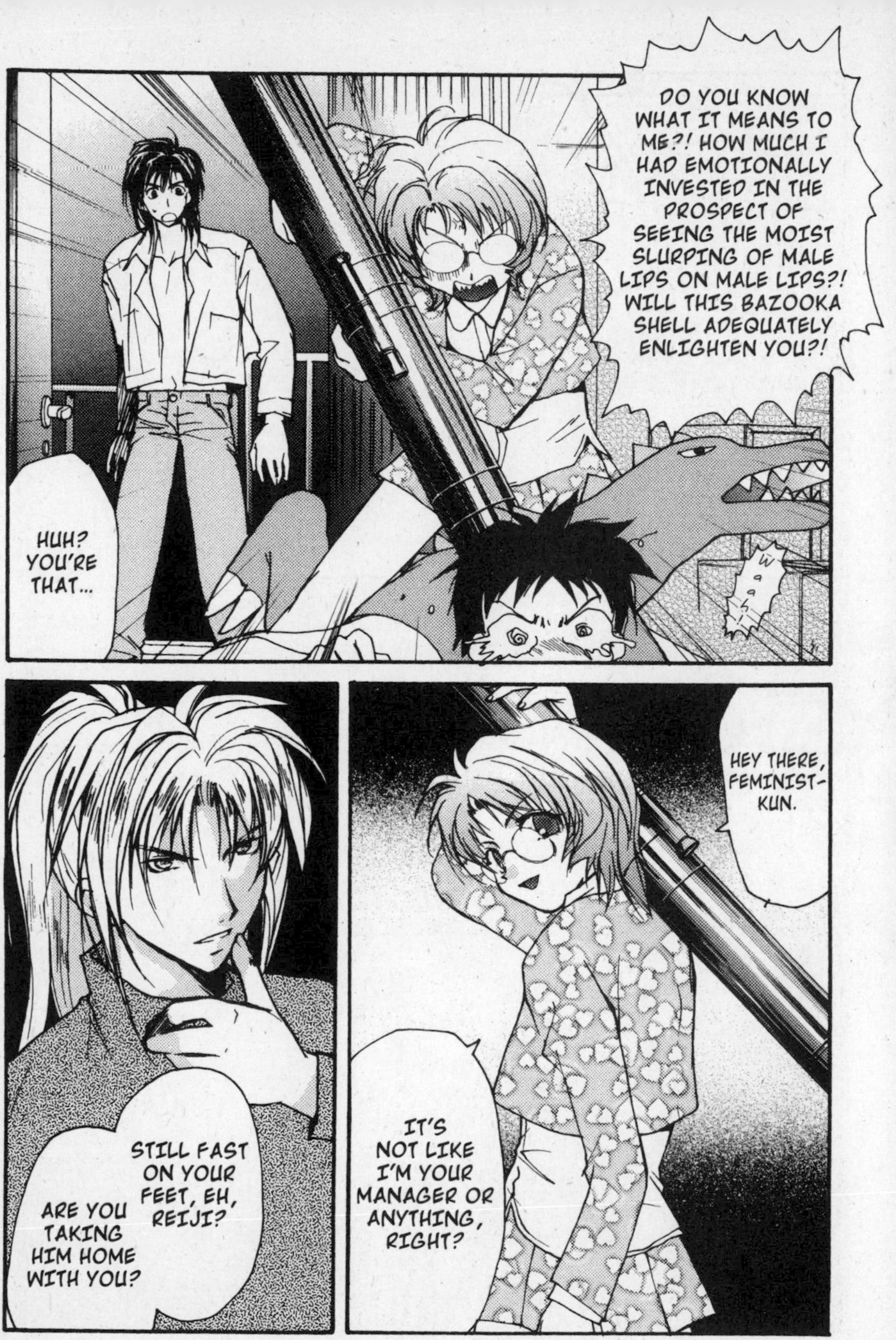
DO YOU KNOW WHAT IT MEANS TO ME?! HOW MUCH I HAD EMOTIONALLY INVESTED IN THE PROSPECT OF SEEING THE MOIST SLURPING OF MALE LIPS ON MALE LIPS?! WILL THIS BAZOOKA SHELL ADEQUATELY ENLIGHTEN YOU?!
Waah!
HUH? YOU'RE THAT...
HEY THERE, FEMINIST-KUN.
IT'S NOT LIKE I'M YOUR MANAGER OR ANYTHING, RIGHT?
STILL FAST ON YOUR FEET, EH, REIJI?
ARE YOU TAKING HIM HOME WITH YOU?

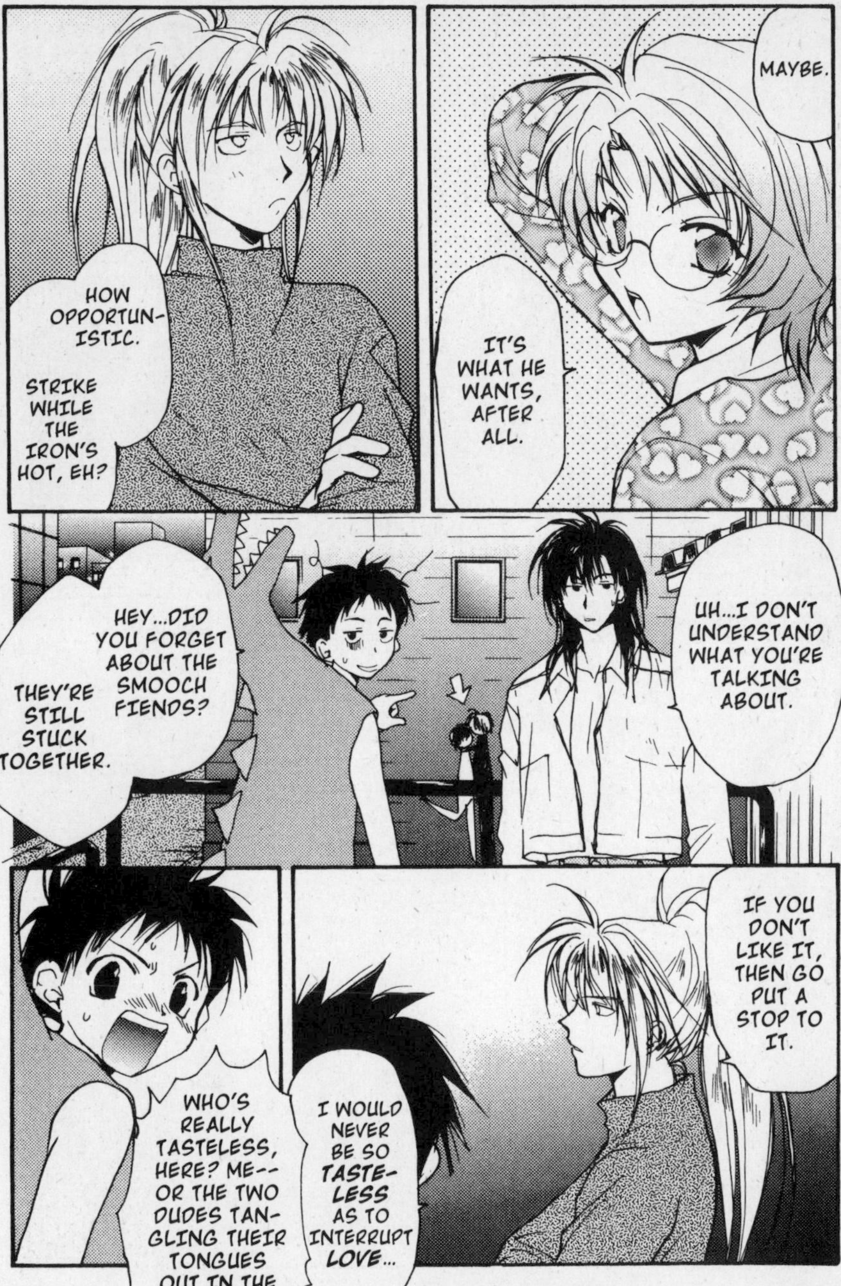
MAYBE.
IT'S WHAT HE WANTS, AFTER ALL.
HOW OPPORTUNISTIC.
STRIKE WHILE THE IRON'S HOT, EH?
UH...I DON'T UNDERSTAND WHAT YOU'RE TALKING ABOUT.
HEY...DID YOU FORGET ABOUT THE SMOOCH FIENDS?
THEY'RE STILL STUCK TOGETHER.
IF YOU DON'T LIKE IT, THEN GO PUT A STOP TO IT.
I WOULD NEVER BE SO *TASTELESS* AS TO INTERRUPT *LOVE*...
WHO'S REALLY TASTELESS, HERE? ME--OR THE TWO DUDES TANGLING THEIR TONGUES OUT IN THE STREET?!

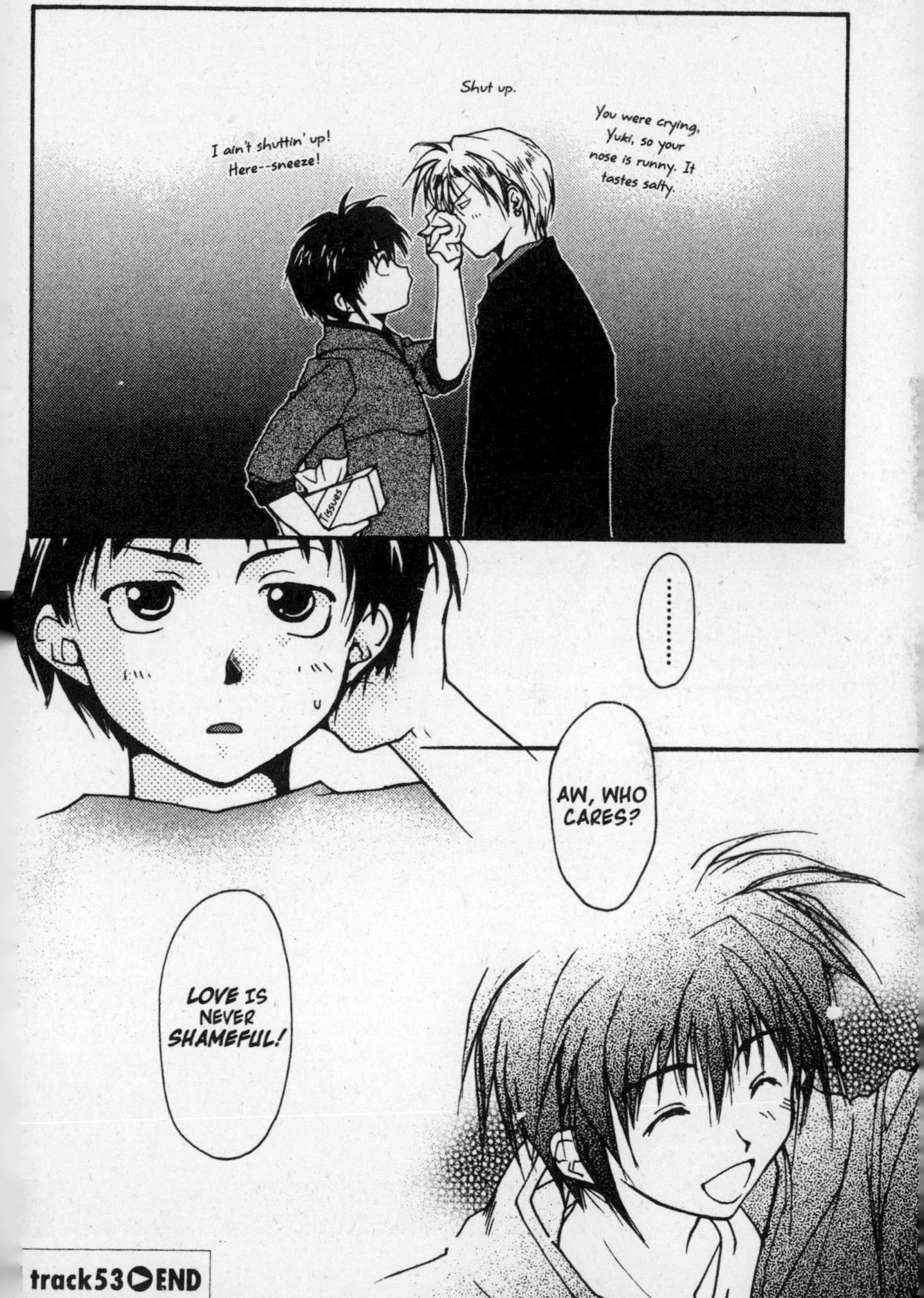
You were crying, Yuki, so your nose is runny. It tastes salty.
Shut up.
I ain't shuttin' up! Here--sneeze!
Tissues
......
AW, WHO CARES?
LOVE IS NEVER SHAMEFUL!

track53 ▶ END

# Gravitation

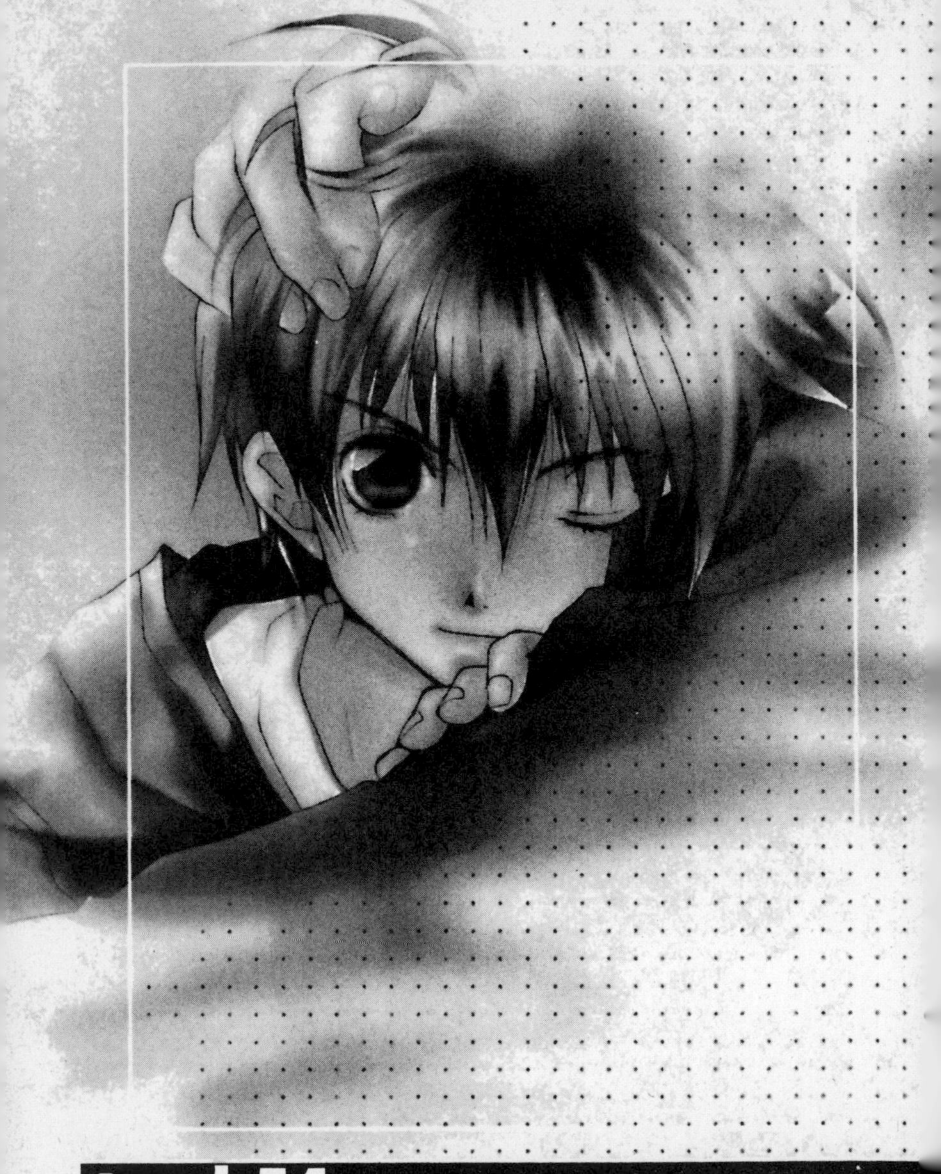

## track54

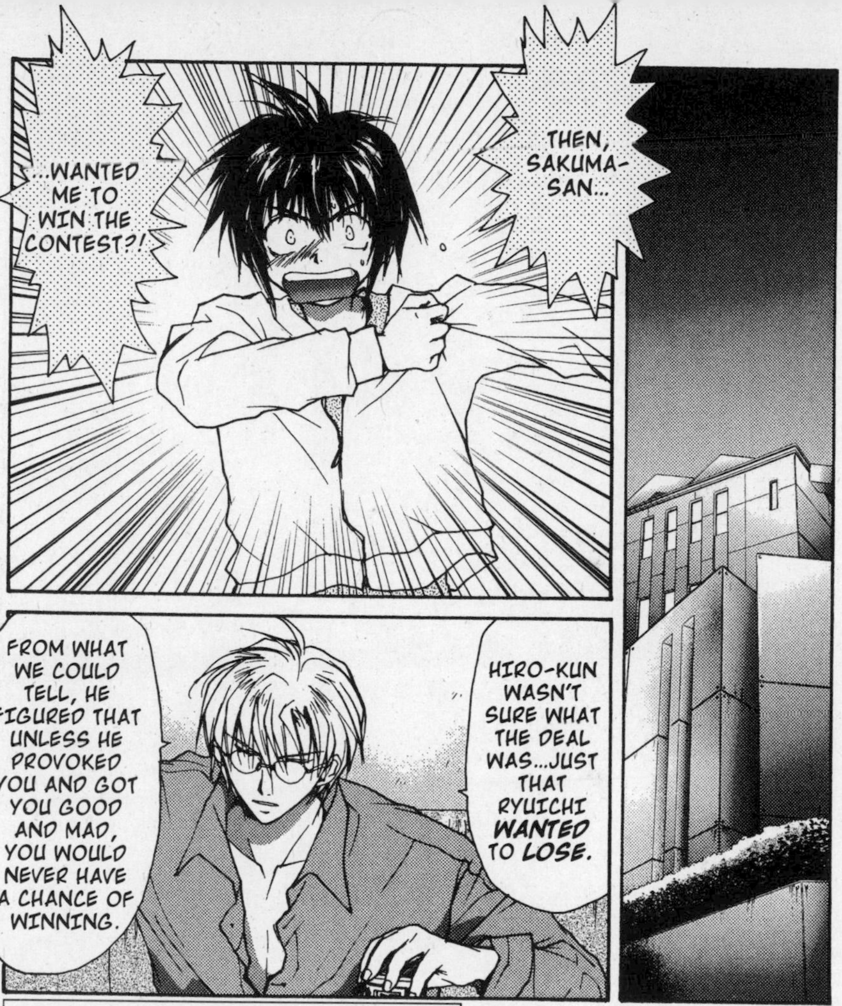
THEN, SAKUMA-SAN...
...WANTED ME TO WIN THE CONTEST?!
HIRO-KUN WASN'T SURE WHAT THE DEAL WAS...JUST THAT RYUICHI *WANTED* TO *LOSE*.
FROM WHAT WE COULD TELL, HE FIGURED THAT UNLESS HE PROVOKED YOU AND GOT YOU GOOD AND MAD, YOU WOULD NEVER HAVE A CHANCE OF WINNING.

## ABOUT GRAVITATION TRACK 54

It's finally here. This is the final episode. I might have another opportunity to draw the same universe that this manga is set in sometime in the future, but *Gravitation* as we know it will end with this chapter. It was like a journey through a long tunnel, and this fifty-fourth chapter feels pretty much like an epilogue. I guess I can only laugh when I think of it all... Still, I just might come out with a *Gravitation EX* or *Gravitation II* in six months or so. I mean... never say never, right...?

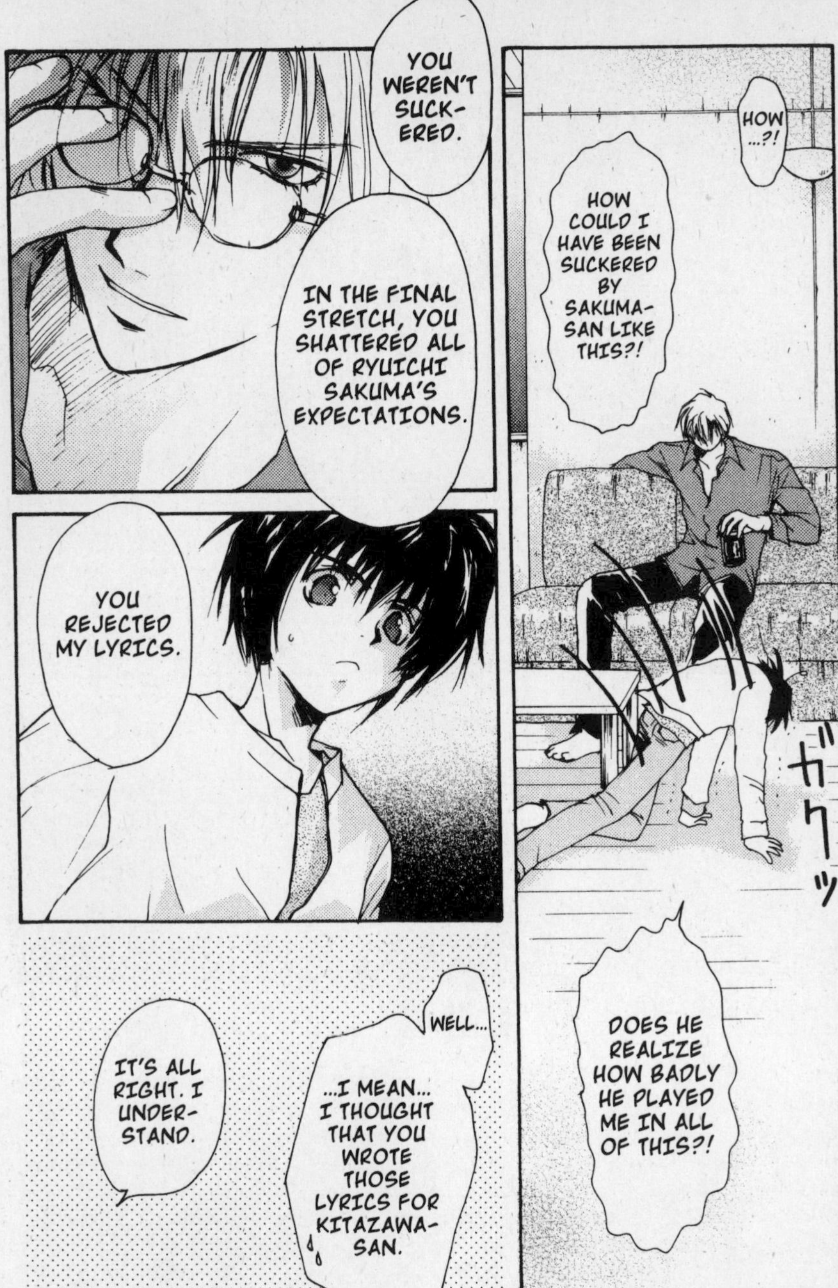
HOW ...?!
HOW COULD I HAVE BEEN SUCKERED BY SAKUMA-SAN LIKE THIS?!
ガクッ
DOES HE REALIZE HOW BADLY HE PLAYED ME IN ALL OF THIS?!
YOU WEREN'T SUCK-ERED.
IN THE FINAL STRETCH, YOU SHATTERED ALL OF RYUICHI SAKUMA'S EXPECTATIONS.
YOU REJECTED MY LYRICS.
WELL...
...I MEAN... I THOUGHT THAT YOU WROTE THOSE LYRICS FOR KITAZAWA-SAN.
IT'S ALL RIGHT. I UNDER-STAND.

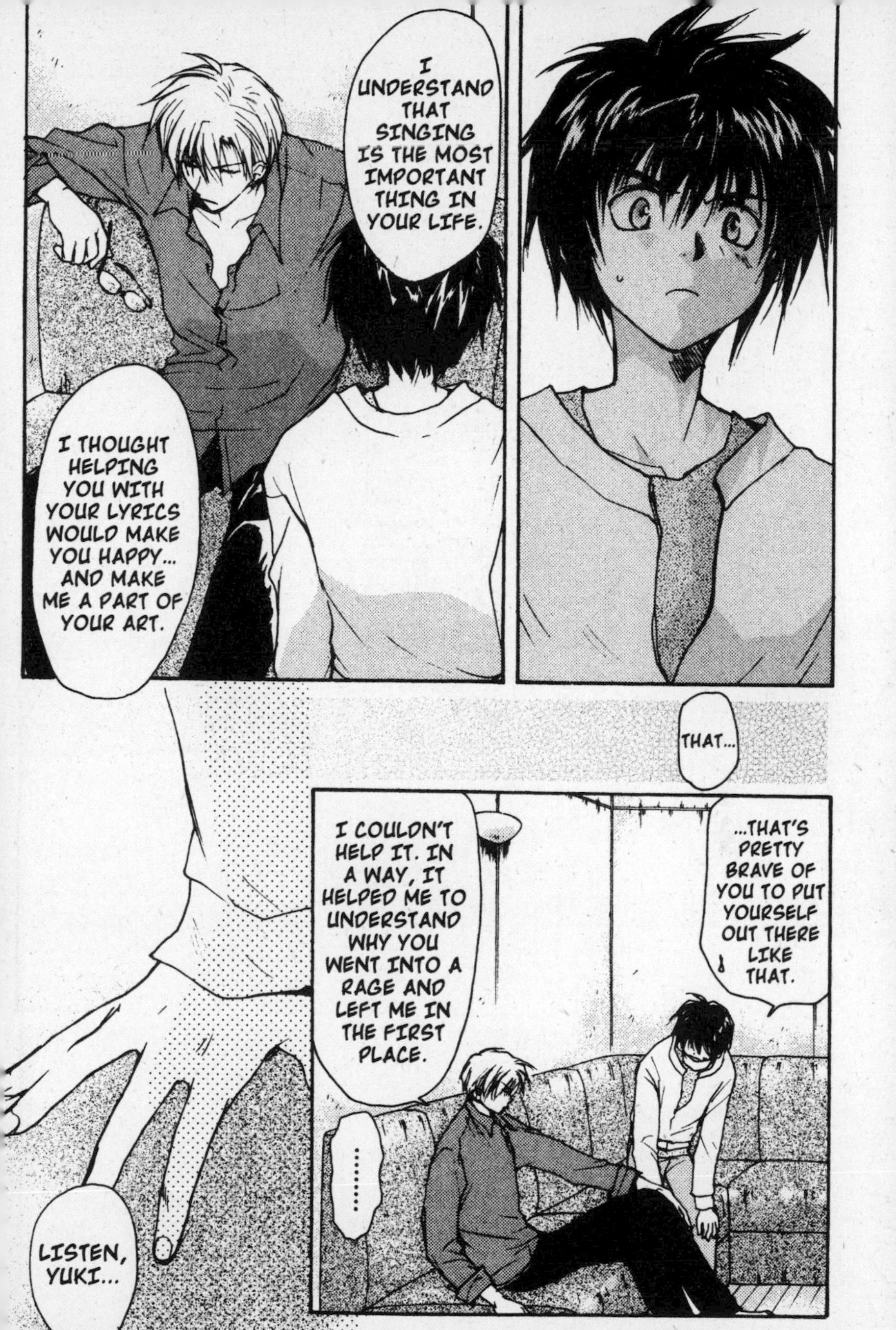
I UNDERSTAND THAT SINGING IS THE MOST IMPORTANT THING IN YOUR LIFE.
I THOUGHT HELPING YOU WITH YOUR LYRICS WOULD MAKE YOU HAPPY... AND MAKE ME A PART OF YOUR ART.
THAT...
...THAT'S PRETTY BRAVE OF YOU TO PUT YOURSELF OUT THERE LIKE THAT.
I COULDN'T HELP IT. IN A WAY, IT HELPED ME TO UNDERSTAND WHY YOU WENT INTO A RAGE AND LEFT ME IN THE FIRST PLACE.
......
LISTEN, YUKI...

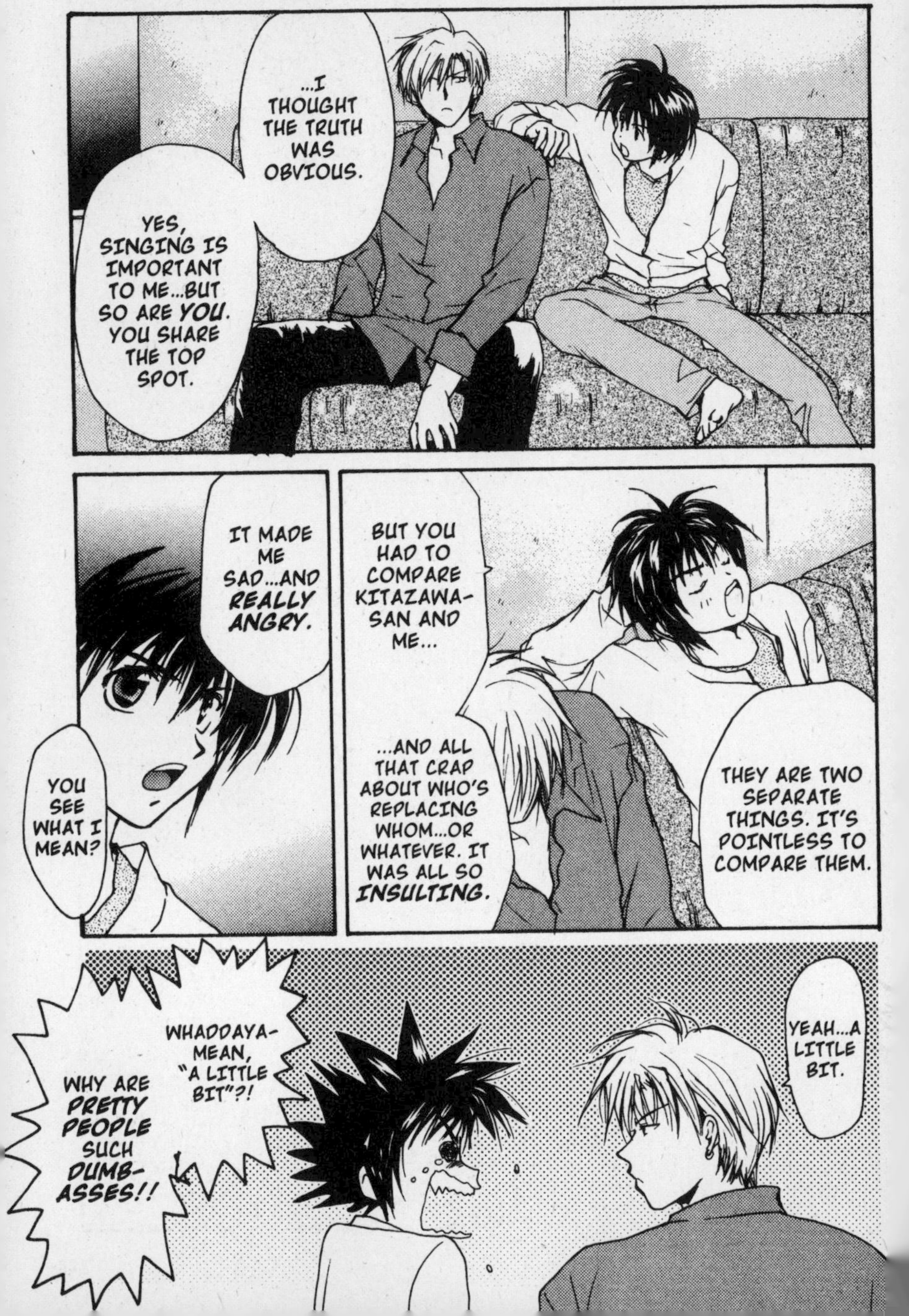
...I THOUGHT THE TRUTH WAS OBVIOUS.
YES, SINGING IS IMPORTANT TO ME...BUT SO ARE *YOU*. YOU SHARE THE TOP SPOT.
BUT YOU HAD TO COMPARE KITAZAWA-SAN AND ME...
THEY ARE TWO SEPARATE THINGS. IT'S POINTLESS TO COMPARE THEM.
...AND ALL THAT CRAP ABOUT WHO'S REPLACING WHOM...OR WHATEVER. IT WAS ALL SO ***INSULTING***.
IT MADE ME SAD...AND ***REALLY ANGRY***.
YOU SEE WHAT I MEAN?
YEAH...A LITTLE BIT.
WHADDAYA-MEAN, "A LITTLE BIT"?!
WHY ARE ***PRETTY PEOPLE*** SUCH ***DUMB-ASSES!!***

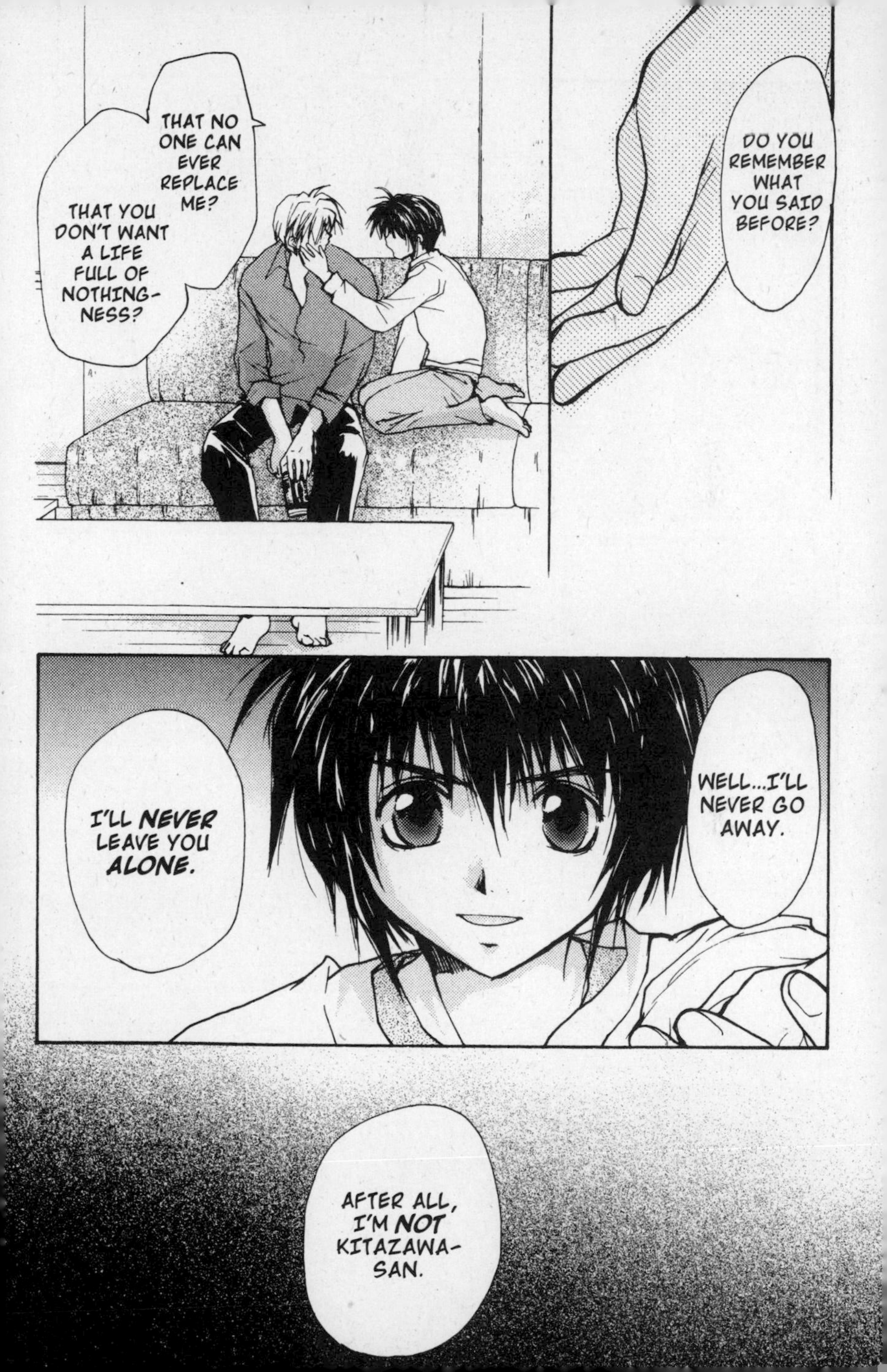
DO YOU REMEMBER WHAT YOU SAID BEFORE?
THAT NO ONE CAN EVER REPLACE ME?
THAT YOU DON'T WANT A LIFE FULL OF NOTHING-NESS?
WELL...I'LL NEVER GO AWAY.
I'LL NEVER LEAVE YOU ALONE.
AFTER ALL, I'M NOT KITAZAWA-SAN.

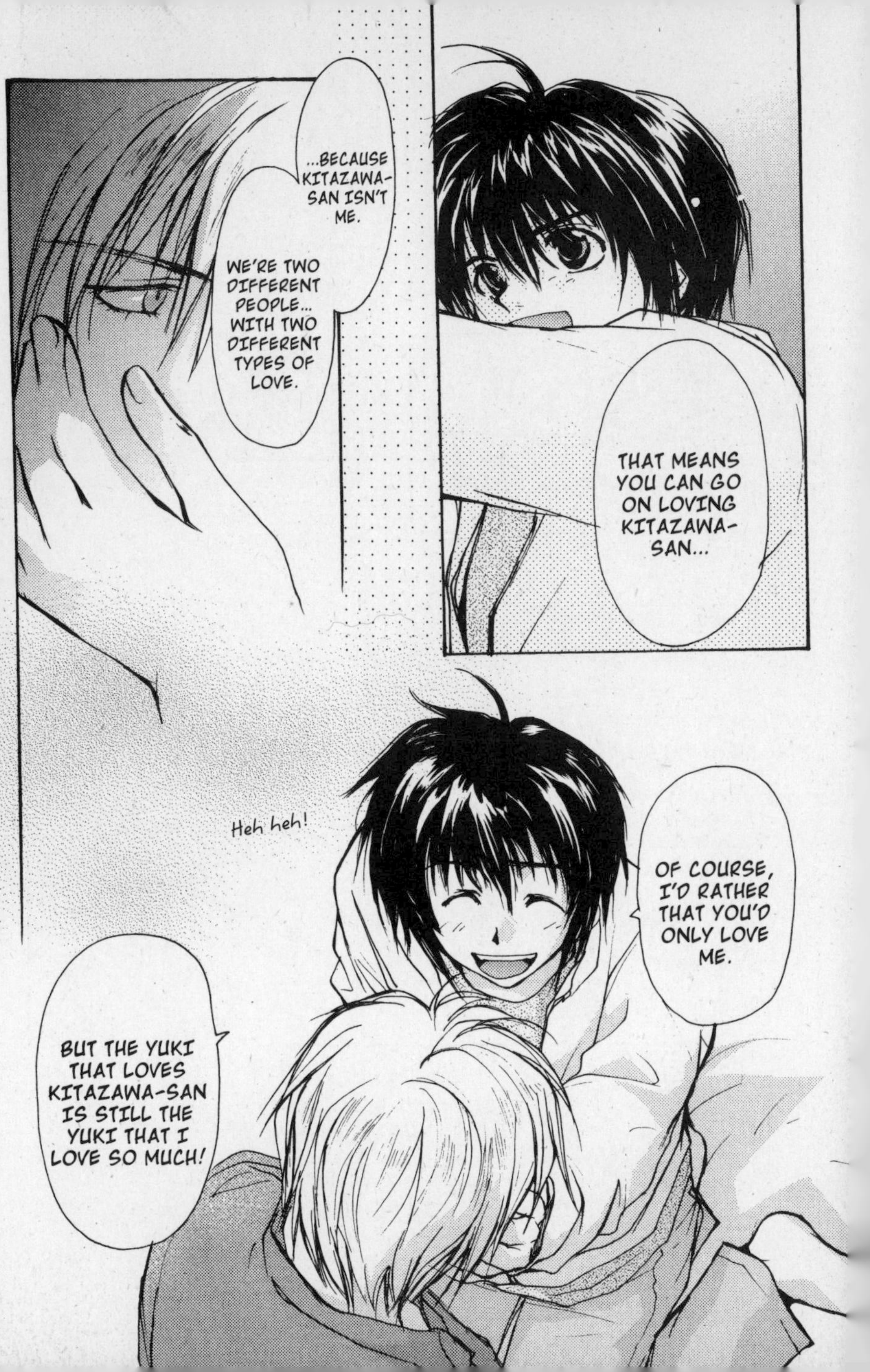
THAT MEANS YOU CAN GO ON LOVING KITAZAWA-SAN...
...BECAUSE KITAZAWA-SAN ISN'T ME.
WE'RE TWO DIFFERENT PEOPLE... WITH TWO DIFFERENT TYPES OF LOVE.
Heh heh!
OF COURSE, I'D RATHER THAT YOU'D ONLY LOVE ME.
BUT THE YUKI THAT LOVES KITAZAWA-SAN IS STILL THE YUKI THAT I LOVE SO MUCH!

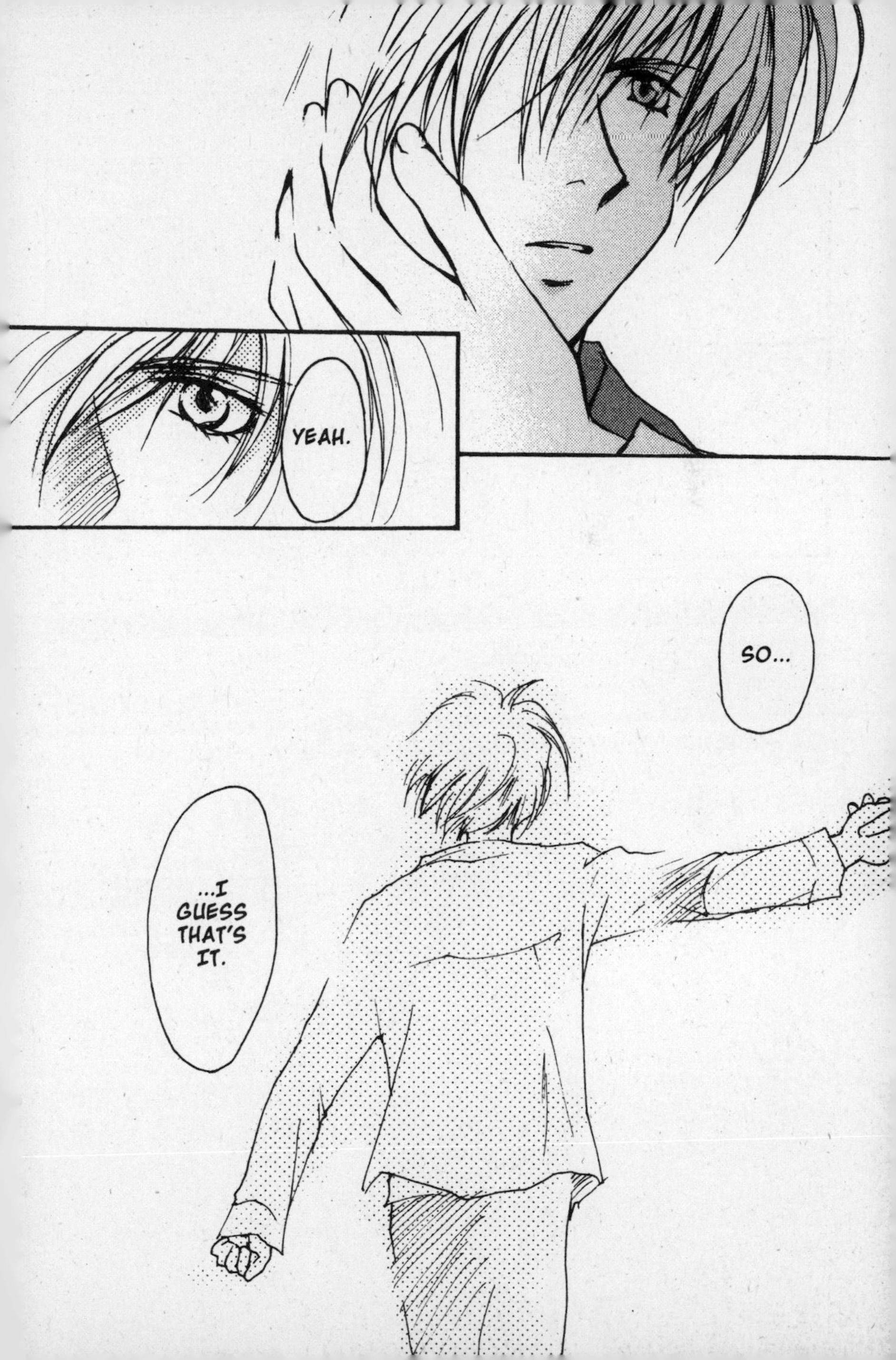
YEAH.
SO...
...I GUESS THAT'S IT.

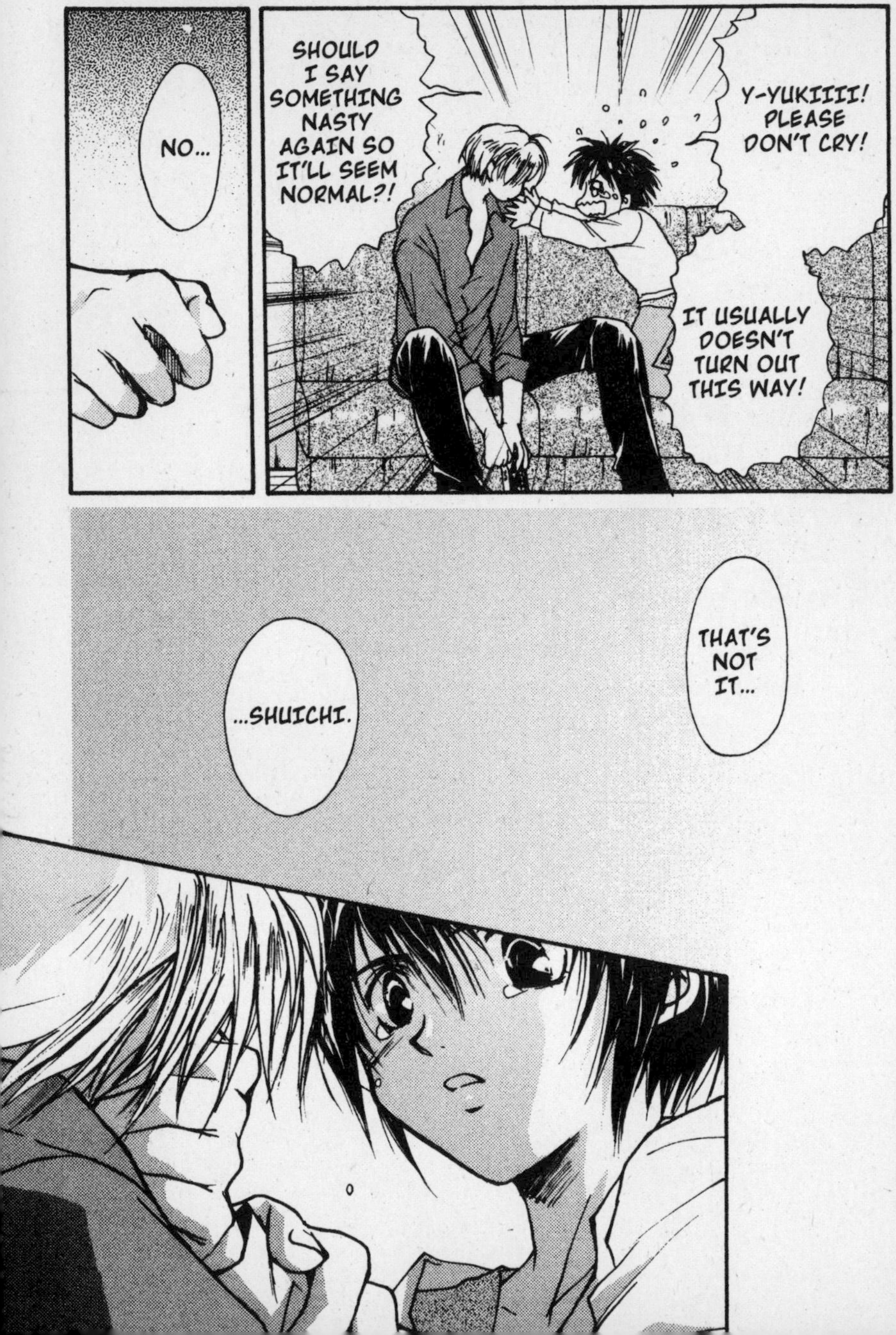
Y-YUKIIII! PLEASE DON'T CRY!
IT USUALLY DOESN'T TURN OUT THIS WAY!
SHOULD I SAY SOMETHING NASTY AGAIN SO IT'LL SEEM NORMAL?!
NO...
THAT'S NOT IT...
...SHUICHI.

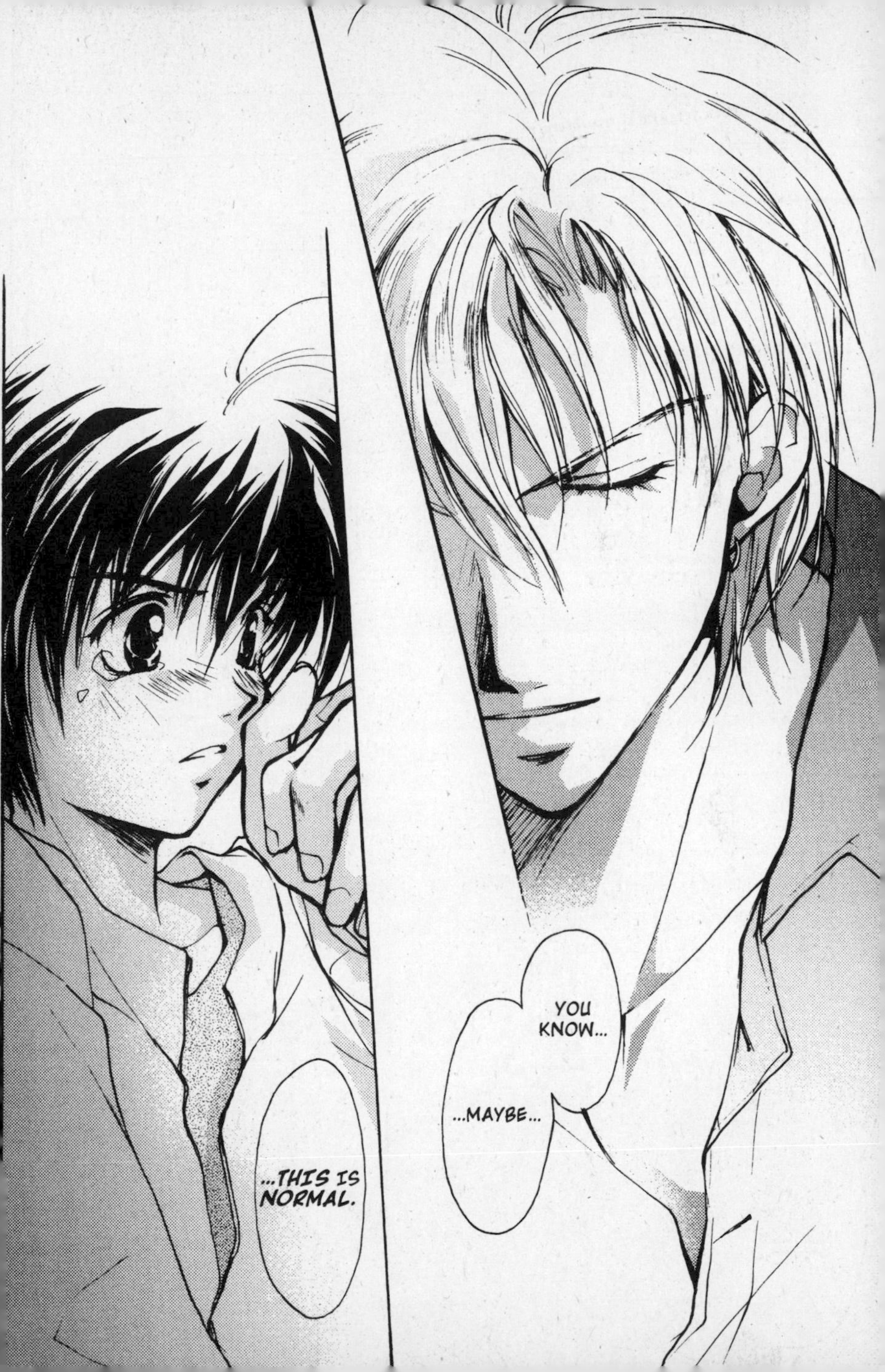
YOU KNOW...
...MAYBE...
...THIS IS NORMAL.

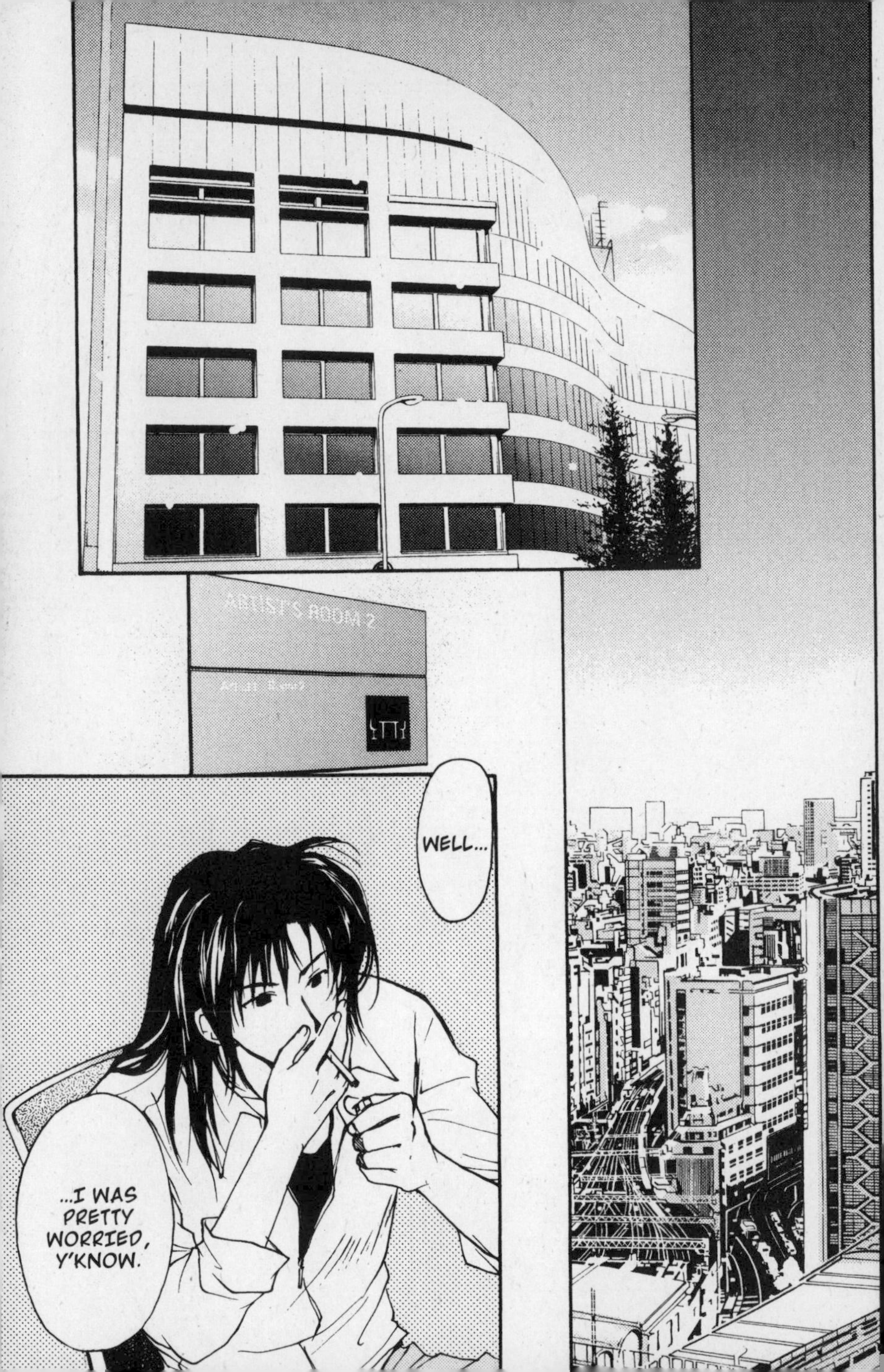
ARTIST'S ROOM 2
WELL...
...I WAS PRETTY WORRIED, Y'KNOW.

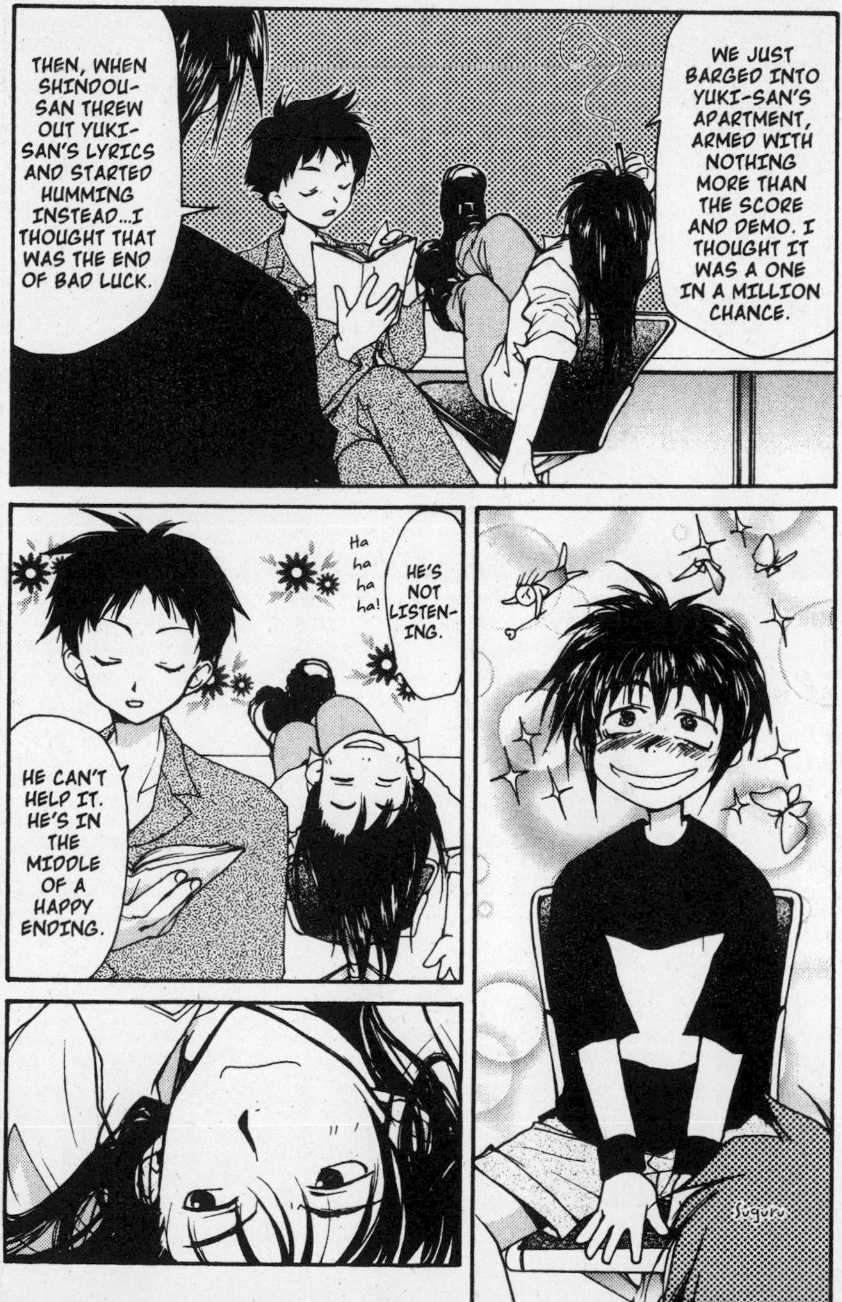
WE JUST BARGED INTO YUKI-SAN'S APARTMENT, ARMED WITH NOTHING MORE THAN THE SCORE AND DEMO. I THOUGHT IT WAS A ONE IN A MILLION CHANCE.
THEN, WHEN SHINDOU-SAN THREW OUT YUKI-SAN'S LYRICS AND STARTED HUMMING INSTEAD...I THOUGHT THAT WAS THE END OF BAD LUCK.
Suguru
HE'S NOT LISTEN-ING.
Ha ha ha ha!
HE CAN'T HELP IT. HE'S IN THE MIDDLE OF A HAPPY ENDING.

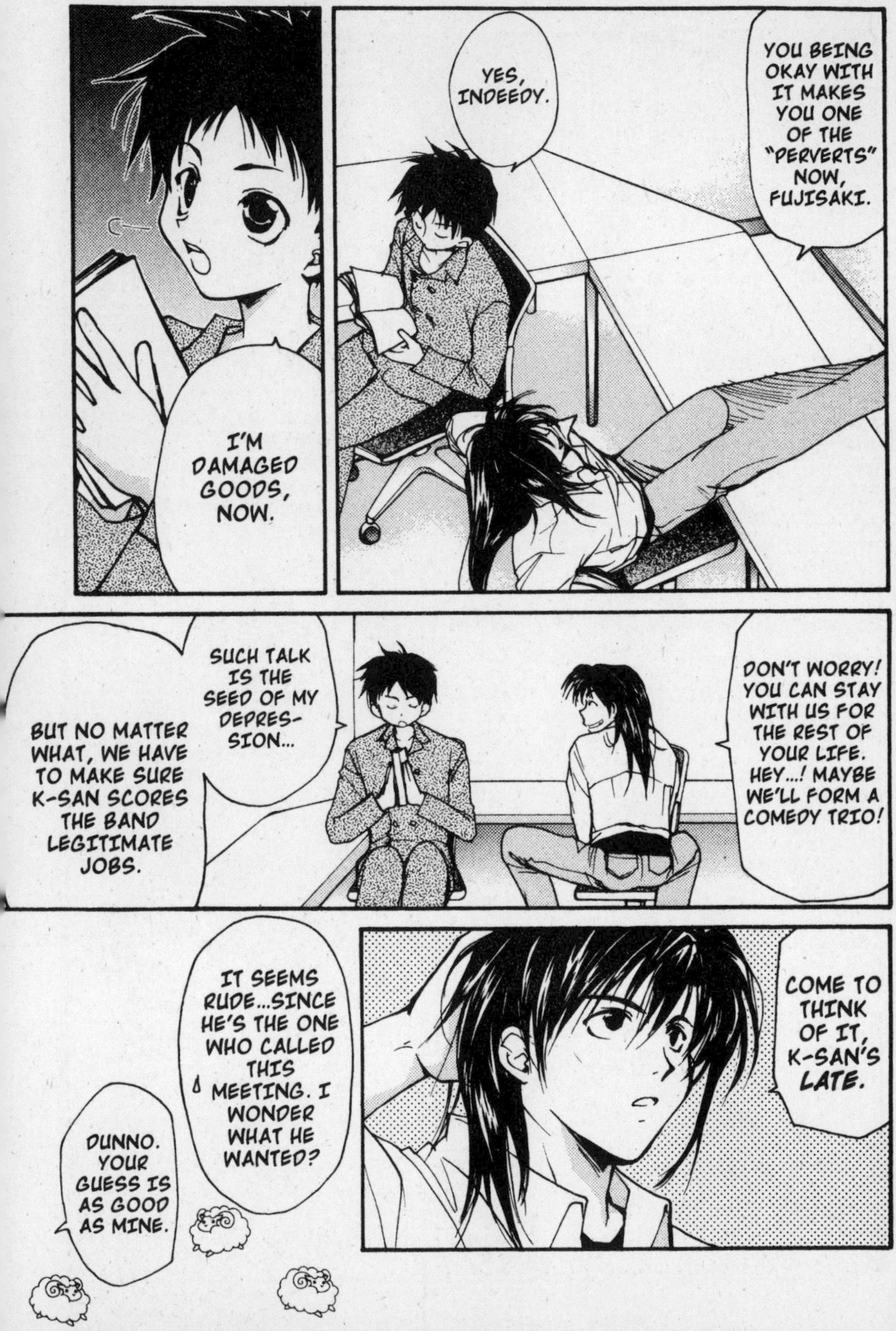
YOU BEING OKAY WITH IT MAKES YOU ONE OF THE "PERVERTS" NOW, FUJISAKI.
YES, INDEEDY.
I'M DAMAGED GOODS, NOW.
DON'T WORRY! YOU CAN STAY WITH US FOR THE REST OF YOUR LIFE. HEY...! MAYBE WE'LL FORM A COMEDY TRIO!
SUCH TALK IS THE SEED OF MY DEPRES-SION...
BUT NO MATTER WHAT, WE HAVE TO MAKE SURE K-SAN SCORES THE BAND LEGITIMATE JOBS.
COME TO THINK OF IT, K-SAN'S *LATE.*
IT SEEMS RUDE...SINCE HE'S THE ONE WHO CALLED THIS MEETING. I WONDER WHAT HE WANTED?
DUNNO. YOUR GUESS IS AS GOOD AS MINE.

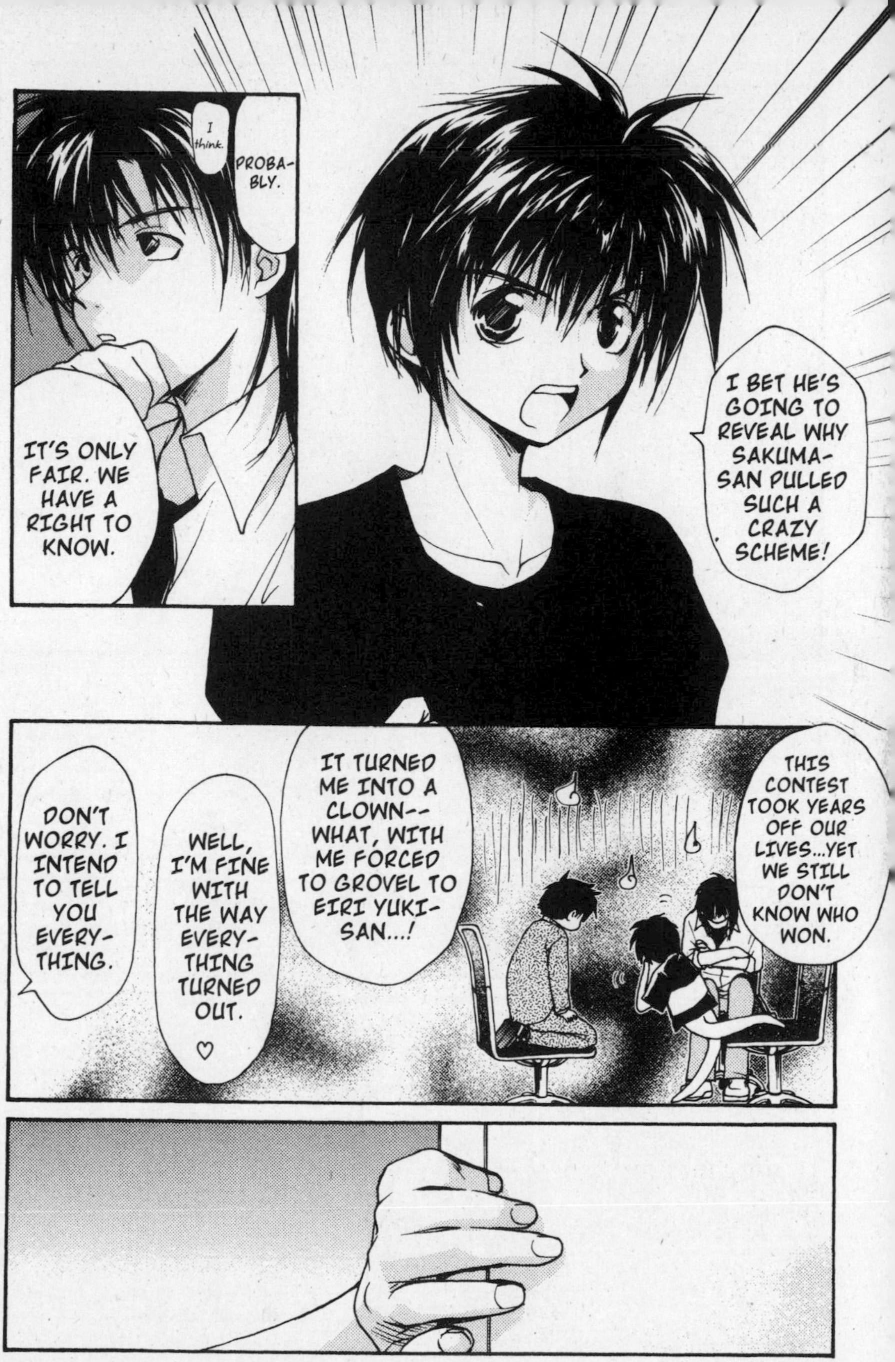
I BET HE'S GOING TO REVEAL WHY SAKUMA-SAN PULLED SUCH A CRAZY SCHEME!
PROBABLY.
I think.
IT'S ONLY FAIR. WE HAVE A RIGHT TO KNOW.
THIS CONTEST TOOK YEARS OFF OUR LIVES...YET WE STILL DON'T KNOW WHO WON.
IT TURNED ME INTO A CLOWN--WHAT, WITH ME FORCED TO GROVEL TO EIRI YUKI-SAN...!
WELL, I'M FINE WITH THE WAY EVERYTHING TURNED OUT. ♡
DON'T WORRY. I INTEND TO TELL YOU EVERYTHING.

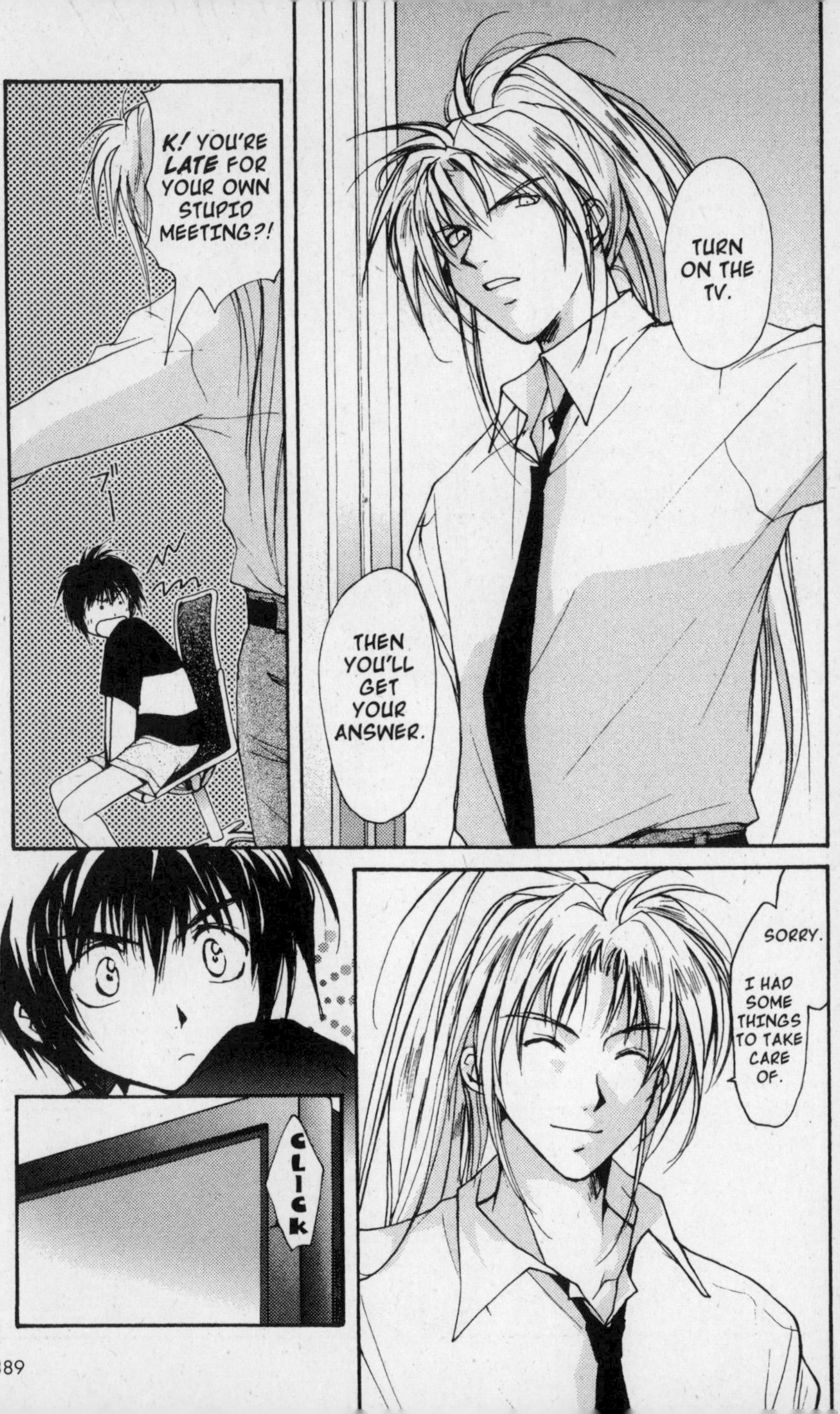
TURN ON THE TV.
THEN YOU'LL GET YOUR ANSWER.
K! YOU'RE LATE FOR YOUR OWN STUPID MEETING?!
ブー
SORRY.
I HAD SOME THINGS TO TAKE CARE OF.
CLICK

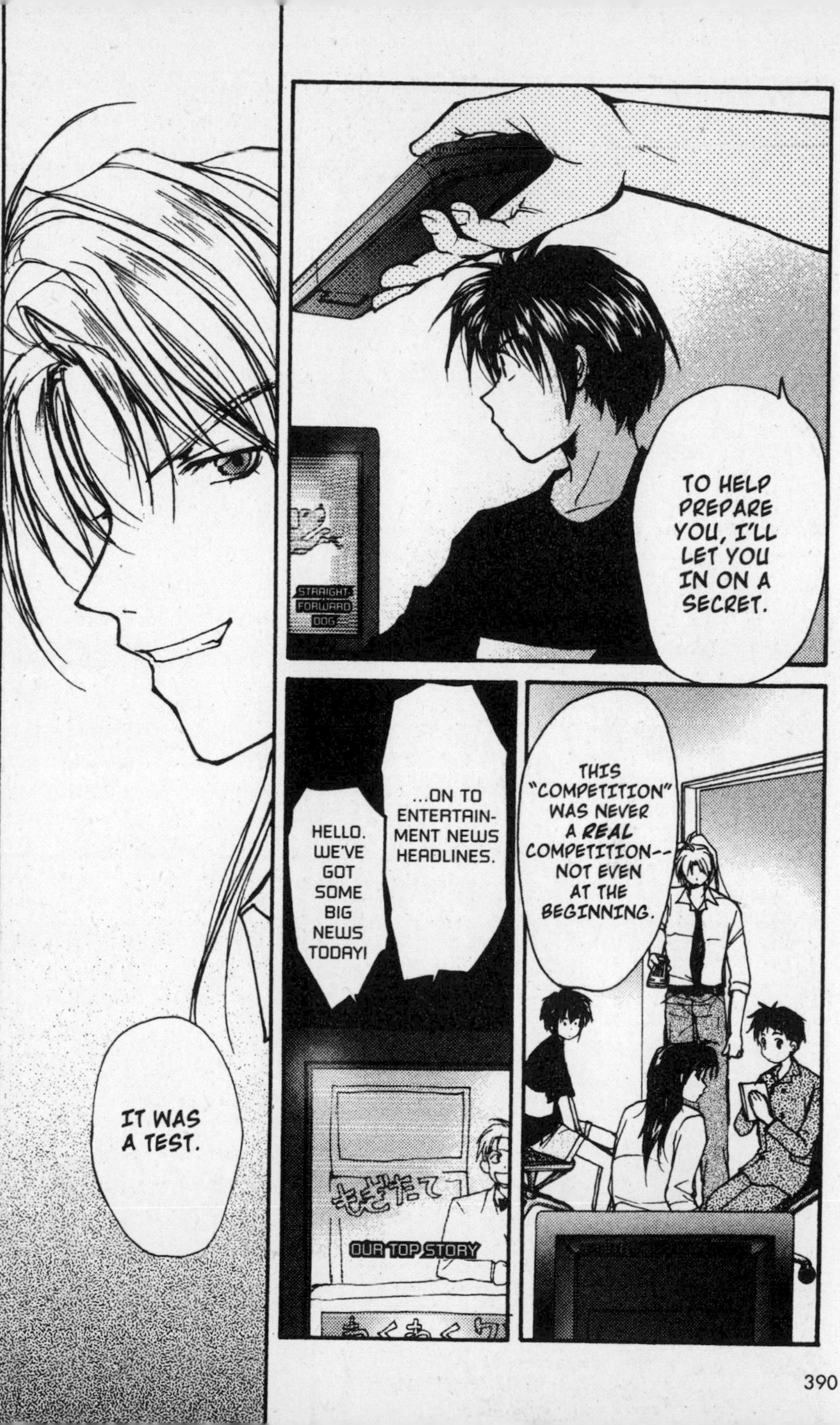
STRAIGHT-FORWARD DOG
TO HELP PREPARE YOU, I'LL LET YOU IN ON A SECRET.
THIS "COMPETITION" WAS NEVER A *REAL* COMPETITION--NOT EVEN AT THE BEGINNING.
...ON TO ENTERTAIN-MENT NEWS HEADLINES.
HELLO. WE'VE GOT SOME BIG NEWS TODAY!
OUR TOP STORY
IT WAS A TEST.

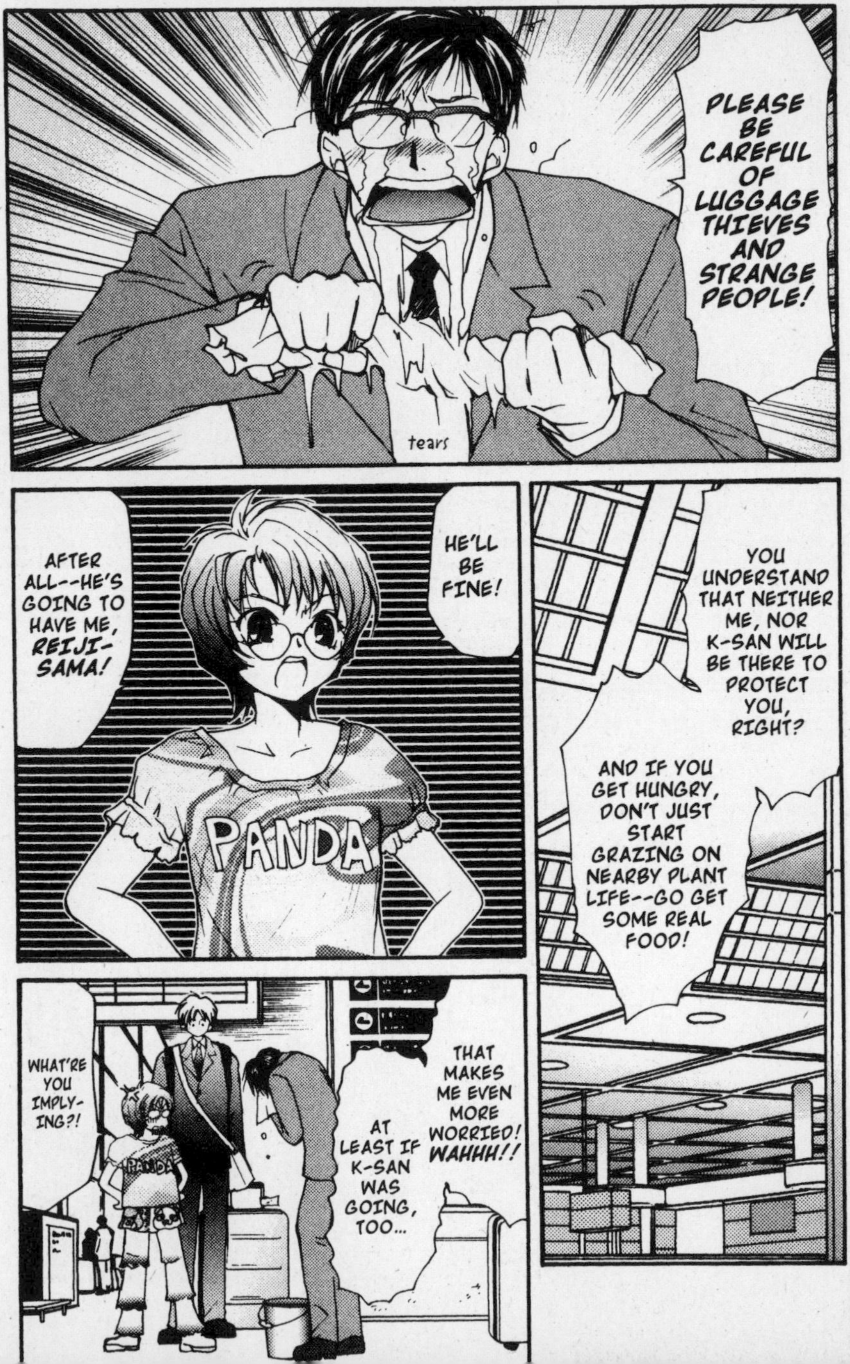
PLEASE BE CAREFUL OF LUGGAGE THIEVES AND STRANGE PEOPLE!
tears
YOU UNDERSTAND THAT NEITHER ME, NOR K-SAN WILL BE THERE TO PROTECT YOU, RIGHT?
AND IF YOU GET HUNGRY, DON'T JUST START GRAZING ON NEARBY PLANT LIFE--GO GET SOME REAL FOOD!
HE'LL BE FINE!
AFTER ALL--HE'S GOING TO HAVE ME, REIJI-SAMA!
THAT MAKES ME EVEN MORE WORRIED! WAHHH!!
AT LEAST IF K-SAN WAS GOING, TOO...
WHAT'RE YOU IMPLY-ING?!

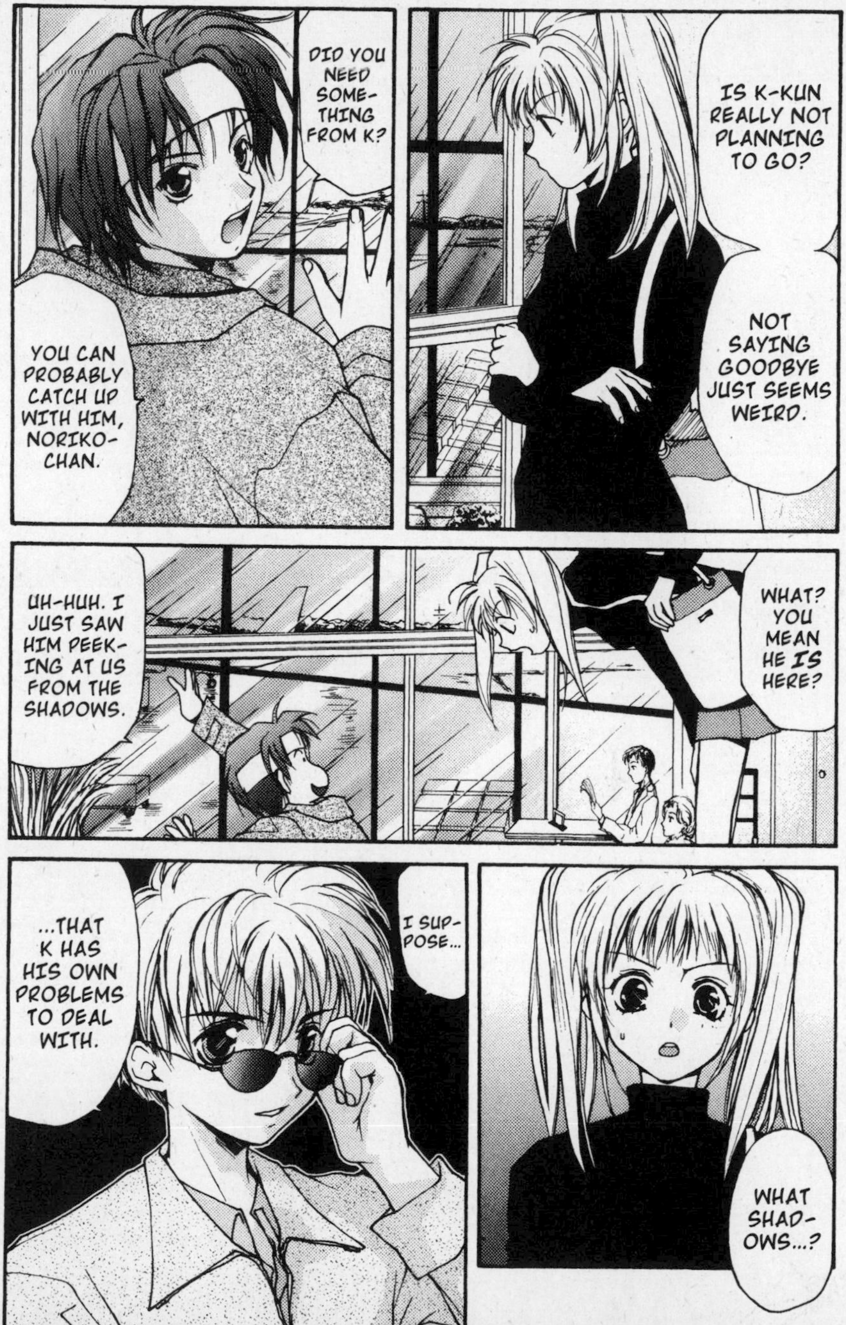
IS K-KUN REALLY NOT PLANNING TO GO?
NOT SAYING GOODBYE JUST SEEMS WEIRD.
DID YOU NEED SOMETHING FROM K?
YOU CAN PROBABLY CATCH UP WITH HIM, NORIKO-CHAN.
WHAT? YOU MEAN HE **IS** HERE?
UH-HUH. I JUST SAW HIM PEEKING AT US FROM THE SHADOWS.
WHAT SHADOWS...?
I SUPPOSE...
...THAT K HAS HIS OWN PROBLEMS TO DEAL WITH.

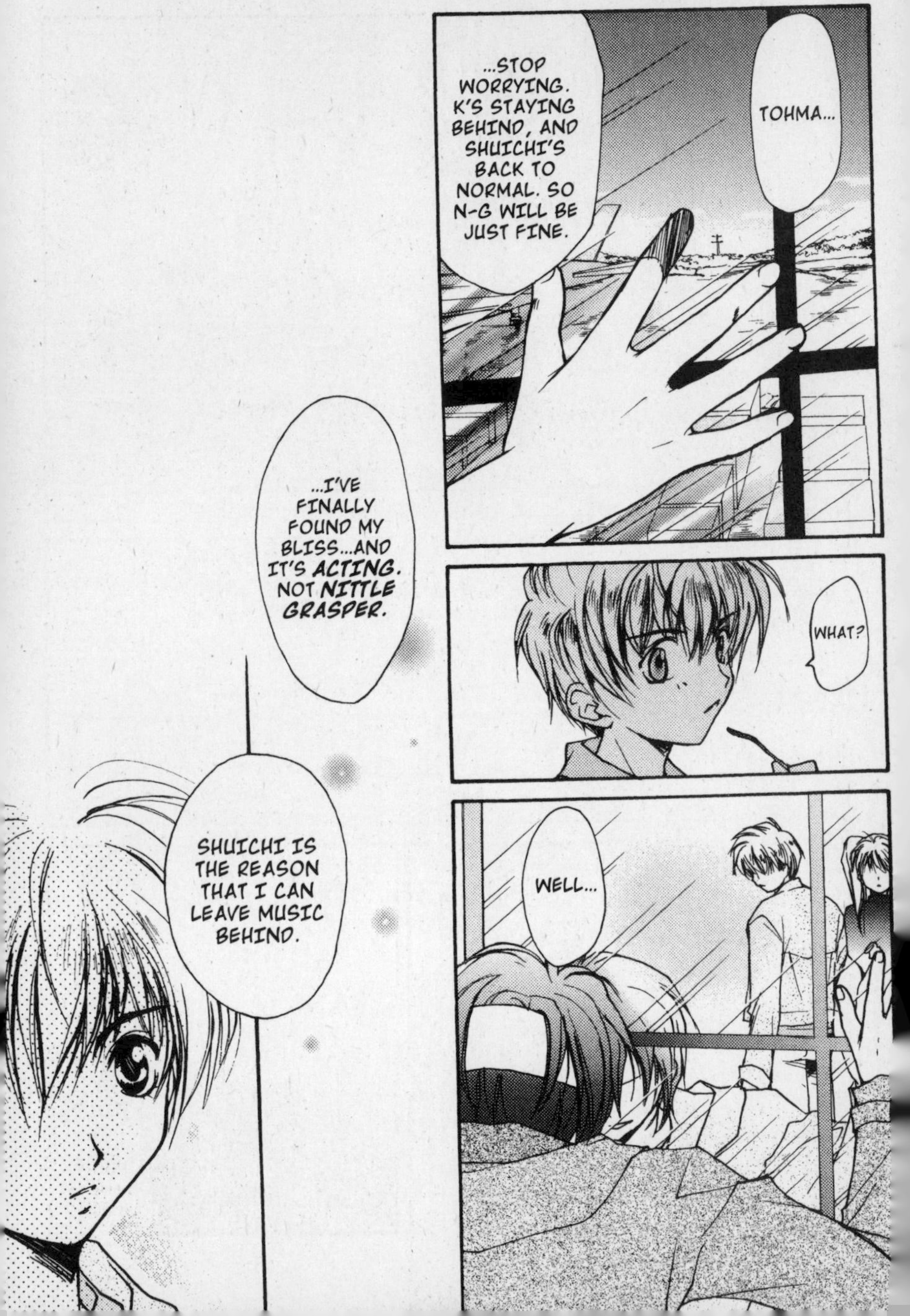
TOHMA...
...STOP WORRYING. K'S STAYING BEHIND, AND SHUICHI'S BACK TO NORMAL. SO N-G WILL BE JUST FINE.
WHAT?
WELL...
...I'VE FINALLY FOUND MY BLISS...AND IT'S ACTING. NOT NITTLE GRASPER.
SHUICHI IS THE REASON THAT I CAN LEAVE MUSIC BEHIND.

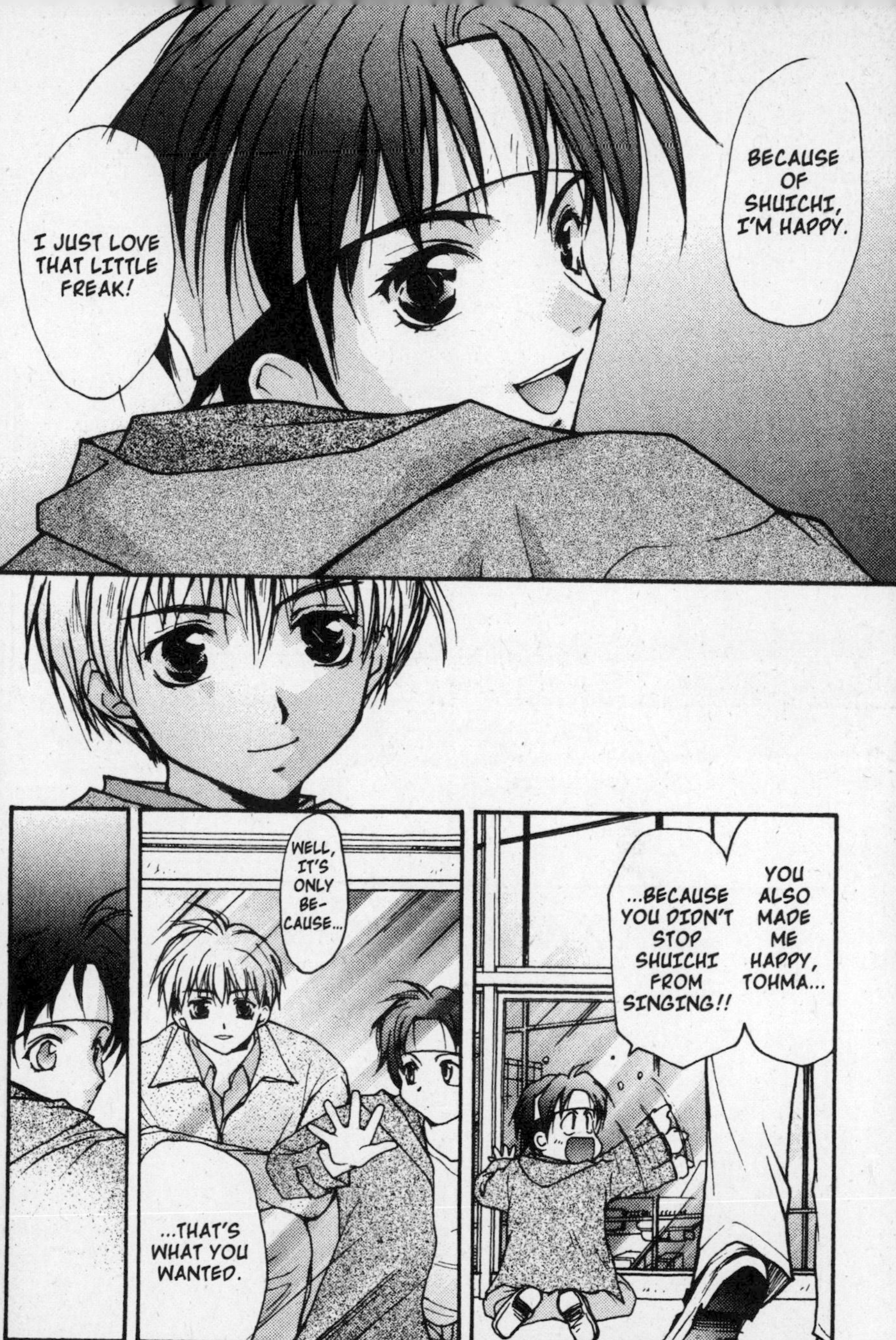
BECAUSE OF SHUICHI, I'M HAPPY.
I JUST LOVE THAT LITTLE FREAK!
YOU ALSO MADE ME HAPPY, TOHMA...
...BECAUSE YOU DIDN'T STOP SHUICHI FROM SINGING!!
WELL, IT'S ONLY BE-CAUSE...
...THAT'S WHAT YOU WANTED.

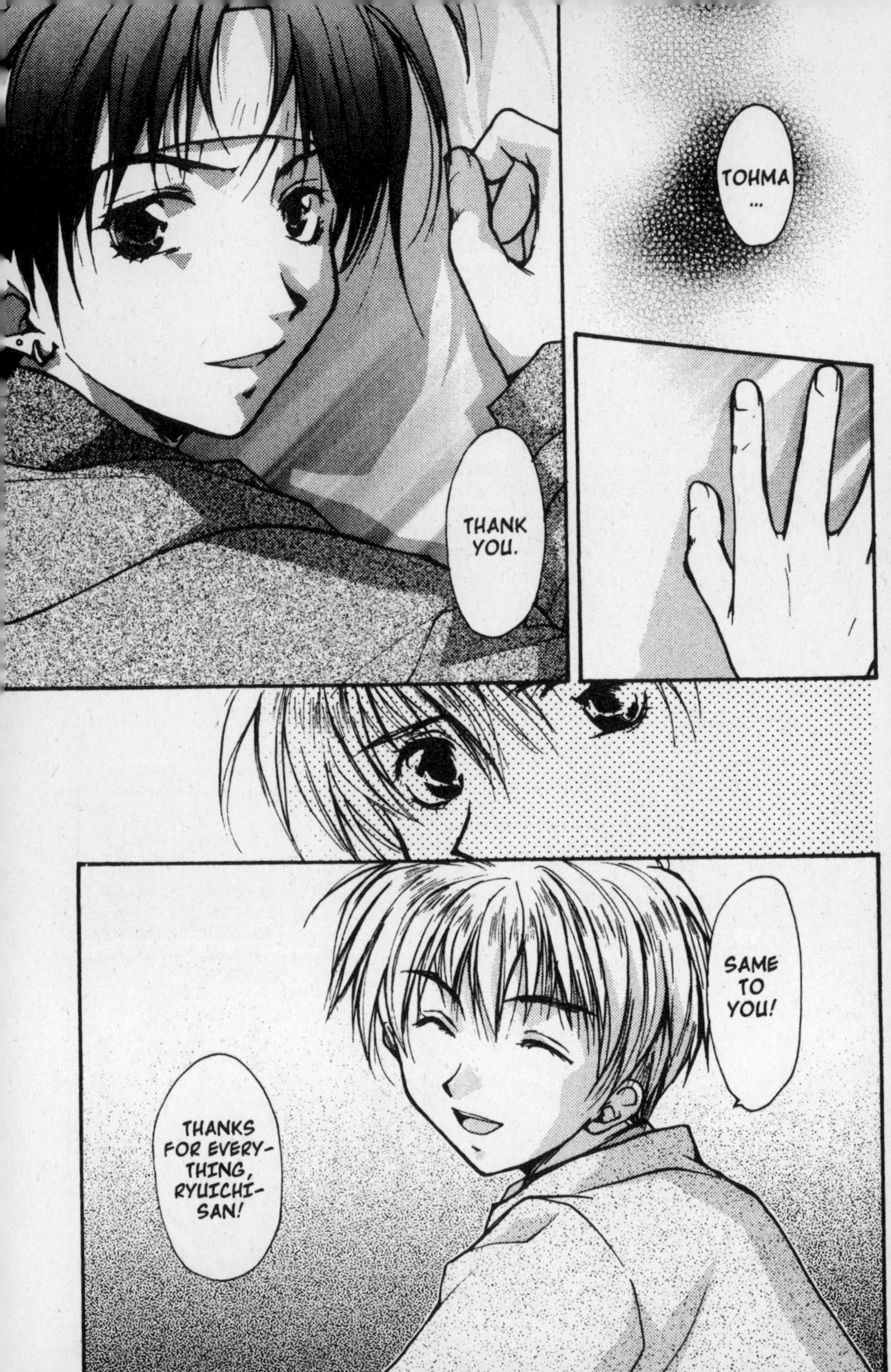
TOHMA ...
THANK YOU.
SAME TO YOU!
THANKS FOR EVERY-THING, RYUICHI-SAN!

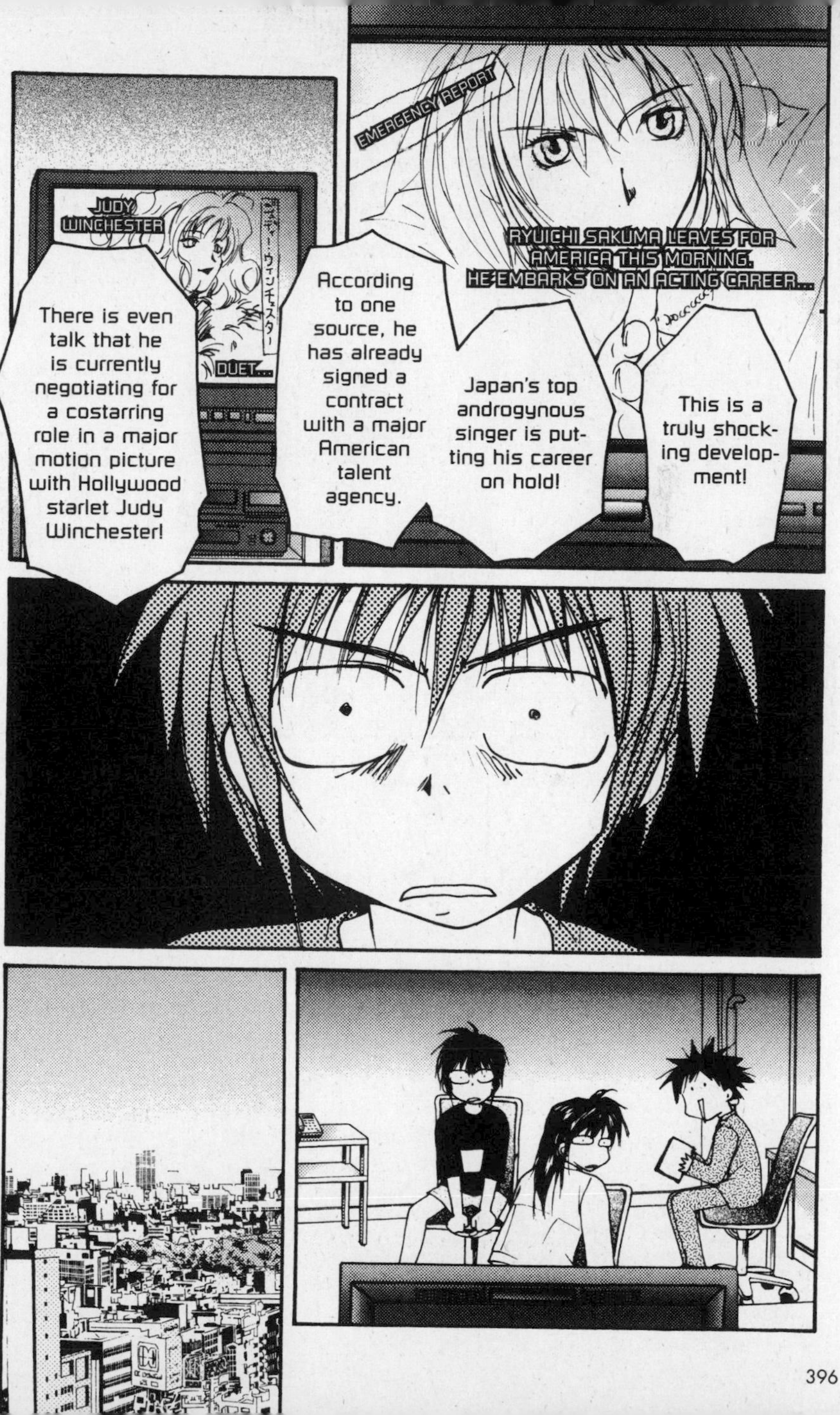
EMERGENCY REPORT
RYUICHI SAKUMA LEAVES FOR AMERICA THIS MORNING. HE EMBARKS ON AN ACTING CAREER...
This is a truly shocking development!
Japan's top androgynous singer is putting his career on hold!
According to one source, he has already signed a contract with a major American talent agency.
JUDY WINCHESTER
ディ・ウィンチェスター
DUET...
There is even talk that he is currently negotiating for a costarring role in a major motion picture with Hollywood starlet Judy Winchester!

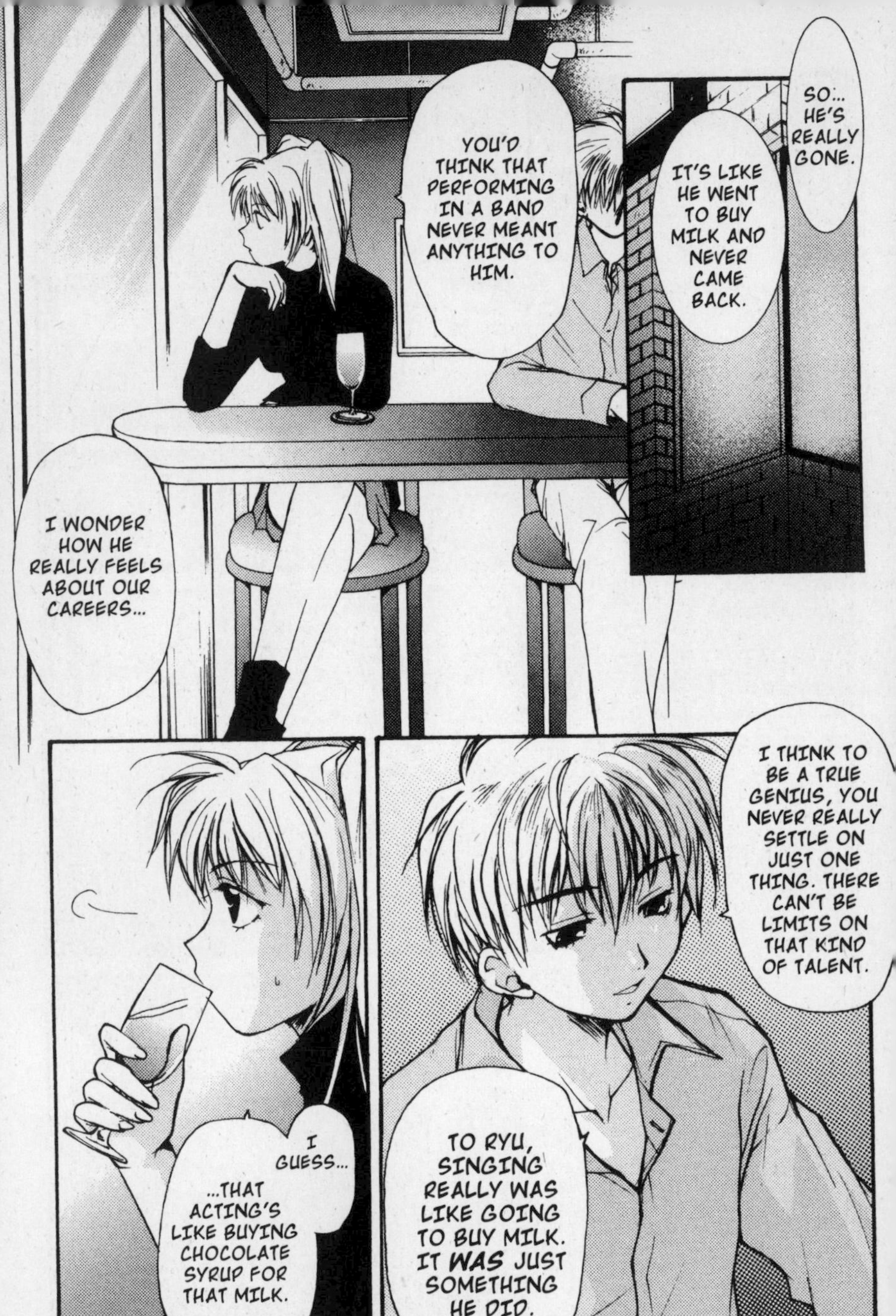
SO... HE'S REALLY GONE.
IT'S LIKE HE WENT TO BUY MILK AND NEVER CAME BACK.
YOU'D THINK THAT PERFORMING IN A BAND NEVER MEANT ANYTHING TO HIM.
I WONDER HOW HE REALLY FEELS ABOUT OUR CAREERS...
I THINK TO BE A TRUE GENIUS, YOU NEVER REALLY SETTLE ON JUST ONE THING. THERE CAN'T BE LIMITS ON THAT KIND OF TALENT.
TO RYU, SINGING REALLY WAS LIKE GOING TO BUY MILK. IT *WAS* JUST SOMETHING HE DID.
I GUESS...
...THAT ACTING'S LIKE BUYING CHOCOLATE SYRUP FOR THAT MILK.

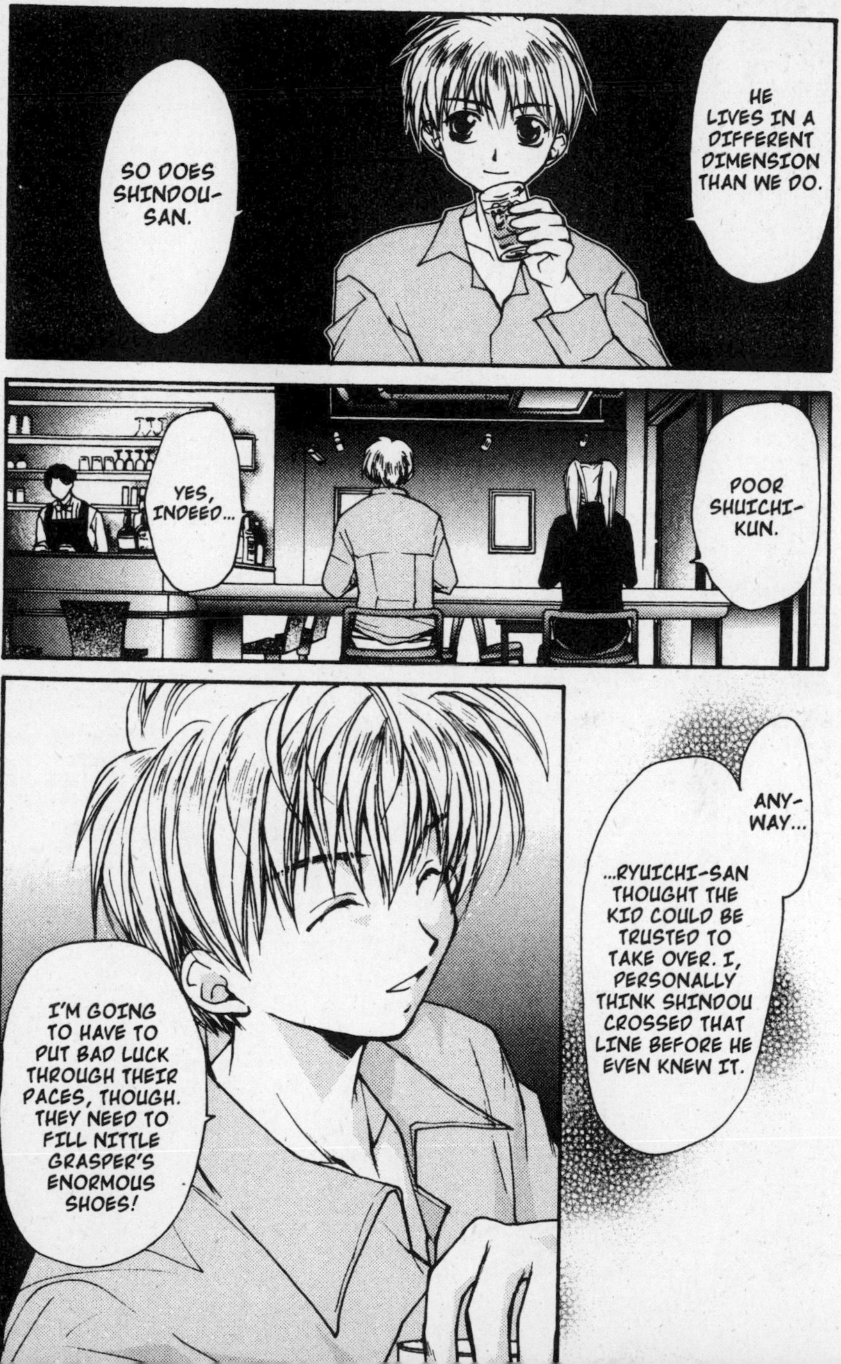
HE LIVES IN A DIFFERENT DIMENSION THAN WE DO.
SO DOES SHINDOU-SAN.
POOR SHUICHI-KUN.
YES, INDEED...
ANY-WAY...
...RYUICHI-SAN THOUGHT THE KID COULD BE TRUSTED TO TAKE OVER. I, PERSONALLY THINK SHINDOU CROSSED THAT LINE BEFORE HE EVEN KNEW IT.
I'M GOING TO HAVE TO PUT BAD LUCK THROUGH THEIR PACES, THOUGH. THEY NEED TO FILL NITTLE GRASPER'S ENORMOUS SHOES!

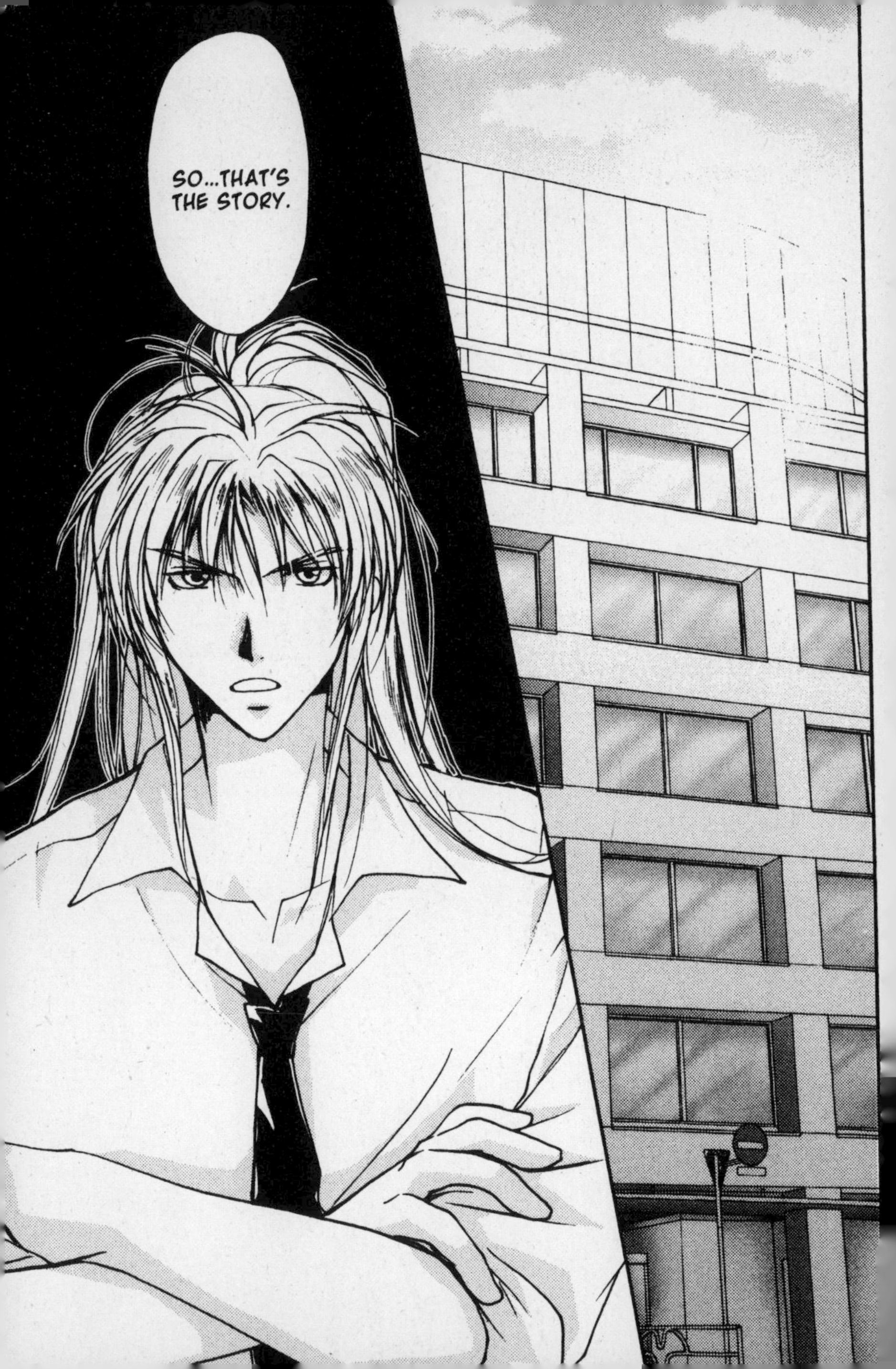
SO...THAT'S THE STORY.

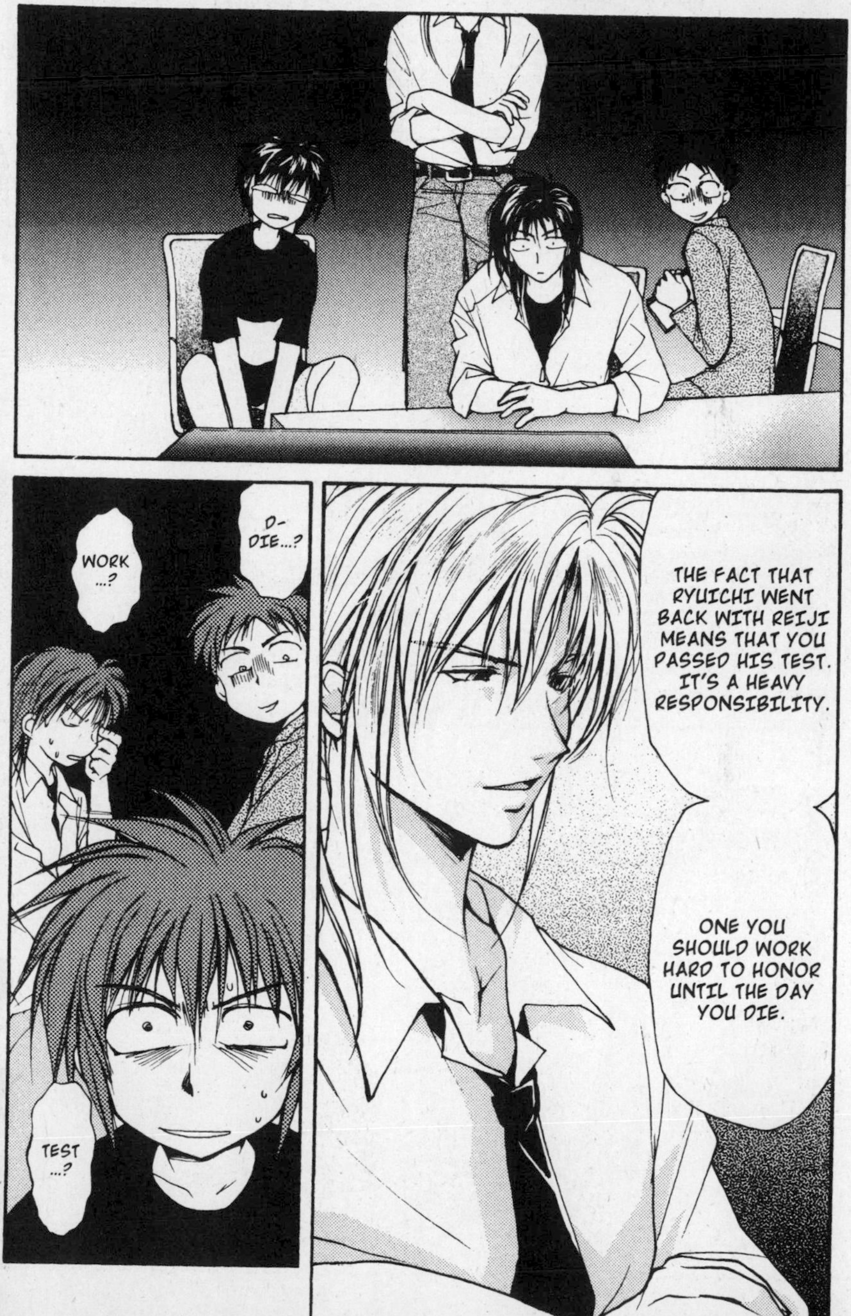
THE FACT THAT RYUICHI WENT BACK WITH REIJI MEANS THAT YOU PASSED HIS TEST. IT'S A HEAVY RESPONSIBILITY.
ONE YOU SHOULD WORK HARD TO HONOR UNTIL THE DAY YOU DIE.
D-DIE...?
WORK...?
TEST...?

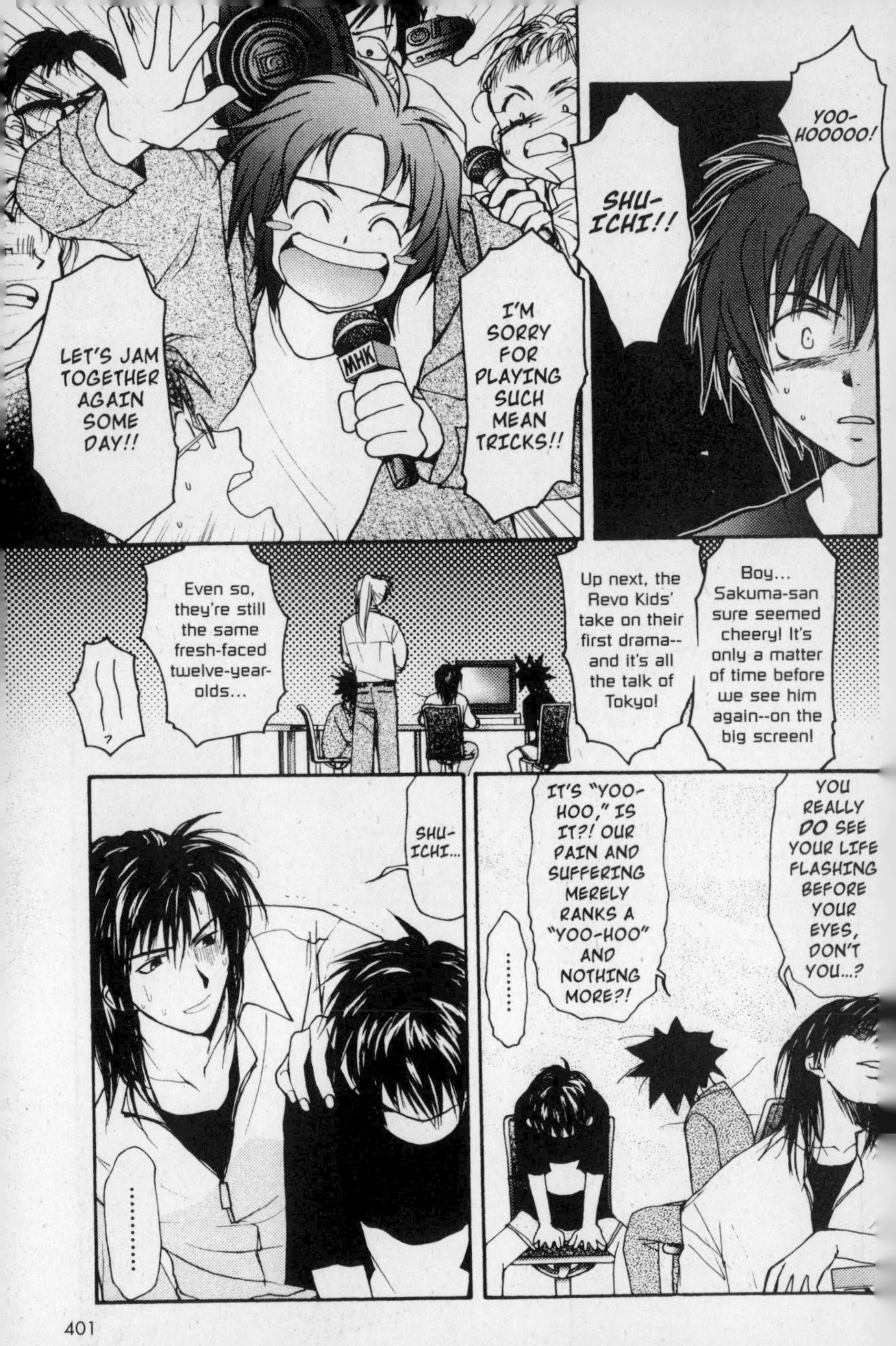
YOO-HOOOOO!
SHU-ICHI!!
I'M SORRY FOR PLAYING SUCH MEAN TRICKS!!
LET'S JAM TOGETHER AGAIN SOME DAY!!
Boy... Sakuma-san sure seemed cheery! It's only a matter of time before we see him again--on the big screen!
Up next, the Revo Kids' take on their first drama--and it's all the talk of Tokyo!
Even so, they're still the same fresh-faced twelve-year-olds...
YOU REALLY DO SEE YOUR LIFE FLASHING BEFORE YOUR EYES, DON'T YOU...?
IT'S "YOO-HOO," IS IT?! OUR PAIN AND SUFFERING MERELY RANKS A "YOO-HOO" AND NOTHING MORE?!
........
SHU-ICHI...
........

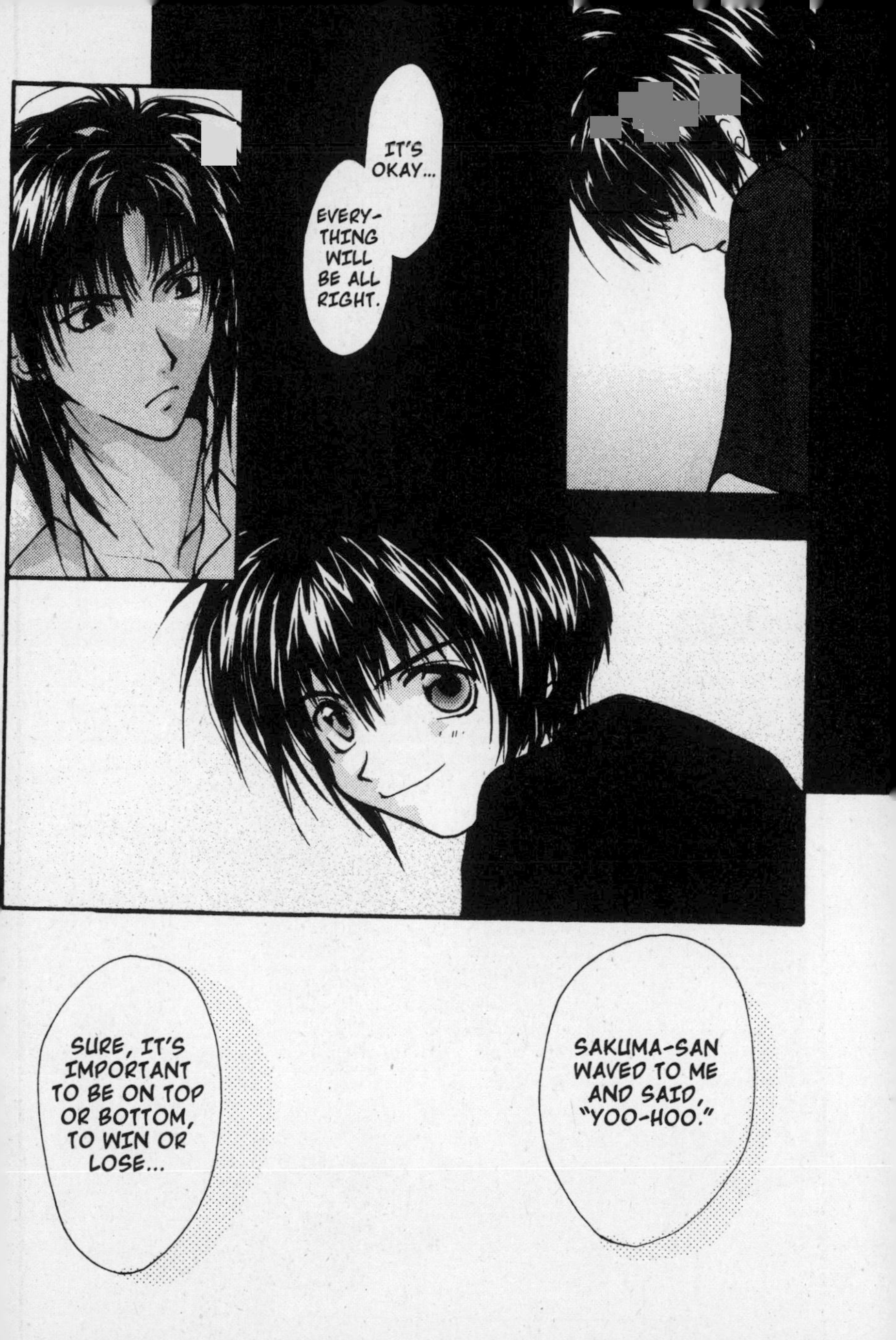
IT'S OKAY...
EVERYTHING WILL BE ALL RIGHT.
SAKUMA-SAN WAVED TO ME AND SAID, "YOO-HOO."
SURE, IT'S IMPORTANT TO BE ON TOP OR BOTTOM, TO WIN OR LOSE...

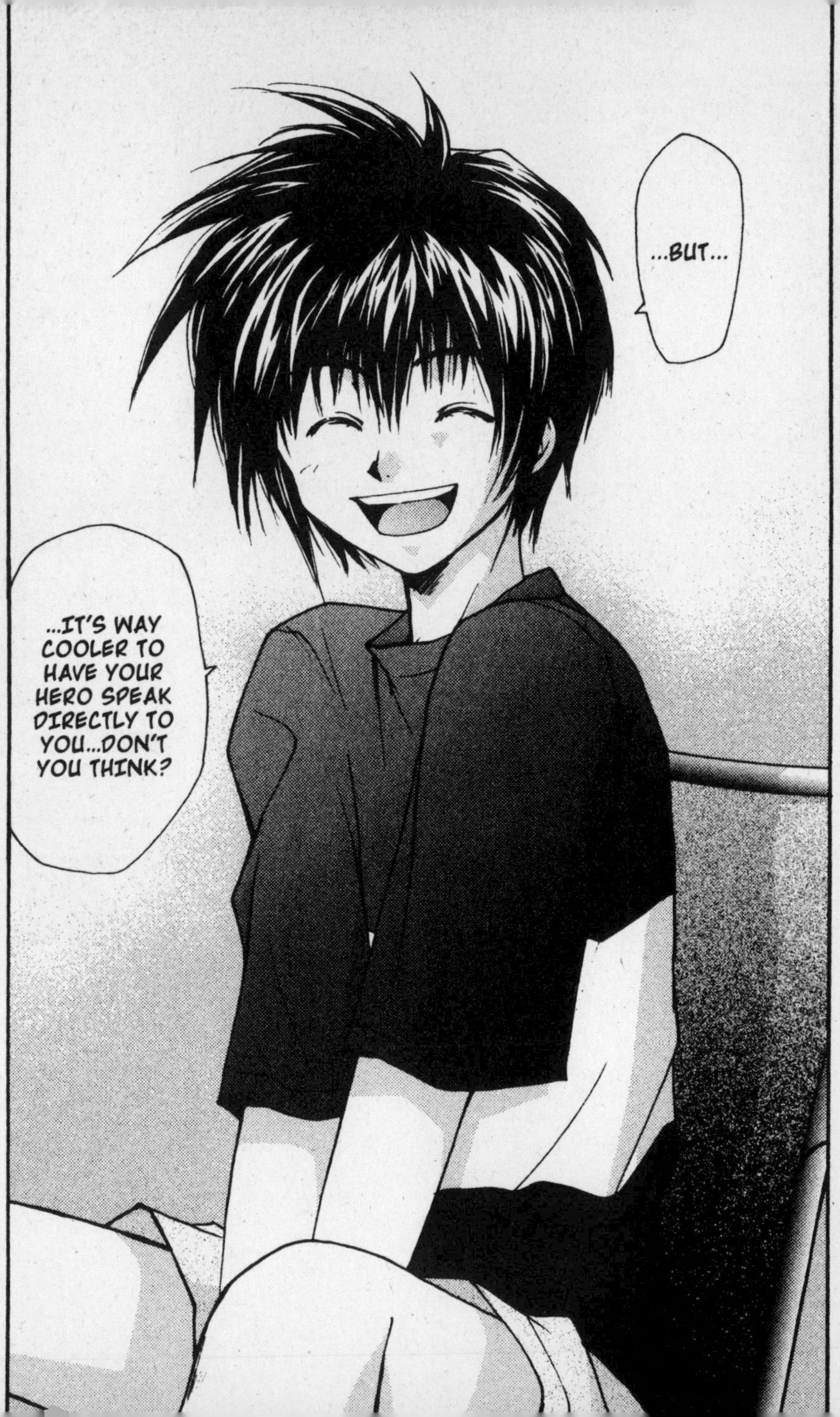
...BUT...
...IT'S WAY COOLER TO HAVE YOUR HERO SPEAK DIRECTLY TO YOU...DON'T YOU THINK?

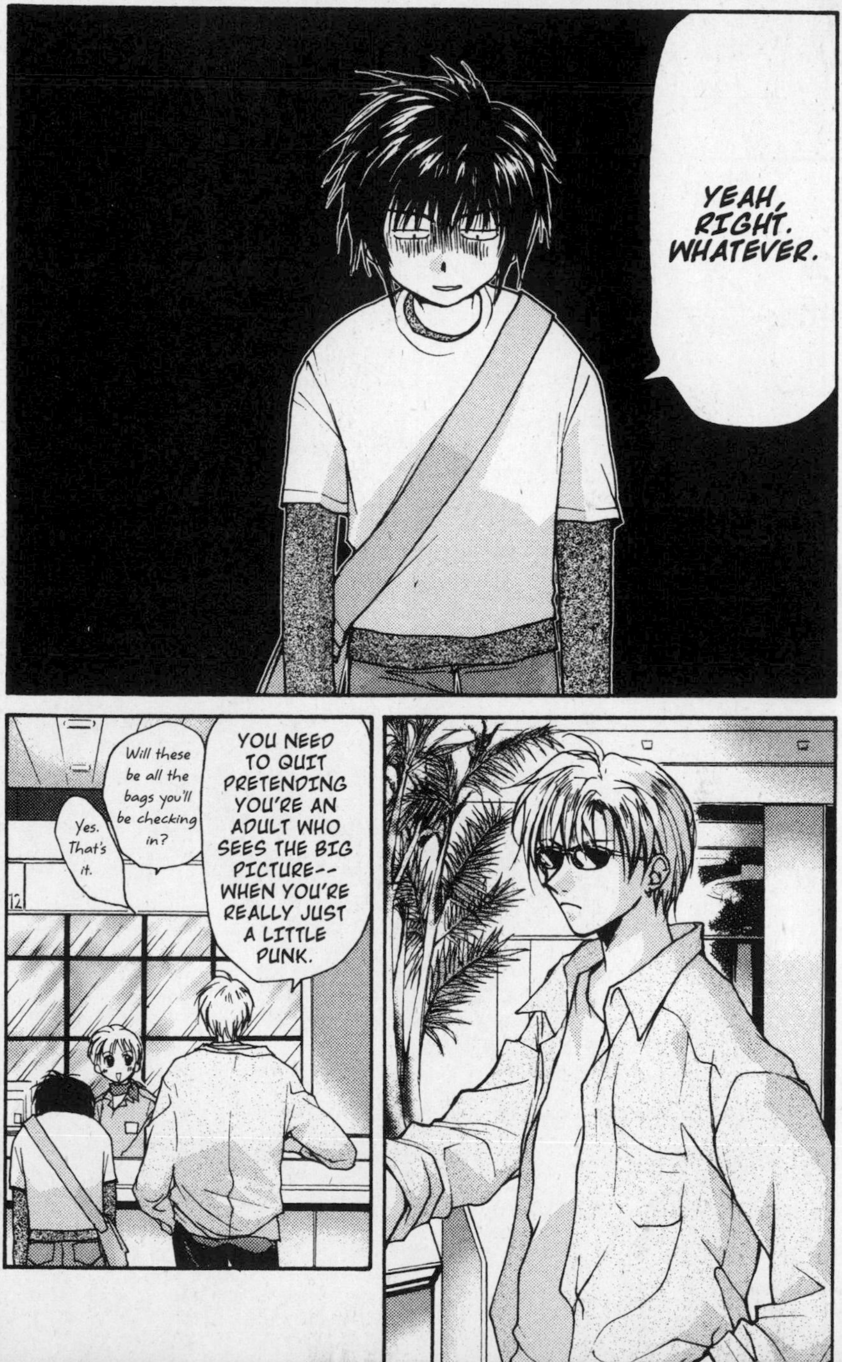
YEAH, RIGHT. WHATEVER.
YOU NEED TO QUIT PRETENDING YOU'RE AN ADULT WHO SEES THE BIG PICTURE-- WHEN YOU'RE REALLY JUST A LITTLE PUNK.
Will these be all the bags you'll be checking in?
Yes. That's it.

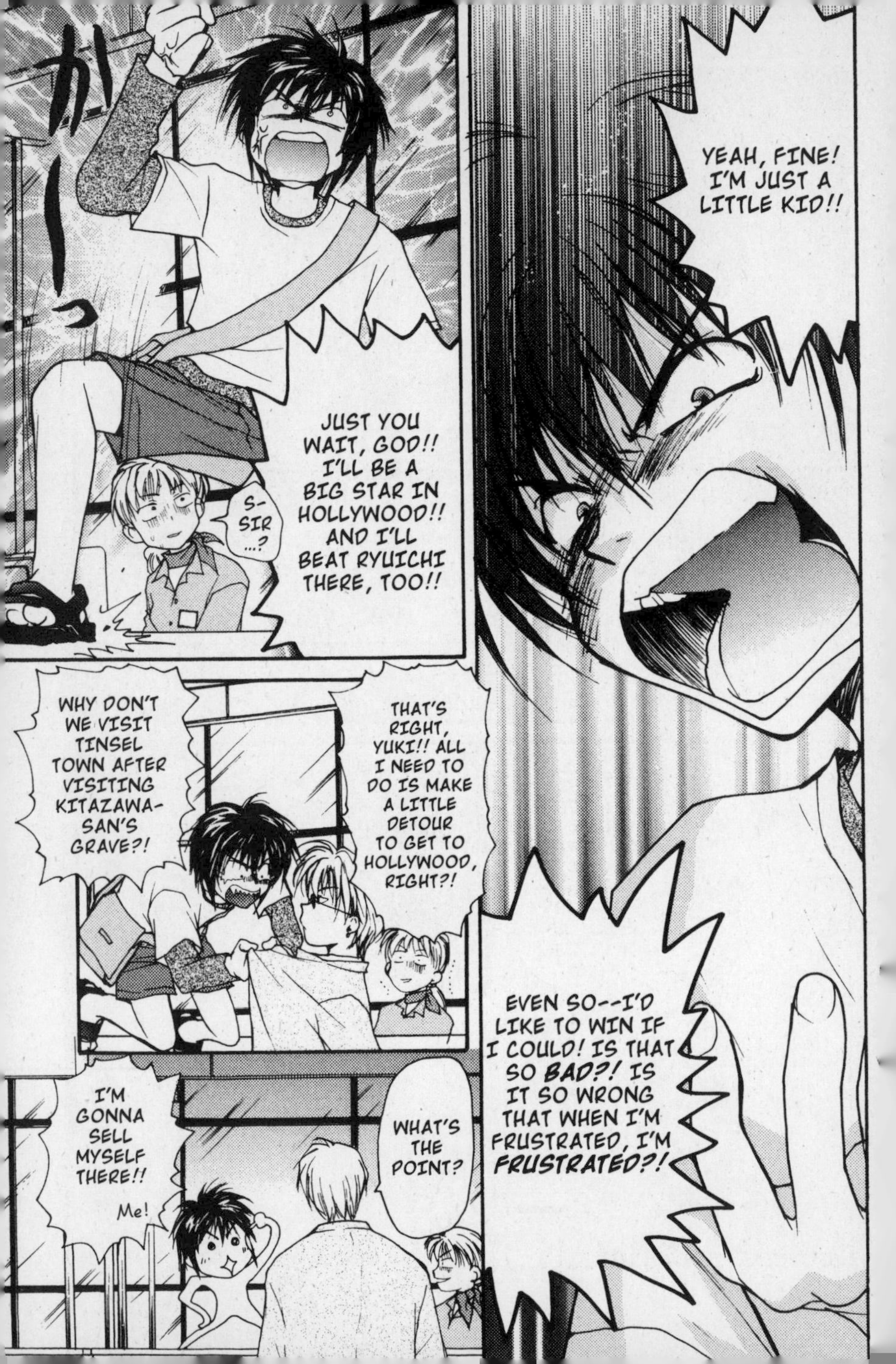

YEAH, FINE! I'M JUST A LITTLE KID!!
EVEN SO--I'D LIKE TO WIN IF I COULD! IS THAT SO *BAD?!* IS IT SO WRONG THAT WHEN I'M FRUSTRATED, I'M ***FRUSTRATED?!***
かーっ
JUST YOU WAIT, GOD!! I'LL BE A BIG STAR IN HOLLYWOOD!! AND I'LL BEAT RYUICHI THERE, TOO!!
S-SIR ...?
THAT'S RIGHT, YUKI!! ALL I NEED TO DO IS MAKE A LITTLE DETOUR TO GET TO HOLLYWOOD, RIGHT?!
WHY DON'T WE VISIT TINSEL TOWN AFTER VISITING KITAZAWA-SAN'S GRAVE?!
WHAT'S THE POINT?
I'M GONNA SELL MYSELF THERE!!
Me!

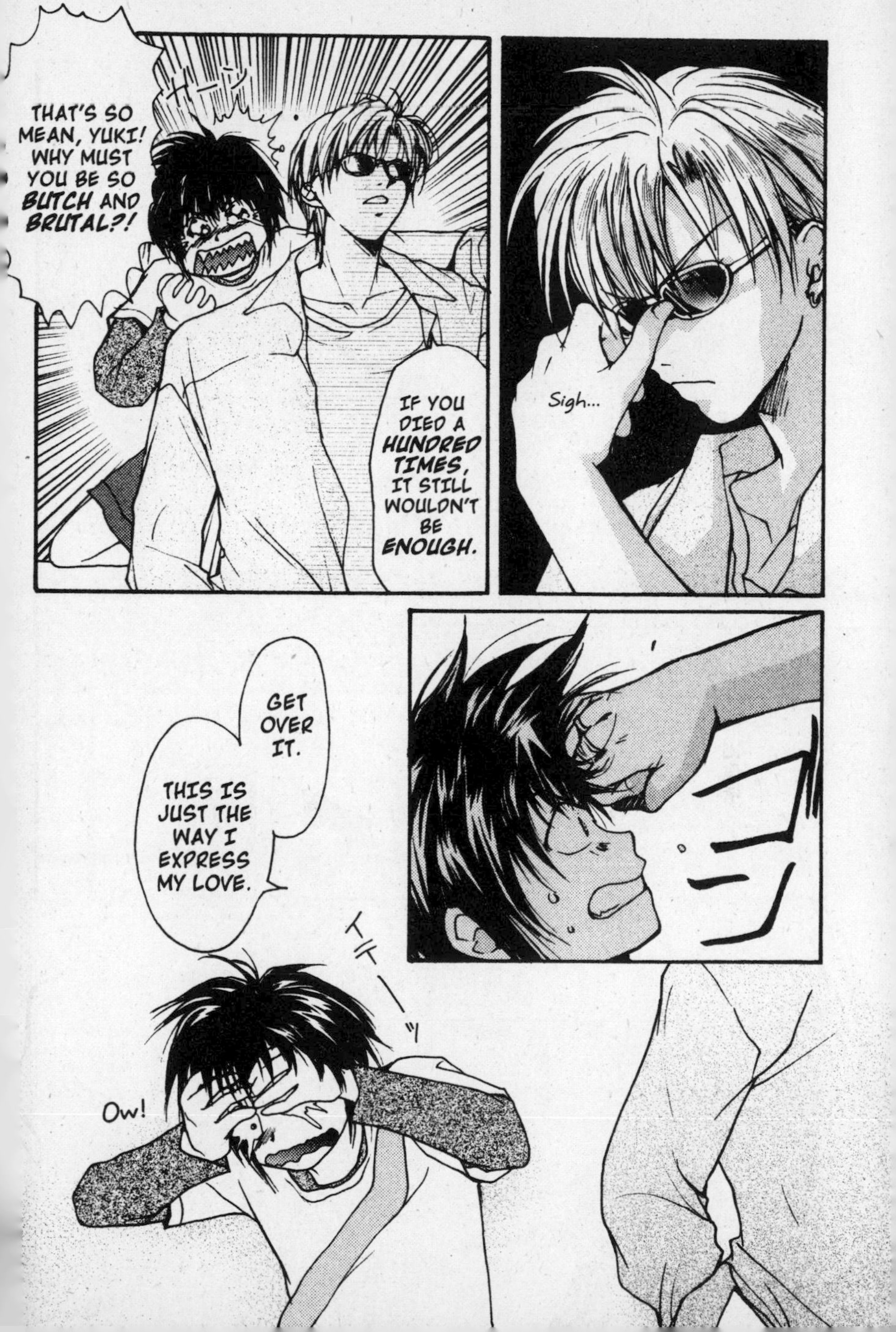
Sigh...
THAT'S SO MEAN, YUKI! WHY MUST YOU BE SO *BUTCH* AND *BRUTAL*?!
IF YOU DIED A *HUNDRED TIMES*, IT STILL WOULDN'T BE *ENOUGH*.
GET OVER IT.
THIS IS JUST THE WAY I EXPRESS MY LOVE.
Ow!

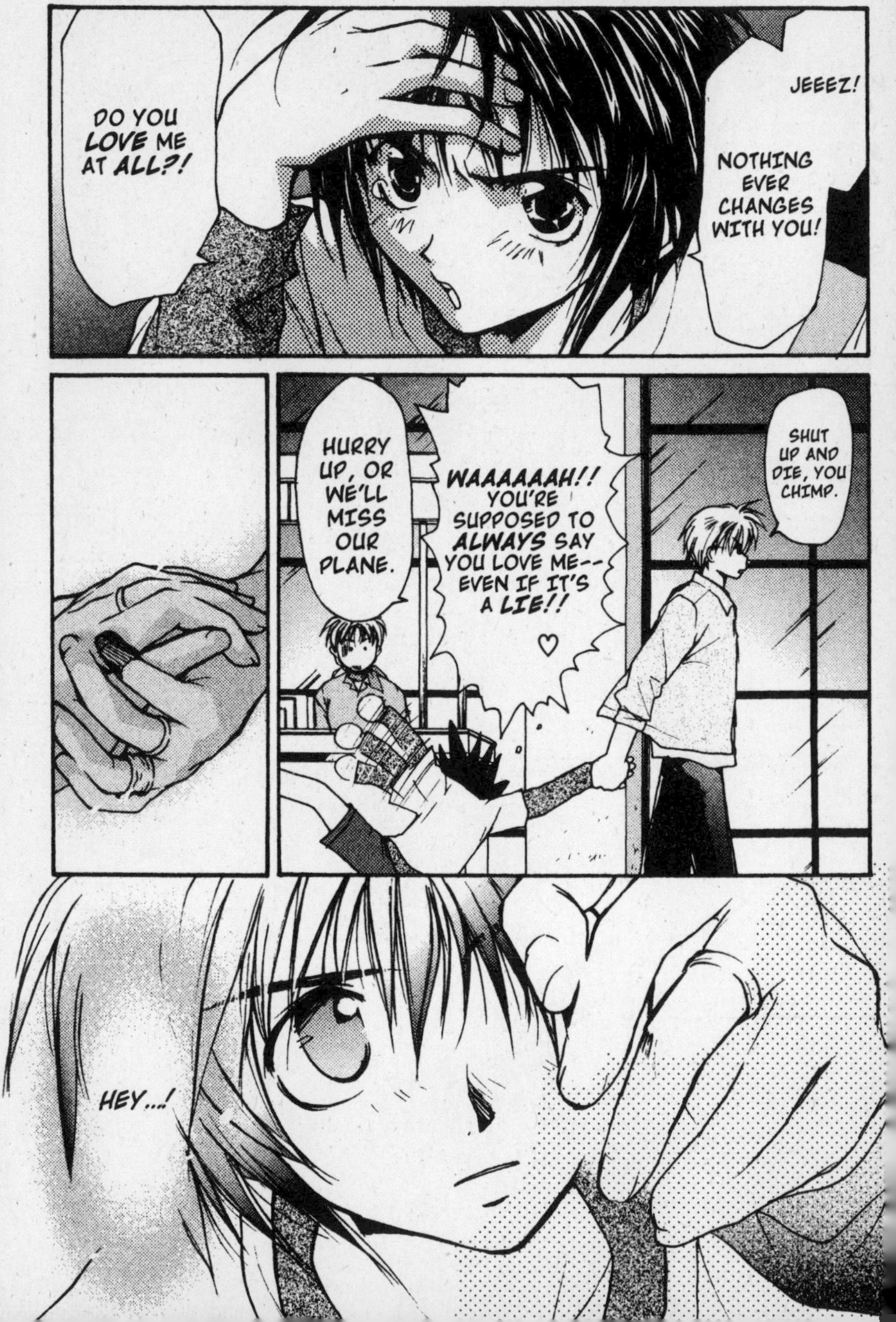
JEEEZ!
NOTHING EVER CHANGES WITH YOU!
DO YOU LOVE ME AT ALL?!
SHUT UP AND DIE, YOU CHIMP.
WAAAAAAH!! YOU'RE SUPPOSED TO ALWAYS SAY YOU LOVE ME-- EVEN IF IT'S A LIE!!
HURRY UP, OR WE'LL MISS OUR PLANE.
HEY...!

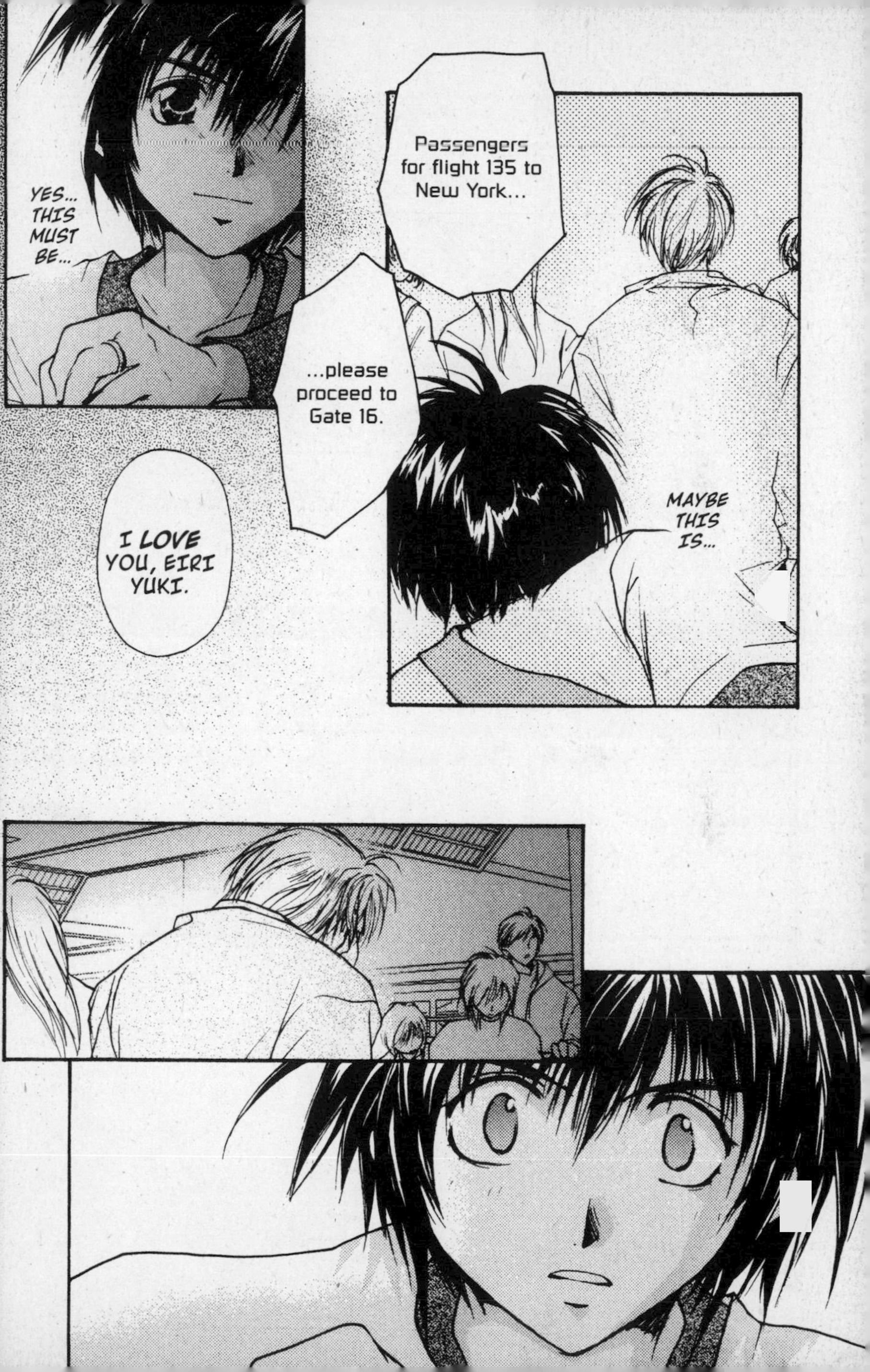

Passengers for flight 135 to New York...
...please proceed to Gate 16.
MAYBE THIS IS...
YES... THIS MUST BE...
I LOVE YOU, EIRI YUKI.

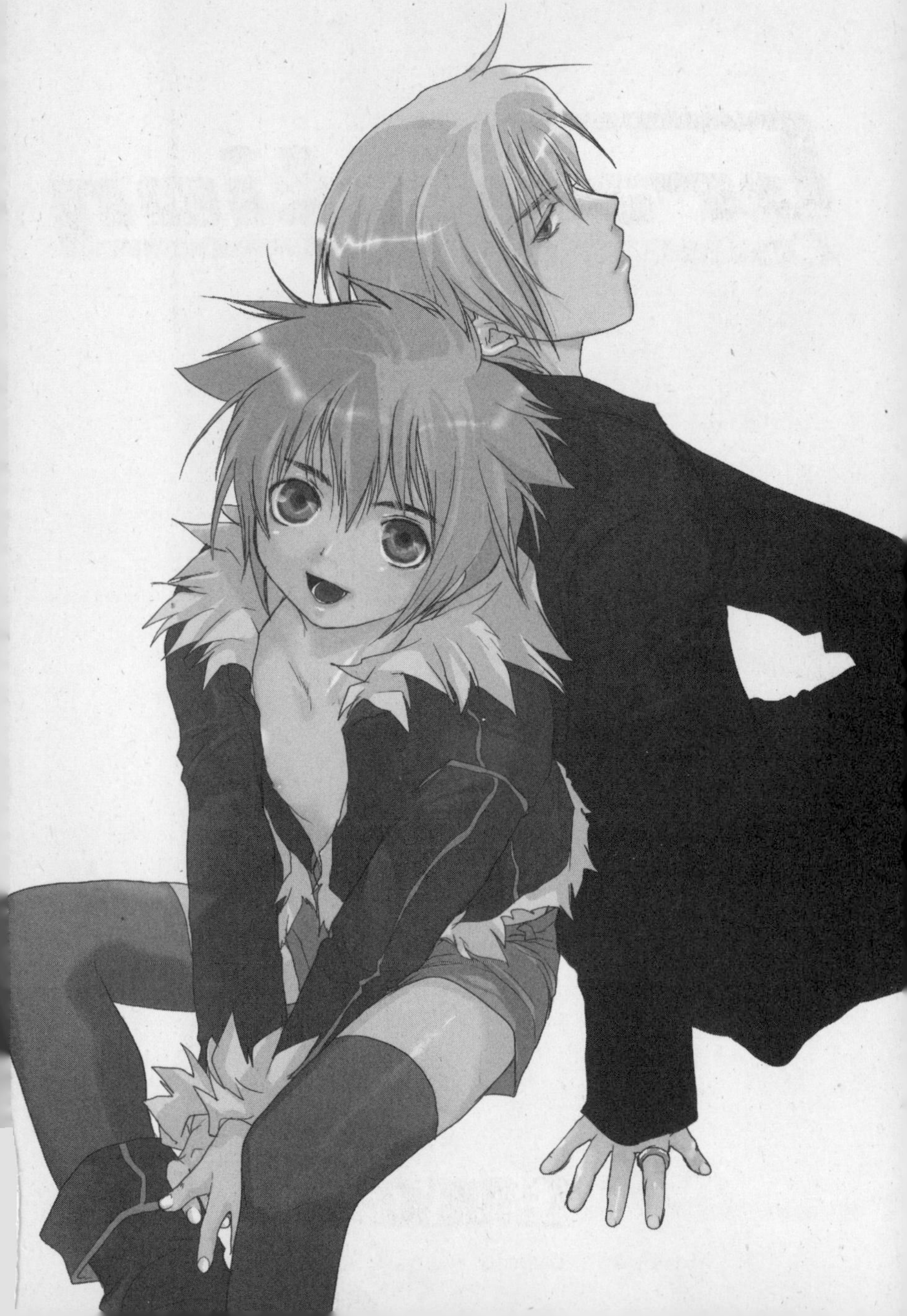

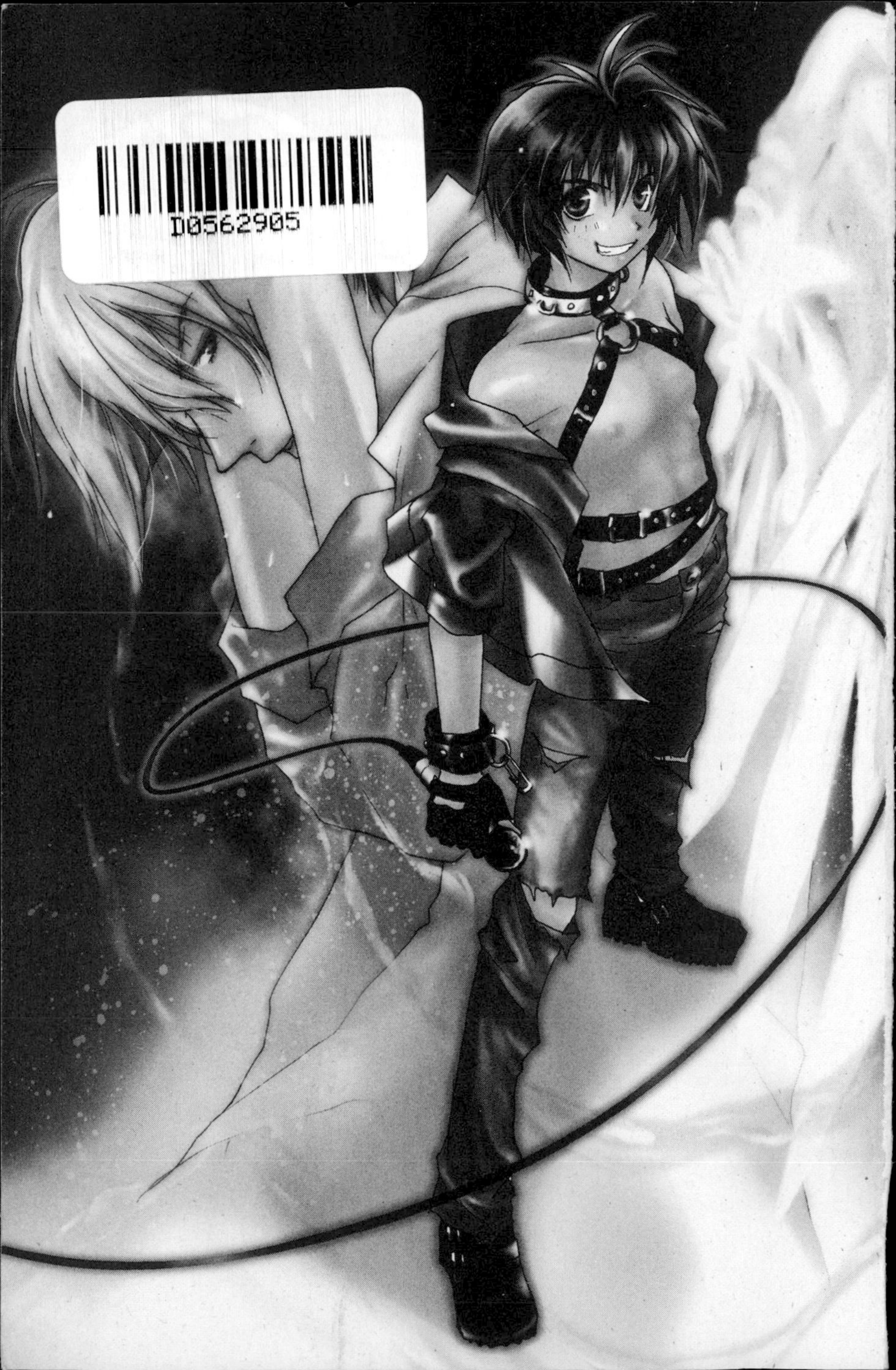